MODERN CRIMINAL INVESTIGATION

MODERN CRIMINAL INVESTIGATION

by

HARRY SÖDERMAN, D.Sc.

*Late Chief Director, National Institute
of Technical Police, Sweden
Reporter General to the International
Criminal Police Commission*

and

JOHN J. O'CONNELL

*Late Chief Inspector,
New York City Police Department
Dean and Founder,
New York Police Academy
Former President,
International Association
of Chiefs of Police*

REVISED BY CHARLES E. O'HARA

New York Police Department

Fifth Edition

FUNK & WAGNALLS
NEW YORK

MODERN CRIMINAL INVESTIGATION

FIFTH EDITION

Completely revised and reset

Copyright © 1962 by Funk & Wagnalls Publishing Co., Inc.

Published in Canada by Fitzhenry & Whiteside Limited, Toronto.

Library of Congress Catalog Card Number 62–9736

Printed in the United States of America

ISBN 0–308–40080–1

9 10

Based on MODERN CRIMINAL INVESTIGATION, copyright 1935, 1940, 1945, and 1952 under the Articles of the Copyright Convention of the Pan American Republics and the United States.

PREFACE TO THE PRESENT EDITION

The present edition has been designed to include the more important developments in the art and science of crime detection while retaining without substantial change the essential elements of the methods and philosophy of the original authors. It would be presumptuous to hope that these changes and additions have been managed without some sacrifice of the unique flavor, felicity of style, and incisive presentation which contributed so greatly to the success of the earlier editions.

CHARLES E. O'HARA

New York City, 1962.

PREFACE TO THE FOURTH EDITION

During the sixteen years which have elapsed since this book first appeared, there have been no fundamental changes in police procedure or basic criminal investigation. During this time, however, new methods have been developed, new answers found to old problems, new skills and techniques have grown out of the advance of science. It was essential, therefore, that this book be completely revised if it was to continue serving as a guide and manual for the alert, intelligent, law-enforcement officer.

My duties in Sweden and with the International Criminal Police Commission have kept me in Europe during the past years, but the death of my collaborator, the late Chief Inspector John O'Connell, placed the burden of revision on my own shoulders. I have crossed the Atlantic, therefore, to bring this book up to date. I have revised all chapters, completely rewritten some in order to include new material, and added several chapters on subjects not included in earlier editions.

In this labor of revision I have sorely missed the inspiration, the rich experience and valued collaboration of the late Inspector O'Connell. I am grateful for the cordial assistance of his old colleagues of the New York City Police Department, of the New York City Medical Examiner's Office, and other American agencies which have made my task easier. To them, and to everyone else who received me so graciously during my stay in the United States, I express my thanks.

HARRY SÖDERMAN

New York City
December, 1951.

ACKNOWLEDGMENTS

Like its predecessors, the present edition is indebted to the New York Police Department for the unfailing spirit of cooperation shown by its members. We wish to thank Police Commissioner Michael J. Murphy, Chief Inspector Francis J. M. Robb, Chief of Detectives Michael E. J. Ledden, and Assistant Chief Inspector Walter F. Henning, and the personnel of the various Central Office Bureaus and Squads on whose fund of specialized knowledge we have constantly drawn. Special thanks are due Mr. Kevin P. O'Brien of the Baruch School faculty of City College, who aided greatly by his extensive knowledge of criminalistics and broad experience in case work.

Acknowledgment for friendly assistance is similarly given to J. Edgar Hoover, Director of the Federal Bureau of Investigation; H. H. Clegg, Assistant Director of the Federal Bureau of Investigation; Bruce Smith, Director of the Institute of Public Administration, New York City; Dr. Thomas A. Gonzales, Chief Medical Examiner of New York City; Fred E. Inbau, Professor of Law, Northwestern University, Chicago; Donald F. McCall, Assistant Professor of Police Science, State College of Washington, Pullman, and John J. O'Connell, formerly Special Agent, Counter Intelligence Corps, U. S. Army, and son of the coauthor of this book.

Also acknowledged are the many fine suggestions for the chapter on Sabotage and Plant Protection of Mr. O. Charles Urton, former member of the Ohio State Police and U. S. Public Safety Official in Germany, and of his collaborator on the chapter on Plant Protection, Lt. Col. Carl E. Grimsley, formerly of the Ohio State Patrol and of civilian and military defense production protection services of Air Force, Ordnance and Signal Corps commands, A. U. S., and Provost Marshal, Stuttgart Military Post, Germany.

Acknowledgment is again made to those who assisted in the preparation of the material that is retained from previous editions. In the Chief Medical Examiner's Office, we wish to thank Dr. Alexander O. Gettler, Toxicologist; Dr. Benjamin Vance; and Dr. Alexander S. Wiener, Chief Serologist.

CONTENTS

ILLUSTRATIONS

MODERN CRIMINAL INVESTIGATION

3-17

I ASPECTS OF DETECTIVE WORK

IN THE MIDDLE OF THE NINETEENTH CENTURY NATURAL SCIENCE BEGAN to develop by leaps and bounds. The mystic theories theretofore advanced to explain the scheme of things began to lose ground as the clear, cold logic of scientific experiment gradually shed a new light on the mysteries of the universe. The change in point of view from the mystic to the scientific soon became apparent in criminal investgation. Justice, which for centuries had been searching for truth, turned to science for assistance. Bertillon, Gross, Galton, Henry, Vucetich, Dennstaedter, Locard, Jeserich, Reiss, Stockis, Heindl, Balthazard, Wentworth, Van Ledden, Hulsebosch, De Rechter, Kockel, Türkel, Kanger, Minovici, Mezger, Osborn, Mitchell, Bischoff, Lucas, Ribeiro, Schneickert, Schmelck, and others began to build the foundation of police science by using the methods of natural and related sciences as aids in criminal detection.

Modern police science may be said to have three phases. The first phase embraces the identification of living and dead persons. The second embraces the field work carried out by specially trained detectives at the scene of the crime. The third embraces methods used in the police laboratory to examine and analyze clues and traces discovered in the course of the investigation. All these methods will be described in the following chapters. *also 4th Interview & interrogation*

Modern police science has had a striking influence on detective work and will surely further enhance its effectiveness in due time. However, the opportunity to use time-honored methods and practical detective work will always exist. Knowledge of the *modus operandi* of criminals and the methods of their apprehension; skill, patience, tact, industry, and thoroughness, together with a flair peculiar to the successful detective, will always be primary assets in detective work.

Modern criminal investigation in a broader sense also has several phases. The first is the requirement of a thorough examination and inquiry into the method and technique used by the criminal in his approach to the commission of the crime. Therefore it is absolutely vital that the

3

X investigating policeman or detective visit the scene of the crime. This he must do in order to act intelligently and logically and to avoid any pre-conceived notions or theories.

When a building has been entered, the place where the entrance was effected must be determined; likewise the means of entrance used by the criminal. If a jimmy, chisel, key, assistance of an accomplice, or bodily force has been used, this must be noted. The object of the crime must be determined. At or during what time, as exactly stated as possible, did the criminal transaction occur? Was it at some special time, such as opening or closing time, or on a holiday or over the week-end?

The investigating officer should also seek to ascertain if any representation was made by the criminal prior to the crime or if an inquiry by any individual was made one or more days before its actual commission. This would include an approach by a canvasser, peddler, mechanic, bogus inspector, gasman, or electrician. In many cases a criminal relies to a great extent on the tale he tells. It almost invariably indicates the calling or trade to which the criminal has been accustomed. It is likewise important to learn whether any individual has approached the victim or the premises ostensibly to locate a missing friend, to secure employment, to hire a room or apartment on the premises, or to make a purchase; and, if so, was opportunity afforded to make observations which would be helpful in planning the crime committed?

Some criminals work with confederates. It is essential for the investigating detective or police officer to be able to decide whether the crime was planned by more than one individual. This conclusion can be arrived at after a thorough examination of the approach and the means used to enter and to attack the person or property.

The search for clues should not be confined to the premises alone. The investigating officer should invariably look for traces of vehicles in the neighborhood of the crime. The marks of vehicles that cannot be accounted for by the ordinary traffic having business at the scene, if discovered, should be noted as having a possible connection with the crime. Many good cases of detection have been attributed to finding traces that indicated the way in which the criminals moved in taking away property or in fleeing after committing a crime.

As criminals are frequently known to commit extraordinary acts not associated with the object of the crime, such as changing clothes on the premises, drinking liquors, smoking cigars or cigarettes, eating food, committing nuisances, poisoning the dog, or preparing a particular getaway, the investigating officer should be careful to note any such peculiarities.

With the criminal's method and technique of entry fathomed, his progress in the premises is to be determined. This can be accomplished by keen observation and examination of the premises and their surroundings. A systematic search should be made for footprints, fingerprints, and any clue that might be of help in tracking the criminal. It is essential that a complete examination and record be made of the *corpus delicti,* which is the body of the crime or the subject-matter which has been the particular objective of the criminal. In simple language *corpus delicti* means the existence of the essential, fundamental fact that a crime has been committed. In murder cases *corpus delicti* means the victim's death together with the fact that it was caused by the wrongful act of another.

Important phases of criminal investigation are the techniques used by the policeman or the detective in establishing the fact that the crime reported is bona fide; in apprehending the criminal responsible; in recovering property stolen, if any; and in gathering and collating statements of facts, circumstances, and clues necessary for the prosecution of the criminal.

Many a crime is simulated for the purpose of collecting insurance or covering up peculations, and so it is compulsory for the investigating officer to establish its authenticity. When this has been accomplished, clues available generally comprise the method of operation, the stolen property, and the traces left by the criminal on the scene.

When a criminal flees after the commission of a crime, his chance of escape will be greatly reduced if an accurate description is secured and immediately broadcast through a general alarm. The matter of description of criminal fugitives is covered in detail in Chapter V. Description of stolen property is covered in Chapter XXI. Emphasis must be laid upon the importance of both of these matters in helping in the solution of cases.

Corroboration of the criminal's identity should be obtained, if possible, from persons other than the victim. This corroboration may be secured from voluntary statements made by witnesses or in reply to questions asked by the investigating officer. When the necessary information has been obtained, pursuit of the criminal should be immediate.

It is well to bear in mind when taking voluntary statements or questioning witnesses that the scope of inquiry should cover matters known, seen, heard, tasted, discovered, smelled, and felt; and that particular attention should be given to the motives of the criminal, both prior to the commission of the crime and subsequently, noting coincidences of presence, absence, and movements, as well as to the sequence of action of witnesses and the connective accuracy of their account. Consideration must also be given to the results of their lines of conduct, suspicious discrepancies, omissions, false statements, unnatural reluctance, extreme prejudice, abnormal desire to volunteer evidence, and the general reliability of witnesses. After covering these aspects, a definite conclusion can be reached on facts, and statements can be substantiated, qualified, or refuted.

The efficient conduct of a criminal investigation requires an effective integration of the resources of modern police science as well as the diligent employment of a number of individual skills. The investigator's knowledge of criminalistics should be sufficiently well grounded to permit ready recognition of opportunities for its profitable application. A thorough training in the methods of recognizing, collecting, and preserving physical evidence is, of course, essential to the work of every criminal investigator. The proportionately greater need for self-sufficiency in the investigating officer for the smaller police department— or, for that matter, the field agent of a large organization whose work places him at a distance from the headquarters—implies additional training in photography, casting techniques, field tests, and other technical aids.

II POLICE ORGANIZATIONS HERE AND ABROAD

THE AUTHORS HAVE OFTEN BEEN ASKED WHETHER AN AMERICAN DETEC-
tive is better than a man from Scotland Yard or from the *Police Nationale*, if the German detective is better than the French detective or vice
versa. We have never been able to answer this question. This is not only
for reasons of tact but because the methods and conditions of work and
the mentality of the people are so different in different countries that the
police of one country must be considered as a product of that very society. An American detective, however good, even if he spoke French
fluently, would most certainly not immediately be an efficient *commissaire de police* in Paris; and a French detective, however smart, would
probably be a failure if put to do the work of a first-grade detective in
New York City.

It has been said with some justice that every country has the police it
deserves. Without attempting in any way to classify the police systems
here and abroad or to deal with the efficiency of the organization or the
individual skill of the detectives and policemen, we shall attempt in the
following pages to give a short survey of the most important police forces
of the world of today.

Before this attempt is made, we must point out the difference between
political police and ordinary police. In olden days these were very frequently mixed up with each other and it was difficult to tell where the
political police ended and the ordinary police started. This was the case
in France, for instance, many years ago, when the decaying monarchy
of the *ancien régime* maintained a net of spies all over the country. This
system subsequently was copied by many rulers in different countries of
the Continent. It was also in France that the forerunner of the political
police systems prevailing in certain countries in our time first saw daylight. This was in the gigantic police organization which existed under the
ill-famed Fouché. In the Napoleonic days Fouché's spies could be found
all over Europe and mention of the name Fouché must then have had

7

about the same effect on our forefathers as mention of the name Himmler or Yagoda on us in our day.

France was also the first country to start a detective organization of the modern type. This was after the downfall of Napoleon, in the days of the restoration, when the ex-convict François Vidocq[1] was entrusted with the building up of a small body of detectives to rid Paris of the gangs of thugs who were rampant in those days.

In the latter part of the nineteenth century, in the calm days of liberalism, a political police in the meaning of our day did not exist outside czarist Russia, and the task of protecting society from fanatics, as, for instance, anarchists, was entrusted to the ordinary police. It was in our century that the idea of an independent political police rose to its full height in the shape of those two formidable organizations the German Gestapo and the Russian Cheka. The Gestapo is dead, but the Cheka, under another name, is still a very flourishing organization and has been copied faithfully in the Russian satellite states.

The defunct Gestapo and the present Russian MVD (the old Cheka) represent pure political police systems. In fact they go farther, because their function was and is not only to preserve the existing order and put its assailants out of the fight but also to preach the gospel of their dictator. To make an historic parallel, the creed of the prophet is not only spread with the sword but also with the gospel.

It is just as well that political police systems of this type are entirely separate from the ordinary police organization and therefore do not mar the reputation of the latter, which, with a changing political regime, may emerge fairly intact out of the turmoils accompanying a change in the national structure. This, for instance, was the case in Germany, where, after the downfall of the Nazi rule, a large percent of the lower ranks of the old ordinary police was used in the new police organization. The ordinary police always disliked the Gestapo.

UNITED STATES

It has truthfully been said that the manifold police forces in the United States may be compared to an intricate mosaic and that there is no American police system in the sense we speak of a French or an English police system. This is due to historical development and to the almost complete freedom which the different communities and States, as well as Federal agencies, have had in solving their policing problems.

The police systems in the United States[2] may be divided roughly into local, State, and Federal. In rural districts and small communities the sheriffs and the constables still represent the local police. In most cases both are elected. Larger communities as a rule have their own local police force under a chief of police, who is under the immediate command of the mayor. State police forces, which nowadays exist in all states, usually patrol the highways but in many cases have modernly equipped detective forces which work anywhere in the State where there is no adequate local force. The Federal police bodies are attached to various Federal departments in Washington. Their scope of work is nation-wide and will be described briefly later.

The basis of the American police system is the sheriff, of whom, since olden times, there is one in each county. As mentioned above, the sheriff is elected, the official term usually being two years. Formal qualifications pertain only to residence, citizenship, and electoral status. Because of the shortness of the term of office, most sheriffs keep their private occupations. The sheriff is also the keeper of the county jail and in many sections has duties to perform in connection with civil suits.

A survey of the sheriffs in the United States shows that their official duties vary to an astonishing degree in different parts of the country. In some parts, especially in the East, the sheriffs seem to confine themselves chiefly to the care of the county jail. In other parts, especially in the West, the sheriffs are more active as peace officers, some of them even heading comparatively large and quite modern police forces. Some counties also have county police forces, which may be independent of the sheriff's office. There is still another type of county police force, namely, the so-called parkway police, which may be found in several sections and which is under the supervision of the county park board or other special authority. In this connection should be mentioned also the prosecutor's detectives, who may be found in many thickly populated suburban counties but mostly in the larger cities. In some cases these detectives are a special and permanent body of investigators. In others they are drawn from the city police and put at the disposal of the prosecutor. Finally, when speaking about county police, the so-called vigilantes or county auxiliary protective units, which were organized in the late twenties by the American Bankers Association to protect rural banks, may be mentioned.

Important parts of the American police are found at all three levels of government—Federal, State, and local. For sheer weight of numbers the police of the larger cities hold special importance. The policeman's art and science is more easily developed to a high degree in a large community. The training facilities[3] for recruits such as offered by larger communities, by the State police, and by certain of the Federal forces also are an important factor. Today every American city of more than 500,000 inhabitants has training establishments for its police.

The organization of the large city forces naturally differs in detail but is on the whole of the same pattern. Promotion is almost always regulated by a civil service system, at least in the initial grades. The patrolman has to pass an examination to become a sergeant, the sergeant has to pass another to become a lieutenant, and the lieutenant has to pass still another

to become a captain. A peculiarity about the American police system is the special career of the detective. The fact that there are certain aspects of police work in the United States which demand a highly developed personal talent as regards trailing and investigation explains this high appreciation of the investigating genius. Patrolmen having special personal qualifications along these lines may advance as detectives without passing any examination, finally reaching a salary status comparable to that of a police lieutenant or captain.

The head of a large police department in the United States is commonly called a chief of police, or, in the largest cities, commissioner of police. In some sections the commissioner of police may be regarded as a kind of ambassador from the mayor to the police, and in such cases there is also a chief of police, who runs the force.

Figure 2. William S. Seavey, founder of International Association of Chiefs of Police.[4]

In the last three decades the State police forces have shown a marked development and many of them are now complete police units whose recruiting, training, and performance of work will stand comparison with any other similar organization. The State police forces are, as regards jurisdiction, territorially limited only by the State boundaries. The administrative head of the State police force, generally called a superintendent or commissioner, as a rule is directly responsible to the governor of the State.

In describing the Federal police agencies we shall follow the classifications made by Bruce Smith, who divides them into those aimed at protecting the national revenue and those aimed at protecting life and property and enforcing the penal statutes.

1. *Protection of the National Revenue:*
   a. Intelligence Unit of the Bureau of Internal Revenue (Department of the Treasury), concerned primarily with investigations of violations of the income tax laws
   b. Alcohol Tax Unit of the Bureau of Internal Revenue (Department of the Treasury), investigates violations of internal revenue laws relating to liquors
   c. Division of Investigations and Patrol, Bureau of Customs (Department of the Treasury), investigates smuggling activities and enforces customs and navigation laws

2. *Protection of Life and Property and Enforcement of Penal Statutes:*
   a. Federal Bureau of Investigation (Department of Justice), investigates all violations of Federal laws except those where enforcement authority has been specifically assigned to some other Federal agency; also investigates all cases of espionage, sabotage, treason, and other matters pertaining to internal security
   b. United States Secret Service (Department of the Treasury), chiefly concerned with investigating the counterfeiting, forging, or altering of any of the moneys or other securities of the United States; also charged with protection of the President and his family, and of the Executive Mansion and grounds
   c. Bureau of Narcotics (Department of the Treasury), investigates all violations of Federal laws relating to narcotic drugs and marihuana
   d. Bureau of the Chief Post Office Inspector, investigates mail losses, mail depredations, unlawful use of the mails, and other violations of the postal laws
   e. Immigration and Naturalization Service (Department of Justice), investigates violations of immigration and naturalization laws, patrols borders to prevent surreptitious entry of aliens, and registers and fingerprints aliens

The eight agencies above do not complete the list of Federal agencies having certain police functions. All in all there are well over forty Federal agencies performing investigative work.[5]

The numerical strength of the Federal police agencies cited above may at first glance compare unfavorably with the large city police forces. It should be borne in mind, however, that the bulk of the large city police forces naturally is made up of patrolmen and that the Federal agencies are made up almost entirely of special agents or investigators. A comparison of the strength of the Federal agencies with the number of detectives and plain-clothes men in the large cities will show that the Federal agencies compare very favorably in number.

Under the able management of John Edgar Hoover,[6] the Federal Bureau of Investigation has developed rapidly in the last few decades. This was due at first to the trend in the 1930's of federalization of many crimes with an interstate aspect, such as kidnaping, extortion, bank robbery, etc., and the duty given to the Bureau by the late President Roosevelt in 1941 of defending the internal security of the country. The FBI also maintains some national and central police institutions which are an absolute necessity to a great and progressive country, i.e., a central fingerprint file, a statistical bureau which records exact figures on the occurrence of crime throughout the United States, a national police academy, and a national crime laboratory.

Figure 3.   J. Edgar Hoover, director of the Federal Bureau of Investigation.

The qualifications for recruits for the FBI require that they be young and of sound physique and graduates in law or accountancy. The FBI recruit undergoes an initial training period of fourteen weeks of intensive practical and theoretical instruction, after which he must take several qualifying examinations. Every third year the FBI agent takes a two- to four-week supplementary course.

The head of the FBI carries the title of director. His nearest men in Washington are called assistant directors. The field offices of the FBI are scattered all over the country and are connected with an effective radio and teletype system. The agent in charge of a field office is simply called special agent in charge, and all other FBI men are special agents.

The other Federal police agencies recruit and train their personnel according to their needs.

A comparison of police work in the United States with that on the Continent points up certain difficulties met with by the American police. It can definitely be stated that the arrest of a criminal in a large American community as a rule involves more police work than would be the case on the Continent. This is a direct result of the freedom of the individual in the United States, which even makes it impossible to exercise a strict control of the hotels. The United States and the Continent differ very much in this respect. The United States exercises a very strict frontier control; but as soon as an individual is let into the country, he enjoys complete freedom of movement and if he chooses to avoid notice it is very difficult to trace his whereabouts. Every American knows that he can register at a hotel as Napoleon Bonaparte without any consequences. On the Continent it is the contrary. As a rule it is not difficult to get past the frontier, but once in a country the individual has to register with the police at almost every step. Some countries even go so far as to ask the foreign traveler to give his passport to the hotel (i.e., the police) for the length of his stay. Native travelers are compelled to register under their true names, and the entries are immediately turned over to the files of the local police department. This is just one detail among the many difficulties met with by the American detective as compared with his Continental colleague. And if the incredible mixture of races, creeds, habits, and morals which are found in many large American communities is also taken into account, the difficulties peculiar to the American detective are easily understood.

ENGLAND

The English police can be divided into the London police, the county police, and the borough police.

London is policed by two separate forces, the Metropolitan Police and the City Police. The Metropolitan Police is the symbol for the public of the English police system, but it should not be forgotten that there are also important police forces in other large English cities. The City of London, i.e., the old City, an enclave of one square mile, has a police force of its own of about 700 officers and men, who are under a commissioner. The Metropolitan Police has jurisdiction over the rest of London, an area of 800 square miles and a population of 8,700,000. The strength of this force is about 16,000 men.

Each county in England has its own police force, with a chief constable at its head. The chief constable is under the authority and control of a standing joint committee, which consists of an equal number of justices who are appointed by Quarter Sessions and of members of the county council. The county police force is divided into divisions, which are commanded by superintendents. The county police in England numbers approximately 25,000 men.

The boroughs also have their own police forces. These too are commanded by a chief constable, but his powers are more limited than those of the county chief constable. The controlling authority in the case of the borough police is the watch committee, which is composed of members of the local town council. The borough police forces consist of about 17,500 men.

The chief of the Metropolitan Police is called commissioner of police, and he and the chief of the City police are the only police chiefs in England carrying this title, the others being called chief constables. The second-in-command to the commissioner of the Metropolitan Police is called deputy commissioner and to the commissioner of the City police, assistant commissioner. The Metropolitan Police is divided into two main branches, the Criminal Investigation Department, commonly called by the abbreviation CID, and the uniformed branch.

The New Scotland Yard is the actual headquarters of the Metropolitan Police forces, though the term is most popularly associated with the CID. The name Scotland Yard, or the "Yard," as the policemen themselves call it, stems from the fact that the original building was believed to have occupied the site of a palace used by Scottish kings and their ambassadors when on visits to London.

The Criminal Investigation Department consists of about 1,500 detectives, of which 1,300 do ordinary detective work. The remaining 200 detectives are employed in the Special Branch, which in many respects is national in scope, first, because it has a staff at every airport and seaport, and, secondly, because it is charged with protecting prominent persons and dealing with movements which might be regarded as subversive to the state.

Other branches of the CID which operate on a nation-wide scale are the following:

1. The criminal record office, which is the only office in the entire country that maintains a central record of all criminals
2. The fingerprint department, which, by statute, keeps all fingerprint records
3. The fraud squad, which is used all over the country by chief constables whenever they think fit, at no cost to themselves

The names of the ranks in the English police system are quite different from those used in the United States. In England the patrolman is called a constable, and then follow consecutively, sergeant (two grades), inspector (two grades), and superintendent (two grades).

It may be mentioned that in the English police practically all higher officers come from the ranks, exceptions being the commissioner of the Metropolitan Police and sometimes his chief assistants and some of the county chief constables. The commissionership is regarded as such an important function that high officials from other branches of government sometimes are appointed to this post.

Police recruits have ten to seventeen weeks of training at Peel House, a police school named after Sir Robert Peel,[7] and special courses for detectives are given at the Metropolitan Police Detective School in Hendon. A national police school, recently established at Ryton, not only has English police students but foreign students as well.

England is now well equipped with scientific police laboratories, one of which is maintained at all important police centers.

FRANCE

In France the minister of the interior is responsible for the maintenance of law and order and the internal security of the state. He commands directly or by requisition all civil and military police forces, i.e., the *Gendarmerie Nationale,* which is charged with patrolling the highways, rural districts, and small towns; the *Police Nationale,* which has nation-wide jurisdiction and is roughly comparable to the FBI in the United States; and the *Préfecture de Police,* whose jurisdiction is limited to Paris and its surroundings.

Of these three services the *Police Nationale* and the *Préfecture de Police* are civil administrations under the direct command of the minister of the interior. The *Gendarmerie Nationale* is a military corps, administered by the minister of defense.

As a rule the patrolling of towns with less than 10,000 inhabitants is done by the *Gendarmerie Nationale.* The gendarmes are grouped into brigades, which consist of from five to ten men living in a cantonment under the command of a non-commissioned officer. The gendarmes may investigate criminal cases but as a rule confine themselves to the less important ones, leaving to the specialists of the *Police Nationale* the complicated affairs.

In all cities with more than 10,000 inhabitants (except Paris) the *Police Nationale* is at work. Its functionaries are called *commissaires de police, inspecteurs, gradés,* and *gardiens de la paix.* The *commissaire de police,* a title which corresponds roughly to that of police captain in the United States, is the chief of police of a city. He has a certain number of police officers and patrolmen (*gardiens de la paix*) at his disposal, as well as a certain number of detectives (*inspecteurs*). In regard to the maintenance of order he must be in constant touch with the mayor and the *préfet* (a title corresponding roughly to that of lord lieutenant of a large county in England and the bearer of which is a representative of the minister of the interior). In respect to the activities of his detectives the *commissaire* of police works under a district attorney.

If a city has more than 100,000 inhabitants, it is divided into *quartiers* (districts), each one having its own *commissaire,* the chief *commissaire* then carrying the title of *commissaire central.*

The plain-clothes men of the *Police Nationale* may be divided into two groups: *renseignements généraux* (general information) and *police judiciaire* (judicial police). The general information detectives are in charge of frontier control and, curiously enough, with the control of horse-racing and gambling houses. Their chief duty, however, is to gather information, political and otherwise, for the heads of the administration, i.e., the *préfets* of the minister of the interior. The judicial police, the detective agency proper of the French police, is divided into seventeen groups, which are scattered throughout the country. Each such *service régional de police judiciaire* consists of about fifty detectives and has territorial jurisdiction over about five (the number varies) *départements* (large counties).

The headquarters of the *Police Nationale* is the *Direction générale de la Police Nationale* in Paris, with a director general as head. The *Police Nationale* has several police laboratories in the principal cities, the best known of which is the one at Lyons. The national police school is also located in Lyons.

A peculiarity of the French police system is that since olden times the city of Paris and its environs (*département de la Seine*) has had its own police, independent of the *Police Nationale.* The head of the Paris police is called the *Préfet de Police,* who, as mentioned above, is directly under the minister of the interior. There are only two police commissioners in England and there is only one *Préfet de Police* in France, and for that matter in the world, because probably nowhere else is there an official with such manifold duties. The *Préfet de Police* is not only the chief of police of Paris but is also charged with such things as sanitary control, passports, immigration authority, the execution of legislative matters pertaining to labor, and so on.

The *Préfet de Police* of Paris has a uniformed branch numbering more than 20,000 men and divided into twenty *commissariats d'arrondissement* for the city proper and twenty-five *commissariats de circonscription* for the suburbs and the rural communities around Paris. He also has 2,000 detectives of all grades. The detective division is divided into eighty *commissariats de quartier* for the city proper and twenty-five for the suburbs; and the director of investigation, as the head of the detective division is called, also has at his disposal several central brigades which specialize in such things as homicide, juvenile delinquency, vice, etc. Attached to the detective division of Paris is the famous *Service de l'Identité Judiciaire,* which includes the central fingerprint collection for all France as well as the central criminal records office for the country. This service was created in 1882 by Alphonse Bertillon, one of the pioneers in police science.

The International Bureau of the International Criminal Police Commission, which is discussed later in this chapter, is located in Paris in the office of the ministry of the interior and the *Police Nationale.*

GERMANY

The police in Nazi Germany was strongly centralized, with headquarters in Berlin. There were three branches, a uniformed branch, a detective branch, and a political branch, the latter known as the Gestapo (an abbreviation of *Geheime Staatspolizei,* secret state police). The detective division (*Kriminalpolizei*) had huge laboratories, second in the world only to the FBI laboratories in Washington and a very good technical outfit. In the turmoil of war and capitulation the German police organization was completely destroyed, and when the three Western allies occupied their parts of Germany, they brought police advisers with them to help build up a new police force. Since 1946 the Germans in the allied sections have been running their own police under allied supervision. The new police organization is characterized by complete decentralization. In 1951, however, there was established in Wiesbaden a Federal Office of Crime Investigation (*Bundeskriminalamt*). This office maintains large laboratories; publishes the Police Bulletin; keeps central files of fingerprints, *modus operandi,* etc.; and sends out specially trained agents to aid the local police if so requested. The Office has limited executive powers. It maintains in the capital, Bonn, a special squad of detectives for the protection of the president, cabinet members, and the diplomatic corps.

The Federal Office of Crime Investigation handles all relations with foreign police and is the connecting link with the International Criminal Police Commission.

RUSSIA AND THE SATELLITE STATES

Just as the Gestapo became the symbol of Nazi Germany's police in the eyes of the rest of the world, so the term for the Russian political police, the MVD (formerly known as the NKVD, the Ogpu, and the

Cheka, which was the original organization), has come to stand for the Russian police. However, there does exist in Russia an ordinary police organization called the militia. The militia is divided into a uniformed branch and a detective branch, which have the same functions respectively as these forces have in the Western world. The detective branch is well trained and well equipped with modern police laboratories, the chief ones being in Moscow, Leningrad, and Odessa.

The overwhelming position of the MVD accounts for the fact that the militia is heard of very little. The MVD is a kind of state within the state and has, in a purely administrative way, power over life and death. Its spies are everywhere, although this is not to say that this is anything new for Russia, because even in czarist days the janitor in every house, and there is a janitor in every apartment house in Russia, was a member of the secret police organization. But it is to say that in Russia if a conspiracy consists of more than three people, it will inevitably leak out, as permanent informers of the MVD are found everywhere. This is a good explanation for the mutual distrust among the Russians. The MVD also has its own troops to guard the frontiers and the forced labor camps and must certainly be regarded as the largest and most peculiar police organization which ever existed. Needless to say, there is no connection whatsoever between the police of Russia and the police of the rest of the world.[8]

ITALY

In Italy the police function is a centralized state function. The Italian organization has no equivalent to the Anglo-Saxon police system, that is, independent local police. There is an ordinary police, consisting of a uniformed and a plain-clothes branch, and the *carabinieri,* whose functions and organization are about the same as those of the French *Gendarmerie.*

Police functions proper are performed by the state organs of Public Safety, divided into provincial and local. The provincial authority is represented by the *prefetto* and *questore* responsible for each of the ninety-one provinces of the Italian territory. The local authority is represented by the head of the Public Safety Field Office (Ufficio di Publica Sicurezza), or, where this office does not exist, by the Mayor of the Commune. At the top of the organization is the Ministry of the Interior's General Directorate of Public Safety, which directs, coordinates, and controls, on a national level, all police services, insuring proper unity and uniformity.

SWITZERLAND

There is no such thing as a national Swiss police. Switzerland is a federal republic, with every canton enjoying almost complete independence within the federal statutes. Defense and foreign affairs are federal matters, of course, but the policing of the cantons is their own affair. Each canton has an independent chief of police, and there is no central police authority. However, in Bern, the capital, there are a few federal offices dealing with police matters, i.e., a central fingerprint and criminal records bureau, a bureau dealing with counterfeiting, and a small political police force.

Questions concerning police matters in Switzerland can be addressed telegraphically to *Interpol,* Zurich, which will direct them to the attention of the proper authority.

BELGIUM

The structure of the Belgian police is really unique. There are a large number of small communal police forces, strictly territorial, following closely the development of urban sections. Brussels, the capital, is an outstanding example, with no less than seven different police forces, each with its own strictly defined territory. There is also a *gendarmerie,* organized much along the same lines as the French *Gendarmerie* and working chiefly in rural districts. In 1919 a central body for criminal investigation was organized, the so-called *police judiciaire* (judicial police), which now has divisions in all principal cities. Formally the judicial police is under the ministry of justice, but it is directed in all its activities by the district attorneys. The judicial police has its headquarters in Brussels and is commanded by a *Commissaire Général aux délégations judiciaires.* Also in Brussels, operating under the authority of the *Commissaire Général,* is the *Bureau Central de Documentation Nationale et Internationale de Police Criminelle,* which maintains all registers concerning criminals and crimes, publishes the police bulletins, and is charged with all liaison with foreign police forces.

A career in the judicial police requires the passing of several civil service examinations; advancement depends to a large extent on seniority. The actual strength of the judicial police is 850.

THE NETHERLANDS

In The Netherlands there are three types of police, the municipal police, the state police, and a military gendarmery called the *Royal*

Marechaussee. One hundred and twenty-seven cities have a municipal police force of their own, administered by the mayor (burgomaster). The small towns and rural districts are patrolled by the state police. The *Royal Marechaussee* is charged with frontier control and is also bodyguard to the royal house. The state police, which is directly under the minister of justice, is by far the most important force in The Netherlands. It is divided into five regional groups, corresponding to the court organization of the country. These five regions are divided into twenty-two districts. Each district has its own detectives and a motorized traffic group. There are also two river police districts, which have a fleet of seventy-five vessels with a total crew of about 400 men. The state and municipal police number about 20,000 men.

There are four police schools in the country for different ranks of police officers.

The Dutch police is headed by a director general, who is also charged with all relations with foreign police. A large scientific laboratory is attached to his offices in The Hague.

SCANDINAVIA

At one time the four Scandinavian countries, Sweden, Denmark, Finland, and Norway, all had police systems which were fairly alike, being built upon the principle of decentralization. Sweden, however, is now the only one of the four countries which has a decentralized police, the other three having yielded to the common Continental trend toward centralization in police businesses. As a rule each Swedish community pays and runs its own police and therefore has a deciding influence on its activities.

Since olden times Sweden has been divided into twenty-five provinces, including the capital, Stockholm, a province in itself. The police of Stockholm is under the command of a commissioner of police (*polismästare*), who is subject to the control of the governor of the city. The police force is communal anl the commissioner a communal employee, although he is appointed by the government. The force numbers about 2,000 men, including almost 500 detectives.

In the other twenty-four provinces there is an official (*landsfogde*) attached to the provincial government who is at the same time chief public prosecutor and chief of police for the province.[9]

All the police forces of a province are subordinate to the provincial public prosecutor, except in a few large cities where the chiefs of police are directly under the provincial governor.

Even in this decentralized police system, however, there are certain central institutions maintained by the national government, i.e., the National Institute of Technical Police and the Police School, both located in Stockholm, and the so-called state police, with headquarters in Stockholm.

The National Institute of Technical Police in many respects has the same functions as the Federal Bureau of Investigation. It keeps central files of fingerprints, *modus operandi,* etc.; serves as the central passport institution for the country and handles all relations with foreign police; publishes the police bulletin; and sends out specially trained agents for the examination of scenes of crime at the request of local authorities. It has extensive laboratories which are considered to be among the best in Europe.

The Police School in Stockholm is one of the most extensive in the world. The passing of its examinations is compulsory for every rank up to commissary of police (superintendent, English style; captain, American style) as well as police chiefs.

The state police set-up is rather unusual. This force is chiefly concerned with policing the rural districts and has branch offices in every provincial capital. The detectives and patrolmen are lent out from the local forces for a certain time but paid by the government, and the different state police forces are mainly handled by the chief public prosecutor of the province. The head of the state police is formally an assistant commissioner in the Stockholm police department.

The police forces of Sweden number about 8,000 men.

The police of Denmark is a governmental police headed by a director general (*rigspolitichef*), the commissioner of police of Copenhagen (*politidirektören*) enjoying a certain independence because of the largeness of the city. Denmark is divided into seventy-four police districts, each one with a chief of police, who is also in some respects a magistrate. The local police chiefs are all subordinate to the director general in Copenhagen.

The Danish police forces total about 3,500 men.

Before World War II, the Finnish police system was much like the Swedish pattern, because the Finnish administration was kept fairly intact after the country was separated from Sweden in 1809. World War II, however, has brought about certain changes. The police was nationalized in 1942 and a director general (*rikspolischef*) was appointed. The functions of this official, however, are more those of a connecting link between the secretary of the interior and the police, and he is not an executive head of the police in the ordinary meaning. In the capital, Helsinki, there is an institution called the Central Office of Criminal Investigation, an independent organization which maintains fingerprint and *modus operandi* files and a police laboratory. The Central Office also handles all relations with foreign police forces.

The Finnish police numbers about 4,500 men.

The police of Norway is nationalized but almost only insofar as salaries are concerned, the different chiefs of police operating quite independently, with the commissioner of police in Oslo (*politimesteren*) as a *primus inter pares*. There is no director general and no central executive head. The police of Oslo is entrusted with certain nation-wide police activities as regards fingerprints and police laboratories.

The Norwegian police numbers about 3,500 men.

THE INTERNATIONAL CRIMINAL POLICE COMMISSION (ICPC)

The shrinking of global distances brought about by the development of modern means of transporation has made it necessary for the police of the various countries of the world to cooperate on an international scale. It seemed obvious many years ago that this was an urgent necessity, and an attempt was made by international conferences to unify the penal laws and to establish a single treaty on extradition. At the first international congress of criminal police in Monaco in 1914 it was decided that these efforts would not be sufficient, and an endeavor was made to establish officially direct contacts between the different national police forces and to create a central office concerned with international criminals.

Figure 4.   F. E. Louwage.

The first world war prevented the immediate realization of these aims, and it was not until 1923, at the second international congress of criminal police of Europe at Vienna, Austria, that any concrete action was taken. At that time, under the auspices of Police Commissioner Schober of Vienna, the International Criminal Police Commission (ICPC, as it is commonly called) was created and its headquarters, together with those of its International Bureau, set up in Vienna, where both functioned for a number of years. By 1938 thirty-four countries were participating in the ICPC.

The activities of the Commission were disrupted by World War II, but after the war international crime increased so alarmingly that restoration of ICPC activities became imperative. In 1946 F. E. Louwage,[10] inspector general of police at the Belgian ministry of justice, initiated the reconstitution of the ICPC, and during the course of a year a reunion was held in Brussels in which nineteen countries participated. There it was decided that the headquarters of the Commission should be transferred to Paris effective June 15, 1946, and set up within the premises of the ministry of the interior, in the headquarters of the *Police Nationale*.

The following thirty-five countries now belong to the ICPC:

Argentina	Greece	Poland
Australia	Guatemala	Portugal
Austria	Hungary	South Africa
Belgium	Iceland	Sweden
Bulgaria	India	Switzerland
Canada	Iran	Tangier
Czechoslovakia	Israel	Trieste (English–
Denmark	Italy	American zone)
Egypt	Lebanon	Turkey
Finland	Luxembourg	United States[11]
France	The Netherlands	Venezuela
Great Britain	Norway	Yugoslavia

The purpose of the ICPC as given in its statutes is to insure and promote the greatest possible mutual assistance between all police authorities within the limits of the laws existing in the different countries and to establish and develop institutions likely to contribute to an efficient repression of common law crimes, strictly excluding all matters having a political, religious, or racial character.

The ICPC includes active members, delegated by their respective governments, as well as extraordinary members, elected because of services rendered to the Commission or because of their technical or scientific knowledge. The Commission has general assemblies once a year at which different problems concerning the prevention and repression of criminality are discussed. Since 1923, eighteen general assemblies have been held. In recent years important questions regarding extradition, juvenile delinquency, narcotics, counterfeiting, and technical police have been taken up for discussion.

The board of the ICPC includes one president and seven vice presi-

dents. The president is assisted by three general reporters and one secretary general, forming the executive committee. This committee exe-
cutes the resolutions made by the general assemblies, supervises the International Bureau and other institutions belonging to the Commission,
and handles preparations for the general assemblies. An assembly of
ten reporters is entrusted with elaborating reports on questions submitted to the general assembly.

All major problems concerning criminality and technical police are
studied by subcommissions of specialists, which are under the presi-
dency of the heads of the most important police forces of the world and
the most eminent technicians. The subcommissions deal with problems
of counterfeiting, narcotics, technical police, air police, etc.

The International Bureau is also joined to the general secretariat in
Paris and constitutes a world center for the solving of international police problems. Its activities include searching for and pursuing international criminals; establishing files containing all information received
from the different police forces, which information may, if requested, be
circulated by means of individual notices; and assisting in the provisory
arrest of international criminals, when extradition is demanded. A
special section devoted to counterfeiting correlates all information regarding genuine and counterfeit money and documents.

The International Bureau thus forms the connecting link between the
different national bureaus existing in each adherent country and concerned with crime problems of their respective countries.

The press and a radio-telegraphic network aid the International Bureau in tracing international criminals. A review of its own, the *International Criminal Police Review,* is published in French and English and
contains articles on criminology and technical police as well as retro-
spective lists of the international criminals appearing in the above-
mentioned individual notices. The lists contain full particulars of identity
and reasons for the inquiry and may constitute real international warrants. Another review, entitled *Counterfeits and Forgeries,* deals with
genuine and counterfeit money. Bank establishments as well as organizations concerned with issuing of currency subscribe to this review.

The radio-telegraphic network, which insures the prompt dissemina-
tion of information, is directed from Paris and at present includes fifteen
stations. All national bureaus of the ICPC have adopted the telegraphic
address of "Interpol." Under present circumstances there is only one exception; namely, for Western Germany, which can be reached under the
telegraphic address "Interpolice" at Hamburg.

The library of the International Bureau supplies the member countries with many interesting technical articles and reports. Here also are filed all documents and reports on questions submitted for the consideration of the International Bureau through the general assemblies and through international conferences at which the ICPC has been represented. Among the latter are conferences held by societies of penal law and, particularly, by the United Nations. This organization usually applies to the Commission on such questions as passports, suppression of crime, treatment of criminals, and white-slave traffic.

1 François Vidocq was born in 1775 in Arras, France, and died in 1857 in Paris. He ran away from his father's home and after an adventurous youth as a soldier in one of the French revolutionary armies was sent to the galleys for forgery. Then for many years he played the role of a Houdini, walking in and out of French prisons. A daring man, with a masterful mind and a thorough knowledge of French criminals, their language, and their methods, he became in time a police spy and in 1816 was promoted to the office of chief of the *Sûreté* of Paris. He worked so efficiently in wiping out crime in Paris that he won the admiration of his contemporaries and became quite a legendary figure. In 1832 Vidocq was removed from office as a result of intrigues among his own collaborators. There are a great number of books dealing with his adventurous life, but most of them must certainly be regarded as pure fiction. Even his so-called memoirs, which appeared during his lifetime, were written by a ghost writer who used much of his own fancy. In 1832 the French parliament passed a regulation prohibiting an ex-convict from becoming a police officer.

2 For a fuller picture of the United States police systems read the excellent book by Bruce Smith.[2]

3 Of particular interest are the excellent training facilities which the Federal Bureau of Investigation offers smaller communities in the National Police Academy in Washington. Some State and municipal police schools offer similar service.

4 William S. Seavey, Omaha, Nebraska, founder and first president (1893–1895) of the International Association of Chiefs of Police. This organization (originally called the National Chiefs of Police Union) was founded in May, 1893, when fifty-one chiefs of police of the United States met in Chicago at the request of Chief Seavey of the Omaha police to discuss matters of mutual interest and take steps toward establishing a nation-wide system of cooperation in the suppression of crime and apprehension of criminals and the forming of a voluntary association of police officials to hold regularly scheduled meetings.

In October, 1897, the Association established in Chicago the National Police Bureau of Identification, a central office for the maintenance of fingerprint records. The Bureau was moved to Washington in May, 1902, and set up at the Metropolitan Police Headquarters of the District of Columbia. For the next twenty years the Association actively campaigned for the passage of legislation authorizing a federally operated identification bureau, and finally, in 1924, the identification bureau of the Federal Bureau of Investigation was created. In the same year the fingerprint records of the IACP, together with those of the Federal penitentiary at Leavenworth, Kansas, were turned over to the FBI. The IACP now has over two thousand members in the United States, Canada, and fifteen other countries.

5 According to Bruce Smith,[2] the following agencies of the United States government have auxiliary police authority:

1. Public Health Service (Department of Health, Education, and Welfare), which prevents the introduction of communicable diseases into the United States and their interstate spread
2. Bureau of Land Management (Department of the Interior), which investigates matters relating to the survey, management, and disposition of public lands and arranges for the protection of surface resources
3. Various bureaus in the Department of Agriculture
4. Various bureaus in the Department of Commerce
5. The Veterans' Administration, which, through a force of field examiners under the Solicitor, seeks to protect the Federal government from fraudulent claims made by veterans and their dependents
6. Two personnel units—the United States Civil Service Commission and the Bureau of Employees' Compensation of the Department of Labor—which also investigate fraudulent misrepresentations as a part of their regular administrative functioning
7. Federal Maritime Board (Department of Commerce), which has assumed some of the functions of the former United States Maritime Commission
8. Various more or less independent agencies concerned either wholly or in part with unlawful trade practices—Federal Trade Commission, Securities and Exchange Commission, Federal Communications Commission, Interstate Commerce Commission
9. National Park Service (Department of the Interior), Bureau of Indian Affairs (Department of the Interior), Office of Territories (Department of the Interior), and the Canal Zone Government. All these agencies exercise police authority but within narrowly circumscribed geographical limits.

6 John Edgar Hoover, Director of the Federal Bureau of Investigation, United States Department of Justice; born in District of Columbia, January 1, 1895; educated at George Washington University. Hoover entered the Department of Justice in 1917 and was appointed Special Assistant to the Attorney General in 1919. From 1921 to 1924 Hoover was Assistant Director, Bureau of Investigation, and was made Director in 1924. He is regarded as one of the foremost policemen of our century, having developed the FBI from an inconsequential body to its present status as one of the largest organizations of its kind in the world.

7 Sir Robert Peel, famous English statesman, 1788–1850. In 1829, as home secretary in the cabinet of Wellington, he got the consent of Parliament to found the Metropolitan Police in London. The idea of a regular police system at first met with much resistance, the public fearing that it would be a means for oppressing them. However, in a few decades the Metropolitan Police, by their kindness, politeness, patience, and honesty toward the public, achieved a popularity unique of its kind.

8 One of the authors had the good fortune to study the Russian militia for about a month in 1931.

9 This is a very doubtful combination and has been subject to much discussion.

10 F. E. Louwage, President of the International Criminal Police Commission. Louwage, who was born in 1888 in Calloo, Belgium, has made his career in the Belgian police, which he entered in 1909. He served as an infantry officer in the first world war and in 1928 became chief of the Belgian CID (*police judiciaire*). Even before World War II, he was a leading figure in the ICPC, and when the Commission was reorganized in 1946, he was unanimously elected its president. Louwage is regarded as one of the foremost policemen of our time and is the author of several treatises dealing with crime.

11 The United States is not an ordinary member of the ICPC, but the United States Secret Service and the Bureau of Narcotics in Washington maintain certain relations with the organization in connection with counterfeiting and narcotics.

III PSYCHOLOGY IN DETECTIVE SERVICE

AN UNDERSTANDING OF PSYCHOLOGY AND OF VARIOUS PSYCHOPATHIC personalities can be of immeasurable assistance to the criminal investigator. It is almost a prerequisite for the interrogator of witnesses and suspects, for he must not only utilize psychology in his interrogations but must also be able to place the proper evaluation on the evidence of the various personality types he may be called upon to question. Such an understanding may be invaluable to the detective also in determining motives for crimes and in tracking down and handling criminals. In this chapter we shall discuss briefly some of the problems and devices of the interrogator and some of the psychopathic and neurotic personalities whose actions and motives may prove puzzling to the detective unless he has a basic understanding of the reasons for their behavior.

GENERAL REMARKS ABOUT QUESTIONING

The interrogation should be conducted as soon as possible after the commission of the crime. Each person should be heard individually, and none of the suspects or witnesses should be allowed to hear the questioning of the others. If possible, the principal witnesses, especially the most trustworthy ones, should be heard before the suspect is questioned, in order that the interrogator may be sufficiently informed.

The method of questioning varies widely according to the mentality of the questioned person, his age and race, sex, religious and political views, social status, and education. A good interrogator must therefore be highly experienced, with a keen comprehension of the psychology of the questioned person, thus being able to understand his mentality and behavior from moment to moment. Seriousness, kindness, and patience also are necessary. To force a witness to give information or a suspect to admit his guilt by threatening him, frightening him, injuring him, or by giving him false information regarding the state of the investigation is discreditable, unnecessary, and unwise.

27

The questioning should be fair, legitimate, and unprejudiced. All circumstances favoring the suspect and apt to prove his innocence should be carefully investigated. It should never be forgotten that a suspect may be innocent even though the adverse evidence momentarily seems to be strong and the interrogator is convinced of his guilt. The ability to be impartial and free from prejudice is a signal virtue of the superior interrogator.

SUGGESTIVE QUESTIONS. The questions should be clear and unambiguous. They should not be so formulated as to lead the questioned person to answer in a certain direction or suggest the answer to him. Such questions are called suggestive questions and should be avoided. For example, if the question is put in this way, "Did the man you met have on a black or a brown hat?" the person is led to think of a hat. The question should be, "What headgear did the man you met have on?" The interrogator must be careful not to infer meaning nor to put words in the mouths of those unable to express themselves clearly. Such questions as, "It was so that—, wasn't it?" should be avoided. With aliens, interpreters can often clarify idiomatic expressions if the meaning is not clear to the interrogator.

THE DENOUNCER—WHO IS HE?

The value of the denunciation has first to be established, and the facts or probabilities checked. The denunciation may be such that no investigation has to follow; it may be due to a monomaniacal idea of the denouncer or he may be insane or a crank. It may also be a mistake, as when, for example, a lost object is still in the possession of the owner, without his knowledge.

The denunciation may also be false, as in cases where the denouncer is trying to harm the antagonist or to protect himself or to gain some advantage, as, for example, by simulated thefts, assaults, and burglaries. When something of this kind is suspected, the statement of the denouncer must be checked up on at the scene (see "Simulated Burglaries" in Chapter XXI) and all persons who may have information to give carefully questioned.

THE SUSPECT

Before the suspect is questioned, the preliminary investigation should be finished, i.e., the scene of the crime examined, evidence of a technical nature collected and examined, the residence and office—or workshop—of the suspect searched, and as much information as possible gathered. The interrogator must know all the facts thoroughly and possess the ability to keep them together. The latter is an art which is not acquired at once.

The interrogation should be made in such a manner that the road to admission (confession) is made easier for the suspect. Such expressions as murder, rape, burglary, etc., should not be used, but more neutral words employed, especially when a young suspect or woman is questioned. People who have already served a penal term as a rule are not so sensitive.

The success of the interrogation often depends on where it takes place. The presence of parents, relatives, or friends may prevent the suspect from speaking openly. The same applies if the questioning is conducted in his house, or in the place where the suspect works, or in the presence of employers or co-workers.

If the suspect confesses wholly or partly or gives important information, the goal of questioning is achieved and the interrogation may then be concentrated on important parts of the events leading to the crime.

If, on the contrary, the suspect pleads innocence, the success of the interrogator depends upon the evidence gathered and his ability to plan and do the questioning. The suspect should never get any information regarding the investigation or the evidence at hand. In many cases he should not even know why he is being questioned. If little evidence is present, the interrogator has to complete the evidence through the suspect. It would be a fatal error to accuse him. He should be handled as a witness. No shadow of suspicion should be apparent.

The interrogation in such cases is founded on the experience that it is difficult to lie consecutively and logically. The interrogation should not consist only of questions from the interrogator and answers from the suspect. The latter should have an opportunity to give his own account of things. If the interrogator knows that the account is untrue he should not show it. The more the suspect lies, the weaker his position becomes later on.

If several persons are suspected of the crime, they should, if possible, be questioned at the same time and in the same manner, but not together. In one case, for instance, a merchant had been robbed and killed. Several years afterward the police got vague information that a waiter, T——, and his wife were probably the murderers. No motive was given. After a careful investigation, the pair were arrested and questioned along the same lines. To start with, they were compelled to give a thorough account of their common lives. The investigation brought to light the fact that T—— had committed some small thefts. The suspects were next questioned about their economic condition and then about the thefts. Not a word was said about the murder. Several facts of importance bearing on the murder were in this manner unconsciously revealed. Finally there was enough evidence to open a murder trial.[1] There is no doubt that if the interrogation from the beginning had been directed toward the murder, the pair would have grown suspicious and never hinted a word which would have served as a guide.

It is a good practical rule that the more meager the evidence, the later the suspect should be allowed to know of it. In another case a girl was assaulted, robbed, and killed. A young man was arrested on no other suspicion than that he had made several large purchases the same day, although he was known to be absolutely without funds. When he was first questioned, the murder was not mentioned, but he told about his life, his means of earning a living, and so on. This did not arouse his suspicions, because he was an ex-convict and accustomed to being interrogated. Under this interrogation it was discovered that he was penniless the day the murder was committed.

If the interrogation had sought to establish where he had obtained the money for his purchases, his attention would have been directed to this point, thus putting him on his guard. By the method used, he was prevented from answering, for instance, that he had won at cards or from admitting some burglary to avoid the murder issue.

If a confession is obtained, the details of the crime must still be proved. For example, in burglary the manner in which the burglar broke into the house and in which he left, what tools he used, in what room the goods were stolen, how the stolen objects were kept and where they were hidden, whether he had accomplices or not, and so on. In important crimes criminals should be taken to the scene of the crime, especially when there is suspicion that guilt will be denied before the courts. Such a reconstruction is a very effective method of proving the value of a confession. Careful notes on the reconstruction and what the suspect said should be kept.[2]

DETECTING DECEPTION—THE LIE DETECTOR

Ideally, the interrogator should be a practical psychologist whose investigative experience, knowledge of human nature, and insight into criminal behavior permit him to discern when he is being misled by fabrications and also when the subject's plea of ignorance of facts has the ring of truth. To distinguish truth from falsehood, particularly in a situation that conduces to lying, is an ability which exists naturally in some investigators and may be developed in others through observation and practice. But the ability carries only a very limited assurance; the interrogator is often puzzled by the subject and sometimes deceived and misled.

Aside from the internal logic and the consistency of the subject's statements, the interrogator frequently has only the visible reactions of the person's features and mannerisms to guide him. In drawing conclusions as to the subject's truthfulness on the basis of physical reactions to key questions, the investigator is unconsciously serving the function of a lie detector. He is relying on the same fundamental principle: the mental state of a person influences the bodily functions. A suspect's emotions will effect certain physiological changes such as a quickened heartbeat, a difference in breathing, blushing, perspiring, and dryness of the mouth. The brain reacts to emotional conditions by transmitting through the nervous system the impulses which regulate the body's vital functions.

The psychological and physical stimulation that are experienced during an interrogation result, then, in autonomic changes—changes which are self-regulating and difficult to control consciously. A number of these changes, moreover, are measurable and can be recorded and interpreted with reasonable accuracy.[3] A mechanical aid for recording these changes is in effect a lie detector.

The results of some fifty years of experimenting in search of reliable indicators of emotional stress have established blood pressure and respiration as the two most useful bodily functions for this purpose. Changes in body chemistry, electrodermal changes, and other stress effects which have been tried do not meet to the same degree the requirements of reliability and facility of measurement. Blood pressure and respiration, moreover, can be measured with conventional medical instruments. Changes in these functions can be recorded by additional instrumentation to provide a reliable pattern of the subject's reactions to emotional stress.

The early experiments of Lombroso and Benussi with blood pressure and respiration symptoms of deception were followed by actual case testing by Marston, Burtt, and Larson. The first instrument for continuously recording blood pressure, pulse, and respiration was devised by

Larson. Several years later Keeler developed a more satisfactory recording unit and also an effective test procedure and method of deception
diagnosis. The contributions of Reid and others have since improved
both the instrumentation and testing technique. The instrument shown
in Figure 5 records changes in blood pressure, pulse rate, and breathing, and in the resistance of the skin to the flow of a mild electrical current.

THE LIE DETECTION PROCESS.[4] The "Lie Detector" or mechanism by which changes in respiration and circulation are measured is
simply an instrumental aid to the examiner. It does not detect lies as
such. By far the more important element in the lie detection process is

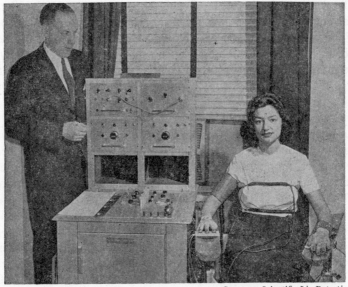

Courtesy, Scientific Lie Detection, Inc.

Figure 5.   The Arther Polygraph, constructed by C. H. Stoelting Co., measures pulse and blood pressure, chest breathing, stomach breathing, galvanic
skin response, and skin temperature changes.

the qualified examiner whose education, training, and experience enable him to determine whether the charts provided by the instrument
contain a meaningful pattern. The interpretation of the recorded charts
is of critical importance. Without a suitable background in psychology,
physiology, and scientific method, the operator of the lie detector may

be little more than a shrewd mechanic, using the instrument to support conclusions already half-drawn on the basis of experience and intuition.

In the process of lie detection the examiner endeavors at the outset to determine the subject's "normal" reactions through a series of questions irrelevant to the issues of the case. From another series, in which key questions have been injected, he can observe the person's reactions to what should be a situation of stress. For example, if a murder has been committed with a knife and the nature of the weapon is not generally known, the examiner, by skillful questioning about the weapon, should be able to elicit a greater change in the respiratory and circulatory charts from a suspect with guilty knowledge, i.e., a person who knows that a knife was used and recognizes a description of the weapon.

From a set of these and other data, systematically obtained from a suspect, the lie detector examiner sifts out the factors of ordinary nervousness and anxiety caused by the implications of the crime, the police setting, and the instrument itself. Finally he makes his judgment as to whether the indications of emotional stress which he observes are the product of fear induced by guilty knowledge. He may be unable to draw any conclusion if the charts present no statistically reliable differences in intensities or rates of reaction.

In summary, then, the lie detector is simply an instrument for measuring certain bodily changes caused by emotion. In the hands of a qualified examiner the lie detector is a valuable aid to interrogation and is often an effective means of detecting efforts to suppress guilty knowledge. The lie detection process involves a thorough and professional examination, requiring extended effort, preparation, concentration, and time on the part of the operator. Hence, the attitude of "Let's put them on the lie box" should be firmly discouraged where the instrument is being used merely for a routine screening process. A lie detection examination is not intended to replace the normal investigative effort whereby unlikely suspects are readily eliminated through a check of activities and background.

OBJECTIVES. We eliminate first the naive notion that the primary function of the lie detector is to establish the guilt of the subject. The purpose for which a lie detection examination is conducted will, of course, vary with the nature of the case and the status of the subject (i.e., whether he is a witness or a suspect), but will, in general, include one or more of the following objectives:

To ascertain if the subject is telling the truth.

To test or compare inconsistent statements.

To verify assumptions made by the investigators and statements made by the suspect before the examination, i.e., the suspect's "story" is tested by the examiner.

To obtain the facts when the test indicates that the person lied or failed to reveal his full knowledge.

To develop leads to important facts of the crime, such as the whereabouts of a wanted person or the location of stolen goods.

SUBJECTS AND REACTIONS. The examiner does not assume that the emotion prompting a strong reaction is necessarily caused by fear of disclosure of guilt. He is aware of the many other causes of fear and anxiety and appreciates the great variations in emotional intensity to be found in any group of people. As part of his examination, he must classify the subject's emotional type and establish a norm of emotional reactions for the subject under the given circumstances. The predominant cause of the subject's emotional condition is fear. It is the source of this fear that is the examiner's concern.

Innocent persons are usually cooperative and often volunteer to take the test in their eagerness to prove their innocence. The fear and nervousness affecting an innocent person in this situation ordinarily decrease as the test progresses.

A *guilty person* is usually beset by an overriding but logical fear of being found out. There is also the associated dread of being disgraced, imprisoned, and committed to a bleak and precarious future. His immediate apprehension, however, is concerned with being trapped in falsehood and inconsistency. These fears will vary, of course, with the guilty person's character, criminal experience, and with the nature of his offense. The hardened criminal, viewing the proceedings more professionally, will devote his attention to the practical problem of "beating the machine." Toward the other end of the spectrum of compunction are those guilty persons who immediately succumb to a dread of the machine—either from an awe of gadgetry or a superstitious belief in the efficacy of science—and make admissions prior to the test.

Suitability of the subject for a lie detector test is a consideration when his condition, mental or physical, might prohibit a reliable examination. A psychologist or a psychiatrist should be requested to resolve any substantial doubts regarding the subject's mental fitness; physical afflictions affecting suitability should be examined by a physician.

Since the lie detector examination relies upon emotional reactions associated with a moral sense of right and wrong, mental illness or excessively low intelligence may render the subject unsuitable by reason of his inability to form moral judgments and his insensitivity to the moral aspects of the offense under investigation and to the ethical implications of lying. Failing to apprehend the distinction between right and wrong or to understand the purpose of the test, such a person cannot provide a stable, intelligible, and significant pattern of emotional reactions.

Physical afflictions of a temporary nature may also affect the subject's suitability. A person who is suffering from a severe injury or from an allergy or a respiratory affection of a serious nature may at the time be unfit to be tested. Obviously a drunken person should not be examined until he is reasonably sober.

PREPARATION FOR THE TEST. Since the lie detector test relies basically on a series of key questions designed to elicit a reaction from the subject, together with a series of indifferent questions designed to establish the subject's normal reactions, the examiner must be provided before the test with information on the details of the crime and the subject's background. The investigator, in briefing the examiner on the known facts, should provide, in particular, those details which have not been publicized and hence are known only to the victim, the perpetrator, and the police.

A pretest interview of the suspect may be conducted for this purpose provided care is taken to avoid the disclosure of any significant details of the crime. Bluffs, tricks, deception, and other ruses also should be avoided at this time. If the subject is questioned extensively on the details of the crime prior to the test, it will become difficult for the examiner later to evoke the strong emotional response that should accompany a first intrusion on guilty knowledge.

Explaining the test and the function of the lie detector to the subject is desirable, since his cooperation is necessary for the test. Emphasis should be placed on the examiner's impartiality and on the fact that the test can serve also to indicate innocence.

Treatment of a suspect before the test should include the normal comforts of food, exercise, and rest, but communication should not be permitted with another suspect. The suspect should not be subjected to stress situations; anxieties and fears artificially created may serve only to add confustion to the test patern. During the test the suspect should be alone with the examiner in a private room, free from noise and interruptions.

TEST PROCEDURES. The exact procedure varies to some degree with the person tested and the facts of each case, but two major techniques are used—the general question test and the peak of tension test.

The general question test consists of relevant (concerning the offense) and irrelevant (not concerning the offense) questions asked in a planned order. The relevant questions are asked in order to obtain a specific response. The irrelevant questions are asked to give the subject relief after pertinent questions and to establish a normal tracing on the test chart. The questions are so arranged that a specific reaction to a relevant question can be compared with a normal tracing made during the answering of an irrelevant question. The reaction may be strong enough to indicate that the subject either did not tell the truth or was unduly disturbed by the question. In the general question test, the subject usually does not know beforehand what questions are to be asked. Repeat tests are used.

The peak of tension test depends on the building up of a crisis of internal emotional disturbance through a series of questions in which the subject knows there is imbedded a key or climactic question, related to a specific detail of the offense. The subject is usually told beforehand the questions that are to be asked. The test chart of a subject who is not telling the truth or who is otherwise unduly disturbed usually shows a rise in the tracing up to the relevant question (peak of tension) and a decline thereafter. The rise is attributable to the subject's anticipation or dread of the question to which he knows he is going to lie. The decline follows the relief of knowing that the dreaded question is past. The peak of tension test is most effective when the examiner has knowledge of some unpublicized details of the crime. It may also be used by the examiner to probe for a weakness in the subject's testimony. Variations of this technique are used as preliminary tests to ascertain if the subject is capable of giving a reliable response, i.e., he possesses an insensitivity, or control of his sensitivity, which will militate against a meaningful reaction.

ILLUSTRATIVE CASE.[5] The questioning techniques described above will best be illustrated by several elementary question series taken from an actual case, in this instance a homicide which took place on a military post. Sergeant Allen Rowe was found dead in the dayroom of Company A, 916 Infantry. He was killed by a bullet fired from a caliber .45 weapon. Rowe's wallet, which, according to friends, contained about $500, was found beside his body, empty. Investigation revealed Private John Simpson as a suspect in the murder and robbery of Sergeant Rowe. Simpson was promptly brought in for a lie detector test.

The examiner decided to test him first by the general question test and then by the peak of tension test.

General question test. The following is a sample series of the questions used: (Note that questions *3, 4, 6, 7,* and *9* are relevant to the case.)

1. Is your last name Simpson?
2. Are you over 21?
3. Do you know who shot Rowe?
4. Did you shoot Rowe?
5. Were you born in Indiana?
6. Did you take Rowe's money?
7. Did you shoot a caliber .45 pistol last night?
8. Is your hair brown?
9. Have you answered my questions truthfully?

Peak of tension test. Since the details of the murder and robbery had not been made public and the investigators had not mentioned specific facts to Simpson, the suspect, the following peak of tension tests were used:

First Test.

1. Did you stab a man?   4. Did you shoot a man?
2. Did you poison a man?   5. Did you hang a man?
3. Did you drown a man?   6. Did you strangle a man?

Second Test.

1. Did you shoot a submachine gun last night?
2. Did you shoot a carbine last night?
3. Did you shoot an M-1 rifle last night?
4. Did you shoot a caliber .45 pistol last night?
5. Did you shoot a cannon last night?
6. Did you shoot a shotgun last night?
7. Did you shoot a caliber .22 rifle last night?

POST-TEST QUESTIONING. It should not be expected that the examiner will be able to reach a positive conclusion in every case, but he will often be able to form some useful opinions from a study of his charts. The test may, for example, indicate that the suspect is innocent and hence that investigative effort would be better employed in other directions. On the other hand, the examiner may conclude that the suspect is untruthful on certain points or that he reacts intensely to certain questions. These points should form the basis of leads and provide examiner and investigator with material for interrogation after the test.

SOURCES OF FAILURE. The two major causes of failure in a lie detector examination are the lack of suitability of the subject and the lack of preparation on the part of the examiner and investigator. A test may be inconclusive for other reasons. Postponing the test until the last minute; employing the test as a last resort when other methods appear to have failed; letting the suspect learn too much about the offense before the test; incomplete investigation of the case; failure to develop background information concerning the subject—all of these circumstances and oversights can render the examination ineffective.

Finally, the results of the test should be properly evaluated. The lie detector does not decide whether the suspect is innocent or guilty. It simply is an aid to determining whether the person is telling the truth. Hence, if the test indicates that the suspect is lying or if the suspect confesses after the test, the work of the investigator is far from completed. As the case now stands, he possesses a number of leads. Testimony of witnesses and other evidence must be gathered to prove the facts establishing the elements of the offense. The lie detector has not eliminated any of the essential work of the investigation; it has, however, provided us with useful leads, and saved us a great deal of investigative time. It may even have induced the suspect to confess.

WITNESSES

The interrogation of a witness must also be formulated according to his mentality. Some witnesses must be handled with sternness, but as a rule best results are obtained through kindness and patience. The difficulty lies in determining when a witness consciously hides or gives false information, because witnesses often unwittingly give false information without any desire to mislead the interrogator. Low intelligence, illness, lack of education, etc., may cause a witness who tries to speak the truth to give false information unconsciously or to recite things known only through hearsay as if they were parts of a personal experience. (See "Criticism of Human Testimony," later in this chapter.)

At times a person may be reluctant because he does not like to be involved in a trial. He may be a friend of the suspect or have business connections with him. He may be unwilling to go before the court and may not like publicity. He may have economic reasons, such as loss of salary for the time spent in court as a witness. He may dislike the police authorities. He may pity the suspect, or he may avoid speaking because of the annoyance it would cause him later. There may be many other reasons why he declares that he has no knowledge of the matter. Such occasions place great responsibility on the interrogator. He must not only attempt to understand the motive for the reluctance but create a new interest for the witness. Tactfulness, diplomacy, and patience will help a good deal in such cases. Generally, very little will be achieved by threats and severity, although, if a real egotistical motive for the reluctance has been established, the interrogator should always proceed with sternness and determination. Here, as always when it is suspected that the witness is hiding something or giving false information, the motive for his acts must be established.

Unreliable persons or liars should always be allowed to talk as much as they like. If such a witness is allowed to give his own account of things related to the investigation, he will finally contradict himself and tell the truth. It is very difficult, not to say impossible, to lie consistently.

From shy and nervous persons it is usually necessary to drag out information piece by piece. There is a lot of uncertainty about such testimony, and it is difficult to get any real facts in such cases. The interrogator should be as gentle as possible. The interrogation should be held, if practicable, in the milieu or environment of the person and in the form of casual questions and conversation rather than as a formal interrogation; i.e., the detective should act as a casual visitor having a chat about the case.

The garrulous person presents many difficulties. Although patience may be strained to a high degree, it is necessary to let him give his own account. The interrogator, through cautious questions, must keep the witness on the right path. The risk of misunderstanding such witnesses is great if they are not allowed to use their own expressions, and they are also apt to give exaggerated and false information. Leads and statements in such cases must be well sifted and controlled.

Children are generally good witnesses when handled with care. They are keen observers, especially boys of ten to fifteen years of age on questions regarding phenomena of nature and girls of twelve to fifteen on personal and intimate occurrences in their environment.

Until recent years it was believed that children were generally extremely susceptible to personal suggestions. Modern witness psychologists, however, have proved that children react very individually to suggestions. A fatherly and friendly tone is used in order to give them confidence and encourage them to talk. They should be told to tell only about their actual experiences and not what they have heard. Children easily confuse their own experiences with those of others.

Persons in their early twenties are not looked upon as good witnesses because they are occupied with themselves and their own affairs and do not care for things which do not pertain to them personally.

Persons of advanced age may have keen powers of observation of details, especially in regard to things in their own sphere of activity.

In all interrogations of witnesses it is best to have a certain amount of suspicion, even if the witness seems to be truthful and serious. As a rule he should first be allowed to give an account in his own way. When he has finished, he should be made to furnish, through cautious questions, details which the interrogator desires to know. The real interrogation then should begin. Details of importance should be examined and eventual contradictions revealed to him if necessary. If memory fails him about the time of an occurrence, it may be jogged by asking him about some associated idea, as, for instance, what he did on the day in question. In order to get precise facts about positions and other details it is better if the interrogation is made on the scene of the crime.

CRITICISM OF HUMAN TESTIMONY

In the preceding pages we have attempted to give some practical advice as to how to conduct the interrogation of suspects, criminals, and witnesses. We have stressed how the interrogator should attempt to adjust himself to the individual in order to obtain the best possible results. In an ideal interrogation the questioner should be able to enter into the process of the criminal action as vividly as possible. There is, however, a link between the actual events and the witness. No matter how well the interrogator adjusts himself to the witness and how precisely he induces the witness to describe his observations, mistakes still can be made. The mistakes made by an experienced interrogator may be comparatively few, but as far as the witness is concerned his path is full of pitfalls. Modern witness psychology has shown that even the most honest and trustworthy witnesses are apt to make grave mistakes in good faith. It is therefore necessary that the interrogator get an idea of the weak links in the testimony in order to check up on them in the event that something appears to be strange or not quite satisfactory.

Unfortunately, modern witness psychology does not yet offer any means of directly testing the credibility of testimony. It lacks precision and method, in spite of worthwhile attempts on the part of such learned men as Binet, Gross, Stein, Lipmann, Gorphe, Locard, and others. It does not therefore lead to definite ways of achieving certainty. At the same time, witness psychology, through the gathering of many experiences concerning the weaknesses of human testimony, has been of invaluable service to criminology. It shows clearly that only evidence of a technical nature has absolute value as proof.

Testimony presents three different aspects. The witness sees the occurrence, fixes it in his memory, and expresses it. In agreement with Locard the testimony may be separated into the following stages: (1) perception; (2) observation; (3) mind fixation of the observed occurrences, in which procedure fantasy, association of idea, and personal judgment participate; (4) expression in oral or written form, where the testimony is transferred from one witness to another or to the interrogator.

Figure 6.   Edmond Locard.

Each of these stages offers innumerable possibilities of distorting testimony. In the following pages we shall study some of these possibilities, following chiefly the ideas of Locard,[6] Gorphe,[7] and Sternack,[8] who have examined the problem from a thoroughly practical angle.

PERCEPTION. This is a stage of testimony which may be verified readily. A witness states, for instance, that a certain occurrence took place in a mill at a certain definite time. "How do you know the exact time?"

"I heard a clock strike the time."

An investigation at the scene of the crime shows that the noise coming from the mill completely drowns the sound of the clock, even to a very sensitive ear. The witness then remembers that he heard the clock strike only on leaving the mill.

Lacassagne, the famous French specialist of legal medicine, describes a case of this kind in which a man was accused of a number of sex offenses. Lacassagne proved that from where the accuser said he had witnessed the occurrence, it was impossible even to see the accused man. Many similar cases could be cited. This example shows clearly that one must place oneself in an absolutely identical situation in order to verify the testimony.

OBSERVATION. Bertillon has wisely said, "One can only see what one observes, and one observes only things which are already in the mind." Unfortunately, there are often many details which are important for the investigation but which were of no interest to the witness at the moment he perceived them. He simply did not pay attention to them and as a rule does not know them or at best has only a meager knowledge of them.

The sense of touch is one of the deceptive perceptions. In most persons it is very slightly developed unless controlled by eyesight. This naturally deceptive perception may lead to serious mistakes. If the witness, for instance, contends that he recognized an object in the dark merely by touching it, his testimony must be regarded with the greatest suspicion. It is an entirely different matter when the witness is blind, for then the touch perception may be so highly developed that his testimony can be regarded as having real value and application.

Figure 7.   Hans Gross.

Olfactory experiences and the *sense of taste* are also unreliable. In poisoning cases, for instance, the witness finds difficulty in determining the various sensations experienced. It is also difficult for him to express himself clearly in definite terminology. The objective sensation of smell or taste is easily replaced by the witness's conception of the good or bad taste which he experienced. It is well known that taste is individual, and as Locard pointed out, "It depends upon the taste of the individual whether the smell of a rotten pheasant makes him think of corpses and cadavers or places him in a condition of culinary happiness."

It is possible also to have a sensation of smell without the presence of any smell. Schneickert[9] reported a case in Berlin in 1905 in which a girl named Lucy Berlin, nine years old, had been murdered and mutilated in a house at No. 130 Ackerstrasse. On the sixteenth of June some boys playing on the banks of Lake Plötzensee found the head and the arms of the child, and on the seventeenth of June her legs and torso were discovered. On the sixteenth of June, however, before the discovery of the legs and torso, several persons reported to the police that they had sensed a strong odor of burnt flesh in the vicinity of the scene of the crime and especially in the neighborhood of Nos. 125-130 Ackerstrasse. The thought prevailed that it must have been the murderer burning the missing parts of the body. Their perception of the smell was therefore a mere suggestion which may have had its origin in the fact that in 1904 a similar murder had been committed and the corpse had been burned.

Aural experiences take an intermediate position between the senses of touch, taste, and smell and the sense of sight, which is the most objective of all human senses. It is necessary, however, to make a careful distinction between mechanical noises and the sound of the human voice. Also the observation of a sound is often unclear and subjective. A loud noise may appear to have been produced nearby, while a weak sound may seem to have been transmitted from some distance. This difficulty of estimating the distance from the site at which the sound is produced to the place where it is heard is increased considerably if the sound is of a nature unknown to the listener. The direction of the sound is a matter which the witness can never fully determine (see "Errors Caused by Acoustics in Determining Direction of Shooting" in Chapter XIV). The sound which the witness perceives is unconsciously compared to a whole series of memories of sounds previously heard, and he attempts to coordinate them in his mind. Locard tells of a man who one night heard a peculiar sound and expressed this series of confused memories by exclaiming, "That dog is not a frog—it is a cartwheel!"

A witness is usually asked whether he can recognize the voice of a person, to tell what language was used, to repeat as carefully as possible the exclamations heard, and finally to state at least the general trend of what was said. This places the witness at a great disadvantage. In order to recognize the voice, for instance, a highly intricate operation is necessary, including an analysis of the loudness of the voice, its intensity and tone, a comparison between these elements and former sound pictures, and then finally the actual identification. If the person is known to the witness, however, identification of the voice is rather certain.

In order to determine the language used in a conversation it is not necessary to possess a thorough knowledge of the language. The knowledge of certain characteristic phrases is sufficient. However, it is not advisable to accept such perceptions without verification.

When we ask a witness to state the content of a conversation, we are confronted with one of the most dangerous parts of testimony. We do not listen to all the sounds which form a spoken sentence, and we either compare unconsciously those which we hear with sound pictures which we already possess or else undertake the more complicated work of forming visions which correspond to the words. When we listen to a conversation, therefore, we are not registering a long series of sounds but rather are reconstructing the talk from separate aural fragments and filling up the gaps with the aid of our power of combination. When a witness repeats a conversation which has taken place, he does not describe what he has heard but what he has reconstructed in his own mind. If he has had a mistaken conception of the conversation from the very beginning, he reconstructs it accordingly, and his testimony is utterly false. The fact that such accounts of conversations are actually interpretations subject to distortions is recognized by the courts in the hearsay rule.

IDENTIFICATION OF LIVING PERSONS THROUGH WITNESSES. Mistakes made by confrontations are innumerable. The following factors especially tend to promote mistakes: *similarity to others, bad light, witness excited, witness not sufficiently alert, suggestions,* and *great lapse of time since day of occurrence.*

It is customary in confrontations to have the witness brought into a room where several persons are lined up with the suspect. The witness is asked to pick out the culprit. Photographs or descriptions of the suspect should naturally not be supplied the witness.

Some psychologists claim that identification of an individual by witnesses *normally* gives false or negative results. Such an opinion may be exaggerated, but it is nevertheless true that the individual to be identified should, if possible, be placed in the same circumstances as when seen by the witness, i.e., the same position, the same light, etc. The best method is to attempt the identification at the scene of the crime at approximately the hour the crime was committed.

IDENTIFICATION OF DEAD BODIES. The interrogator may also have to deal with false testimony, given unconsciously, in the identification of dead bodies, as well as of living persons. It is not always easy to recognize a dead body, especially if it has been subjected to putrefaction or mutilation, and many errors occur in this respect. Hellwig[10] reports an interesting case which shows that even relatives may be mistaken under the most favorable circumstances. A German railroad man named Kirstein quarreled one evening with his wife. The wife left the room. Soon afterwards Kirstein was informed that a woman had thrown herself in the neighboring river and been drowned. He rushed there, certain that his wife had committed suicide; under the light of a lamp, he thought he recognized the body, wept and was greatly grieved. His brother and sister, who had accompanied him, confirmed his recognition. The body was carried home and artificial respiration was applied for some time. After the excitement had waned, suddenly Kirstein remembered that his wife had had more money on her and had worn different clothes. He rushed upstairs to see if she had changed her clothing, saying, "I wonder what clothes she had on today?" One can imagine the shock when he heard the voice of his wife answer, "The clothes which I had on today are hanging here." Kirstein ran down terrified, crying, "Now I believe in God. The ghost of Emma is in the bedroom!" No one dared to enter the room until Mrs. Kirstein herself came out. It was at once apparent that there was not the slightest resemblance between her and the drowned person. The case can only be explained by the supposition that Kirstein had been the victim of powerful autosuggestion. It is peculiar that the husband, who had been at work applying artificial respiration to the dead body, had not been able to perceive the difference between this woman and his wife. His agitation apparently obscured all other observation.

In Chapter V, methods of reconstructing dead bodies are described. Such methods will without doubt diminish the possibility of mistakes in identifications.

IDENTIFICATION BY PHOTOGRAPHS. A witness should never be shown a single photograph and asked if he recognizes the person. On the contrary, the photograph should be put among several others and the witness asked to pick out the person in question. Even such a procedure does not eliminate mistakes, as the witness may previously have seen a picture of the suspect in newspapers or elsewhere. The identification by photographs involves another danger: If the witness's mind-picture of the criminal is vague and unclear, he may complete the mental picture erroneously by looking at a photograph of a person having some slight resemblance to the suspect. When this mind-picture becomes fixed, in later confrontations the witness may identify the wrong person or fail to identify the right person because he looks like or does not look like the person in the photograph.

MENTAL ABNORMALITIES

Every good detective should have a general knowledge of mental illnesses and constitutional abnormalities of the mind. In the course of his investigations he will often meet persons whose actions and motives may seem puzzling to him if he is not equipped with some knowledge of psychiatry. He should, in fact, be somewhat familiar with the common mental illnesses and abnormalities so as to be able to make a tentative preliminary diagnosis for his own information. This fact has also been recognized by several police and medicolegal institutions in which the subject is taken up not only in theory—in didactic lectures, etc.—but also in practice, by giving students the opportunity to make observations in insane asylums and psychopathic wards.

A knowledge of the signs and symptoms tending to prove mental illnesses is, of course, necessary. Familiarity with the personality make-up of neurotic persons, of epileptics and hysterics, should be of particular interest to the interrogator, as these conditions often affect suspects as well as witnesses.

An individual who is not insane in the true sense of the word, but who nevertheless shows great divergences in character and emotional reactions from those of a normal person, may be classified as a psychopathological person. The intelligence of such a person is often quite satisfactory and at times highly developed. However, it exercises entirely too little control over his actions, which, instead, are generally influenced by compulsive emotional reactions or more rarely by previously acquired mental diseases in which delusions play a prominent part. Among these persons we encounter many criminals.

In this group are found sexual perversions and the so-called moral insanities. This latter term covers a group of abnormal individuals in which students of psychiatry usually include many criminals. To the psychic abnormals belong also persons suffering from feeble-mindedness, pathological liars and swindlers, and highly emotional (explosive) persons. For practical reasons it is customary to regard all these as one group.

A general knowledge of all these illnesses and abnormalities will be of enormous aid to the interrogator. Such a knowledge should be of a practical nature, designed to recognize irregularities of behavior and mental processes which would affect the validity of a person's observations or testimony. The interrogator should acquire a working grasp of elementary psychology, but he is ill advised to burden himself with the elaborate terminology of the Freudian school of psychiatry. He should, for example, know that a psychosis differs from a psychoneurosis in that the mental disturbance is of such a magnitude that the mind is distorted more or less in entirety. The psychotic person displays inability to correct his misconceptions about what is real and what is unreal and hence is not a fit subject for ordinary interrogation. The terms by which the various psychotic disorders are distinguished—e.g., schizophrenia, paranoia, manic-depressive psychosis, and so forth—are the concern of the psychiatrist and serve no useful purpose in the conversation of the investigator.

Persons suffering from a psychoneurosis, however, are a problem of immediate concern to the interrogator, since their mental condition does not necessarily prevent them from apparently normal participation in work and social life, and experience has trained them in most cases to disguise and adjust to their condition. Yet the testimony of such a person may be basically unreliable; his statements may be motivated or colored by malice or his original observations may have been invalid. The most common of the psychoneuroses, hysteria, is discussed below. Another and equally difficult problem for the interrogator is the sexual pervert, who is described below in some of his forms without any extended reference to the psychology of his condition.

Sexual perversions play a role, directly or indirectly, in the planning as well as the execution of many major crimes. Most frequently the word perversion is used to describe homosexuality, but it is also used to describe sadism, fetishism, transvestitism, and other abnormalities. Let us establish at the beginning the fact that all sexual perversions are related either to normal sexuality (heterosexuality) or to homosexuality. The pernicious belief that homosexuality is inborn (and consequently incurable) is all too common. Modern evidence, with few exceptions, contradicts this belief. G. W. Henry,[11] in the most intensive medical-anatomical study that has ever been made of homosexuality, concluded that three general factors were of significance in this condition: (a) constitutional deficiencies, (b) the influence of family patterns of sexual adjustment, and (c) lack of opportunity for psychosexual development. Of the "constitutional deficiencies" Henry found that "Structural deficiencies are the least evident; the psychological [deficiencies] are the most readily demonstrated. . . ."

We may define homosexuality as sexual desire directed *primarily* toward someone of the same sex, whether or not it is consummated in actual sexual relations. The homosexual is an inhibited personality whose tendencies are the result of early conditioning in the home and by his environmental experiences. An active homosexual is a likely victim of the blackmailer and the robber, since his condition leads easily to involvement with relative strangers of questionable character. Thus, the homosexual is notoriously a poor security risk.

To the investigator, the homosexual's condition is of interest mainly when it has led him to become the victim or the perpetrator of a crime, especially a crime of violence for which the motivation is obscure. In the military establishments, however, the condition of the homosexual as such is a matter of importance to the military investigator from the point of view of security and morale. One homosexual in a military organization can often create a number of others, particularly among the border-line personalities who are originally ignorant of his intentions.

SADISM. This form of perversion, first described by the Marquis de Sade (1740–1814) consists in the association of sexual pleasure with the infliction of punishment, mental or physical, on the sexual partner. Among the sadists may be found not only sex murderers but also the perpetrators of many brutal acts notorious in the pages of history. Sadism, like other sexual perversions, runs the whole scale from thoughts and wishful thinking to murder. The sex murderer can be divided into two types: (1) the person who attains sexual satisfaction only by torturing, killing, or mutilating the victim, without sexual intercourse, and (2) the person who commits the murder in connection with sexual intercourse. The former condition could also be called transferred sadism, and as such it represents sadism in its purest form. Many cases of this kind have been known in the history of crime.

MASOCHISM. Named after the Austrian writer Leopold von Sacher–Masoch (1835–1895), this form of perversion is characterized by an association of pleasure with pain. Through conditioning a person can eventually come to connect a sensation of pleasantness with an experience that is actually unpleasant—the person is uncomfortable without his hair shirt. The masochist in sexual relations derives sexual pleasure from being whipped or otherwise mistreated. It is easy to see how a sexual relationship between a sadist and a masochist can develop into a crime, since the mutual encouragement of perversions would lead to an excess of violence. In general, however, law enforcement is rarely concerned with the masochist. He is an inhibited personality for whom failure and frustration have become a habitual lot. He wills to be unhappy. It is an oversimplification to say that the masochist "enjoys" his pain; nevertheless, his reaction systems don't feel complete without it. In many large cities the brothels, phony massage institutes, and prostitutes have devised various methods to take advantage of the peculiar inclinations of the masochist.

FETISHISM. This is the collective name for a number of perversions all of which have one thing in common: sexual desire is abnormally fixed upon one part of the body (such as the foot) or on some object of apparel. An erotic attachment to some object such as a handkerchief or a glove is the result of association; through conditioning the fetish becomes an objective in itself.

TRANSVESTITISM. This term refers to an overwhelming desire to wear the clothes of the opposite sex. It must be assumed that this indicates a strong homosexual trend, although this may not be evident.

EXHIBITIONISM. The exhibitionist obtains sexual gratification by exposing and attracting attention to his private parts. In large cities exhibitionists are not an uncommon police problem. Railway stations and public parks are their usual operating grounds. This type of pervert becomes dangerous when he attempts to lure children into an automobile.

NECROPHILISM. In this perversion sexual desire is concentrated on dead bodies. Morgue attendants and funeral parlor assistants occasionally succumb to this morbid attraction to corpses.

SODOMY. This term is commonly used to include fellatio as well as buggery. Bestiality, a sexual offense upon an animal, is treated in the same manner as sodomy. The investigation of these offenses is similar to that of rape with respect to the physical evidence required.

HYSTERIA. Of the various mental conditions affecting the reliability of a witness' testimony, hysteria is probably the most frequently encountered by the investigator. Hysteria is classed among the psychoneuroses —a group of relatively benign mental disorders that are substitutive reactions in which the symptoms play some concealed but protective role within the mental life of the person. While the symptoms in the psychoneuroses are for the most part subjective, there may be objective physical manifestations as well. Involuntary movements, for example, may occur in major hysteria. One seldom sees pure hysteria, however, or pure compulsions, or phobias, but rather syndromes in which there is a little of each, although one particular phase may predominate sufficiently to warrant a classification. A symptom of conscious anxiety will usually be found in all of these conditions and will be especially pronounced in anxiety hysteria.

Naturally the investigator is not expected to appraise the significance of anxiety reactions or to consider them as symptomatic of a psychoneurosis. Borderline and transition cases exist, not only between the various psychoneuroses, but between the neuroses and psychoses as well. An investigator must resist the temptation to engage in facile diagnoses; he should restrict his professional interest to the evaluation of the person's reliability as a witness. He should, however, have a practical knowledge of the most common forms of abnormality so that he may recognize indications of unreliability in a witness. Where the testimony is of a critical nature, he should secure the advice of a physician.

There is no other neurosis that causes the interrogator as great and as many difficulties as hysteria. This illness exists more generally than one might suspect. It is not easily recognizable in its milder forms, and sometimes it is quite difficult to recognize even in its advanced stages, because of its multiform symptomatology. All kinds of mistakes, misjudged actions, and formal injustices may well be ascribed to it.

Hysteria occurs both in women and in men. It may be characterized by paralysis, emotional outbreaks, or convulsive attacks. The hysterical convulsion differs from the epileptic in that the unconsciousness is not so profound and usually does not display the real elements of a true convulsion.

Hysterical persons often have many characteristic traits which make them highly dangerous both as accusers and as witnesses. They frequently lack deeper ethical feelings, are extremely egocentric, mendacious, and malicious. They also have an unusual ability to simulate and a lust for intrigues. Hysterical women sometimes accuse men with whom they have had only a casual acquaintance of personal attacks of a sexual nature. Young physicians are cautioned against being alone in a room with a hysterical woman. Similar advice may also be given to the interrogator. In fact, it is always advisable to have a third person present during an interrogation.

As hysteria is an illness which is difficult to recognize, the following signs, which are given by Gross, should be remembered: the ill person believes himself disdained, thinks himself a martyr, has sudden changes of moods, has exaggerated sensitivity, and is abnormally receptive of external influences. If these symptoms are not marked, the interrogator may attempt to ascertain through cautious questions whether the person under examination has severe headaches, a sensation of choking, stomach-aches, or fits of uncontrollable laughter. If these symptoms are present, it is necessary to obtain the advice of a physician, because if a person afflicted by hysteria is called as a witness his testimony will be extremely unreliable.

False accusations by hysterical persons may result from their lack of ability of perception and also from their suggestibility.

SUGGESTION AND HYPNOTISM

Suggestion and hypnotism are both important to criminology insofar as they may serve to influence or utilize individuals for criminal purposes.

SUGGESTION. Suggestion is a term covering all those mental influences, good or evil, which exercise a certain degree of compulsion upon our thoughts and actions. The suggestive influence is in direct opposition to any influence resulting from reasoning. In order to understand the phenomena of suggestion we must bear in mind that human beings have a natural tendency to believe or—to be more accurate—to assume everything as true that does not awaken conflicting ideas or emotions; generally everything is assumed to be true and real provided there is no reason to doubt it. Suggestion can arouse emotions and feelings, can cause actions to be performed, and can bring about changes in an individual's bodily and mental functions—even within fields which are otherwise not under the control of the human will.

Hysterical and nervous persons are particularly susceptible to suggestion and are easily influenced in an evil direction. And persons lacking in moral character have no ethical promptings to prevent suggestions from exercising their full power.

Other types of influence similar to suggestion are *habit* and *example*. People do what they are in the habit of doing, without paying any particular attention to it; and often an individual does just as other people are doing, without being aware of it. As regards *example,* mass suggestion seems to play a certain role.

MASS SUGGESTION. While sporadic suggestion usually plays only a minor part in the life of a normal person, even the most intelligent often cannot escape the influence of mass suggestion. Human beings influence each other through mutual suggestion when they are gathered in dense crowds. The power of independent thought is then weakened. In its stead there is formed what may be called a collective mass will, which is not the sum total of the mental wealth of the members of the group but a new and independent phenomenon. This mass will lies on a far lower plane than do the mental powers of each individual. This explains the savage acts and the very credulity which characterize the mass.

HYPNOTISM. Hypnotic conditions are caused by suggestion, and the person who is under the influence of hypnotism is highly susceptible to suggestive commands from the hypnotist. In cases of deep hypnotic trance only those things which the hypnotist permits can be observed and thought about by the person under his influence, and this person follows and obeys almost every command. Furthermore, the subject may preserve the impressions of the hypnotic influence even after he has awakened (post-hypnotic influence). So it is easily understandable that it is within the realm of possibility to make use of hypnotism for criminal purposes.

Although sensational news items dealing with hypnotic influence are common, cases of this kind really are rather rare. Most of those in the newspapers are cases of simulated hypnotism, in which the culprit is trying to escape the consequences of his act by claiming to have been under hypnotic influence. Insane persons also frequently insist that they have been under the influence of hypnotism.

Crimes in which hypnotism plays a role may be divided into two categories: (1) cases where attempts are made to utilize a person for criminal acts while he is under hypnotic influence, and (2) crimes in which the culprit has made use of the fact that a person is in a state of hypnotic coma in order to commit a crime against him. If the culprit in the first case should utilize the hypnotic condition of the other person, he would have to make use of so-called post-hypnotism, such as to command the hypnotized man to shoot a particular person the first time he meets him. Here, of course, the same rule as mentioned before prevails: that it is not easy to make a person perform an act by suggestion if such an act is something for which that person has a definite distaste. In spite of the power of suggestion we find in most persons of high moral standard several hampering factors springing from the ethical personality of the individual which counteract and prevent the suggestion from being transformed into action. Very few crimes of this kind are known.

Crimes of the other category are also very rare. However, they are particularly dangerous, as the victim can be made to forget what has taken place. An incident is related in which two young men hypnotized a young girl, raped her, and then through suggestion compelled her to forget what had happened. Cases have also been reported in which a person has been robbed and then compelled by suggestion to forget his own personality and his entire previous life.

If it is suspected that a person has been subject to hypnotism or suggestion, it is of course necessary to obtain the advice of a psychiatrist. Regarding the manner in which hypnotism may be applied, it is important for the interrogator to know that it can be done in several ways, such as by making the subject gaze into a crystal for some time or into the eyes of the hypnotist, or by massaging the forehead of the victim. Hypnotic influence achieved by a quick look or a short command cannot, with few exceptions, be easily brought about except with persons who have on several previous occasions been under the influence of the same hypnotist.

SLEEP AND DREAMS

Criminal attacks are sometimes committed while the culprit is in a state of somnolence. The observation has been made that as a rule such attacks are committed by young persons who before retiring to sleep have been through severe physical or mental exertions. Often the attack is directed against the first person they encounter, such as a roommate. During these attacks the culprit develops tremendous power—usually far above his normal physical strength.

From a psychiatric viewpoint this condition is regarded as an abnormal transition stage between being asleep and awake. It is characterized by a slower awakening of the intellectual faculties as compared to the faculties of motion. It is, of course, most pronounced when it occurs after a deep sleep. According to investigations made by Pick, Michelson, and others, a person's sleep is deepest after the first hour and becomes lighter and lighter until a minimum is reached in the sixth and seventh hour, whereupon it grows once more deeper as the morning approaches. It is quite natural that somnolence should exert an influence upon a person's capacity for perception, so that one must regard observations made by persons who have just awakened after profound sleep with a certain degree of caution.

Dreams may often be so intensive that one believes them to be real experiences or, in other words, true. It is known that epileptics are subject to such particularly vivid dreams.

The modern science of psychoanalysis attempts to interpret dreams. It is most uncertain, however, whether such analyses of a person's dreams can be of any practical value to the criminologist, as dreams can be related only very incoherently. It may also happen that important matters are added to the continuity of the dream through sheer imagination on the part of the narrator. In such a case there exists no possibility of testing the accuracy of the information.

Listening to a person talking during his sleep is an entirely different matter. Some persons have a habit of revealing what they wish to keep secret when, during sleep, they lose control over their actions. Often such talks are incoherent and difficult to understand. Criminal history shows, however, that some people have disclosed their secrets while sleeping.

SOUND RECORDING

The detective who secures oral statements from a witness, suspect, or defendant is often placed in a poor position in court by having no record of such statements. In recent years a compact, efficient, and economical device has been developed which assists the investigator in court by making it possible for him to present a recorded transcription of his subject's remarks.

At 8:45 P.M. John Brown was found dead on the floor of his apartment by his daughter. The clues pointed to murder. The police surgeon stated that Brown had been dead for approximately two hours, which fixed the time of death at around 7 P.M. Witnesses testified that a Mrs. Smith had visited Brown that same afternoon at 5:15, that a Mr. Jones had joined them in the apartment at 5:50, and that Mrs. Smith and Mr. Jones had left together at 6:15. About 6:45 a messenger boy had delivered the laundry to Brown's apartment and had been paid by Brown. Around 7:15 Brown's daughter had called her father on the telephone and not received any answer. The owner of the store on the ground floor of the same building had noticed an unknown man leaving the house at approximately 7:30. Some boys playing on the street claimed that they had seen somebody moving behind the blinds in the lighted room in Brown's apartment sometime around 8 P.M.

(Solid lines indicate checked statements; dash lines indicate uncertain information.)

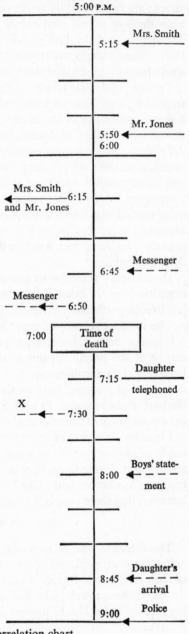

Figure 8.   Time correlation chart.

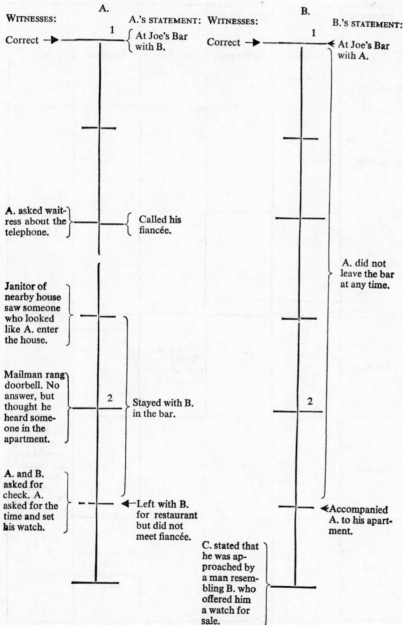

Figure 9. Statement time-check chart.

Information about:	Baldwin	McDermott	Brodsky	Peterson	Arlen
Statements of:					
Baldwin					
McDermott					
Brodsky			Was at Blue Moon Café when fire started		
Peterson					Arlen appeared to be nervous during the fire; stuttered, made no sense, etc.
Arlen				Saw Peterson participate in extinguishing the fire	

Figure 10.   Statement and information cross-check chart.

The early bulky devices by means of which voices were recorded on discs or records have been replaced by paper tapes containing magnetized iron particles (usually ferric oxide) or wire devices. By either of these methods it is possible to record a forty-five minute conversation.

In the hands of an inexperienced operator the tone quality will not be true enough to identify the individual. It requires but little practice, however, to balance the instrument to the extent that the voices are identifiable. The microphone should be of an extremely sensitive type and therefore very small in size so that it may be placed in an inconspicuous position or concealed, e.g., under papers or a hat, in a paper bag, in a lampshade, waste-paper basket, ceiling lamp, etc.

Such instruments are also of value for recording conversations of possible co-defendants when they believe their conversations to be secret, as in a waiting-room or a detective office or in adjoining cells, etc.

GRAPHIC COMPARISON OF TIME ALIBIS

Sometimes when comparing information given by suspects and witnesses, it may be very useful to put down the information in the form of graphs. Graphs were frequently used one hundred years ago on the Continent in countries where the so-called inquisitive form of procedure was still prevailing. According to the law, the court of the first instance was the only one in which perpetrators and witnesses could give oral testimony, and therefore the cases had to be carefully prepared in writing to make it possible for the courts of appeal to judge the case from documents alone. Recently there has been a revival of interest in graphs and a growing recognition of their value as an investigative aid. The charts shown on pages 54, 55, and 56 illustrate the utility of these graph forms in the analysis and presentation of evidentiary facts and testimony in a relatively complex homicide. The investigative supervisor will also see in these charts a control mechanism for the management of the case. Additional chart forms will suggest themselves after a study of these illustrations. A set of leads, for example, can be used as the basis of a lead-control chart; lead assignments will then suggest themselves, as well as an assignment-investigator chart. The desirability and usefulness of such charts will be determined by the importance of the case and its complexity, i.e., the number, character, and degree of involvement of the persons associated with the crime as suspects, witnesses, or simply "leads"; the nature of the physical evidence available and the extent to which the crime-scene topography enters as a factor in understanding the criminal occurrences; and finally the number of investigators assigned to the case—a consideration by no means negligible in a large city, and one which can be further complicated through multiple jurisdiction, by reason of the nature of the offense or the location of the crime scene. Granted, then, the complexity of the crime, the usefulness of such charts is not to be gainsaid. Certainly, they would appear to be more profitable than the construction of miniature models of the scene or house wherein the crime was committed, since the latter is merely a presentation of physical facts whereas the charts deal with ideas, the relationships existing among the facts.

1 Related by Gennat, late chief of the homicide squad of the police department, Berlin, Germany.

2 See also Ernst Fontell on the technique of interrogation in Söderman–Fontell.

3 One of the first scientific efforts in this direction was the series of experiments begun in 1879 by Francis Galton which led to the development of the word association-reaction time test through the work of Jung, Wundt, Wertheimer, Klein, Binswanger, Freud, Gross,[3] Gorphe,[2] and Munsterburg. In one form of the method a number of words that are related to the crime are placed strategically in a long list of irrelevant words. The words are read to the suspect in the order in which they appear on the list. The suspect is instructed to respond with synonyms as rapidly as possible, giving the first word that comes to his mind. The answers are noted as well as the elapsed time between questions and answers. The criminal will answer less rapidly to the *critical* (related) words than to the *indifferent* (unrelated) words and still less rapidly to the *post-critical* words which follow immediately after the critical or stimulus words. Among the indices of emotional disturbance are (1) overlong reaction time; (2) extremely short reaction time; (3) repetition of the stimulus word; (4) repetition of a response word previously used; (5) response word unrelated to stimulus word; (6) pretended misunderstanding of stimulus word. Since the thoughts of a guilty person are circling around the crime, he reacts unconsciously to the stimulus of a word related to the crime.

4 Inbau–Reid and Lee.

5 U.S. Army *Tech. Bull.* PMG, No. 10.

6 Locard.[8] Edmond Locard was born in 1877 in Saint-Chamond, France. A Doctor of Medicine and a Master of Law, in 1910 he became director of the scientific laboratory of the police department of Lyons, France. Locard was vice president of the International Academy for Criminal Science and chief editor of the *Revue Internationale de Criminalistique.* For the development of many new methods in police science as well as for his contributions to its literature, Locard is regarded as one of the foremost criminologists in the world.

7 Gorphe.[2]

8 Sternack.

9 Schneikert.[1]

10 Hellwig.[1]

11 Henry. G. W.

IV TRACING THE FUGITIVE

ABILITY TO SECURE INFORMATION ABOUT A FUGITIVE CRIMINAL HAS always been and will lastingly be an asset for success in the work of a policeman or detective. This ability can be attained and developed by tact in the performance of duty; by becoming acquainted with residents, owners, managers, and employees of business concerns, storekeepers, proprietors of licensed premises, hotel managers, chauffeurs, clerks, porters, taxicab starters, taxicab drivers, truckmen, and other persons following divers vocations in the territory in which the officer is working. This knowledge should be enhanced at every opportunity throughout the municipality.

SOURCES FOR INFORMATION

Aptitude for receiving information can be stimulated by friendly intercourse and cooperation with other officers working in the same or other districts. The habit of jotting down and keeping permanent notes regarding aliases, places of residence, hangouts, habits, and police records of potential and professional criminals will be found invaluable. For this purpose a small card 3 by 5 inches in size may be kept on which memoranda can be written. In all but the smallest police departments there is a central office in which a file of criminal records is kept and displayed for official inspection. Sometimes detectives do not avail themselves as fully as they should of this service, resorting to it only when a crime occurs in the territory to which they have been assigned. In some metropolitan police departments nowadays refresher courses in training are given to the personnel in service. Such courses include visits to local bureaus of criminal information and identification at headquarters so that observations can be made and knowledge secured of the *modus operandi* file, photograph gallery, and criminal record and fingerprint classification files. Here police officers and detectives have recourse to the index of crimes and criminals. Information is obtainable as to the identity, history, and methods of criminals, all of which is of practical use in solving problems of crime.

With the identity of the fugitive criminal established, the first step to be taken in the pursuit is transmission of an alarm. A complete description of the individual should be given in the alarm. Likely places in which the fugitive may be found should be visited, kept under surveillance, and searched if circumstances demand it. These include his residence; former residences; places or hangouts frequented; residences of relatives, close

friends, or associates; and places of employment. Inquiries under suitable pretexts can be made of members of the family, relatives, friends, and shopkeepers who would be likely to know of the whereabouts and movements of the person wanted or with whom he would probably communicate.

The habits of the fugitive should also be considered. Many criminals of the so-called accidental type, as well as of the potential and professional types, frequent gambling places, night clubs, pool parlors, dance halls, burlesque and motion picture theaters, saloons and restau-

Figure 11.   Hugo von Jagemann, rants, and hotels of the bizarre type.
pioneer of modern investigating Frequently residence is located or
methods.[1] sought in a neighborhood which has
undergone a transition in type from the better-class private home to a furnished-room type of dwelling.

THE MOTIVE. The motive for the crime is often helpful in tracking the fugitive. Motive may be said to include the elements of gain, sex, revenge, anger, homicidal mania, and sex perversion. *Cherchez la femme*—"seek the woman"—is an axiom that has been followed successfully in tracking criminals in many cases. Many acts of criminals before and after the commission of a crime, as well as in supplying the motive for a crime, have been done at the urge of or on account of a woman. Often the woman is innocent of the criminal transaction. The present era, however, has brought to public notice repeatedly the participation by females in bold and daring crimes, including murder, kidnaping, robbery, extortion, and other felonies.

AIDING AGENCIES AND IDENTIFICATION THROUGH PHOTOGRAPHS. Of

the many aids in tracking and identifying the fugitive criminal, one of the most valuable is found in the records of the criminal record office or bureau of criminal identification maintained by municipal and State police departments and by national governments. Here also application should be made for search to be instituted of the *modus operandi* or crime index. If the offender can be identified, arrangements should be made for the victim and witnesses to attend and inspect photographs of suspects or persons likely to have committed such a crime. There are two aims to be achieved in this respect: (1) to establish identity and (2) to trace the perpetrator.

Figure 12.   The line-up or show-up.

Photographs of suspected persons should not be shown to a witness if the criminal himself can be arrested and placed on view for identification nor in cases where it is intended to arrest the person at once for having committed a crime. But if the criminal cannot be found or if a person is still merely under suspicion, there should be no objection to placing his photograph among a dozen others and showing them to a victim or witness, with the object of selection. Care should be exercised to see that no assistance is given, that no consultation is permitted with other victims or witnesses, and that names, aliases, or other indices to identity are kept out of view.

When a felony is under investigation, it often becomes essential to locate the fugitive or a suspect or to find stolen property under conditions which necessitate a search beyond the territorial jurisdiction of the precinct, district, or zone in which the crime occurred. Inquiries in adjacent or remote precincts, districts, or zones are desirable. Places are usually specified, such as pawnshops, second-hand jewelry stores, rooming houses, garages, warehouses, or others. It is of the utmost importance that these inquiries be made promptly, intelligently, tactfully, and conscientiously, because the solution of a major crime and the arrest of its perpetrator often depend on the speed with which inquiry is made. Cooperation is essential to success. It must be given willingly and thoroughly.

If the fugitive sought is a member of a mob or gang and has a criminal record, it is reasonable to expect that records on file at the central information or identification bureau will show with whom he was arrested previously. Check should be made to determine if these persons are at liberty. By locating them, the fugitive, whether he has or has not a criminal or police record, may be found. Should they be in prison, it is possible that they may write letters to the fugitive you are seeking. Such addresses are a matter of record. Parole and probation boards cooperate with police departments in taking into custody parolees who have returned to the field of criminal operations. Contact should be made with the appropriate boards or officers thereof immediately when it is found that the fugitive is on parole or probation.

It is possible that a fugitive may attempt to leave the country on a steamship either as an employee or passenger. Information regarding persons who apply for passports may be obtained from the passport bureau maintained in some cities by the Federal government or through the Passport Bureau, State Department, Washington, D. C. The United States Shipping Board maintains a record of persons going to sea on American ships in various jobs. Steamship companies also print, post, and distribute sailing lists of passengers and crews.

ALIEN FUGITIVES. If the fugitive is or was an alien, information on his personal history, destination, and friends may be obtained from the Immigration Bureau of the Department of Labor. Knowing the port of entry into this country is an aid to making a rapid search. Every steamship from foreign ports files with the Immigration Department a list of passengers and crews.

Aliens seeking first or second papers of citizenship are required to produce witnesses who have known them for a number of years. The names of these witnesses are on file at Naturalization Bureaus. If the fugitive is an alien, it is possible to locate him through such witnesses.

Tickets and Checks. When a railroad ticket for any distant point is purchased at a station, including perhaps a Pullman chair or berth, a sales ticket filled out by the agent gives the number of the ticket, the car, and the berth. Collected tickets are returned to the office of the railroad company. Punch marks on the tickets identify the conductor in charge of the train. Locating the conductor will lead to locating the trainman and the Pullman porter. These are means by which identification of fugitive criminals using railroad transportation can be made. There is also the possibility that travel insurance was purchased from the ticket agent by the fugitive.

Helpful information regarding fugitive criminals who have been depositors may at times be secured at banking institutions. Canceled checks supply information and leads. Entry to safe deposit boxes generally is secured through a court order. In many jurisdictions an order from the Supreme Court is required before examination of the contents of the box can be made. Subsequent to such an examination, if anything found in the box is wanted, an order of replevin generally is issued.

A fugitive criminal whose identity is known may carry insurance or may have been rejected as a risk. Aid in locating him may be secured from information given at the time of applying for insurance.

Crime Index. The important work of assisting in the detection of criminals through a crime index or *modus operandi* (that is, by method of crime committed) and by description is carried out in practically all metropolitan police departments and in central bureaus of criminal information and statistics located in a number of States. In Canada a central repository along these lines is maintained at Ottawa. In European, South American, and other countries central bureaus are likewise maintained. Most police departments as well as most sheriffs, prisons, and jails have their fingerprint records of criminals cleared through the Federal Bureau of Investigation, United States Department of Justice, Washington, D. C. Therefore, it is important to report fully on the identity and aliases of persons wanted and to make inquiry through official channels of the FBI in Washington for the purpose of determining whether any information is already recorded. In the event of the individual wanted being taken into custody elsewhere there will be on file a record showing that he is wanted locally. It is also advisable to consult police reports of aided and accident cases and to consult hospital records.

Various techniques are used in different sections of the country in tracing fugitives on information secured from spoken or written communications. These channels will be discussed in subsequent chapters. When cases of sufficient notoriety or importance occur, investigating officers should consult with their supervisory heads to see that such channels of intelligence, including the mail, telegraph, telephone, Dictaphone, various license and permit bureaus, water, gas, and electric lighting corporations, tax and assessment bureaus, school systems, election board records, divers mailing lists and directories, fraternal, veteran, and labor organizations, laundry and dry-cleaning establishments, bonding and loan corporations, auto rental agencies, bus, airplane, and other transportation agencies, and social service and welfare organizations are approached and the facilities thereof used to the fullest measure.

To the laundry industry has come an invisible, indelible identification system. A mark that cannot be seen under ordinary conditions is placed in the fabric at the laundry. The mark is visible only when exposed to ultraviolet rays. Police officers and detectives should see to it that all fabrics, including tablecloths, napkins, handkerchiefs, doilies, towels, washcloths, bath towels, knit underwear, etc., found under circumstances having or suspected of having a relationship to a criminal operation or to investigations of missing persons or other police cases are examined by means of ultraviolet light to determine whether an invisible laundry mark has been placed in the fabric and what aid may be obtained therefrom.

TRAILING

The ability to trail an individual without arousing his suspicions is a very valuable talent for the detective. It must also be regarded as one of the most strenuous jobs carried out in the police department, tiring both to body and soul and demanding sometimes an almost supernatural gift of patience and alertness. It should be remembered that a hunted man is often very suspicious and sometimes develops quite a sense of clairvoyance in spotting his trailers.

The following are some rules pertaining to trailing which have been found useful in the New York Police Department. They do not by any means cover the whole of the subject but will give some useful hints to the investigator.

1. *Act naturally.* This is most important. The subject may not detect you, but someone else may tip him off. A person acting unnaturally is both conspicuous and suspicious, and these are two things to avoid. Most trailers are self-conscious at first but become accustomed to the task as they gain experience.

2. *Dress conservatively but appropriately.* Unusual attire or loud colors attract attention and must be avoided. A person wearing loud clothing is conspicuous and stands out even in crowds. Bright-colored neckties, scarfs, and sports clothing, light-gray hats and striking-colored suits, over-coats, topcoats, shoes, etc., should be avoided, unless at a resort, sporting event, etc.

3. *Disguises.* This method of concealing identity is tabu and belongs only to fiction. Changes of suit, hat, tie, or scarf will alter one's appearance greatly, as will eyeglasses or sunglasses. A useful change can sometimes be made simply by removing the hat or overcoat. Reversible topcoats are useful.

4. *Other suggestions.* A trailer should have coins readily available for use in entering subways, making telephone calls, and the like. He should have a plausible story ready if stopped and asked for an explanation of his actions. The trailer should avoid coming face to face with the subject too often and should never look him in the eye. Do not become flustered, however, if you do come face to face with the subject. Ignore any sign of recognition made by him and do not become startled under such circumstances. Good judgment, proper distance, and luck play important parts. It is far better to lose the subject temporarily or discontinue the surveillance than to have the subject recognize you. You can always take up the surveillance again if your identity is not revealed. When following automobiles, watch his rear-view mirror; in following taxicabs watch his left-side mirror. Obtain a good look at the person to be trailed so as to be able to remember him. A few days' surveillance will usually determine the subject's residence, business address, type of employment, associates, habits, hobbies, hangouts, etc.

5. *Observation.* Study the face of the subject so that you will know him weeks later. Make a mental note of his age, height, weight, build, hair, eyes, and mustache and glasses if any. Note particularly his walk, gestures, and peculiarities. Study his manner of dress, paying particular attention to his choice of coat, hat, suit, shoes, ties, shirts, scarf, etc. Notice habits such as smoking and so forth. Attention to all of these items will facilitate picking the subject out of a group and ready recognition under any circumstances. Photographs, even movies, can often be taken from an automobile while the subject is on foot. If an automobile is to be trailed, memorize the type, make, color, and model and license number and State. Record also any damage to or peculiarity of the car. This serves to differentiate cars of the same model.

6. *Be careful.* Be wary of the subject's neighbors, friends, employer, or

employees. Do not arouse the suspicion or inquisitiveness of the police or taxi drivers. Have a logical reason prepared for being at a certain spot. Do not make inquiries, for it focuses attention on you; leave the gathering of information to others. Your job is to observe and record only.

7. *Methods*. Keep off the streets as much as possible and out of automobiles. If it is necessary to use a car, then use two of them and alternate the leads. Let one trail for a while then alternate with the other. Always park cars in opposite directions. Never follow against a one-way street. If working with a partner, do not contact each other too often; stay apart as much as possible. Always arrange a contact point in case you become separated. Have a telephone message center, as two-way radio may be heard. The location of your cover point largely depends upon the neighborhood and the individual. In large hotels you may use the lobby; if the hotel is a small one, however, you must take up the surveillance from the outside. When in the suburbs, you may have to locate from one to five blocks away. In cities you may set up your cover from a garage, a subway or El station, or a bus stop. In small towns you may use the railroad station or bus depots. The distance the trailer stays from his subject is most important and varies greatly, depending on the neighborhood, the size of crowds, time of day or night, etc. The trailer must stay close enough to the subject not to lose him yet must remain far enough away so as not to arouse suspicion.

8. *On entering a building*. The type and size of the building materially determine the technique used in maintaining a surveillance over a person within. A quick survey should be made to see if there are more ways than one to enter or leave. In larger hotels, department stores, office buildings, restaurants, amusement places, etc., it is necessary to enter after the subject; while in smaller places it is best to remain on the outside to prevent running into him too often. Patience is needed at times such as these, since the subject may remain in a building anywhere from a few minutes to several hours.

WAYS OF LOSING A TRAILER

1. *Act naturally*. Do not run or look back. Do not be crude in your actions. Jumping from a moving train or bus should be tabu, as you not only allow the trailer to know you are suspicious of him, but you may also be picked up by someone else who, unknown to you, has seen your unnatural actions. If you act naturally, the trailer has absolutely no means of knowing that you have lost him intentionally and usually will blame himself for not having been more alert. Try to elude him by entering a

place by one entrance and leaving by another, such as: through stores from the street, with a rear entrance leading into hotels, office buildings, apartment houses, etc.; through hotels with more than one entrance; through hotel bars from the street, with an exit through a hotel lobby; through arcade buildings, office buildings, apartment houses, etc., where there are two or more entrances, particularly buildings that run through to the next block; through department stores by going to the upper floors then working your way to the second floor and leaving by a stairway to the street.

Use elevator and observe others occupying it with you. Go to the top floor and then return to a lower floor. Try going through large parks, where it is necessary to be given exceptionally long leads, and through corner stores or L-shaped stores with two or more entrances. Make appropriate use of telephone booths, doubling back, change of clothing, taxicabs, and automobiles.

2. *Make thorough survey.* After arriving in a strange city, make a survey for the purpose of finding places where you can readily lose a tail or to determine if being tailed. Study particularly hotels, apartment houses, office buildings, large stores, and places of amusement; also railroad and bus terminals and other transportation. Change hotels frequently (because of employees, house detectives, telephone records, tapped phones, microphones, baggage, etc.). Beware of strangers attempting to make your acquaintance.

3. *Other suggestions.* Men doing trailing usually work in pairs but are seldom if ever seen together. Care should therefore be taken to insure that they always appear to be total strangers and that any identity with their jobs is entirely lost. Passes, badges, or other identification should never be shown to gain admittance to transportation, amusement places, or anything else.

---

1 Jagemann was born in 1805 and died in 1853. He was a judge in Baden, Germany. Jagemann is regarded as the foremost early pioneer of tracing and investigating methods and of the technique of interrogation. His textbook on legal investigation, which appeared in 1831, is regarded as a classic.

V IDENTIFICATION OF
INDIVIDUALS

POSITIVE IDENTIFICATION OF INDIVIDUALS HAS ALWAYS BEEN A PROB-
lem of vital importance in the maintenance of law and order. Years and
years ago, means of identification were of the crudest sort, but down
through the years tremendous strides have been made, and today personal identification is a science in itself.

HISTORICAL SURVEY

In ancient times criminals were punished by mutilation and branding.
This may well be looked upon as the first attempt toward subsequent
identification, as the limb which had sinned was frequently the one subjected to mutilation; thus the hand of the thief would be amputated or
the tongue of the slanderer would be cut off.

Branding disappeared less than a century ago—in Russia, for example, not until 1860 or thereabouts. Life-timers sent to Siberia were
branded on the forehead and on each cheek. By the time this barbaric
method of identification was finally abolished from the Russian scene,
it had already disappeared from the rest of Europe. In France, branding
was abolished at the end of the Revolution, was later reintroduced, and
was finally abolished in 1832. It had already disappeared in Germany,
but Holland continued to employ it until 1854 and China until 1905.

Descriptions of wanted criminals were used as far back as the Egypt
of the Ptolemies and in the days of the Roman Empire; and the system
used then has a surprising similarity to the *portrait parlé* of today. The
German criminologist Heindl, after studying these Egyptian descriptions,
came to the interesting conclusion that centuries before the birth of Christ
a very complicated method of description similar to the original *portrait
parlé* was used and that the Egyptians later gradually simplified it to
embrace only the most important signs. This is in complete accord with
modern police methods, a very simplified *portrait parlé* now being used.

In medieval days and until the middle of the nineteenth century the descriptions used were in no way better than those of the Egyptians. They were planless, unmethodical, and gave rise to serious mistakes. Contemporary accounts from the beginning of the nineteenth century of the "identification parades" in London gave a good picture of the conditions which existed in olden times. Owing to the heavy penalties dealt to second offenders, criminals made every possible effort to appear as first offenders. In order to check up on these persons certain days of the week were designated for a parade of the newly arrested criminals. They were lined up in the prison yard, and experienced policemen from the different districts of the city scrutinized them carefully to discover whether criminals were posing under assumed names.

Figure 13. Alphonse Bertillon. From an anthropometrical photograph made in Paris in 1914.

ANTHROPOMETRY. About 1840, the Belgian statistician Quetelet[1] stated that there are no two human beings in the world of exactly the same size. This theory is said to have been used for the first time for criminological purposes by Stevens, the warden of the prison in Louvain, who in 1860 proceeded to measure hands, ears, feet, breasts, and lengths of bodies of criminals.

Stevens then should be credited with having been the first man to identify criminals scientifically. However, his measurements had only the character of a trial and were soon discontinued. The invention of a system of identification founded on the thesis of Quetelet and the then existing knowledge of anthropology was left to another. This man was Alphonse Bertillon,[2] a young clerk in the police department of Paris who had many opportunities to convince himself of the unreliability of the old methods of description. Bertillon originated a new method of classifying criminals according to bodily measurements. At first he met with strong opposition from the chief of the Paris detective division, Macé, but finally the Bureau of Identification was established in 1882 with Bertillon as its director. The new method of identification, which was called anthropometry or *bertillonage,* gave very good results, and on the fifteenth of February, 1889, the famous *Service d'identité judiciaire* was founded and soon became known the world over. The method of anthropometrical measurement of the human body was based on the following principles:

1. The human skeleton is unchangeable after the twentieth year. The thigh bones continue to grow somewhat after this period, but this is compensated for by the curving of the spine which takes place at about the same age.
2. It is impossible to find two human beings having bones exactly alike.
3. The necessary measurements can easily be taken with the aid of simple instruments.

The anthropometrical measurements may be divided into three categories:

1. Body measurements: height, width of outstretched arms, and sitting height.
2. Measurements of the head: length of head, breadth of head, bizygomatical diameter, and length of the right ear.
3. Measurements of the limbs: length of left foot, length of left middle and left little finger, and length of left arm and hand from the elbow to the top of the outstretched middle finger.

Each of these eleven measurements is classified into three main groups, small, medium, and large. The subclassification begins with the length and breadth of the head and is subdivided into nine groups. Each of these nine groups is again divided into three new groups according to the length of the left middle finger, and these twenty-seven groups are divided into three new groups according to the length of the left foot. The division continues with the elbow measurements (three groups), the height of the body (three groups), the length of the small finger (two groups), the length of the ears (three groups), etc. Later, of course, the system was extended to include personal characteristics, such as the color of the eyes (five groups), and so forth.

Boys and young men, in whom the measurements of the bones are not constant, were classified by Bertillon according to the color of the eyes and details of the ear. The classification of women was very superficial; the measurements of the head, the left foot, and the elbow were excluded.

The anthropometrical system gave immediate good results. During the first year of its application, in 1882, 49 individuals giving false names were identified. During the following year, 241 were identified, and in 1892 as many as 680. However, the system had serious drawbacks. It was limited to adults, and there was often a marked difference in the measurements of a person who had been measured in different police departments or for a second time in the same department. A table of measurement allowances was introduced, but serious mistakes still could not be avoided. Persons having the same anthropometrical measurements as others already registered occasionally were arrested. The anthropometrical description has now been replaced almost everywhere by the fingerprint description or simply exists as an additional aid, as in France, where an old law compels the recording of anthropometrical measurements in the identification books issued to Gipsies, vagrants, etc.

Bertillon devised also the *portrait parlé,* a clear and precise method of describing a person, as well as the method of photographing criminals practiced today.

BEGINNING OF CRIMINAL PHOTOGRAPHY. Before the English physician Maddox invented the photo-

Figure 14.
Rudolph Archibald Reiss.

graphic dry plate which made photography inexpensive and simple in its application, others had already succeeded in photographing criminals with Daguerre's process (the first photographic method), using wet plates with the exposure lasting several minutes and each print requiring a new sitting. Reiss[3] showed that this method was already in use in Switzerland in 1854 and that by 1860 important scenes of crimes had already been photographed. Paris was the first city in the world to establish a special photographic studio for the police. To Léon Renault, the Commissioner of Police, belongs the credit for adopting it.

The first photographs of criminals were taken front view, and the scale was very arbitrary. Bertillon made them uniform and introduced a fixed scale, so that bodily measurements could be calculated from the photographs. He finally photographed the criminals in both front view and profile, simplifying identification enormously.[4]

DESCRIPTION OF WANTED PERSONS

A knowledge of how to obtain a description of a wanted person from statements of witnesses, how to identify a wanted man from a photograph, and how to give a description of a prisoner for future use is necessary for the detective. In spite of all progress in police science one cannot get along without a knowledge of personal description.[5]

The first accurate system for description of prisoners, also called *portrait parlé* (spoken picture), was devised by Bertillon. In its original form the *portrait parlé* was divided into four categories:

1. Determination of color (left eye, hair, beard, and skin)
2. Morphological determinations (shape, direction, and size of every part of the head)
3. General determinations (grade of stoutness, carriage, voice and language, dress, social standing, etc.)
4. Description of indelible marks (scars, tattooings, etc.)

The *portrait parlé*, with its hundreds of exact definitions and details, was, however, altogether too complicated for detectives. Some parts are still used, but the great bulk of it has been discarded. It is, however, regarded as one of the classic subjects of police science, and at least the members of the identification bureau ought to be familiar with it.[6]

Coverage of the following items in descriptions of wanted persons will prove to be adequate in most cases:

Name
Sex
Color
Nationality
Occupation
Age
Height
Weight
Build—Large; stout or very stout; medium; slim; stooped or square-shouldered; stocky.
Complexion—Florid; sallow; pale; fair; dark.
Hair—Color; thick or thin; bald or partly bald; curly; kinky; wavy; how cut or parted; style of hairdress.
Eyes—Color of the iris; bulgy or small; any peculiarities.
Eyebrows—Slanting, up or down; bushy or meeting; arched, wavy, horizontal; as to texture, strong, thin, short- or long-haired; penciled.
Nose—Small or large; pug, hooked, straight, flat.

Whiskers—Color; Vandyke; straight; rounded; chin whiskers; goatee; side whiskers.

Mustache—Color; short; stubby; long; pointed ends; turned-up ends; Kaiser style.

Chin—Small; large; square; dimpled; double; flat; arched.

Face—Long; round; square; peg-top; fat; thin.

Neck—Long; short; thick; thin; folds in back of neck; puffed neck; prominent Adam's apple.

Lips—Thick; thin; puffy; drooping lower; upturned upper.

Mouth—Large; small; drooping or upturned at corners; open; crooked; distorted during speech or laughter; contorted.

Head—Posture of: bent forward; turned sideways to left or right; inclined backwards to left or right.

Ears—Small; large; close to or projecting out from head; pierced.

Forehead—High; low; sloping; bulging; straight; receding.

Distinctive marks—Scars; moles; missing fingers or teeth; gold teeth; tattoo marks; lameness; bow-legs; pigeon toes; knock-knees; cauliflower ears; pockmarks; flat feet; nicotine-stained fingers; freckles; birthmarks.

Peculiarities—Twitching of features; rapid or slow gait; long or short steps; wearing of eyeglasses; carrying a cane; stuttering; gruff or effeminate voice.

Clothes—Hat and shoes: color and style; suit: color, cut, maker's name; shirt and collar: style and color; tie: style and color; dressed neatly or carelessly.

Jewelry—Kind of; where worn.

Where likely to be found—Residence; former residences; places frequented or hangouts; where employed; residences of relatives, etc.

Chronic diseases—Obtain information from family physician and neighborhood druggist concerning disease, also addresses given to them by patient.

Personal associates—Friends who would be most likely to know of the movements or whereabouts of the person wanted or with whom he would be most likely to communicate.

Habits—Heavy drinker or smoker; drug addict;[7] gambler; frequenter of pool parlors, dance halls, cabarets, baseball games, resorts, etc.

How he left scene of crime—Running; walking; by vehicle; direction taken.

Regarding the details of the above list, the following should be noted:

Height—When questioning a witness about the height of a wanted person, one should ask the witness to compare the height of the person with the height of another person familiar to the witness. It cannot be expected that the witness will be able to tell more than the average height of the body, i.e., distinguish between small, medium, and tall persons. A small person is between 5 ft. and 5 ft. 3 in., a medium person between 5 ft. 4 in. and 5 ft. 7 in., and a tall person 5 ft. 8 in. to 6 ft. and over.

Complexion—Peculiarities such as freckles, pockmarks, pustulous skin, etc., are noted.

Hair—The hair may be: (a) light blond, (b) blond, (c) dark blond, (d) brown, (e) black, (f) red, (g) white, (h) mixed gray, (i) gray. Baldness should be specified, i.e., it may be *frontal, occipital, cover the whole top of the head,* or be *total.* Hair of buried corpses sometimes turns red owing to the action of the humus in the soil.

Eyes—Seven distinct colors may be seen in the iris: (a) blue, (b) gray, (c) maroon, (d) yellow, (e) light brown, (f) brown, (g) dark brown. Peculiarities such as *pronounced bloodshotness; different colors in the two eyes* (multicolored iris); *white spots on the iris; albinos* (blue eyes with red pupils); *arcus senilis* (a glossy ring surrounding the iris); *squinting, large, pear-shaped,* or *eccentric pupils; amputations; artificial eyes;* and *watery eyes* are noted. Peculiarities of the eyelids, such as *skin folds at the greater canthus* (inner eye corner), one or both eyelids *hanging, long* or *sparse lashes* and *pronounced pouches under the eyes,* should also be noted.

Figure 15.   The three principal forms of baldness. From left to right: *frontal, occipital,* and *covering the whole top of the head.*

Eyebrows—The color should be especially noted when it differs from the hair.

Nose—The nose is without doubt one of the most important parts of the face from the viewpoint of recognition, although its form may undergo changes due to accidents, disease, or plastic surgery. Some peculiarities are: *The root of the nose,* or the nose saddle, which may be *very narrow* or *very wide; the bridge of the nose,* which may be *broken, flat, very wide,* or *deviating to the left* or *to the right; the point of the nose,* which may be *blunt* or *split; the nostrils,* which may be *very thick* or *very thin, flat to the left* or *to the right, higher to the left* or *to the right,* or *strongly revealed.*

Whiskers and mustaches—This part of the description generally has little value because of the facility with which it may be changed.

Ears—The ears constitute the most characteristic part of the body next to the patterns of the friction ridges. They remain unaltered from birth until death. In cases where an arrested person has to be identified by photograph they play a deciding role.[8]

The principal parts of the ear are the *helix,* the *lobule,* the *tragus,* the *anti-tragus,* the *anthelix,* and the *concha.*

The *helix,* which is generally divided into *beginning helix, upper helix,* and

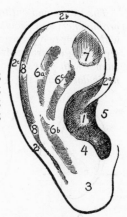

Figure 16. The principal parts of the ear: 1, concha; 2a, beginning helix; 2b, upper helix; 2c, rear helix; 3, lobule; 4, antitragus; 5, tragus; 6a, upper anthelix; 6b, lower anthelix; 6c, lower branch of upper anthelix; 7, *fossa digitalis;* and 8, *fossa navicularis.*

rear helix, may be *flat* (when the fold is missing) or form different *angles,* or the rear helix may be *fused* with the anthelix. Among peculiarities we find the *Darwinian extension,* the *Darwinian tubercle, frostbitten ears,* and *cut helix.*

The *lobule* may or may not be adhering to the cheek. The border furrow of the ear may or may not be continuous with the lobule. Some peculiarities are the *pierced, split,* or *twisted* lobule.

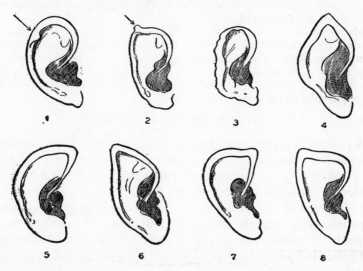

Figure 17. Peculiarities of the helix: 1, Darwinian extension; 2, Darwinian tubercle; 3, frostbitten ear; 4, upper helix with acute angle at top; 5, upper helix with acute angle in front; 6, upper helix with acute angle in rear; 7, upper helix with right angle in front; and 8, upper helix with right angle in rear.

The tragus and antitragus. The antitragus is examined as to *sloping, profile, prominence,* and *peculiarities.* Among peculiarities there may be noted *tragus with one or two protrusions, tragus* and *antitragus hairy, tragus missing, ridge separating* antitragus from the rest of the ear, *very small concha, fossa navicularis with pit* (a round cavity instead of the sharp angle in which the *fossa navicularis* generally ends).

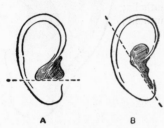

A   B

Figure 18.   Slant of the antitragus: A, horizontal;
B, oblique.

The *anthelix* is examined as to its *prominence.* It may be markedly *flat* or very *prominent* and *broad.* Peculiarities are: *upper anthelix in several branches, upper anthelix fused with upper helix,* and *upper helix with some growth.*

It goes without saying that the *general form* of the ear (oval, rectangular, triangular, or round), as well as the *protrusion from the head* and the *position on the head* (vertical or oblique), should be noted.

Distinctive Marks—One of the best features of Bertillon's *portrait parlé* was the accurate description of scars, moles, tattooing, and other marks upon the surface of the body. They were examined as to shape, dimensions, and position. This system of description, however, was initiated in the 1880's, when fingerprints were not yet used. Today tattooing, except on the hands, neck, and face,[9] has very little importance for identification.

Almost all distinctive marks can nowadays be removed by plastic surgery or other cosmetic methods. If surgery has not been used, however, there is always a possibility of at least locating the place where a tattoo mark has been removed. This is done by rubbing the suspected part of the skin until it reddens. The scar of the tattooing will then blanch in contradistinction to the surrounding red skin.

PHOTOGRAPHING PRISONERS

A prisoner is always photographed in an anterior view and in profile. The anterior photograph permits ready recognition of the individual, but the profile is necessary for certain identification. We are so accustomed to viewing our fellow citizens from the front, that it is quite possible, at first sight, not to recognize someone if a profile photograph is shown. Experience shows that the public will easily recognize front-view photographs in the *modus operandi* photographic file, but the trained observer will prefer the profile photograph when attempting to identify an individual.

Front-view photography shows very little of the most important details of the description, i.e., the profile of the nose and the details of the ear, but gives a good survey of the general appearance of the person

Figure 19. Photographic section of the Philadelphia Police Department Laboratory.

Photographic Unit, New York Police Department

Figure 20. Equipment for photographing prisoners. In addition to the usual black-and-white photograph, prisoners arrested for certain specified offenses are photographed in color with the 70mm. camera shown on the right.

and in some cases shows up peculiarities which are not apparent in profile.

The correct position of the head when photographing is of importance. In order to obtain this position, two lines crossing each other at an angle of 75 degrees may be drawn on the ground glass with a pencil. The head in the profile photograph should then occupy such a position that the intersection of the lines is at the outer corner of the eye and the horizontal line passes through the center of the ear.

The negative of a criminal's photograph should not be retouched. Scars and other marks must show sharply and clearly.

A black or dark-maroon background is often used for white people and a gray background for colored people. If possible, the light should be uniform for all photographs. This can only be obtained by the use of artificial light, which should come chiefly from above and the rest from the front and side. The light should play on the ear so as to bring out its details very sharply. Triangular lighting (floodlights) should be used for best results. The speed and lens opening can best be determined by test.

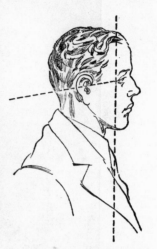

Figure 21. The correct position of a prisoner's head for photographing. The line passing through the tragus is at a 75° angle with the vertical line.

At times additional photographs are taken, front view with hat on or the whole figure or both. If several persons have been arrested in the same case, they are photographed in a group, with a seven-foot stake marked off in inches behind them.

The number of the photograph and the date are marked on a strip and photographed with the prisoner so that it is not necessary for the operator to make any marks on the negative. This may be important in court to offset any charge of altering the picture.

All identification photographs should be taken in proper alignment, and special consideration should be given to the ear. When a female is the subject, her hair must be arranged to expose her entire ear.

In this country a 4 by 5 studio camera equipped with a portrait lens is used. To facilitate identification, both front and profile views are taken on the same film. This is accomplished by covering half of the film with a mask, so that only one half is exposed at a time. If no mask is available, the two views can be taken on two separate films and printed side by side on one sheet.[10]

The camera is placed on a studio camera-stand, and the person to be photographed is seated in a studio-type chair. The camera lens should

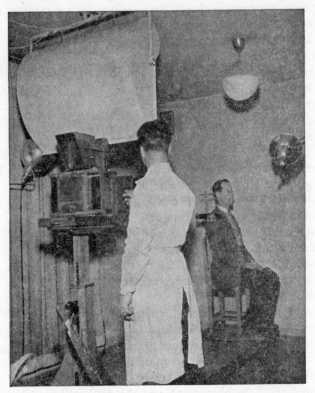

Figure 22.   Photography setup in a smaller police department.

be approximately on a level with the eyes of the person to be photographed. The picture should be sufficiently large to bring out the facial characteristics. It is always important to make certain that the camera has been properly focused. The positions of the camera and the chair should be marked on the floor when the right distance between them has been determined.

The New York City Police Department is now using speed-lights. This is a special type of electronic flash tube that has inside the tube a modeling light of low intensity for posing and focusing, but which, at the time of flash, produces a high-intensity, high-speed flash at the instant of shutter opening. The modeling light may have the low intensity of a 60-watt bulb. The speed-light is synchronized with the shutter and flashes in 1/5,000 of a second. This requires the fastest type of panchromatic film.

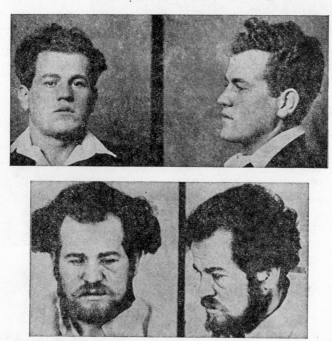

Figure 23. A human face may change completely in a short time. Top: Photograph of a prisoner twenty-three years old. Bottom: The same prisoner five years later, having passed the interim in the prisons of several European capitals. His moral by this time was, "If you would have a good time in prison, be as bad as possible."

Some Continental police forces use a special camera and a special chair mounted on a jointed platform. The camera has two lenses mounted over one another, the upper lens being for the ground glass. By means of this arrangement, the man to be photographed may be observed during the exposure. The seat of the chair is as small as possible and is framed with wooden slabs surrounding the sides and divided evenly. In order to sit more comfortably the subject instinctively tries to sit erect. The chair is supplied with a head support to insure that the head is in the correct position. The head support also serves to keep in place the numbers to

Scotland Yard
photographing
criminal in
1872.

Old, once widely used, but now obsolete method
of photographing the front and profile views at
the same time. The mirror picture is naturally
reversed.

The method of police
photography introduced
by Bertillon in the 1880's
and still used in the greatest part of the world.

Modern police pho-
tography, in which
three views are taken;
the method in use to-
day on the Continent.

Figure 24. Stages in the development of police photography.

be photographed with the subject. The chair revolves by the action of a lever attached to the camera.

IDENTIFICATION OF THE INDIVIDUAL BY MEANS OF FINGERPRINTS

The greater portion of the human body is covered with hairs. Most of these are very rudimentary, the fully developed ones being found on a few parts only. Some parts of the body are completely devoid of hairs— namely, the palm of the hand and the palmar surface of the fingers, as

 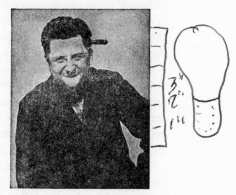

Figure 25. Old-time con men trying to disguise their faces while being photographed by the police.

well as the soles of the feet. On these parts we find friction ridges which form different patterns. Such friction ridges, more or less developed, will be found on corresponding parts of the body in all mammals.

The skin consists of two principal layers, the epidermis and the corium. In the upper portions of the corium are the so-called corium papillae, forming the pattern of the friction ridges. The nerves of sensation terminate in the furrows between the ridges.

If a friction ridge is examined through a magnifying glass, one finds that on each ridge there is a row of pores, the mouths of the sweat glands. They are equally distant from each other.

One sweat pore with the surrounding part of the friction ridge is called an *island*. There is reason to believe that the friction ridges are formed by the fusion of such islands. The number of sweat pores therefore represents the number of islands fused into a ridge.

From the viewpoint of identification, friction ridges are divided into three groups: *fingerprints,* meaning the patterns on the tips of the fingers;

palmar prints, or prints of the palm of the hand; and *sole prints,* or prints of the sole of the foot.

Of these, the fingerprints are the most important. Nowhere are the patterns so intricate and complicated as in the fingerprints; the friction ridges on the two lower joints of the finger and the palm of the hand are comparatively monotonous. The chance impressions found at scenes of crimes in most cases originate from the fingertips. This fact adds to the importance of their patterns.

EARLY HISTORY. The history of the use of fingerprints is fairly meager, although there are some early accounts of interest about them. These, curiously enough, come from the Far East. So far as the records show, there were only a few occasions in which our ancestors in Europe or America showed interest in fingerprints.

A prehistoric tomb was discovered in 1839 on the island of Gavr'Inis, Brittany, France. Peculiar patterns in the form of arrows, rings, and snakes were found on its stone walls. It is now believed that these represented stylized designs of patterns of friction ridges. Another early record, probably aboriginal, is an Indian pictograph showing representations of finger patterns carved on a rock at Kejemkoojic Lake, Nova Scotia.

We also know that in the first century after Christ a Roman lawyer named Quintilian was the defending attorney for a blind man who was prosecuted for having killed his father. At the scene of the crime there were bloody palm prints on the walls, which were thought to have been made by the blind man after the murder. The defense attempted to show that the real murderer was the stepmother of the defendant and that she had made those palm prints on the wall in order to cast suspicion on her blind stepson. The Roman lictors must have been very near to a discovery of the palmar patterns as evidence, but no attempt at identification was made.

When the famous Italian anatomist, Marcello Malpighi (1628–1694), examined different parts of the human body with the then recently invented microscope, he also discovered the patterns of the friction ridges; but neither Malpighi nor Purkinje, a professor of physiology at the University of Breslau, Germany, who in 1832 wrote a book in which he dealt with the patterns of the skin, had any thought whatsoever of using those patterns for the purpose of identification.

The credit for having adopted fingerprints for commercial purposes belongs to the East. Fingerprints were found on Babylonic clay plates. The Babylonians, in order to protect themselves against forgeries, pressed a fingerprint into the soft clay when they wrote receipts and other important documents. It appears that even before Christ the Chinese used fingerprints as seals for personal identification.[11]

The German criminologist Robert Heindl [12] has thoroughly studied the history of fingerprints in the Far East and found that they were already commonly used for identification purposes during the Tang dynasty (618 to 906 A.D.). Later the Chinese developed a classification of fingerprints based upon loops and whorls for the identification of criminals. This Chinese system of classification was described by a Dr. McCarthy in an American journal in 1886, and Galton learned of this. Heindl is convinced that Galton derived his classification system from the Chinese. The Galton–Henry system, the one most widely used, is therefore said to be derived from China.

Figure 26.   Robert Heindl.

DISCOVERY OF MODERN DACTYLOSCOPY. Dactyloscopy, or identification by means of fingerprints, was discovered simultaneously, but independently, by two Englishmen living in Asia. They were Sir William J. Herschel, administrator of the Hooghly district in Bengal, India, and Dr. Henry Faulds, on the staff of the Tsukiji Hospital, Tokyo, Japan. Both denied that they had had any previous knowledge of the use of fingerprints in Asia for identification purposes, but it seems more than a coincidence that dactyloscopy was born in Asia, the classical continent of fingerprinting.

Herschel's first attempt to use fingerprints was made when he compelled two natives who wrote their names on a contract to press an inked finger on the paper after the signature. This mystical procedure is alleged to have been carried out in order to frighten the natives so they would not later deny their signatures. At this time, 1858, Herschel had no thought of the individuality of fingerprints. Very soon, however, he realized their importance as a medium of identification, and used them in his district to prevent pensions from being paid out to impostors, a common crime in India at that time.

Herschel, in 1877, sent a semi-official report on fingerprints to the in-

spector general of Indian prisons, requesting him to introduce fingerprinting in the prisons of India. This gentleman, however, did not accept
Herschel's suggestion, and the latter continued to work without publishing the results achieved. We can imagine his astonishment when in 1880
he read in *Nature,* a journal of popular science, an article signed by Henry
Faulds, describing fingerprints and pointing out their usefulness for tracing criminals by chance impressions left at scenes of crimes. Dr. Faulds
had begun to study fingerprints of living persons after having become
interested in fingerprints found on prehistoric Japanese pottery. It is
interesting to note that Faulds' studies led him to the discovery of chance
impressions, while Herschel, on the contrary, looked upon fingerprints
as a dependable means of identification. Herschel answered immediately,
in the next issue of *Nature,* and while making no claims of priority, stated
that he had used fingerprints for more than twenty years and had introduced them for practical purposes in India.

If we compare Herschel's work of twenty years, during which he established the usefulness of fingerprints as a means of identification, and
Faulds' brief work resulting only in general speculation, we must certainly regard Herschel as the pioneer of modern fingerprinting.

The ideas of Herschel and Faulds were adopted by an English scientist,
who gave fingerprinting its scientific foundation. Sir Francis Galton (born
1822 in Birmingham and died 1911 in London) was a famous English
anthropologist. He worked out the foundation of the Galton–Henry system of classification, the final touch being added by Sir Edward Richard
Henry, who had studied with Herschel in India and later became the
police commissioner of the metropolitan district of London. The Galton–
Henry system was first introduced in India, and later—in 1901—was
adopted by Scotland Yard. This latter step definitely put an end to the
anthropometrical system of Bertillon.

Bertillon's enthusiasm for fingerprinting was lukewarm, because he
looked upon it as a rival of anthropometry. A fingerprint system, in the
modern sense of the word, was therefore not introduced in Paris until
after the death of Bertillon in 1914. In view of these facts it is odd that
Bertillon is sometimes credited with having been the father of the fingerprint system.

A contemporary of Galton, the Argentinian Juan Vucetich, also devised a system of fingerprint classification. In 1898 he introduced in
Argentina a system very similar to Galton's original system. Later he
accepted Galton's subclassification with ridge tracing and ridge counting.
The system of Vucetich has found widespread use, especially in Latin

countries, and is used in the original or modified form in all South America; in Lyons, France; Geneva, Switzerland; Oslo, Norway, and other places.

FIRST RULE OF DACTYLOSCOPY: THERE ARE NO TWO IDENTICAL FINGERPRINTS. When fingerprinting was first used as a means of identification, defending attorneys would sometimes object to its use, claiming the possibility that identical fingerprints could be found. Galton, in his book *Fingerprints,* showed mathematically that there could not be two identical fingerprints; but opponents raised the objection that these calculations were purely theoretical and that a sufficient number of fingerprints had not yet been examined.

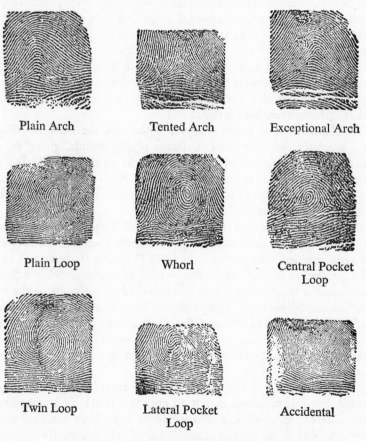

Plain Arch	Tented Arch	Exceptional Arch
Plain Loop	Whorl	Central Pocket Loop
Twin Loop	Lateral Pocket Loop	Accidental

Figure 27. The fingerprint patterns.

Today, however, after the fingerprinting of millions and millions of individuals over a period of fifty years, one can offer a convincing demonstration that two identical fingerprints do not exist. Fingerprints, like other physical objects, obey Quetelet's rule: Every nature-made thing shows unlimited and infinite variations of forms. Nature never exactly duplicates one of her works. We may, for instance, search in vain for two identical leaves. If we found two which seemed alike to the eye, a microscopic examination would immediately show a formidable unlikeness. Galton calculated that 64,000,000,000 different patterns were possible, i.e., almost three times the numbers of fingers existing in the world on the basis of a total population of 2,350,000,000.

A South American scientist calculated that if only twenty characteristic points in each pattern were recorded and these were compared with the present population of the earth, there would be the possibility of getting the same pattern only once every 4,660,337th century. There is a saying that one should not force biological facts into a mathematical straitjacket, and this is certainly true about such calculations. Much more important is the fact that two identical fingerprints amongst the millions registered have never been found.

THE HEREDITY OF FINGERPRINTS. Sometimes the daily newspapers print articles concerning the inheritance of fingerprints, giving the impression that fingerprints may be inherited in all their details and that they may even be used to determine paternity. Such opinions conflict with one of the fundamental principles upon which dactyloscopy rests, namely, the absolute individuality of fingerprints.

Galton's researches on the inheritance of fingerprints conclusively showed that they are *not* inherited. After Galton, several scientists studied the same problem. For instance, in 1892 Forgeot's studies down to the third generation in different families where intermarriages had occurred demonstrated that patterns were not inherited. Senet came to the same conclusion after having examined several families down to the fifth generation. In 1908 Cevidalli found that there existed a certain tendency to heredity. After Cevidalli, several research workers—Helweg, Harster, Sommer, and others—expressed the opinion that fingerprints are not inherited.

These dissimilar opinions may lead one to regard the question as perplexing, but it is necessary merely to note that it has been looked upon from different viewpoints. Anthropologists have been satisfied with a mere similarity in the general arrangement of the patterns, thereby drawing their conclusion that inheritance plays a part. On the contrary, criminologists who have dealt with the problem have sought an absolute identity, and this has never been found.

All researchers unanimously state that identity, from the dactyloscopic viewpoint, has never been found between parents and their children or between brothers and sisters.

During the past, the question of the heredity of fingerprints has been extensively debated, and several scientists, such as Ethel M. Elderton, K. Bonnevie, Poll, and others, have found that there is a tendency to heredity in certain patterns. However, the question of proving paternity is a different matter. Though research in a very large number of cases may give interesting results for the science of heredity, it is unlikely that it will prove possible to determine fatherhood from fingerprints.

SECOND RULE OF DACTYLOSCOPY: FINGERPRINTS ARE NOT CHANGE-ABLE. Fingerprints are already formed in the fourth month of pregnancy, between the 100th and 120th day of the development of the fetus. A three-months-old fetus has absolutely smooth fingers. From this stage on, the friction ridges begin to grow on the fingertips and finally cover the whole finger. During further intra-uterine growth, as well as after birth, the patterns enlarge, but no changes take place in the number or arrangement of the friction ridges. The same relation exists between the fingerprint of an infant and the fingerprint of the same individual when an adult as exists between a photograph and an enlargement of it.

The best proof of the unchangeability of fingerprints is found in those taken of the same person at different ages. The oldest known print of a friction-ridge pattern was made in 1856 by the German anthropologist Welker in Giessen, Germany. At thirty-four he recorded a print of his palm. In 1897, at the age of seventy-five, he made a similar print. There is an absolute identity between the prints. Herschel also made prints of his own hands at an interval of twenty-eight years, and these likewise show an absolute identity. All bureaus of identification tell the same story.

The pattern is not influenced by illnesses—except by leprosy. Fingerprints of infantile paralysis patients and rachitic and acromegalic persons (an illness which enlarges the face, hands, and feet) have established the fact that, although the distances between the friction ridges can be changed, the patterns as a whole will not show any alteration. If the skin on the fingertips is wounded or burned, the whole pattern, with all its details, will reappear when the wound heals. Locard and Witkowski, of Lyons, who performed rather painful experiments on themselves by burning their fingertips with boiling water, hot oil, and hot metals, showed that after the healing of the epidermis the original patterns reappeared,

If the wound is deep, the resulting scars constitute no obstacle to identification. On the contrary, the scars are characteristic clues of high value. It has been observed that scars on a fingerprint will make a much deeper impression on the judge and jury than the entire pattern.

Recent attempts of criminals to alter or destroy the skin on the fingers by plastic operations have also proved unsuccessful.

The friction ridges disappear only after death, by the decomposition of the body. It can truthfully be said of them that they are an indelible signature which we carry with us from the cradle to the grave.

EQUIPMENT FOR TAKING FINGERPRINTS. In order to make impressions of fingerprints for registration or comparison the following materials are needed: paper, printer's ink, rubber roller, and plate.

All smooth white paper can be used except blotting paper. The best paper for fingerprinting purposes is absolutely white, as glossed as good writing paper, and perfectly smooth. Paper with a rough surface, with watermarks, or with printing on the back should be avoided. The ink should be of the best type used for Mimeograph or neostyle and in tubes.

The plate can be a glass plate or a polished metal plate about 6 by 10 inches. It should be covered when not in use and should be cleaned daily with gasoline or turpentine. The regular Mimeograph rolls are the best, but the hard rubber rollers employed in photography can also be used.

The taking of good fingerprints requires a certain amount of experience, although the actual process is in itself very simple.[13] The fingerprint should be rolled, so as to show the whole pattern from one side of the finger to the other and to bring out all deltas.[14] The determination of the delta is of great importance for classification and identification of many chance impressions, when only one side of the pattern may be had.

The ink is spread in a thin layer on the plate with the aid of the roller. The person to be fingerprinted must have clean fingers. Perspiring hands are cleansed with ether, benzol, or soap and hot water to avoid spotty prints. The person is told to relax both the fingers and the hand, and under no circumstances should he be allowed to exercise any pressure on the paper himself. The fingers are now printed in order, generally from the right thumb to the right little finger, and from the left thumb to the left little finger. The tip of the finger to be printed is placed on the plate with the right edge of the nail downward and then is rolled slowly, with a light pressure, to the left edge of the nail. The finger is then rolled on the paper from the right to the left. It should never be rolled back again.

If a finger is mutilated or curved, it is inked directly with the roller and the paper then pressed against the finger. Persons who resist fingerprinting may be fingerprinted in this manner.

FINGERPRINTING PERSONS WITHOUT THEIR KNOWLEDGE. In cases where the person is to be fingerprinted unknowingly it may be arranged for him to touch a clean bottle or a glass, although a special trap will give the best results. Such a trap may consist of two heavy thick glass plates, about 6 by 10 inches in size, whose corners are held together by screws. There should be no frame, and the plates should hang by a chain fastened to two of the screws. A photograph is sandwiched between the plates. The suspect is asked if he has seen the photograph before, the plates being carelessly swung toward him at the same time. He is then forced to grasp the plates with both hands, leaving prints of all ten fingers on the glass. These fingerprints are powdered and photographed.

REGISTRATION OF FINGERPRINTS. The registration of fingerprints may be divided into *principal registration* and *single-fingerprint registration.* In the principal registration the fingerprints are classified in such a manner that only with the aid of the ten patterns is it possible to look up a certain registration card in order to establish the identity of the fingerprints. The principal registration is intended to identify a second offender with the aid of *all ten fingerprints.* The single-fingerprint registration (see Chapter IX) is intended to identify chance impressions left at the scene of a crime, something which is almost impossible to accomplish by means of the principal register. The average detective is not supposed to be familiar with the registration of fingerprints, although in our opinion a rudimentary knowledge of this subject is absolutely necessary in order to understand the fingerprints and their identification.[15]

DELTA AND LOOPS. The delta is a triangular-shaped detail of the pattern which is found in all fingerprints. It is not found in the arches. A delta is formed by the bifurcation of a ridge or through the wide separation of two ridges which have, up to the point of the delta, run side by side. For the subclassification the determination of the point of the delta or outer terminus is very important. For this there are the following rules:

Figure 28.   Determination of the inner and outer terminus and ridge counting

If the delta is formed by the bifurcation of a ridge, the point of the delta is the place where the line becomes divided. If there is more than one point of division, the one nearest the core is the point of the delta. If the delta is formed by the separation of two parallel ridges, the point nearest the place where the lines separate is the point of the delta. In this latter case the point of the delta may be an isolated island on the outermost loop in a loop pattern.

The core is the center of the pattern. It may consist of a loop or a rod, or be composed of whorls of concentric figures, circles, or ellipses. The point of the core or inner terminus is of importance for the subclassification. If the core consists of a single loop, the point of the core is on the part of the loop farthest from the delta and where the curving begins. If the core is a rod, the tip of the rod is the point of the core, and if there are an uneven number of rods, the point of the core is the tip of the middle rod. If the rods are even in number, the two inner rods are considered to make a loop and the point of the core is determined as above described. In whorls the point of the core is the middle of the innermost circle or the innermost part of the spiral.

There are five principal patterns:

1. *Arches,* in which the ridges go from one side of the pattern to another, never turning back to make a loop. In the arches, as a rule, there are no deltas.

2. *Tented arches* are modifications of simple arches, and they are also devoid of real deltas. In the tented arches one line goes more or less straight upward in the center of the pattern and the other lines are grouped in pointed angles around this axis.

3 and 4. *Radial loops and ulnar loops* are characterized by the turning of one or more of the ridges to make a loop. There is only one delta in the loop. If the opening of the loop is directed toward the ulnar side of the hand, the loop is called an ulnar loop. (The ulna is one of the two bones of the forearm—the one located on the same side as the little finger.) If the loop opens toward the opposite direction, it is called a radial loop (named from the radius, the bone of the forearm on the same side as the thumb). It is impossible to determine if a loop is ulnar or radial from a single fingerprint without knowing which of the two hands you are dealing with. The following rule should then be followed: On right-hand prints ulnar loops have the delta to the left and radial loops have the delta to the right. On left-hand prints, ulnar loops have the delta to the right and radial loops have the delta to the left.

5. Whorls. To this group belong all patterns with two deltas and patterns too irregular in form to classify. The following patterns belong to the whorl group.

   a. *Simple whorls,* which have two deltas, with the core consisting of circles, ellipses, or spirals turning to the right or left.

   b. The *central pocket loop,* which looks like a simple loop; in the core, however, we find at least one ridge which forms a convex curve toward the opening of the loop. This can be looked upon as a tendency to whorl formation with a second delta. In order to distinguish between loops and central pocket loops, the following rule should be applied: If a straight line is drawn through the axis of the loop, at least one ridge which is convex to the side of the opening should cut the line at a right angle.

   c. *Lateral pocket loops,* in which there are at least two loops opening at the same side.

   d. *Twin loops,* in which there are two loops opening at different sides.

   e. *Accidentals.* For these patterns, no rules can be made. They are very rare and often have more than two deltas.

RIDGE COUNTING. In this procedure an imaginary line is drawn from the point of the delta to the point of the core and all ridges which cut this line are counted. The two points should not be included in the counting. Lines close to the imaginary line are not included if they do not touch it, but very small fragments of ridges which cut it are included.

An amateur may need to draw the line between the point of the delta and the point of the core with a lead pencil, but the experienced person will not find this necessary. For counting, a magnifying glass and a needle should be used.

RIDGE TRACING. Through ridge tracing the whorl patterns are divided into three groups. When the left and right deltas have been located, the ridge be-

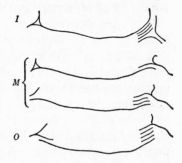

Figure 29.   Ridge tracing.

ginning on the lower side of the left delta is traced toward the right delta. If the ridge bifurcates or ends, the line underneath it is followed. If the ridge actually meets the right point of the delta, the pattern is called a *meeting whorl.* If the ridge passes inside the right point of the delta, the pattern is called an *inside whorl.* If the ridge passes outside the right turn of the delta, the pattern is called an *outside whorl*. At least *three ridges* must separate the traced ridge and the right point of the delta in order to classify the pattern as outside whorl or inside whorl. If there are only two ridges between them, the pattern is known as a meeting whorl.

PLASTIC SURGERY AND CRIMINAL IDENTIFICATION

The desire to change the appearance of the face in order to escape recognition by the police has since time immemorial tempted criminals. In most cases these alterations have been confined to the dyeing of the hair, growing or cutting off of mustaches and beard, wearing of spectacles, etc. Cases are known, however, in which criminals endeavored to alter the appearance of the face by means of more or less crude operations. A certain member of the gang of the ill-famed Bonnot, the French automobile *apache,* for instance, made slits along the inner corners of his eyes in order to make them appear longer. This operation changed his appearance very little. The notorious John Dillinger is supposed to have had surgical operations performed on his face, but the changes these made in his appearance were actually very slight.

There is no doubt that a good plastic surgeon may be able to work wonders by altering the facial appearance; it must be pointed out, however, that such changes will prove to be of little value if the criminal cannot cut off all his connections with his old surroundings and start anew.[16]

There are two reasons why attempts to conceal identity by resort to plastic surgery are likely to be unsuccessful. One is that in a normal face it is difficult to make changes that will really deceive, and if they are made the surgical traces are not obliterated within the time that a hunted criminal can count upon. The other is that he finds it difficult to locate in a place where he is a stranger and to stay there unobserved long enough to allow the healing influence of time to be of aid. He must do more than alter his face. His posture, his manner of walking, may expose him to scrutiny. Short-sighted people recognize their friends not by their features but by some familiar movement when they walk. Time is therefore an essential, and time the hunted criminal cannot command. When he is found, the evidence of what has been done is readily detected. Where there has been surgical incision there is some scar or trace of scar for skilled eyes to see.

The situation is somewhat different when the person sought is known to have had some definite deformity. The photographs of him may show a broken nose, or peculiar eyebrows, or protruding ears, a burn scar, a

Figure 30. A small portion of the fingerprint classification unit in the FBI Identification Division, Washington, D. C.

birthmark, the scar from a knife wound, a harelip, an injured eyelid, or any one of a score of disfigurements to which attention is immediately attracted and whose absence will divert attention. The changes resulting from correction of these disfigurements may be significant. Moreover, the effort is made, and properly so, to leave no visible trace of the surgery that has effected the improvement. But there are traces to be found when sought for, if an opportunity to seek them is afforded.

The framework of the nose may be reconstructed with no surface incision, but there will be the mark of an incision within the nose. A protruding ear may be laid back against the head, but the skin had to be incised to get at the cartilage whose removal made this possible. This scar may be looked for behind the ear. The sunken lip that goes with harelip may be well out in place, but the means of holding it there can be quickly discovered. Even a protruding jaw may be shortened, but not without leaving evidence within the mouth of how it has been done. Perhaps the only exception to the rule is in the case of an absent fingernail. It can be replaced from another fingernail, but that donor nail must have time to grow. If it does, no trace is left of what was done.

It is true, also, that these betterments produce changes that influence not only the appearance of the whole face but even the general bearing of the person. Back of these, however, are the personality, the individuality, the history, the movements from place to place, by which identity may primarily be disclosed. Surgery cannot disguise these. It may be necessary first to catch your hare, but once caught the recipe for treating it is at hand. Like all camouflage, surgery may for the moment deceive, and so constitute a measure of defense, but it is not in itself a perfect defense. It may be somewhat of an obstacle to criminal investigation, but it is an obstacle that intelligent observation can overcome.

1 Lambert Adolphe Jacques Quetelet, statistician, astronomer, and mathematician, was born in Ghent in 1796 and died in Brussels in 1874 while director of the Observatory in Brussels. Quetelet is looked upon as the father of modern statistics.

 2 Alphonse Bertillon, born 1853 and died 1914, was founder and leader of the bureau of criminal identification of the Paris police department. He invented anthropometry, the *portrait parlé,* the photography of criminals, and metrical photography. Accounts of the priority of Stevens regarding anthropometry are given by Heindl,[2] who, however, does not do Bertillon full justice. Heindl regards anthropometry as a detriment to the development of dactyloscopy. It is true that Bertillon was against dactyloscopy, but anthropometry had been used for decades before dactyloscopy had won recognition worth mentioning. No one can deprive Bertillon of the honor of having been a pioneer in the technique of identification.

 3 Rudolph Archibald Reiss was born in 1874 in Baden, Germany, and died in 1929 in Belgrade, Yugoslavia. Reiss was professor of police science at the University of Lausanne, Switzerland, until 1915. From 1920 on he directed the laboratory

of the Yugoslavian National Bank in Belgrade. Reiss is the author of numerous works on police science and especially on photography.

4 The New York City Police Department adopted the Bertillon system in 1896 and did photographic work in conjunction with it by employing outside civilian photographers. In 1901 the photographic gallery was established. Photos were taken of the full face and the right-side profile, and each picture was numbered consecutively beginning with No. 1. In 1906 the then Lieutenant Faurot, who later became deputy police commissioner, was sent to Scotland Yard to learn and adapt their fingerprint methods. He brought back the Galton–Henry system of identification by fingerprints. Police departments throughout the United States sent men to New York to learn the system. The system was commercialized in the Middle West.

5 Sannié.[5]

6 Bertillon's classic[2] is recommended.

7 It is worth while to remark that some addicts generally are recognized at first glance by the experienced detective especially immediately after they have had the dope. Their bright, shiny eyes, air of self-confidence, and loud, self-assertive speech betray them immediately. For details see chapter on drug addiction.

8 An interesting case in which the ears were used for identification purposes was that of the false Grand Duchess Anastasia of Russia. Some years after World War I a woman, after an attempt at suicide in Berlin, Germany, declared herself to be a daughter of the murdered Czar Nicholas. She said she had escaped the execution of the Czar's family in Ekaterinburg, Siberia, had lost her memory as the result of a blow on the head, and after many adventures had finally come to Berlin. She had a superficial similarity to the real Anastasia, but Professor Marc Bischoff, the head of the Scientific Police Institute of Lausanne, Switzerland, established her non-identity by means of the ears—by comparing profile photographs of the impostor and of the real Anastasia.

9 French criminals or persons associating with *apaches* have quite often one or several blue points tattooed at the outer corner of the eye.

10 Decades ago a mirror was sometimes placed alongside the head of the criminal when he was photographed, so that the front view and the profile were photographed simultaneously. This method, however, is to be rejected, chiefly because the profile is reversed, so that, for instance, a mole on the right cheek will appear on the left cheek in the photograph. This may give rise to serious mistakes.

11 In China and Japan seals are used by all classes of people from the mandarin to the laborer and are necessary for all kinds of signatures. The laws regulating the use of seals are very elaborate, and seals must be registered by the police in order to be valid. It is still very common in China for a signature to be made valid by putting a fingerprint in India ink on the paper. These fingerprints generally are so blurred that their use for identification is impossible.

12 Dr. Robert Heindl, last head of the Bavarian Central Police Institute of Munich, is the author of a book[2] which is unique in the literature of identification. Through his initiative fingerprint classifications were introduced in Germany at the beginning of this century, and he has made extensive researches on fingerprints and their history.

13 Sannié–Guérin.[2]

14 The Greek letter Δ, which looks like a triangle and signifies the meeting place of three ridges.

15 The standard book by Henry is recommended for this purpose.

16 See J. Eastman Sheehan, M.D., F.A.C.S.; also Maliniak.

VI PROBLEMS WITH MISSING
PERSONS

OF THE INNUMERABLE SERVICES THAT A POLICE DEPARTMENT FURNISHES the public, the tracing of missing persons is one of the most important. Here all the records of the police, the services of experienced detectives, and much of the technique of the crime laboratories, which is otherwise important in tracking down criminals, may be put to use to relieve suffering persons from anxiety regarding their kin or friends. In the following discussion the organization of this work in New York City will be described. Even if it may be said that the conditions in New York are on a greater scale than anywhere else in the world, the principles governing this type of work there can certainly be applied anywhere.

In New York City the Missing Persons Unit (formerly Bureau) is a branch of the Detective Division, which operates from police headquarters and has city-wide jurisdiction. Its functions are:

1. To locate and return runaway children under eighteen years of age.
2. To locate persons who disappear under circumstances indicating an involuntary absence; that is, where the disappearance might be caused by death, accident, kidnaping, homicide, or insanity.
3. To establish identity and to notify relatives in all cases where a person is brought to a city hospital or a body is moved to the morgue.

To understand the procedure in a missing persons case, it must be realized that the Communications Division of the New York City Police Department is notified whenever an ambulance or a morgue wagon is required. Communications notifies the hospital or morgue and then the local police precinct, which dispatches a patrolman to make a report on the case. This report is telephoned to the Communications Division, and if the person or the body is unidentified or the address of relatives is not known, the case is relayed to the Missing Persons Bureau by telephone.

The local precinct also prepares a card under the name of the person hospitalized or body found (if known) and every twenty-four hours forwards all such cards to the unit at headquarters known as the Bureau of Information, where they are filed alphabetically. Included in this file are not only the hospital and morgue cases but also arrests and summonses.

Thus if a man fails to return home after a day's work and his wife makes inquiry to the police, the local officer first checks with the Communications Division to see if the man has been hospitalized or found dead during the day. For a check of previous days, inquiry is made at the Bureau of Information. This double check is necessary because the record cards are forwarded only once every twenty-four hours.

When a person is believed missing, a relative usually goes to his local police precinct. There a detective lists the necessary information on a special form. He first checks with the desk officer of his own precinct, since the missing person could have been arrested or hospitalized in that precinct. Then he checks with the Communications Division and with the Bureau of Information to see if the missing person or anyone answering his description has been removed to a hospital or morgue. If none of these calls produces any results, he telephones the information he has recorded on the form to the Missing Persons Bureau, where the same form is prepared in triplicate. For confirmation, he forwards a copy of his own report to the Missing Persons Bureau the following day.

At the Missing Persons Bureau an index card is prepared under the name of the missing person and filed alphabetically. One copy of the special form is filed according to date, the second according to physical description (that is, first by sex and then by age), and the third is given to a member of the Missing Persons Bureau so he can proceed with his investigation. Thus we have the three points covered which are necessary in any missing persons bureau file: a file by name, by date, and by physical description.

After the necessary records have been prepared, a teletype alarm is sent throughout the city and to adjacent police areas. In addition a daily mimeographed list of missing persons is prepared and distributed to railroad and bus terminals, hospitals, homes, and shelters where runaways might seek refuge, etc. In the meantime the missing persons detective interviews the relatives and follows up any leads established by this interrogation.

It has been found that almost 85 percent of all missing persons eventually return home of their own volition, usually within a short time; others are picked up by the police or occasionally found in hospitals or morgues. Eventually 99½ percent of all missing persons are located; the balance remain missing. One case in three thousand proves to be a homicide case.

The third type listed above—the aided case—is handled from the other end in the following way. Patrolmen report all ambulance and morgue cases to their local precincts. Where relatives are unknown, the pertinent information is telephoned through the Communications Division to the Missing Persons Bureau. If the name of the person is unknown, the physical description is given. At the Missing Persons Bureau a card giving the name of the person is prepared and filed. If identity is not known, a card is prepared and filed under a classification such as "unknown man," "unknown woman," etc. A copy is also filed by date and by physical description if identity is unknown. A third copy is given to the missing persons detective assigned to the case, whose duty it is to establish identity and notify the relatives. Sometimes this is accomplished by an interview with the patient in the hospital, through papers in the person's possession, through checking the files to see if he has been reported missing, or by sending a teletype to other police departments, giving name, if known, and physical description, and asking such departments to check their records to ascertain if the person so named or described has been reported missing to them.

If the case in question is a morgue case, an expert of the Missing Persons Bureau draws up a new and particularly accurate physical description, giving special attention to scars, tattoos, identifying characteristics, laundry marks, dry cleaners' marks, etc. An ultraviolet lamp is used to detect invisible laundry marks. The body is then photographed and fingerprinted. Fingerprints are checked with city, State, and Federal authorities. Many identifications are established by this means. From an annual average of 2,500 cases in New York City, 97 to 98 percent are usually identified. The remainder are interred in the city cemetery and their photographs placed in the unknown-dead file in the Missing Persons Bureau. These are open to inspection by persons seeking long-lost relatives, but caution must be exercised in accepting such identifications because many persons would make an identification either for the purpose of collecting insurance or for remarrying.

In those cases where a person is declared insane and is committed to an institution a photograph and physical description is also maintained in the unidentified-insane files of the Missing Persons Bureau.

Some interesting data in regard to missing persons are disclosed by statistics such as the following:

1. On the basis of thirty years' experience the peak age for missing persons is age fifteen.
2. There are usually about 25 percent more male than female.
3. May is always the peak month and September the second peak month.
4. The majority of missing persons travel to other cities. Most of the missing persons picked up in New York have been found to come from other cities.
5. A thorough search should always be made at the point where the missing person was last seen; many bodies have been located in the attics and cellars of their own homes, or on roofs or in air shafts, or at their places of employment.

Where the missing person is a child, the necessary information and description are immediately dispatched by radio to patrol cars in the area, in order that a supervised search can be made. This has proved effective, particularly in cases where the child has been killed by a sex maniac. If the case is one of a lost child, he is usually found by a patrol car wandering somewhere in the area.

Where the circumstances indicate that the missing person may be the victim of a homicide, copies of his fingerprints should be obtained, if possible, and placed on the wanted file with city, State, and Federal authorities. A copy of a dental chart should also be secured, if possible, and kept on file. In the event that the body is later found so badly decomposed that fingerprinting is precluded the dental chart may make identification possible. Records of medical histories should be included also. In one case of a decomposed body identification was established by comparing X-ray plates taken in life with stomach ulcers and blood clots found on remains. The following cases will further illustrate the use of records such as the foregoing to establish identification.

A "floater" (dead body floating in water) was found on the rocks at Governors Island, New York, in April, 1949. It could be established that it was the body of a man approximately thirty-five years of age, 5 ft. 7 in. in height, and weighing about 145 lbs. The hair had been completely washed away, but judging from the pubic hair, which was dark brown, it could be assumed that the head hair might have been black. The teeth were in good condition, with no fillings or cavities, although the upper front teeth had been lost in the water. The body was nude except for a pair of white shorts. The body was decomposed and was estimated to have been in the water for about four months. The epidermis of both hands was lost. After treatment of the dermis for several days, it was possible to obtain an impression of all fingers, and it was thus possible to identify the body.

In the treatment of fingers in cases such as the foregoing good results may be obtained by cutting the fingers from the hands and drying them over an open flame. Each finger is individually and very carefully treated. The drying should be done by passing the finger over the flame with a sweeping movement until it has shrunk and dried. Thereafter printer's ink is applied lightly and impressions taken. This method, however, requires a certain amount of skill on the part of the operator, and it is advisable to follow the method described on page 108.

In another case a male floater was exhumed in March, 1949. The man had been dead for sixteen months; the body had been in water for six months and interred for ten months. The combined findings pointed to missing person "A.L.," who had disappeared from his home in December, 1947. For comparison the following table gives the data on the missing person and the data on the unknown deceased person:

Missing person	Body found
38 years of age	34–38 years of age
5 ft. 7 in. height	5 ft. 8 in. height
155 weight	145 weight
Brown eyes	Eyes decomposed
Brown hair	Few strands of brown hair
Teeth in good condition; denture completed while in the armed forces	Teeth in good condition
Laundry marks on shirt collar	Label of shirt disclosed laundry marks M–1782–1333 x c x
Tattoo mark believed to be an eagle	Tattoo of spread eagle, partially decomposed, traced to A.L. by the police research laboratory

It was possible here for the technical research laboratory of the New York City Police Department to trace the deceased through the laundry marks, which were traced to A.L., a war veteran. Parts of the body were devoid of flesh, and it was impossible for the family to identify the remains; the hands had been eaten away by the water so fingerprinting was impossible. The tooth chart of the deceased was compared with the dental chart of A.L., and the findings were sent to the veterans' branch of the Department of the Army, where a further comparison of dental charts and the report of the roentgenologist covering a fractured right ankle was made with the records on file in that department. The doctors were unanimous in their decision that the reports made on the remains of the deceased man as checked with the records of their office referred to one and the same person, A.L. The family was satisfied with the identification beyond a reasonable doubt, and the deceased was buried in the military cemetery on Long Island.

Another floater was found in the North River, New York City, in May, 1949. Both hands and feet were destroyed by the water. The body was estimated to have been in water approximately twelve to sixteen months. The head had fallen from the body when the scoop of a ship picked it up when dredging the river. The findings finally pointed to one "A.S.," who had been reported missing in November, 1947. Here are the data on the missing A.S. and on the body found in the North River:

Description of missing A.S.	*Description of unknown deceased person*
35 years of age	35 years of age
5 ft. 11½ in. height	5 ft. 11 in. height
130 weight	140 weight
Hernia and ulcer scars	Postero-gastro-enterostomy, indicating scars
Heart condition	Mitral valvular disease
Dark suit	Black-gray portions of trousers
Treated at Polyclinic Hospital, and carrying a clinic card with signature A.H.S.	Card on deceased proved to be clinic card. Letters S and L were exposed by ultraviolet rays, which also exposed initials A.H.S. on folder of wallet. Belt buckle with Army officer's emblem.
The name of missing person was A.... H.... S.... L....	

The family stated that the deceased had tried to enlist in the Army and was always wearing some military emblem.

The case was concluded even to the extent of the life insurance.

IDENTIFICATION AND RECONSTRUCTION OF DEAD BODIES

When an unknown body is found, the following items should be noted:

1. Place where the body is found
2. Time when found
3. Cause of death[1]
4. Time when death occurred[1]
5. Supposed age

6. Supposed profession
7. Description of body (see "Description of Wanted Persons" in Chapter V)
8. Description of clothing (with special attention to laundry and dry-cleaning marks)
9. Jewelry and other objects on person

Hands and nails may give important information as to the profession of the person. Cobblers, blacksmiths, musicians, seamstresses, etc., have characteristic callosities on the hands. The appearance of the nails may give information. We should note their shape, length, and cut, and whether or not they are torn, bitten, manicured, or well kept. Bleeding under the nails caused by blows or clamping persists for a long time and extends forward to the tip of the nail. Fingernails will grow about $\frac{1}{25}$ of an inch in a week, and the toenails about one-fourth as fast. A characteristic appearance of the nails will be seen in laundrymen on the thumb and index finger of the left hand, in cobblers on the left thumb, in engravers and jewelers on the right thumb, and in lacemakers on the right index finger. Dyers, photographers, and pharmacists usually have brittle nails.

All unknown dead should be photographed in the same manner as a criminal, i.e., front view and profile.

For photographing purposes it is necessary to have the face of the dead person appear as natural and with as lifelike an expression as possible because of the difficulty encountered by most persons in recognizing a dead relative or friend from a post-mortem photograph. The eyes are in most cases shut, or if open, they are sunken and covered with a gray film. There is no contrast between the color of the skin and the lips, and finally the rigid, unnatural appearance of the face gives the impression of something unreal. In order to make the face more lifelike the appearance of the eyes and the lips should be improved. Numerous methods have been proposed for this purpose. Generally a mixture of equal parts of glycerin and water is inserted in the eye-sockets with the aid of a syringe with a fine tip. The eyelids are then raised. The lips are covered with a mixture of carmine in alcohol, which is applied with a small brush. If the body has been submerged in water for a long time and the skin is already partly gone, the face can be given a more natural appearance by powdering it with talcum, which is gently massaged over the flesh and the remaining skin. Rubber gloves should be used for this purpose.

If putrefaction is so far advanced that large portions of skin and flesh have disappeared, one may be able to reconstruct the face even in seemingly impossible cases. The putrefaction ceases when corrosive sublimate solution is used as an external wash. Plastelina, clay, or cotton fixed with collodion and covered with the proper shade of wax may be used to replace the lost flesh. As the eye-sockets are generally empty, glass eyes are inserted. The missing hair is replaced by a wig, and the face is made to assume its natural color with make-up.

Dead bodies, or parts of them, that have become mummified as a result of being buried in dry places may be returned to their natural shape by putting them in a 3 percent potassium hydroxide solution. They should be allowed to stay in the solution until they have resumed their natural contour. Then they should be soaked for a short time in water and preserved in a weak solution of alcohol or formalin.

Attention should be drawn to the possibility of making lifelike casts of the faces of dead persons through the moulage process (see "Casting Methods" in Chapter XXVII). In certain Continental police laboratories, as, for instance, in Vienna, casts are made of the heads of practically all unknown dead bodies. The casts are painted in natural color and placed in a gallery for future identification. A cast is superior to a photograph for identification purposes, and should be made, if possible, in all cases where a major crime is suspected. Continental police records show that such casts have frequently aided in solving crimes. The assistance of a sculptor is employed when reconstructions or repairs are needed. The results obtained through casts sometimes are quite remarkable.

In cases where teeth have been treated by a dentist there is a possibility of identification if the dentist can be located. Fillings, crowns, bridges, and other items of dental work are mainly individual and may sometimes be traced to a certain dentist through his records and teeth charts. The teeth are the hardest and most lasting of tissues. Heat and chemicals have little influence on them.

When a skull is found, the possibilities of identification are indeed small if the teeth are missing. However, a method invented by the German anatomist Wilhelm His may be of aid in such cases.[2] When the supposed skull of the famous composer Johann Sebastian Bach was found, Professor His modeled a head, in clay, over the skull of Bach in order to bring out the similarity with contemporary portraits. To determine the average thickness of the layers of flesh on the face, measurements were made on dead bodies in a normal state of nourishment. The measurements were made by introducing a needle deep into various parts of the face. The thickness of the fleshy portion was thus obtained. With the aid of the average measurements determined, a table was computed which was utilized by the sculptor. The same method has been advantageously used for the reconstruction of other faces.

The method, though, has its weak points. By modeling the ears, no clue to their original shape can be obtained. If the individual who is to be reconstructed was unusually stout or unusually thin, the similarity would not be very striking. It is also quite difficult to reproduce the lips and the contour of the mouth, both of which give the face its characteristic countenance. The reproduction of the nose appears difficult, but the results are good because of the distinctive length of the nasal bone.

The La Rosa murder, which occurred in New York in 1916, is a good example of resourceful reconstruction.[3]

On September 12, 1916, a skeleton of a human being was found in a house on Hegeman Avenue at Powell Street, Brooklyn. It appeared to belong to a man about twenty-five years of age and 5 ft. 6 in. tall. There was a small amount of brown hair on the scalp, and the lower jaw contained two gold teeth. The body was dressed in trousers and coat of a blue fabric, with a black belt around the waist. The only article found in the pockets was a briar pipe. The wisdom teeth had not yet grown. Some dark-brown hair was also found on the neck. The autopsy showed that the skull had been fractured in four places. Since the investigations as to the identity of the man proved fruitless, it was decided to attempt a reconstruction of the face.

A sculptor remodeled the face with plastelina. Dark-brown hair was obtained from a barber, and two brown glass eyes were bought, on the assumption that the man was Italian. Rolled newspapers covered with plastelina formed the neck. The eyes were put in place, eyebrows were made of brown hairs, and a quantity of hair was put on the top of the head and down along the neck. This reconstructed piece of work was photographed.

A few days later, a new skeleton was found in the same vicinity, together with a check payable to a certain Rosario P. The Bureau of Missing Persons reported that a man of that name had been missing. The skeleton was identified by a sister, together with the clothing and the contents of the pockets. When friends of P. were questioned, they were also shown the reconstructed head of the first skeleton, and one of them quickly cried, "This is Domenico La Rosa," whereupon he tried to open the lips of the head saying, "Domenico had two gold teeth besides being inclined to baldness." Another witness testified that he had known La Rosa for many years and that the reconstruction was similar, although

La Rosa's face had been stouter. When this omission was corrected with plastelina, the witness declared that the reconstruction was now absolutely similar to La Rosa's facial appearance.

Naturally a skull with teeth is the most valuable part of a skeleton for identification purposes, but most of the bones will give some information.

The height of the person, relative size, relative age, and very often the sex may be determined from the bones. Diseases of the bones, their shape, and fractures may also give information.

For the determination of sex the skull, the hip bones, and the sacrum are most important. Each may, in most cases, reveal the sex; but if all three are missing, the determination is uncertain. In such cases the size and proportions of the other bones may, however, be of help.

The age of a skeleton, during the first eight to ten years of life, can be determined within approximately one year; and under one year of age, examination of the skull may determine the age within approximately one month. The older the individual, the less precise must be the determination of age. During growth, and until twenty-five years of age, various changes in the bones and teeth are still going on. This fact may give good clues to the age of the person. In the adult stage no such changes take place. In the aged slight and very approximate changes may be noticed.

There are numerous tables and calculations worked out by anthropologists for determining the height of a person from various portions of the skeleton. The length of the thigh bone, for instance, multiplied by 3.7 (in women 3.6) is equal to the height of the body; the length of the whole skeleton plus 1 to 1½ inches is equal to the height of the person, etc.

Determination of race can only be made from the skull, and even here the conclusions are far from certain if the racial characteristics are not distinct. Examinations of this kind should be made only by experienced anthropologists.

FINGERPRINTING DEAD BODIES

Fingerprinting dead bodies is necessary in murder cases and should always be done. Experience shows that a number of dead bodies found are those of tramps or criminals previously fingerprinted. Identification from their fingerprint records is then quite easy.

In the case of a fresh dead body the fingers are unclenched and each one is inked individually with the aid of a small rubber roller. A piece of paper is put on a spoon-shaped piece of wood and slowly and evenly rolled over the pattern. If the fist is too tightly clenched, a small incision may be made at the base of the fingers. The contraction may also be overcome by dipping the hands in hot water.

To fingerprint floaters that have been in the water for only a short time —and if the so-called washerwoman's skin is not too marked—the finger is dried off with a soft towel and glycerin is injected with a syringe under the skin of the fingertips in order to smooth the surface. The fingerprints are then taken as described above.

If the floater has been in the water a longer time and the friction ridges have disappeared, the skin of the fingertip is cut away (an area corresponding to the part of the pattern necessary for the classification). This area of skin from each finger is placed in small labeled test tubes contain-

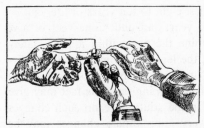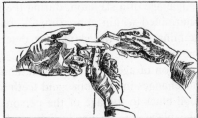

Figure 31.   Fingerprinting a fresh dead body. The ink is applied directly on the finger with the aid of a small roller; then a piece of paper attached to a semilunar-shaped piece of wood is rolled over the inked finger.

ing formaldehyde solution. These tubes are kept in a small box made for the purpose. If the papillary ridges are still preserved on the outer surface, the person taking the prints places the portion of the skin on his right index finger, protected by a rubber glove, and takes the prints. That is to say, he first rolls the finger on the inking plate and then on the fingerprint record form. If the papillary ridges on the outer surface have been destroyed, as often happens, the portion of skin should be fastened carefully on a cardboard, inner surface out, and photographed. As is well known, the entire papillary pattern may be found on the inner surface, and it remains until the skin is totally destroyed. It should be photographed with oblique light to get the relief.

In cases of putrefied or burned bodies one should use the same techniques described above, applying them according to the circumstances.

RAMIFICATIONS OF MISSING PERSONS WORK

Here is an example to show the ramifications of missing persons work. During the recent war, a girl disappeared from a large government reservation in Tennessee. Her father, a key employee, threatened to leave to search for her, despite security restrictions and the need for his uninterrupted skill on this project. A description of the girl was sent out to all police departments. Several days later, the parents received a postcard from the girl postmarked Brooklyn, New York. The illustration indicated the postcard might have been purchased near the Brooklyn Navy Yard. Detectives immediately started checking hotels in that area, finally locating a hotel where a girl of her description had stayed with another girl for two days. A teletype to neighboring States and cities resulted in the girl's being picked up by the Massachusetts State Police two days later while hitchhiking a ride. Her return home, unharmed, not only permitted her father to continue his work in the industrial war effort uninterrupted but also led to some interesting disclosures regarding plant protection, with resulting improvements from a security standpoint.

1 These questions should be answered by the medical examiner or coroner.
2 For more comprehensive information see Wilder–Wentworth.
3 In the last years several attempts have been made by Dr. W. M. Krogman of Chicago to identify bodily remains of persons. No actual identification has been made, however, and the La Rosa case still seems to be a unique one. See Krogman–McGregor–Frost, Krogman,[1] and Krogman[2] in *FBI Law Enforcement Bulletins*. As Dr. Krogman assures us in one of the articles that "the science of anthropology offers its services," it is hoped that the value of the methods described will in time be tested in real life.

VII SKETCHING THE SCENE
OF A CRIME

OFTEN THE SCENE OF A CRIME PLAYS AN IMPORTANT PART IN GATHERING evidence necessary for the prosecution, and a clear picture of it serves to outline evidential facts and circumstances to court and jury. The appearance of the scene should be presented and recorded in such a manner that witnesses, prosecutors, attorneys, jury, and judges can see it clearly. The history of criminal investigation shows some cases which have been unsuccessfully prosecuted because an accurate description of the scene of the crime was not made immediately. It is therefore essential that an accurate, objective description be made before anything can be altered, removed, or destroyed.

There was a time when long and intricate descriptions of scenes of crimes were written. Such descriptions, being too complicated, fail to give the imagination enough substance to form an accurate picture of the scene. A good sketch and photographs will provide this substance.

After the discovery of the daguerreotype about one hundred years ago, photography began to be used on rare occasions to record scenes of crimes. Twenty years later, with the creation of the dry plate, this method came into common use by metropolitan and national police forces. Today sketching and photography, individually or combined, are used to record the scene of a crime. They are related in such a way that one might compare the sketch to the skeleton and the photograph to the flesh and blood of the record. The sketch furnishes information about distances; the photograph presents the details.

Sketching and photography combined should as a rule be used in recording the scenes of homicides and felonious assaults, fatal and critical vehicular traffic accidents, arson, major burglaries, and other major felonies.

Attention is drawn to the fact that in the last decade a rather handy photogrammetric apparatus has been designed with which it is possible to draw an accurate sketch from a photograph. Several police departments on the Continent, particularly in Switzerland, use this method in recording the scene of traffic accidents.

GENERAL RULES FOR SKETCHING

All measurements should be taken with equal accuracy in order to prevent distortion. For instance, one distance should not be judged by footsteps and another by mensuration. A common error is to measure a distance by pacing and to express the result on the sketch in feet and inches.

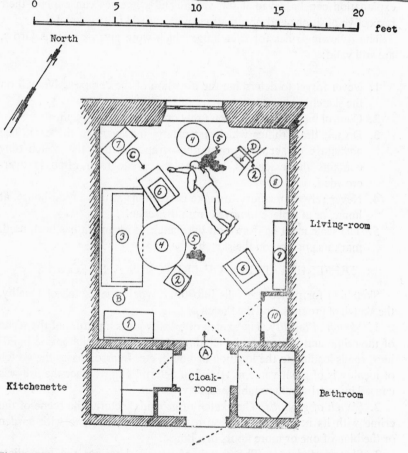

Figure 32.   Sketch of the room in which a homicide was committed. The letters indicate the placement of the camera for taking the photographs, the numbers as follows: 1, chest of drawers; 2, chair; 3, sofa; 4, table; 5, pool of blood; 6, armchair; 7, table for radio set; 8, sideboard; 9, bookshelves; 10, closet.

Another frequent mistake is to draw the outlines of a room from accurate measurements and then put furniture into the sketch by mere visual estimate when the placement of the furniture is the major factor.

Decide what is to be sketched before the work of sketching is started. This is especially important when sketching an outdoor site. Sketching cannot begin until one is sufficiently familiar with the scene, but on the other hand it may be of great help if at least the first rough sketch is ready before the victim or witnesses are interrogated. Time and considerable explanation can be saved if the victim and witnesses can explain their respective positions and observations with the aid of the sketch.

The following rules for sketching, which were given by Hans Gross, are still valid:

1. Never forget to determine the direction of the compass. Draw it on the sketch.
2. Control measurements. Don't rely on others to give them.
3. Do not draw things which are clearly irrelevant to the case. The advantage of sketching over photography is that the sketch only contains the essentials, whereas the photograph often is overcrowded.
4. Never rely on memory to make corrections at the station house, at home, or at a place removed from the scene.
5. The scale must be drawn on the sketch. If a camera has been used, mark its position on the sketch.

DIFFERENT TYPES OF SKETCHES AND SCALES

Sketching for police use falls into three types: the sketch of locality, the sketch of grounds, and the sketch of details.

1. *Sketch of locality.* The sketch of locality gives a picture of the scene of the crime and its environs, including such items as neighboring buildings, roads leading to the location or house, etc. In arson cases the sketch of locality is of great value as an aid in determining whether the fire was caused by nearby inflammable property.

2. *Sketch of grounds.* The sketch of grounds pictures the scene of the crime with its nearest physical surroundings, e.g., a house with garden or the plan of one or more floors in a house.

3. *Sketch of details.* The sketch of details describes the immediate scene only; for instance, the room in which the crime was committed and the details thereof. Nowadays the sketch of details of a room is generally carried out by what is known as a cross-projection. In this method walls

and ceiling are pictured as if on the same plane as the floor. The accompanying picture shows how a cross-projection is made (Figure 33). The cross-projection method gives an especially clear impression of the scene in cases where bloodstains or bullet holes are found on walls or on the ceiling. This method of describing a room was further augmented by Kenyeres, who developed the plastic cross-projection. In this method the cross-projection is drawn on cardboard and cut out. Light cuts are

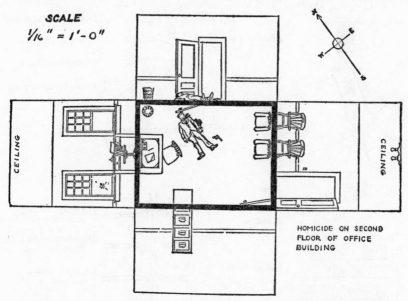

Figure 33.   Sketching the scene of a homicide by cross-projection.

made along the junctions of walls, floor, and ceiling, so that the cardboard may be bent. The folding of the cardboard walls in proper relation to one another reproduces a model of the interior of the room. One of the walls is left hanging to permit looking into the room.

It is important to determine a scale suitable to the locality or scene to be sketched and also to the size of the paper being used. Suitable scales for use in police work are:

½ inch = 1 foot (for small rooms)
¼ inch = 1 foot (for large rooms)
⅛ inch = 1 foot (for large rooms and small buildings)
½ inch = 10 feet (for large buildings)
½ inch = 10 feet (for buildings with surrounding gardens)

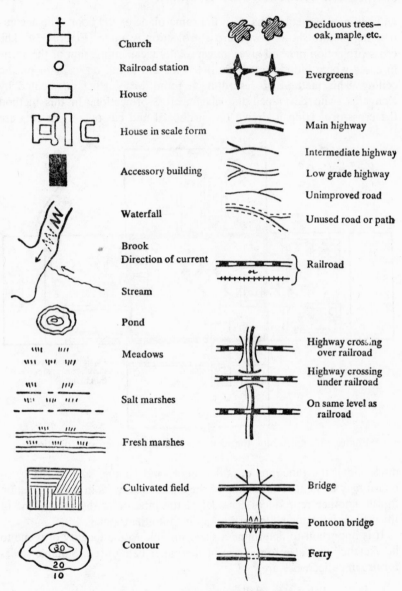

Church

Railroad station

House

House in scale form

Accessory building

Waterfall

Brook
Direction of current

Stream

Pond

Meadows

Salt marshes

Fresh marshes

Cultivated field

Contour

Deciduous trees—
oak, maple, etc.

Evergreens

Main highway

Intermediate highway

Low grade highway

Unimproved road

Unused road or path

Railroad

Highway crossing
over railroad

Highway crossing
under railroad

On same level as
railroad

Bridge

Pontoon bridge

Ferry

Figure 34.   Common conventional signs.

⅛ inch = 10 feet (for large areas with several buildings; for instance,
    a village)
⅛ inch = 100 feet (for a region with a length of at least one mile in
    each direction)

The work of sketching is made easier by using cross-section or graph
paper. The scale, together with the title, date, time, and the sketcher's
name, must always be recorded in the corner of the paper in traditional
fashion.

When sketching large outdoor sites, the conventional signs used on
maps can be used advantageously. The most common are shown in Figure 34.

MATERIALS

A police force should be equipped with adequate materials to make
sketches. Such paraphernalia should be kept in a small case always available for immediate use. A sketchboard consisting of a square of soft pine
attached to a photographic tripod, as
shown in Figure 35, will prove very useful.[1] A small alidade is desirable, although a common wood ruler can be
used. Other items required for field
work are a good compass, preferably of
the military type, graph paper, a soft
lead pencil, india-rubber, common pins,
a wooden triangle with scale, a scale,
and a tape measure. A flexible steel ruler
is also useful.

Figure 35.   Sketchboard with
alidade.

To finish the sketch (this may be
done at a location other than the scene
of the crime), a drawing-board, white drawing paper, a drafting outfit, and multicolored crayons should be on hand. Coloring a sketch
should serve to make it clearer. For example, to show how a motor vehicle proceeded after a collision, use different color crayons for before
and after. Be careful not to use too many colors. A sketch is not a
painting.

SURVEYING METHODS

Sketching must be done in a logical and methodical manner. Some
draftsmen without previous technical training develop individual methods
which are quite accurate. When comparing the self-taught methods of old

policemen with standard surveying methods used in modern police and detective service, one is struck by the resemblance. However, it takes time before this state of self-development can be attained.

Sketching consists of determining the position of one point in relation to another point. The method most commonly used for this purpose is the *coordinate method*[2] (Figure 36). This consists of locating points by perpendicular distances from a common base line.

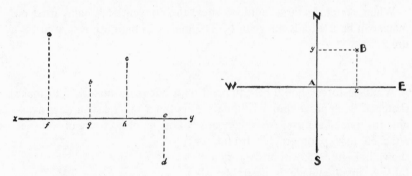

Figure 36. The principle of the coordinate method.

Figure 37. Determining the position of Point *B* in relation to Point *A* by the coordinate method.

Let us suppose that the position of Point *A* in relation to Point *B* is to be determined (Figure 37). Two lines are drawn at right angles to each other through Point *A*. Let one of these lines represent north-south, and the other east-west. From *B* draw two straight lines perpendicular respectively to north-south and east-west. These lines, *By* and *Bx,* are termed coordinates of Point *B* in relation to *A*. *AxBy* is a rectangle; therefore *By* equals *Ax* and *Bx* equals *Ay*. In order to determine the position of Point *B* in relation to *A* measure the distance *Ax* on the line *AE* and the distance *xB* at right angles from *x*.

When performing this operation, measure eastward from *A* to a point directly opposite *B,* then determine the distance from this point to *B*. Point *B* may then be plotted. When buildings, rectangular fields, cross-roads, or right-angled ditches are in the area to be sketched, it frequently simplifies matters to use them as coordinates instead of north-south and east-west.

To sketch the interior of a room, a tape measure is stretched across the room as a coordinate and the ordinates to pieces of furniture, footprints, bloodstains, and so on, are determined (Figure 38).

Figure 39 shows how a road is sketched by the coordinate method. The sketching-table is set up by *A*. A stick is set at *B*. An additional stick is set at each point where the road crosses *AB*. Care must be exercised to set the most distant sticks first in order not to obstruct the line of sight as each stick is located. Measure ordinates from the different parts of the curve to the base line.

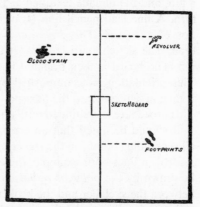

Figure 38. Sketching the interior of a room by the coordinate method.

A method related to the coordinate method is the *polar coordinate method* (Figure 40). In order to determine the position of a Point *B* in relation to Point *A,* at which the sketching-table is set, one draws a line of known direction, for instance, east-west (use the compass), through Point *A. A* is then connected with *B* by a straight line, following which the angle *BAE* is measured. The distance *AB* and the angle *BAE* are termed the polar coordinates of *B* in relation to *A*. The whole is called a polar coordinate system. When using this method, Point *A* is marked on the sketchboard with a pin, around which the alidade is swung and aimed at *B*. Distances are measured with the tape measure.

Figure 39. Sketching a road by the coordinate method.

Sometimes the coordinate method takes too long. Sometimes it cannot be used. In such cases the *traverse method* is used (Figure 41). To sketch a road by this method, proceed thus: The base line, *AB,* is marked and measured, and the sketchboard

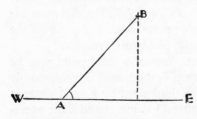

Figure 40. The polar coordinate method.

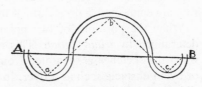

Figure 41. The traverse method.

is set up on Point *A* and oriented with the compass. The table must be horizontal. Point *A*, at which the sketchboard is located, is marked with a pin, and the alidade is aimed at Point *a*, where the road makes its first turn. A fine lead pencil line (traverse line) is drawn to mark the direction of *a* from *A*. This direction is now fixed. The distance *Aa* is measured. The sketchboard is now set up at *a* and the place marked with a pin. The board is then oriented in the same compass direction as in *A*. This orientation is accomplished by aiming back from *a* to *A*. A sight is then taken from *a* to the next point, *b*, and the distance *ab* is measured. This procedure is continued until all points have been located.

It should be noted that an error in the traverse method carries on to all succeeding points on the traverse.

Broken lines—for example, the edge of a forest—may advantageously be drawn by the *polar or radial method*, provided there is an open field between the sketcher and the broken line. If, for instance, the forest edge *AF* is to be drawn, the drawing-table is put up at Point *P* and oriented with the compass (Figure 42). Point *P* is marked on the paper with a pin.

Figure 42.   The polar or radial method.

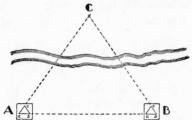
Figure 43.   Triangulation.

With the aid of the alidade, rays are drawn to the more important points of the edge, namely, *PA, PB, PC, PD, PE,* and *PF*. The distances are measured and recorded in a suitable scale on the paper. If the ends of the rays are connected, a projection of the edge of the forest results.

When the positions of two points are known, a third point may be determined by *triangulation*. This method is used most advantageously when the sketcher is separated from the third point by a great distance or by an obstacle such as a river. In Figure 43 Points *A* and *B* are accessible to the sketcher. The position of Point *C* is to be determined. The sketchboard is set up horizontally at *A*. This point is marked on the paper with a pin as *a*. Point *B* is then aimed at with the alidade, the line *ab* measured and drawn, and the direction of the compass marked on the paper. Point *C* is now aimed at, and the aiming line *ac* is drawn. The sketchboard is next set up at Point *B*. The alidade is set on the line *ab* and the board rotated until Point *A* is in the line of sight. Then the aiming line *bc* is drawn with the aid of the alidade. The point where the lines *ac* and *bc* cross each other is *C*.

By this method the position of several unknown points may be determined from two known points without direct distance measurement. Care must be taken that the angles at which the lines cross each other are never smaller than 35 degrees or larger than 145 degrees; otherwise the possible margin of error will be greatly increased. If several lines are drawn from one point, the aiming lines should not be drawn on the paper; only the part where the crossing-point is supposed to come should be shown.

Measurement of Height. Sometimes it is necessary to measure heights. Appliances required are a sketching-table and two straight sticks, one of which is graded. A simple graded stick can be made by fastening a tape measure to a stick by means of thumbtacks. When measuring, the sketching-table is set up before the object to be measured. The graded stick is put about two yards in front of the table. Aim on a slant from the near edge of the table to the top of the object and read the measurement on the point of the graded stick that is cut by the aiming line. The distance between the table and the object is also measured. This gives us two triangles, *acd* and *abe*. We know the measurements of *abe* and the ground-line distance, *G*. The two triangles are similar because their three angles are equal. The sides are therefore in proportion to each other according to formula:

$$\frac{h}{g} = \frac{dc}{G} \; ; \; dc = \frac{hG}{g}$$

If the ground is horizontal, add the height of the sketching-table, *bf*, to get the real height.

If the ground is sloping, take two aiming lines and measure the distances h_1 and h_2. The side h_1 in the small triangle corresponds to the side H_1 in the large triangle. This is also the case with h_2 and H_2. It is also possible to compare directly the triangles *abc* and *adf*, as they are similar. The real height, *H*, equals H_1 plus H_2.

$$\frac{h_1 + h_2}{g} = \frac{H}{G} \; ; \; H = \frac{(h_1 + h_2) \, G}{g}$$

In the latter example it is not necessary to know the height of the sketching-table.

The following examples will specifically illustrate this method of measuring height:

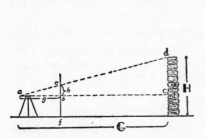 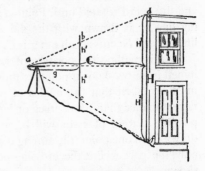

Figure 44. Measurement of height when drawing-board and object to be measured are on the same level.	Figure 45. Measurement of height when drawing-board and object are on different levels.

1. The height of a flagstaff on horizontal ground is to be measured. The sketchboard is set up 30 yards from the flagstaff and is 1.5 yards high. The vertical graded stick is 2 yards from the table, and the aiming line is cutting the graded stick at a height of 1.5 yards above table level.

$$\frac{1.5}{2} = \frac{X}{30}; X = \frac{30 \times 1.5}{2} = 22.5 \text{ yards}; H = X + 1.5 = 22.5 + 1.5 =$$

$$24 \text{ yards} = 72 \text{ feet}$$

2. The height of a tree which grows on a hillside is to be measured. The sketchboard is 72 yards distant horizontally from the tree and is 1.5 yards high. The upper and lower aiming lines intercept an interval (h_1 and h_2) of 40 inches on the graded stick, which is 2 yards away from the table.

$$\frac{\frac{40}{36}}{2} = \frac{H}{72}; H = \frac{72 \times \frac{40}{36}}{2} = \frac{2 \times 40}{2} = 40 \text{ yards}$$

1 The military-type traverse table, with its attachments, is convenient for this purpose.

2 For further details on the coordinate system see Griffin or other standard texts on analytic geometry and trigonometry.

VIII PHOTOGRAPHING THE SCENE
OF A CRIME

THE APPLICATIONS OF PHOTOGRAPHY TO LAW ENFORCEMENT ARE TOO numerous for treatment here beyond a brief discussion of its use at the crime scene. In criminal investigation photography can be used as an additional mode of communication wherever the investigator is concerned with identification, reporting, recording evidence, or presenting court testimony.

In Chapter V, photography was seen to be an invaluable aid to personal identification. Historically, this was the first use of photography in criminal investigation. Soon after this innovation, the value of the camera became apparent as a means of recording the appearance of the crime scene and of objects of evidence. A photographic supplement to an investigative report is now expected as a matter of routine, particularly in crimes of violence. With the development of the scientific aspect of photography, the camera in the hands of the laboratory expert became a means of discovering new evidence by rendering visible the hidden aspects of clues through the use of magnification, directed lighting, filters, and special emulsions. Finally, photography is indispensable to the effective presentation of certain types of court testimony. Exhibits of handwriting and fingerprint comparisons are considered integral parts of the expert's testimony. In a serious criminal case the verbal accounts and descriptions by witnesses become more vivid and meaningful if the jury has become acquainted with the scene through the medium of black-and-white or color photography.

The usefulness of photography at the scene of the crime is obvious. The photograph is a sort of artificial memory, often very sorely needed by the policeman. Many small details may escape the investigator at the first examination of the scene, and these may later prove of great importance. In most cases it is impossible to examine certain details repeatedly, because the scene of the crime has been altered, furniture has been moved, floors have been washed, etc. As an illustration, let us suppose that a dead man is found in his bed, shot through the forehead. A pistol is still clasped in his hand. The investigator makes the usual examination, sees no traces of violence, and draws the conclusion that he is confronted with a case of suicide. The body is buried. After some time, doubts about the suicide arise and the person is believed to have been the victim of a clever murderer. It is no longer possible to examine the hand that held the pistol to determine if the position of the fingers was natural or unnatural. It is no longer possible to determine whether there were suggestive traces of violence on the bed or on the carpet. Good photographs of the scene of the crime and of the body will help enormously in such a case.

There are cases in which remote developments compel the investigator to reconstruct, for instance, a room in detail, exactly as it was at the time of the crime. It can be said that a good photograph of the scene is a permanent reconstruction which is always available. It is sometimes a good idea to have a print made of the plate in the usual way and another print made of the plate reversed. Thus the scene is pictured as it actually looks and as it looks in reverse, with the right side to the left and the left side to the right. When the two pictures are compared, a quite different impression of the room will be obtained.[1] In many cases the reversed picture is almost unrecognizable, but in many other cases attention will be focused on details and objects which were not particularly noticeable in their normal positions.

Paul[2] illustrates the immediate influence which photography may have on a trial. A farmer, in building a barn, used old materials in order to economize. The beams and boards were quite decayed, and one day when a farmhand ascended to the second floor, a board gave way and the unfortunate man fell through the floor and was killed. The farmer was prosecuted for manslaughter in the third degree, but soon after the accident, in order to avoid judgments and expenses, he substituted new boards for the defective ones. However, the police had photographed the scene immediately after the accident. The photograph clearly showed that the death of the farmhand was caused by the old building material used. Furthermore it brought out the fact that the farmer had replaced the boards after the photographs had been taken.

In another case, reported by Balthazard, the Paris police had photographed the interior of a room which was suspected to have been the scene of a homicide. No bloodstains were found during the search. When the photograph was developed, however, a large washed stain on the carpet, invisible to the eye, was revealed. Here, as in many other cases, the photographic lens saw more than the human eye.

In Vienna some years ago, a young woman was found dead sitting on a bench in a public park. She had apparently shot herself through the head with a pistol which was lying in a natural position where it had presumably slipped from her hand. The scene was immediately photographed—in the early morning before sunrise. Later in the day, after developing the plate, the police photographer discovered that a person had been sitting close to the woman. This was shown by the marks in the dew which had collected on the bench. The marks were very faint, but the photographic lens had caught them before evaporation had taken place. Investigation brought out the fact that a homicide had been committed.

It goes without saying that the photograph has a psychological influence on the defendant and the jury as well as on the court. No description can tell the horrors of homicide as forcefully as a photograph can.

EQUIPMENT

Equipment for crime-scene photography should be selected to provide close-up photographs as well as medium-distant views. A press-type or view camera accepting 4-by-5-inch or larger film is most practical. An 8-by-10-inch negative size is excellent for black-and-white pictures, but a 4-by-5-inch or smaller film size is used for color photographs.

Two lenses for each camera will meet the requirements of most crime scenes—a wide-angle lens for interior photographs and a normal-angle lens for outdoor photographs and other purposes. The following focal lengths are suggested:

	4-by-5-inch camera	8-by-10-inch camera
Normal Angle	80mm. (3.2-inch) f/6.3	12-inch (30.5cm.) f/4.5
Wide Angle	152mm. (6-inch) f/4.5	135mm. (5.3-inch) f/6.3

Other essential items of equipment include a tripod, an exposure meter, a selection of filters, and an appropriate lighting system. Photoflood, photoflash, or electronic flash lamps can be used.

To photograph fingerprints developed at the scene, it is convenient to use a special fingerprint camera of the fixed-focus type with a built-in lighting chamber. Alternatively, a 5-by-7 view camera or 4-by-5 press-type camera with a long bellows extension may also be used for this purpose. By extending the bellows to twice the focal length of the lens a

1:1 size image can be obtained directly on the film. For greater convenience a close-up attachment is available to convert any late-model 4-by-5 Speed Graphic into the equivalent of a fixed-focus fingerprint camera.

PROCEDURE AT THE CRIME SCENE

The importance of the camera at the crime scene as an investigative tool requires no detailed explanation. The basic function of the crime-scene photograph is to aid the investigation in its search for truth, that is, the nature of the events that took place, their sequence, and causal relationships. This is accomplished, first, by providing an accurate pictorial representation of the appearance of the scene, together with the location of relevant objects at the scene. The photograph aids the investigator in reconstructing the crime and equips him with background knowledge for the questioning of suspects and witnesses. Finally, by presenting the court with a reliable visual record of the scene, the photograph enhances an understanding of the evidence and promotes an intelligent evaluation of testimony concerning the events that took place.

The aim of the photographer at a typical crime location is to record a series of scenes and objects which will acquaint the viewer with the place where the crime was committed and thus enable him to understand the manner in which it was accomplished. Since the relevance or significance of crime-scene objects is not always apparent, the photographer ordinarily takes more photographs than necessity would seem to dictate. By photographing from different viewpoints, different aspects of the same scene are presented.

The general procedure of crime-scene photography aims at obtaining views of broad areas of the crime locale, supplemented by closer views of sections containing important detail. The scene should be first photographed in its original, undisturbed state. The point of view of the camera lens may be selected as that of a typical observer. A series of views should be taken at this height and at an angle directed toward the most important object in the scene. If a room is to be photographed a set of at least four views will be required to show the room adequately. The number of photographs is usually determined by the nature, gravity, and circumstances of the crime. The number will be further influenced by the complexity of the criminal events and the amount and variety of physical evidence present.

In planning a series of photographs the elements of the offense can serve as a guide to the kind and number of views required. The prosecution's objective will be to show that a particular crime was committed and that the accused perpetrated the act. Thus, the prosecutor must establish the elements of the offense and adduce evidence associating the defendant with the crime scene and the events. This program can provide the photographer, too, with a useful frame of reference.

In a burglary, for example, the elements of breaking and entering would suggest photographs of the exterior of the building with close-ups of the window, showing where the jimmy had been applied. Views of the ransacked room or the rifled safe would aid in showing the intent of larceny. Photographs of footprints and fingerprints would tend to link the suspect to the scene.

In a homicide the manner of death should be shown with views of the room in which the body was found; areas of access to this room; evidence of struggle; signs of activities prior to the fatal event, such as drinking glasses, liquor bottles, or playing cards; and any trace evidence such as cigarette butts, bloodstains, or broken glass.

The circumstances of death can be illustrated by various views of the body, including close-up photographs of wounds and bruise marks. The weapon, of course, should be photographed, and the place from where it may have been taken.

PERSPECTIVE AND DISTORTION

To be acceptable for court purposes, a photograph should be a conventional representation of the scene or object. The perspective and tonal relationships should not tend to deceive the average person. In conventional perspective, vertical lines remain parallel while horizontal lines appear to converge at some distant point. Hence a photograph of a building in which the camera bed is tilted back may give the viewer an erroneous impression of the height of the building. Where it is necessary to tilt the camera bed in order to obtain a satisfactory field of view, compensating adjustments can be made on a view camera by using the various degrees of freedom of the lens board provided by swingbacks and swivels. Some restorations of perspective can be made in the enlarging process if the enlarging lens can be tilted as well as the easel.

A common misconception attributes many photographic distortions to the lens, particularly the wide-angle and the long focal-length lenses. Actually these lenses do not distort the perspective. Photographs made with these lenses appear distorted only because they are viewed from the wrong distance. As a general rule, a contact print should be viewed from a distance equal to the focal length of the taking lens. Thus, a con-

tact photograph taken with a two-inch focal-length lens will appear distorted when it is viewed at the normal distance of ten inches. In general,
the distortions can be readily corrected by enlarging proportionally, i.e.,
a negative from a two-inch lens will require a 5X enlargement to produce
a print suitable for viewing at ten inches.

MARKING DEVICES IN THE FIELD OF VIEW

Rulers, identifying letters, and similar marking devices are excellent
aids to an understanding of crime-scene photographs. When a series of
photographs is used as a supplement to the written report, markings in
the field of view are invaluable to the supervisor reviewing the investigation. In court exhibits the significant evidential points can be marked
so their relationship can be readily grasped by a jury, ordinarily unfamiliar with the subject matter.

Occasionally the admissibility of a photograph showing markers is
contested on the grounds that it does not truly represent the original
scene. As a precaution, then, the crime scene and its objects should be
photographed first in its original state. Markers—that is, devices which
aid the interpretation of a photograph—may then be placed in the scene
and another photograph taken with the same camera settings. Typical
marking devices are rulers and tape measures placed to show the relative
size of an object such as a rifled safe, or white arrows placed along a
skidmark to show points of discontinuity. A ruler when placed at the
side of a shoe impression, for example, serves as a guide in the enlargement process. At the time of taking the photograph the ruler may also
help in adjusting the camera so that it is parallel to the surface of the
shoeprint.

It should be noted that a ruler placed near the margin of the field of
view can be blocked out in printing, if necessary. Location markers,
however, cannot be deleted from a photograph easily. These are usually white sticks or numbered signs placed in the field of view to show the
exact location of important objects. Persons should not be used as markers; the objection of a "posed" picture may be raised against such a photograph. If a lettered board is placed in the picture for identification, care
should be exercised to avoid the expression of opinion, e.g., the label
"Burglary" or "Murder" should not be included in the identifying data
since it expresses a conclusion or opinion.

Many of the difficulties associated with marking devices can be eliminated by the use of a transparent overlay. The photograph can be taken
without any markers and the necessary inscriptions can be made on the

transparent overlay so that the information is conveyed to the viewer when it is placed on top of the photograph.

NEGATIVE MATERIALS

Fast panchromatic sheet film will serve for most purposes in black-and-white photography at the crime scene. Color photographs should also be taken of the scene. The rapid development of color photography in the last decade has made the process sufficiently reliable for routine use in crime-scene photography. A color photograph of a homicide scene, for example, is more informative for the average juror. Stains, such as those of blood, can be more readily seen. The marks of wounds and bruises are more easily identified through the additional contrast provided by color.

With regard to the admissibility of color photographs, it appears that the general rules hitherto applied to black-and-white photographs will apply also to color films. "That a color is gruesome does not render it inadmissible per se where the medium is relevant and material to prove the point in issue. It is only where its inflammatory nature outweighs its relevancy and materiality that courts will exclude color films."[3]

MOTION PICTURE CAMERAS

Certainly in the larger police departments the motion picture camera will find many applications. A 16mm. motion picture camera is ideal for certain kinds of surveillance work. Concealed within an ordinary commercial truck, the photographer may be able to record the movements and criminal acts of a group of automobile thieves. In a stationary surveillance, the identity of persons entering and leaving a house under observation can be more easily established by a motion picture camera concealed in a room across the street. Photographs of rioters and participants in certain types of parades can be obtained in this manner. The motion picture provides an ideal record, also, of the reenactment of a crime by the defendant subsequent to a confession.[4]

1 Reiss.[2]
2 Paul.
3 Scott.
4 Eastman Kodak.[2]

IX FINGERPRINTS AT THE SCENE
OF THE CRIME

IDENTIFICATION OF INDIVIDUALS FROM THEIR FINGERPRINTS AND THE fundamentals of dactyloscopy have been treated in Chapter V. In addition to providing a sure means of identification, fingerprints are invaluable from the viewpoint of trace evidence, since they are the most reliable of the common forms of evidence left at the crime scene.

TYPES OF CHANCE IMPRESSIONS

Chance impressions may be left on an object by any of the body surfaces which bear friction ridges, viz., the fingers, palms, toes, and soles of the feet. The techniques of searching for, developing, photographing, and preserving fingerprints and other impressions are essential skills for the investigator. Chance impressions may be divided into three kinds:

Plastic prints, which are actual impressions formed by pressing the friction ridges into a plastic material. Melted candle wax, putty, tar, and soap are typical of these materials. Ordinarily these prints require no development. They are photographed with oblique lighting.

Visible prints, which are a deposit of a visible substance or stain left by a soiled finger. Blood and dirt are the most common substances. The burglar in his climb down a fire escape acquires considerable dirt on his hands. As he enters the apartment he may leave a deposit of this dirt on the white woodwork bordering the window. Similarly, in a homicide the assailant may acquire blood on his fingers in the course of the struggle and leave a blood-stained print on some object in the room. Visible fingerprints are seldom clear, since the pressure of the fingers tends to spread the material into the spaces between the ridges. Moreover, a slight sideways movement of the fingers will produce an illegible smudge. Nevertheless visible fingerprints more often attract the attention of amateurs and untrained policemen than latent fingerprints, which usually yield better results. Where characteristics are discernible in the visible print, a photograph should be made. Ordinarily a visible print requires no special developing methods.

Latent fingerprints, which are not readily visible to the unaided eye but can sometimes be seen with the aid of indirect light. On hard, smooth, nonabsorbent surfaces they can be developed, that is, made visible, by the use of fine-grain powders.[1] Where the surface is rough and absorbent, latent prints are invisible. Although they may be developed by powders in rare instances on such surfaces, the best results are obtained through the use of silver nitrate, iodine, and other chemical reagents. Latent fingerprints have been developed on objects made of bare wood, such as wooden boxes, barrels, ladders, hammer and ax handles; on paper objects such as letters, envelopes, checks, cardboard, cardboard boxes, etc.; on cloth such as shirts, collars, cuffs, handkerchiefs, bed sheets, pillow slips, etc. In some cases they have been developed on human skin and on fingernails and toenails.

Latent fingerprints are impressions made by the colorless substances that are transferred from the skin to the surface of an object when the fingers come in contact with that object. Under normal conditions, the fingertips are always more or less covered with a colorless residue of oil and perspiration. The natural secretion from the fingers and palms of the hands and from the toes and soles of the feet, unlike that from other regions of the skin, contains no oily matter. The minute quantity of fat or oil found on the skin of the fingers and palms comes from frequent and unconscious contacts with the fatty portions of the skin, i.e., the hair, the face, etc.

The secretion from the sweat pores on the fingertips contains 98.5 to 99.5 percent water and 0.5 to 1.5 percent solid material. Of the latter, about one third is composed of inorganic matter, mainly salt, and two thirds of organic substances, mostly urea, volatile fatty acids (formic, acetic, and butyric acids), and at times a very small quantity of albumin (0.045 percent).

That there are generally some chance impressions to be found at the scene of a crime is frequently due to the fact that the skin of the fingertips of the perpetrator is usually dirty, even if he avoids all contact with blood or obvious dust. When committing a crime, the criminal is generally nervous and the perspiration on his hands is more abundant than normally. This perspiration, mixed with the dust on dusty objects and with dirt, produces the film and the impression. Frequently his hands also become greasy from contact with his tools and weapons; and in drilling, the criminal often uses oil. We must also consider the fact that the criminal type is not prone to be very clean.

TRANSPORT OF OBJECTS CONTAINING FINGERPRINTS ·

Objects containing fingerprints should, if possible, be taken to the identification bureau. At the scene of the crime only the presence of fingerprints on the object is ascertained; powdering and photography should be done at headquarters. Even if transportation proves to be difficult at times, the advantage gained is great enough to offset the work undertaken. If objects are too large to be moved in their entirety and the gravity of the crime warrants the trouble, it is sometimes possible to excise just that portion on which the prints appear. Furniture can be taken apart, portions of windowpanes can be cut out, etc. If such an operation will destroy the prints or if it is impossible to excise the portion on which the prints appear or transport the object, as, for instance, when the fingerprints are on a large safe or wall, they should first be photographed and then transferred to a foil, or lift (see section on the use of foils later in this chapter).

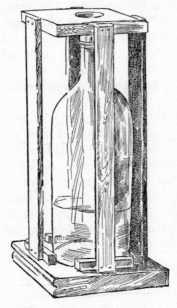

Figure 46. How a bottle bearing fingerprints is protected during transportation.

Objects to be transported should be packed with the utmost care to avoid breakage. Also, they should not be exposed to friction from the wrapping material; and of course the prints themselves should never be touched. It is a serious mistake to wrap pieces of glass or put them in paper or fabric.

The packing varies according to circumstances and the resourcefulness of the policeman, but in most cases there is enough material at the scene of the crime to pack any object. Figures 46, 47, 48, and 49 show some of these packings. Bottles are put in a wooden crate, which is fastened in a strong cardboard or wooden box. Glasses are put between two squares of wood and made firm by driving four nails in each square, after which the whole thing is fastened in a small cardboard box. Pieces

of glass are put in a pasteboard box with the corners of the glass penetrating the sides of the box so that it is held securely; and a string is
tightened around the box so that the whole thing will remain firm. Pieces
of glass may also be put in an upright position in a wooden box, where
they are fastened with nails and slabs. Knives and pistols are fastened to
a board or a piece of strong cardboard, with strings threaded in holes
made in the cardboard or board and tied to hold them in place.

HOW TO DEVELOP AND PHOTOGRAPH OR
OTHERWISE RECORD LATENT FINGERPRINTS

COLORING THE FINGERPRINTS. The most valuable of the chance impressions are the latent ones, which must first be made visible before they
can be photographed or transferred to lifts.
They are developed through the medium of
colored powders which stick to the more or
less smeary fingerprints.

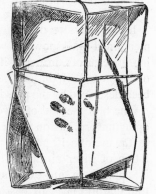

Theoretically, it is not very important what
powder is used as long as it be fine-grained
and devoid of lumps. It should be a different
color from that of the background. If, for
instance, fingerprints appear on a white background, such as porcelain, the use of any of
the commercial black powders is advisable.
For dark objects and for glass, white lead,
aluminum powder, or the commercial white
powder marketed for developing purposes is
generally used. The aluminum powder has
the advantage of having very fine grains and
great power of adhesion. Its disadvantage lies

Figure 47. How a piece
of glass bearing fingerprints
is protected during transportation.

in its lightness. It is blown about by the slightest whiff and soils the
fingers.

If fingerprints are detected on both surfaces of a glass plate, it is necessary to develop them separately. The print on one of the surfaces is first
treated with white lead, then photographed, and finally colored black by
allowing the vapors of ammonium sulfide to act on it for a few minutes.
Then the print on the opposite surface is covered with the white-lead
powder, a dark-colored paper is applied against the print previously
blackened, so as to render it invisible, and a photograph of the second
print taken.

Powders are deposited over all spots where prints are visible or suspected to exist. The spots should be completely covered and the excess powder then removed by allowing it to fall on a sheet of paper. The print is then carefully gone over with a fine camel's-hair brush or an ostrich feather until all the details are brought out. Should the object bearing the

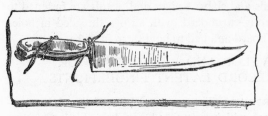

Figure 48. How a knife bearing fingerprints or bloodstains is protected during transportation.

prints be too large to be moved, the brush or the feather may be dipped in the powder and passed directly over the suspected place. This latter method, by the way, is used by many fingerprint experts on all occasions.

DEVELOPMENT OF FINGERPRINTS ON PAPER. Any of the previously mentioned black powders will give a fairly satisfactory result in developing fingerprints on paper if the fingerprints are not more than a couple of hours old. If this method is not successful, the paper will not have been destroyed by the powder and silver nitrate may then be used.

The best method of developing fingerprints on paper is by the use of a 10 percent solution of silver nitrate.[2] This is applied in an extremely thin uniform layer by passing the paper between two rollers moistened with the solution. The paper is allowed to dry and is then exposed to sunlight or ultraviolet light, which reveals the prints in a few sec-

Figure 49. How a pistol bearing fingerprints is protected during transportation.

onds. Ordinary daylight will develop the prints, but the time required is longer. Such prints photograph extremely well and can be preserved for a year or more if kept in absolute darkness. The process used to fix the prints for permanent record requires considerable skill and training and should be attempted only by those who have had instruction in it.

A very good method of developing fingerprints on paper is by the use of iodine fumes. Some fingerprint bureaus recommend the use of hot iodine fumes. Crystalline iodine has the property of evaporating at common room temperature, and if a little heat is applied to it, the evapora-

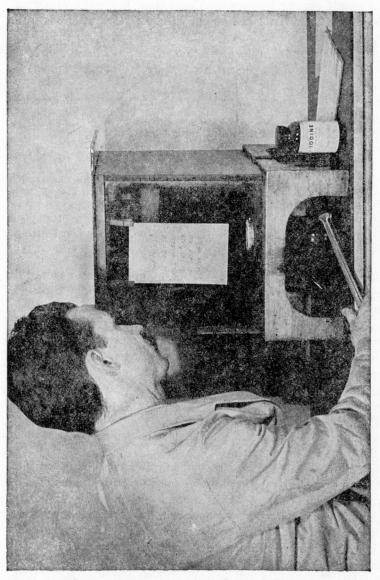

Figure 50. A technician in the FBI laboratory, Washington, D. C., developing latent fingerprints on an extortion note with iodine fumes.

tion is greatly increased. When the fumes come in contact with paper, a thin coat of iodine spreads over the surface. The organic content of the paper is simultaneously affected. Stains on the paper, especially those of a greasy nature, and even impressions, show up brown against the paper. The success of the process depends upon the length of time the iodine is allowed to act on the paper.

The use of Ninhydrin as a developing agent has been found especially effective for latent fingerprints on some forms of paper, particularly cellophane. Ninhydrin is used in the same way as silver nitrate.

Figure 51.   Latent impression on white cloth, natural secretion. Developed by silver nitrate process and fixed. (Technical Laboratory, New York City Police, Dr. E. M. Hudson collaborating.)

PHOTOGRAPHING FINGERPRINTS. Visible prints are photographed directly, but latent prints must first be developed. Side lighting will aid in photographing plastic prints. It should be noted that when white powder is used on a black surface the friction ridges will appear white in the picture. A reversal negative or transparency should then be made to render the ridges black for purposes of comparison and classification.

Sometimes fingerprints may be found on backgrounds that make development and photography by the common methods impossible. The aid of a specialist should then be sought, but if a detective is called upon to do the work, he should first perform experiments on his own fingerprints produced on the same material before attempting to do anything with the suspected fingerprints.

Fingerprints against a colored background are often difficult to photograph because of the lack of contrast. A suitable choice of powder color will provide some degree of subject contrast—white powder for a dark background. A filter can be used to lighten the background for black-powder prints or to darken it for white powder. If panchromatic film is to be used, the simplest way to determine the proper filter is to view the fingerprint through a filter test chart.

Ultraviolet fluorescence will provide contrast for multicolored backgrounds. The prints are processed with a fluorescent powder, as, for instance, anthracene. Photography in ultraviolet light is described on pages 475–479. Fingerprints on mirrors or reflecting backgrounds—for instance, on glossy metals—often give blurred photographs. Many complicated methods have been proposed to improve such photography, but they do not give any better results than a rational light and good focusing. If the mirror is of little value, a simple procedure is to scrape off the reflecting surface and use a black background.

Fingerprints should always be photographed. Only a photograph gives effective proof that fingerprints have been found on a certain object. This is of great importance in court proceedings. The photograph should always be made in natural size and later enlarged to convenient proportions.

Because of its simplicity of construction and operation, the fixed-focus camera with a built-in light source is now widely used to photograph fingerprints at the crime scene. When a fingerprint is developed it can be photographed within a few seconds by means of this camera. If the investigator is assured that he has obtained a satisfactory photograph, he may then lift the print. A portable object bearing a print of significance should be transported to the identification unit.

USE OF LIFTS OR FOILS. Lifts or foils are used to record prints at the crime scene by transferring them to another surface. Their use is recommended as a supplement to photography and also as a method of obtaining an image of a print which is inaccessible to the camera. The typical lifting material is an elastic, tacky substance which when pressed against a developed print will pick up by adhesion a powder outline of the print without absorbing the powder into the lifting surface. The lifting surface is protected by celluloid which can be pulled back to expose the surface for lifting and subsequently smoothed back over the lifted print. When a foil is used—more accurately, there are two celluloid foils, with a layer of transparent paste between—the thinner cover is removed to expose the paste layer, which is then pressed gently against the developed print. On withdrawal the celluloid cover is carefully replaced. Rubber lifts are applied in much the same way. These materials resemble tire patches with a celluloid covering. They are available in black and white to provide a contrasting background for either kind of powder.

Lifting materials are also used to transfer footprints in dust on a linoleum or similar surface. Especially effective for this purpose is Lift-Print, a material specifically made for lifting faint dust prints, even from paper surfaces, and providing them with a suitably contrasting background for photography.

Facility in lifting fingerprints can be readily acquired with practice. The investigator should not, however, look upon the lifting process as a substitute for a photograph of the original print *in situ*. Photography should always precede the transfer of a fingerprint to another surface, except of course when the location of the print prevents taking a picture. Lifting will be found especially valuable for prints which are developed on a surface which does not offer adequate photographic contrast.

EXAMINATION OF THE CHANCE IMPRESSION

The chance impression has now been powdered and photographed or transferred to a foil and is ready to be identified. There may be one or more suspects from whom comparison prints have been taken, but generally reference is made to the single-fingerprint registration. In all cases it is necessary to determine from which hand and from which finger the chance impression originated.

DETERMINING THE FINGER AND HAND

Chance impressions seldom appear alone. They usually occur in groups, the most common combinations being the index and the middle finger or the middle, ring, and small finger. One of the most difficult tasks in fingerprinting is to determine which of the fingers of the hand we are dealing with. This involves visualizing the manner in which the criminal touched the object and the different positions his fingers assumed during the maneuver. To gain experience, it is advisable to practice with one's own prints, placing the fingers of the hand in various positions on bottles, glass panes, etc.

The following rules—with few exceptions—may be useful:

If the fingerprints are loops and have one of the following patterns, they in all probability originated from the index finger, middle finger, ring finger, and small finger of the right hand:

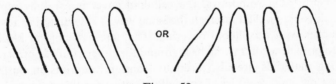

Figure 52.

If the prints are loops and have one of the following patterns, they in all probability originated from the index finger, middle finger, ring finger, and little finger of the left hand:

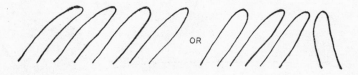

Figure 53.

Statistics show that generally all fingers have ulnar loops, or the index has a radial loop and the other fingers have ulnar loops. Statistics also show that whorls usually appear on thumbs and ring fingers and that the little finger almost always has ulnar loops. The most certain signs, however, are the position of the fingers in relation to each other and the size of the prints.

In order to determine the origin of the single print both a trained eye and long experience are necessary. The following advice will be found useful:

THE THUMB. This is recognized by its large size and by the distance between the core of the pattern and its tip, which is conspicuously greater than in the other fingers. The upper ridges in the print always slide in the same direction as that of the hand. The ridges on the right thumb will slide to the right and the ridges on the left thumb will slide to the left. If the pattern of the thumb is a loop, the loop will open to the right on the right thumb and to the left on the left thumb.

Figure 54. Right thumb and left thumb respectively.

If the pattern on the thumb is a twin loop, the *under* loop opens to the right on the right-hand thumb and to the left on the left-hand thumb.

If the pattern on the thumb is an egg-shaped whorl, the egg slopes to the right or left, according to which hand the print is from.

If the pattern of the thumb is a common whorl, the spiral turns to the right when made by right thumbs and to the left when made by left thumbs.

THE INDEX FINGER. This finger is curved to the left or to the right according to the particular hand. All types of patterns may occur here.

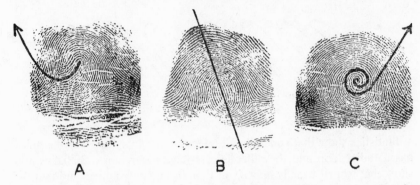

A   B   C

Figure 55. A, left thumb, twin-loop pattern: the under loop opens to the left; B, right thumb, egg-shaped-whorl pattern: the egg slopes to the right; C, right thumb, ordinary-whorl pattern: the spiral turns to the right.

THE MIDDLE FINGER. These prints are recognized by the length and size of the pattern. It is not possible to confuse them with prints from the index finger, but they may be confused with prints from the ring finger.

Figure 56. Left index and right index fingers respectively.

THE RING FINGER. The print of this finger can easily be confused with the middle finger if it occurs singly.

THE LITTLE FINGER. The little finger is recognized by its small size.

ANALYSIS AND IDENTIFICATION OF FINGERPRINTS

The characteristic points found in the patterns of friction ridges are shown and described in Figure 57.

By the identification, the patterns naturally are compared first and their similarity must be established. If the patterns are not the same, identity is out of the question. Outward similarity, however, does not prove anything, and it is necessary, in order to definitely establish identity, to make a careful examination of the characteristic details. Such examinations can be made with the aid of a magnifying glass, although most fingerprint experts use the naked eye. In difficult cases the magnifying glass is indispensable.

In determining the ridge characteristics their positions in relation to one another must first be ascertained. This is done by counting the ridges between two characteristics. The shapes of certain details play a less important role. Forks, abrupt endings and beginnings, and especially lake formations, may not be the same in appearance in different prints from the same person. If dirt, small fibers or the like find their way between the fingers and the object, a ridge may, for instance, appear as one or two islands, etc. As a rule fingerprints from the same individual are nearly

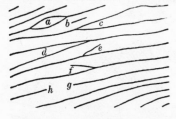

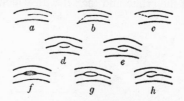

Figure 57. The characteristic points in the pattern of the friction ridges: a, the eye; b, the island; c, the fork; d, the contrafork; e, the hook; f, the contrahook; g, the abrupt beginning; h, the abrupt ending.

Figure 58. Possible changes of characteristics in chance impressions: An abrupt ending (a) in some cases may form a fork with the lower ridge (b) or with the upper ridge (c). The eye (g) may form an island (d), a thick point on the ridge (f), or may look like two different ridges (e, h).

always alike as to the shape of the friction ridges, but there are exceptions which teach us to show a certain tolerance toward the absolute form of the characteristics.

The most important parts of the pattern from the viewpoint of identification are the core and the delta. The ridges between the points of the deltas and the points of the cores are counted first. The result of the ridge counting is a good foundation for further identification. Very valuable signs are scars and other constitutional or accidental deformations of the patterns. It should be noted, however, that some temporary markings, like warts, often disappear completely.

Fingerprints should not be expected to correspond closely in absolute size, although relative measurements will remain substantially the same. Differences in applied pressure, curving of the finger, and even gross bodily changes can affect fingerprint size, while the basic pattern is unaltered. Because of these variations the older identification methods founded upon conformity of size and requirement that the two prints cover each other are now extinct.

HOW TO PRESENT FINGERPRINT TESTIMONY

When the identity of the fingerprints has been established—by examination of the patterns, by the characteristics and their positions in relation to each other, and, if present, by the constitutional or accidental deformations—both sets of fingerprints (i.e., the set found at the scene of the crime and the set with which identity was established) are photo-

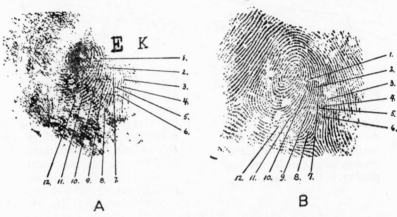

Figure 59.   Identification of fingerprint: A, fingerprint developed with iodine on envelope from scene; B, perpetrator's fingerprint.

graphed and enlarged. The enlargements, which are generally five to six times the natural size, are pasted side by side on cardboard and the distinguishing characteristics marked with corresponding numerals written on the edge of each enlargement. The numbers are connected with the characteristics by fine lines in red or black ink.

VALUE OF FINGERPRINTS AS EVIDENCE

The first rule of dactyloscopy holds that there are no two identical fingerprints. This of course only applied strictly to the well-prepared rolled fingerprints taken at the various bureaus of identification. But can we say the same about the blurred or indistinct chance impressions found at the scene of the crime?

We have already described how the fingerprints are analyzed and how the conclusion on identity is arrived at by considering the similarity of the patterns and the shape and position of the characteristic points. How great must this similarity be in order to draw a conclusion of identity between the chance impression and the real print?

It has been a long-standing rule that a minimum of twelve identical and characteristic details must be found. One should not, however, adhere too closely to this rule. The identification does not consist only in searching for identical points, such as forks, abrupt endings, and abrupt beginnings, but also in estimating the angles of the forks, the length of the ridges forming the forks, etc. When the core of the pattern is missing, the appearance of the details must be examined with the utmost care. In such cases only one difference (not originating in the above-described natural alteration of certain details) is sufficient to declare that the impressions are not of identical origin.

The demand for twelve similar prints stems from the tradition of Galton, Remus, Balthazard, and others. Recent authorities, such as Steinwender and Cooke, tend to the opinion that eight to twelve check points may suffice for identification, depending upon the nature of the points and the overall pattern. Although there is no international agreement concerning these minimum requirements, the courts of a number of European countries use a national standard. In Spain, from 10 to 12 points are required; Switzerland, 12 to 14; Austria, at least 12; England, at least 16; France, at least 17; Germany, 8 to 12. In the United States, although no standard has been set by law or court decision, "Most experts consider eight check points as sufficient, but . . . some regard twelve as required."

Thus we see that even in judging fingerprints a certain subjectivity must be exercised where the fingerprints are fragmentary. In other words, one must, to a certain degree, rely on the judgment of the fingerprint expert as to the rarity and value of evidence of the different details.

Three sets of conditions are possible:[3]

1. If twelve or more characteristic points are the same and the fingerprint is clear, there is absolute proof of identity.
2. If eight to twelve points are the same, the value of identification as evidence depends on:
   a. The clearness of the impression
   b. The rarity of the pattern
   c. The presence of the core or the delta of the pattern to be examined
   d. The presence of pores
   e. The obvious identity between the breadth of the ridges, the direction of the ridges, and the angles of the forks

Figure 60. A rare case of identification of a fingerprint on a revolver. Patrolman John W. was shot and killed while trying to prevent a robbery on Fulton Street in New York City. The patrolman was struck on the head with a blunt instrument; as he fell the criminal seized his revolver and then dropped it, leaving a finger impression thereon. This impression was classified and identified as that of a criminal recorded in the New York Police Department files. The perpetrator was arrested and convicted of murder in the first degree and sentenced to be executed. At the above left is the revolver, showing the fingerprint on the frame; and below are enlargements of the print found on the gun and a comparison print, with a list of the characteristics establishing the identification.

RIDGE CHARACTERISTICS

1	Ridge ending—upward trend	7	Ridge ending—upward trend
2	Bifurcation—downward trend	8	Ridge ending—upward trend
3	Ridge ending—upward trend	9	Ridge ending—upward trend
4	Ridge ending—upward trend	10	Ridge ending—upward trend
5	Ridge ending—upward trend	11	Ridge ending—upward trend
6	Bifurcation—downward trend	12	Ridge ending—upward trend
		13	Ridge ending—upward trend

14	Ridge ending—upward trend
15	Short ridge line
16	Scar
17	Bifurcation—upward trend
18	Island
19	Ridge ending—upward trend

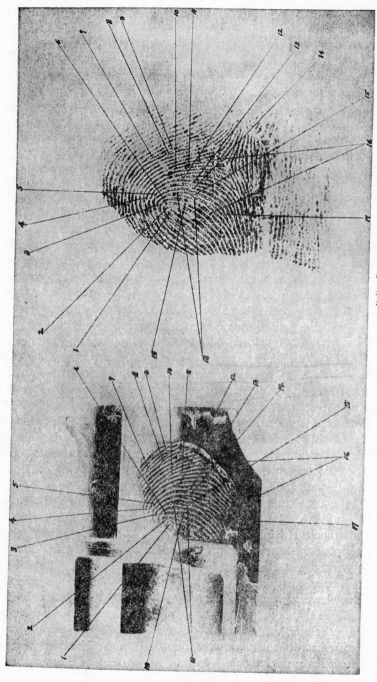

Police Department, City of New York, Bureau of Criminal Identification

3. If only a small number of similar characteristic details are found, the fingerprint has no absolute value as evidence, but identity can be surmised with a degree of probability proportionate to the number and the clearness of the characteristic points.

If there is a series of impressions and no one print is of sufficient value as proof, the total value of the evidence is figured in the following manner:

1. Let us suppose that the same finger has left several chance impressions. If certain details can be seen on one print and not on another, they may be added. Suppose, for instance, that the right index print is found on a bottle three times. One impression has ten characteristics; the second has seven, five of which are present in the first impression, but two of which are additional characteristics. The third has four characteristics present in the first and second impressions but also three new ones. The identification is then complete because we have fifteen details altogether. The identity is only probable with the first print but becomes a certainty when all are examined.

2. Let us suppose that there are several different impressions, each of which—with a degree of probability but not certainty—is identical with the fingerprints of the suspect. It is impossible, however, to determine the fingers from which the fingerprints originate. Such an occurrence is common, for example, when one impression is found on the neck and another about the middle of a bottle. From the position of the impressions it is impossible to determine if they originate, say, from the index and middle finger or from the ring finger and little finger. If the first impression has six characteristics which are identical with the suspect's right index finger and the second impression has four characteristics identical with his left ring finger, identification may be a probability but not a certainty. It may simply be a matter of chance occurrence.

3. Let us assume that there are impressions of several fingers in their natural positions. These cases are the most frequent and occur when an object is touched with the whole hand. There then may be found, in natural order, the impressions of the index, the middle, the ring, and the small finger, and on the other side of the object the impression of the thumb. One of these impressions taken alone may not lead to identity; but if they have respectively seven, nine, eight, and eleven characteristics identical with those of the impression of the suspect, it may be concluded without hesitation that the identity is established. In such a case the proof is not only based on the characteristic details in the individual impressions, but also upon the coincidence of two series of the same details.

SINGLE-FINGERPRINT REGISTRATIONS

A good single-fingerprint classification where each finger is classified by itself is an absolute necessity. The ordinary ten-finger classifications are not, as a rule, suited for single-fingerprint search. The suitability of the ten-fingerprint registration for the search of the single fingerprint varies, however. For instance, in the large registration of the Galton–Henry system, it is almost impossible to search for a single fingerprint because the patterns from the ten fingers are transformed into a formula which pays very little attention to the patterns of the single fingers and none at all to the details of those patterns. Successful attempts at identification have been made, but the tremendous amount of labor involved constitutes a great handicap. When several impressions from the same hand are found, there is some possibility that the Galton–Henry system may be of help; but in any event much time is required.

The system of Vucetich and its modifications have more possibilities for identifying a single fingerprint because the patterns of the individual fingers are noted in the principal formula. Identifications can sometimes be made without much loss of time, but if the impression from the scene is of a very common type—for instance, a loop—much time is needed.

Attempts to register single fingerprints are of quite long standing. The Spaniard Oloriz[4] and the Belgian Stockis[5] were the pioneers, but their systems were not practical and did not meet with much favor. The first usable single-fingerprint registration was devised by a Dane, Hakon Jörgensen.[6] His ideas were first made public at the Conference of Legal Medicine in Brussels in 1921. Since then other systems have been developed.[7]

A good system which in the past few years has been adopted by most identification bureaus was devised by Harry Battley,[8] chief inspector in charge of the fingerprint bureau of Scotland Yard.

The value of the single-fingerprint classification is proportional to the number of prints classified; i.e., the fewer the prints, the more effective the classification. For this reason, only those categories of criminals who leave fingerprints on the scene are classified: burglars, certain classes of thieves, etc.

As this manual does not deal with classifications of fingerprints, we refer those interested in further details to the works mentioned in the footnotes and also to *Practical Fingerprinting* by B. C. Bridges, Funk & Wagnalls Company, Inc.

POROSCOPY

The sweat pores, which in many chance impressions appear as rows of small white pinpoints on the ridges, may also be used in identifications,

especially in fragmentary impressions where the number of characteristic details is not sufficient. Identifications by means of sweat pores have been made when only a minute part of the pattern could be utilized. Identification through the sweat pores is called poroscopy and was discovered by Locard.[9] The sweat pores have the same properties as other details in the

Figure 61.   Friction ridges in strong enlargement.

patterns of the friction ridges, i.e., they are absolutely individual as to shape, size, position, and number for each human being and for each finger. They do not change during life, and if the skin is injured in any manner they will reappear in identical form after the skin has completely healed.

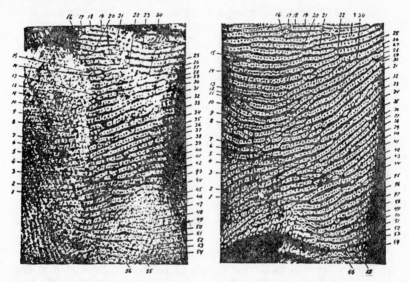

Technical Police Laboratory, Lyons, France

Figure 62.   Poroscopical identification of a fingerprint left by a burglar on a piece of furniture.

The sweat pores have another important property. Contrary to the alterations occurring in details of the fingerprint pattern, they are not subject to any changes resulting from the pressure used. They keep their form under all circumstances. On prints taken with ink the shape of the sweat pores can be seen only with difficulty. They may be seen quite clearly on uncolored fingerprints or on fingerprints taken by special methods.

The size varies greatly, even in the same individual. The diameter varies between the 0.08 and the 0.25 part of a millimeter and is much smaller in women than in men.

The arrangement of the sweat pores on the ridges varies to a great extent. In some individuals they are placed so close together that the distance between them is less than the diameter of the opening. In other cases, the distance between them is seven to eight times larger than the openings. They may be placed in the middle of the ridge, or so far out to the sides that the edge of the ridge has a ragged appearance. According to Locard, in normal cases there are from nine to eighteen pores on each millimeter of a ridge.

As already mentioned, the common impressions made with printer's ink are not suited for poroscopical identifications and a special method must be used. One formula used consists of the following:[10]

> 4 grams of yellow wax
> 16 grams of Greek resin
> 1 gram spermaceti
> 5 grams tallow

The mixture is allowed to solidify in a flat receptacle of glass or metal, where it can be kept for some time if the container is covered. The finger, which has been cleaned with ether or xylol, is rubbed against the surface of the mixture and then against a highly glossed paper or against celluloid. The print is colored with oxide of cobalt. If it seems advisable, the final print may be fixed with a mixture composed of the following:

> 25 grams of gum arabic
> 10 grams of alum
> 5 grams of formalin (40%)
> 300 grams of water

In order to smooth the surface of the wax before use, it may be passed over a flame.

Instead of this somewhat complicated method, Heindl recommends the rolling of the clean finger against a glass plate and the developing of the print with iodine fumes.

PERSONAL TRAITS IN FINGERPRINTS

Many dactyloscopists, as Forgeot, Pottecker, Galton, and others, have tried to gather information about the personality of the criminal by studying his fingerprints. Such information would be of great value in cases where the fingerprints originated from an unknown person. The results, however, are insignificant. Most valuable, from a practical viewpoint, are the examinations made by Forgeot on the size of the friction ridges.[11]

We have already remarked about the growth of the friction ridges during the normal development of a person, although nothing is altered in the relative proportions of the fingerprint. Forgeot drew a perpendicular line over a certain number of parallel friction ridges and calculated the number of intersecting lines on five millimeters of the perpendicular line. On this length of line newborn infants had fifteen to eighteen ridges; children of eight years, thirteen ridges; children of twelve years, twelve ridges; and adults, nine to ten ridges. Adults with very large hands often have only six to seven ridges. There is then the possibility of approximately determining the age of the person, even by fragmentary impressions.

Determination of race, intelligence, etc., by fingerprints is not possible, although numerous efforts have been made to establish such relationships. Some have tried to determine the profession of the person by marks on the fingerprints and on the hands. Only in very pronounced cases (see "Identification and Reconstruction of Dead Bodies" in Chapter VI) is such a determination possible.

TRICKERIES EMPLOYED BY CRIMINALS TO AVOID LEAVING FINGERPRINTS

Cases are on record where arrested criminals have tried to avoid having their fingerprints taken by continuously rubbing their fingertips against the rough walls of the cell until the friction ridges were worn off, leaving only a smooth surface. Other criminals have injured their fingertips with incisions, scarifications, and burns. In such cases it is only necessary to put the persons in handcuffs and gloves for a few days until the friction ridges have grown back or the wounds have healed. The friction ridges will normally regrow in a few days.

In past years newspapers have dealt extensively with attempts of criminals to have the skin of their fingertips removed and new skin transplanted to them by means of plastic surgery. Three such cases were reported in New York City in 1934. On closer investigation the newspaper reports in all three cases proved to be entirely without foundation in fact. The arrested persons simply had scars on their fingertips as the result of accidents.

The notorious felon John Dillinger and some of his accomplices were reported as having made *unsuccessful* attempts to alter their finger patterns by plastic surgery.

While operations in which skin from other parts of the body is grafted onto the fingertips have been performed successfully, the procedure is not usually effective in serving the criminal's purposes. Very little imagination is needed to picture how closely an arrested person is scrutinized if his fingertips have been tampered with. Also the questions of expense, time wasted, difficulty in obtaining a skilled surgeon, and last but not least the physical courage and stamina to withstand these ten painful operations will always prove deterrents to this method of procedure.

The cases mentioned above are very rare, but this cannot be said of the methods used to avoid leaving chance impressions at the scene of the crime. The most common method is the wearing of gloves. It is difficult, however, to find one's way in the dark or to use tools with gloved hands, and many criminals who at the beginning of the act have used gloves have finally been compelled to discard them, leaving fingerprints behind. It cannot be denied, however, that the use of gloves has hampered investigations not a little. Modern criminals seldom leave fingerprints unless drunk, very excited, or very inexperienced.

Many attempts have been made, especially abroad, to identify criminals from glove impressions. The gloves are often greasy and may in many cases leave a perfect impression of the glove fabric on smooth surfaces. The pattern of the fabric, especially the presence of possible defects due either to the manufacture or wear or accidental tears, is used for identification. In such cases the glove prints are either photographed directly, if visible, or colored with white powder or white lead. Comparison prints from the suspect's gloves are made by inking them with a roller and pressing them gently against white paper.

In this regard attention is called to the necessity of examining the dust on the suspect's gloves. In one case, for instance, a man was arrested for burglary. The dust found on the gloves, when examined, contained a small quantity of glass particles. A windowpane had been smashed by the burglar and the glass from the gloves was compared with the glass from the pane. It was finally determined that the glass on the gloves did

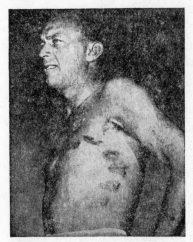

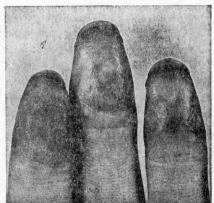

Figure 63. Roscoe Pitts, North Carolina criminal, had an operation performed by a Union City, New Jersey, doctor to remove the friction ridges of his fingertips by having patches of skin from his sides grafted onto his fingers. His arms were taped across his chest for two weeks while the skin was being transplanted. Picture at left shows where the skin was removed; picture at right shows results of the operation on the first three fingers of his right hand.

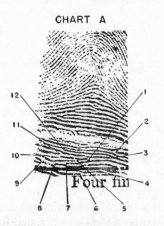

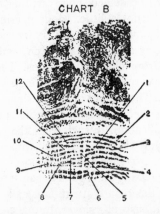

CHART A

CHART B

CHARTED ENLARGEMENT OF THE
LEFT RING FINGERPRINT SHOWING
HOW IDENTIFICATION WAS EFFECTED
BY USE OF CHARACTERISTICS OF THE
SECOND JOINT *(NOTE APPEARANCE
OF FIRST JOINT BEFORE MUTILATION)*

CHARTED ENLARGEMENT OF THE
LEFT RING FINGERPRINT SHOWING
HOW IDENTIFICATION WAS EFFECTED
BY USE OF CHARACTERISTICS OF THE
SECOND JOINT *(NOTE APPEARANCE
OF FIRST JOINT AFTER MUTILATION)*

Federal Bureau of Investigation

not come from the windowpane in question. Hence it was assumed that the burglar had also committed other burglaries and had smashed other glass panes. In this case the glove gave more information than would a chance impression found at the scene.[12]

Small quantities of paint, fibers, etc., may also be found on the gloves

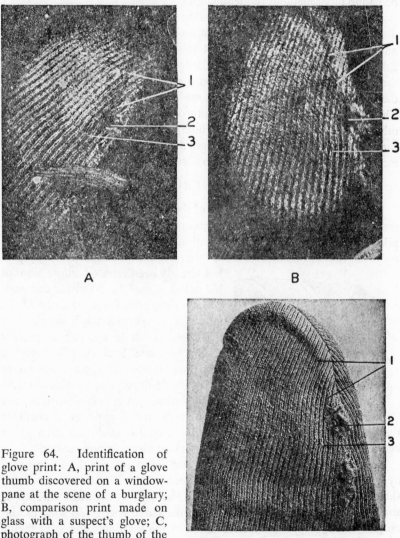

Figure 64. Identification of glove print: A, print of a glove thumb discovered on a window-pane at the scene of a burglary; B, comparison print made on glass with a suspect's glove; C, photograph of the thumb of the glove. Conviction was obtained.

and may give valuable information as to past burglaries committed by the thief. As a rule, therefore, all gloves found on arrested burglars should be thoroughly examined.

There are also other known methods to avoid leaving fingerprints; in cases where the possibility of such a situation is indicated, recourse must be had to other methods of identification.

During the last decade the question of forged fingerprints has been discussed quite frequently. Even before World War I, Reiss in Lausanne and Minovici in Bucharest studied this question. Later, Wehde[13] published a book describing methods of forging fingerprints. In all these cases the fingerprints were reproduced on a stamp which was pressed against the object. However, such forgeries must be considered rare occurrences. They not only require a large amount of skill but the fingerprints of another person must be available. Enlargement of the forged print will surely bring out the fact that the ridges do not have the same fine arrangement of pores as the natural print possesses.

PALM PRINTS

Chance impressions of the palm of the hand will be seen very often at scenes of crimes, either alone or accompanying fingerprints. If the fingerprints alone do not lead to identification or if the palm impression is the only one found, one must use the latter for identification. If the suspect

has already been arrested, impressions of his palms should be taken for comparison with the print from the scene of the crime. If the perpetrator is unknown, a thorough search in the palmar register should be made. Such classifications are very rare, though they are as necessary as the single-fingerprint classification. At the moment palm classifications are found only in a few places. Sometimes

Figure 65. Stockis' device for the taking of palm prints.

the classification of palm prints is also used to subclassify arch prints because of the inability to subclassify the latter by common methods.

The best method of taking palm prints is to use the device invented by the Belgian criminologist Stockis, which is shown in the accompanying sketch. The block is of common wood, about 15 by 6 inches. The upper surface of the block is curved. Half of the curve is covered with an aluminum or copper plate which is inked in the same manner as in taking fingerprints. The other half of the curved surface is covered with a piece of white paper. The hand is pressed lightly against the inked plate and then against the paper. The fingers must be slightly spread and pressure must be exerted, especially against the knuckles and the wrist. To get the right degree of pressure, the operator's hand is generally pressed across the hand which is being printed. Some bureaus of identification use a rubber air pillow instead of the device just described.

The identification is made in the same manner as with fingerprints. It is very common to have more than one hundred characteristic points in an identification; but, on the other hand, the interpretation of the

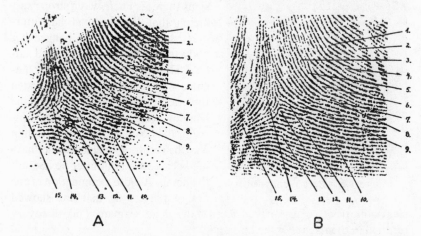

A   B

Figure 66. Identification of the palm print of a burglar wearing gloves who left a print through a slit in one glove while opening a door: A, print from the scene; B, perpetrator's palm print.

palmar print is difficult for the untrained, especially if only fragmentary evidence is available.

Palm prints have been specially studied by Stockis,[14] Ferrer,[15] and Wilder and Wentworth.[16] The study of some of those classification systems is recommended, especially the one of Wilder and Wentworth. Such a study will lead to a better knowledge of the patterns in the palm and will simplify identifications.

PRINTS OF THE SOLES OF THE FEET

From the viewpoint of criminology, sole prints are not as important as finger and palm prints, but occasionally they may have some measure of importance. One of the authors of this book knows of a suicide case where a sole print solved the problem.

A recently married pair had frequent quarrels which were noticed by the neighbors. One morning the nude body of the young wife was found hanging from a rope attached to an iron hook in the wall. The body was

swinging. The husband had left the house a few hours earlier, following a violent quarrel which had been overheard by the neighbors. He had, without doubt, mistreated his wife, whose body and clothing showed signs thereof. There was a strong suspicion that the husband had murdered his wife and then hanged her body to simulate a well-planned suicide. He was arrested. A sewing machine with a highly polished wooden top was standing on one side of the hanging body. According to the husband, the death of the young woman was the result of suicide, the act having been carried out after he had left the home. A close examination of the top of the sewing machine showed clear sole prints of the naked feet of the dead woman. This discovery resulted in the release of the husband.

Figure 67.   Bert Wentworth.

The burglar or murderer may also at times remove his shoes and socks, thus making sole prints important in such cases.

Prints of the sole of the foot are being used in some maternity hospitals for identification purposes. Classifications for this purpose have been devised by Wilder and Wentworth and by Dr. Emil Jerlov of the Maternity Hospital of Halsingborg, Sweden.

The importance of recording the footprints of newborn babies was emphasized by two recent kidnaping cases in New York in which the courts accepted the hospital records as conclusive proof of the identity of the infants. Although the footprints in these cases had been satisfactorily recorded, a subsequent review of hospital files revealed that many of the prints were worthless for purposes of identification because of blurring, excessive inking, and other faults arising from inexperience and ineptness. Hospital personnel responsible for recording infant footprints should be trained for this duty by experienced identification experts. The records of the hospital, moreover, should be periodically inspected to insure that prints are being satisfactorily recorded.

The footprint of a baby consists in general of a network of flexure creases. Friction ridge areas may or may not be present in the sole print. The complex of lines and creases, however, is always present and will serve the purposes of identification. Some of the lines are permanent, while others disappear after about seven months. In recording an infant's footprint, excessive inking should be avoided, as well as heavy pressure. The recorded print should be checked for clarity specially in areas containing friction ridges.

1 There are quite a few cases on record where fingerprints on glass have been developed after having been in water for several days. They were first dried and then developed in the usual manner.

2 The recommended percentage of silver nitrate in the solution varies with different laboratories. The Federal Bureau of Investigation in Washington uses a 3 percent solution, for instance.

3 See also E. Locard.[8]

4 Ferrer.[2]

5 Stockis.[1]

6 Jörgensen[1] was commissioner of police of Copenhagen, Denmark, and may be regarded as the foremost criminologist of Scandinavia. He was born in 1879 and died in 1927.

7 C. S. Collins (London, 1921), J. L. Larson (New York, 1924), Fr. Born (Bern, 1926). See also Sannié–Guérin[1] and Sannié–Guérin.[3]

8 Battley.

9 E. Locard.[5]

10 This method originated from the Spanish dactyloscopists Maestre and Lecha Marzo.

11 Forgeot.

12 Lochte.

13 Wehde–Beffel.

14 Stockis.[2]

15 Ferrer.[1]

16 Wilder–Wentworth. Harris Hawthorne Wilder, professor of zoology at Smith College, famous anthropologist, known for his extensive researches on various problems of identification, died in 1928. Bert Wentworth, former police commissioner of Dover, New Hampshire, invented a code for distant fingerprint identification and can be regarded as one of the foremost experts on fingerprints.

X FOOTPRINTS

KNOWLEDGE OF FOOTPRINTS AND THEIR NATURE IS NOT AS WIDESPREAD among policemen as it should be. Footprints are generally not used sufficiently by investigators of crime. Practical work is needed to gain an understanding of footprints. Theoretical speculations, however clear, can neither explain the mechanics of walking and running nor impart knowledge of the traces. Experience is needed, and the only way to gain it is to carry on practical experiments under different conditions. It is especially important to study footprints while out walking. At first they will not reveal much information, but once the eye has become accustomed to observe minute details, a composite picture of interesting facts will stand out very clearly.

The investigator often satisfies himself with a mere examination of the footprints at the scene of the crime or in the immediate neighborhood, not taking into account the fact that curious onlookers or perhaps the criminal himself may have walked upon and destroyed the prints. The chances of finding the footprints of the criminal are greater in a suburban or country neighborhood, and here the difficulty of differentiating from footprints not pertaining to the crime is less. The criminal, during his escape, will be quite likely to use unfrequented roads. In rural districts a check-up of the restricted numbers of persons responsible for making the footprints is easily made. Prints left by a running person are more suspicious, especially if he has tripped over stones or bushes, an indication that he does not know the neighborhood.

THE WALKING PICTURE

In walking, the heel of the foot is first brought down to the ground, to be followed by the sole, which is pressed to the ground from the heel forward to the toes. The foot is then raised by exerting a final pressure against the toes. The pressure is strongest against the heel and the foremost part of the foot.

In walking, the weight of the body exerts greater pressure on the outer and rear portions of the heel and sole. Examination of a group of soldiers, for instance, disclosed that the greater percent wore their shoes out along those parts, while the remaining small percent wore them out on the inner and anterior portions of the heel and sole. This latter peculiarity should be kept in mind.

Footprints produced by someone running are less visible because of the sliding of the foot and because dirt and sand are thrown over the print by the rapid movement of the foot. Many persons run on their toes only, but experienced runners, especially when tired, put down the whole foot.

By the expression *walking picture* is meant the whole ensemble of footprints left by the walker. The principal components of the walking picture are the direction line, the walking line, and the foot line.

The *direction line* indicates the direction in which the walker is moving.

The *walking line* is an imaginary line which in normal and ideal walking fuses with the direction line and runs along the inner sides of both heelprints. The walking line, however, is often irregular, varying with each step because of the manner of putting down the foot. It is more broken by stout persons and by pregnant women, who walk with their feet unusually far apart in order to maintain their equilibrium. In general it can be said that the broken walking line is especially suggestive of phlegmatic persons, strollers, and women.

The *foot line* shows the angle at which each foot is put down. This is a straight line through the longitudinal axis of the footprint. The angle between the foot line and the direction line is called the *foot angle*. It can be very characteristic and does not normally change much except when the subject is standing still, runs, walks up and down slopes, or carries heavy weights. The foot angle of a man is often larger than that of a woman. The normal foot angle is 30 to 32 degrees.

The *step length* is the distance between the centers of two successive heelprints. It depends upon the size of the walker, the habits of the walker, and the speed of the walk. Generally a large person takes longer steps than a small one walking at the same speed. However, one should not arrive at positive conclusions too readily. Persons with hernia or pelvic disorders often take steps which are very short in proportion to the length of their legs. Railroad workers, on the contrary, are accustomed to taking exceptionally long steps because of walking on railroad tracks. The step length varies from 20 to 40 inches. It is said that 27 inches is the average for slow walking and 35 inches for fast walking. Step lengths over 40 inches are in most cases taken by persons running.

A changing step length in the same walking picture is an indication that the person limps. The normal leg takes a longer step than the shorter one.

In the accompanying sketch it will be seen that an imaginary line drawn along the inner sides of both right and left heelprints will be straight and parallel with the direction line. If those lines are also broken —that is to say, if the distance between the heelprints on the left and those on the right side changes—there is some fault with the walking apparatus of the person. The simplest explanation is to assume that the

Figure 68.   Normal walking line.

gait is that of a drunken person, but it may also be caused by wounds or illness, such as paralysis. Certain diseases such as syphilis or Parkinson's disease, in which there is interference with body equilibrium, give fairly characteristic walking pictures.

When the walker has stood still in one place, it may be possible to determine if he has stayed there for some length of time by noticing the number of times he has shifted his weight from one foot to the other.

Figure 69.   Broken walking line.

Jumping to one side, sudden changes to a slow walk, steps taken previous to jumping, turnings, etc., may be of great importance and should be noticed.

MEASURING THE WALKING PICTURE. In recent years many attempts have been made to measure walking pictures and record them in a formula. In cases where the footprints themselves are plain and without characteristic details the formula of the walking picture may be of value as evidence. At least two consecutive footprints of the left and right foot are necessary for such measurements.

For measuring, two squares and a compass are used. Each square is a right angle operating on a hinge. One of the two has a scale marked in inches. When a usable picture is found, the graded square is put in such a position that the longer side lies against the outer and longer side of the left foot and the short side touches the front tip of the right foot. If the right foot is in the rear of the picture, the procedure should be reversed. Then the second square is put so that the short side touches the rear tip of the left foot and the long side touches the outer side of the right foot, or the contrary if the right foot is in the rear. The squares should frame the feet in such a manner that they make four right angles.

The compass is now placed so that one arm is parallel with the longitudinal axis of the left footprint and the other arm with the longitudinal axis of the right footprint. The axis may be determined by putting a right angle against the straight line which connects the two corners of the heel. The angle of the arms gives the position of the feet in relation to each other. Experience has shown that the two feet often make different angles with the walking line of the individual, and the angles which the arms of the squares make with the footline are then measured. These angles are called l for the left foot and r for the right foot.

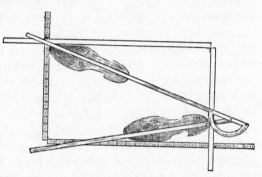

Figure 70. Müller's[1] method of measuring the walking picture.

The following measurements are also made:
1. The step length, measured from the rear edge of the left heel to the rear edge of the right heel
2. The breadth of the step, measured from the outer edge of the long side of the left foot to the outer edge of the long side of the right foot
3. The length of the left foot, and the greatest width of the left foot
4. The length of the right foot, and the greatest width of the right foot

Experience shows that walking pictures are highly individual and that one can often identify without difficulty the person who makes them. For instance, several persons have been made to walk side by side. It has then been possible to determine the walking picture of each person after having taken comparison prints of them.

SURFACE FOOTPRINTS

The slight interest shown by policemen in footprints may be attributed partly to the fact that almost all shoes are of the ready-made type, which vary very little in the design of the sole. Apart from exceptional sole designs on fancy shoes, most soles vary only slightly from one another. In olden times it was quite different. Shoes were usually made to order and often not only repaired many times but also studded with nails, protected with heel irons, etc. Such shoes may still be found in rural districts and may leave footprints which are as valuable as fingerprints for identification purposes. With the ever-increasing use of rubber soles and rubber heels, new and highly valuable means of identification have been added to the identification of prints. Millions of rubber heels will be quite uniform in the manufacture when sold in the shop, but after only a few days of wear will develop individual characteristics.

Prints from rubber heels can be left on almost all floor coverings, e.g., linoleum, parquet, or painted wooden floors. Papers bearing heel prints are commonly found at the scene of a safe burglary. The search for surface prints should be conducted with an oblique light, since they are often invisible when viewed directly. On discovery, a surface print should be photographed and then lifted. The plane of the film (as well as the lens board) should be parallel to the surface of the print. A ruler should be placed at the side of the print and included in the view. Footprints which are not readily visible can be photographed effectively by means of side lighting and filters.

If the footprint is on a portable object, this can be removed and protected. Alternatively, a portion of the background surface can be cut out and removed. Prints on immovable objects can be lifted by means of an ordinary rubber lift or by the use of a material such as Lift-Print.[2] A sheet of photographic film or paper can also be used for this purpose, if it is first fixed, washed, and dried. When it is moistened after this procedure, the film or paper offers a suitably tacky surface for lifting.

Comparison prints from the suspect's shoes may be obtained by inking them with a common fingerprint roller and requesting the suspect to walk over a strip of white paper. Additional comparison prints should be made by pressing the heel carefully against a sheet of paper by hand.

FOOTPRINTS IN PLASTIC MATERIALS

Impressions of the foot found in plastic materials should be reproduced by casting. As in the case of surface footprints, impressions should

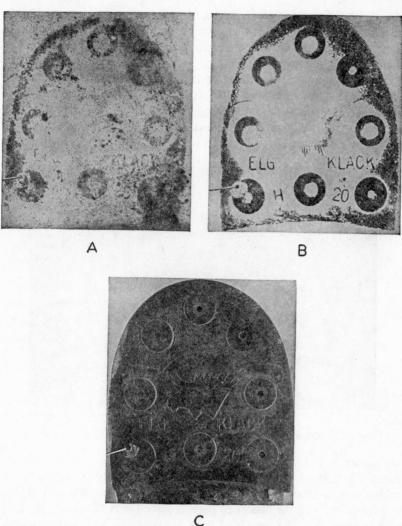

A   B

C

Figure 71.   In a blow job the insulating material of the safe was spread over the floor in a fine dust and adhered to the burglar's shoes, one of which left a rubber heelprint on the linoleum. The print was transferred on a piece of adhesive tape. An examination showed that there was a defect in the manufacture of the heel, the metal ring over one of the right holes not being in place. A shows heelprint from scene, B is a comparison print from the suspect's shoe made with printer's ink on paper, and C is a photograph of the heel. Confession was obtained.

also be photographed before they are processed in any way. A 4-by-5-inch film size is suitable for this purpose, especially since plastic impressions are often found on uneven ground and their ground-glass image should be checked for parallelism.

The technique used in making casts differs according to the nature of the footprints. Some authors—for instance, Gross, Reiss, Frecon, Hofmann, and Hugoulin—recommend plaster of Paris and different materials such as wax, sulfur, glue, concrete blends, etc. Our experience still shows that plaster of Paris is the best medium.[3] Only the very best plaster—

Figure 72.   Plaster cast of print made by a rubber-soled shoe in flour.

art plaster of the finest grade—should be used. The technique used by dentists in mixing plaster of Paris with water should be followed. A rubber cup is filled with one pint of water (approximately enough for one footprint) and the plaster of Paris is spread over the water. No stirring is permitted. The plaster of Paris is allowed to sink to the bottom spontaneously. Enough should be added until the water is unable to absorb any more. The mixture is then ready for use.

Before using, it should be stirred thoroughly, and then placed on the footprint. When a layer about one third of an inch thick has been applied, portions of twine, sticks, twigs, or some similar material should be put on for reinforcement. This reinforcing material should not extend past the print, and should be put on carefully and without pressure to prevent it from touching the bottom of the print and thus destroying the details. A new layer of plaster is then put upon the reinforcement and the cast allowed to harden completely before it is taken away. A sure sign of hardening is that the plaster is getting warm.

If rapid hardening is desired, a small quantity of salt may be mixed with the plaster. On the other hand, if slow hardening is desired, some sugar or dextrose should be added. In order to prevent the spreading of the plaster of Paris over the sides, a frame of cardboard, wood, or similar material is built around the print. To prevent air bubbles, the first layer of plaster should be put on slowly and carefully, preferably with the aid of a spoon.

About twenty ounces of plaster of Paris are needed for one footprint. In cases of great emergency, sulfur, tallow, lard, porridge, or flour and water may be used.

It is always advisable to prepare the surface of the footprint before the plaster cast is made, and this is especially the case when the footprints are in dust, fine sand, or other soft material. This is done by spreading a thin coat of shellac over the surface. The shellac hardens quickly and renders even a very sensitive surface hard enough to bear the weight of the plaster. In order to spread the shellac a Flit can or other spraying device may be used, but it is advisable to have a special sprayer for that purpose. The complete outfit used by the New York City Police Department for preparing the surface of footprints and for making the casts is shown in Figure 73.[4] It consists of the above-described sprayer, from which the shellac can be easily removed and the outlets kept clear by inserting pieces of wire in them when the sprayer is not in use; one container for shellac and another for oil, both of which can be screwed to the sprayer; one shaker for talcum powder; two containers for the plaster; one container for water; a rubber cap; a spoon; and a spatula.

Footprints in soft or hard earth, dry marshland, and sand are prepared in the following manner: A thin coat of shellac is spread upon the surface of the print. The sprayer should be kept at a distance of about one yard so that the shellac may fall like a soft cloud on the surface. Care should be taken that the air stream from the sprayer does not disturb or carry off particles from the print. The shellac dries in a few minutes; a thin coat of talcum is then shaken over the print, and the plaster cast is made in the manner described previously.

Footprints in dust, fine sand, or other soft materials are prepared in the following manner: A coat of shellac is spread with great care over the surface, and this is followed by a thin coat of oil, which is spread over the dry shellac by means of the sprayer. The plaster cast is made in the ordinary manner, although the mixture of the first layer should not be so thick and should be applied in small portions with a spoon. When the plaster cast is dry, it is possible, in many cases, to peel off the coat of shellac and oil very easily. If the coat sticks to the plaster, it can be placed on a hot stove and in most cases loosened. If necessary, the cast may also be cleaned by immersing it in alcohol.

Footprints in sand may also be cast by using melted paraffin wax. Water is sprayed over the print until the sand is thoroughly moistened. At the side of the print a trough is built, the bottom of which should be

Figure 73. Complete kit
for casting footprints.

Figure 74. Spraying the surface
of a footprint with shellac.

about one inch higher than the highest part of the footprint. From the trough a small ditch down to the print is made. The place where the ditch enters the footprint should be chosen judiciously so that the ditch does not touch any important detail or contour. Also the trough and the ditch should be thoroughly moistened. If necessary, the footprint should be surrounded by a piece of cardboard or a flexible copper-plating so that the paraffin cannot escape at the sides. The paraffin is melted in a pan and should be cooled off, while stirring, until a finger can be dipped in. Just before the cast is made the footprint, the trough, and the ditch are moistened once more. The paraffin is now poured into the trough so that it flows in an even stream into the print. A small wooden stick should be handy with which to lead the paraffin into difficult places. No reinforcement is necessary. The ready cast should be about one-half inch thick.

Footprints in snow may be prepared in the following manner: A thin coat of talcum is first shaken over the print. Shellac is spread over the talcum, and talcum is again shaken over the shellac while it is still wet.

This operation is repeated three times. By this time a thin skinlike layer of talcum and shellac protects the print. The plaster cast may then be made in the regular manner.

In the last years the method of Karlmark, which is the use of melted sulfur, has attracted attention. By this method a trough is built just as described above, but the footprint is not prepared. Powdered sulfur is melted in a pan while stirring. The heating should not be done too quickly because the sulfur then takes on the consistency of syrup and cannot be used. It melts at 115 degrees centigrade and will then be almost like water. Care must be taken that the sulfur does not burn while melting because this would destroy it. It is difficult to see the fire, but the dark, sticky smoke will tell. When all of the sulfur is thoroughly melted, it should be allowed to cool off, being stirred continuously. The stirring is very important, particularly in cold weather. The cooling should continue until small crystals form on the surface of the sulfur. A last stirring is made, and the sulfur is poured into the trough. The part of the sulfur which touches the snow hardens almost immediately, and it is therefore possible to pour the last of the sulfur directly on the top of the last layer of the footprint. The cast should be about three quarters of an inch thick and should be taken up as soon as possible. To start with it is fairly brittle, but it will soon harden.

In cases where water covers the footprints, as at the seashore, plaster of Paris should be spread on the water over the print with the aid of a piece of gauze, which acts as a sifter. The plaster will sink to the bottom of the print and form a hard crust.

When it is raining, the footprints should be protected pending the arrival of the men from the police laboratory. Empty boxes, etc., may be used for this purpose. If there is a small quantity of water on the prints it should be carefully drawn away with a blotter or filter paper.

PRINTS OF NAKED FEET

Prints of naked feet are seldom found, although the history of crime shows that quite a few cases have been reported where a criminal has taken shoes and socks off in order to operate more silently and to avoid contaminating his shoes with blood. In the well-known murder of the banker Remy,[5] when Bertillon made a very ingenious reconstruction of the crime, the two murderers, Renard and Courtois, had undressed completely and operated in the nude.

In most indoor cases surface prints on floors, tables, chairs, etc., will be found; and more seldom prints in plastic materials, earth, ashes, etc.

Prints of naked feet can be colored or colorless. In the first case the feet are soiled with blood, dust, soot, etc. The prints are then visible. In determining the size of the foot care should be exercised, as the pressure and coloring material have a large influence on the size of prints. One should look for malformations and flat feet.

Colorless prints of naked feet are dealt with the same as latent fingerprints. (See "Prints of the Soles of the Feet," at end of Chapter IX.)

TRACES OF SOCKS

Frequently it is possible to identify traces of socks. They may be visible or latent. Latent traces of socks are dealt with as fingerprints, inasmuch as the latent mark is due to perspiration. The identification is based on the structure of the fabric, which can be very characteristic, especially if there are holes or darns.

IDENTIFICATION OF FOOTPRINTS

COMPARISON PRINTS. For the identification of naked feet and socks the foot is pressed against a glass panel or tin plate covered with a thin layer of fingerprint ink and the suspect is made to walk on a sheet of white paper. In order to get a true picture of the formation of the foot in different positions, it is necessary to take four different footprints; namely, in normal standing position, in walking, in a standing position with pressure on the outer portion of the foot, and in a standing position with pressure exerted on the inner part of the foot.

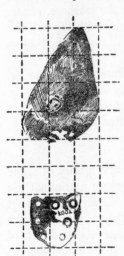

Figure 75. Causé's method of identification.

In making comparison prints of shod feet the suspect is made to walk, if possible, on the same plastic material as that in which the footprints are found. Casts are then made at the scene. If the prints found on the scene have been made with wet shoes, the shoes of the suspect should also be wet when making the comparison prints. However, it is often possible to make the identification by direct comparison of the cast made at the scene and the suspect's shoes.

THE IDENTIFICATION. For identification it is necessary to have definite starting-points for measurements. For naked feet these points are the rear border of the heel and the tip of the large toe, and for shoes the rear border of the heel and the tip of the shoe. With the aid of these starting-points a Causé's net, which is shown in the accompanying figure, is drawn. It is advisable to photograph the two prints (suspect and comparison) side by side, including the graduated scale, on the same plate; to enlarge them to natural size; and then to draw the net on the photograph. It is also possible to photograph the two prints separately in exactly the same size and make the comparison between the two prints.

In the identification of naked feet differences of 1/100 of an inch are not important, because the foot becomes larger or smaller according to whether the person stands or walks.

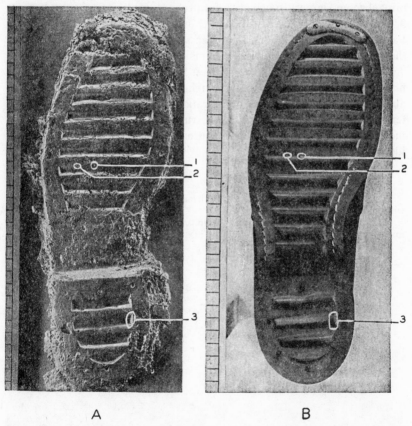

A   B

Figure 76.   A, sulfur cast of footprint in snow; B, suspect's shoe. In this case a burglar was surprised and fled, leaving several footprints in a thin layer of snow in a courtyard. Corresponding and characteristic points are marked on the pictures. Confession followed.

Shoe prints seldom are exactly the same size as the shoes which made them. This is due to the various movements in walking. Differences of some hundredths of an inch in length or width are no indication of non-identity. The substance in which the print has been made is also subject to alterations. Wet earth, for instance, contracts in drying, and this contraction in clay can be more than one half an inch for a footprint. In such cases experiments must be made and the contraction carefully studied. The drying process is also very often not uniform; this is especially the case with earth which has been wet and dried several times. Traces in snow can also be subject to changes. In warmer weather the prints become larger. In one case, for instance, footprints in snow became 3/100 of an inch longer with a rise in temperature of only 9 degrees Fahrenheit in half an hour. The process of casting in snow also enlarges the prints, and it is then advisable to make the comparison prints in snow.

In the identification of shoe prints it is a general rule that the size has little value for identification, although it certainly must fit within the above-mentioned limits. The identification is usually based on the characteristic signs of wear, repairs, nails, rubber heels, heel irons, etc. The measurements of the walking picture also add a great deal to the identification.

1 Müller.
2 Watson.
3 Some commercial preparations such as the albastone have also been used with success.
4 This outfit was constructed for the units of the Swedish State Police by Söderman in collaboration with Ivan Lindell, instrument-maker to the faculties of the School of Science, University of Stockholm.
5 See Söderman.[4]

XI TRACES OF TOOLS

ON APRIL 28, 1930, THE SUPREME COURT OF THE STATE OF WASHINGton, in an opinion written by Justice Millard and concurred in by Chief Justice Mitchell and Justices Parker, Beals, and Tolman, stated:

Courts are no longer skeptical that by the aid of scientific appliances, the identity of a person may be established by fingerprints. There is no difference in principle in the utilization of the photomicrograph to determine that the tool that made an impression is the same instrument that made another impression. The edge of one blade differs as greatly as the lines of one human hand differ from the lines of another. This is a progressive age. The scientific means afforded should be used to apprehend the criminal. [Case of Washington vs. Clark.]

Any tool, such as jimmies, hatchets, axes, hammers, cutters, pliers, knives, chisels, and drills, will leave markings on material softer than the tool itself. In a burglary, for instance, there may be jimmy marks in the paint or wood of windows, doors, cabinets, and drawers. A cut telephone wire will carry markings of the cutter. A hatchet with characteristic marks of wear will leave traces on the cut branch of a tree or even on the skull of a murdered person. It must also be remembered that in some cases the criminal may inadvertently leave a piece of the tool itself or

Figure 77.   While trying to open a desk with a knife, a burglar broke off a small piece of the knife in the lock. Picture shows how the piece from the lock fitted the suspect's knife.

169

another implement at the scene of the commission of a crime (for example, see Figures 77 and 78).

The identification of tools is especially common in burglaries, and it can be said that the technique for bringing out miscroscopic evidence in such cases represents one of the most valuable aids that has been added to police science since the perfection of forensic ballistics.[1] Today it is often possible, after a miscroscopic examination of the surface of a trace of a tool, to identify the tool with the same accuracy with which a bullet is identified as coming from the weapon from which it was fired.

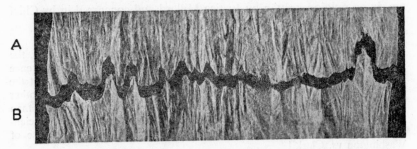

Figure 78.   Identification of paper string used by a poacher: A is the piece
left at the scene; B was found at the suspect's home.

If a screwdriver, a jimmy, or any other tool is examined under a suitable miscroscope, preferably in oblique light, a slight enlargement will show innumerable ridges and irregularities on the surface of the tool. These are caused by the grinding of the tool and by wear and may be looked upon as being as characteristic as are the ridges and grooves of a fired bullet.

When the tool is pressed against a plastic material, generally paint, these characteristic ridges will be molded into the paint, leaving a more or less perfect cast of themselves. These casts can be identified as having been caused by the tool in question.

The procedure to be used in caring for the marks caused by the tools depends entirely upon the manner in which the identification is going to be made. In any case, the position of the trace should be marked on the sketch or photograph of the scene, and a detail photograph showing the whole trace should be taken. A graduated ruler should be placed beside the trace and on a level with it before photographing. If there are easily interpreted characteristics of the mark, a cast of the trace may be made. If the case is very important and there is reason to believe that a microscopic examination will yield results, the trace should be cut out and taken to the laboratory.[2]

MAKING CASTS OF THE IMPRESSION. The most commonly used casting method consists of pressing a piece of plastelina against the trace. Before its application the plastelina should be kneaded in the hand until

Figure 79. Identification of the trace of a screwdriver left on a lock: A, markings on the lock; B, comparison marks made with the suspect's screwdriver in lead. Conviction was obtained.

it becomes soft. In order to prevent the plastelina from sticking to the trace it is generally moistened with water, although quartz powder is recommended for this purpose.

The quartz powder should be sprayed with the aid of a small rubber sprayer over the surface of the trace. The plastelina is then pressed gently but firmly into the trace and removed. The cast is transported in a small cardboard box (often an empty matchbox will do) to the laboratory, where a cast of plaster of Paris is made of the plastelina cast. A mixture of plaster of Paris and water is made and put into a small container, whereupon the plastelina cast is placed on the surface of the plaster mixture and allowed to sink to the necessary depth. It can be kept in position by a string attached to a support. In order to avoid air bubbles, which cause holes in the plaster cast, a thin coat of plaster should be spread over the surface of the plastelina with the aid of a fine brush before sinking it into the plaster. The plaster should be allowed to harden completely before the plastelina is removed.

Comparison can be made between the plaster cast and a plastelina cast of the tool (negative against negative) or directly between the original plastelina cast from the scene and the tool (positive against positive). If

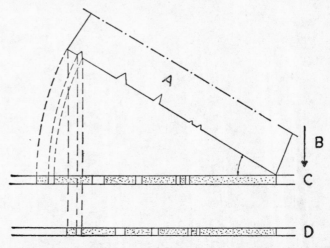

Figure 80. The distance between the characteristic marks of wear in the trace left by a hatchet is related to the attacking angle of the tool. A, hatchet with marks of wear; B, direction of cutting; C, trace on surface when attacking angle is zero; D, trace on surface when attacking angle is larger than zero.

the trace of the tool can be removed and transported to the laboratory, a cast of the trace can be made there and compared directly with a cast of the suspected tool. Before the tool is cast, it must be examined microscopically for minute traces of paint, copper, lead, etc.

In all identification of traces of tools the angle at which the tool was held when the trace was formed plays a great role. This angle may be ascertained by pressing the tool at different angles against flat cakes of plastelina. Each cake of plastelina should be marked and labeled with a note of the angle used. Instead of plastelina, paraffin may be used. The paraffin should be melted and put in a flat bowl. Then aluminum powder should be placed on the surface of the melted paraffin. The powder will

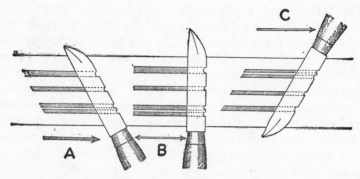

Figure 81. If a knife is kept at right angles with the object being cut, the distance between the traces of the marks of wear will be larger than if the knife is held at an oblique angle. The appearance of the trace will also differ according to whether the user is right- or left-handed. A, direction of cutting; B, right-handed person; C, left-handed person.

immediately spread over the surface, forming a glossy, metallic layer in which the comparison marks can readily be made. Before the paraffin hardens, the comparison traces are cut out. These may be put side by side with the trace from the scene and the two photographed together. This method gives excellent results because of the ease of photographing and because the paraffin is more resistant than the plastelina cast.

Figure 82. Microscopic identification of marks left by a burglar's tool on a painted window frame.

THE MICROSCOPIC METHOD. The microscopic method of May and Madsen is founded on the normal occurrence of fine ridges on the surface of the tool. These ridges cannot be seen by the naked eye, because some of them are as fine as 1/100 of a millimeter. A direct comparison of the tool and the trace in the microscope is difficult, because the ridges in the trace are naturally found to be raised, while they are sunken in the tool. The trace represents a reflected picture of the tool. The examination of such a large object as a tool under the microscope is also difficult —another reason for not examining the tool directly. For these reasons a cast of the tool in soft lead is made. The tool is wrapped in a piece of soft, thin lead plate and tightened in a vise. The two jaws of the vise are covered with lead so that the pressure may be spread evenly. If necessary, the working angle of the tool should be ascertained as described above.

The trace from the scene and the comparison proof of the tool are now matched under a binocular microscope. When the identity is established, photomicrographs of both are made in exactly the same enlargement. Microsummar or Microtessar lenses should be used. A very oblique light will give good results. In order to avoid reflections in the photography the

Figure 83. Identification of a hatchet used when stealing wood: A shows marks of the hatchet found on a stump at the place where the wood was stolen; B shows comparison marks made with the suspect's hatchet. Note the perfect identity. Confession followed.

lead plate may be dipped for several seconds into diluted nitric acid and then for one minute into a sulfide ammonium solution until the lead turns black.

An enlargement of about ten times is generally appropriate. When showing the similarities to the court, a characteristic strip of the photograph of one print may be cut out and, by mounting it directly above the other print, the similarities directly and visibly pointed out.

Figure 84.   Identification of the markings left by a circular saw: A is a piece of stolen wood found at the suspect's home; B is the corresponding piece found at the scene.

It is strongly recommended that traces of tools from burglaries committed by unknown perpetrators be classified in the police laboratory. The classification is founded on the manufacture, composition, dimensions, and impressions of the tool. Notes on the *modus operandi* of the perpetrator should be added. When tools are found on suspects, they should be delivered to the laboratory, for this may be instrumental in establishing whether or not the same tools have been used in previous burglaries.

1 May, Madsen, Burd–Greene, Koehler.
2 Davis.

XII THE EXAMINATION OF PAINTINGS

MUCH HAS BEEN WRITTEN ABOUT THE CREDULITY OF THE WEALTHY American art collector and about the questionable authenticity of many of his acquisitions. "Of some 700 pictures known to have been painted by Corot, over 2,000 of them are now in the United States." Similar remarks have been made about the excessive number of Rembrandts catalogued in the United States and Canada. Enthusiasm and inexperience can readily lead to serious errors in buying a work of art. Determination of authenticity is a difficult matter even for the professional art critic, whose career has been in great part devoted to the development of the capacity to discriminate and recognize the genuine works of the Old Masters. The ease with which Jan van Meegeren's forgeries of Vermeer passed the scrutiny of European museum directors and various art experts forcefully demonstrated that something more than esthetic sophistication and a trained eye is needed to detect a fraudulent "old master." A scientific examination of the materials and structure of a questionable painting is indispensable to a reliable authentication of an old painting. The methods of the physical scientist are best illustrated in their application to a representative work of the Renaissance.

From the point of view of the scientific examiner, and of the forger, a classical painting is a stratified object consisting typically of four layers: support, ground, paint film, and varnish film. The task set for himself by the forger is to simulate each of these layers in a manner consistent with the imputed age of the painting and the known practices of the master.[1]

The *support* ordinarily is made of wood or canvas. On this was placed the *ground* or layer on which the picture was to be painted. Great care was given to the preparation of the ground; the Italians favored a ground of either coarse or fine *gesso* (gypsum) in a glue medium, while chalk was preferred by the Dutch and Flemish. For special purposes other ma-

176

terials were used, such as bole, an aluminum silicate, which served as a ground for gold leaf.

The *paint film* consisted of pigment particles dispersed in a suitable medium or vehicle. Tempera painters, for example, at first used egg yolk as a medium but later shifted to linseed oil. Since the success of the picture depended in great part on the character of the paint film, considerable care and knowledge were brought by the masters to its preparation. In their own terms they were aware of the critical importance to visual effect of such factors as the particle size of pigment, the proportions of pigment to medium, and the refractive indices of the resulting combinations.

The *varnish film,* a topmost layer that served as a protective covering, could also be made to impart an additional brilliance to the painting. Natural resins (mastic, colophony, copal, and sandarac) were mixed with oil to produce varnishes well into the late Renaissance, when they were supplanted by spirit varnishes using turpentine or alcohol as a solvent.

THE PROBLEMS OF THE ART FORGER

From this brief description of the structure of the classical painting we can at least conclude that the successful simulation of an Old Master requires depth of knowledge, extraordinary technical competence, and artistic gifts of an exceptional order. For Jan van Meegeren to create the "lost" Vermeers, it was essential to bring to his task artistic talents that would not have been considered mean at the side of the Dutch master's. The subject matter of each painting, the theme, and the level of its esthetic appeal were required to be consistent with the standards of Vermeer's accepted works. The iconography, colors, perspective, brush work, and other elements of style and execution had not only to be free of inconsistencies but had also to meet the positive requirements of technical excellence.

But the interest of the scientific examiner lies not in the artistic success of the fraudulent painting but in the materials and processes which the forger has used to simulate the structure of a painting of the attributed period and authorship. From a knowledge of the forger's technical methods and materials the investigator can learn the pitfalls and the trace evidence of forgery. The nature of the clues will suggest the procedure of detection.

The problem of producing a support of suitable age and materials is met by using a support from a painting of a minor artist of the same period. The uniformity of weave would betray the modern canvas as the product of a machine—although it is not uncommon to have an old painting transferred to a new canvas, a circumstance that can be detected by the experienced eye as well as by the X-ray. The forger must clean his old canvas of all traces of the original painting. Despite the great care exercised by van Meegeren in cleaning the genuine seventeenth-century supports which he had purchased for his Vermeers, X-ray examination revealed in all eight works traces of the original paint, indications not only of forgery but of the extraordinary difficulty of removing all traces, especially from areas where paint containing white lead was used. In one painting, a fake Vermeer *Last Supper,* a partial image could be discerned in the radiograph from which it was possible to identify a work of Hondius, a minor contemporary of Vermeer. Further investigation revealed that van Meegeren had purchased Hondius' *Hunting Scene* in 1940 for £90 to provide a suitable support for the *Last Supper,* which was sold for £150,000.

Other inconsistencies revealed by X-rays include defects in the wood and the presence of anachronistic nails. A painting after the style of Luca di Tommé (Metropolitan Museum) was detected as a forgery by a study of a radiograph of the old frame, in which it was clear that the ground had been applied over already existing worm holes and a split in the knotty wood. No major artist would have painted over such a surface.

The *ground* will receive the same careful attention from the experienced forger. A material such as *gesso* or chalk will be laid on the support, using a sizing of parchment and glue or of carbonate of lime or perhaps all three in combination. The forger would be guided in his use of a priming coat by his knowledge of the typical X-ray picture of a painting executed by the master who is to be simulated. He would be aware of the critical requirement for fourteenth, fifteenth, and early sixteenth-century paintings in this regard—namely, the absence of a white lead priming coat. Radiographs of paintings of this period have a characteristic clarity; the figures are clearly delineated, even modeled, and reveal to the experienced eye the methods by which the master achieved his effects. White lead and vermilion are ten times more effective than ultramarine or chalk with respect to their stopping power for X-rays. In particular the effect of pigments containing white lead predominates in an X-ray so that, as Burroughs[2] has said, in a radiograph "one studies the use of white in painting." White lead was used from the

Figure 85. Painting photographed in polarized light.

early Renaissance to raise the tone of pure colors and to provide high-lights and enhance luminosity.

The use of white lead as a priming coat, however, did not come into general use until the latter half of the sixteenth century. The effect of such a primer is the heavy absorption of X-rays, resulting in a relatively thin negative with a few of the characteristics described in the previous paragraph. Thus, the forger who wishes to produce a sixteenth-century master must first ascertain the character of the radiographs of accepted works of the painter, since a white lead priming coat applied to the ground will radically alter the X-ray picture.

The *paint film* should, of course, be made with materials consistent with those used by the painter and his contemporaries. In medieval days, and well into the Renaissance, a distinguished artist was expected to use the very best pigments. The painting itself would have considerable intrinsic value simply because of the materials used. The use of ultramarine (*lapis lazuli*) for the blue of the Madonna's robe is urged upon painters of excellence by Cennino Cennini, a contemporary writer on pigments and their preparation. At that time *lapis lazuli* was as valuable as gold since it could be obtained only by import from Asia in limited quantity.

The knowledgeable forger, then, would provide himself with genuine ultramarine for the blue of his "Renaissance" painting and would be careful to avoid any of the blue pigments which were introduced into the art world in later centuries, e.g., Prussian blue, discovered in 1704; the cobalt blue of Thénard, discovered in 1802; or even artificial ultramarine, which first appeared in 1824. Genuine ultramarine is distinguishable from the synthetic product by means of its natural impurities and its irregular particle size.

Similarly, in the choice of a pigment for a red robe, the forger would use genuine vermilion, i.e., mercury sulphide prepared from cinnabar.[3] He would avoid the use of red earth or red lead pigment as substitutes for the true vermilion, which was without exception used for the red in all fine paintings, especially in the fifteenth century.

In his choice of the various pigments the accomplished forger would be especially careful to avoid the "dating pigments," that is, the pigments such as Prussian blue which, because of the known date of their discovery or first use in the art world, set a definite limit on the age of the painting. A painting containing Prussian blue (retouches excepted) could not have been made earlier than the eighteenth century.

Since lists of these dating pigments and their years of discovery have

Figure 86. Photograph using fluorescent light.

been compiled,[4] it would appear a simple matter for the forger to select his pigments in accordance with the period of the painting. In the art world, however, the purity of the dealer's pigments can not always be assured. Van Meegeren, who purchased his ultramarine from an English dealer to insure his use of the genuine pigment, proved a victim of this pitfall. In one of his paintings it was found that the ultramarine contained an admixture of cobalt in the blue. It was necessary, however, for the expert to distinguish between two forms of cobalt—smalt, a cobalt silicate used from 1550 to 1750, and cobalt blue, the relatively modern pigment discovered in 1804. Refractive index tests were used to eliminate smalt. X-ray diffraction is a more direct approach to this analysis.

Having procured the correct pigments for his picture, the forger must now prepare his paint with a suitable medium. The proportions of medium to pigment must be adapted to the degree of translucency desired in the picture. Finally, the forger must manage to impart the desired appearance of age to his paint film. Authentic craquelure, the result of unequal reactions in the various layers of the painting to changes in humidity and temperature, is difficult to simulate. If it is artifically induced, a fresh appearance may be visible along the edges of the cleavage. Attempts to camouflage these fresh cross-sectional areas may result in a telltale running or absorption of the stain by areas beyond the exposed craquelure. More subtle aspects of the aging of an oil paint must also be understood to avoid incriminating errors. The translucency, for example, of an old oil paint may be greater than that of one recently made, because of the increase of the refractive index of the oil medium with the passage of time.[4] If the varnish and top layer of the paint are transparent, a state of translucency may be reached where under images or *pentimenti* become visible. These alterations in composition made by the artist are sometimes visible in ordinary light but are more commonly seen in an infrared photograph.

The major problem, however, is the production of a paint film which has the hardness and resistance to organic solvents that is acquired with true aging. Van Meegeren successfully produced a resistant paint by using as his medium a synthetic resin of the phenol-formaldehyde type. The appearance of age was achieved by baking the painting. The contraction of the resin resulted in a network of fine cracks that convincingly simulated the true craquelure. Nevertheless, under a low-power microscope the hand of the forger could be detected in the blurred edges where he had applied India ink to give the appearance of dirt.

METHODS OF EXAMINATION

Repeated references have been made to the work of van Meegeren, not only because of his preeminence in the field of fraudulent painting but also because of the lessons to be learned by the scientific examiner from a study of the technical *modus operandi* of the forger at his best. A description of the forger's techniques suggests the appropriate method of examination or analysis. It should be noted, however, that van Meegeren's forgeries were exposed not as a result of critical examination or scientific analysis but rather as an outcome of a police interrogation conducted for an entirely different purpose. The defects of his faked Vermeers were revealed only by examinations conducted subsequent to his confession and self-exposure. Art critics and connoisseurs had already accepted the forgeries as authentic Vermeers. The case serves again to point up the importance of a scientific examination—a lesson that should have been learned several decades earlier from a study of the expert testimony presented at the Hahn v. Duveen trial.[5] At that time Justice Black had noted that the only substantial expert testimony was that of the scientific examiners and that the testimony of art critics and similar experts tended to be insubstantial and inconsistent, if not at times actually self-contradictory.

The scientific methods may be roughly divided into the physical and chemical. The physical methods—especially those employing radiography, photography, and the various forms of visual examination—are applied first, because of their nondestructive nature. The subsequent use of chemistry is restricted to micro-methods for obvious reasons.

RADIOGRAPHY. Both hard and soft X-ray regions are useful. Most generally helpful is a radiograph taken at about 35 kilovolts. The exposure time will vary with distance as well as current. The distance will vary with the size of the area which is being X-rayed. As we have seen, X-rays can reveal information about the structure of the painting: the nature of the support and its condition; the existence of damage beneath the visible surface; retouches; the relative density of the pigments (mass-absorption coefficients); the manner in which the painter has used white lead (and zinc white) and whether a white lead priming coat has been used; the presence of latent images where the artist has painted over an already existing image; and other information relevant to particular cases.

In the matter of latent images, it should be noted that their existence does not necessarily imply deception. A later artist may have been commissioned to finish the painting in a different manner or to make specific alterations. In some paintings the presence of an under image may provide excellent evidence of authenticity. In these instances the under image is simply a slightly displaced version of the visible figure. The artist, dissatisfied with his first effort, reworks the area to achieve a more pleasing composition. A copyist would hardly concern himself with doubt and decisions of this nature.

SECONDARY RADIATION. Some paintings are difficult and even impossible to X-ray satisfactorily because of the blocking effect of the support. Wooden panels and cross-pieces obstruct the desired image. In these situations secondary radiation may be used to provide information concerning the lower layers of the painting. An electron radiograph (i.e., an image made by secondary radiation) is also a useful supplement for the conventional radiograph. A 150-kilovolt source is used to emit X-rays which are too short to affect the photographic film but which will excite some of the materials of the painting (in particular, the metallic substances) so that they emit a radiation which will be recorded on the film. The film, then, may be placed on top of the painting. The X-rays are then sent through the film where they impinge on the painting and cause it to emit a radiation which will affect the film.

Since the emitted electrons are easily absorbed by air, the operation is conducted in a partial vacuum (4mm.) by placing both the painting and the film in a polyethylene bag which can be attached to a vacuum pump. The problems associated with a vacuum can be obviated by displacing the air in the bag with helium, an inert gas which has little absorptive effect on electrons.

PHOTOGRAPHY. The whole range of scientific photography has proved useful in the examination of paintings. Infrared photographs are the most helpful in revealing under images, deciphering inscriptions, and providing general information on the nature of the pigments. Fluorescent ultraviolet will show alterations and retouches. Polarized light penetrates the topmost layer to give a clearer picture of the various forms, figures, and colors. An excellent treatment of the various uses of visible and invisible light in the examination of paintings will be found in Hours-Miédan.[6]

MICROSCOPY.[7] In addition to low-power microscopical examination of the surface and photomacrography, a study of a cross-section of a small sample of the paint will be found valuable in obtaining information about the various distinct layers. A small, sharp-pointed knife is inserted in an already existing crack and a fragment is carefully levered up.

Figure 87.   Radiograph showing double image.

The point of extraction is located on a photograph and also by means of coordinates. The fragment is mounted in a suitable medium ("Marco" resin, a synthetic, cold-setting polyester is considered excellent), and a cross-section prepared and polished. The sample may now be studied under the microscope (30X to 150X) using the suggestions of Gettens.[8] With a micrometer eyepiece the thickness of layers and the particle size of coarser pigments can be measured. Color, particle size, refractive index, crystalline form, and other characteristics of the pigments can be determined to limit the range of subsequent chemical tests. A comparison with specimens from an extensive collection of reference samples is of great assistance.

CHEMICAL ANALYSIS.[7] The paint section is now subjected to solvent tests, stain tests, and other chemical tests. A series of identifying solvents is used for this purpose. In summary, the Feigl microchemical tests are applied. Partition chromatography is considered more suitable for testing the varnish layer.

A spectrographic examination is an effective method of chemical analysis of paint specimens in view of the minuteness of the sample. X-ray diffraction analysis, however, is the instrumental method of choice, since the sample is not destroyed and the critical area of the investigation is concerned with crystalline materials. Professor I. Fankuchen has demonstrated the effectiveness and rapidity of X-ray diffraction in distinguishing true ultramarine (*lapis lazuli*) from the chemically identical synthetic form.

SUMMARY

The discussion of art examination has been limited in this chapter to Renaissance paintings not merely for reasons of space but also because of the relative simplicity of the subject matter. The multiplication of painting techniques and materials in the last century has greatly increased the difficulty of determining the authenticity of more modern paintings. The use of such methods as dating pigments and radiography is far more fruitful in examining the Old Masters.

No mention either has been given to such newer methods of determining age as the use of radioactive carbon and the magnetometer. Dating by means of carbon 14 is impractical for paintings because of the quantity of the sample that must be used (and is consumed). Magnetometer methods fix the age of the painting by means of the magnetic force lines whose position is fixed at the time of execution, a period which can be compared with other periods in similar locations, for which a record of the direction of the earth's magnetic field has been determined. Extrapolation, however, is required beyond 1550.

Finally, the investigator should bear in mind that scientific examination is only one of three major requirements of proof of authenticity. The importance of documentation must be emphasized. The historicity, or truth of such a painting's existence as a historical fact, is in the province of art historians. Some documentation should exist to establish the fact that the painting was known to have been made or to have been catalogued at one time. A full pedigree or complete history of its title and location is, of course, the ideal.

Nor should the other requirement be neglected—namely, that the artistic achievement is consonant with the attribution, i.e., if it is claimed that the painting is the work of Rembrandt, then the subject matter, style, and level of skill should compare favorably with known works of Rembrandt. Much has been said in derogation of the esthetic critic with respect to the reliability of his testimony, but the last word must inevitably be his in these judgments, since his opinion relates to those qualities of the master which differentiate him from all other painters.

The scientific witness can claim the advantage of objectivity over the art critic, who often is testifying to the nature of his own impressions. The physical evidence provided by the painting must be free of inconsistencies and wholly in accord with what is known of the painter and his times. A favorable outcome of the scientific examination is a necessary condition for authenticity. It is not, however, a sufficient condition; it must be supplemented by some degree of documentation and the favorable opinion of a number of reliable art critics.

1 The only medieval written account of this process in full detail is that of Cennino d'Andrea Cennini of Colle di Val d'Elsa, a pupil of Agnolo Gaddi.

2 Burroughs.

3 Thompson. It should be noted again that the discussion is here limited to medieval and Renaissance practices and that many of the statements are not applicable to modern pigments or paints. Thompson draws heavily on Cennino Cennini.

4 de Wild.

5 An entertaining and informative account of this trial is given in H. Hahn's *The Rape of La Belle*, Frank Glenn Pub., Kansas City, 1946.

6 Hours–Miédan. In her *A La Découverte de La Peinture* (*pour les méthodes physiques*), Hours–Miédan provides the reader with a concise but thorough treatment of the application of photography to criminalistics.

7 Plesters.

8 Gettens.

XIII   HAIR

THE EXAMINATION OF HAIRS IS AN IMPORTANT ASPECT OF CRIMINAL investigation. At the scene of the crime, and especially at the scene of a homicide, a careful search for hairs should always be made.

PLACES WHERE HAIRS MAY BE FOUND

In homicides where a struggle has occurred between the victim and the murderer hair from the murderer may be found in the hands or on the clothing of the victim or hair from the victim may adhere to the clothes of the murderer or to his weapon. Fingernails should be carefully examined, particularly in cases of sex crimes. Hair may be found on all kinds of things—clothes, combs, brushes, beds, floor, carpets, and furniture. It has happened that some of the burglar's hairs have been caught by a safe door. In rape and other sex offenses the persons of the victim and of the perpetrator should be searched by a physician for foreign hairs.

Hairs may play a role in robbery, assault, illegal hunting, and generally on all occasions where it can be shown that a human being has been at a designated place or has had anything to do with a certain object. A stolen coat may, for instance, carry hairs of the thief and a stolen fur coat will sometimes leave traces of the coat's hair on its bearer.

As will be shown later, the identification of hairs is not as easy or as sure a matter as is generally thought, although the importance of a search for hairs at the scene of a crime should not be underestimated. The floor of any room when cleaned with a vacuum cleaner will probably yield hair from dozens of persons. Places where one can reasonably expect to find hairs from the perpetrator should be searched.

Examination of hairs in criminal investigation was made for the first time when the Duchesse de Praslin was murdered in Paris in 1847. An examination was made of a hair which clung to the pistol used, although the examiner satisfied himself with making some general remarks about the character of the hair and did not make any attempt at identification.

TRANSPORT OF HAIR

Specimens of hair, like specimens of blood, must be delivered to the laboratory examiner in an unaltered and exact manner. This is necessary to establish the chain of identification from the place of the crime, or from the place where the specimen was obtained, to the police laboratory. Unless this is done, the court will not admit the testimony of the laboratory examiner as evidence. Furthermore, the hair specimens and their original containers must be presented in court by the examiner and identified by him and by police officers who had a part in transporting the specimens.

Hair should be kept in either a clean white paper folded in the same manner as druggists fold powders or in test tubes. Hairs to which blood or sperm is attached should be kept with great care so that they will not be subjected to friction. If the hair has become brittle and dry, it can easily be broken and damaged. In such cases when the hair is examined, false conclusions may be reached as to the manner of assault.

COMPARISON HAIRS

Comparison hairs should be taken at each autopsy of a person who is the victim of an unknown murder or when the investigation is not yet completed. The comparison hairs should be as complete as possible. Hairs from the head, beard, eyebrows, eyelashes, and genitals should be kept in containers, properly labeled.

The necessity for taking comparison hairs before burial of the body cannot be too greatly emphasized. For example, in an actual case in which a woman was murdered with a hatchet the woman lived for a few hours and was taken to a hospital where all the hairs on her head were shaved previous to the performance of an operation. This hair was thrown away. A few days after burial the hatchet was found with some hairs attached to it. In order to get comparison hairs it was necessary to search the murdered woman's hairbrushes and hats. Unfortunately, she had had a girl friend living with her who had hair of the same color. This friend had also worn some of the murdered woman's hats. It became almost impossible to connect any of the hairs found with those of the dead woman. This part of the evidence, therefore, had to be discarded.

THE STRUCTURE OF HAIR

Among mammals, including human beings, there are two kinds of hair: real hair (here called hair) and fuzz. Hairs are generally long and stiff compared with fuzz, which is short, fine, and at times curly or woolly.

OUTER ASPECT

The hair consists of the root, tip, and shaft. The root does not give much information as to the origin of the hair. Often the root is missing on hair found on clothes at the scene of the crime, on weapons, etc.

There are two kinds of roots, living and dry roots. The living roots, which are often found on hair in full growth, are very different from the roots of hair that is dry and dead. An examination of the root gives the clue to a very important question, namely, whether the hairs have been pulled away by force or have fallen out. There are three possibilities:

1. *All hairs have living roots.* In this case they have not fallen out themselves but have been pulled away by force.
2. *All hairs have dry roots.* In this case they have probably fallen out.
3. *Some hairs have living and some dry roots.* In this case they have been pulled away by force, the living hairs with the dry ones.

The tips may be natural or cut. In animals that live in freedom and whose hair has never been cut the original primitive form of the tip can be seen. The same is the case with certain domestic animals and also with women whose hair has never been cut.

The form of the tip varies greatly on different parts of the body and on different animals. In some animals the hair has the same thickness from the root to the tip. Sometimes it has a very fine point. Between these two extremes there are all kinds of variations.

A cross-section of a hair of a human being differs according to the part of the body from which it is procured. Hairs from the head are generally round, although curly hairs are sometimes oval. The hair of the beard is triangular, with concave sides. Hair from the torso is usually oval or kidney-shaped. These characteristics should not be looked upon as final, as the appearance of the cross-section is fairly variable. On animals many different types of cross-sections can be found.

INNER STRUCTURE OF THE HAIR

If a hair is examined under a microscope, three parts may be observed: the medulla, the cortex, and the cuticle. Of these three the medulla is the most important from the viewpoint of investigation.

Certain hair has no medulla. Therefore, hair can be divided into two categories—that without medulla and that with medulla. The hair of a very few animals belongs to the first category.

The medulla begins more or less near the root. In hairs that are full grown and nearly falling out the medulla begins fairly high up, its appearance varying to a high degree. In some animals it starts with a row of cells which continue the whole length of the hair to the tip, or the medulla makes one or more bifurcations and continues in several rows of cells side by side.

The medulla can be *continuous* or *interrupted*. It is continuous in a large number of animals and very often interrupted in humans, monkeys, and horses. The diameter of the medulla can be absolutely constant but may also at times be alternately narrow and broader in the same hair. The actual diameter of the medulla is of very little importance, but the relation between the diameter of the medulla and the diameter of the whole hair is of great importance. This relation should always be calculated at the point where the hair is thickest. The diameter can be measured under the microscope with an eyepiece micrometer or by microphotography with a ruler. The relation between these two diameters is designated I ($=$ medullary index).

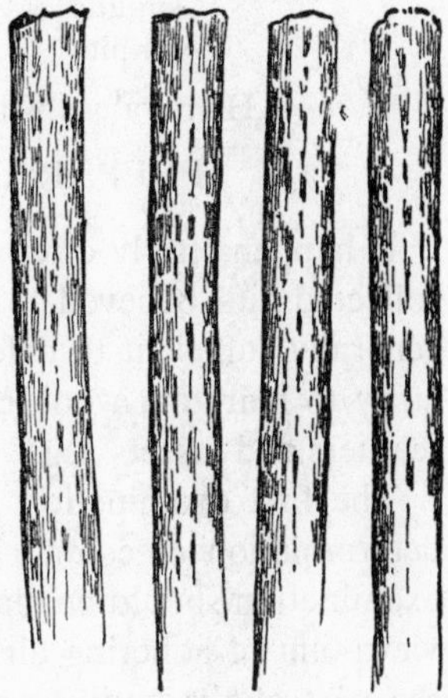

Figure 88. From left to right, tips of hair cut twenty-four hours, two, eight, and twenty days previously.

THE MEDULLARY INDEX. According to this index, hairs may be divided into three general groups.

1. Hair with narrow medulla (i.e., less than 0.5). In this group belong human and certain monkeys' hairs.
2. Hair with medium medulla (i.e., approximately 0.5). In this group belong the hairs of the cow, horse, and some other animals.
3. Hair with thick medulla (i.e., larger than 0.5). The hairs of almost all other animals belong in this group.

Certain human hairs show a narrow and often interrupted medulla; others, especially hairs from women's scalps, are often without medulla. In the table on page 192 the values of I are approximate:[1]

The cuticle consists of translucent scales, laid one on another as shingles on a roof, with the free end pointed toward the tip of the hair. In humans about four fifths of each scale is covered by the adjoining scale.

	Man	Woman
Neck	0.115	0.163
Forehead	0.132	0.148
Eyebrows	0.236	0.233
Eyelashes	0.095	0.146
Beard	0.260	
Genitals	0.153	0.114
Armpits	0.102	0.179

High values will be found in most domestic animals.

PREPARATIONS FOR EXAMINATION

It happens fairly often that at the scene of a crime hairlike fibers are collected and believed to be hair. A simple microscopic examination is generally sufficient to determine their origin. Fibers which show a similarity to hairs are wool, cotton, silk, hemp, linen, straw, and sometimes feathers and insects' legs.

The first examination is made with the naked eye and includes the determination of color, curliness, and length. Thereafter a microscopic examination should be made. The hairs are examined especially from the viewpoint of adhering dirt, which often gives valuable information as to the part of the body from which the hair comes, the profession of the bearer, and the nature of the crime. Many professions leave characteristic dust on the hair. The mechanic will have metal dust; the miller, flour dust; the bricklayer, brick dust, etc.

For the microscopic examination the hair should be mounted on a glass slide. In most cases mounting in water or in a very diluted solution of gelatin or glycerin is quite sufficient. If there are several hairs to be examined, they may be placed on the slide side by side so that they can be studied at full length. If the hairs are very long they should be cut in pieces, and in order to avoid getting them mixed they should be marked with small lumps of different colored wax. Sometimes it may be necessary to wash the hairs before the final examination if they are very dirty. They are washed with alcohol or ether, but this should not be done until a thorough examination of the adherent dirt has been made. In some cases the hairs are so strongly pigmented that the cells in the interior and the details in the cuticle do not show up. The strongly pigmented hair may best be studied by cross-section or, if the cuticle is in question, by the method of Moritz.[2]

Hairs on dead bodies at times assume a reddish color on account of the action of the humus in the soil.

Cross-sections of hair may also be valuable for the examination, particularly in cases where it is necessary to distinguish between human and animal hairs. For this purpose the hairs may be mounted for sectioning in blocks of liver tissue, hardened in chloroform, and sliced by the ordinary sliding microtome.[3]

DEFORMATION OF HAIRS

Deformation of hairs sometimes leads to very interesting conclusions as to the kind of weapon used. If the head of a person has been hit only once with a hatchet or an ax, there are seldom deformations of the shaft of the hair in the longitudinal direction but it can very often be broken in the neighborhood of the root. The condition of the hair may disclose whether more than one blow has been struck; if so, longitudinal splits can be seen in the shaft. Such splits, then, are a sign of several blows.

The following description of conclusions which can be drawn from deformation of hairs may serve to show the importance which they may have in an investigation.[4]

DEFORMATIONS CAUSED BY CUTTING. Sharp, right-angled, or oblique cutting surface without splits denotes a sharp cutting tool, such as a knife or scissors.

Uneven, stepped cutting surface, with splitting or crushing of the end of the shaft, denotes a blunt cutting tool, such as a dull knife, hatchet, ax, or similar weapon.

DEFORMATIONS CAUSED BY SHOOTING. Here sometimes particles of powder and metal may be found and also the natural consequences of burning, such as blackening, curling, and charring.

DEFORMATIONS CAUSED BY BURNING. These can be the result of an open flame, lightning, electric current, curling iron, and, as above mentioned, shooting. Singeing only causes curling, a slight swelling, and a gray color. Burning in all its degrees up to complete charring leaves an odor like burnt horn, great swelling, gray, brown, red, or black color, brittleness, and transparence. Sometimes air bubbles, arranged like the beads of a necklace, can be seen in the interior of the hair. Treatment with a curling iron often gives these results, although generally it only splits the hair.

DEFORMATIONS CAUSED BY SCALDING. These deformations are caused by hot water or steam. In the latter case, if the temperature has not gone above 350 degrees Fahrenheit, the hairs are reddish and show streaks in the longitudinal direction caused by the shriveling of the cells of the medulla. Up to 480 degrees Fahrenheit the hairs curl and become brittle, the reddish color becomes red-black, the hair is more transparent, and air bubbles form the typical "necklace."

DOES THE HAIR COME FROM A HUMAN BEING OR AN ANIMAL?

When studying this problem it should not be forgotten that none of the properties described below are alone and of themselves absolutely certain indices of origin. One or more of them can be found in hairs of certain animals but never all together. The following table gives a survey of the principal differences between human and animal hairs: [5]

TABLE OF THE MAJOR DIFFERENCES BETWEEN HUMAN AND ANIMAL HAIR

HUMAN	ANIMAL
Medulla	
Air network in fine grains	Air network in form of large or small sacks
Cells invisible without treatment in water	Cells easily visible
Value of *I* lower than 0.3	Value of *I* higher than 0.5
Fuzz without medulla	Fuzz with medulla
Cortex	
Looks like a thick muff	Looks like a fairly thin hollow cylinder
Pigment in the form of very fine grains	Pigment in the form of irregular grains—larger than the human
Cuticle	
Thin scales, not protruding, covering one another to about four fifths	Thick scales, protruding, not covering one another to the same degree as the human

Collections of mounted specimens of animal and human hair and of photomicrographs will aid in these examinations.

IS THE HAIR DYED?

In order to answer this question a microchemical examination must be made. It is possible to determine if it has been dyed with salts of bismuth or lead, nitrate of silver, permanganate of potassium, pyrogallic acid, paraphenyldiamine, henna, etc.

DOES THE HAIR BELONG TO A
CERTAIN INDIVIDUAL?

Identification of hairs is very difficult, especially if only a few hairs or, as it often happens, only a few pieces of hair are at the disposal of the expert. In almost all cases it is only possible to reach conclusions with great difficulty. The length of the hairs and the average diameter of the medulla are measured, and the colors compared. The diameter should be measured at the thickest places, and this has in itself little value for identification. *I* should be calculated. The color is determined after the *portrait parlé*. Cross-sections may be made and compared. If all these signs are alike, there is a probability of identity, but only a close examination can strengthen this probability. Examination of the medulla is important; likewise that of the root, the point, and the pigmentation of the cortex.[6] Although a strong similarity can be shown by hair comparison, efforts to establish identity have thus far been unsuccessful. Refinements of color analysis appear to offer promise in this direction.

The results of hair examinations should only be taken as confirmatory evidence and must always be supported by additional proof.

1 Lambert–Balthazard.

2 See Smith–Glaister and Boller. The methods outlined in the latter's article (use of ultraviolet and infrared rays) may in time be useful but at present are in the experimental stage. The same is true of polarized light and similar tests.

3 For details of this technique see Vance.

4 Leers.

5 This table is taken from the excellent work of Lambert–Balthazard, *Le Poil de l'homme et des animaux*. This book is recommended for anyone who desires to enter more deeply into this study. Of special value are the illustrations showing microscopic studies of the hairs of almost all animals.

6 Note also the possibility of studying the structure of the cuticular layer by casting the hair. See Kirk–Magagnose–Salisbury.

XIV PROBLEMS OF ATTACKS
WITH FIREARMS

THE FIRST ATTEMPTS TO IDENTIFY A BULLET AS HAVING BEEN DIS-
charged from a certain firearm[1] were made hundreds of years ago, and
it is quite possible that some such identifications may have been successful simply because the projectiles in those days were usually manufactured by the shooter himself. However, when factories began to produce
ammunition, the possibility of identification on that score disappeared,
at least as far as pistols and revolvers were concerned.

COLLECTING AND PRESERVING THE EVIDENCE

Never touch the arm (weapon) on the scene of the crime before its
location has been recorded by photographs and sketch. The surroundings
of the arm can also be of importance; for instance, in cases where markings on the floor show that the arm was dropped, giving support to a
theory of suicide: In such a case there should be some marks on the arm
too. The location of empty shells and the entrance holes of bullets in walls
should also be recorded by photographs and sketch. Fingerprints may be
found on the polished surfaces of the arm, on the magazine, and also on
the butt. It must be pointed out, however, that cases where fingerprint
identification was possible have been relatively rare. No additional
processing for fingerprints should be done until the weapon has been
examined by a firearms expert. If the firearms specialist is expected at
the scene, the weapon should, if possible, be left untouched. If the arm
must be moved, it should be picked up by some safe part such as the
checkered grips. Great care should be exercised, since some pistols may
be easily fired by careless handling. The weapon should not be lifted by
placing an object inside the barrel or within the trigger guard. This
procedure can be dangerous and, moreover, may destroy minute clues.

Make notes immediately and in detail of the condition of the arm. Pay
special attention to such things as the position of the safety catch, the
marks of a defective cartridge in the barrel, evidence that the arm did not

196

function because a cartridge was stuck, etc. Such points may later be of great importance.

Manipulate the arm as little as possible before giving it to the expert! If it is necessary to manipulate the arm in order to take out a loaded cartridge from the chamber of an automatic pistol, this information should be given to the expert in all details. When unloading an automatic pistol, the magazine in the butt is lowered so that a new cartridge cannot enter the barrel. The cartridge taken from the barrel should be marked with a label fastened to the rim and should be transported in a small box so that it will not be marked additionally.

In describing a firearm, all available identifying data should be given. As a minimum the description should contain the following: caliber, make, model, type, serial number, and finish. The make is the manufacturer's name, usually stamped on the barrel of revolvers and on the slide and frame of automatics. The model designation is essential since two revolvers of the same caliber and make can have identical serial numbers. Colt "Official Police" and Iver Johnson "Trailman 66" are examples of model designation. The type describes the manner of operation, e.g., revolver, semiautomatic, or single shot. Serial numbers are located in various areas on handguns. Both the letters and the numerals constitute the complete serial number. The finish, i.e., color and surface of the arm, are described by terms such as *Blue* and *Nickel*.

TYPES OF REVOLVERS AND PISTOLS

The revolver is a hand firearm having at the rear of the barrel a revolving cylinder provided with a number of chambers which, by the revolution of the cylinder, are brought successively into alignment with the barrel and the firing mechanism for successive and rapid firing.

In modern revolvers the cylinder-revolving mechanism is connected with the firing mechanism, the cocking of which automatically revolves the cylinder.

In double-action revolvers the pulling of the trigger performs the double function of cocking the hammer and revolving the cylinder to present a fresh cartridge to the firing mechanism.

An automatic pistol is a firearm from which the shell of a fired shot is ejected and a fresh cartridge pushed from the magazine into the breech by means of the gases generated by the preceding explosion. The magazine usually fits into the butt or frame of the pistol but may also be a permanent part of the mechanism.

From the viewpoint of construction revolvers can be divided into **four** categories:

1. Revolvers with barrel firmly fixed to the frame and a revolving cylinder which may be swung out to the side for the purpose of loading
2. Revolvers with barrel hinged to the frame and carrying a revolvable cylinder which may be broken open to load by releasing the barrel latch
3. Revolvers with barrel firmly fixed to the frame and a revolving cylinder which may be removed by taking out the cylinder pin on which it rotates
4. Revolvers with barrel firmly fixed to the frame and a revolving cylinder operated by the gas pressure

An obsolete type of revolver known as the pepperbox had a group of barrels which was revolvable.

From the viewpoint of identification the revolver should be classified first by caliber and secondly by percussion. We then have the three following primary groups:

1. Revolvers with center fire, where the percussion cap is placed in the center of the cartridge
2. Revolvers with rim fire, where the percussion composition is placed around the inside of the rim of the shell
3. Revolvers with pin fire, where the hammer strikes a needle which is placed at the rim of the shell and presses on a percussion cap in the interior of the cartridge (this type is obsolete now and is very rarely found)

Revolvers with center fire are most prevalent for individual purposes. In the United States the following are the arms using center-fire revolver and pistol cartridges:

Firearm		Diameter of bullet	
.25	Automatic Colt	.251	inch
.32	Smith & Wesson	.315	"
.32	Smith & Wesson Long	.315	"
7.63	mm. Mauser	.3105	"
7.65	mm. Luger	.3095	"
.32	Short Colt	.315	"
.32	Long Colt	.313	"
.32	Long Colt	.300	"
.32	Colt N.P.	.314	"
.32	Automatic Colt	.3125	"
.32	Winchester	.312	"
9	mm. Luger	.3555	"

Firearm	*Diameter of bullet*	
.38 Short Colt	.375	inch
.38 Colt N.P.	.359	"
.38 Colt Special	.358	"
.38 Colt Long	.358	"
.38 Automatic Colt	.359	"
.38 Automatic Colt Super	.356	"
.380 Automatic Colt	.357	"
.38 Smith & Wesson	.3585	"
.38 Winchester	.3595	"
.41 Short Colt	.406	"
.41 Long Colt	.387	"
.44 Smith & Wesson Am.	.420	"
.44 Smith & Wesson Russ.	.431	"
.44 Smith & Wesson Special	.431	"
.44 Winchester	.4255	"
.45 Colt	.455	"
.45 Colt Automatic	.4505	"
.455 Colt	.458	"

On the Continent the following calibers are found:

	Diameter of bullet	
5 mm.	.1968	inch
5.6 mm.	.2165	"
6.35 mm.	.250	"
7 mm.	.276	"
7.63 mm.	.300	"
7.65 mm.	.302	"
8 mm.	.315	"
9 mm.	.354	"
11 mm.	.433	"
12 mm.	.472	"

Revolvers with rim fire are not much in evidence today, although the rim-fire .22 caliber cartridge is used to a large extent in target practice. Single-shot pistols are used by professional shooters in target practice. The Derringer .41 caliber may be found in many places throughout the United States.

It should be added that some of the above-named revolvers with rim or center fire can be loaded with birdshot, but the custom is by no means common.

Automatic pistols may be classified according to the number of grooves and impressions made on the bullets (see "Possibilities of Determining the Make of an Unknown Firearm by a Bullet" later in this chapter). The common calibers in the United States are as follows:

.25	caliber	.251	inch
.32	"	.315	"
.35	"	.350	"
.357	"	.357	"
.38	"	.356	"
.380	"	.356	"
.45	"	.451	"

On the Continent the following calibers are used:

6.35	mm.	.250	inch
7.63	mm.	.300	"
7.65	mm.	.302	"
9	mm.	.354	"
11.25	mm.	.451	"

Of these the 6.35 mm. and the 7.65 mm. are the most generally used. The 7.63 is a special type of cartridge used only for the Mauser automatic pistol of military type. The 9 mm. is almost exclusively used for military and police purposes. The 11.5 is rare on the Continent and only used for imported pistols (.45 Auto Colt for the Colt M. 1911 and .455 Auto for the Webley & Scott), except for the Norwegian military Colt 11.5, which is manufactured on license in Norway and which during the occupation of the country was spread all over Scandinavia. Also found on the Continent are some other calibers of automatic pistols—the Lilliput 4.25 mm., the Clement 5 mm., the Steyr and Roth 8 mm. (.315 inch), etc.—but these are now becoming obsolete. In the U.S.S.R. and surrounding countries may be found the Tokarev automatic, caliber 7.62 mm., as well as the Nagant revolver, caliber 7.62 mm., both used in the Soviet army.

Calibers are calculated differently in English, American, and Continental firearms. In order to understand this important difference we will introduce the terms "real caliber" and "nominal caliber." In Continental arms (with the exception of arms without rifling—as, for example, for buckshot) the real caliber, i.e., the diameter of the bore, is measured between two opposite lands. In other words, the bore is looked upon, in measuring, as having no grooves. The measurement is taken at the muzzle and not at the breech, where the cartridge chamber is located. The nominal caliber is purely a conventional measurement which has only an indirect relation to the bore. American and English calibers are nominal and are expressed in decimals of an inch. The following table shows the relation between American, English, and Continental calibers:

American caliber		English caliber		Continental caliber in millimeters
.22 inch		.220 inch		5.6
.25 "		.250 "		6.5 (6.35)
.28 "		.280 "		7
.30 "	(.32 Rev.)	.300 "	(.303)	7.65
.32 "		.320 "		8
.35 "	(.351)	.350 "		9
.38 "		.360 "		9.3
.38 "		.370 "		9.5
.38-.40-.41 inch		.410 "		10
.405 inch				10.5
.44 "		.440 "		11
.45 "		.450 "	(.455)	11.25

In converting mm. to inches, multiply the mm. by .03937 or divide by 25.4. To convert inches to mm., multiply by 25.4 or divide by .03937.

There are now semi-automatic pistols of .22 caliber. These are the Walther Mod. PP, Walther Olympia, Walther duel pistol, Parabellum (Luger), Colt, High Standard, and the Spanish Star. In Switzerland there is now manufactured a semi-automatic pistol called Neuhausen, which has an interchangeable barrel so that it can be used for either 9 mm. or 7.65 mm. Parabellum cartridges. Also manufactured at present are the following small arms for .22 caliber: Ruger automatic (American), Baretta Olympic Model (Italian), Hammerli Automatic Olympic Model (Swiss), Tompkins single-shot target pistol (American).

THE CALIBER OF A FIRED BULLET

WHEN THE BULLET HAS ITS ORIGINAL SHAPE. One would perhaps expect a bullet to have a caliber absolutely corresponding to the arm. This is not the case. If an attempt is made to introduce the bullet back again into the firearm after it has been fired, it will be found to be impossible. If the lands are to make markings on the bullet, the latter must be larger than the bore. In bullets of small caliber (.22–.32) the difference between the diameter of an unfired bullet and the real caliber of the arm is about .008 inch. In the arm of larger caliber (.35–.45) the difference may be as great as .015 inch.

The caliber is determined with the aid of a micrometer, calibrated to .0001 inch, and measured on two opposite grooves.

WHEN THE BULLET HAS BEEN DEFORMED. If a bullet has partly lost its original form, there is a possibility of determining its caliber by measuring the width of the land or groove and in some cases of foreign bullets by noting the letters affixed to the bottom and by the weight.

In order to determine the caliber and the origin by the weight there should be available a complete collection of information about all bullets. The weight of the bullet varies with the manufacturer and the materials used.[2]

If the bullet has been split in the body, all parts should be carefully collected at the autopsy. When weighing these parts, there are three alternatives. In the first case the weight may tell the supposed caliber if, for example, the firearm has been seized. This is at any rate interesting information. In the second case the parts may weigh more than a bullet from the suspected arm. In this case no identity is possible. Finally, they may weigh less, in which case identity is not excluded because all the small parts may not have been collected.

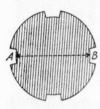

Figure 89. Schematic cross-section of a fired bullet. The caliber is measured between A and B.

To try to determine the origin of a bullet by chemical analysis is almost useless. In some cases special alloys are used, notably in jacketed bullets, but this is rare. As a rule both bullets and jackets from different manufacturers are of fairly uniform composition.

Bullets are made either of lead or, with regard to jacketed bullets, of hard metals, generally of gilding metal coated with nickel, and with a lead core. There are also jackets consisting entirely of copper and zinc, and coated with nickel or tin, and of steel and iron.[3]

THE IDENTIFICATION OF BULLETS

Examination of a bullet should lead not only to the determination of identity with the firearm from which it has been fired but also to a thorough knowledge of the marks produced on it by its discharge. Under certain circumstances it might be possible to identify a bullet by examination of an object which it has touched on its way. De Rechter and Mage,[4] for instance, succeeded in identifying a bullet by studying a tooth which it had hit. Lead bullets may also be identified by the marks left on them by the fabrics which they have pierced.[5]

All modern small arms have rifled bores. The grooves are necessary because modern bullets possess a long or cylindrical section and a more or less conical shape. If they were not put in rotation around the longitudinal axis through the pitch of the grooves, they would probably turn end-over-end in the air. The number of grooves varies according to the manufacturer, but there are generally five or six. In modern firearms the grooves are made with an automatic cutter and by broaching, and it would seem natural to assume that all barrels of a certain serial would be absolutely indentical.[6] However, this is not the case. While irregularities might have no influence whatever on the value of the arm, they have great importance in criminological examinations.

Another important fact is to be considered. The tools used become worn while in use and produce numerous microscopic ridges in the grooves, which are still more accentuated when small metal alloy particles are ground between the cutter and the steel. Defects in the material may also make characteristic marks. All in all, the width, the depth, and the pitch of the grooves, the ridges in the grooves and other peculiarities due to defective material, wear and tear, and accidents individualize the barrel and render possible the identification of the bullet which has passed through it. On a bullet we find *the sum total* of the peculiarities of the particular barrel. Generally speaking, it is useless to compare the barrel or its parts directly with the bullet as was formerly done. The comparison should be made with comparison bullets.

The bullet to be examined is at first inspected for adhering particles, and these, if necessary, should be analyzed microscopically. Such an analysis may give important information. If the bullet is deformed, an attempt should be made to determine how the deformation came about— eventually by performing practical experiments. If the bullet is deformed to such a degree that it has completely lost its original form and does not show any grooves, it may only be possible to determine the caliber and perhaps the make.

If, on the contrary, the bullet has retained its shape or is only partly deformed, the grooves are examined with the comparison microscope.[7] The comparison microscope is double—two separate microscopes fitted with a comparison eyepiece, which, when placed on them, merges them together like one microscope. The comparison eyepiece fuses the images of two bullets or shells into one image. On may see the front half of one and the rear half of the other bullet, and they appear to be one in the microscope.

When a fatal bullet or shell is set in the microscope with a test bullet or shell fired from the arm used, they can be rotated either independently or together; and any marks left on them by reason of any condition of the rifling of the barrel used, or any marks left on the primer of the shell from the breechlock or firing pin, are bound to match in the composite image of the two bullets or shells, thereby making identification positive. This eliminates any possibility of guesswork.

This instrument was first used to identify bullets by the Americans

Graville and Waite, but many modifications, especially concerning the bullet-holders, have been made. It goes without saying that a great deal of experience is a prerequisite to complete success. The able expert may often detect signs of identity or non-identity where the amateur sees nothing at all.

Comparison bullets should be obtained by shooting them into cotton. This applies, however, only to coated bullets and to lead bullets fired by pistols and revolvers or by rifles of small calibers, as for instance caliber .22. Lead bullets shot from rifles of larger calibers must be shot into water because they would be polished by the friction of the cotton.

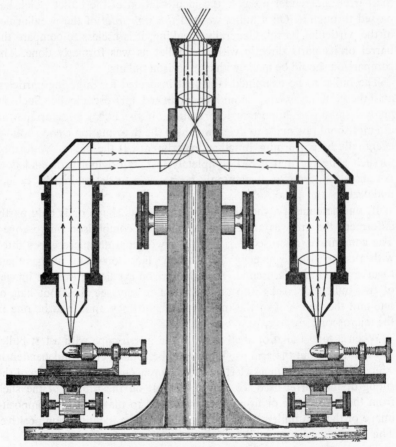

Figure 90.   Comparison microscope, shown schematically.

Two cases from the Ballistics Bureau of the New York City Police Department will illustrate the use of identification of firearms.

At about 10:35 P.M. on March 19, 1949, the body of Benjamin Klein was found on the floor of the store of the Steinberg & Dubin Memorial

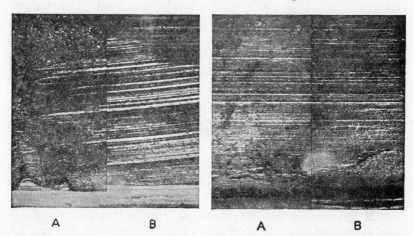

Figure 91. Identification in the comparison microscope of pistol bullets: A, fatal bullet; B, test bullet.

Figure 92. Identification of bullets: A, fatal bullet; B, test bullet.

Works at 245 Houston Street. He had been shot and killed by some unknown person or persons. No arrest was made or gun recovered at the time. A discharged cartridge case was recovered at the scene and after examination at the Ballistics Bureau was identified as having been fired from a 9 mm. Baretta automatic pistol. The Homicide Squad was informed of this fact, and after diligent detective effort, the perpetrator was arrested. Upon being questioned, he informed the police that he had committed the homicide during a robbery and that he had used a 9 mm. Baretta automatic pistol. He further stated that he had thrown this pistol into the East River. The pistol was not recovered. The suspect was convicted.

At about 6:50 A.M. on February 8, 1949, one Rafael Almodover was shot and injured in his grocery store at 123 Ellery Street, Brooklyn. He stated that he was shot by one of three men who attempted to rob him. No arrest was made at the time as the suspects had escaped. A .32 caliber discharged cartridge case was found at the scene of the shooting. A .32 caliber metal jacket bullet was removed from the injured at the hospital but was too deformed for comparison. On February 14, 1949, at 2 P.M., two police officers engaged in a shooting with three robbery suspects on Madison Avenue in Manhattan, New York City. The suspects were escaping after the robbery of a grocery store located at 1460 Park Avenue. One suspect was shot and the other two were arrested. Two firearms were recovered from them. One, a 7.65 mm. Unique Automatic pistol, was found, after test and microscopic examination, to have been the pistol used to shoot Almodover. The comparison was made from the cartridge case recovered at the store of Almodover. The suspects were identified and several robberies solved.

POSSIBILITIES OF DETERMINING THE MAKE OF AN UNKNOWN FIREARM BY A BULLET

In order to determine the make of an unknown arm from which a bullet has been fired a classification of bullet marks must be at hand. Early attempts at such a classification were begun in the United States by Charles Waite and continued by Lieutenant Colonel Calvin Goddard. In 1926 in Lyons, France, Dr. Söderman began a classification of European automatic pistols, and at the same time Professor Mezger, Dr. Heess, and Inspector Hasslacher in Stuttgart, Dr. Kraft in Berlin, and Major Wittman in Nuremberg, Germany, undertook a similar classification. The work of Mezger, Heess, and Hasslacher has been published in an *Atlas of Arms,* which contains photographs of more than a hundred different automatic pistols and can be classed as one of the achievements of police science in modern times.[8] In many police departments of the United States there now exist, however, comprehensive classifications of revolvers, pistols, etc. In New York City, for instance, the following classifications are used: The arms are classified according to caliber, according to direction of twist of the rifling, and by the number of lands and grooves. When a gun not previously recorded is entered in the file, a description of the appearance of the gun, barrel length, over-all length and cartridge capacity, type of operation, manufacturer's name, serial number, country of origin, and proof marks are typed on the card. The test bullet is then rolled on a piece of carbon paper so that a reverse impression showing the width and length of the rifling mark is transferred to the file card. The roll may be protected from smudging by covering it with a piece of transparent cellulose tape. It may be noted that in practice it is even possible to note differences in rifling characteristics, as they appear on the impression, between guns of the same caliber and twist and the same number of lands and grooves.

When a bullet is recovered in a case in which the gun is missing, a rolled impression is taken of the bullet and this compared with the specimen cards. When the rolled impression compares favorably at first sight with the evidence bullet, a microscopic comparison of measurement is made with the best bullet in the file. Fired cartridge cases from the scene may also be compared with test cases from the file as to the firing-pin impression characteristics.

Determining the make of an unknown firearm is accomplished by examining the grooves on the bullet, their number and width, as well as the direction (right-hand or left) and the degree of twist of the spiral. These four factors will be found constant in the same make of pistols, or at least in the better-known ones.

Unimportant European manufacturers of pistols will often have the barrels made by a "barrel-maker" (home industry). In these cases the measurements are seldom exact, and home manufacturers do not record changes in measurements. This gives rise to uncertainty regarding the date of manufacture and the exact calibers. In addition, when large orders have been received, the manufacturers frequently begin a new series of numbers for arms, beginning with No. 1, or some other low number, to avoid the extra work of making four ciphers.

For the sake of simplicity almost all pistol barrels have an even number of grooves. In the .25 and .32 caliber automatics there are usually 6 lands (smooth surfaces between the spiral grooves). Only about one half of the Continental pistols of the .25-caliber group and only one third of the pistols of the .32-caliber group have 4 lands. Very few pistols of European make have 5, 7, or 8 lands. In the survey made by Mezger and Heess there were only eight automatics having 5 lands. In the .25-caliber group there are the Express, Floria, Pickert, and Princeps & Waldman. In the .32-caliber group there are the F. N. Model 1900, Helios, and the Stenda pistols. The Schmeisser Model No. 2 .25 caliber has 8 lands. Up to No. 105,000 the Schmeisser pistol had 6 lands. Such variations have also been noted in the Walther Model 5 and 7 and in the Stenda. Walther has changed from 4 to 6 lands.

Pistols with the same number of lands may also be differentiated by the direction of the twist of the rifling, which may be either to the left or to the right. The direction of the twist is figured from the breech to the muzzle. There are very few automatics with twist to the left, with the exception of Spanish pistols of .25 and .32 caliber. The Bayard and Colt, calibers .25, .32, .38, and .45, also have left twist. All pistols known so far to have left twist have 6 lands.

The twist can be expressed by measuring the distance a land must travel to make one full revolution, or it may be expressed by the angle of twist. The angle of twist is the angle which the land forms with the longitudinal axis of the bullet. If that angle is large, the twist is small. To measure the angles, a special measurement microscope has been manufactured. A complete description of the technique of measuring is given in the above-mentioned work of Mezger and Heess.

The angle of twist is an important sign, but it is not always constant. Small defects may arise by a readjustment of the cutter. The angle of twist will, however, often give sufficient information for distinguishing different makes of pistols.

The width of the lands must be judged even more carefully than the angle of the twist. This is necessary because of the manufacturers' practice of making the cutter about .002 of an inch wider than standard and using the cutter until it has worn down to .002 of an inch below standard, causing a difference of .002 plus or minus. Therefore, differences in the same make of pistol may occur. The width of the lands is measured with the same microscope mentioned above.

In the classification the bullets are divided first by the caliber and then according to the number of lands and the direction of twist. The following classification may be found in the *Atlas of Arms:*

Table No.	Caliber		No. of lands	Direction of pitch or twist
1	.25	with	6	right
1A	.25	"	6	left
2	.25	"	4	right
3	.25	"	5, 7, or 8	right
4	.32	"	6	right
4A	.32	"	6	left
5	.32	"	4	right
6	.32	"	5	right
7	.38 / .380	"	4, 6, or 7	right and left

In these tables the individual makes are arranged according to the degree of the twist. In tabulating, the authors of the *Atlas* have considered only the smallest angle of the twist. If two pistols of the same make vary more than .3 degree (angle of twist), the pistols are tabulated separately. The minimum and maximum width of the lands will also be found in the tables.

The possibilities of determining a certain make when dealing with the most common combinations—for instance, .25 caliber, with 6 lands and right twist—are small, and only in exceptional cases are results obtained. The possibilities of determining the makes of rarer combinations in the table, such as 1A, 3, 4A, 6, and 7, are greater. As a rule, it may be said that only in a few cases is it possible to determine an individual manufacturer.

The following is a table of rate of twist and groove diameters of American-made pistols and revolvers:

TABLE OF RATE OF TWIST AND GROOVE DIAMETERS OF AMERICAN-MADE PISTOLS AND REVOLVERS

Name and caliber	Make	Twist in inches	Groove diameter in inches
.22 Long Rifle	S. & W.	15R *	.2235
.22 Colt	Colt	14L †	.222
.25 Automatic	Colt	16L	.251
.32 Colt Automatic	Colt	16L	.311
.32 Smith & Wesson	S. & W.	183/4R	.313
.32–20 Colt	S. & W.	12R	.312
.32 Colt	Colt	16L	.312
.38 Smith & Wesson	S. & W.	183/4R	.357
.38 Smith & Wesson Special	S. & W.	183/4R	.357
.38 Colt Special	Colt	16L	.354
.38 Colt Automatic	Colt	16L	.356
.38 Colt Revolver	Colt	16L	.354
.38–40 Colt	Colt	16L	.402
.41 Colt	Colt	16L	.402
.44–40 Colt (old models)	Colt	16L	.424
.44–40 Colt (new models)	Colt	16L	.427
.44 Smith & Wesson	S. & W.	20R	.431
.44 Colt	Colt	16L	.427
.45 Automatic Colt Pistol	Colt	16L	.451
.45 Colt	Colt	16L	.452

 * R indicates right or clockwise rifling twist.
 † L indicates left or counterclockwise rifling twist.

The Colts have six grooves. Most of the Smith & Wesson have five grooves, except Smith & Wesson Government 1917 model and Smith & Wesson Automatic, which have six grooves.

IDENTIFICATION OF SHELLS

In order to understand the process of identification[9] of shells it is necessary to know what happens when a shot is fired.

The revolver is a firearm with a rotating chamber which allows the successive firing of five or more shots. The chamber is put in rotation by a hand or pawl, often connected with the trigger. It is the shooter himself who makes the necessary movement to fire the cartridge from the revolver and to introduce a new cartridge.[10]

In the automatic pistol, on the contrary, as the name implies, this series of movements is absolutely automatic. The cartridges here are in a magazine which is lodged in the butt. When a cartridge is fired, the empty case is forced backward by the recoil; the slide around the barrel is movable and retreats a certain distance, due to the pressure of the recoil. This causes the slide to open, thus permitting the empty shell to come out. The empty shell is drawn backwards with the slide and the extractor. At the moment when the slide is opened the cartridge strikes the ejector and is thrown free of the extractor and slide. The slide goes back to its original position with the aid of a spring. The spring of the firing pin has in the meantime been contracted again, and it is now only necessary to pull the trigger in order to repeat all the movements of firing, recoiling, throwing out the empty case, and contracting the spring of the firing pin.

Because of the difference in the construction of pistols and revolvers the examination of the fired shells differs according to the arm. We will first deal with automatic pistols, which from the viewpoint of identification are the more interesting.

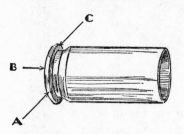

Figure 93. Automatic-pistol shell: A, rim; B, head; C, front of rim.

AUTOMATIC PISTOLS

Let us assume that a murder has been committed and that some empty shells have been found by the side of the victim. These are given to an expert to be compared with the automatic pistol seized from the suspect. The first step to be taken is to determine whether the shells belong to an automatic pistol and whether the calibers are equal. Both facts may be determined without difficulty, but care should be taken not to introduce the incriminating shell in the pistol while making the comparison, as the small scars found on the shell, which are necessary for the identification, may be destroyed during the manipulation. Anyone who is familiar with firearms is usually able to tell the caliber at a glance. Should there be any doubt about the caliber, as, for example, calibers 7.63 mm. and 7.65 mm., Mauser and Parabellum pistols, respectively, measurements on a special test shell should be taken, the test shell being fitted into the incriminating pistol and then compared with the incriminating shell. Knowledge of the calibers commonly used in different countries is of importance to the expert on firearms.

When the caliber has been determined, the actual examination takes place. We have already sketched, superficially, the procedure of firing an automatic pistol. It goes without saying that all those operations must leave marks on the shell. Of these the following are of importance:[11]

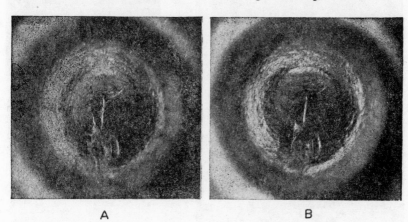

A   B

Figure 94. Identification of rifle cartridges by the markings of the firing pin on the percussion cap: A, incriminated shell; B, test shell.

MARKS FROM THE FIRING PIN. The pin leaves an impression in the percussion cap which is sometimes characteristic of the arm but often varies according to the hardness of the metal in the cap.

MARKS FROM THE EXTRACTOR. These are of great importance because they are the starting point in observation of the shell. The position of the shell previous to being fired is determined by the trace of the extractor. The trace of the extractor is found in front of the rim of the shell and will show up bright and glossy, in an oblique light, against the sooty background of the shell.

This sootiness around the trace will enable one to differentiate between the trace of the extractor which is made when the shot is fired and such traces as will occur when a cartridge is inserted in the weapon and later extracted but not fired. The fact that no soot is present at the opening of the breech where the extractor is located may be explained by the fact that the powder gas finds its way out at this point and is not condensed.

Sometimes the extractor when extracting the shell will slip over the rim and make distinctive scratches on it. Only the traces in the front of the rim should, however, be taken into consideration. Other traces may easily be mistaken for scratches from the magazine.

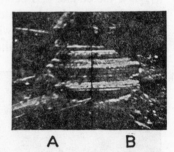

A   B

Figure 96 (above). Identification of cartridge cases in the comparison microscope by the markings of the ejector: A, incriminated shell; B, test shell.

A   B

Figure 95 (left). Identification of cartridge cases in the comparison microscope by the markings of the extractor on the rim: A, incriminated shell; B, test shell.

TRACES FROM THE EJECTOR. The trace of the ejector is found on the head of the shell. When examining these traces it is essential to have a clear idea of the position of the shell previous to the firing. This will, as already mentioned, be determined by the trace of the extractor on the rim. The shell is thrown backward a relatively long distance before it is pivoted against the extractor, thus altering its position to some minute degree on its way.

Sometimes the marks of the ejector will be distinctly imprinted, sometimes it will touch the edge only very slightly, and in some cases it will not leave any marks at all. Owing to such variations, the amateur will probably have difficulty in finding these traces, although it is always possible to note where the marks of the ejector should be found by looking for the marks of the extractor. Generally the ejector has a position directly opposite the extractor, although this may not be the case in all instances.

MARKS FROM THE BREECHBLOCK. These are most important. The breechblock is very often finished by hand and bears the characteristic ridges from the file or from other tools used. These ridges are pressed into the soft metal of the shell and often give identification marks of great value.

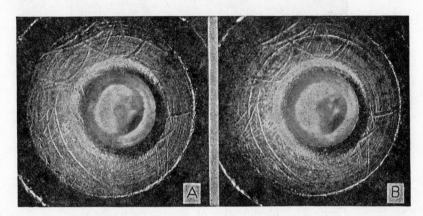

Figure 97.   Identification of rifle cartridges from the marks of the breechblock: A, incriminated shell; B, test shell. Note the almost complete conformity.

The identification is made in the following manner. A few shells are fired from the incriminating arm and collected and marked. The incriminating shell is also marked to avoid confusion. They are then carefully washed, first with soap and water, and then with diluted ammonia, to free them from all adhering grease and dirt.

With the aid of a strong magnifying glass or a low-power microscope, preferably of the binocular type, the traces of both the ejector and the extractor are compared. If they are in the same position in relation to one another and their general appearance is the same, one may conclude that they have been fired from a pistol of the same make. An absolute conclusion about the origin of the shells, however, can be reached only after a microscopic examination of the markings from the breechblock on the rear of the shell or from the ejector and extractor, depending on which ones are most developed.

In order to photograph the microscopic findings on the shell head a common photomicrographic apparatus of vertical type with a special shell-holder is used. A Mikrosummar with a focus of about 65 mm., or similar lens, may be used.

Usually it is sufficient to photograph the incriminating shell and two comparison shells.

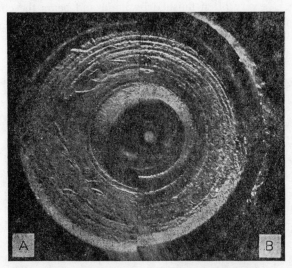

Figure 98.   Identification of pistol cartridges in the comparison microscope by the markings of the breech-block: A, incriminated shell; B, test shell.

Each shell is placed in the holder so that the head is absolutely parallel to the lens. In order to facilitate the identification care should be taken that the markings from the ejector have an absolutely identical position before photographing each shell. A line mark may be made on the shell and holder with a fine lead pencil. The lines should touch each other when the shell is inserted in the hole.

Oblique light from a small, powerful spotlight should be made to fall on the shell. There should be as much relief as possible. A magnification of ten is adequate; higher magnifications may detract from the identification.

To show the microscopic findings with the aid of the enlargement should not prove difficult. The characteristic scratches can be seen easily. A photograph of the incriminating shell and one of a comparison shell should be pasted side by side on cardboard, and the characteristic marks should be recorded with lines and ciphers, following the same method as that used in the identification of fingerprints. To meet any special requests or objections in court, an unmarked exhibit should also be made.

The identity of the shells may also be shown by printing photographs of the shells on negative films instead of on paper. If, when the negatives are held up to the light, the details cover each other, the identity may easily be shown. When the identification is made from markings from the ejector or the extractor, the findings may be photographed directly in the comparison microscope. In some cities nowadays the comparison microscope is brought into the courtroom itself and the findings are shown directly to the judge and the jury. The procedure has little to recommend it.

REVOLVERS

When a shot is fired from an automatic pistol, the shell, in most cases, will be found on the scene, as the criminal seldom thinks of disposing of this important piece of evidence. On the other hand, when a revolver is used, the empty shell remains within the chamber. It is seldom thrown away on the scene unless the criminal is forced to reload, in which case the empty shells will be found in numbers at the spot.

REVOLVERS WITH CENTER FIRE

Cartridges of calibers .32 and .45 for automatic pistols may in some cases be used in revolvers, just as revolver cartridges may, with some alterations, be used in pistols, and it may even happen in the latter case that there are repeats. Often, however, the shell will burst. But a doubt about the type of firearm used should never arise because of the presence of traces from the ejector and the extractor when an automatic has been fired. Mistakes are possible with certain automatic pistols, as, for instance, the German D-pistol, where the firing pin serves as ejector and where the usual marking on the edge of the rim is missing. A careful examination, however, will disclose a microscopically small oval scratch on the percussion cap near the mark of the firing pin. This scratch is due to the second striking of the firing pin against the shell, denoting clearly that the shell has been fired from an automatic pistol.

In the United States Army special clips are used to shoot pistol cartridges caliber .45 in revolvers of the same caliber. On account of the reduced space between the shell head and the breechblock the latter will make typical bow-shaped scratchings on the shell head by the rotation of the cylinder.

The identification of a shell with the revolver from which it has been fired is often difficult. The following characteristic marks are available for identification: the mark of the firing pin and the mark of the breech-block, and the mark of the firing-pin hole.

The mark made by the firing pin varies according to the shape of the pin, the hardness of the metal in the percussion cap, and the force of the blow dealt by the firing pin. If all these three factors were constant, characteristic marks should be found on all fired shells, but this is not the case. On account of the varying degrees of hardness of the metal in the cap the depth of the mark changes often, and if the ignition cap is not deformed in some manner, it is in most cases difficult to arrive at positive conclusions. By firing some cartridges from a revolver and then comparing the marks, the difference in the shapes of the marks will be easily seen. Some of them are fairly similar, but some show such great variations from the true form that they cannot be identified. Some of the marks may be similar to those on cartridges fired from other revolvers, and some are so different that they may lead to the conclusion that no identity is possible. It is therefore necessary to make a very painstaking investigation to determine the true shape.

REVOLVERS WITH RIM-FIRE CARTRIDGES

The identification is based upon the markings of the breechblock. In rim-fire revolvers the markings of the hammer may sometimes be characteristic.

POSSIBILITY OF DETERMINING THE MAKE
OF AN UNKNOWN ARM BY A SHELL

In order to determine the make of an unknown arm from which a seized shell has been fired a classification of marks on shells must be available. Such a classification of automatic pistols will be found in the *Atlas of Arms* by Mezger, Heess, and Hasslacher.[12]

The shell receives the first marks from the sharp guide lips of the magazine in the form of very fine scratches on two opposite sides of the cartridge, parallel with its longitudinal axis. When the cartridge enters the chamber, there will be one more mark caused by the magazine slide or the following cartridge, which presses the first cartridge down. This trace consists of a faint mark between the two aforesaid marks. None of these marks has importance from the viewpoint of examination, but it is necessary to know them so as not to confuse them with other marks.

If the cartridge is inserted directly into the chamber, a secondary extractor mark will occur which comes from the extractor touching the rim when the slide is going forward.

Other marks are the above-mentioned impressions of the breechblock.

In order to be able to judge the possibilities of determining the pistol system the different phases of the procedure of repeating must be studied. The traces may be studied by covering the shell with a coating of black enamel containing a little resin oil to make it more elastic. All the traces on the shell will then be easily seen.

The traces of the extractor may sometimes serve as a basis for the determination of the system, as there are at least two automatic pistols made without extractors—the Steyr .25 and .32. This fact is very interesting. It shows that the extractor in reality is not needed to draw out the shell after firing. The pressure exerted by the powder gas will do that by itself. The extractor is useful only when the cartridge misfires, or in pistol instruction.

The extractor varies a great deal in different pistols, and a distinctive print of the extractor will often afford some ground for the determination of the pistol type. Generally speaking, there are four principal forms of extractors. Figure 99 shows graphically these forms which are seen at the front of the rim of the cap.

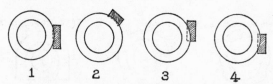

Figure 99. The principal forms of extractors.

Starting from the mark of the extractor and looking at the rim on both sides, a trace of the rear of the chamber, in case the shell has rested against it, will be seen. In many pistols the marks of the rear of the chamber will be found whether the cartridge has been deposited in the chamber by hand or had slid up from the magazine automatically.

The lower part of the rear of the barrel is cut in a certain fashion in order to facilitate the sliding of the cartridge from the magazine to the chamber. There is also a notch for the extractor. The shell does not rest against these two latter portions of the rear of the barrel, hence no marks are produced. The presence of the above-mentioned marks will determine whether the extractor has been in the middle or to the right or left.

This observation is of highest importance in determining the pistol system. There are eight principal forms of the rear of the barrel. They are shown in Figure 100. In the illustration the shells are in the chambers.

and that part of the rear of the barrel which will cause markings is indicated by a dotted line.

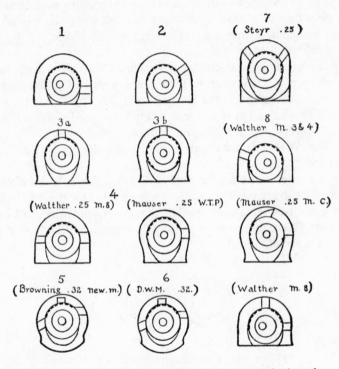

Figure 100.   The principal forms of the rear of the barrel.

If we now turn to the marks on the head of the shell, we notice first the marks of the ejector. As already mentioned, its position is determined by the trace of the extractor. The drawings in Figure 101 show the different principal forms of the traces of the ejector and their relationship to the extractor. The extractor is marked *E*.

About two thirds of the automatic pistols on the market have a special ejector, and the different systems of relationship of ejector and extractor will serve to differentiate them.

Examination of the head of the shell can be looked upon as an attempt to reconstruct the picture of the breechblock. The traces of the extractor and the ejector, as well as the outline of all holes in the breechblock— for example, the hole for the firing pin, notches in the periphery of the breechblock for the extractor, ejector, etc.—will aid in this reconstruction.

The print of the firing pin on the primer is important in determining the pistol system. The diameter of the firing pin is distinctive in different makes of automatic pistols and its width is approximately constant in the same make. If the firing pin has left a clear mark on the primer, it is measured directly with the measuring microscope. If only sections of the marks are found, the measurement may be made in the following manner: The shell is placed before the photographic apparatus and enlarged ten times on the ground glass. A cellophane paper upon which concentric circles have been drawn with India ink is then placed on the ground glass. An attempt must now be made to pick out a circle corresponding with the mark on the primer. With this method the measurement can be taken to within plus or minus .002 inch.

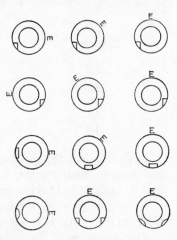

Figure 101. The principal forms of the traces of the ejector.

Traces of tool marks on the breechblock may also be characteristic for certain pistols. These traces may be arranged in three different categories: (1) parallel linear traces, (2) concentric traces, and (3) irregular traces of the file.

Some of the above-described marks may not be found at all on a cartridge, while at times other traces, characteristic of certain makes of pistols, will be found. There is, for example, the Swiss Chylewski pistol, .25 caliber, which leaves a broad resting mark across the primer.

The first classification of shells is based on the caliber and on the presence or absence of the ejector. In the *Atlas of Arms* the following tables will be found:

Table No.	Caliber	Description
8	.25	with ejector
9	.25	without ejector
10	.32	with ejector
11	.32	without ejector
12	.38	

In Table 12 are included all pistols of .38 caliber, because of their rarity. In all the tables the cartridges of the same caliber and the same marks caused by the ejector are arranged according to the diameter of the mark of the firing pin on the primer. In cases where the mark of the firing pin is not clear another classification based on the principal form of the rear of the chamber may be used.

Table No.	Caliber	With principal form of rear of barrel
13	.25	1
14	.25	2
15	.25	3
16	.32	1
17	.32	2
18	.32	3

In these tables the shells are divided into two categories: those with and those without ejector. A simpler and more practical division than that in Tables 8 to 11 is obtained.

A separate classification is given to the pistols which have right-angled traces of the ejector of principal form No. 3.

The possibility of determining the pistol system from a fired shell is in direct relation to the construction of the arm and the clearness of the impression. If the automatic pistol system is characteristic with some individual markings, the work is not only greatly facilitated but the identification can be made with a greater degree of certainty.

Automatic pistols which cause individual marks on the shells making them easy to identify, are:

Sauer & Sohn, .25, .32 caliber; the Spanish pistols, Victoria, .25, .32 caliber, Astra, .25 caliber, Alkar, .32 caliber, Ydeal Waldman and Kaba-Speziel, .25 caliber; the Swiss Chylewski, .25 caliber; the German Titanic and Walther Model 2, .25 caliber; as well as the Belgian F.N., .32 caliber. The Mann pistols with a broad extractor embracing about one fourth of the rim of the shell, and the Steyr, .25 and .32 caliber, both without extractor, are also easily identifiable. The principal forms of the rear of the barrel 4, 5, and 6 can also give information concerning the following pistols: Mauser Vest-pocket Model, Walther Model 8, German D.W.M., and the Belgian F.N. Model 1910. Fairly easy of identification are the following pistols, characterized by their ejectors; Oewa (principal ejector form 4), Webley without hammer (principal ejector form 6), the pistols Delu, .25 caliber, and Praga, .32 caliber (principal ejector forms 5), as well as the pistols with the ejector to the right (principal form 2), as in the German Walther, Models 3 and 4, and the Spanish Star pistol. Other characteristic pistols are the Frommer Stop and the Frommer Baby, Savage,

Walther Model 9, .25 caliber; and Stock, .25 caliber; F.N., .25 and .32 caliber, Model 1900; Bayard, .32 and .380 caliber; Schwartzlose, .32 caliber, and Ortgies, .32 and .38 caliber.

The photographs in the *Atlas of Arms* give clear information about the above-mentioned characteristic details in the pistols. In conclusion it may be stated that the determination of the pistol system is, in most cases, not difficult. The difficulty arises when the make of the pistol is to be identified.

THE POWDER RESIDUES AND WHAT THEY WILL TELL

There are two different types of powder used in firearms, black and smokeless powder. Black powder is still employed in some revolver cartridges, especially in those used for revolvers of Continental make, but the smokeless powder is now almost exclusively used.

The composition of black powder is classical: nitrate of postassium, sulfur, and charcoal. The proportions of these ingredients vary in different countries within the following limits:

> 60 to 78 % nitrate of potassium
> 10 to 18.5% sulfur
> 12 to 21.1% charcoal

The base of all smokeless powders is generally nitrocellulose and nitroglycerin. There may also be included non-explosive ingredients, as, for instance, stabilizers to absorb traces of free acids and nitric gases, substances which facilitate gelatinization of the powder, or substances to prevent muzzle flame or to render the powder less sensitive to friction and less inflammable. There may also be substances to lower the temperature and speed of combustion.

The smokeless powders may be divided into two large groups: (1) powders containing nitroglycerin gelatinated with nitrocellulose and (2) powders containing pure nitrocellulose as an active ingredient.

The necessity for analyzing powders in criminological investigations may arise when:

1. Powder is found on the victim or otherwise on the scene of the crime
2. Powder grains are found in the so-called "tattooing" around the wound, to establish the kind of powder employed and the distance of the shooting

3. Residue is found in the interior of the barrel, to establish the sort of powder employed and the probable time elapsed from the firing of the shot
4. Powder grains are found on a suspect's skin or clothing

ANALYSIS OF POWDER. When a substantial quantity of powder is to be analyzed and compared with another powder, there are numerous chemical and microchemical methods at our disposal. Such an analysis may in many cases lead to the identification of the manufacturer. A collection of comparison powders would be advisable for the laboratory.[13]

ANALYSIS OF POWDER TATTOOINGS. In spite of the high temperature and the instantaneous combustion of the powder in the barrel the unburnt or partly burnt powder grains are in most cases flung out so violently from the barrel that they become deposited on nearby objects, as in shooting cases, on the clothing or the skin.

The black powder produces the heaviest deposits. Owing to the similarity to real tattooing (particles of charcoal are deposited in the epidermis), this is called "powder tattooing." There is no possibility of mis-

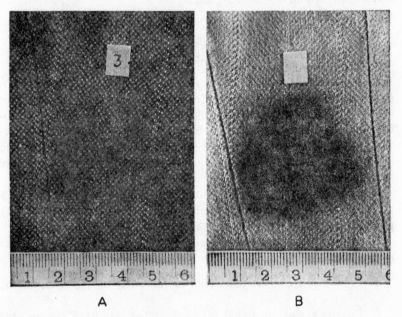

A   B

Figure 102.   Entrance hole of a bullet in cloth photographed (A) with ordinary plate and (B) in infrared in order to bring out the powder tattooing. Note that even the number on the label has disappeared.

taking the characteristic tattooing of black powder for that of smokeless powder.

Owing to the uniformity of the composition of black powder, an analysis would be fairly useless. The skin is examined under the magnifying glass, and the grains may be picked out with forceps and examined under the microscope in order to determine the minuteness of the grain.

The tattooing produced by smokeless powder is very insignificant in comparison with that inflicted by black powder. This is due to the nearly complete combustion of the smokeless powders. However, smokeless powder will produce tattooing at short distances, i.e., less than ten or twelve inches, grains may be found with the magnifying glass during the examination of the surface fired upon. The search for powder grains may sometimes be of the utmost importance, as, for instance, in cases of doubtful suicide.

When the shot has been fired from a very short distance, several powder grains from the tattooing may in most cases be retrieved. Generally a microscopic examination is sufficient to determine with certainty the powder used. At times some of the grains may be broken or only partly burned. The color and the size of the powder grains is often very characteristic for a particular manufacture.

ANALYSIS OF POWDER RESIDUES. Only a very minute residue of the combustion products will be found inside the barrel. Black and smokeless powders are easily distinguished, but the only possibility of determining the specific powder used is to carry out a spectrographical examination. Spectrography, however, gives useful results especially when dealing with powders containing metal constituents.

In collecting the residue, the barrel is cleaned with a small piece of cotton soaked in alcohol. The quantity of cotton should be as small as possible to avoid dispersing the residue which is already present in very minute quantities. The cotton is incinerated at the lowest temperature possible in a platinum crucible. The ashes are now evaporated by the electric spark in the spectrograph and the spectrum is photographed.[14]

TIME ELAPSED SINCE SHOOTING. Before the above-mentioned cleaning of the barrel takes place, the residue in the barrel should be examined for the possibility of determining the time elapsed since the firing. Chavigny[15] has studied this question carefully. The expert will in most cases establish approximately whether the weapon has been fired recently or not, especially when black powder has been used; the visible changes in the residue are not typical and characteristic enough, however, to permit decisive conclusions.

If essential, tests to determine the time necessary for the experimental residues to assume the same physical characters as the incriminating one should be carried out. Such tests should be made under the same circumstances as the incriminating residue was supposed to have been subjected to, but even under such conditions the conclusions concerning the time elapsed can only be made with great reserve.

DETERMINING THE DISTANCE FROM WHICH THE SHOT WAS FIRED

The examination of the wound and its aspects in relation to the distance from which the shot was fired should be left to the medical examiner or coroner. Among the duties of the expert on forensic ballistics is that of determining by the powder tattooing the distance from which the shot was fired.[16]

The tattooing consists of three zones:

1. The first zone, also called the flame zone
2. The second zone, where the real powder tattooing is to be seen
3. The third zone, where powder grains and combustion products are sparsely scattered

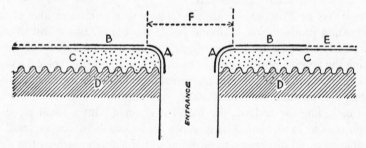

Figure 103.   Schematic cross-section of a bullet wound (after Chavigny): A is the flame zone, B is the second zone, and E the third zone. C represents the powder grains embedded in the corneum, which can be washed away; and D represents the powder grains embedded in the mucosum, which cannot be washed away. F is the diameter of the bullet.

The second and third zones will change entirely if the wound is washed. Washing will alter the color and aspect of the second zone and may entirely dispose of the third zone. It is therefore important to ascertain whether the powder tattooing to be examined has been subjected to washing or not.

The aspect of the three zones will alter with the slant of the shot and the distance. Only practical tests can guide in cases where the distance is to be determined. The tests are generally carried out on white paper or linen sheets, using the same firearm and ammunition as those used in the original shooting attack.

The distance which a bullet has traveled can only be determined within the limit in which powder tattooing will occur.

In recent years much research has been done concerning the determination of shooting distances from a microchemical examination of the area around the hole of the bullet.[17]

By examining the metal content of the area surrounding the bullet hole, much may also be learned about the shooting angle. This research work has mostly concerned the constituents of the primer and not of the bullet. The primer constituents are transferred to the object together with the powder smoke. Modern munition almost always contains organic lead compounds (for instance, lead azide and lead styphnate); and owing to the fact that the amount of lead transferred to the object is fairly proportional to the shooting distance, a quantitative determination of the lead content of the area around the bullet hole may be helpful in setting an upper limit to the distance from which the shot was fired.

Small pieces of the tissue around the bullet hole are cut out, ashed, and dissolved in nitric acid. The acid solution, containing the lead of the smoke, is then made to react with a dithizone solution, which is a very sensitive and highly specific reagent for lead. A brick-red color results, the intensity of which is proportional to the lead content. The intensity of the color is read in a colorimeter and the lead content estimated from the value obtained here.

For purposes of comparison bullet holes which have been caused by the same arm, the same munition, and on the same tissues at different shooting distances are produced. The comparison areas are analyzed as described above and the results compared with the value obtained in the actual case.

In the case of buckshot, birdshot, etc., there are two methods of determining the distance; namely, by the powder tattooing as described above and by the dispersion of the pellets. When the tattooing is found to be of no importance the dispersion of the pellets or shot may still, with a certain precision, give information about the distance. When leaving the barrel, the group of pellets or shot may be regarded as a large bullet that will immediately start to disperse in a fairly regular manner. The scheme of the dispersion can be established experimentally and will be highly characteristic for various distances and for types of ammunition.

ERRORS CAUSED BY ACOUSTICS IN DETER-
MINING DIRECTION OF SHOOTING

When a shot is fired, the air in front of the barrel is driven away so forcibly by the bullet and the powder gases that the sound vibrations produced are heard as a report. This report is usually called the muzzle blast and occurs in all cases. Sound vibrations travel spherically with the speed of 1,090 feet per second.

When a person hears the muzzle report, he gets an idea of the approximate direction of the sound, i.e., the place of the shooting. The person perceives the source of the sound from a direction which is at right angles to the sound waves. The exactness with which the direction of the sound is determined depends very much upon the development of the sense of hearing of the person in question (a person who is deaf in one ear cannot as a rule tell the location of the shooter) and upon his experience.

Bullets which have a very high initial velocity, higher than the velocity of sound, will, as long as the speed is great enough, hurl aside the air particles along the trajectory with such a speed that sound waves are produced. An ear against which these vibrations are directed will perceive a sharp report, called the bow-wave report. This report, from some point in the trajectory, travels like other sounds, spherically, and with the same speed of 1,090 feet per second. Because the person perceives the source of sound to be at a right angle to the sound waves, this bow-wave report does not tell the shooter's position but only the direction from which the sound originates. If a person is placed in such a relation to the shooter that the bow-wave report will be perceived by his ear before the muzzle report, the person will first hear the bow-wave report and the direction from which it came. If the ears under this act of perception also are encountered by the muzzle report, the person has no time to perceive the direction from which the latter came. Most persons do not know of the existence of the bow-wave report and therefore, trusting their ears, assume that the direction whence the first sound came is the one leading to the shooter.

A practical example may illustrate this. If a gun has been fired at a victim, designated by *B* in the accompanying sketch, the phenomena of sound in different moments will occur as follows: The gun is 160 meters distant from *B*. The bullet will then reach the victim in 0.25 second after it has left the muzzle. By this time the muzzle report has traveled 85 meters in all directions, the speed of sound being about 340 meters per second. The bow-wave report at this moment has the form of a cone with its apex directed toward *B* and its sides aiming at the circumference of the muzzle report. After one tenth of a second, the radius of the muzzle report is 34 meters larger and the bow-wave report from each point of the trajectory has also traveled 34 meters, but it is now mutilated and without apex, because the bullet has reached its destination. The bow-wave report is still a cone tangential to the circumference of the sphere of the muzzle report. The observer in the sketch gets the impression that the shot was fired from a direction far away from the true one.

Figure 104. Acoustic errors in perceiving direction of shooting: A, gun; B, victim; C, person hearing bow-wave report; D, muzzle report at the moment the bullet hits the victim; E, bow-wave report at the moment the bullet hits the victim; F, muzzle report 1/10 second later; G, bow-wave report 1/10 second later; H, direction from which the person believes the shot to have been fired; J, point in the trajectory where sound perceived by the person originated.

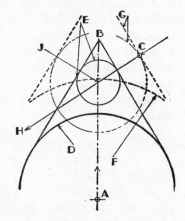

The bow-wave report does not occur when pistols and revolvers are fired because the speed of the bullet is too slow.

The sound of the bow-wave report will deaden the whizz of the bullet. At first, at long ranges, on account of the resistance offered by the air, the speed of the bullet is less than the speed of the sound; hence the bow-wave report disappears and the whizzing can be heard. If, for instance, a bullet fired from a military rifle passes close to a person at two thousand meters from the point where the shot was fired, he will first hear the bow-wave report originating from the first path of the trajectory of the bullet, then the whizzing of the bullet, and finally the obtuse sound of the muzzle report. At short ranges, when the speed of the bullet is higher than the speed of sound (for military rifles on ranges less than eight hundred meters), the sound of the friction of the bullet against the air, the whizzing, is deadened by the bow-wave sound. If the bullet has touched any object on its way so that its speed is less than the speed of the sound, it may also be heard at shorter distances, especially if it travels more or less transversely to the direction of the wind.

RESTORING OBLITERATED NUMBERS

Experience shows that professional criminals nowadays generally file the numbers off the machine guns, pistols, and other weapons used in order to keep their origins from being traced. Stolen motorcars also very often have the motor numbers filed off or changed.

In most cases the numbers may be brought out again, even if the filing has penetrated deeply. When the original numbers were punched into the steel, its molecular structure underwent changes which were not confined to the immediate vicinity of the numbers but extended also to the portion underneath. By grinding down the surface with emery, highly polishing it, and then treating the smoothed surface with one of the etching fluids generally used in metallurgical work, the numbers can be made to reappear.

The process of restoring the obliterated numbers involves three operations:

1. *Cleaning.* The site of the numbers should be carefully cleaned; all oil, dirt, grease, and paint should be removed with gasoline, xylol, and acetone.
2. *Polishing.* This operation is by far the most important. The whole surface should be polished smooth, using a fine file followed by a medium to fine grade Carborundum cloth. When the area is large or the scratches are deep, a mechanical polisher may be used to save time. The time of polishing depends on the hardness and granularity of the metal. However, the area should always have a mirrorlike surface.
3. *Etching.* For all iron and steel materials the following etching solution may be used:

Hydrochloric acid	80 cc
Distilled water	60 cc
Ethyl alcohol	50 cc
Copper chloride	10 grams

The solution is swabbed on continually until the numbers appear. This may take several hours.

P. Law[18] has described various methods which may be used for the restoration of obliterated numbers on different metals.

1 This chapter deals chiefly with small arms, i.e., revolvers and pistols. Identification of bullets and shells fired from rifles and sub-machine guns is founded on the same principles and differs in no essential respect from the methods here described.

2 Fairly complete tables regarding the weight and chemical composition of bullets are given in Söderman's book.[5] Some stocks of old cartridges no longer manufactured are even now, without doubt, in the possession of some individuals.

3 During World War II, the Germans manufactured bullets from powdered iron dust under hydraulic pressure.

4 De Rechter–Mage.

5 Piédelièvre. See also Sannié.[3]

6 Howe.

7 E. Locard.[4]

8 See Söderman.[1]

9 Sannié.[1]

10 There is, as formerly mentioned, one make of revolver called semi-automatic where the cylinder is revolved by the recoil action, for instance, the Webley Fosbery automatic, calibers .38 Rim and .455.

11 See also Burrard, Hatcher, and Goddard.

12 See Söderman.[1]

13 For more detailed information see Brunswig and Söderman.[5]

14 For detailed information about spectrographical analysis of powder residues see Söderman.[5]

15 Chavigny. See also Fleury–Silvera.

16 Piédelièvre–Desoille.

17 Von Neureiter–Pietrusky–Schütt and Brüning–Schnetka.

18 Law.

XV PROBLEMS OF BROKEN WINDOWS

SOMETIMES IT MAY BE OF THE UTMOST IMPORTANCE TO DETERMINE whether a bullet has entered a windowpane or whether a windowpane has been smashed from within or without. The latter question frequently arises in connection with arson cases and insurance frauds in the form of faked burglaries. These questions were first studied by Gross and subsequently by the Russian criminologist Matwejeff.[1]

Generally it may be said that the hole produced by a bullet with a strong charge has the sharpest edges; but if a bullet has been fired from a very long distance and hits the window at a low speed, it will break the pane in the same manner as will a stone. A shot from a very short distance will produce the same result, because the pressure of the powder gas itself will smash the glass. In important cases test shootings should be made on the same sort of glass and under as nearly identical circumstances as possible.

It is easy to determine the direction from which a shot was fired. On one side of the hole only, numerous small flakes of glass will be found to have been blown away, giving the hole the appearance of a volcano crater. Such an appearance indicates that the bullet was fired from the opposite side of the hole from which the flakes are missing. If the bullet strikes the glass at right angles, the flake marks are evenly spread around the hole. If the shot is fired from the right of the pane, very few flake marks will be found on the right side of the hole. Most of them will be on the left side. It is even possible to calculate approximately the angle of the shooting. The more acute the angle, the more flakes will be blown away. It should be added that bullets passing through glass generally deviate and continue their flight spinning around their longitudinal axis, thereby causing large, more or less rectangular wounds in the case of pointed bullets, and oval wounds, larger than the caliber of the bullet, if the latter is round. This fact is important from a medicolegal point of view.

It is not so easy to determine from what side a blunt object—a fist

230

or a stone—has smashed a windowpane, although the experienced can still solve the problem.

If test shots are made on a windowpane and then the broken glass pieced together, it will be seen that the fractures produce a network consisting of radial rays running out from the center (the bullet hole), crossed by concentric lines. The radial fractures precede the concentric ones, as may be seen by noting that the radial rays are continuous while the concentric are interrupted at the crossings.

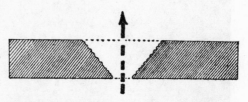

Figure 105. Determination of the direction from which a shot was fired through a windowpane. A cross-section of the hole.

If the same experiment is carried out by smashing a windowpane with a blunt object it will be found by putting the pieces together that an analogous pattern of radial and concentric fractures occurs, although it is not as regular. To facilitate matters, the glass may be marked on the side which receives the blow with a net of rays and circles made with grease crayon. The surface of the glass gives no evidence as to where the blow was struck; but if a cross-section of one of the pieces of glass is examined a relief consisting of a series of curved lines will be found. Sometimes this relief is very evident, at other times quite difficult to detect, but with a little training it can always be found.

Studies of these curved lines will show that they are not uniformly developed throughout. For example, on a particular piece of glass the left and top portions of the line may be strongly developed while its right portion may be barely visible. In other panes the contrary may be true. By the left portion we mean the part of the line nearest the surface struck by the blow. The right portion is nearest the opposite side of the glass.

On the cross-section of the glass which is within the concentric fracture lines, the left portion of the curve, i.e., the part nearest to the surface which is struck, is well developed and the right one feebly. On the cross-section which is within the radial fracture lines it is just the opposite. The part of the curve nearest to the surface struck is in the latter case feebly developed while the other part is strongly developed. Figure 108 shows this graphically. The arrows indicate the direction of the blow. Tests made at the New York police laboratory confirm these findings.

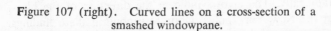

Figure 106 (above). Typical appearance of the exit
side of a bullet hole in a windowpane.

Figure 107 (right). Curved lines on a cross-section of a
smashed windowpane.

It is obvious that the pattern of the curves on the cross-section of the fractures is related to the missing fragments on the surface of the glass. The pattern of the curves on the cross-section has no relation, however, to the structure of the individual glass. This is corroborated by the fact that if tests are made on windowpanes cut from the same large piece of glass, different patterns are obtained. The direction of the blow and the location of the pattern determine whether the curves are feebly or strongly developed.

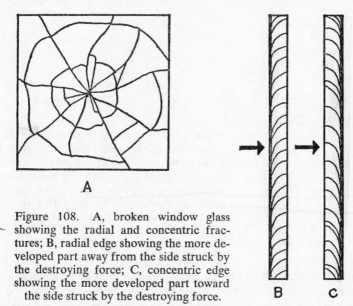

Figure 108. A, broken window glass showing the radial and concentric fractures; B, radial edge showing the more developed part away from the side struck by the destroying force; C, concentric edge showing the more developed part toward the side struck by the destroying force.

The difference in the development of the curves is explained by Matwejeff in the following manner: When the blow strikes the glass on one of its surfaces—the front, for instance—the glass first bends a little, owing to its elasticity. When the limit of its elasticity is reached, the glass breaks along radial lines starting from the point where the destroying force is applied. These radial fractures originate on the opposite surface of the glass, because this is the surface which is more subjected to stretching by the bending. The front surface is only pushed in. This may be illustrated by folding a piece of thick cardboard; its back side breaks first.

While the radial fractures are taking place, the newly created glass triangles between the radial rays will also bend away from the direction of the destroying force. By this bending the glass is stretched along the front surface, the limit of elasticity is reached, and the glass breaks in concentric lines. These concentric fractures originate on the front of the glass, because of the stretching. This occurrence may be illustrated in the following manner: Radial lines running in all directions are drawn on a piece of thick cardboard. These are then cut out with a sharp knife. If pressure with the finger is exerted at right angles against one of these triangles so that it is pushed backward as far as possible, the cardboard will break anteriorly in a concentric manner.

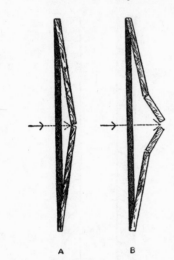

Figure 109.   Schematic drawing of the order of occurrence of the radial and concentric fractures in the smashing of a windowpane with a blunt object: A shows how the radial fractures occur first at the side opposite the destroying force; B shows how the secondary concentric fractures occur at the same side as the destroying force.

A   B

Only fractures which can be shown to be radial or concentric should be utilized. Small fractures occurring near the frame should not be considered, as the resistance offered by the latter complicates matters. Matwejeff is of the opinion that only fractures showing their points of origin (where the destroying force has been applied) should be considered. In these cases it should be possible to determine immediately whether the glass has been broken from within or without.

The pieces of glass should be collected as soon as possible and an attempt made to reconstruct the whole windowpane. Dirt or an aged surface will occur on the outer side of the glass, thus facilitating the solving of the puzzle.

Sometimes it is advisable to reconstruct the whole windowpane by pasting it together with paper on one side. The reconstructed pane should not be transported to the laboratory for during the move fractures of the glass may be subjected to dangerous friction; instead it should be carefully photographed. If it is possible to determine the two sides of the glass, the pieces should be marked accordingly with ink. Some experts demand that the corresponding numbers be marked on the photograph. The pieces should then be wrapped in paper and packed in a box.

Windowpanes which have burst from being exposed to heat have very characteristic wave-shaped fractures. The fracture will not show any—

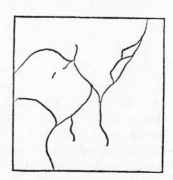

Figure 110.   Typical appearance of a windowpane which has been burst by heat. In such cases the curved lines are very feebly developed and generally the glass splinters fall in the direction of the source of the heat. This is an important point to remember in the investigation of arson cases, because the discovery of glass splinters inside a room may lead the investigator to believe that the window was smashed from the outside.

or at least only very weak—curve patterns on the cross-sections. Generally the pieces will fall down on the side of the source of heat. If pieces of glass are found on the floor of a room, this may be due to fire and it should not be taken for granted that the window was smashed from the outside. If the windowpane was directly exposed to a blowtorch, pieces of glass corresponding to the shape of the flame will break out.

If at the moment when two vehicles meet on a road, or when one vehicle passes another, a windowpane is cracked, a stone from the road is generally the cause. In these cases the interior of the vehicle should be carefully searched for stones or bullets. The hole in the window should be examined microscopically and spectrographically. If the whole window has been smashed, the investigation usually will produce no results.

Fragments of glass have proved to be of great importance in criminal investigations, and their identification may present convincing testimony in a case at trial. A common way of identifying glass fragments is by the comparison of their physical properties, such as the refractive index, specific gravity, and hardness. Spectrographic analysis of minute glass particles may also furnish valuable information about the chemical composition. A number of surveys have been made of glass comparison methods.[2]

1 Matwejeff. For a full list of references see O'Hara–Osterburg.
2 Tryhorn,[1] Gamble–Burd–Kirk, and Kirk–Roche.

XVI STAINS OF BLOOD,
SEMEN, ETC.

BLOODSTAINS ARE OFTEN DIFFICULT TO DETECT OR RECOGNIZE. BLOOD-stains on walls sometimes do not have their usual reddish-brown color but may be black, green, blue, or grayish-white. This change of color is due to the fact that the dyes in wall paper and paint sometimes are dissolved in the bloodstains, with the result that the latter change color. Bloodstains on golden-brown wallpaper, for instance, often turn green, because of the forming of oxide of copper. Blood on certain fabrics turns gray if it is exposed to the action of the sun.

On a dark background bloodstains are often difficult to recognize. When searching for bloodstains in such cases, one should use a searchlight, even in the daytime. Under artificial light the dried bloodstains will appear against the dull background as a glossy varnish.

WHERE BLOODSTAINS MAY BE FOUND

Blood is often found in places which are not directly visible, e.g., under the edge of a table, where the criminal may have wiped his hands, a common custom in rural districts; under drawers in a table or cabinet where the criminal may have searched for money; or in the drain of a sink where the criminal may have washed his hands and where there still may be blood remaining in the water. In this latter case the remaining water in the drain should be drawn off by unscrewing the valve under the drain and letting the water drop into a clean bottle. Blood may also be found on paper, on stoves, toilets, waste-paper baskets, etc.

Of great importance are the bloodstains on the body of the suspect, where especially the fingernails, the edges of the beard, and the hairline should be searched. For this sort of examination a magnifying glass is used, and the blood is scraped with a knife onto white paper. Pockets should be carefully searched. On clothing that has been recently washed the seams should be cut open to ascertain if any blood may be there.

In certain cases it is also possible to ascertain the presence of blood on a scrubbed floor, although such an examination must be made with great care. When the floor has been scrubbed, blood may still be present in the cracks between the floor boards. It is especially important if it is determined that the floor has been scrubbed with some etching substance, such as strong lye, sulfuric acid, etc. The position, size, and form of the bloodstains should be carefully determined (see section "What the Shape and Position of Bloodstains Will Tell" in Chapter XVIII).

TRANSPORT OF BLOODSTAINS

When the stains are very large and are located on easily transported articles, only a part of them is used at the examination; in this case it is not necessary to describe them so carefully, because one can always, with the aid of the remaining blood, reconstruct the original appearance of the stains. Smaller stains, where all the blood must be used for the examination, should be photographed or sketched and their position noted on the photograph or sketch of the scene. (Instructions for some methods of photography of bloodstains on dark or otherwise unsuitable backgrounds are given in Chapter IX, where the photographing of bloody fingerprints is described.)

Smaller objects carrying bloodstains are transported in clean cardboard boxes or in glass containers, which are packed in wooden boxes with straw or sawdust. On larger objects bloodstains are protected by clean white paper, which is kept over the stains with thumbtacks or strings and the whole object is carefully packed in thick wrapping paper. On wearing apparel the pieces of clothing are rolled tight and the stains are protected by tissue paper. Clothing should be rolled after the stains are *dried;* with moist stains a mold may grow and interfere with tests. Firearms or other weapons which carry bloodstains are packed as described in the transport of fingerprints.

When the object cannot be transported, the dry blood is scraped away with a clean knife and put on clean white paper, which is folded in the same manner as a druggist folds powders. This paper is put in a glass container. The place where the bloodstain was found must be photographed or sketched before this operation takes place.

As a general rule, the whole object which carries the stains should be given to the expert. Following this principle, wallpapers should be torn down, pieces of wood cut away, parts of floor sawed away or surfaces of floors planed, pieces of stucco taken away, etc. In many large cities as well as in other localities specific instructions are followed as to the proper procedure in delivering promptly to the medical examiner or coroner articles for examination and analysis, especially in homicide cases.

Blood that has been absorbed by earth is dug up and put in glass or enameled containers. All the blood should be collected, because sometimes it may be important to make quantitative blood tests in order to determine the quantity of the blood.

ANALYSIS OF THE BLOODSTAIN

Several questions are put to the expert in connection with bloodstain examinations. These will now be dealt with in a definite order.

DOES THE STAIN CONTAIN BLOOD OR ANOTHER SUBSTANCE

There are two different groups of methods to determine the character of the stain. The first group embraces the preliminary tests, often carried out at the scene of the crime; the second embraces the microscopic and spectroscopic methods used in the laboratory.

PRELIMINARY TESTS. The preliminary test may be made by a policeman or detective in cases of emergency and provided that there is enough blood left for a later expert examination. The most commonly used are the benzidine test, the leuco-malachite test, and the reduced phenolphthalein test. It should be mentioned that these are only presumptive tests and not necessarily specific for blood.

The benzidine test is sensitive (1 to 300,000). The reagent is made fresh each time by filtering a saturated solution of benzidine in glacial acetic acid added to a few drops of a solution of perborate of sodium (0.1 N) or hydrogen peroxide, which is more easily obtained. The entire mixture is used diluted with water or a saline solution.

In making the test blotting paper soaked in water is carefully pressed against the stain, whereupon a few drops of the reagent are put on the part of the blotting paper that was in contact with the stain. If there is blood, the paper turns blue or green. However, fresh fruit and milk give the same color.

The leuco-malachite test is very sensitive and fairly specific and is looked upon by some as the best test. The reagent is prepared according to the following formula: [1]

Leuco-malachite green	1 gr.
Glacial acetic acid	100 cc
Distilled water	150 cc

The reagent has a slightly greenish color. The stock solution should be kept in a dark-brown bottle with a paraffin cover over the glass stopper. It will then keep indefinitely.

When making the test, 8 cc of the stock solution are mixed with 2 cc of a 1 percent solution of peroxide of hydrogen. This mixture will keep for a few days. Before making the actual test, the reagent is tested on a minute quantity of old blood, which is put on absorbent paper soaked with a drop of the reagent. After ten seconds at most, a green stain should appear which should become a dark greenish-blue after the lapse of not more than one minute.

When performing the actual test, a piece of filter paper is placed as near the bloodstain as possible and with the aid of a knife a small amount of dried blood is scratched from the stain onto the paper. With the aid of a glass rod a drop of the reagent is placed on the side of the powdered blood, and in a short time the latter will be soaked with the reagent. The coloring of the stain should then follow in the above-described manner.

Owing to the surprising sensitiveness of the reaction, the articles used (knife and glass rod) must be absolutely clean in order to avoid error. Even an infinitesimal amount of blood adhering to them from a former operation may lead to false conclusions.

The reaction is so sensitive that small traces of blood may be detected by the following procedure: A thin glass rod is moistened in water and pressed for a few seconds against the trace, whereupon the glass rod is pressed against the filter paper soaked with the reagent. A green stain is immediately produced in the presence of blood. Small isolated green points, which may appear on filter paper of bad quality when soaked with the reagent, should not be mistaken for the reaction.

In searching large surfaces, such as the mudguards of an automobile in hit-and-run cases where no blood is visible, a filter paper soaked with distilled water should be pressed against the surface and then against another paper soaked with the reagent.

As a check on the reagent, when blood is found, a test should be made with a drop of the stock solution only. No stain should then appear, but when a drop of peroxide of hydrogen is added a green stain should appear.

In order to be perfectly sure, the hematoporphyrin test should be added. A minute drop of blood or a small quantity of blood dissolved in a drop of water is allowed to dry on a glass slide. After the preparation is thoroughly dry, it is placed under ultraviolet rays and a drop of concentrated sulfuric acid is added. If the stain is blood, there will gradually develop a beautiful brick-red luminescence due to hematoporphyrin.

LABORATORY TESTS. On the Continent the microchemical tests of

Teichmann and Strzyzowski are used in the laboratory to determine if the stain is blood. In this country (for instance, in the laboratory of the chief medical examiner of New York City) the phenolphthalein test, which is a fairly specific preliminary test, is used. If this test is positive, the precipitin reaction test of Uhlenhuth is then made.

In some places the laboratory examination is made with the aid of the microspectroscope. Only a very small amount of blood is needed. The blood is dissolved in a 30 percent potassium hydroxide solution, a drop of sulfhydrate of ammonia is added, and the preparation is examined with the microspectroscope. In the presence of blood the spectrum of the hemochromogen is seen.

IS THE BLOOD OF HUMAN OR ANIMAL ORIGIN

An early method used to determine the origin of blood was a microscopic examination of the shape of the red blood corpuscles. With this method, however, it is only possible to differentiate between mammalian and avian or saurian blood, and this usually only if the bloodstains are fresh.

Numerous methods have been devised for the determination of the origin of the blood. The commonly used one is the precipitin reaction of Uhlenhuth. In this method some blood from a stain is scraped off and dissolved in a saline solution for a few hours, centrifuged so as to obtain a crystal-clear liquid, and then carefully mixed with the so-called human antiserum obtained from a rabbit previously injected with human blood.

TECHNIQUE OF PRECIPITIN REACTION. A clean capillary tube is examined against a dark background to determine its cleanness. Its lower end is brought in contact with the crystal-clear saline extract of the bloodstain, and a column of approximately one-half inch is drawn into the tube by capillarity. This amount represents about one eighth of a drop of the unknown blood extract. The lower end of the tube is next allowed to draw up about the same amount of the antiserum, without shaking the tube. Some prefer to use narrow (3 mm.) tubes and capillary pipettes for layering. If the bloodstain is human blood, a white ring will appear at the junction of the two liquids within two to five minutes. This gradually becomes more dense, and at the end of twenty minutes a white precipitate forms. The reading should be taken against a dark background.

If this precipitin reaction is not obtained, the stain is not due to human blood. Of course, control tests must be carried out to demonstrate (1) that the antiserum will produce the white ring and the precipitate wher mixed with known human blood; (2) that the extract of the stain will not give the reaction with known normal animal serum; and (3) that both antiserum and stain extract will not react with normal saline solution.

It is imperative that the human antiserum be powerful enough to give a distinct reaction within the specified time. It should be capable of detecting human serum in dilutions as high as 1 to 1,000.

This test is highly specific, and it is only between closely related animals such as the horse and the mule, the dog and the fox, the hare and the rabbit, the hen and the pigeon, and the goat, the sheep, and the cow that any doubt can arise. Though the reaction may be positive with the blood of such other primates as the chimpanzee, the gorilla, or the orangutan, it will not be had with high dilutions, as is the case when dealing with human blood.

It must also be remembered that if the blood has undergone putrefaction or has been heated or altered chemically by soaps, peroxide of hydrogen, or tannic acid from leather, the reaction will not be obtained.

FROM WHICH PART OF THE BODY DOES THE BLOOD ORIGINATE

A murderer will often try to explain the presence of bloodstains on his body or clothing by claiming that the blood originated, for example, from the nose, from shaving, or from various accidental causes. In cases where blood grouping does not give results it is important to verify such a tale. It may be verified if the form and the position of the stains correspond with the tale. On the other hand, it is difficult to believe that bloodstains on the rear of a coat or under an apron could come from the nose.

A microscopic examination of the blood may sometimes disclose the origin of the blood through the presence of foreign particles. In blood from the nose mucus from the nose or hairs from the nostrils may be found. In the blood by rape semen and hairs from the genitals may be found. In blood from menstruation epithelial cells from the vagina are found.

Questions of this kind arise often. In a trunk murder case, for example, where a woman was killed, bloody linen was found after a search of the suspect's home. The woman had lived with him. He denied any knowledge of her fate and explained that the bloodstains were menstrual blood. This was corroborated by the result of the examination.

The presence of such elements or particles in the blood may lead to a definite conclusion about the origin of the blood, but their absence does not prove that the blood does not originate from the part of the body from which it was said to come.

This problem can only be solved in a negative way. One can determine that the blood *does not* originate but not that it *does* originate from a certain individual. It should not be forgotten that negative proofs are often just as valuable from the viewpoint of the investigation as positive ones. For this examination blood grouping tests are used.

Human blood of all races can be divided into definite groups because of the ability of the blood serum of one person to clump, or agglutinate, or bring together the red blood cells of certain other individuals. Landsteiner discovered this phenomenon, which is due to certain properties in the blood corpuscles and serums of the various bloods. The properties contained in the red blood cells are called *agglutinogens*. and those contained in the serums (liquid portion of the blood after it has clotted) are called *agglutinins*.

The agglutinogens have been named *A* and *B* and the agglutinins alpha (or anti-*A*) and beta (or anti-*B*). The *A* and *B* agglutinogens may occur separately, that is, *A* alone or *B* alone, or they may be found together, that is *AB*, or they may be entirely absent, that is, *O*, in the blood of an individual. The same applies to the agglutinin content of the serum of an individual. According to the absence or presence of both agglutinogens and agglutinins, we have the formulas indicating the various blood groups, of which there are four.

CLASSIFICATION AND COMPOSITION OF BLOOD GROUPS

Group	Red Blood Cells (Agglutinogen)	Serum (Agglutinin)
O	—	α and β
A	A	β
B	B	α
AB	A and B	—

Cells of Group O do not contain agglutinogen, but the serum contains both agglutinins. Owing to the fact that the agglutinogen is absent, the red cells of this group cannot be clumped by any serum with which it may be mixed. On the other hand, as anti-*A* and anti-*B* are found in this serum, when it is brought in contact with another blood, there will be clumping of the opposite red cells as the result of the action of α (anti-*A*) and β (anti-*B*) on the agglutinogen therein contained. Consequently we must conclude that the red blood cells of a person belonging to Group O cannot be agglutinated by the serums of the remaining three groups, while its serum will agglutinate the red cells of all groups.

Red cells of Group A are agglutinated by serums from Group O and Group B bloods.

Red cells of Group B are agglutinated by serums from Group O and Group A bloods.

Red cells of Group AB are agglutinated by serums from all other groups, while its serum, lacking agglutinin, is unable to clump the cells of the other groups.

Bloods of the same group cannot agglutinate each other, i.e., Group A or B cannot agglutinate Group A or B, respectively. Landsteiner formulated the following law: "In a given blood containing a given agglutinogen, the serum will also contain agglutinins which are incapable of acting on the said agglutinogen and thus bring about agglutination."

The following table will elucidate further:

Red Blood Cells	Serum			
	O $(\alpha\beta)$	A (β)	B (α)	AB (o)
O	−	−	−	−
A	+	−	+	−
B	+	+	−	−
AB	+	+	+	−

The plus sign indicates agglutination.
The minus sign indicates no agglutination.

Group O corpuscles are not agglutinated by any of the serums, while its serum agglutinates corpuscles of all other groups. Group A corpuscles are agglutinated by serums O and B, while its serum agglutinates corpuscles B and AB. Group B corpuscles are agglutinated by serums O and A, while its serum agglutinates corpuscles of groups A and AB. Group AB corpuscles are agglutinated by all serums, while its serum does not act upon the red cells of the other groups. Notice that no red cells are agglutinated by the serum of their own group.

The group to which a person belongs is permanent and remains unchanged throughout life. In other words the blood group is hereditary, and since it is hereditary, it is immutable. It can no more change during life than the color of one's eyes or the form of one's physiognomy. An individual born in Group O will die in Group O, etc.

To determine the group to which an individual belongs, we must have serum A (anti-B) and serum B (anti-A) at our disposal. These serums must be prepared by experts in the laboratory and must be powerful enough (high titer) to agglutinate susceptible blood corpuscles within a very short period of time and in an unmistakable manner. The technique is the following.[2]

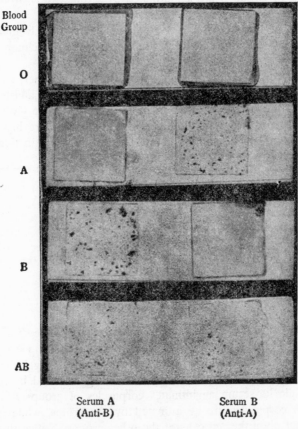

Figure 111. Blood grouping on glass slides. From *Blood Groups and Transfusion,* by Alexander S. Wiener, Charles C. Thomas, publisher.

A small drop of serum *A* (anti-*B*) is placed on the left extremity of a glass slide, and a drop of serum *B* (anti-*A*) is placed on the opposite extremity of the same slide. A finger of the person to be tested is pricked with a needle, and with its eye some of the blood is transferred from the finger to the serum *A* (anti-*B*) and intimately mixed with it. With another clean needle the same procedure is carried out with serum *B* (anti-*A*). The slide is then agitated from side to side for a few minutes until the presence of agglutination, if there be any, is detected. The clumps of red cells may be seen either with the naked eye or microscopically. The reading of the reaction should not be taken until one-half hour has elapsed. The reaction should be interpreted in the following manner (see Figure 111):

1. Group O   — no agglutination in either serum
2. Group A   — agglutination in serum *B* (anti-*A*) only
3. Group B   — agglutination in serum *A* (anti-*B*) only
4. Group AB — agglutination in both serums

The above technique is carried out only in cases where the liquid fresh blood may be obtained from the individual to be tested and with fresh bloodstains represented by large quantities of blood soaked into a fabric (cotton, linen, gauze, towels, cloth, etc.). In these cases the red blood cells, still intact and retaining their normal contour, may be extracted from the soaked stain with a normal saline solution, examined under the microscope to be certain of their presence, and finally tested against the known serums anti-*B* and anti-*A,* as described above. On the other hand, when we are dealing with old bloodstains (weeks and months old), we find that the red cells have been destroyed and can no longer be seen under the microscope. In other words, they have been broken up or hemolyzed, and in that condition they are unable to be agglutinated if the grouping test is carried out. What we find in the stain is the liberated hemoglobin (red coloring matter previously contained in the intact red blood cells). Nevertheless, the stain still contains the various blood group properties, unless they have been destroyed by age, prolonged exposure to the sun or heat, putrefaction, or by other chemical or physical agents. Experiments have demonstrated that the agglutinogens are often more resistant to extraneous influences than the agglutinins.

In cases of old bloodstains or clots, therefore, to establish the individual diagnosis, we may follow two courses:

1. Extraction of agglutinins and determination of the group by testing directly against red cells *A* and *B*
2. Determination of the agglutinogen present in the dried blood by the absorption method

The methods of these techniques are given in the excellent work of Dr. Alexander Wiener, *Blood Groups and Transfusion.*

The result of the blood grouping, however, depends entirely on the ability of the expert. It can be said that the value of the method as evidence stands or falls with the expert. Through too popular introduction of the method, the public is of the mistaken opinion that blood group determinations are easily carried out. On the contrary, they require extensive practice and experience. There are so many sources of error that control tests, a thorough knowledge of the properties of the serums used, and, above all, a full knowledge of all reactions which may be confused with true agglutination (false agglutination, self-agglutination, rouleaux formation, cold agglutination) are absolutely necessary. It goes without saying that accurate knowledge of the mechanism involved is a prerequisite if scientific as well as practical deductions are to be drawn in work as delicate as this.

In the white race the blood groups A and O are most common, the former occurring in 40% and the latter in 45% of the individuals examined. Group B is found in 10% and Group AB in the remaining 5%.

As above stated, a positive conclusion can be drawn only if an extract of a human bloodstain is found to agglutinate the cells of a given suspected individual. In this case the stain cannot be due to this person's blood. If no agglutination occurs, there is always the possibility that the blood may have come from the suspect, but nothing can be proved because there are millions of individuals belonging to the same group. In the latter case, however, the probabilities are greater if the blood belongs to Group B or to the still rarer Group AB.[3]

The heritable agglutinogens M and N discovered by Landsteiner and Levine[4] in 1928, which become evident by a delicate technique using serum obtained from rabbits previously injected with human red blood cells, give promise of valuable aid in the individual diagnosis of bloodstains. According to the discoverers, besides the four classic groups discussed above, individuals may belong to any one of three other groups —M, N, or MN—bloods not belonging to one of these groups do not exist. There is no doubt that in examining fresh bloodstains the combined search for A and B and for M and N facilitates matters a great deal. It is not possible to demonstrate M and N reliably in dried blood.

Further specific factors aiding the identification of blood individuality have been discovered—the Rh-Hr factors and the P factor—but have not yet come into accepted forensic use.

It must again be stressed that mere identity of blood groups does not prove a bloodstain came from a specific person because of the possibility of coincidence, but when the blood groups are different, this proves the stain could not possibly have come from that person. Owing to certain recent publications which are not based on fact, this has to be strongly emphasized.

DETERMINATION OF NONPATERNITY BY BLOOD GROUPING TESTS

During the past few years the problem of determining fatherhood from blood grouping has been greatly debated, but there is absolutely no doubt that by examination of the blood a negative proof can be obtained, i.e., in certain cases it may be possible to show that a man is *not* the father of a certain child, but it can never be proved that he *is* the father of a given child. This fact is of importance and interest to the police and legal authorities, and its possibilities will be briefly brought out. In order to understand the problem fully it is necessary to be familiar with Mendel's laws of heredity, on which the entire structure of blood group transmission is based. These are described in any comprehensive encyclopedia.

The agglutinogens A and B are dominant properties, and the absence of agglutinogens, i.e., the property $O,$ is said to be recessive. The fundamental law is that these properties cannot occur in a child unless at least one of the parents has them. Innumerable experiments[5] and extensive work have definitely shown that unions of:

Parents			Offspring				
O x O	give only		O	but cannot give A, B, AB			
O x A	"	"	O, A	"	"	"	B, AB
O x B	"	"	O, B	"	"	"	A, AB
O x AB	"	"	A, B	"	"	"	O, AB
A x A	"	"	O, A	"	"	"	B, AB
A x B	"	"	O, A, B, AB				
A x AB	"	"	A, B, AB	"	"	"	O
B x B	"	"	O, B	"	"	"	A, AB
B x AB	"	"	A, B, AB	"	"	"	O
AB x AB	"	"	A, B, AB	"	"	"	O

Exceptions have been reported, but they are said to be due to faulty technique, to incorrect interpretation of the tests, or to incorrect information as to the actual parents of the particular child.

While it is true that blood grouping reactions cannot determine paternity, a man accused of being the father of a child will be able to establish his innocence, according to Hooker and Boyd,[6] once out of six times. But the work of Landsteiner and Levine on the new agglutinogens M

and *N* has made it possible to help to establish innocence in one third of the cases if all the known factors are studied.

Parents			Offspring			
M x M	give only	M	but cannot give			N, MN
M x N	" "	MN	"	"	"	M, N
M x MN	" "	M, MN	"	"	"	N
N x N	" "	N	"	"	"	M, MN
N x MN	" "	N, MN	"	"	"	M
MN x MN	" "	M, N, MN				

Following the discovery of the *Rh* factor by Landsteiner and Wiener, Dr. Wiener[7] found that there are actually three principal types of *Rh* factors, designated as Rh_0, *rh'*, and *rh''*, which determine eight blood types, *rh*, *rh'*, *rh''*, *rh'rh''*, Rh_0, Rh_1, Rh_2, and Rh_1Rh_2. Moreover it was later found that there are three contrasting *Hr* factors, Hr_0, *hr'*, and *hr''*, related to the *Rh* factors like *M* and *N*. The *Rh-Hr* factors in all determine twenty-seven types of blood, of which tests of eighteen are in actual use. As a result, a falsely accused man now has a better chance than ever of proving himself not the father, provided that all tests for *Rh-Hr*, as well as *A-B* and *M-N*, are performed.[8]

BLOOD GROUP ANTIGENS IN TISSUES OTHER THAN BLOOD

The substances *A* and *B* are not confined to the red blood cells but are present in practically all the cells of the body. They have been found in saliva, tears, sweat, urine, exudates and transudates, bile, milk, etc.

The ability to secrete the *A, B,* and *O* antigens in the saliva is not present, however, in all individuals of groups A, B, AB, and O. It has been shown that two distinct types exist, namely, secretors and non-secretors, and that they occur in approximately 70 and 30 percent respectively of A, B, AB, and O individuals. According to Putkonen[9] and Sasaki,[10] the presence of blood group antigens in body fluids other than blood occurs only in salivary antigen secretor individuals. The power to secrete blood group antigens in the saliva is a constant and constitutional property of the individual and is inherited as a Mendelian dominant.

As the quantity of blood group antigens in the saliva and semen of secretors is much greater than the quantity found in the red blood cells, it is often possible to type successfully even very small stains of saliva and semen. Traces of saliva on gummed edges of envelopes, on stamps,[11] and on cigarette stubs[12] have been typed in several cases.

STAINS OF SEMEN

In cases of rape, sexual assault, and bestiality the presence of a semen stain can provide excellent corroborative evidence. Semen, a colorless, tenacious fluid of the male reproductive organs, may be found as a stain on clothing, bedding, or similar articles associated with the scene of the offense. Fresh, undried seminal fluid has a characteristic alkaline odor and ordinarily contains millions of minute organisms known as spermatozoa. In drying, the stain loses its odor, acquires a grayish-white, sometimes yellowish appearance, and imparts a starchy stiffness to the fabric. The spermatozoa die in the drying process.

As the identification of the actual spermatozoa is considered by many experts the only specific test for semen, articles suspected of bearing seminal stains should be handled with great care. The stained area should not be rolled or folded. For transmission to the laboratory, the articles should be placed between sheets of cardboard and secured to prevent friction.

The procedure for identifying semen consists of an examination under the microscope (about 400X) for an intact spermatozoon. The stain is usually located readily by visual observation. The ultraviolet lamp is also useful for this purpose, since seminal stains emit a strong fluorescence. The examiner can locate these areas under ultraviolet light, but he must later differentiate them from other stains, such as urine, which also fluoresce.

Most commonly the stain is dry when it reaches the laboratory and a water extract must be obtained for the microscope slide. The stained area is cut out of the garment and placed on a watch glass, stained side down. Distilled water is added dropwise until the stain is thoroughly moistened. After a period of thirty minutes a stain of recent origin will have been adequately extracted. Several hours are required for older stains. The fabric is then picked up with a pair of tweezers and applied to several microscope slides. After the slides have dried and have been given cover glasses, they are ready for the microscope. They may be stained —Giemsa's stain, Loeffler's methylene blue, or carbol fuchsin—to facilitate the location and identification of spermatozoa.

For the identification of the stain as semen a complete spermatozoon must be observed under the microscope to satisfy the requirements of most medicolegal textbooks. The organism consists of a head, neck, body, and tail; it varies in length from 50 to 70 microns; the head is about 1/10 of the total length. When viewed flat the head is egg-shaped; in profile it appears pear-shaped. Some cytologists state that the differential staining of the head and its characteristic form are sufficient for identification, even though no tail is present. Insistence on the presence of an intact spermatozoon, however, is a precaution appropriate to criminal investigation, where the occurrence of contaminating substances is not uncommon and the danger of confusing certain spores for the head or certain bacteria for the tail is more likely to be present. Dried stains often contain pus, feces, vaginal discharge, blood, sweat, saliva, and confusing underlayers such as fruit and vegetable stains. Fibers, bacteria, trichobacteria, and molds suggest the tails of spermatozoa; yeast blood cells and spores may be mistaken for heads. Conditions of zoospermia and aspermia (absence of spermatozoa) further contribute to the number of cases in which there is a failure to demonstrate semen although it may actually be present.

A specific and sensitive chemical test would permit the identification of stains in which the spermatozoa were initially absent or subsequently destroyed. To this end many attempts have been made to base a reliable test on such semen constituents as choline, spermine, fructose, and citric acid. Until recently, tests for choline were the most popular. The Florence test, for example, depends upon the formation of brown crystals which may correspond to acetycholine. No absolute conclusions, however, can be drawn from either a positive or negative result.

In fact none of these tests is specific for semen. Some of them may be useful screening procedures, but none can singly provide proof that the stain in question contains semen.

Physical and serological methods have proved even less successful than the chemical tests. Ultraviolet irradiation of the stain will induce a characteristic fluorescence with a maximum intensity near 4200 mμ. The fluorescence is not, however, specific and varies widely with the substrate material. Serological procedures, in which the precipitin test is used to identify semen, are impractical because of the prohibitively high specific titer required. They are useful, nevertheless, in differentiating human from nonhuman semen.

The Acid Phosphatase Method of identifying seminal stains has made the closest approach to the requirements of a satisfactory chemical test. In 1935 Kutscher and Wolberg,[13] investigating cancer arising in the prostate gland, had found that normal prostate tissue contains an extraordinary amount of acid phosphatase. Riiesfeldt[14] and Hansen[15] in 1946 reported their experiments in using acid phosphatase for the identification of semen. A practicable method for measuring the amount of phosphatase was developed from the work of King and Armstrong,[16] who found that the estimation of phenol liberated from a substrate of disodium phenyl phosphate provides a reliable measure of the extent of the substrate's hydrolysis by phosphatase. Modifications of this method, relating mainly to color indicators of phenol, buffers, and optimal pH, led to its practical application to semen identification.

Acid phosphatase values of seminal fluid are expressed in King–Armstrong units. A value greater than 30 units would indicate the high acid phosphatase activity associated with semen. Sidney Kaye, in an extensive study of the specificity of the phosphatase method, analyzed a number of common body fluids and food stains that might be encountered in a semen stain examination and found their acid phosphatase values to be well below those indicative of semen.

The medicolegal significance of the acid phosphatase method may be seen in Lindquist's report on 346 legal cases (in Denmark) in which an acid phosphatase and spermatozoa examination was conducted. In 9 of the first 140 cases, high acid phosphatase levels were present in the absence of demonstrable spermatozoa. Of the next 200 cases, 32 showed positive acid phosphatase activity when the specimens were negative for spermatozoa. After scrupulous reexamination, 20 of these 32 cases were found to show spermatozoa. In 21 of the total 346 cases, the suspected stains were identifiable as semen, although no spermatozoa were demonstrated.

Although the question of whether the test is specific to the degree where it may be used as a positive test in cases of court testimony has not been satisfactorily resolved at this point, the practical worth of the test seems well established. There is no doubt of its great value as a screening test, and it has been shown to be additionally useful as an indicator of stains worthy of reexamination after negative spermatozoa findings.

The differentiation between human and animal semen is difficult. There is no relation between the size of the animal and the size of the spermatozoon. Certain insects have spermatozoa that are larger than the human ones; and the whale, on the contrary, has smaller spermatozoa than humans. Generally speaking, the spermatozoa of the common domestic animals are larger than those of the human being, and the heads have a slightly different shape.[21]

In cases of sexual offense where no seminal stains are found on the woman's clothing, a search for other stains on the man's clothing should always be made. These stains may contain the characteristic vaginal epithelial cells and bacteria, the presence of which conclusively shows that the man has had intercourse with a woman. The vaginal epithelial cells are identifiable by a microscopic examination, using high magnifications with an oil immersion lens.

OTHER STAINS OF IMPORTANCE [17]

OBSTETRICAL AND GYNECOLOGICAL STAINS. Examination of the scene of abortion, infanticide, and sex offenses may lead to the discovery of bed linen, towels, handkerchiefs, nightgowns, pajamas, underwear, slips, shirts, mattresses, blankets, etc., which have stains. It is often important to determine the composition of the stains. The medical examiner or a skilled physician should be employed for these examinations.

EXCREMENTS. Excrements may be found at the scene, on paper as stains or together with obstetrical stains in .the investigation of sex offenses. Especially in cases of burglary it is not unusual to find excrements at the scene. These may have been left there on account of superstition or revengeful desire or more often on account of real need due to the nervousness of the perpetrator.[18]

Excrements of adults are normally yellowish-brown and solid. The excrement of infants is greenish-yellow, contains undigested cheesy lumps, and under the microscope shows lumps of milk and fine needles of fatty acid. A thorough analysis of excrements is very difficult and seldom carried out for the purposes of police science. Generally, a microscopic diagnosis of the components is sufficient.

Many times characteristic parts of the excrement, such as fruit cores, parasites, etc., have led to the apprehension and conviction of a criminal.

PAINT STAINS. The perpetrator, in committing a crime, may have brushed against a newly painted wall or a wall with loose whitewash and may carry some of the paint or lime on his clothing. Or the tools used by the perpetrator may carry small adherent particles of paint from the scene. Microscopic diagnosis, microchemical analysis, and especially a spectrographic examination in case inorganic matters are present may lead to identification of the paint, as even extraordinarily small quantities can be analyzed. The possibilities of such identification should never be overlooked.[19]

URINE. It may be important in some cases to identify stains of urine. Such stains are sometimes mistaken for seminal stains in a preliminary examination, as they produce a slight fluorescence. Urine stains can be easily identified, however, by microchemical methods.[20]

MISCELLANEOUS STAINS. Naturally, numerous other stains may play a role in criminal investigation, although in many cases the most important step is the differentiation between stains of blood and semen. Among other stains which may be of interest in criminal investigation, those of meat, vegetables, fat, sugar, oils, candles, rust, mud, etc., may be mentioned.

 1 Medinger and J. Locard.[7]
 2 Wiener[3] and Schiff–Boyd.
 3 Lattes.
 4 Landsteiner–Levine.
 5 Wiener,[3] Schiff–Boyd, Schatkin, and Harley.
 6 Hooker–Boyd.
 7 Wiener.[2]
 8 Wiener,[1] Schatkin, and Keefe–Bailey.
 9 Putkonen.
10 Sasaki.
11 Kunkele.
12 *American Journal of Police Science.*
13 Kutscher & Wolberg.
14 Riifeldt.
15 Hansen.
16 King & Armstrong.
17 Sannié.[4]
18 Reuter, Abderhalden, and Sannié.[4]
19 J. Locard.[6]
20 Balthazard–Rojas and Hanson.

XVII MISCELLANEOUS TRACES

ALMOST EVERYTHING IMAGINABLE MAY CONSTITUTE A CLUE IN A CRIMinal investigation. In the following pages we shall describe briefly some traces which are not treated in the other chapters but which have frequently been found of value.

TRACES OF CLOTH. The perpetrator of a crime may at times leave negative prints of his knee or his forearm in clay, soft earth, dust, etc. If the fabric has a characteristic pattern or has been repaired, the traces can be of importance. They are photographed, and if possible a cast is made of them. In order to get comparison prints the same method is used as that used in taking fingerprints. The fabric is inked with the fingerprint roller and fingerprint ink and pressed against white paper.

FEATHERS. The question of examination of feathers arises in illegal hunting, theft, unnatural acts against animals, etc. The feathers may be divided into down and contour feathers.

Contour feathers are characteristic in shape and color. They grow out of the feather sacs, and their lower part, which is hollow and hard, is called the quill. The quill is continuous with the shaft, which generally has a square cross-section and is composed of a porous hornlike material. Barbs protrude from both sides of the shaft. The barbs are supplied with two rows of barbules carrying fine hooklets which serve to connect the barbs and make it possible for the contour feathers to offer resistance to the air during flight. The shape and number of these barbules are different in different classes of birds and serve for identification of the feathers along with the color and general form of the feather.

Birds of the Gallinae order (hen, turkey, partridge, etc.) have hooklets which are short and close together. Hooklets usually number from four to six. Pigeons have a similar arrangement. Feathers of marine birds and wading birds have long, fine hooklets which are covered with hair up to the tips. Sparrows and song birds have fine, haired hooklets which end in fine, fork-shaped tips.

The down differs from the contour feather because of the fine, soft shaft, with round cross-section. The barbules have no hooklets and consist of small joints with knotlike projections at their junctions. The form and position of these knots are very characteristic in the various orders of birds and aid in the differentiation of the orders.

In the order of the Gallinae and in the wading birds we find conical, pointed knots, varying in number from four to six. The barbules are hard and haired.

In the order of pigeons the feathers have long knots, consisting of several protruding tips. The aquatic birds have strong knots with dull points, and the climbing birds have strongly protruding knots with four tips.

In the sparrows the knots are conical and close to each other. They have a darker pigment than the barbules, which are covered with very fine hairs.

The down of birds of prey has nothing characteristic.

In each case comparison feathers from the suspected order of birds should be used. It is strongly recommended that a collection of common feathers and down be kept at the police laboratory for comparison purposes.

The examination of feathers is very simple. The feathers are placed in hot soapy water for a short time, washed in running water and then in alcohol, and examined microscopically. If they are to be photographed microscopically, they should be dyed.[1]

TRACKS OF SKIS. Identification of the tracks of skis is of very little importance because almost all skis are of standard type and of the same size and pattern and are used by the thousands. However, study of the tracks can answer a few questions, such as, whether the ski-runner has gone uphill or downhill, whether one or more persons have run in the same tracks, whether the tracks have been made by a man or a woman, and whether they are old or new.

If the two tracks do not show straight, fleeting lines but often draw closer together, and if it is seen that the person has slid backward, the runner has gone upward. The traces are quite different if he has gone downhill. The lines are then straight and fleeting if the slope has not been so steep that the runner has been forced to break the momentum by pointing the skis inward. This movement gives the tracks quite another appearance than that caused by the regular position of the skis when going upward.

The appearance of the traces of the ski pole suggests immediately the direction in which the runner has traveled when on level ground. Through these traces it is also possible to determine how many persons have run in one track. Good runners leave even and uninterrupted ski tracks, and the traces of the ski poles succeed one another at fairly even intervals. The inexperienced ski-runner often runs with legs spread apart, avoids steep slopes, and makes bad turns. He may also leave traces of many falls.

It is more difficult to determine whether a man or woman has made the tracks. Women, however, take very short steps when going uphill, and the tracks of the skis follow each other at short intervals. Going downhill, men are generally bolder than women.

Old tracks are recognized by the fact that the edges are never sharp but are rounded by the wind and sun. The small heaps of loose snow produced around the tracks when running are never seen in old tracks. If new traces of wild animals cross the tracks, the latter are likely to be old. If the traces of animals break before the tracks of the skis, the tracks still carry the human odor and must have been made recently.

EARWAX. If a person has been subjected for some time to dusty environments, the dust will find its way into the interior of his ears and be deposited on the wax. This dust will remain attached to the wax even after the most careful cleansing of the ears. The question has been especially studied by Severine and Jean Maurel;[2] they obtained some remarkable results by examining longshoremen who had worked at unloading coal about one year previously. In spite of this lapse of time small particles of coal were still present mixed with the wax. Other laborers had coffee-bean particles in the earwax (coffee roasters), hairs (barbers), flour (bakers), sawdust (laborers in sawmills), particles of copper (workers in copper), etc.

The finding of insignificant quantities of dust is of no great importance. In order to arrive at definite conclusions fairly large quantities of the dust in question must be found. If the particles are abundant and originate from rare substances, important conclusions may be drawn.

A small quantity of the earwax is put on a glass slide and examined microscopically. If foreign matter is found, a microchemical analysis may be necessary.

TRACES OF ANIMALS. In some rare cases it may be necessary to examine traces of animals—horses, donkeys, dogs, cats, monkeys. The animals may leave traces of their feet, teeth, hair, and excrement.

Certain animals leave traces of their friction ridges, as the monkeys and some dogs. The shape of the feet will permit identification of the animal in question.[3]

DUST. Dust and dirt which are in or on the suspect's apparel, shoes, hair, under the nails or in fissures, or on weapons or tools may give some clue as to where the suspect has previously been or what he has done.[4] The possibilities of dust analysis are not sufficiently exploited by detectives. By such examinations the presence of what is called professional dust may be determined, as glue and sawdust (carpenters and laborers in sawmills), lime (bricklayers), etc., and also dust from places where

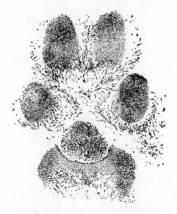

Figure 112. Trace of a dog's right forefoot (E. Goddefroy, Brussels, Belgium).

Figure 113. Part of Figure 112 enlarged.

the suspect has made a brief visit, such as safe insulation material (safe burglaries), flour (flour mill), fibers or parts of vegetables (from a barn). Shoes and cuffs of the trousers should also be examined for the presence of certain dirt, soil, insulating material, etc.

Such examinations sometimes play a helpful role in an investigation, and yet they are still regarded by many investigators as too imaginary and too romantic to be considered.

Dust is generally characterized as being composed of microscopic particles so small that they can float in the air. From the viewpoint of police science the collective term dust may also include other particles of importance which are either too small to be collected in the usual manner or are later discovered accidentally by collecting the dust to be examined. These particles (splinters, sawdust, hair, feathers, seeds, etc.), especially if they have settled on the surface of a fabric, may be collected by very simple methods, such as, for example, with a magnifying glass and forceps or by beating the article of clothing in question. In the latter case the article of clothing is put in a large, clean paper bag and beaten forcefully for five minutes, whereupon the dust which falls to the bottom of the sack is collected. Dust from the pockets should be collected and kept in envelopes labeled as to their origin.

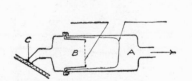

Figure 114.   Söderman-Heu-
berger filter, to be attached to
a vacuum cleaner.

Figure 115.   Gathering
dust with the special filter
when attached to the vacuum cleaner.

If the dust clings to the surface of the fabric or the dust in the interior of the fabric is to be examined, a special vacuum cleaner must be used. The vacuum cleaner collects the dust on filter paper, on which it may be examined microscopically.[5]

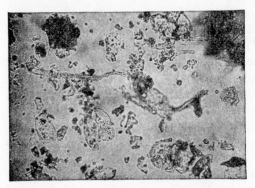

Figure 116.   Photomicrograph of dust.

A complete analysis of dust is very complicated and requires some experience, although the determination, for instance, of certain metals is fairly easy and can be made in any police laboratory. The analysis of dust has been especially studied by Locard in his excellent *Traité de criminalistique,* which gives a thorough description of the methods used.[6]

FINGERNAIL SCRAPINGS. Sometimes important clues may be found by examining the fingernail scrapings from suspected persons. Hairs, fibers, drugs (poisoning, drug addiction), epithelial tissues from the vagina in cases of sexual offense, and many other objects may turn up in the scrapings. The fingernails should be cleaned by means of a pointed glass rod and each sample of dirt put into a small separate test tube. In scraping the nails of a suspect it is necessary to avoid causing any lesions.

WOOD PARTICLES. Small particles of wood and sawdust often are important in investigations. When doors, windows, locks, or drawers have been forced, particles of wood may be found on wearing apparel or on the tools used by the criminal.

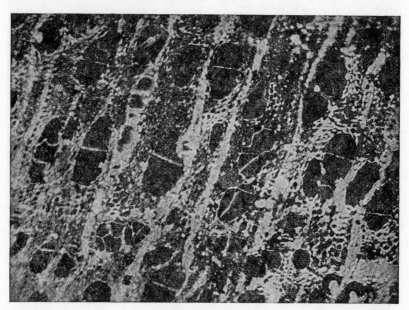

Figure 117. Microscopic identification of the origin of a tree from a piece of charcoal. The picture shows the characteristic structure of aspen.

In one case, for example, microscopic examination showed that sawdust from a handsaw had not originated from a cherry tree but from a pine tree. This proved to be of great importance in the investigation. In another case the wife of a barber was found murdered and the husband was suspected of having committed the crime. A particle of wood was found in one of the fissures of his pocket knife. The prosecuting attorney showed, with the aid of expert evidence, that the barber had carved away all traces of blood from the hammer he had used to kill his wife.

The determination of the origin of particles of wood may sometimes be very difficult when the question of related trees arises. However, it is easy even for the amateur to differentiate evergreen from leafy trees.[7]

TOBACCO AND TOBACCO ASH. Since the days of Sherlock Holmes,

the examination of cigarette and cigar ashes has been regarded, at least by the layman, as having some value in investigations. As a matter of fact, however, the differential diagnosis of tobacco ashes gives very meager results.

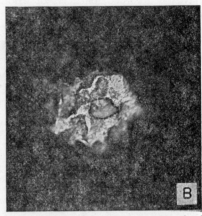

Figure 118. A man was accused of having shot another man. The accused maintained he had shot into the earth and the bullet had ricocheted. A microscopic examination of the bullet corroborated his story, because a small piece of quartz was embedded in the metal jacket. A, bullet; B, quartz particle.

Microscopic examination of tobacco and ashes shows dark, almost black, particles which under high magnification show as cells filled with small crystals of oxalate of calcium. These so-called crystal sand cells are found in all sorts of tobacco, with the exception of snuff.

Cigar and cigarette ashes are differentiated by the presence of paper ash in cases where cigarettes have been used. The paper ash is easily recognized under the microscope.

BRAIN SUBSTANCE. When a skull has been smashed, part of the brain substance may be found not only in the immediate vicinity of the body but also in other places not suspected during the first few moments after the discovery of the crime. The brain substance may be mistaken for numerous other substances, and the detective should have a certain amount of knowledge of its appearance. A preliminary examination may be made with the aid of strong magnifying glasses.

Figure 119. The analysis of a soil specimen in the FBI laboratory by means of the petrographic microscope.

The brain is composed of two different substances, white and gray matter. The white seldom plays a role in murder cases. It gets its color from the nerve filaments which run through it and are kept together by connective tissue. The gray substance, which may have all kinds of colors —yellow, red, blue, and even dark brown—consists of small quantities of fine-grained connective tissue and nerve filament.

The gray matter represents the outer layer or cortex. It encloses the white matter, or inner portion, and covers the entire brain proper at the surface, dipping down even into the depths of the many convolutions of which the brain is composed.

POLLEN ANALYSIS. In connection with dust analysis it may sometimes be of importance to identify pollen grains adhering to the clothes of a criminal. The presence of pollen grains from a certain plant may furnish conclusive proof that a person has been in a certain vicinity.[8] The pollen grains may be identified by a microscopic examination.[9]

1 Kockel.[1]
2 Severine–Maurel; also E. Locard.[10]
3 Goddefroy.[1]
4 E. Locard[1] and Britton.
5 See Söderman.[2]
6 Duquenois.
7 Further information may be obtained from Eames–MacDaniels.
8 E. Locard[8] and Türkel.[3]
9 Erdman.

XVIII   INVESTIGATION OF HOMICIDE

GREAT DEMANDS ARE PUT ON THE POLICEMAN WHO FIRST ARRIVES AT the scene of a homicide or any other major crime. The final result of the investigation often depends completely on the preventive or preliminary measures which this policeman immediately has to plan and carry out. The seemingly easy task of informing his superiors and keeping watch over the scene until the experts arrive is often complicated by difficult problems which require the ability to analyze the situation and quickly and immediately thereafter undertake the measures called for by the circumstances. The following general rules for the behavior of the policeman first arriving at the scene are universally applicable though not exhaustive. Every crime, of course, has to be individually approached and handled.

DUTIES OF FIRST POLICEMAN ON SCENE

1. Try immediately to make the situation clear to yourself. If the scene is indoors, proceed to the room where the crime took place. Enter the house cautiously and watch for and be careful not to destroy footprints or other traces on the floor. The room of the crime should be entered with the greatest caution. First determine if the supposedly murdered person is dead (corpus delicti). If the corpse is already in a decomposing state (smell), the room should not be entered by anybody until the arrival of the experts. The policeman should later be able to report every movement he makes on the scene of the crime. Remember always that fingerprints may be present on door handles, light switches, telephones, etc. The least and seemingly unimportant change in the arrangement of the furniture, the position of curtains and doors, etc., should be noted. The scene of the crime should then be closed off and nobody allowed to enter, not even colleagues, before the experts have arrived. Even if the scene is a room in a house, the outside surroundings should also be closed off if possible (in case of footprints, etc.). Use only dependable persons for help.

   If the scene is located outdoors, the space to be watched has to be determined. The size of the space should be as large as possible, depending on the number of guards available.

2. Notify your superior as quickly as possible and do not leave the scene unguarded during this time (handle telephone carefully or call elsewhere).

3. Proceed immediately to carry out measures which cannot be postponed, such as arresting the suspect and taking down names and addresses of witnesses and information about persons who may have entered the scene of the crime.

4. Take down the time of discovery of the crime, your arrival at the scene, and the arrival of your superior.

5. Try to keep the resident witnesses separated, and as far as possible try to prevent any discussion between them regarding the crime.

6. Do not discuss the crime with witnesses or any other person present.

7. Listen carefully to the remarks of the people around without appearing to do so.

The ideal condition for examining a scene is to have *only one man,* and the best qualified one, enter the scene carrying a flashlight. This "scout" should walk very carefully, being conscious of every movement he makes, and he should systematically search the scene from beginning to end without missing one single detail. The scout should then dictate his findings to a stenographer outside. During this first orientation, the scout should make up his mind about the method the criminal has used, how the criminal entered the scene, his movements during his presence at the scene, and his method of exit. If it can be determined, it is of great importance to investigate the method of the criminal thoroughly. Only when this is done should the photographer and the sketcher be allowed to enter cautiously and work according to the directions of the scout. The object of the crime is now carefully investigated, and finally the investigation is expanded to the ground around the scene. Water, piles of stone, bushes, etc., are searched for hidden objects.

The authors are fully aware that the above-described method of letting only one man enter the scene at the beginning of the investigation in most cases will prove Utopian, but it is their firm conviction that in places where it is possible and where this first alert scout has a chance to work in peace and with time to ponder the problems, this method will help the examination a good deal. In most cases in this country and also on the Continent, altogether too many policemen will enter the scene, and the technical man, who is generally surrounded by superior officers, will only be a minor part in the set-up. It is firmly believed that the work on the scene of a homicide would be much improved if district attorneys, squad commanders, and detectives of all grades would abstain from entering the scene until the technical scout has finished his job. This applies also to the medical examiners, who, if the victim is dead, could well wait a few minutes to examine the body, allowing the technical part of the investigation to be finished.

GENERAL RULES AND SCHEDULE OF INVESTIGATION

The methods of investigation in murder cases have been greatly improved during the last score of years. In training schools for detectives conducted by Federal, State, and large municipal police departments and in the so-called zone schools conducted in many States under various auspices for smaller municipalities, young detectives have been given the benefit of the experience of older men and of experts in related fields. In most of the large departments a special squad has been organized, known as the homicide squad, composed of detectives who have shown special ability in murder cases. Such steps supplant the old system of assigning to a murder case any detective who happened to be on duty, regardless of his ability and knowledge of this type of crime.

Among improvements in methods of operation have been (1) speed in getting to the scene of a crime, (2) arriving at the scene with all necessary appliances, and (3) conducting the necessary preliminary investigation with system and planning.

The specialists of the homicide squads are on duty every hour of the day and night, together with a stenographer, a photographer, a fingerprint expert, and a technician particularly qualified to develop traces and clues at the scene of the crime.

The necessity for having proper appliances resulted in the establishment of a homicide kit containing every conceivable article which experience had shown might be helpful. (See "Portable Outfit" in Chapter XXVII.) A powerful portable light is carried to illuminate cellars, areaways, and other large spaces.

In New York City and other metropolitan centers the medical examiner or his deputy or assistant, and a toxicologist, if necessary, speeds to the scene with the experts from the police laboratory to investigate the crime and to secure every possible scintilla of evidence. They make and preserve an accurate report of the scene of the crime, proceeding in an orderly and businesslike way throughout. This is essential, as the evidence obtained must afterward stand a legal test. With a dominating mind in authority, the delicate work of photographing, sketching, sifting out the material witnesses, obtaining statements, and searching for fingerprints and other traces and clues of evidential value proceeds without confusion and in an orderly and authoritative fashion.

In examining the scene the detective should look not only for the usual, standard traces—fingerprints, footprints, etc.—but should also keep his eyes open for details which at the first glance may not seem to have any connection with the crime. A few examples will illustrate this.

On a highway in France a woman had been violated and slain. The only thing found on the scene was a piece of bread. By questioning the workers in the neighboring bakery, it was found that this piece of bread had been given to a tramp who had asked for it. The bread was recognized by the fact that it was burned. A stone was missing in the oven of the bakery, and the portion of the loaf nearest to this particular place had been burned. The murderer was arrested on the description furnished by the baker.

Some years ago a homicide was committed in the neighborhood of Oslo, Norway. No traces were found at the scene, but the chief of detectives ordered a combing of the surrounding terrain. A piece of paper, part of a printed blank issued by prisons, was found along the banks of a stream. This paper gave the information that a certain man had been released from a prison on a certain day. The man was arrested and admitted his guilt.

A servant girl was found murdered in an apartment in a town in Germany. The murderer had left his own clothing in the apartment and had donned new clothing found there. An examination of his clothes furnished very good descriptive material. A red-blond mustache hair was found on the lapel of the coat, blond head hairs were deposited on the collar, and particles of tobacco, crumbs of white bread, debris of vegetables, some fish scales, and two phosphorus matches with blue tips were found in the pockets. The much worn and rather filthy clothing had been repaired in several places and apparently by expert hands.

With the aid of the above-described findings the following description of the murderer was developed: He had blond hair and a reddish mustache; smoked strong tobacco; the repairing of the clothing showed that he was familiar with the handling of needle and thread, but not to such a degree as to classify himself as a skilled tailor; he had probably learned the trade in some prison; the remains of the fish, bread, and vegetables showed that the man was a tramp who carried his food in his pockets.

The description was very accurate. Blue-tipped matches were rather rare and were found in two municipal lodging houses in Cologne. After two days the murderer was arrested.

It cannot be sufficiently stressed that the suspect and his clothing be thoroughly searched. Some examples of investigations where such examinations have had great success are the following:

A woman had been murdered in the neighborhood of Lyons, France. An examination of the body and the scene revealed no clues. A few days later some tramps were arrested for other reasons and subjected to a close search. Some seeds were found in the clothing of one of them. Examination by an expert botanist showed that these seeds were those of a plant rarely found in the neighborhood. Such plants were found on the scene of the crime, and the arrested man finally confessed.

In a burglary the burglar had forced his way into a cellar through a narrow corridor. Some electric cables were suspended on the walls of this corridor. The perpetrator must have touched them, because the under surface of his fingernails were filled with the same pitch with which the cables were covered.

In another case[1] the shoes of a man suspected of having burglarized a flour mill were examined. The shoes were covered with dirt consisting of three layers, first earth, then a thin layer of flour, and finally another layer of earth. The arrangement of these layers disclosed that the man had walked through the muddy road leading to the mill and had returned on the same road.

In still another case a person was suspected of having hidden stolen money in the neighborhood of a small stream. Sand from the banks of the stream, found on his shoes, gave him away.

It is almost impossible to visualize and comprehend the manifold duties devolving upon a police officer or detective investigating a homicide. Many detectives are peculiarly qualified to perform the mechanics of an investigation in a homicide case, but if asked to enumerate the steps taken, they would be at a loss to do so. It is deemed advisable to list in an orderly fashion here the complex duties devolving upon the investigator at the scene of a murder. Such a schedule naturally cannot cover the whole field. Crime is ever changing in its aspect, and each case will present its individual sides, to which the successful detective must adapt himself.

Upon arrival at the scene:

Ascertain who the perpetrator is and arrest immediately if possible.
Note time of arrival.
Prevent anyone from touching body or disturbing anything pending arrival of homicide squad, technicians from police laboratory, and medical examiner or coroner. Prevent destruction of evidence such as fingerprints, footprints, etc.[2]
Show shield and hold everyone at scene for questioning.
Prevent unauthorized persons from entering the scene.
Notify station or headquarters, giving a brief outline of case.
Take names and addresses of all persons present and endeavor to ascertain name of perpetrator or perpetrators and a detailed identifiable description for immediate alarm.
Keep room and immediate area clear of all but authorized persons present upon official business or detained on case.
Keep witnesses separated to prevent conversation.
Assign specific task to each detective, proceeding in a systematic manner. Keep record of all assignments and detail of work.

Examination of scene:

The position of the body is examined.

The clothing and its position are noted.

Traces on the body and on the clothing are noted, photographed, and sketched.

Take photographs to show body in original position with relation to stationary objects, the route of the murderer, etc. The photography should be carefully planned (see Chapter VIII).

Make diagram of scene (see Chapter VII).

(If something has been altered before the arrival of the homicide squad, the original position of objects sketched and photographed should be established with the aid of witnesses.)

(*Only after the above steps have been taken should the body be allowed to be moved or its position altered.*)

The wounds are examined by the medical examiner. The back of the body is examined, and the ground under it.

The weather (1) when the crime is discovered and (2) when the homicide squad arrives should be noticed, especially in rural crimes. (Position of sun and moon, rain, snow, frost, thaw, visibility, direction of wind, force of wind, etc.)

Examination of doors and windows, furniture, etc., will disclose the probable direction of entry and exit of the perpetrator. Note position and whether doors are open, closed, or have been moved.

Look for bullet holes, empty shells, and bloodstains. Note and mark location.

Search for visible and latent fingerprints, plastic and surface footprints, traces of tools, cut telephone wires, traces of teeth, strands of hair, bits of cloth, buttons, cigarette butts, etc.

Search for other traces and clues.

Determine if traces come from victim, murderer, or third party. (Remember the possibility of false clues having been deliberately planted.)

Search terrain about premises or vacant lot, noting vegetation, condition of soil, footprints, etc. Determine movements of victim and murderer.

Officer in charge should dictate to stenographer complete and detailed description of scene.

Try to visualize what has taken place, with the aid of the position of the victim, traces of violence, position of bloodstains and weapon, etc.

Search for clues. Follow to the end. Investigate every theory.

Preserve evidence.

Record findings in memorandum book.

Suggestions if homicide was committed elsewhere than where the body was found:

It may happen that the homicide was not committed in the place where the body was discovered, but that:

1. The body was dragged to the place of discovery. (Watch for traces of dragging and footprints; note pattern of bloodstains.)

2. The body was hanged or shot or stabbed after the homicide (see "Suicide or Homicide?" later in this chapter).
3. The body was cut up and the parts disposed of in different places; the body was placed in a trunk and checked in a luggage room; the body was sunk in a lake. (Note the nature of wrappings around the body, i.e., rare materials, faults in the weaving, pieces of newspapers from which origin and date may be ascertained, etc. Watch for peculiar notes, particles sticking to the body, dust, professional butcher work. For identification purposes note fingerprints, laundry marks, watch-repair marks, labels on clothing, dental work, signs of disease, etc. Don't forget the possibilities of X-ray examinations, reconstruction of face, and anthropological examination.)
4. Body was thrown from a car or carried to the scene where it was found. (Watch for traces of tires and footprints.)

Remember that after having inflicted serious wounds upon himself a suicide may still have enough strength left to carry out complicated actions or walk long distances.

Determining perpetrator:

Statements of eyewitnesses. Information.
Motive.
Number of murderers.
Weapons.
Route of murderer. Search for traces along the road or surrounding the scene. Reconstruction of the movements of the murderer is all-important.
Was the murderer wounded or his clothes soiled?
If suspect is arrested, search clothing, fingernails, etc., for blood. If scene had peculiar dust, soil, or other substances, search suspect's clothing, fingernails, shoes, etc.
Diaries, journals, letters, addresses, telephone numbers, photographs.
Associates, relatives, sweethearts, friends, enemies, etc.
Places frequented, hangouts.
Habits.
Wearing apparel, laundry marks thereon, etc.
Traces and clues found on the scene or elsewhere linking the suspect with the crime.
Description of vehicle, if any used.
Stolen property. Secure complete list and description.
Poisons (search for container on suspect or in his dwelling; seize suspicious glasses, bottles, etc., on scene; gather vomited substances and excrement of deceased; never allow family or friends to aid in the search).
Unguarded statements of witnesses or bystanders.
Fingerprints found and photographed at scene compared with those on file.
(Unless impractical or not expedient, question witnesses at station house. It may be necessary to take witnesses to bureau of identification to view photos on file.)

Direction of escape of perpetrator:

Inquiries should be made concerning means and direction of escape.

Detective should familiarize himself with roads, streets, routes of public conveyances, for alarm and other purposes. Notify desk officer at station or headquarters.

If outside of state or city limits, headquarters will give alarm.

If direction is to a distant point, headquarters will telephone and teletype.

Notification:

1. Ordinary homicides:

   a. Chief of police
   b. Commander of detective division or bureau
   c. Borough (New York City) and district commander, detective division or bureau
   d. Squad or precinct commanding officer
   e. Medical examiner (or coroner)
   f. District attorney
   g. Telegraph, telephone, or teletype bureau at headquarters
   h. Homicide squad, specialists
   i. Police laboratory
   j. Photographers
   k. Stenographers

2. Homicides caused by explosions: in addition to above notify special squad of detectives concerned.
3. In other cases, such as accidents on railroads, elevated transit lines, etc., notify transit commission, building department, or Public Service Commission or other public authority having jurisdiction.

Treatment of evidence:

Articles requiring analysis are delivered to the proper experts (medical examiner or coroner, police laboratory, and ballistic expert).

Preserve and transport the articles carefully. (For treatment see the different chapters on traces.)

Mark for future identification, secure against tampering, label, wrap, and forward evidence to property clerk.

Tag and wrapper should include:

1. Date of arrest and marking
2. Charge
3. Nature of evidence or sample
4. Name of prosecuting authority (State or national)
5. Name and address of deceased person
6. Name and address of the defendant
7. Rank, name, shield number, and command of the officer
8. Time and place of court examination

Res Gestæ:

Circumstances and things said at the instant of the homicide are the *res gestæ*.

Wearing apparel worn by deceased and weapon or instrument showing marks of violence are *res gestæ* evidence.

Motives (facts showing):

Revenge
Feud
Jealousy
Crank
Gain, financial or otherwise
Civil suit
Sadism
Sex motives other than sadism
Moral turpitude
Mental deficiency or insanity
Self-defense

Preparation before committing homicide:

Attempt to determine whether defendant or fugitive wanted was armed shortly before crime or had in his possession means for its commission.

Try to determine if defendant or fugitive wanted was near the scene of the crime under suspicious circumstances, such as disguised, armed, uttering threats, etc.

Dying declaration:

Questions to be asked (statement signed in presence of witnesses, if possible):
What is your name?
Where do you live?
Do you now believe that you are about to die?
Have you no hope of recovery from the effects of the injury you have received?
Are you willing to make a true statement of how you received the injury from which you are now suffering? (Dying declaration is competent evidence. Admitted only when person has no hope of recovery.)

Identity of deceased:

Complete and correct name of deceased.

Complete and correct names of witnesses and memorandum as to what is expected to be proved by each.

First member of the force to arrive at scene must identify body of deceased for medical examiner or coroner as body of person found at scene of homicide.

Officer must produce witnesses (preferably relatives of deceased) at autopsy to identify the deceased in presence of medical examiner or coroner as body of person whom they knew during life.

Officer should record in his memorandum book a record of identification for future use.

Clothing, letters, photographs, moles, birthmarks, conformation of teeth are aids in identification (see Chapters III and V).

Conduct of accused subsequent to crime:

Study actions and demeanor carefully. Flight, attempt to commit suicide, false statements, concealment are considered indications of guilt.

Question him at opportune time.

Steps to arrest:

If perpetrator is known, forward alarm, giving name, address, description, also peculiarities, habits, associates, and places where he might be found.

Determine movements of perpetrator for days prior to crime.

Keep home and place of employment under surveillance.

Supervision over all channels of communication.

Trail associates, sweetheart, and family.

Look for information at hospitals and doctors' offices (if circumstances warrant).

If indicted, mail a circular with picture to principal cities.

(See Chapter IV for further steps.)

Alibi:

Question prisoner as to his whereabouts at the time of the crime. Check up immediately.

Determine movements of perpetrator for days prior to crime and on day of crime.

Disposal of body:

Medical examiner or coroner determines cause of death, pending autopsy at morgue.

Tag placed on all dead bodies in homicide cases.

Do not remove body without permission of medical examiner.

Remove body to morgue.

Fingerprint deceased. If circumstances warrant, have samples of head hair and beard taken from the body. In sex murder also hair samples from the torso. Examine clothing.

In the case of a female notify policewomen's bureau. Assigned member will assist.

Clothing must be removed from body and taken care of by detective.

Mark each article and place in sealed package as per regulations and deliver to property clerk.

Forward valuable property to desk officer.

Burial cannot take place until district attorney and medical examiner release body.

Autopsy:

Only the medical examiner or coroner is qualified to testify as to cause of death.

The medical examiner or coroner aids investigation by disclosing types of wounds and manner of infliction.

Officer should know location of the wounds, condition of clothing, and surrounding property in order to give accurate description.

Expert and non-expert evidence as to bloodstains (see Chapter XVI):

Stains found upon person or clothing of accused.

Stains found upon person or clothing of deceased.

Expert's opinion is competent evidence.

Non-expert may testify as to existence and color of stain.

SUICIDE OR HOMICIDE?

In the investigation of homicides the boundary line between the work of the criminologist and the medical examiner or coroner is difficult to draw so far as concerns the exterior examination of the body. Theoretically, the criminologist should confine himself to traces of the murderer, while the medical examiner or coroner should give the exterior description of the body and perform the autopsy. Experience shows, however, that such a strict limitation of duties gives very limited results. Sometimes the medical examiner or coroner, as a pathologist, may, aside from the autopsy, confine himself to a formal description of the exterior of the body. The report is often made out in such a professional manner that the average detective has very little use for it. On the other hand, if the coroner or medical examiner happens to be personally interested in the detectives' side of the question—and in many localities he is—he can, as experience shows, be of enormous service to the investigator. The latter must, however, know something of legal medicine and its possibilities so that he can meet the medical examiner or coroner on the same ground, at least as far as the exterior examination is concerned. It is here, in the exterior examination, that we meet the vague boundary line between police science and legal medicine. It is also here that many of the most difficult problems in homicide investigations will be encountered, as, for example, the determination of whether it is a case of homicide or suicide. Intelligent cooperation between the medical examiner or coroner and the skilled investigator is the best means of solving such problems. The examiner or coroner should have an understanding of the problems and work of the investigator; the investigator, on his part, must recognize the point where the examiner's work ends and his own begins.

GENERAL INDICATIONS OF SUICIDE

IF SUICIDE HAS OCCURRED BEFORE IN THE FAMILY. This is an indication which supports the theory of suicide, because family history seemingly plays a great role. Note, too, that according to Continental statistics 40 percent of the women committing suicide are in a menstruating period.

THREATS TO COMMIT SUICIDE. Sometimes such threats are reported to the police to cover a homicide. It also often happens that suicide threats are denied by relatives who want to show that the suicide was committed "while of unsound mind."

SUICIDE NOTES. These are certainly a strong indication of suicide. particularly if written by hand and the identity of the handwriting can be proved.

CIRCUMSTANCES IN WHICH COMMITTED. Remember that a weapon may be put into the hand of a dead body and retained there by the action of *rigor mortis,* and that in spite of the fact that a door is locked from the inside of a room, this can have been accomplished from the outside.

DETERMINATION BASED ON SPECIFIC METHOD

SHOOTING. In shooting cases the wound caused by a bullet fired from a short distance must have a typical appearance—and so must the immediate surroundings—to lead to a conclusion of suicide. One cannot fire a shot at oneself at a greater distance than about twenty inches. Generally the suicide will press the muzzle of the firearm directly against the skin or at least keep it very close to make the result certain. The entrance to the wound in such cases is always larger than the diameter of the bullet. Hairs surrounding the hole are singed, and the skin around the hole is burned to a reddish-brown or gray-brown color. The skin around the hole will be covered with unburnt powder grains, and if the shot has been fired from less than eight inches, a smeary, black coat of powder residue will be found. This is especially abundant if black powder has been used, and less apparent if the smokeless type has been employed. All these signs are missing when the shot has been fired from a long distance, although unburnt powder particles can be carried fairly long distances.

If the direction of the canal in the body seems plausible and the wounded part of the body (heart, forehead, temple, mouth) is so situated that the suicide may have fired the shot from a comfortable position, a conclusion of suicide may be well founded, especially when the wounded part of the body has been uncovered. There are, however, quite a few cases where suicides have shot themselves by firing through their clothing.

Naturally attention should always be paid to fingerprints, footprints, traces of violence, etc., which may indicate murder. If several bullet wounds are found in a dead man, a conclusion of homicide may be reasonably drawn, but it should be kept in mind that suicides may and sometimes do shoot themselves several times. There is a case on record where a man inflicted five head wounds upon himself. A case of this sort will naturally supply the investigator with plenty of food for thought.

In normal suicides the entrance to the wound will be smaller than its exit. This is natural, because the bullet on its way through the body encounters resistance which alters its form. The margins at the entrance are as a rule turned inward, and those at the exit outward. There are, however, exceptions to this rule. The wounds of entrance and of exit may look quite alike, especially if the shot has been fired from a fairly long distance and the bullet has traveled at high speed. Putrefaction and drying may also completely alter the original appearance of the wound.

EXPLOSIVES. Suicides by means of dynamite or other explosives occur among miners, road workers, etc. The explosive may be placed either on top of the head or in the mouth. In the first case only the head, or parts of it, will be blown away. In the second case, as a rule, the whole neck and part of the breast will also suffer. A similar result may be achieved by using a shotgun whose barrel is filled with water. The suicide puts the end of the barrel in his mouth, pulls the trigger, and a blank cartridge is discharged. The column of water produces enormous damage to the head.

HANGING. Strangulation is one of the most common methods of suicide, owing to the ease with which the act is performed. Ropes of all kinds, towels, handkerchiefs, suspenders, aprons, belts, gauze bandages, electric wires, etc., can be used. It is not necessary that the body swing free to bring about the desired result. During the act of strangulation, the arteries of the neck which carry blood from the heart to the brain are pressed upon. This immediately shuts off the blood supply, causing almost instantaneous unconsciousness because of the resulting anemia of the brain. The effect on the brain is further aggravated by the fact that the return flow of blood—through the veins to the heart—is also interfered with by the pressure on these veins. This interference increases the pressure within the skull and contributes to the production of unconsciousness. Comparatively little pressure on the neck is necessary, and this accounts for the peculiar positions in which hanged persons may be found (sitting, standing, lying). Strangulation proper—asphyxia—then sets in and causes the death of the unconscious person.

In cases of strangulation signs of the rope will be found around the neck. There will be an interruption in the mark at the place where the knot was tied. If the knot was made at one side of the neck, the face will often be found to be red because of the complete compression of the

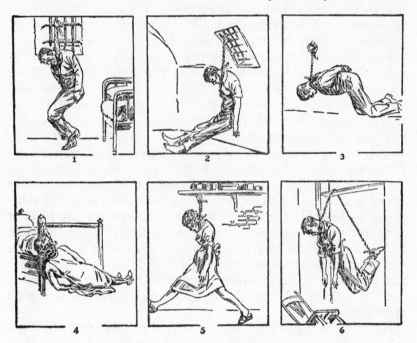

Figure 120. Some cases of suicide illustrating the fact that the body does not have to swing free. No. 6, of course, is an unusual case, but the presence and position of the chair indicate suicide.

arteries and veins on that one side only. This is so often the case that a suspicion of homicide has some foundation if the face is found to be pale while the knot has been tied at the side of the neck. In most hangings where the knot has been tied at the nape of the neck, the face will be pale.

Generally differentiation is made between two types of markings found on the neck, namely, the soft and the hard. The soft marking consists of a pale groove with purplish, swollen borders. Such markings are produced when a soft and broad object has been used for strangulation. The hard markings result from the use of hard and rough instruments, such as hard ropes, electric wires, etc. Such marks are generally leather-brown. The horny layer of the epidermis has been scraped away by the rope, causing drying of the epidermis. Sometimes the soft markings may entirely disappear, especially when the body has been hanging only for a short time and a soft material has been used. Fat persons, because of the pressure from the collar or shirt after death, may have marks on the neck which can be mistaken for strangulation marks. This is also the case in new-born in-

Figure 121.   Hanging in a sitting position.

fants, whose normal furrows of fatty tissue may at times be mistaken for strangulation marks.

By hanging a murdered person practically the same marks as those caused by strangulation may be produced. There is no sure way, either by autopsy or by microscopic examination of the marks, of determining whether a person was hanged after death or not. Hanging of a living body by murderers does not occur very frequently, although a few cases are on record. In such cases traces of violence almost always will be found if the hanged person is an adult. On the other hand, outer signs of violence on children and drunk or aged persons may not be found at all. In most cases strangulation will be used to simulate suicide, although poisoning and especially choking may have caused death. In such cases not only the scene must be carefully studied but also the probabilities of voluntary strangulation. For example, if the body hangs free, there must have been a place from which the person could have jumped—a chair, a table, a ladder, etc. Such objects should be carefully examined for traces of the suicide's feet, and in more doubtful cases reconstructions should be attempted.

The examination of the rope used may reveal most important information. (This question has been studied by the Belgian detective E.

Goddefroy, and such examinations have led to the solution of quite a few crimes on the Continent.) The fibers of the rope will lie in the opposite direction to that of the pulling. If a person slides down a rope, the fibers will be directed downwards. If what appears to be a voluntary strangulation is in fact murder and the murderer has pulled the body up, the fibers will be directed upward on that part of the rope which was pulled by the murderer because of the contact of the rope with the substructure. A dead person is a very heavy and limp mass, hence it is difficult to raise the body and put the head in the noose. Experience shows that the murderer will in some cases pass the rope over the branch of a tree, for instance, put the sling over the head of the body, and proceed to pull it up (see Figure 122). On the other hand, if the fibers of the rope maintain their normal direction this is no proof of suicide, because the murderer may have raised the body and put the head in the

Figure 122. Schematic drawing showing Goddefroy's method of determining whether a person found hanging was pulled up.

sling. The knots on the rope may give valuable information and should not be untied when removing the body. The rope should be cut with great care instead (Figure 122 will show what parts of the rope must be protected against friction in an examination). It is advisable to get a long, strong, wooden box for the transportation of the rope, which should be placed in the center of the box and held there by a string arrangement to avoid friction. It goes without saying that the part of the rope which has been in contact with the substructure, as well as the ends of the rope (in case the rope has been cut), should be marked in some manner; for example, with labels fastened to the rope with strings.

CHOKING. In choking, the markings on the neck have a different appearance from those produced by hanging. They run almost horizontally around the neck, and there is no such interruption in their continuity as may occur in hangings, where interruption is due to the knot of the rope. An interruption may be found, however, if a collar or something similar has prevented the formation of the markings. Self-choking with the hands is obviously impossible because the hands gradually become powerless as unconsciousness develops. The markings by choking are generally deeper than those found in hangings. Traces of violence found on other parts of the body and not brought about by previous, unsuccessful attempts at suicide indicate homicide.

SLIT WOUNDS. Slit wounds in suicides generally occur only on certain parts of the body and have a certain direction, since the intention of the suicide is to bleed to death as quickly as possible from some main artery. The wounds, either one or more, are found, then, on parts of the body which can be reached with comfort by the arm, i.e., on the front part of the neck, the middle of the upper arm, the elbow, the wrists, or the thighs. Wounds on the abdomen are seldom found in suicides. Persons mentally deranged, however, sometimes have self-inflicted wounds on parts of the body more difficult to reach. Very often, besides the deadly incision of an artery, superficial wounds, the result of the first unsuccessful attempts, are found.

In normal cases the direction of the wounds in a suicide should indicate that a left-handed or right-handed individual has been able to make them himself with enough pressure and in a normal position. If, for instance, we assume that a right-handed person has cut his own neck, the wound should begin on the left side behind or under the left ear and run obliquely over the front of the neck to the right. If the line of incision runs in the opposite direction and the suicide is known not to be left-handed, strong reasons for a suspicion of homicide must be entertained. This is especially the case when the bloodstains are found mostly on the posterior portions of the body, i.e., the nape of the neck, the back of the head, the shoulders and back. In authentic suicides the bloodstains are generally found on the anterior part of the body, on the front part of the neck, on the breast and abdomen. Several incisions in the neck will often be found, and some may be very deep. On the other hand, if the wound extends to the vertebræ of the neck, this is a sign of homicide. Sometimes in suicides, besides the fatal wounds, typical wounds running across the fingertips and the nails will be found. These arise from the fact that the suicide, in stretching the skin with the fingers of one hand over the area which he has selected to incise, involuntarily cuts them with the knife carried across by the other hand. These finger wounds may also be due to the grasping of the knife-blade with both hands so as to exert more pressure during the performance of the act. These wounds are not to be mistaken for the defense wounds found in the palm of the hand, which are signs of homicide.

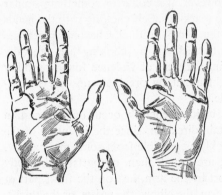

Figure 123. Typical defense wounds in a homicide.

Suicides will almost always uncover the part of the body on which they intend to inflict the wound. This is the case in slit wounds as well as in stab wounds and shootings. If the clothing of the person has been cut through, a suspicion of homicide is justified, especially if the injured area has been uncovered later to make the crime look like suicide.

So much for the appearance of the cuts in typical cases. It may be extremely difficult to arrive at definite conclusions as to whether we are dealing with a suicide or homicide merely by the appearance of the cuts. It cannot be determined with absolute certainty whether a wound has been made from right to left or from left to right. Experience shows that

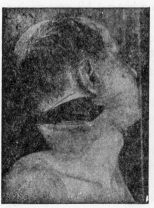

Figure 124. Unusual wound in the rear of the neck by a suicide.

the area where the weapon has been inserted may look identically the same as the place where it has been withdrawn. There is also no possibility of drawing conclusions on the basis of the number of cuts on the neck, because in both homicides and suicides one or several cuts may be found. Neither from the depth of the wounds nor from their direction may any certain conclusions be drawn. Suicides in many cases inflict wounds upon themselves which appear totally different from the above-described classical types.

Figure 125. Another unusual suicide wound.
The man was right-handed.

In conclusion it may be said that it is not possible to arrive at definite conclusions on the question of homicide or suicide solely from the appearance of the cuts. There are certain things besides the fatal wounds, however, which differentiate to a certain extent. A sign of suicide is the presence of one or more parallel cuts over the temples, wrists, elbows, or thighs—often superficial ones. Signs of homicide are several irregular deep cuts, especially if accompanied by bruises, contusions, abrasions,

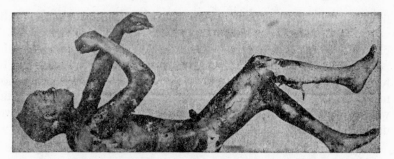

Figure 126.   Typical fighting pose of a burnt body which may lead the inexperienced investigator to believe that the deceased died while fighting.

or scratches. Defense wounds on the hands and underside of the arms, as already stated, are almost sure signs of homicide.[3]

CHOP WOUNDS. Chop wounds are seldom found in suicides. When found, they are almost always on the forehead or on the scalp, are of varying depth, and are parallel and close together. In homicides chop wounds on the head run in different directions and are larger.

Figure 127.   Typical parallel wounds in the head in a suicide with a hatchet.

STAB WOUNDS. Stab wounds in suicides are as a rule close together and on the anterior part of the body. Typical of suicides are small superficial holes in the vicinity of the deep wounds, as the result of the first attempts. Scattered wounds indicate homicide. The above description of slit wounds applies to stab wound also.

DEATHS DUE TO TRAFFIC ACCIDENTS AND TO LEAPS FROM GREAT HEIGHTS. Such deaths may result from homicide as well as from suicide, a fact which renders it very difficult to determine whether the death was voluntary or not. Signs of homicide are impressions on the skin which, because of their shape and position, indicate that they originated from another person, e.g., impressions of nails, of kicks, of cane blows, etc. Suicides often previously disclose orally by telephoning friends, family, police, for example, or in writing their intention of committing the act.

Occasionally it may happen that the murderer attempts to hide the nature of his act by making it appear like a traffic accident or a death resulting from a leap. An interesting case was reported in France. A contractor and two of his engineers were motoring at night on a highway running parallel with the railroad tracks. They were traveling at high speed in spite of the fact that the headlights of the car were in a bad condition, only lighting the road for a few yards ahead. As a result they ran over a farmhand of Polish extraction who was walking along the side of the highway. In order to hide the accident the motorists put the victim across the rails and continued their journey. A fast train which passed soon afterward beheaded the Pole and mutilated his body. During the examination of the body, traces of motorcar tires were found on the leg of the dead man, and an investigation resulted in the discovery of the motorists and their car. They unanimously denied their guilt, but the police found traces of human blood on one of the mudguards of the car. This fact brought about a confession.

DROWNING. Drowning is the most common form of suicide. Direct homicide by drowning is unusual and can hardly be accomplished on a male adult in possession of his full powers and knowing how to swim. It is often extremely difficult to determine whether an apparent case of death by drowning is the result of suicide or of a disguised previous homicide, since even the most unusual bruises and mutilations present may be due to the body's colliding with different objects in the water—for instance, propellers, etc. Of common occurrence, however, is the hiding of homicide by throwing the body in the water after the crime.

The sodium chloride content of the blood in the right and left chambers of the heart in death from drowning may show a distinct difference and should therefore be determined in suspected cases. The principle of this test,[4] developed by Gettler in 1921, is based on the fact that, when drowning occurs, water tends to pass from the lungs into the blood and therefore if the water in which the drowning occurs has a low chloride content, as in fresh water, the blood in the left side of the heart will show a chloride content lower than usual. On the other hand, if the drowning should occur in sea water, the chloride content should be above normal. The difference between the chloride content of the right and the left sides of the heart is thus a fairly good criterion for drowning. According to Smith,[5] no water can get to the left chamber of the heart if the person is dead when thrown into the water.

The water of ponds, ditches, and streams often contains debris which is characteristic of the area, and in cases of drowning the water in the lungs should contain debris of a similar nature to that in the water in which death occurred. Very often characteristic plant fragments and diatoms may be found in the lungs by a microscopic examination and may furnish conclusive evidence in fixing the place of drowning.

POISONING. Poisoning is often a means of committing suicide, and the investigator ought to be familiar with the more common poisons and their action. As a rule the murderer will not use poisons which, because of their color, smell, or taste, may awaken suspicion. On the other hand, the suicide may take any evil-tasting and evil-smelling poisonous substance. In homicide or suicide by poisoning special attention should be paid to the appearance of the skin, to the smell, and to changes in or around the mouth, genitals, and anus.

When there is a suspicion of poisoning, all bottles and drugs in the house must be seized. Food which the poisoned person has eaten, glasses, cups, dishes, vomitus, excrements, and urine are collected and sent for examination. The collecting and transportation of these substances and objects should not under any pretext be taken care of by the family or neighbors of the dead person, because death from poisoning is often a family affair. It is of greatest importance to act speedily, because the evidence is perishable and easily destroyed.

Special circumstances which may arouse suspicion of poisoning are:

1. Quick death without special symptoms (prussic acid and cyanide of potassium)
2. Vomiting of coffee-brown substances with odor of onions or garlic (phosphorus)
3. Black vomitus (sulfuric acid)
4. Greenish-brown vomitus (hydrochloric acid)
5. Yellow vomitus (nitric and chromic acid)
6. White vomitus which turns black in daylight (silver salts)
7. Vomiting of substances with a sharp smell (strong vinegar or ammonia)
8. Bluish-green vomitus (sulfate of copper)
9. Colic and pronounced diarrhea (arsenic, sublimate, and lead salts)
10. Cramps, paralysis, unconsciousness (carbolic acid, Lysol, strychnine, nicotine)
11. Drowsiness (morphine and opium)
12. Excitation and delusions (belladonna and atropine)

The most common poisons and their actions on humans will be briefly described in Chapter XIX.

AT WHAT TIME DID DEATH OCCUR?

This question will be answered by the medical examiner after observing the temperature of the body, the *rigor mortis,* the post-mortem lividity, and the degree of decomposition.

In some rare cases, for instance, typhoid fever, cholera, and deaths caused by certain poisons, the temperature after death may rise for two or three hours and then drop. Normally, however, the temperature becomes gradually lower until it approaches the temperature of the surroundings—within six to eight hours. It is possible, then, to determine approximately the time elapsed since death by measuring the fall in temperature with a thermometer inserted in the rectum. The temperature is said to drop one degree centigrade for each hour after death. This, however, depends very much upon the conditions of the individual case, and the assumption is always hazardous. It is dependent on whether the body is obese or thin, whether clad or nude, whether the exterior temperature is exceedingly low or high, etc.

The *rigor mortis* generally occurs two to six hours after death. The stiffening usually begins from the head and gradually spreads down over the whole body. After a time which varies from eight to twenty hours (in most cases ten to twelve) the *rigor* is complete. It disappears after two to three days, although in some cases it may last until the fifth day. The time for the appearance and disappearance of the *rigor mortis* is dependent upon many factors, especially the temperature and the strength of the muscles. In cold weather it appears sooner and the stiffness is more pronounced than in hot weather. Poorly developed individuals and children do not show as pronounced *rigor mortis* as strong persons.

The post-mortem lividity occurs three or four hours after death, although it may sometimes occur earlier or later. It occurs sooner in cases of instantaneous death, such as by strangulation, and later in slower deaths, such as by arsenic poisoning. Post-mortem lividity is due to the action of gravity, which causes the blood to sink to the lowest level of the body. When the position of the body is altered during the first few hours after death, the lividity appears in other places if the blood is still liquid. This may be very important in homicide investigations, hence the necessity of always carefully noting the position of the lividity.

The first signs of decomposition are seen twenty-four to forty-eight hours after death and consist of a greenish-blue coloration of the veins in the skin and a diffused greenish-blue coloration of the abdomen. The presence of insects on the body will also give indication. In summer, if the body is lying in the open, after a few hours there will already be eggs of insects in the corners of the eyes and mouth and in the nostrils; larvae will form after forty-eight hours, the pupae after eight days, and a new generation of flies after two weeks. If empty pupae are found on the body, the person must have been dead at least three weeks. In summer maggots may completely eat away the soft tissues in four to six weeks.[6]

In "floaters" the "washerwoman's skin" will appear on the fingers after a few hours and on the entire hand after forty-eight hours. The skin does not begin to loosen from the flesh before six to eight days.

The rare adipocere formation, in which the fat of the body is turned into a whitish, waxy substance, does not occur before six to eight weeks, and a complete transformation of the whole body into wax requires at least half a year.

The condition of the stomach when the autopsy is performed may permit the drawing of certain conclusions as to the time when death took place. These conclusions are only approximate, however, because the stomach continues to digest food for twenty-four hours after death. If death takes place immediately after a meal, the post-mortem digestion will be found to be very slight. If the amount of the stomach content is small, it may signify that the person has been dead for a considerable time. The stomach of a living person empties in two to six hours. An empty stomach therefore indicates that death has occurred at least two to six hours after the last meal.

When skeletons are found, the degree of the decomposition of the clothing may give certain information. Cotton fabrics fall to pieces after four to five years, woolens after eight to ten years, and silk and leather after twenty years or more.

WHAT THE SHAPE AND POSITION OF BLOODSTAINS WILL TELL

The appearance of the bloodstains can often give important information concerning the circumstances of the murder. Blood drops and blood sprinkles will have a different appearance according to the height from which they have fallen. If the distance is short, they appear as round drops, provided the surface on which they fall is not rough. If the height of the fall is greater, the blood drops have jagged edges, the jaggedness having relation to the height. The greater the height, the more jagged the blood drops will appear (see Figure 128). If the drops fall from a considerable height, say two or three yards, the contents of the drop will be sprinkled in many small drops.

The above applies only to blood drops which fall at right angles from a stationary object. If the drops fall from a person who is moving, their form will be quite different. The movement of the drop in this case consists of two components:

1. A vertical movement due to gravitation
2. A horizontal movement due to the forward progress of the person

When the first part of the drop touches the floor, the remaining portion is still moving in a horizontal direction and splatters over the first part, thereby forming toothlike projections. The direction of these teeth denotes the direction toward which the person is moving. The more rapid

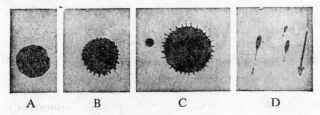

Figure 128.   Shape of blood drops falling from different heights: A, from three inches; B, fifteen inches; C, fifty inches. The shape of the drops also indicates the direction of fall (D).

the walking, the longer and narrower are the blood drops and their teeth. It should be pointed out, however, that such an appearance may also be had under other conditions. If, for instance, while a murder is being committed, an ax smeared with blood is raised during the act of delivering a second blow, drops of blood may fall from the weapon and assume the characteristics described above. It is necessary, then, to examine carefully all bloodstains on the scene, because the position of the different stains in relation to one another may throw some light on the crime.

Hasty conclusions should not be drawn concerning the direction taken by the person from the appearance of the blood drops. The person walking may have moved the blood-smeared or wounded hand in a direction opposite to the one in which he was walking. He may also have remained quiet and moved only the limb. In such cases the blood drops and their teeth will extend in the opposite direction. In most cases, however, such drops are characterized by small teeth.

If a blood drop is quickly spouted at an angle against an object, blood sprinkles will form. As a result of the rapidity of the movement of the drops in touching the object, the last portion of the drop will continue over the first part with such speed that a stain resembling an exclamation point will be formed. The pointed end of this exclamation mark will reveal the direction of the moment. The more obtuse the angle at which the blood spout meets the object, the thicker the exclamation point; the more acute the angle, the longer and narrower is the shape of the exclamation point.

If a blood spurt from a long distance touches a vertical wall obliquely, the direction of the exclamation point may lead to false conclusions. What has been said above concerning the thickened part of the exclamation point representing the source and the point representing the direction of the movement holds good only for sprinkles originating from a short distance. If the distance is great, the individual drops will very soon gravitate toward the floor. Then even if the blood spurt originally was going in an absolutely horizontal direction, the stain on the wall may show these exclamation points at an opposite direction to that of the movement.

The source of blood sprinkles may vary. They may originate from injured arteries, giving highly characteristic sprinkles, although this occurrence is rather rare. More often the sprinkles occur when a bleeding wound is struck with violence or when blood drops fall from the quickly moved bloodstained weapon of the murderer. The number, relative position, and appearance of the individual stains will in many cases allow conclusions as to their origin. It has many times been possible to tell the position of the murderer and the manner in which the weapon was handled by simply examining the bloodstains.[7]

When examining the appearance of bloodstains, a reconstruction with the aid of ox blood (or any other blood easily obtained) is recommended.

The surface upon which the bloodstain is found is important inasmuch as it may alter the original shape of the stain. If the material is smooth metal, tile, smooth or hard wood, glass, porcelain, leather, or a similar material, the bloodstain will keep its original form. On the contrary, if the material is porous, such as, for instance, cotton, wool, blotting paper, hairs, porous bricks, soft wood, etc., the original form will be altered by absorption of the blood into the material.

No bloodstain is so characteristic that it can have originated in only one way. Wide experience is needed to draw correct conclusions. The position and shape of the stains are to be carefully recorded by photographs and sketches.

The shape of bloodstains on the clothing is also important, since it affords a means of testing the explanations of the defendant as to the presence of the stains on his clothing. When, for instance, a defendant claims that the presence of blood sprinkles on his clothing is due to the fact that he has touched such clothing with bloody hands, it can immediately be concluded that he is lying.

In Chapter XVI we deal with the search for bloodstains and how carefully the weapons, clothing, and body of the murderer must be searched for very minute traces. It should be added that an important part of the clothing to be searched is the opening of the trousers, because the murderer will often urinate involuntarily after the crime.

PROBLEMS OF LOCKED DOORS

Formerly if a door was found locked from the inside, this was looked upon as a certain sign that no one had left the room by the door. Many times in investigations detectives have looked upon this sign as infallible, and if no special circumstances suggested homicide, the result of the investigation was inevitably a concluson of suicide. A door with a common lock, however, is easily locked from the outside after leaving the key on the inside. Locksmiths, professional criminals, and trained amateurs can pick many patented locks from the outside and, by leaving the pick in the lock, can relock the door after leaving. However, careful examination of the lock will disclose small loose particles of metal filings as a result of the lock-picking. Unusual scratches will also be found on the tumblers. Traces of carbon within the lock indicate that the perpetrator of the act tried carbonized blank keys to enable him to file the blank to fit the tumblers. Thus his own key might have been used to enter and leave.

On doors with common locks the criminal will use one of two methods to lock the door from the outside after leaving the key on the inside. He will either use a tool known to international hotel thieves by the French slang name *ouistiti* or a simple device consisting of a string and a small piece of wood.

The *ouistiti* may change in form, but in principle it is always the same. A pair of thin semilunar tongs, rifled to prevent sliding, is inserted into the lock, and the tip of the key is grasped and turned in any direction. In order to determine if the *ouistiti* has been used a careful examination of the key is necessary. In many cases the rifling of the tongs will leave marks on the key which can be seen without difficulty by slight enlargement.

The other device, consisting of string and a piece of wood, requires more time for its application; but it has the advantage that the needed materials can almost always be found on the scene. A small piece of wood, a short lead pencil, a match, or some similar object is inserted in the handle of the key. A loop of the string is fastened loosely around the object used, and the two long ends of the loop are then carried along the line of closure of the door to the outside. The object is kept in its place by carefully pulling on the string. The door is now closed, and by further pulling the key is made to turn. The string is completely pulled away from the outside, and the object falls on the floor on the inside of the room, where it will in most cases attract the attention of the expert. In any event the door should always be examined very carefully for string marks in the paint.

In addition to the methods discussed above, which were first described by the Germans Nelken and Jeserich,[8] there are many other techniques of surreptitious entry and departure which leave meager traces and are ordinarily detected only by investigators with some knowledge of the methods of by-passing locks. The chain lock, for example, which most householders consider trustworthy, is readily by-passed through a simple expedient involving only a thumbtack, rubber band, and pencil. Descriptions of these techniques can be found in literature privately circulated among locksmiths but available to investigators.

In conclusion it must be stressed that it is always necessary to examine the door and lock very carefully in cases where the theory of suicide is based to a great extent on the fact that the door was locked from the inside.

INVESTIGATIONS OF SPECIAL CASES

HIT-AND-RUN ACCIDENTS

Vehicular homicide is by far the most common form of violent death. In the United States over 40,000 persons are killed each year. In some of these deaths criminal negligence is a factor. Although all vehicular homicides are of interest to the police, there is a special interest—as well as special and severe sanctions—attached to the hit-and-run (or hit-skip) homicide, the accident in which the driver, whether through fear, folly, or calculated self-interest, leaves the scene without identifying himself. From the testimony of witnesses and the physical evidence in the area of the collision, the investigator tries to identify and locate the vehicle, and eventually its driver.

Initial procedure

A fairly standard procedure for accident investigation is followed in the beginning:

1. Proceed promptly to the scene.
2. Care for the injured and summon medical assistance.
3. Isolate the accident scene to the extent necessary.
4. Maintain guard until the scene has been photographed and searched.
5. Safeguard property.
6. Establish traffic control.
7. Identify witnesses.
8. Obtain statements.
9. Photograph the scene.

Immediate action

A basic step in most investigations is the verification of reported facts and the identity of the person reporting. The following information should be acquired and checked as early as possible:

1. *Verifying facts to determine the nature of the accident:*

   a. The accident may not be a hit-and-run but may be being reported as such for other reasons. Thus, the person, witness, or victim alleging the hit-and-run should be questioned carefully, and his statements should be checked for consistency with information given by others or derived from the physical evidence.
   b. The motor vehicle operator may have given all the necessary aid and information at the scene and still be accused of "leaving the scene" by an excited witness or distraught victim.
   c. In questioning witnesses and victims to verify facts, the investigator should use a discreet approach until he detects positive evidence of misrepresentation of facts. Allowance must be made for some inaccuracies in the statements of an excited witness.

2. *Identifying the vehicle:*

   A description of the wanted vehicle and its operator should be obtained as quickly as possible:
   a. Make of vehicle: Ford, Cadillac, Jaguar, and so forth.
   b. Type: four-door sedan, station wagon, or convertible coupe.
   c. Color: maroon body and white top.
   d. License plate.
   e. Special features: ornaments, statuettes, antenna, decals, or permits.
   f. Special defects: defective lights in front or rear, missing parts, damage or markings existing prior to the collision.
   g. Collision damage: broken fenders, lights, or other damage acquired in the accident.
   h. Occupants of vehicles: number and appearance.
   i. Direction of travel and location where last seen.

Gathering evidence

The information sought by the investigator can be related to five major objectives: to identify the driver; to locate the vehicle and driver; to determine the manner in which the accident took place; to acquire evidence of the fact of the collision; and to acquire evidence of any criminal negligence. The sources of this information are: the witness; the physical evidence at the scene; marks on the victim or his car; and marks or signs of damage on the suspect car.

1. *Witnesses:*

First the eyewitnesses should be sought out; then persons whose attention was called to the scene by the sound of the collision or the ensuing cries. Persons at some distance from the scene may have observed the fleeing vehicle. Residents of the neighborhood, especially those in buildings with floors above street level, may have witnessed the accident. Injured persons, of course, should be questioned. Finally, an effort should be made to determine whether a car of the description given has been seen in the neighborhood or is known to pass through the area at the time in question.

Witnesses should be completely identified and questioned as soon as possible. Interviewing each witness separately is desirable. In this way the witness is made to feel that his statements and observations are being given the attention he feels they deserve. As a consequence, he is more likely to give full cooperation if his testimony is needed later. Separating the witnesses, moreover, will provide a truer picture of what each witness observed.

2. *Recording the scene*

Measuring, sketching, and photographing the scene are of great importance in a motor vehicle homicide, especially where more than one vehicle is involved. The exact position and orientation of each vehicle and victim should be meticulously recorded, as well as the location of small articles of physical evidence such as pieces of metal and glass, and accumulations of dirt.

a. Sketching the accident scene will usually require two drawings— one of the immediate scene of the accident and one of the overall scene, on a different scale, to show the approaches to the scene and the course of the vehicle after impact. In addition to the objects previously mentioned, the sketch should show the skid marks, obstructions to driver's vision, vehicles parked at the scene, objects bearing signs of collision, and other elements of the scene that have significance in the case. The sketch should indicate only those objects present at the scene after the collision.

If it is desired to show, as part of expert testimony, a reconstructed version of the accident, a separate sketch should be used. In this drawing the probable path of the vehicle would be drawn with consecutive arrows. Other vehicles traveling through the scene at the time would also be indicated in accordance with available testimony. This sketch, however, is the hypothetical version of the accident—it is the expert's opinion or, rather, a training aid with which the expert can illustrate his testimony. Other training aids are available for this purpose, such as boards on which the elements of the scene in miniature can be laid out to illustrate the testimony of witnesses.

b. Photographs should be taken as soon as possible after the accident, so that obstructions, such as parked cars, will still be in place. If it is necessary to take additional photographs at a later date, it is well to photograph under similar traffic and weather conditions. One or more of the following views will be found useful:

Overall views of the scene from the direction of each vehicle.

Overall view from a sufficiently high point of view to show clearly all elements of the scene.

Photos taken with the camera at the level of the driver's eye and from the distance at which the driver would have become aware of the danger situation. The view of a pedestrian victim should also be used.

Medium-distance views to show the immediate area of the collision.

Close-up views of significant objects of evidence found at the scene—headlight glass or car ornaments, for example.

Overall views of each set of skid marks. A polarizing filter may be helpful here.

Examination of the vehicle

The search for clues on a vehicle should follow a definite procedure to insure thoroughness in the examination. The car should be examined piecewise as indicated in the illustration (Figure 129). The techniques applied will vary with circumstances. If the identity of the owner, operator, or occupants of the car is a matter of investigative interest, the car should also be processed for latent fingerprints.

In a hit-and-run case the search should concentrate on evidence of contact with the victim (or the victim's car), evidence of a recent accident, or indications of collision or contact with objects at the scene of the accident. Clues of possible value include fragments of clothing, hair, blood, tissue, marks in paint, paint from the victim's vehicle, dust or grease, impressions of fabric, marks made by the victim's clothing or vehicle.

In examining the victim's vehicle, the exterior surface is of primary importance. Paint streaks and other marks which could have been made by the hit-and-run vehicle should be carefully noted.

1. *Exterior surfaces*

   a. Examine and check each portion in the following order:
     Front; left side; right side; rear; top; and underneath.

   b. Check the following:
     License plates. Were securing bolts and nuts recently replaced? Is license data the same as reported by victim or witnesses?
     Engine or radiator. Warm?
     Grillwork, radiator ornament, and radiator (core and shell). Breaks? Fractures? Bent parts? Parts missing? Adhering foreign substances, such as fabric or blood?
     Tires. Evidence of recent skidding? Bent rims? Note location. Record make and tread pattern of each tire, noting location: right front, left front, etc.
     Door handles, bumpers and bumper guards, hinges, and other protruding parts. Adhering foreign substances, such as fabric or blood?
     Windshield, left and right windows, hood, left and right fenders, and running boards. Fabric or fiber impressions?
     Headlights, foglights, stoplights, spotlights, parking lights, turn or signaling lights. Working properly? Bright or dim? Broken lenses? Recover and retain all broken particles of glass found. Keep separated as to sources.
     Light rims. Bent? Recently replaced?
     Grease fittings, crankcase pan, axle housing, differential, spring shackles and bolts, and steering assembly. Fabric abrasion marks? Pieces of fabric or fiber? Blood?
     Color of paint. Solid or two-tone? In taking standards for comparison, remove paint flakes to base metal, including primer coat.

2. *Interior surfaces*

   a. Record motor and body numbers, make, year, and model.
   b. Take odometer mileage totals. Was speedometer operating?
   c. Note whether foot and emergency brakes were operating. Note condition.
   d. Note whether gas gauge was operating. Check contents of gas tank.
   e. Note whether horn was operating.
   f. Check recent servicing stickers (lubrication or oil change). Note date and mileage recorded on the stickers.
   g. Check evidence of ownership, registration, or insurance that may be attached to some interior part of the vehicle or may be in an interior compartment.

Evidence at the scene

A planned and orderly search of the scene should be made to collect any physical evidence which can aid in identifying the wanted vehicle or in reconstructing the manner in which the collision took place. Ordi-

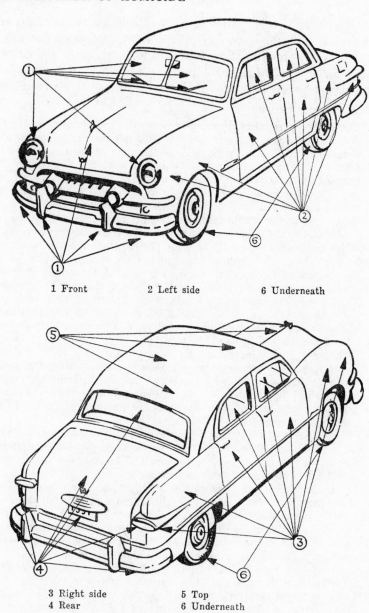

1 Front   2 Left side   6 Underneath

3 Right side   5 Top
4 Rear   6 Underneath

Figure 129.   Order of searching a hit-and-run car.

narily the search is begun with the point of collision as the center and branches out until the immediate area is entirely covered. The search should then be continued along logical paths indicated by the circumstances of the accident. Perishable evidence, such as tire marks and stains, should be given attention first. The following are the most common types of evidence:

1. Tire marks, particularly impressions in mud, dirt, tar, or snow. In addition to photographing and measuring the impression, the investigator should request that a cast be made of the more characteristic sections. Occasionally the direction of travel of the vehicle is not certain. An examination of a soft-surface road will show the direction, since the soil is lifted stepwise in the direction of travel of the wheel. To even the track we would have to visualize the car backing up.

2. Skid marks are helpful in reconstructing the manner in which the accident took place. On hard surfaces the skid mark indicates the point at which the brakes were fully applied. The length of the skid mark can be used to determine a minimum value of the speed of the vehicle at the moment of full application of the brakes.[9] A theoretical computation can be made if the coefficient of friction of the surface is known. More commonly, comparison marks of approximately the same length are made with the suspect's vehicle, if it is operable. An instrument such as the decelerometer can also be used for this purpose. Naturally the brakes of each vehicle should be tested.

3. Dirt may be shaken loose from the fenders by the force of the collision. Characteristic soil present in these loosened masses sometimes provides a clue to the neighborhood of origin of the vehicle. Impacted masses which fall to the ground without crumbling should be preserved intact, since their contour will correspond to the outlines of the space left underneath the fender.

4. Chipped flakes of paint should also be preserved without breaking, for the same reason. Paint is especially useful since it provides a tracing clue to the car and can later be compared microscopically and spectrographically with samples from a suspect car.

5. Broken equipment and fragments of headlight glass are valuable pieces of evidence both for tracing the vehicle and associating it definitely with the scene of the collision. A broken door handle or radiator emblem will provide a clue to the make and year of the car. Although headlight glass has lost much of its identifying value with the widespread adoption of the sealed beam unit, there has been a tendency in recent years toward the use of characteristic headlight shapes. Parking lights and rear lights on the newer cars vary widely in shape and size. The glass fragments should be pieced together if possible. In any event, all fragments of glass should be preserved for later comparison with pieces found on a suspect car. Even though the evidence fragments cannot be shown to match the pieces found on the suspect vehicle on

the basis of shape or outline, the composition of both samples can be compared by physical and spectrochemical methods.

6. Blood, tissue, and hair should be preserved. In particular their exact location and their relation to other evidence at the scene should be recorded as an aid to reconstructing the manner in which the accident took place.

Marks on the victim

1. *Glass.* If a headlight was broken as a result of the collision, pieces of glass may be found on the victim's clothing or embedded in his skin. The glass pieces, including even slivers, should be preserved for possible comparison with broken glass from a suspect vehicle.

2. *Grillwork or radiator.* The pattern of the grillwork or radiator may sometimes leave clear marks on the victim. As the grillwork and radiator are characteristic of particular makes, these marks constitute a good clue in the search for the missing vehicle and are valuable for comparison purposes. The nature of the victim's clothing will affect the clarity of the marks; the examination for these traces, however, should extend to the body itself, where marks that were but faintly discernible on the clothing may be observed clearly impressed on the skin. These marks should be photographed to scale.

3. *Tire marks.* The tire patterns may leave distinctive marks on the clothing. As in the case of radiator marks, it may be found that the impressions are even clearer on the skin surface. Again, the marks should be photographed to scale as soon as possible. Some difficulty may be encountered in the interpretation of tire marks on clothing. The grabbing action of the wheel may fold a shirt, for example, on itself so that it is necessary to study the tire mark in relation to the manner in which the clothing was pulled and folded by the wheel before any reliance can be placed on measurements of the width and other aspects of the tire pattern.

4. *Grease.* If the understructure of the vehicle passed over the victim, a sample of grease may be obtained from the clothing.

5. *Paint.* Ornaments, buckles, buttons, and other hard surfaces on the clothing may have retained traces of paint from the vehicle.

RAILROAD ACCIDENTS

In railroad accidents where strong forces of nature such as fire, water, steam, etc., play a role many valuable traces and clues will be destroyed during or after the catastrophe.[10] A derailed rapidly moving locomotive, for example, will destroy everything in its path. The cause of the derailment does not have to be negligence on the part of the railroad employees; in many cases it is purely an accident. It is very difficult, however, to determine if the accident is the result of criminal intention, negligence, or otherwise, because of the scarcity of evidence. The investigator must then possess the ability to draw conclusions from the scanty clues at his disposal. His sources of information should be the employees of the division in question, the train crew, the trackwalkers, and foremen, as well as other employees of the railroad company. Since the search for traces is hindered by the necessity of clearing the line as soon as possible, the investigator must be able to gather all traces and clues in a very short time.

Fairly long distances surrounding the tracks on both sides of the scene should be examined. The position of the switches at the critical moment should be ascertained, as well as the position of the steam regulator, the slide regulator, the brake handles, etc., on the locomotive.

Furthermore, several other questions are to be answered: How many cars were derailed? On which side did the derailment occur? Are the derailed cars upright or overturned? Were the wheels worn out? Who are the dead or injured? Were prominent persons on the train? Was a robbery committed, either of the train or persons on it? What is the condition of the roadbed?

In the examination of the roadbed only actual damages are described. Damages may also result from the derailment. When examining the condition of the roadbed, it is advisable to mark the different sleepers with crayon. If tools used to derail the train are found, they should not be touched before examination by an expert. The broken stone of the roadbed is examined as to displacements. The displacements may be shown by the fact that the blackened upper surface is turned downward. Footprints may be found on the slope of the roadbed in the broken stone or in the grass. A criminal may also leave other traces. He may, for instance, lose or throw away things. It has often been proved that too little attention is paid to the necessity of searching all terrain within the range of vision. In many cases the criminal will encamp a hundred yards or more away from the tracks in order to view them before and after the accident has taken place. Here he may leave pieces of paper, wrappings, cigarette packages, etc. Fingerprints and other traces may be found on any of these articles.

During the examination of the scene, the position of all objects should be noted and marked on the sketch. It is never known what role they may play later. The position of articles found on the roadbed and scratches on the rails should also be noted. Photographs of the scene and its surroundings should be made.

If an obstacle was caught by the train and dragged along, it should be ascertained, if possible, where it was first caught.

ABORTION AND INFANTICIDE

Investigations of abortion and infanticide often arise in detective work. Abortion is by far the more common of the two, even though it seldom comes to the attention of the police.

The investigation of abortion can be divided into two categories. The first embraces the cases in which women are suspected of having provoked abortion with their own hands or with the aid of a second party. Direct evidence is represented only by the remaining portion of poisons which may have been used, injuries on the miscarried embryo, or injuries on the woman's genitals. In most cases there is only circumstantial proof. One of the strongest signs of abortion is high fever in relation to a miscarriage. In many cases, however, the fever will drop immediately after the expulsion of the infected egg, so that the physician who later examines the woman is unable to detect any rise of temperature. High temperature and chills before and during the miscarriage constitute a very important sign of abortion. Another proof is the possession of a sound, or probe. It should be pointed out that a soft catheter may be made rigid by the introduction of iron wire in its cavity.

The second category embraces the cases where professional abortionists are concerned. Here only direct confession by the woman on whom the abortion has been performed is of any value.

Naturally all the investigations and examinations above described should be made in close collaboration with the proper medical authority, such as the medical examiner or the coroner.

In infanticides the mother will almost always try to get rid of the dead infant by throwing it away in a sewer, river, forest, etc. The remains and especially the wrappings should be carefully examined as to fingerprints on the paper, laundry marks on lingerie, etc.

Before any conclusions are formed concerning the cause of death, the findings of the autopsy surgeon and the results of the pathological examination must be considered. The information of the autopsy surgeon will bear on a number of important aspects of the offense. The question of viability should be answered by his examination: was the baby likely to live had normal care been provided? A viable infant is one that fulfills the criteria of normal formation and a gestation period of at least seven months in the uterus. The birth must, of course, have been a live birth, a matter which the autopsy surgeon determines by examining the lungs to see if the baby had breathed. Finally, the surgeon can discover the cause of death and determine whether the infant died of natural causes, accidental birth injuries, or criminal violence. Accidental smothering and nonbacterial food poisoning are possibilities to be considered in the deaths of children under two years of age. Smothering by accident, however, is unusual if the child is more than three weeks old.

In recent years many women have died from abortions. Their deaths caused relatives to complain to police. Excellent investigation and interrogation of boy friends revealed the location and operation of "abortion mills" conducted by a group of one or two doctors and a few nurses or midwives. Generally the doctors were unlicensed, or, if licensed, at the bottom of their profession in competence. Unsanitary, vile conditions and poor medical practice caused the deaths. The detective must apprehend these individuals when actually in operation, getting pre- and postoperative patients to confess and identify the malefactors.

1 Tage–Jensen.
2 The importance of instructing patrolmen in the elements of police science and criminal investigation so that they may avoid the destruction of traces cannot be overemphasized.
3 See Rehfeldt and Kippel.
4 Gettler and Moritz.
5 Smith.[6]
6 Smith–Glaister and Von Neureiter–Pietrusky–Schütt.
7 See also Jeserich, where the shape of bloodstains is fully described.
8 Jeserich.
9 U. S. Army Tech. Bull., PMG 18.
10 The engineer in many cases is killed. Should he escape, experience shows that often he is in such a mental state that no accurate information can be obtained for a considerable time.

XIX ELEMENTS OF TOXICOLOGY[1]

TOXICOLOGY IS THE SCIENCE OF POISONS. IT IS NOT AN EASY MATTER to define a poison in specific words, for almost any substance exerts deleterious effects upon the body when taken in a sufficiently large amount. Perhaps the best definition is that given by Taylor in 1865, which runs as follows: "A poison is a substance which, when taken into the mouth or stomach, or when absorbed into the blood, is capable of seriously affecting the health or of destroying life by its action on the tissues with which it immediately, or after absorption, comes in contact."

For legal purposes, however, the definition of a poison is unimportant, as the wording of most law statutes dealing with poisoning is so broad that a criminal cannot escape on the ground that the substance taken was not a poison.

TYPES OF POISONING

ACUTE POISONING. Acute poisoning is produced by taking an excessive single dose of poison. This is most often the case in suicidal poisoning. Several smaller doses, when taken with such frequency as to result in sudden illness, coma, or unconsciousness, may also produce an acute poisoning.

CHRONIC POISONING. Chronic poisoning is caused by taking small doses of poison over a long period of time, resulting in gradual but progressive deterioration of body functions. Poisoning by arsenic, for example, is usually of a chronic nature.

CUMULATIVE POISONING. Cumulative poisoning is caused by the sudden increase in intensity of the action following slow additions of the poison. Some of the cardiac glucosides, e.g., digitalis, are typical cumulative poisons.

ACTION OF POISONS

The modes of action of poisons may be classed as follows:

LOCAL ACTIONS. These are poisons such as the strong mineral acids, which only injure or destroy the tissues with which they come directly in contact.

REMOTE ACTION. Poisons which act only after they have been absorbed into the blood, e.g., morphine, carbon monoxide, etc.

LOCAL AND REMOTE ACTIONS. Poisons which affect the tissues they come into contact with and have a further action after absorption, e.g., arsenic.

CONDITIONS MODIFYING THE ACTION
OF POISONS

Certain conditions which have great influence on the effect of poisons include the following:

DOSE. The larger the dose, the more rapid and certain is the action as a general rule. Furthermore, a large dose may produce shock symptoms before the appearance of the typical symptoms.

The amount of poison known to induce poisoning to such a degree that death results is called the fatal or lethal dose. This term should be distinguished from the toxic dose, which merely causes symptoms of poisoning.

METHOD OF ADMINISTRATION. Symptoms of poisoning usually appear most rapidly when the poisons are administered directly into the blood by injections. Poisons taken into the mouth generally act more slowly, as they have to be absorbed from the stomach or small intestine. Poisons may also be introduced into the rectum or vagina. The absorption from these organs is relatively slow, however. Gaseous or volatile poisons, for example, carbon monoxide, hydrocyanic acid, and chloroform, which are inhaled through the lungs, are rapidly taken up by the blood. Poisons placed on, or rubbed into, the unbroken skin are but slowly absorbed.

HABIT AND TOLERANCE. Many poisons when constantly taken tend to lose their effects, and large doses have to be given to produce the actions desired. Such tolerance is seen in drug addicts (morphine, cocaine, etc.)

IDIOSYNCRASY. Idiosyncrasy may be defined as an individual hypersensitivity to the action of a poison.

AGE. As a rule children are more susceptible to poisons than adults.

DISEASE. Pathological conditions in the body have a marked influence on the action of poisons. As a general rule a poison is more likely to produce serious effects in a person weakened by disease than in one in good health.

SYMPTOMS OF POISONING

General symptoms and signs are of value in cases of suspected poisoning. Certain diseases, however, will produce the same signs.

Symptoms	Poisons	Diseases
Vomiting	Arsenic, antimony, acids, alkalies, copper, iodine, mercury, phosphorus, alcohols, sulfonamides, and others.	Gastrointestinal disorders, uremia, brain tumor, and many infectious diseases.
Convulsions	Brucine, strychnine, nicotine camphor, cyanides, carbon monoxide, and others.	Tetanus, epilepsy, eclampsia, uremia, meningitis, and other acute cerebrospinal affections.
Coma	Barbiturates, opium derivatives, chloral hydrate, chloroform, alcohol, cyanides, CO, CO_2, atropine, scopolamine.	Cerebrovascular accidents, brain diseases and injuries, diseases listed above for "Convulsions."
Contracted pupils	Opium derivatives, physostigmine, pilocarpine, muscarine.	Diseases of the central nervous system, e.g., tabes dorsalis.
Dilated pupils	Belladonna and its derivatives, barbiturates, amphetamine, cocaine, scopolamine, nicotine.	Epilepsy, glaucoma, fear.
Paralysis	Cyanides, CO, CO_2, arsenic lead, and barium.	Stroke, brain tumor, botulism, and meningitis.
Cyanosis	Cyanides, opium derivatives, aniline, acetanilide, nitro-benzene.	Cardiac and respiratory diseases.
Rapid breathing	Atropine, cocaine, CO_2, strychnine, amphetamine.	Respiratory diseases, anemia, and hysteria.
Slow breathing	Opium derivatives, hypnotics, CO, cyanides.	Uremia, brain compression.

DIAGNOSIS OF POISONING

Suspicion of poisoning arises if a person who has been in apparent good health suddenly manifests marked pathological symptoms which rapidly become intensified and result in death. This suspicion becomes strengthened if the symptoms appear a short time after the person has taken some food or drink which has a strange odor, taste, or appearance.

The first important step in the investigation of a suspected fatal poisoning is a thorough examination of the location where the body was found. An intensive search should be made for containers from which the poison may have been taken, such as cups, plates, medicinal bottles, etc. Any remaining drink or food should also be confiscated and subjected to analysis.

HISTORY. An accurate history of the case should be obtained from relatives or friends. A written record of all observations should be made at once.

SYMPTOMS. A record of the symptoms and signs associated with any particular poisoning case is of great aid to the analyst in making the toxicological examination. Preliminary information concerning the symptoms may be of help in excluding or taking into account large groups of poisons which might or might not be present.

POST-MORTEM EXAMINATION (AUTOPSY). Post-mortem examination of the dead body should be made to establish the previous diagnosis made on the case. A thorough autopsy and histological examination would eliminate the chance of mistaking natural diseases for poisoning. The post-mortem appearances are sometimes characteristic of poisoning. For example, poisons like the strong acids and alkalies and irritant poisons such as arsenic and mercury leave fairly typical signs. In every case, however, the presence of the substance should be proved by a toxicological analysis. Therefore, following the autopsy, specimens should always be taken for analysis.

TOXICOLOGICAL ANALYSIS.[2] A careful toxicological analysis should be made of the organs and excretions of the body in order to determine the presence or absence of any poisonous agent.

The methods employed in tracing the cause of poisoning and in determining the nature and quantity of the poison involved may be divided into four classes:

1. *Physical methods.* Various optical instruments such as the spectrograph and the infrared and ultraviolet spectrophotometer are employed in the detection and estimation of poisons.

2. *Microscopic methods.* Small solid particles of the poison may be recognized among the debris of food, etc., by a microscopic examination. If fragments of leaves or seeds are found, an endeavor should be made to identify them.

3. *Biological methods.*[3] These methods are of importance because of their great sensitivity. Biological tests are in constant use, in addition to chemical tests, as corroborative evidence of the presence of poison. For example, it is usual in strychnine poisoning to inject a small quantity of the substance into a white mouse and observe the typical convulsions.

The biological tests can be made generally with substances less pure than those required for chemical tests.

4. *Chemical methods.* The examination by the toxicologist consists chiefly of chemical analysis of the organs, excretions, or tissues. Poisons are chemical compounds and thus exhibit characteristic properties on the basis of which they can be isolated, purified, and identified.

All material confiscated at the location of a poisoning or preserved at the autopsy should be packed in clean containers covered with glass. Intestinal contents, stomach contents, brain, liver, blood, urine, hair, etc., should be placed in separate containers. All specimen containers should be sealed in a safe manner because of the possibility of wilful and malicious tampering. Even during post-mortem examinations, attempts have been made to interfere with specimens intended for toxicological analysis.

In instances where a person is found dead under obscure circumstances and the autopsy discloses no significant gross or microscopic changes and no typical symptoms point to a certain poison, the toxicologist must have ample material with which to perform the large number of analyses that may be required. Therefore it is always wise to preserve too much material at an autopsy rather than too little. S. Kaye[4] has suggested the following guide for the collection of material best suited for toxicological analysis.

Specimen	Minimum amount	Poison for which best suited
Urine	All available	In nearly all types of poisoning
Stomach contents	All available	For cases in which poison is known or thought to have been taken by mouth within a few hours
Intestinal contents	All available	For cases in which poison was taken by mouth within one or two days
Blood	At least 10 cc (preferably 200 cc)	All gas poisons, sulfonamides, bromides, and many other poisons
Brain	500 grams	Volatile poisons, barbiturates, alkaloids, and acute alcoholism
Liver	300 grams	Metals, barbiturates, fluorides, oxalate, and many other poisons
Kidney	1 kidney	Metals, especially mercury, and sulfonamides
Bone	200 grams	Lead, arsenic, etc.
Lung	1 lung	For inhaled poisons (proof of entry)

Specimen	Minimum amount	Poison for which best suited
Hair and nails	5 grams	Chronic arsenic poisoning
Muscle	200 grams	In most acute poisonings and when internal organs are badly putrefied

SOME COMMON POISONS

In the following paragraphs some of the most common poisons and their actions will be briefly described.

PHOSPHORUS

Phosphorus occurs in two forms, the colorless and red varieties. The red phosphorus is not poisonous. On the other hand, the colorless phosphorus, which is among the better-known non-metallic poisons, is such a powerful poison that 0.1 gram to 0.3 gram will cause death. The symptoms of phosphorus poisoning vary. In most cases there is a burning feeling of thirst, pain in the abdomen, belching, vomiting, etc., and toward the end bleeding from the intestines, muscular twitchings, etc. The time elapsing between the ingestion of the poison and death depends on the quantity administered and on the individual resistance to its action; but death usually supervenes in from two to seven days, and in rare cases it takes place in only a few hours.

Phosphorus is decomposed relatively soon in the dead body. However, it is still possible to detect its presence there after three months—in the form of phosphoric acid. Here, as in all cases of poisoning, the composition of the soil surrounding the coffin plays a large part in determining the presence of the poison in the dead body.

Antidotes for phosphorus poisoning are stomach lavages and sulfate of copper, 1 gram in 500 cc of water. The administering of milk and fatty foods should be avoided, as the phosphorus will be dissolved and the condition aggravated.

METALLIC POISONS

ARSENIC. Normally traces of arsenic are found in the urine, milk, menstrual blood, nails, skin, etc. This fact must be considered when examining a dead body if poisoning is suspected. Quantities of arsenic less than 0.02 mg in 100 grams of tissue may be regarded as originating from the body itself.

The symptoms of arsenic poisoning as a rule do not appear immediately but usually after half an hour or an hour. The person poisoned has a burning sensation in the throat, vomits substances which are either colorless or have the color of the arsenic preparation, and complains of acute pains in the abdomen, accompanied by diarrhea. This last, however, may not occur in very severe arsenic poisoning. The urine is bloody and diminished in quantity, and the agony is extreme. Death almost always occurs during the first twenty-four hours. When large quantities of arsenic have been administered, death, preceded by vomiting, may follow within a few hours.

Arsenic has always played an important role in the history of poisonings because of its odorless and almost tasteless qualities. Chronic arsenic poisoning is not uncommon in certain metallurgical plants and in glass factories. Some horse dealers feed arsenic to horses in order to improve their appearance. Arsenic is also an ingredient of many medicinal preparations for anemia and nervousness. The lethal dose varies from 0.1 gram to 0.5 gram.

It is very important to determine in what part of the body the arsenic is to be found; the organs to be examined are therefore divided into three categories. The first consists of the stomach and its contents; the second, of the intestines; and the third of the liver, the kidneys, the spleen, the lungs, and the heart. In arsenic poisoning the examination of the hair, nails, and skin may be important, because they may also contain arsenic. In analysis of the hair for its arsenic content some analysts claim that it is sometimes possible to fix the time of administration of the poison,[5] although others claim that it is only possible to determine by this analysis whether it is a chronic or an acute case.

The separate examination of the different organs of the body will show whether the whole system was impregnated with arsenic, as in chronic poisonings resulting from excessive and prolonged use of medicines, such as subcutaneous injections of arsenical preparations, etc., or whether the greatest amount of the arsenic was in the stomach and intentines. This latter fact indicates that death resulted from the oral ingestion of the poison.

Arsenic remains in the body unbelievably long after death; its presence may be determined several years after burial. It has even been possible to show the presence of arsenic in the ashes of cremated bodies.

In exhuming for the purpose of determining the presence of arsenic, the soil around the body should always be analyzed; also all objects in the coffin or in its surroundings which may contain arsenic, such as artificial flowers, paint on the coffin, etc. When large quantities of arsenic are present in the body, some of the arsenic may, during the process of putrefaction, reach the soil under the coffin. The soil around the coffin must therefore be tested in different places.

ANTIMONY. Antimony salts have sometimes been used in poisonings, especially in the form of tartar emetic (tartrate of antimony and potassium). The poisonous actions consist of its local effects on the gastrointestinal tract, with further toxic effects on the kidneys, liver, and central nervous system.

Acute and chronic poisoning by antimony salts is characterized by symptoms similar to the toxic actions of arsenic. The fatal dose of tartar emetic is usually 0.5 gram to 1 gram, but survival may follow upon the taking of much larger doses if the vomiting starts early, as is likely with the emetic.

The stomach and its content and the liver are satisfactory for toxicological analysis.

LEAD. Nowadays lead salts are very seldom used for criminal purposes. In medieval times, however, they were commonly used in homicides.

Lead acetate is the most common salt to produce poisoning when taken by mouth. The symptoms of acute poisoning are metallic taste, dry throat, cramps, persistent vomiting, and diarrhea. The feces are bloody and dark, due to the lead sulfide. The urine is scant, and cramps in the legs are common. Death may follow in a day or two. If the person survives, a blue line may develop on the gums and signs of anemia, epileptiform convulsions, and paralysis appear.

The fatal dose varies from 10 to 20 grams. For toxicological analysis the stomach contents, feces, urine, liver, kidneys, and bones are most important.

Chronic poisoning by lead compounds is of great importance owing to its industrial incidence.

MERCURY. Two forms of salts, the mercuric and the mercurous, exist; and as the former are more soluble they are the more poisonous. Mercuric chloride (corrosive sublimate) is by far the commonest mercurial poison and is often used in suicides and homicides.

The symptoms of acute poisoning are metallic taste, violent purging, thirst, soreness in the throat, nausea, and diarrhea, with bloodstained stools. Death may occur within an hour from shock, or the person may die of toxemia after several days. In the latter case profound salivation develops on the second or third day, the gums become swollen and inflamed, and the breath foul. A kidney lesion soon becomes pronounced, and suppression of urine follows. Collapse and death usually result.

The fatal dose of mercuric chloride is 0.1 gram to 0.5 gram. The best materials for toxicological analysis are urine, stools, kidney, liver, etc.

STRONG ACIDS AND ALKALINE (CORROSIVE POISONS)

The mineral acids, such as sulfuric acid (H_2SO_4), nitric acid (HNO_3), and hydrochloric acid (HCI), and the caustic alkalies, such as potassium hydroxide (KOH) and sodium hydroxide (NaOH), have been used both for criminal and suicidal purposes.

The symptoms of poison by these agents are corrosion or destruction of the parts touched by the poison, intense burning pain in the mouth, throat, and stomach, vomiting of threads of mucous membrane and bloody matter, difficulty in swallowing, lividity of face, and shock.

On the skin sulfuric acid gives a brown color; hydrochloric acid, a grayish-white; and nitric acid, a bright-yellow color.

The fatal dose of the mineral acids varies between 5 and 10 cc.

GASEOUS POISONS

CARBON MONOXIDE. Carbon monoxide (CO) is an inodorous and very deadly gas formed by the oxidation of carbon at high temperatures or in a limited supply of oxygen. It is a constituent of coal gas, water gas, and exhaust gas from motorcars. Carbon monoxide is by far the most important of the poisonous gases and causes more deaths than all the other poisons combined.

Most poisonings by carbon monoxide are suicidal or accidental. Homicidal poisonings occur frequently, however. The suicidal and accidental poisoning usually results from exposure to household gas or to exhaust gas from motor vehicles.

The toxic action of carbon monoxide is due to the fact that the gas unites with the hemoglobin in the blood, forming a very stable compound known as carboxyhemoglobin. This prevents the blood from performing its functions as an oxygen carrier, and death occurs from asphyxia.

The symptoms of carbon monoxide poisoning are lassitude, shortness of breath on exertion, slight headache, giddiness, nausea, dyspnœa, muscular weakness, paralysis, and coma.

Death occurs rapidly when a person is left unaided in an atmosphere containing the gas. Death in a few hours is caused by 0.25 percent of carbon monoxide in the atmosphere.

The post-mortem changes of carbon monoxide poisoning are rather characteristic. The whole body may be of a rosy-red color. Bright-red patches are often present on the breast, abdomen, and inner surfaces of the thighs. The areas of post-mortem lividity are pinkish. Internally, the striking feature is the bright cherry-red color of the blood.

In cases of carbon monoxide poisoning the presence of the poison may be detected in the blood by optical methods (spectroscopy).

HYDROCYANIC ACID. Hydrocyanic acid (HCN) is a colorless, transparent fluid with an odor of bitter almonds. It is very volatile and for this reason is placed with the gases. The most common salts of cyanogen are potassium cyanide (KCN) and sodium cyanide (NaCN), which are both very poisonous.

Poisoning by the cyanides in most cases is caused by their ingestion for suicidal purposes. Three to four percent of all suicides are thought to be caused by cyanides.

The cyanides act as cell asphyxiants, and the symptoms are characterized by sudden onset, collapse, convulsions, and deep and rapid respiration, which may be followed by death. Death may occur in a few seconds or minutes from respiratory paralysis. The symptoms usually appear more slowly in poisoning by cyanides than in poisoning by hydrocyanic acid, as the cyanides have to be split in the stomach by the gastric juice.

The fatal dose varies. A concentration of 0.2 to 0.3 percent of hydrocyanic acid per liter of air is immediately fatal. The fatal dose of potassium and sodium cyanide is 0.1 gram to 3 grams.

On autopsy the tissues of the body show a characteristic bright-red color.

ALKALOIDAL POISONS

The group of alkaloidal poisons includes many compounds present in various plants and a great number of synthetically prepared substances. In the following such poisons as morphine, heroin, cocaine, strychnine, atropine and scopolamine, which are those most often encountered in criminal investigations, will be briefly described.

OPIUM AND MORPHINE. Acute poisoning may follow oral or hypodermic administration. Opium and its derivatives are frequently employed with suicidal or homicidal intent.

The initial symptoms are those of mental stimulation, physical ease, and rapid pulse. These are followed by dizziness, suppression, perspiration, drowsiness, slow rate of respiration, with cyanosis, and pinpoint pupils. The victim becomes cold and clammy, the temperature of the body is diminished, coma supervenes, and death soon follows because of respiratory paralysis. The duration of the acute poisoning is from five to eight hours.

The fatal dose is from 0.2 gram to 0.5 gram, although drug addicts are known to have taken as many as 5 grams every twenty-four hours without fatal effects.

The post-mortem signs of opium or morphine poisoning are not characteristic, and a toxicological analysis has to be performed in a suspected case.

HEROIN. Heroin acts like morphine but differs in that it is more stimulating and depresses the cerebral centers less and the respiratory center more. Heroin is a highly addicting drug usually taken by injection in the form of a watery solution.

The toxic symptoms are headache, restlessness, cyanosis, slow respiration, coma, and finally death by respiratory paralysis.

The fatal dose is approximately 0.2 gram and the fatal period varies from a few hours to a few days.

COCAINE. Cocaine is a crystalline alkaloid found in the leaves of the coca shrub. Most cocaine poisonings follow an accidental overdose.

Acute cocaine poisoning resulting from toxic amounts of cocaine leads to a variety of symptoms such as mental confusion, delirium, heart and respiratory embarrassment, thirst, paleness, dilated pupils, headache, etc.

The fatal dose is highly individual and ranges from 0.04 gram upward. Death due to respiratory or cardiac failure may follow within a few minutes or be delayed for hours.

STRYCHNINE. Strychnine is a white, crystalline, and very bitter powder. Cases of strychnine poisoning are relatively rare; most of them are suicidal, some are accidental, and a few are homicidal.

Strychnine is quickly absorbed from the intestine, and the onset of the toxic symptoms may appear in five to fifteen minutes. The symptoms are a sense of suffocation, difficulty in breathing, and twitching of the muscles which rapidly passes into tetanic convulsions. The head jerks, the neck becomes stiff, the body is arched backward, resting on the head and the heels. The face is congested, countenance anxious, eyes staring, lips retracted and livid; jaws are clenched. There is usually an interval during which the mind is clear, then the spasms return. Convulsions recur every five to fifteen minutes, and death is due to asphyxia or exhaustion.

The fatal dose is about 0.1 gram and death usually occurs within two hours.

The post-mortem changes are not characteristic, and the poison has to be detected by a toxicological analysis. The urine, stomach contents, and liver and the most satisfactory materials for such an analysis. Strychnine is a very stable alkaloid and will remain in the dead body for a long time. Its presence may be determined months and even years after burial.

ATROPINE. Most poisonings by atropine are accidental; a few are suicidal or homicidal. Accidental poisoning very often is attributable to eating the poisonous berries of belladonna.

Atropine is fairly rapidly absorbed from the stomach. The symptoms of poisoning are dilation of the pupils, which are immobile, dryness of the mouth and throat, indistinct articulation, difficulty in swallowing, nausea, giddiness, delirium and convulsions ending in stupor and coma. The skin is flushed and dry. Death results from respiratory paralysis.

The fatal dose varies from 0.01 gram to 0.1 gram, and death usually occurs within twenty-four hours.

The post-mortem changes are not characteristic, and toxicological analysis must be performed. Atropine rapidly decomposes by putrefaction and the possibility of detection is therefore limited.

SCOPOLAMINE (HYOSCINE). Scopolamine acts like atropine, but depression of the central nervous system is more marked, giving symptoms of drowsiness and stupor. Scopolamine has sometimes been used for homicidal purposes. During recent years it has also been employed in lie detection. In the twilight sleep produced by scopolamine the criminal is interrogated and, according to certain authors, is apt to tell the truth. This method, however, is of questionable value.

MISCELLANEOUS ORGANIC POISONS

ETHYL ALCOHOL. Alcohol is widely used in beverages in many countries of the world. The different alcoholic beverages vary widely in their alcoholic content. Beer contains 3 to 6 percent; unfortified wines (claret, etc.), 10 to 17 percent; fortified wines (port, sherry, etc.), 20 percent; spirits (whisky, brandy, etc.), 45 to 50 percent. The toxic action of these beverages is due chiefly to ethyl alcohol.

Alcohol is rapidly absorbed from the stomach and small intestine and soon becomes evenly distributed throughout the body. Only a small part of the alcohol is excreted; most of it is metabolized.

Alcohol is commonly regarded as a stimulant, but careful analysis has shown that its action is a purely depressant one on the central nervous system.

The subject of alcoholic intoxication has been divided into *acute* and *chronic alcoholism.*

Acute alcoholism.[6] The symptoms of acute alcoholism vary in severity from ordinary drunkenness to acute alcoholic poisoning, depending on the individual's resistance to alcohol and the amount taken. In humans acute alcoholic intoxication is commonly divided into four stages.[7]

1. The *first stage* of intoxication is the only stage in which the person feels pleased with himself and is characterized by a temporary release of the inhibitory influence. The person's behavior becomes more spontaneous, more childish, and less critical. Self-confidence may be temporarily increased. Logical thought is difficult, and reflexes are slower and weaker.

2. In the *second stage* of intoxication the novice loses all self-control and the experienced drunkard consciously pulls himself together and speaks and moves with exaggerated care.

3. In the *third stage* the subject is dead drunk and unconscious, with flushed face, active sweat glands, red eyes, and dilated pupils.

4. In the *fourth stage* he is' in danger of death from paralysis of the respiratory and vasomotor centers in the medulla. He passes into a coma; his skin is cold and clammy. The limbs are flaccid, and muscular twitchings are common. It is not uncommon to meet cases where the individual passes into a coma without any of the preceding stages of intoxication being noticed. This is usually the case when large quantities are consumed within a short period, especially when the stomach is empty.

To aid the memory, these four stages are sometimes called dizzy and delightful, drunk and disorderly, dead drunk, and danger of death. The corresponding concentrations of alcohol in the blood are, very roughly, 0.1, 0.2, 0.3, and 0.4 percent.

In the course of a criminal investigation it is often important to find out whether or not a person was under the influence of alcoholic intoxication. When a motor accident has occurred, it is often necessary to decide legally whether the driver was drunk or not. Clinical tests are easy to apply, but they fail to detect minor degrees of intoxication which may still have interfered with the person's behavior. Also the results of such tests depend on the man who makes them. Besides, it is not always easy to distinguish the effect of alcohol from those of barbiturates, carbon monoxide, and head injuries. A competent chemical estimation of the concentration of alcohol actually present in the blood or urine can be made, however, when clinical tests show nothing. (This statement is only true regarding the quantity of alcohol consumed; it is not true in regard to the alcohol content of the brain.) The difficulty with chemical tests lies in the interpretation of the results; owing to human variation, a concentration of alcohol which has no obvious action on one man will produce an obvious intoxication in another. Nevertheless, chemical tests for alcohol play an important part in criminal investigation.

Figure 130.   FBI technician determining the amount of alcohol in blood.

In cases of homicide it is often of importance to know if the deceased was intoxicated at the time of his death and if the intoxication might have been a contributory factor in the fatal issue. If an autopsy is performed, specimens of blood, urine, and tissues should always be obtained for chemical analysis.

The blood alcohol in states of drunkenness is usually between 0.2 and 0.4 percent, and a proportion over this is likely to be associated with complete stupor. Under 0.1 percent is seldom associated with more than emotional instability. Widmark[8] has shown that the blood alcohol level is related to the amount taken on a fairly straight line, subject only to the conditions affecting the rapidity of absorption and other less important factors. The urine reflects the concentrations of the blood, but the urine values are usually 30 percent higher than the blood values.

It should not be forgotten that in fatal cases the effects of alcoholic intoxication may be complicated by other conditions which may be the immediate cause of death; e.g., it very often happens that intoxicated individuals die from asphyxia due to aspiration of food into the air passages.

The fatal dose of alcohol is variable. However, 250 to 500 cc of alcohol is generally considered a fatal dose.

Chronic alcoholism. The constant drinking of alcohol injures the central nervous system, so that the drinker becomes careless, untidy, forgetful, irritable, and may eventually develop delirium tremens. In this condition he is very restless and terrified by imaginary sights and sounds. Delirium tremens may lead to insanity and death. Besides the central nervous system, other organs may be affected. The liver, kidneys, heart, and skeletal muscles may show fatty degeneration.

METHYL ALCOHOL (WOOD ALCOHOL). Methyl alcohol is a strong poison, and as an adulterant for ethyl alcohol it has given rise to numerous cases of poisoning. The symptoms are those of alcoholic poisoning, but vomiting and delirium are more persistent and a fatal result not infrequently follows. Methyl alcohol is very slowly excreted or metabolized in the body, and repeated doses tend to have a cumulative action. It may cause degeneration of the optic nerve, with consequent blindness. The fatal dose varies between 1 and 4 ounces.

CHLOROFORM. Chloroform is rarely used nowadays as an anesthetic. It is highly toxic and acts rapidly. Due to its quick action chloroform has at times been used for homicidal purposes. A cloth wet with chloroform has been held forcibly over the victim's face until enough has been inhaled to cause death. In other instances chloroform has been used as the anesthetic in cases of criminal abortion and sometimes has caused the death of the patient.[9] Most cases of chloroform poisoning are accidental, however.

The symptoms of chloroform poisoning are pale or cyanotic face, cold and clammy surface, pupils insensitive to light and frequently dilated, stertorous breathing, and slow and weak pulse. Death occurs from paralysis of the respiration system or from cardiac failure. When a person has been forced to inhale chloroform, slight abrasions and excoriations are usually present over the lips, nose, and cheeks.

CHLORAL HYDRATE. As a hypnotic, chloral hydrate is used in medical practice to induce a condition closely resembling natural sleep. The drug is commonly known as "knockout drops" or "a Mickey Finn" when it is used for a criminal purpose. Most cases of chloral hydrate poisoning, however, are accidental or suicidal. The fatal dose varies from 2 to 30 grams.

DIGITALOID POISONS. The most important of this group are digitalis and strophanthin. An overdose of either of these is characterized by slowing of the heart beat, nausea, persistent vomiting, headache, thirst, abdominal pain, roaring in the ears, disturbances of vision, and delirium. Later the heart becomes rapid and irregular, with dyspnea and collapse following. The effects of digitalis are cumulative; hence, poisoning may be accomplished by minor doses over a long period of time.

BARBITURATES. The barbiturates are the most common hypnotics encountered in poisoning cases. The growing popularity of barbiturates has led to the marketing of many proprietary derivatives. The following are some of the barbiturates and trade names: *Veronal, Luminal, Amytal, Nembutal, Seconal, Ipral, Alurate, Dial, Neonal, Phanodorn, Tuinal.*

INVESTIGATIVE ACTION

The initial stages of the investigation should establish whether the poisoning was intentional or accidental, whether a crime or other offense was committed, and the jurisdiction to which the occurrence logically belongs.

Intentional poisoning is usually associated with a suicide. In recent years relatively few murders have been attempted with poison. Suicides, however, have shown increasing favor toward the use of commonly prescribed hypnotics or sleeping pills, painless but toxic in overdose. In particular, suicides of the upper-middle class are characterized by an overdose of barbiturates preceded by a few drinks of whiskey to accelerate and insure their dispatch.

In cases of suspected suicide the exact intent of the victim should be established before a conclusion is reached. Even in cases where the poison was voluntarily self-administered and the person was aware of its toxic and potentially lethal nature, it is not always safe to assume an intent of self-destruction. A person may, for example, risk the hazard of poisoning in drinking an obviously unfit alcohol. Impelled by an intense craving for a stimulant, a person may chance the toxic effect of a narcotic of questionable concentration. Or, to take an instance of more calculated intent, a harmful substance may be ingested to induce an abortion.

The circumstances attending self-poisoning by means of barbiturates are usually more obvious. Ten to twenty times the prescribed dosage may be taken. The effects of the barbiturate are greatly intensified by the synergistic ("working together") action of alcohol, that is, the combined effect is far greater than the sum of the separate effects.

The investigation of murder by poison has been treated in Chapter XVIII.[10] A homicide charge may be brought also where the poisoning is the result of criminal negligence as in the sale of a bootleg liquor containing a toxic alcohol, or may be incidental to the commission of a crime such as a robbery or kidnaping in which a substance such as chloral hydrate is administered to inactivate the victim.

Accidental poisoning—that is, poisoning which is unintended and which is not associated with any illegal act—is commonly caused by contaminated food, toxic substances mislabeled at home or otherwise mistaken, or by a medicine taken in overdose. Individual or idiosyncratic reactions to medication and even food must also be considered. Industrial poisoning, that is, the inhalation or ingestion of a toxic substance such as mercury or lead, is usually a long-term occupational hazard which, though negligence may be involved, is not a matter for criminal investigation.

Since the element of intent is of critical importance in poisoning cases, the investigator should seek information which will answer the following questions:

Who administered the poison?

What was the exact nature of the poison administered?

How, when, and where was it administered?

What was the intent of the person administering the poison? From his own statement and from those of others, what was his motive?

How was the poison obtained? From whom was it received or from what place was it taken? When was it taken or received? In what quantity?

1 See also McNally,[2] Underhill–Koppanyi, Thienes–Haley, Davison, Fabre, Lucas, and Gonzales–Vance–Morgan–Helpern–Milton–Umberger.
2 Bamford, Kohn–Abrest, and Simmons–Gentzgow.
3 Ther and Simmons–Gentzkow.
4 Kaye.[1]
5 Van Itallie[1] and Van Itallie.[2]
6 Newman, Derobert–Duchene, Casier–Delaunois, and Goodman–Daniels.
7 Gaddum.
8 Widmark.
9 Gettler–Blume.
10 Kirk, Lucas, and O'Hara.

XX DRUG ADDICTION

To SIMPLIFY THE FOLLOWING DISCUSSION OF NARCOTICS OR DRUGS OF addiction, it is necessary to oversimplify the concept of addiction. The physiological and psychological conditions that constitute the state of addiction are too complex and varied to be treated here with any degree of thoroughness.[1] For our purposes the distinguishing element in the state of addiction is the condition of physical pain and mental anguish that characterizes the addict's reaction to the withdrawal of the drug.

Habituation is a state of psychological dependence on a drug such as marihuana or cocaine, or even tobacco. A person, through habit, may come to associate a feeling of well-being with the use of marihuana or tobacco. His reaction to the withdrawal of these stimulants is predominantly psychological in nature, i.e., he exhibits signs of restlessness, nervousness, and even anxiety, primarily because of his inability to recapture the sense of well-being which he associates with the drug.

Addiction is a state of utter dependence on a drug for a sense of physical and mental well-being. Addiction includes habituation. The test of true addiction is the *abstinence syndrome,* i.e., the characteristic symptoms of severe physical and mental distress following withdrawal.

Narcotics are drugs of addiction, specifically the opium derivatives, such as heroin and morphine, and those synthetic analgesics which are known to have the addicting properties of opiates (opium derivatives). A synthetic analgesic is simply a manufactured pain-reliever, such as Demerol or Methadon, as distinguished from opium, which is part of a plant. It should be noted that the term narcotic is used here in a limited sense, related to the purposes of law enforcement.

Synthetic analgesics are drugs with a narcotic effect which have been synthesized from inexpensive chemicals. The research of pharmaceutical chemists, in pursuit of a harmless drug which would have the beneficent qualities of the opiates without their addicting properties, has led to the development and marketing of a number of synthetic analgesics which have all been placed under Federal and State regulation as narcotics. In the past the development of a new drug, such as Demerol, has sometimes

318

led to a vigorous dispute within the medical profession on the issue of the drug's potential for addiction. Since opiates are of unquestioned value in treating certain sicknesses and especially in mitigating the terminal ordeals of cancer and tuberculosis, the synthesis of a pain-relieving drug free of the dangers of addiction would be a boon to the practice of medicine. The social implications of such a drug are too great to evaluate at this time. A drug of this nature would provide a safe and relatively painless mechanism for the regimen of withdrawal. At present the "cure" or the process of "kicking the habit" is a protracted procedure which must be conducted under medical supervision, usually in confinement, over a period of several months. One of the milder synthetic narcotics, such as methadon, is administered in gradually diminishing doses as an essential part of this weaning process. On release the former addict finds that he is able to conduct his life and engage in normal activities without the aid of a narcotic. His mental state, however, is characterized by a nervousness and often a mild depression that yields readily to the longing for the old sense of well-being. The temptation to resort to a narcotic stimulant "just this once" is overwhelming, and only the exception is given the intelligent care or possesses the firmness of will that can prevent a relapse into the state of addiction.

The need, then, for a non-habit-forming drug of an otherwise narcotic nature is obvious in both the prevention and cure of addiction. The century-old search for such a remedy provides a history of scientific zeal and optimism, punctuated periodically by triumphant announcements of success which are followed inevitably by an admission of failure. In the early part of the last century some physicians believed that morphine administered by means of a hypodermic injection would not be addicting. As each derivative of opium was discovered it was believed or hoped to be nonaddicting, until at the end of the century, in 1889, the discovery of heroin, diacetylmorphine, was announced as the ultimate success of alkaloidal medicine—a non-habit-forming substitute for opium and morphine which would also serve as a mechanism for the cure of those addictions. Heroin proved to be "four times as addicting" as morphine and among addicts of the twentieth century became the drug of choice, almost to the exclusion of other opiates.

In the field of synthetic drugs a similar optimism attended the discovery of Demerol, and an equal disillusionment grew with the awareness of its addicting powers. Nevertheless, Demerol was less addicting than morphine and had proved its usefulness as a practical analgesic and as a suppressant for asthma sufferers. Many other synthetic drugs of a similar nature, notably the methadones, have been developed without achieving the desideratum of being nonaddicting. Within the last few years, however, definite indications have been given that the goal is within reach. A synthetic narcotic which relieves pain to the same degree as the opiates and which is also nonaddicting would no doubt include among its side effects some degree of euphoria. It is difficult to conceive of such a drug as an unmixed blessing. Although free of the addicting property, the drug would probably lead to habituation.

Tolerance to a narcotic drug is increased by habitual use. More of the drug is required to give the same degree of exhilaration or relief from pain. The body, moreover, acquires an increased capacity to absorb the larger dose. Thus, the confirmed addict eventually finds himself taking doses of the narcotic in amounts that would formerly have proved fatal.

Withdrawal [2] of the narcotic from a confirmed addict results in acute physical and mental suffering, a complex of fairly characteristic symptoms (the *abstinence syndrome*) which provides the most reliable way of identifying an addict. Within twenty-four hours after being deprived of the drug the initial symptoms appear—the addict's eyes water, he begins to yawn and sneeze and gradually develops a condition of sweating and tremors. Within forty-eight hours the addict becomes subject to cramps, nausea, and retching. Characteristic pains in the back of the legs are experienced. The symptoms, after reaching a maximum in forty-eight hours, continue intense until about the seventy-second hour, and thereafter gradually decline. In seven to ten days the acute manifestations subside but the addict will complain of weakness, insomnia, and nervousness for several months. The withdrawal symptoms following abstinence from the synthetic narcotics are similar in nature but usually somewhat milder in degree.

Identifying the addict is not a simple matter since in his normal state —that is, when he has not been deprived of the drug—his behavior is not differentiable from that of other persons and no visible signs are apparent in his features or movements. Physical examination of an addict in custody, however, will usually reveal the puncture marks left by repeated injections or, in the case of an addiction of long standing, ulcerations from continued injections in an area on the arms or legs. The most reliable indication of addiction is the person's reactions to deprivation of the drug for a period of days. Unfortunately, this method of detecting the addict is available ordinarily only to prison guards. A formal determination of a suspected addict's condition obviously should be referred to a qualified physician. In addition to the observations described above, some physicians use the Nalline Test,[3] in which the reactions of the subject's pupils are observed after an injection of Nalline.

Causes[4] of addiction are best deduced from studies of the younger addicts. The notion that many addicts are created inadvertently in the course of some medical treatment requiring repeated use of opiates or analgesics is no longer given credence. In a study brought to the attention of a Senate Subcommittee the following picture was drawn:

The addiction story as told by addicts in general is remarkably uniform. Almost invariably the addicts state that they learned about drugs from friends or associates. In many cases the first trial came about in a most casual way by the novice expressing curiosity and the user offering a shot. All addicts admit to a false sense of self-control in thinking to themselves that they can play with drugs and stop at will.[5]

Other interesting findings of the same study included the following: 70 percent of the subjects studied acquired the addiction before the age of twenty-five; 85 percent showed criminal tendencies and 64 percent had criminal records prior to their addiction; the addict is rarely a violent person, as the fears, worries, indecision, and dependency associated with his condition usually prevent him from doing anything more aggressive than petty thievery such as hall-letterbox larceny and pocketbook theft; addiction is contagious in the sense that an active addict in a group will tend to infect the others; the average age of the addict coming to the attention of the courts is steadily decreasing; addicts for the most part exhibit immature personalities marked by feelings of insecurity and inferiority; over 80 percent appear to be constitutional psychopaths.

It should be noted that this last diagnosis might be given to most persons who are confined to an institution, particularly the recidivists. Although this study was based on a sample of some 83 addicts, the findings are fairly representative of other studies. One of the weak points of any study of this nature is the necessity of relying heavily on the statements of the addicts themselves. Nevertheless, the investigator will be able to draw some useful conclusions from some of the data presented.

It is apparent, for example, that the same factors which tend to cause delinquency must be considered in a discussion of the reasons for addiction. Beyond the causes initially leading to addiction, consideration should be given to the criminal milieu in which the addiction must be maintained and financially supported. Taking the number 80,000 as a reasonable estimate of the number of addicts in the country and the amount $25 per day as the cost of the individual daily dose of narcotics, it is obvious that a great number of addicts, to support the habit, must resort to crimes—crimes not always confined to the area of petty thievery.

It is obvious too that considerable illegal activity is involved in the supply lines by which the narcotic, drawn from an opium plant in Asia and converted to heroin in some European factory, is shipped into this country and distributed, greatly diluted, throughout the large cities.

Smuggling narcotics into the United States has become an organized part of international trade. New York, one of the largest ports in the world, is the heart of this illegal traffic, and, in addition to being the largest consumer of the narcotics, serves as the major distribution center for the other cities of the United States.

The estimated quantity of heroin required to meet the daily needs of some 60,000 addicts is approximately 5 kilograms (11 lb.) per day. Hence, the amount of heroin smuggled into the United States annually is at least 1,800 kilograms (2 tons). The Bureau of Narcotics of the U. S. Treasury Department believes that its annual seizures of heroin, which average about 70 kilograms, represent less than 5 percent of the heroin that is smuggled in.

The determination and energy with which this illegal traffic is pursued can be better understood by a glance at the financial side of the narcotics picture. The average strength of the heroin reaching the addict at the street level ranges from 1 percent to 7 percent. The cost of an ounce of heroin of this dilution is about $200. Hence, an ounce of pure heroin ultimately brings about $5,000, and the final retail value of the annual import of two tons will be about $300,000,000. These estimates, it should be noted, are definitely conservative.

At the other end of the smuggling business, the opinions of experts point to Asiatic countries such as China and certain parts of the Near East. Most of the heroin encountered in the eastern part of the United States is processed in clandestine laboratories in France and Italy from morphine paste smuggled into those countries from Lebanon and the opium-producing countries of the Near East.

The pattern of the smuggling operations changes in adjusting to the rigors of law enforcement. Although New York is still the main terminus, some of the smuggling has shifted to Mexico and Canada, whence the heroin is transshipped to New York across the respective border. After reaching the New York distributors some of this heroin is smuggled back into Canada to supply important distributors in that area. The drugs are then illegally brought into this country for sale and distribution. All aspects of the operation are illegal because heroin, the smuggler's staple, is not permitted in this country, either by import or manufacture.

All aspects of this traffic have been fought with intelligence and sincerity by law enforcement agencies at every governmental level. Before 1950, however, the number of investigators assigned to narcotics work was scandalously inadequate. On the Continent the International Criminal Police Commission in Paris has a special section which deals with the drug problem. The United Nations also aids in this work. For example, the Permanent Central Opium Board makes available through a U.N. publication the statistics and other facts on the licit production of opium and its divergence to utilization and export.

But the fact remains that every ounce of illegal narcotics in this country has eluded international control and national scrutiny. The difficulties of the narcotics problem have been concisely presented by a United States Attorney in his testimony before a Senate Subcommittee:

The narcotics traffic is run by people who operate on an international scale, and in this country on an interstate scale. They are professional criminals. They have lots of money. They have powerful allies. They have expert knowledge as to how to evade the law and to escape detection. They are not themselves addicts. In fact, they seldom handle drugs. They have no bank accounts. They deal only in cash. Their errands are run by others. Their messengers do the transporting and selling. . . .

As a rule, we get nowhere near the big operator when we simply arrest the pusher and the small dope peddler. We are just at the bottom of the ladder. There may be 8 or 10 rungs of the ladder before we get to the big dealer who has been responsible for the importation of the drugs.

As you can see, the profits from importing and selling narcotics are so enormous that the business supports a great many levels of distributors, wholesalers, retailers, all of whom make a very large profit.[5]

COMMON DRUGS OF ADDICTION [6]

For law enforcement purposes there is actually only one narcotic of importance—heroin, the most stimulating and addicting of the opiates. The use of opium is rarely encountered. Morphine and the other derivatives of opium are occasionally used by the addict of the criminal world when he is cut off from his source of heroin and the substitute is available through theft or deception. The same is true of the synthetic narcotics.

OPIUM. The drug consists of the dried latex from the unripe capsule, or fruit, of the opium poppy (*Papaver somniferum*). Raw opium has the appearance of compressed vegetable matter. It is dark brown in color and has a characteristic earthy odor. To transform the raw opium into an extract suitable for consumption, it is dissolved, boiled, roasted, and fermented. The prepared opium may be smoked, chewed, or eaten. Opium develops a characteristic sweetish odor. The practice of chewing or eating opium is confined to the Asiatic countries. In this country opium is used for medicinal purposes, as in cough syrups, although in the last century a decoction of opium called *laudanum* was freely dispensed by pharmacists.

The smoking of opium, an addiction of the Chinese, induces a deep sleep accompanied by pleasant dreams and hallucinations. The opium is formed into small pills which are held by a needle or some similar device in a small hole in the pipe. As opium does not burn by itself, a piece of glowing charcoal or a light is used to heat it. Every time the smoker puts the pipe to the flame, he takes a deep breath and inhales the smoke. The conventional Chinese opium pipe may be improvised by a small bottle with a rubber hose. A small hole in the bottle corresponds to the pipe opening.

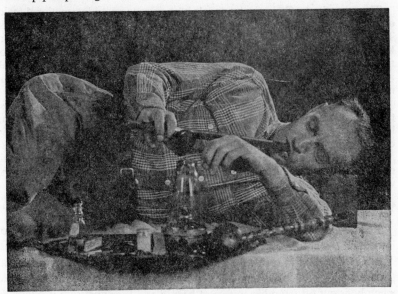

Figure 131.   Opium-smoking equipment.

MORPHINE. The derivatives of opium are the basis of the drug problem. Of some twenty or more different alkaloids that have been isolated from opium, three have had a special significance for both the world of medicine and the half-world of the addict. Morphine, the principal alkaloid of opium, is responsible for the major effects of opium. To be accepted medicinally opium must contain not less than 9.5 percent morphine; it sometimes contains as much as 20 percent morphine.

The common forms in which morphine is used are morphine hydro-chloride, morphine sulphate, and morphine tartrate. These compounds are prepared pharmaceutically in several ways—as small white powdery cubes, white crystalline powders, in capsules, or in solutions. When sold illegally morphine usually appears as a white powder in highly diluted form. Addicts in Continental Europe still use morphine as the drug of

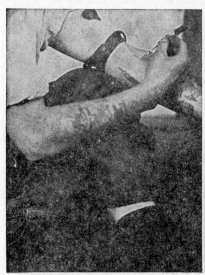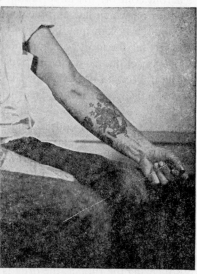

Figure 132. A "mainliner" show-ing how the drug is applied with an eyedropper. This man has been a drug addict for thirty-five years and has always applied the drug in the same place.

Figure 133. Same "mainliner" as in Figure 132. Being clean, he has not developed ulcers; but a deep cavity in his left-upper forearm shows the results of application of the drug.

choice. Morphine is ordinarily taken by injection; the techniques used are the same as those described in the discussion of heroin. The effects of morphine are similar to those of heroin but of less intensity.

CODEINE. Another familiar alkaloid of opium is codeine, which is marketed as codeine sulphate and codeine phosphate and is a common ingredient of pills, powders, and cough syrups, serving as a pain-reliever or as a repressant. It is usually encountered as a white powder when it is occasionally used by an addict deprived of his source of heroin. Codeine is much milder than morphine and addiction to it is negligible.

HEROIN. The most important and the most dangerous of the drugs of addiction is heroin (diacetylmorphine), an opium derivative obtained by synthesis from morphine. The importation or manufacture of heroin is prohibited in the United States; nevertheless, the narcotic effect and addicting power of this drug is so great that it has come to be used by criminal addicts in this country almost to the exclusion of all other narcotics. The problem of drug addiction is synonymous with the problem of heroin control—its importation, distribution, sale, and use are illegal activities on which law enforcement efforts have been focused.

Although heroin may be taken orally, sniffed, or even rubbed on the gums, by far the most common mode of using this drug is through hypodermic injection. Since the hypodermic syringe is not easily concealed and its unlicensed possession is illegal in some states, the addict has devised a satisfactory, but often unsanitary, substitute which he terms his "outfit." The typical outfit consists of a safety pin, an eyedropper, a spoon, and a piece of cotton. The safety pin is inserted at an angle into the arm or some other part of the body to a depth of about one-eighth of an inch. Women prefer the thigh area unless they are "mainliners." The safety pin is left in the skin during the preparations. A small piece of cotton is placed in the spoon, together with the needed amount of heroin and a small quantity of water. When the spoon is heated the heroin is dissolved in the water, which is then absorbed by the cotton. The eyedropper is now filled with the liquid expressed from the cotton, the safety pin is removed from the skin, and the eyedropper is placed in its stead. By squeezing the rubber, the drug is injected; and by massaging the area, the liquid is made to enter the tissues. Repeated abuse of the skin in this manner develops characteristic ulcers and scars. The constant inserting of the syringe into the same place by some addicts ("mainliners"), results in a permanent deep cavity, usually in the upper left arm.

When a juvenile is introduced to heroin, his injection usually takes the form of "skin-popping," that is, the injection is made just under the surface of the skin, where it produces a small swelling. As he becomes addicted he begins to resort to a deeper injection as described above. The difference in effect is one of intensity and immediacy. To achieve the greatest stimulation (or relief) in the shortest time, the addict resorts to injecting the drug directly into the vein (the "mainline"), a procedure that is effective within seconds.

Heroin is a white, sometimes yellowish, fine crystalline powder, extremely bitter to the taste. At the street level it is sold in highly diluted form. Most commonly it is mixed with milk sugar. Thus, the addict purchases a small quantity of white powder which is wrapped in cellophane to make a "deck" about one inch square and which contains approximately 4 percent heroin, 96 percent milk sugar.

OTHER OPIUM DERIVATIVES. When deprived of access to heroin, the addict may resort to other opium derivatives for relief. These include: Dionine, Dilaudid, Metopon, Dromoran, Pantopon, Eukodal, and Dicodide.

SYNTHETIC NARCOTIC DRUGS.[7] Various synthetic equivalents of the opium derivatives have been developed in recent years to provide a cheap source of narcotics without relying on the importation of opium. As these drugs appear on the market a decision is made on their addicting effects, and, where this effect is found, the drug is placed by the U. S. Treasury Department under the same legal controls and prohibitions as the opiates. Demerol (*meperidine hydrochloride*) was one of the first synthetic analgesics to attract attention. This drug is also known as Isonipecaine and Pethidine. During World War II the Germans developed a class of synthetic narcotics which are termed methadones. Methadon (one of the methadones) has proved to be addicting and is now classified as a narcotic drug. Methadon appears commercially under the trade names Methadone, Amidone, Adanon, and Dolophine.

OTHER DANGEROUS DRUGS

From the point of view of the investigator the significance of the addicting drugs such as heroin lies in the compulsions created by the addiction. The contagious aspect of addiction leads to an ever-increasing demand for more narcotics and the growth of a criminal class controlling the drug traffic and indirectly controlling other criminial classes.

There are, however, a number of other drugs which affect the behavior of the user while he is under their influence but which are relatively free of the other undesirable social implications. The unrestricted use of these drugs is harmful to the user's health and can lead to a state of great psychological dependence on the drug that is sometimes the equivalent of a minor addiction. Sleeping pills, "pep" pills, and marihuana are the most important offenders in the class of nonnarcotic drugs.

COCAINE.[8] Although cocaine is still classified with the narcotic drugs under Federal law, it has since been found to lack the addicting property of the opiates. It is, however, a great stimulant, which in some cases can lead to hallucinations and provide the initiative for criminal behavior. Cocaine is a white crystalline substance with a shiny appearance. Although cocaine was used by criminals earlier in this century, its use has practically disappeared as a law enforcement problem.

MARIHUANA.[9] The hemp plant is known in various forms in India as *bhang* or *charras* and in Arabic-speaking countries as *hashish*. So widespread is its use that a dozen or so other colloquial names might be listed for as many countries. In the United States, Canada, and Mexico the accepted name is *marihuana* (or *marijuana*). There is only a single botanical species of hemp, however, and its technical name is *cannabis sativa*. It includes all the various types encountered, although they are often described by such names as *cannabis indica, cannabis mexicana,* and *cannabis americana*. These are simply varieties obtained under varying climatic conditions and cultivated for different purposes.

In the United States the drug is nearly always smoked in the form of cigarettes ("reefers"). In Mexico the alcoholic extracts are a common form. In India, Iran, Egypt, Syria, Greece, and Arabia, the raw resin is sometimes collected from the sticky, glutinous flowering tops of the

hemp plant and mixed with other ingredients to form cakes, spice sticks, or sweetmeats. Marihuana, whether smoked or eaten, acts as an intoxicant with effects that vary greatly with the individual and which form no set pattern of behavior. In general, the drug perverts perception and distorts the user's concepts of time, distance, and sound. Delightful, often sensuous dreams are experienced. The smoker becomes talkative, easily given to laughter, and tending to indulge in elaborate gestures. In the advanced stages of intoxication, the smoker's muscular coordination and vision are affected. Some smokers may become hysterical and even develop homicidal tendencies. The relationship between marihuana and criminal behavior is not well established, but it is generally agreed that marihuana leads the user into company that will tempt him to try heroin.

Figure 134.   Typical marihuana leaf.

The hardiness of the hemp plant permits its growth in most climates, and its commonplace appearance prevents its recognition by any but a thoroughly trained eye. Crops of marihuana have been grown in empty lots bordering elevated railways in New York. The physical appearance, then, is that of a common weed, ordinarily about five feet high, with compound palmate leaves bearing from five to eleven lobes, most commonly seven, and almost always an odd number.

No special skill is required to extract the drug from the plant. Practically all parts of the plant can be used with varying narcotic effect. In the United States the tops, leaves, flowers, seeds, hulls, and twigs are dried, crushed into a coarse powder, and rolled into cigarettes.

In its crushed form, marihuana can be identified by a microscopic examination, called the Beam Test, or by a simple chemical test, the Duquenois reaction.

BARBITURATES.[10] The most commonly prescribed sleeping pills or sedatives are the barbiturates—derivatives of barbituric acid of which the more familiar are phenobarbital, Seconal, and Nembutal. The annual consumption of barbiturates in the United States is approximately 750,-000 pounds, equivalent to 25 doses per capita. Persons habituated to these drugs use them as stimulants rather than for sedation. In larger doses intoxication appears to take place with an accompanying confusion and loss of coordination. The effect is greatly intensified by alcohol.

AMPHETAMINES. The so-called "pep" pill is ordinarily one of the amphetamines, either benzedrine or dexedrine. Amphetamine is produced as a colorless liquid and also as a white, odorless, crystalline powder. The powder when pressed into tablet form is often orange-colored and heart-shaped. The effect of amphetamine is to dispel fatigue, create an illusion of great energy, and provide a temporary feeling of well-being. The danger lies in the extreme reactions of unstable personalities which occasionally find their outlet in acts of violence. Abuse of amphetamine can also lead to physical collapse through over-exertion, since the safety signals of fatigue and sleepiness are absent.

1 Lindesmith.
2 Merck's Medical Manual.
3 Brown.
4 Lindesmith and Maurer.
5 Senate Subcommittee on Improvements in the Federal Code.
6 U. S. Army Tech. Bull. PMG 8.
7 U. S. Army Tech. Bull. PMG 13.
8 Merck's Medical Manual.
9 U. S. Army Tech. Bull. PMG 1.
10 Camps–Purchase.

XXI INVESTIGATION OF
BURGLARIES

THERE ARE A FEW IMPORTANT QUESTIONS THE EXPERIENCED DETECTIVE will always ask himself when investigating a burglary.

What has been stolen? Are the objects supposed to be stolen, misplaced, or lost? (For description of items see section on this subject later in this chapter.) The possibility of a simulated burglary must be considered.

When did the burglary take place? Determine the time when the object was last seen and the time when the burglary was discovered. If the burglary took place in a rural area and a tree was used for climbing or a hedge has been broken through, note the condition of broken and dying branches, rust formations on metal shavings, or marks of rain water, which may give approximate information about the time of the burglary. The date and time the stolen goods were disposed of is always an indication of the time when the burglary took place as far as professional criminals are concerned. They invariably try to sell the loot at the earliest possible moment.

Who committed the burglary? Is a description of the suspect available?

What was the motive? Endeavor to establish the reason for the crime. Is it a case of professional burglars, of need, mischief, greed, or revenge?

How did the burglar know where to find the stolen object?

How did he know that the time chosen for the burglary was the most favorable one? [1]

How did the burglar dispose of the stolen loot? Consider receivers, pawnshops, own use, through peddling in the street, etc.

How did the burglar know the premises? Was it necessary for him to search out the point of burglary himself?

Does the technique employed point to an amateur or professional? This question may be difficult to answer as far as simple burglaries go, because the burglar may have used tools found on the scene. Amateurs will generally cause more damage than experienced criminals. The trade

330

Generally under 25 yrs old
most 15-17 yr old —

of the burglar will show in his work. For instance, if he is a carpenter, he will preferably work with wood, etc.

Were there one or more burglars? This may be determined by the traces left, such as footprints, fingerprints, etc., and by the method used in certain operations. The lifting of heavy furniture, the breaking of furniture in two places simultaneously, etc., indicate that two men have been at work.

GENERAL REMARKS ABOUT BURGLARIES

In investigating various types of burglaries too much emphasis cannot be laid on an exhaustive search for fingerprint impressions on doors, doorknobs, glass in doors and windows, on window frames and sills leading to and in the premises burglarized, and on telephones. A thorough and systematic search of the building burglarized and the building adjoining it must be made. Record a full description and all identifying marks of the stolen merchandise or property.

A preconceived notion that the goods have been removed should never be held. Cases are on record where parallel investigations conducted by detectives specializing in the apprehension of safe, loft, and residence burglars have by diligent search located the stolen property in a vacant apartment, office, or loft in the burglarized building and have traced the criminals through a trunk which they purchased to transfer the loot or through information given by owners or lessees of nearby apartments or rooming houses from which the approach to the scene was made by the criminals.

A knowledge of the technique or *modus operandi* employed by burglars is essential in order to conduct a successful investigation. Of great aid is the perseverance of the criminal, i.e., his unbelievable adherence to a certain method or technique. The ingenious and wise criminal is rarer than he is believed to be. Instead the common burglar shows a marked narrowness of thought and a peculiar inability to vary his actions. Having once invented or learned a method, he believes it will do. He is a specialist who seldom goes out of his field.[2] If he has started to enter houses by the roof, he will in all probability follow the same course throughout his career. If he has found it convenient to become familiar with the premises by making the acquaintance of servants, he will probably continue to do so as long as he is at liberty to follow a career of crime.

The listings under "Burglary" (besides miscellaneous) in the *Annual Report* of the New York City Police Department illustrate the general categories used for classification purposes:

Burglary—attempted
        residence, day
           "   night
        basements—cellars of apartments
        unoccupied houses
        stores or lofts, day
           "   "   "   night
        safes—blown, ripped, forced
           "   other means
        R. R. cars

INVESTIGATION OF THE SCENE OF BURGLARY

In burglaries where the scene may be of importance it should be photographed and sketched. The path of the burglar must be determined. Traces such as fingerprints, footprints, toolmarks, and objects left on the scene by the burglar should be looked for. Locks, doors, windows, and alarms should be examined. Remember that burglars are known to have concealed attacks on doors and windows by putting putty of the same color as the surroundings in the hole left by their work. If it is suspected that locks have been picked, they should be taken apart by an expert. If the lock is of a good make, the modern burglar will most likely go directly through the door instead of bothering to pick the lock. The most common method is the one in which the burglar drills holes around the lock and through the surrounding woodwork, after which he saws off a piece of the wood with a compass saw. The drillholes may be identified, and the handle of the saw may leave valuable identifying marks in the places where it has been pushed against the wood. Examine also the taps of the hinges in cases where locks and doors are seemingly untouched. The possibility of simulation should not be overlooked.

If several burglaries of the same type are committed in the same neighborhood in a rural area, a map may be drawn from which it may be possible to determine whether the thefts could all have been made by the same burglar traveling between the different points. This may give a clue to the approximate location of his hideout.

Always keep in mind that paint, grease, and dust from the scene may stick to the burglar's clothing and to his tools. If necessary, take samples of such materials and keep them for further reference.

METHODS USED ON LOCKS AND WINDOWS. Very few ordinary locks on the market show any resistance to picking.

The good investigator should make himself familiar with locks used in his part of the country. Learned locksmiths or safe experts are certainly the best teachers in this respect, and the investigator should be acquainted with such persons. He should also be familiar with lock-picking tools, and the use of them, and with the use of the celluloid strip and all the other manifold methods of opening locks.

Other methods of burglars may also leave traces, such as that of making a wax case of a key. Sometimes this is done by dipping a blank key in molten wax or other substance. This leaves a thin coating on the blank, which is then introduced into the keyhole and turned so that it touches the mechanism of the lock. The points of contact will leave marks on the wax, making it easy to file the blank to the desired shape. This operation leaves traces of wax in the interior of the lock and can easily be discovered. Blackening blank keys with carbon has also been used. Nowadays, of course, these methods can only be used on old-fashioned locks or in other unusual cases.

The searching movement of a tool for lock-picking will leave traces on the coat of oil and grease on the inside of the lock, where only the parts regularly reached by the key are shiny. In cases where Yale locks have been picked with a strip of lead, particles of lead may be found. Sometimes such things as broken skeleton keys, knife-points, and nails may be found in the interior of the lock and identified with corresponding parts far away from the scene.

In order to avoid the removal of the lock a small apparatus which consists of a tiny tube with a minute bulb and mirror at its end (Figure 135) can be used to advantage.

Figure 135. Device for examining the interior of a lock for traces.

The bulb is lighted by a battery. With this instrument all cavities may be searched. In a larger size it may be used for searching houses when articles are supposedly hidden in the interior of walls, etc. Instead of breaking down the walls or destroying the furniture a hole is opened in the suspected place and the interior explored with the instrument.

The *ouistiti* also leaves characteristic marks when it is used by a burglar to turn a key from the outside of the door.

In Chapter XI we deal with burglars' tools and how to make casts and photographs of the traces they leave. The possibility of such identification should never be overlooked.

Windows may be forced either by breaking the windowpane or by drilling a hole through the window frame near the catch and lifting the catch with a steel wire. If the burglary is simulated, the window may be broken from the wrong side. How to determine from which side a window has been broken is explained in Chapter XV. In order to avoid the use of a soaped handkerchief or a tarred paper, to which pieces of the glass would stick, amateurs will sometimes try to cut a hole with a dia-

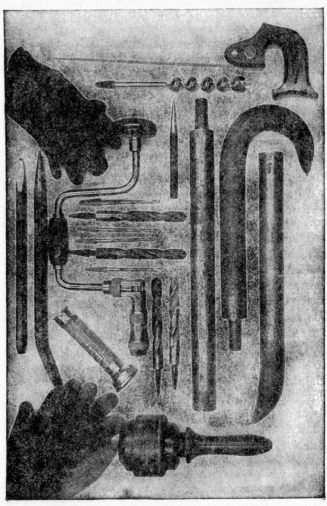

Figure 136. A typical kit of burglar's tools.

mond. This will prove useless, however, because a piece of glass which has been circumscribed with a diamond can only be pulled out by pressure exerted from the inside of the window. It has happened, though, that professional burglars have cut out a piece of glass just at the side of the frame, after which they have forced a pointed, thin steel tool through the putty. The tool acts as a lever on the interior of the glass. The glass will then break in the lines of the diamond cut. Sometimes windowpanes have been heated with a glow lamp, which causes the glass to break. When glass has been handled by the burglar it should be painstakingly searched for fingerprints. It should be noted that minute particles of glass may be found on the clothing of the suspect. These particles should be removed with a vacuum cleaner with a special filter and examined.

TECHNIQUES OF BURGLARY

In the following pages the *modus operandi* of different present-day American burglars will be described.

SAFE BURGLARS

There was a time when almost every safe burglary was committed by some yegg or safecracker fairly well known to the police, but today this type exists only in fiction. The modern safe men may be of any race, creed, color, or occupation, and of any age between twelve and seventy-five.

As already told, the professional finder does not exist today. The mob itself finds the job. The information necessarily includes the size and make of the safe; the time when cash is left in it and the amount; the best method of entrance and escape; and the habits of neighbors, of patrolmen, and of watchmen. Countless other items of knowledge are also necessary for the undisturbed completion of the theft.

Formerly if the mob members feared being caught with burglars' tools in their possession, they would have them planted or hidden in a definite spot in or near the building during the late afternoon or early evening preceding the night set for the commission of the crime. This is seldom done today. Modern safe burglars take their tools with them.

Various methods are used to carry tools to the job. They may be carried in a suitcase or in a case used to carry a musical instrument, such as a violin, saxophone, and so forth. One of the mob may carry one part of a sectional jimmy and another the other part. Or the sectional jimmy may be hung on a rope or cord from the neck and concealed by the clothing. A neat merchandise package may be simulated at times to transport the tools. On the other hand, they may be hidden under the seat or in the toolbox of an automobile or taxicab.

Sometime after dark and before daybreak, depending upon the type of building and character of the neighborhood, the mob will enter the office and begin their attack on the safe or "can," as it is called. The word "attack" is used advisedly, for it well describes the methods used by modern safe men. Gone is the phantom of the novel, sensitive-fingerd "Jimmy Valentine," famous in romance and song—and probably only there. He, together with his more mortal companion, the gentleman who with a well-placed charge of soup, or nitroglycerin, could unhinge the doors of the strongest safe, has almost vanished.

His successors now rip the bottom or back out of a safe with the aid of brute strength and a sectional jimmy or a fair amount of skill and the cumbersome equipment of an acetylene torch. Or on safes of older makes they bludgeon the dial from the front of the safe with a small sledgehammer and are then free to punch out the combination and open the doors. Modern safes are punch proof.

The loot or swag consists of money, jewelry, precious stones, negotiable bonds, or other property easily disposed of through a fence and difficult to trace and identify.

A recent case well illustrates the methods used by detectives in apprehending safe burglars. In Brooklyn an observant patrolman's suspicion was aroused by the actions of a seller of used cars who spent money lavishly but obviously did not do any business. The policeman reported his suspicions to the Safe and Loft Squad. The man was tailed for some weeks and was often seen in the company of people with criminal records. One Saturday afternoon he left for a remote part of Brooklyn accompanied by several friends and a woman. The mob used two cars. They drove to a big plant on the outskirts of the city, and five of the men entered the building carrying all the paraphernalia necessary for a "rip." One man and the woman waited in the cars keeping watch.[3] After a while the tailing detectives closed in on the place. They found the watchman tied and the burglars at work. Some shooting followed, and one criminal was killed and another wounded.

Because safe burglars generally steal only money or jewelry, it may be difficult to get enough evidence to convict them. If there are no definite traces left at the scene of the crime and no witnesses to make an identification, the only method left to pursue for apprehension and conviction is through information and the process of trailing. It should be pointed out that trailing is a very tedious job, in fact, one of the most difficult assignments in any police department. For methods of trailing see Chapter IV.

Before giving details of the technique of safe burglars, it is necessary to give some elementary information about the construction of safes. Different makes of safes are differently constructed, however, and we shall therefore discuss only the general principles used in ordinary makes.

Two main types of safes are manufactured today: the fire-resistant safe and the burglar-resistant safe. The fire-resistant type is made out of sheet steel between the plates of which is found a layer of fireproof insulation material generally consisting of siliceous earth and plaster of Paris. The insulation material is a most important clue with which to link the safe burglar with the scene. It has been used as evidence on the Continent for some twenty years. Particles of safe insulation material may be found in the clothing and shoes of a suspect, and tools used in safe-breaking may have quantities of insulation material adhering to them. The American safe manufacturer either makes the insulation himself or buys it from a special firm. While it is usually characteristic of the make of the safe, some insulations have a very similar composition. The research laboratory of the New York Police Department, as well as the laboratory of the Federal Bureau of Investigation, maintains files of safe insulations.

Most often the fire-resistant type safe is equipped with relocking devices and burglar-resistant locks. A fire-resistant type can readily be opened in a short time by an experienced burglar. The burglar-resistant safe or chest is constructed of laminated or thick steel and will usually withstand the efforts of a safe burglar for quite some time. The burglar-resistant safes in this country, contrary to the Continental ones, are usually not provided with fire-resistant insulation. The fire protection is supposed to be supplied by the walling in of the safe itself in concrete or by placing it in a larger fire-resistant safe. An ordinary burglar-resistant safe should withstand any attempts of drilling and any ripping job because of the hardened steel plating. However, it is not safe against burn jobs and blow jobs.

When it comes to more expensive constructions, it is necessary to differentiate between safes and vault doors. Doors and walls in an expensive modern safe consist of a tough plating of special steel inside of which is a layer of reinforced fireproof insulation and inside of this still another steel sheet plate. The lock has a safety catch which will function by explosions and sometimes by heating with the acetylene torch, thereby automatically locking the mechanism of the lock. This gives a relatively good protection against dynamite and against the ordinary acetylene torch. The latter will easily cut the outer plating, but there will be much resistance from the reinforced filling, which has to be broken up piece by piece. The reinforcing iron pieces must be cut by a torch. While the above-described construction will not give enough resistance to an acetylene torch, often a thin copper plate will be found in the interior. Owing to its capacity for conducting strong heat, the copper plate will quickly conduct the heat away from the torch, making it difficult to accumulate enough heat in one spot for melting and cutting. Regardless of this improvement, it is still possible with the aid of an acetylene torch and suitable tools to penetrate a safe of the latter type within a few hours.

The development of vault-door construction in cases where weight, size, and cost do not play a great role has, during the last few years, been under the threatening shadow of the acetylene torch. Until a few years ago a normal construction consisted of outer plates of special steel inside of which was fireproof insulation reinforced with special steel rods. After that came special steel plate and then another thick cast-iron plate, sometimes reinforced with special steel, with finally a special steel plate. The cast-iron plate would provide resistance against the acetylene torch. However, there are now acetylene torches which will use up to ten thousand gallons of oxygen per hour, and the cast-iron plates will give very little protection in such a case. To safeguard against the large acetylene torches, the designers have developed different constructions. In some of these the thickness of the reinforced cast-iron plate has been augmented and they have been given copperplating to lead off the heat. In other cases, instead of cast-iron plates, thick copper plates reinforced with manganese steel have been used. Thick armor-plates with a high melting point have also been used. All these three constructions will give excellent protection, but even doors so constructed are not burglar-proof if they are left unguarded for a long time or if the burglar has a chance to assemble unlimited supplies of oxygen tanks. Even the best door must have an additional protection in the form of wiring, control by watchman, electric eyes, etc.

The walls of modern vaults are nowadays made of specially reinforced concrete. It seems to be much easier to force entrance into a modern vault through the walls, with the aid of chisels, sledges, and acetylene torches, than to force entrance through the doors. On the Continent several attempts have been made to force entrance through the walls, and sometimes these have been successful. The burglars have dug a tunnel through the ground, for instance. As protection against such attacks,

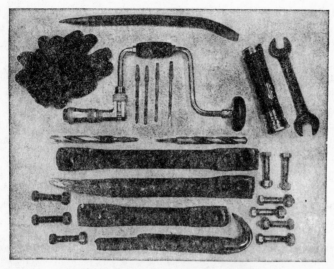

Figure 137. Safe-breaker's outfit.

modern vaults are surrounded by narrow inspection passages which should be inspected during every beat of the watchman.

It may also be worth while to mention the modern electric alarm systems. There are three principal types, namely, the open circuit, the closed circuit, and a combination of the two. The open circuit is the simplest and cheapest. The alarm is sounded when the current is closed. In the

Figure 138. Tools used in a safe burglary.

closed circuit there is always a weak current in the wiring, and the alarm will sound when the current is broken in the contact. By the combination of the two the alarm will be given when the current is broken as well as when contact is established. The latter method is undoubtedly the best of the three. Different manufacturers have constructed many different electrical contacts, such as door and window contacts, devices with infra-red rays, photocells, television camera eyes, etc.

The open circuit system will be put out of action simply by cutting the wiring, and the closed contact system through cross-contacting. In cases where the combined systems are used the criminal may lay open the wiring, but the wires carrying a current must be determined with the aid of a compass and cross-contacted. The other wires must be cut. The weak spot of any alarm system is the wiring. This should be made as invincible as possible by embedding it in the walls and floors.

Figure 139.   A ripping job and the can opener and other tools used.

The technique used today by safe burglars may be any of the following methods, listed in the order of their frequency. Regardless of technique, there are certain instruments common to all safe burglars which are used to force entrance to the premises, i.e., jimmy, bolt cutters, saws (hacksaw and compass saw), brace or electric drills, and bits, chisels, keys, and flashlight. They will also carry gloves to avoid leaving fingerprints.

RIPPING JOBS. The chief piece of equipment used is a sectional jimmy.

There are many kinds of jimmies, among them the one-piece type with one of its ends chiseled and the two- or three-section type with one of its ends like the point of a pencil and the other end chiseled. The latter is commonly called the sectional jimmy.

The safe burglar usually drills a hole in the upper left-hand corner of

New York Police Department

Figure 140. Safe burglary: a punch job.

the door—or one of the doors—with an electric drill, inserts the pencil point of the jimmy into the aperture, and rips in an upward or downward direction until the front steel plate is off. Sometimes, however, he makes an opening large enough to insert the jimmy merely by pounding a corner of the door. (See Figure 139.)

PUNCH JOBS. This is a type of safe job frequently perpetrated today. The dial is knocked off with a sledge hammer, the spindle is punched back with a center punch and mallet, and the small sockets are broken, allowing the release of the lock. Tools carried by the burglars will be sledge hammer, steel punches, or driftpins. (See Figures 140, 141, and 142.)

New York Police Department

Figure 141.   Punch job with the dial punched out.

BURN JOBS. In jobs of this kind one of the criminals must be trained to know the proper amount of air and acetylene gas that has to be applied to heat and burn the steel of the safe. It is necessary to transport an oxygen and gas tank, a burner, and an adequate footage of hose.

CARRY-AWAY JOBS. The mob will use an ordinary automobile, station wagon, or truck, depending on the size of the safe. The motive for this method is to be able to work at ease at their own hideout. The empty safe will be thrown into a lake or river or be dumped in the woods.

COMBINATION JOBS. When the investigator of a safe burglary finds that the safe has been opened by the combination, it is evident that the safe was not locked properly or that someone knew the combination or had gained access to where it was kept and committed the crime. While such a case calls for a check of the movements of employees of the concern and of the building in which the concern is located, the possibility of a professional sneak's gaining access to and searching drawers of desks in offices and obtaining the combination from written memoranda pasted to the side or bottom of a drawer or otherwise left exposed to view must not be overlooked. The combination lock manufacturers always have a few men who are able to open a combination lock without knowing the combination. It is done by a mathematical method and will take several hours for experienced men. A handful of burglars in this country have reached the professional height of being able to open a combination lock. They are very rare, however, and as far as is known the few burglars who are able to do this are at present in public custody. The tool sometimes carried by high-class combination men is a small device which looks like a fountain pen from the outside. Under the

Figure 142.   Tools used in a punch job.

upper screwed-on part, instead of the pen, is an almost microscopically thin steel rod. An extremely thin hole is drilled above the lock and the thin steel rod inserted in the hole to aid in manipulating the lock.

BLOW JOBS. This type of safe job is almost extinct in New York City today. It is extensively used in other parts of the world, however, especially in Scandinavia. The modern blower will use dynamite, although only a few decades ago nitroglycerin was predominant. The criminal who employs this method must know the proper amounts of explosives to use. In many cases he does not, and the content of the safe will be destroyed.

If dynamite is used, about twenty-five grains is enough to open a small, old-fashioned safe. It may be necessary for the burglar to drill a hole to insert the explosive. A fulminating cap is used with the dynamite and a safety fuse or an electric wire connected with the fulminating cap. All crevices are covered with ordinary kitchen soap, clay, or some similar material. In order to avoid the sound of the explosion the safe is wrapped in cotton, clothes, or covers. The wrapping material is often soaked in

Figure 143. A blow job in which nitroglycerin was used.

water. The windows are opened for two reasons: to prevent them from bursting from the pressure of the explosion, causing noise, and to let the gases from the explosion escape. The gases would otherwise give the burglar a terrible headache. It should be mentioned that cases are known in which burglars have put Oriental carpets valued at several thousand dollars around a safe which contained $20. Dynamite, when not too close to a fulminating cap or when frozen, is a fairly harmless material. Nitroglycerin, on the other hand, may explode on the slightest provocation. It is interesting to note that the old "blow jobber" used to carry the nitroglycerin in a hot water bottle under his overcoat. Quite a few instances of accidents are known in which burglars were disfigured or dismembered. In the old nitroglycerin jobs a hole was drilled in the door of the safe a little to the left over the dial, and a piece of cotton saturated in

Figure 144.   Modern safe-blower's outfit.

nitroglycerin was wrapped around the fulminating cap, which was inserted in the hole. The crevices were covered with kitchen soap, and the connecting wire run from the fulminating cap to a battery or electrical outlet at least fifteen feet away.

CHOPPING JOBS. In these cases the safe is turned upside down and the bottom or one of the walls is chopped out. This must be regarded as very crude amateur work.

LOFT BURGLARS

The loft man nowadays plies his trade the year round. In the Middle Atlantic States this sort of theft is most often committed by persons who were formerly employed in loft buildings or who, having received their early training as small-store thieves, were led to the newer field of endeavor by glittering accounts of the profits in looting lofts. Their jobs, however, are distinguishable by the fact that they usually take a large quantity of finished goods without distinction as to quality.

As in the case of safe burglars, the loft men work in mobs of from two to six members, depending upon the type of job and the bulk of the merchandise. They are active between seven o'clock in the evening and daylight, while the loot may be transported from the scene at any time during the succeeding day and night.

Because of the precautions taken by business houses which store furs, silk, or other valuables, a loft mob must carefully plan the crime. They have to discover the best method of gaining entrance and of carrying off the swag; whether the loft is wired or "bugged" or "muzzled" by a protective agency or some other company, and if so, whether there are any unwired spots in the doors, walls, floors, or ceiling through which an opening can be cut.

Tools used by loft burglars depend on the kind of job to be done. If entrance is to be gained through a door, a gooseneck jimmy may be used. (The trade name is can opener or ripping bar.) If entrance is to be gained through a wall or through a floor or ceiling, the tools consist of a jimmy with a sharp point on one end for knocking or chipping out concrete in floors or ceilings, a brace and wood bit, or an electric drill for boring several holes in the wooden floor. An opening of sufficient size is made to gain entrance and to pass the merchandise through.

Continental burglars, when making a hole in the ceiling while working on the floor of an upper room, will very often use a large umbrella. The catch of the umbrella is removed so that it will open easily. A string is fitted to the handle and another string is fitted to the top of the umbrella.

As soon as the first hole through the ceiling has been made, the umbrella is lowered through into the room beneath and is kept open under the hole in the ceiling. It serves the purpose of collecting plaster and concrete which would otherwise fall down on the floor underneath and create some noise. As soon as the umbrella is filled up, it is lowered to the floor and

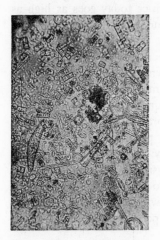

Figure 145. Photomicrograph of safe insulation. In blow jobs Diatomaceae, a typical component of safe insulation, are spread like fine dust all over the immediate area and also penetrate into the burglar's clothes. The traces in the clothes can be collected with the special filter shown in Figure 114.

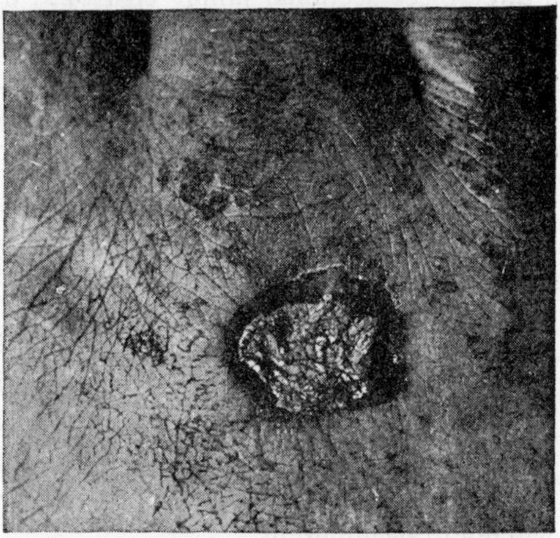

Figure 146. In the investigation of a burglary in a jeweler's shop a piece of human skin about ¾ of a square inch was found. When a suspect was arrested, he had a wound on his right hand which the piece of skin fitted exactly. He finally confessed.

the other string attached to the top is pulled so that the umbrella tips and empties its contents on the floor. The umbrella is again pulled up by the string attached to the handle so the work can continue.

Other paraphernalia may include flashlight, canvas or cloth gloves to protect hands from injury and to avoid leaving fingerprint impressions, and black cloth or burlap bags in which to carry away plunder. Sometimes a chisel—with the aid of a copper hammer or a gut or leather mallet—is used to cut away concrete. Sound is lessened when the chisel is struck by a leather or gut mallet.

The sectional jimmy is made in blacksmith or machine shops. The burglar makes a sketch of the tool he desires and brings it to a blacksmith whose respect for law and order is nil. The unscrupulous blacksmith knows he is making a burglar's tool and charges accordingly. Several years ago it cost $10 for a two-piece sectional jimmy. A can opener and a three-piece sectional jimmy cost $25; the price today goes as high as $100. A small hook jimmy, brace and bits, and other tools may be purchased in any hardware store. The need for thorough investigation at such stores is obvious. Many cases have been broken by information obtained from collaborative hardware store owners.

The technique used today by loft burglars may be any one of the following methods, listed in the order of their frequency:

LAY-IN JOBS. The mob obtains the collaboration of a legitimate businessman and uses his premises as a starting point for their operations and also for a hiding place for their loot. They enter the building in daytime, hide in the loft or office of the businessman, and after dark start looting the neighboring lofts, taking the loot to the starting-point of their operations, where it is hidden. The mob awaits daytime, leaving the building the next morning when it is full of people and their departure will not draw attention.

BORE JOBS. The mobs carrying out this sort of job will invariably bore through the walls, floors, or ceilings. To attack a "muzzled" or protected storeroom, the mob obtains permission from a neighbor who is not very particular as to his source of income to use a loft above, below, or adjoining the one containing the property about to change hands. After some drilling and excavating, an aperture approximately eighteen inches square appears in the lightly constructed ceiling, floor, or wall of the treasure-house. This hole must be carefully drilled, so that no alarm wires are met and broken. The details of the technique of bore jobbers is told above.

KICK-IN JOBS. In this case the mob usually consists of three or four men operating late in the evening, about midnight, or shortly before or after the opening hour of the business day. It is immaterial whether the place is wired for protection. They drive up to the curb in front of the premises, the driver-accomplice keeping the motor running. His confederates force or jimmy the street door, if locked, step into the vestibule or hallway, and there force or jimmy the inner door or smash a window, enter and grab armfuls of valuable furs, ladies' coats, or garments, and then escape in the waiting automobile. Generally the premises selected for attack are on the ground floor.

A lone kick-in burglar may operate on any floor and if there is a commotion will hide in the same building until the alarm subsides, then sneak down the stairway to the street, hail a taxicab, and leave with the loot.

AERIAL JOBS. This technique is used when entrance to the loft can be gained through a window which has no protective wiring. Such a window will be one located on the roof of the building (skylight) or on some upper floor which cannot be reached by a fire-escape. This kind of window is mistakenly thought safe against attacks by loft burglars. The mob will gain access to the roof and hook a rope or a rope ladder to a chimney or to some similar part of the roof. One of the mob will undertake the hazardous task of entering the window by this means, and the rope will be used to hoist the loot to the roof to the waiting members of the mob.

SECRETION JOBS. A member of the mob secretes himself in the loft or building before closing time and makes a careful selection of the desirable goods. When his confederates arrive, they pack his choice in specially prepared swag bags and carry them to the street. Here a truck, cab, or private car receives the loot for transportation to the "drop" or hiding place. If there is danger in this rather open method, the swag is sometimes hidden in a vacant loft in a neighboring building or in the very building in which the burglarized loft is located, in the cellar, on the roof, in the tank house or motor house, or in another loft with the permission of its tenant.

STORE BURGLARS

Generally two or four men work together in store burglaries. The amateur store burglars are usually young men residing in or near the area in which they operate. Stolen goods are disposed of locally to unscrupulous dealers or pawned.

The regular or professional store burglar uses great care in planning and executing jobs. Finders are sometimes employed to locate jobs, or tipsters furnish information. This type of burglar is usually an ex-convict who gets together a mob of younger men with less experience than himself. He inspects places to be burglarized, plans the job, secures tools, and arranges for sale of stolen merchandise to a fence. The place selected to be burglarized is observed and inspected during business and closing hours for one or more days prior to the crime, which is committed during late night or early morning hours. Habits of owners, employees, persons in the neighborhood, policemen on post, private watchmen, and passersby are noted. Opening and closing time of the store is observed, and it is determined whether the premises are wired for burglary protection or not.

When the crime is completed, the loot is placed in the yard or the hallway or near the front door. A lookout signals when the way is clear; another accomplice in an automobile then draws up to the premises, and the loot is taken away in the car. The other criminals follow in another car or leave the scene afoot.

Tools selected depend on the entry to be effected. Eighteen- to thirty-six-inch jimmies are used for doors and windows. If there are bars on windows, a Stillson wrench, a setting pipe cutter, a hacksaw, or an auto jack may be used to cut or spread the bars. To enter through the floor or ceiling or through a side wall from the hallway or an empty adjoining store, braces, wood bits, or cold chisels are employed. Tinsmith's snips are used to cut sheet-iron ceilings.

WINDOW SMASHERS. Window smashers are usually young men. These criminals may have a car, with motor running and an accomplice driver on the seat, parked around the corner from the store selected. In jewelry store cases the job is done during business hours, while the jewelry is on window display. The criminal, carrying a brick or stone wrapped up in a paper or cloth, approaches the window, knocks or throws the missile against the glass, breaking a hole in it, inserts his hand, grabs a tray of jewelry or its contents, runs to the waiting automobile, and flees. Success depends upon suddenness and surprise of attack and boldness of action.

Another type operates in mobs of three or four. They also use a car. Their specialty is fur shops, department stores, and dress shops where valuable merchandise is on display. The hour of attack selected is when stores are closed and not many persons are about. Midnight is a favored time, when patrolmen on post are walking or riding in to the station house or waiting near relieving points, with their thoughts concentrated on going off duty. Other favored times are when street lights are extinguished in early morning or when a policeman leaves his post for duty or for relief of personal needs. Originally the thief would throw a milk can or ashcan to smash the window, but today a brick or some similar missile is used. The thieves then grab the merchandise and take flight in an automobile.

The lone window smasher operates as a rule in the winter season, during late night or early morning hours. While some lone workers might be classified as mental defectives, the urge for sustenance and shelter has furnished the motive for some normal men to commit this type of crime in recent years.

RESIDENCE BURGLARS

Types of residence burglaries may be said to include those committed in flats or apartment houses, those committed in vacant houses, and—a type prevalent in recent years—those committed in penthouses.

FLAT AND APARTMENT HOUSE BURGLARS. The day burglar usually operates in the mornings and afternoons. The night burglar operates in the evenings from midnight to daybreak.

Many burglaries are committed by youths who are without funds to satisfy their desire for pleasure or recreation, although many burglars may be older. Youths of this class usually frequent candy stores and cheap pool parlors; sometimes they fly kites and pigeons from roofs. Their criminal operations are as a rule confined to their neighborhood; they seldom go very far from their rendezvous. Loot is often bought by the owner of the store which they use as a hangout or is pledged, pawned, or sold at a pawnshop or secondhand dealer's establishment by the owner of their hangout or by one of the burglars or by an older boy who frequents the store. Nowadays, however, many of these burglaries are made on a large scale by more professional mobs, and the loot is disposed of in a more businesslike fashion.

Another class of youths committing flat burglaries in the daytime are those not residing at home but living in cheap furnished rooms. They may be found lounging in pool parlors, dance halls, coffee restaurants, bakeries, parks, or around cheap motion-picture theaters. They start out in the mornings from their rendezvous or hangout.

Different methods are used to ascertain if the occupant of a flat or apartment is not at home. The inexperienced thief may be observed looking up at the front windows of the house selected, from the opposite side of the street. When an apartment is spotted where the shades are down full length, the vestibule of the building is entered and the bell of the flat or apartment rung. If there is no answer, the thief either uses a passkey or rings another tenant's bell to gain entrance. Proceeding to the apartment he intends to burglarize, a knock is given on the door or the buzzer or bell is pushed. If there is no answer, the door may be opened with a passkey if it has a common lock. If the door has a patent lock, a jimmy is used to effect entrance or a panel of the door is cut out and a hand inserted to unlock it. Contents of bureau drawers, sideboards, and other pieces of furniture are dumped on beds, on dining-room and other tables, or on the floor. Everything of value is sorted and placed in a suitcase, handgrip, or pillow case. Escape is made by way of the roof or by walking boldly out the front door. If a pillow case is used to carry the loot, it is swung over a shoulder to simulate a laundry bag.

HOUSE MOB. Sometimes a flat burglar works with two or three accomplices. They compose what is known as a house mob. One is a lookout. A faked letter is placed in the letterbox of the apartment selected. Persons entering the hall are checked by the lookout. If the letter is removed, the lookout signals by ringing the bell of the apartment as the tenant starts upstairs. The burglars either escape by way of the roof or walk downstairs past their victim, being careful to conceal the face by tipping the hat in such a way as to cover it or by using a handkerchief. Gaining the street, they proceed to the nearest public conveyance or may use a "drive-your-own car" and return to their hangout or rooms.

Jewelry, silverware, and wearing apparel are usually pawned or sold late in the morning or afternoon. Clothing may also be disposed of by pledge or sale to a dishonest proprietor of a secondhand-clothing store, who immediately removes labels and other marks of identification. Attention to such suspected or known places should be given by police and detectives during business hours.

There have been cases where burglars of this type have kept clothing and wearing apparel in their rooms until a quantity was secured and then sold to a cast-off-clothes man.

In criminal argot the burglar who does not have a place set to burglarize when he starts out but chances to find one is referred to as "going on the blind" or "peddling a flat."

The burglar who works on tips has advance information about the flat or apartment to be burglarized and knows where valuables are kept. Such tips may be given by a laundry, grocery, hall, or telephone boy; by a janitor; possibly by a son or daughter of a janitor; by an employee of a merchant who is in the habit of keeping his money at home; or by a relative of the victim. In cases of the last type the person who gave the tip may make it convenient to be present in the apartment burglarized when the police or a detective is called to investigate. The tipster listens to what is said about efforts that will be made to solve the crime and observes the officer examining articles for fingerprints. The tipster then may try to smudge every fingerprint impression.

SUPPER BURGLAR. The suppertime burglar uses methods similar to those of the day burglar to determine if occupants of an apartment are at home. He ascends the stairs and opens or forces the door. Sometimes he uses the fire-escape, enters through a window, and places a chair under the knob of the door leading from the room he is in to other rooms in the apartment or to the hall—to afford time to leave by way of the fire-escape should the occupant discover his presence.

THE NIGHT BURGLAR. A nighttime burglar of one class works evenings, alone or with a partner, in residential sections comprised of apartment houses, while owners are away from home. Such criminals are shrewd and artful and will visit a residential section making observations to select likely places to burglarize. These observations may be made from adjoining or adjacent houses, occupied or in course of construction, or from areaways or roofs of occupied houses. Some may even inspect the victim's house during the daytime to plan approach and getaway. Suitable pretexts are assumed by them in such instances; they often pose as canvassers, salesmen, or inspectors, or pretend to be looking for a relative or friend. Should there be an empty apartment in the house, the burglar may secrete himself there until nightfall. If not, he returns later, stopping before entering the house to make sure he is not being shadowed or observed. To effect entrance to the selected apartment, he may use a skeleton key, a lock pick, or a jimmy. Or he may ascend or descend the fire-escape to a window leading into the apartment. Gaining entrance, he places chairs across doorways and in the private hall of the apartment, so that warning will be given him if the absent occupants return, and the latter will be impeded in any attempt at pursuit.

This type of night burglar at times operates on tips and may park an automobile in the same or next street to that in which he operates.

The after-midnight burglar uses a technique in many ways similar to his colleague who commits burglaries during the hours before midnight. Gaining the roof or the fire-escape, he removes his shoes. He enters the selected apartment by way of a window leading to the fire-escape, by a rope ladder dropped from the roof, or by means of any available physical abutment or contrivance which is attached to the building.

He listens for the breathing of sleeping occupants. Cautiously stepping into the bedroom, he removes trousers, coat, vest, purses and bags found there to the dining room, kitchen, or other room or to the fire-escape, roof, yard, areaway or cellar, and extracts money and jewelry therefrom. He may also place chairs across doorways or in the private hall of the apartment so that if the occupant or occupants awake and attempt pursuit they will trip and fall and afford time for escape. Seldom does he reach the street by way of the house entered. Exit generally is by way of an adjoining house, or the next street is reached by climbing over a fence.

Generally an automobile is parked at a convenient location. In instances where an automobile is not used, operations are usually confined to localities adjacent to transportation systems.

Some after-midnight burglars operate by inserting a mechanical contraption through the window from the fire-escape which will pick up trousers and wearing apparel placed on chairs, etc., near windows. Others immediately cut the telephone wire upon entry. After-midnight burglars may be classified as the most dangerous type. They have been known to be armed with pistols and to carry lethal and nonlethal agents (chloroform, etc.) or other substances to assist them in their operations. Sometimes they wear masks.

Paraphernalia used by night burglars comprise flashlight, jackknife, small jimmy, screwdriver, glass-cutter, false keys, and picklocks.

PRIVATE DWELLING BURGLARS. 1. *Town and City Type.* While private dwellings in towns and cities are often entered by day and night burglars using a criminal technique along the lines used by flat and apartment house burglars, attention should also be given to the professional private dwelling burglar in urban areas who operates while the occupants are away on vacation, abroad, or absent for a protracted period. Information may be secured by use of the telephone, by tips from delivery boys, from gossipy tradesmen, or from an artisan or servant employed on the premises. In instances where a tip is furnished details of where jewelry, money, bonds, and other valuables are kept are also supplied. Skeleton keys are used or entrance is gained by breaking through a window or door, generally in the basement, areaway, or yard.

2. *Supper Men.* Then there is the supper man, who robs private dwellings exclusively between 7 P.M. and 9 P.M., while the occupants are in the dining room. Search is made in rooms on upper floors only. Money, jewelry, furs, and valuable coats comprise the plunder taken. This type climbs to the roof of the private dwelling from the roof of an adjoining house and enters by way of skylight or scuttle or by climbing up or down a drainpipe to an open window. Before going to work, he arranges a getaway, perhaps by placing a ladder or table under the skylight. In investigating such cases the detective should carefully examine the walls around scuttle or skylight entrances for fingerprint impressions or for articles or memoranda which may have been dropped by the burglar in making entrance or getaway. The roof should also be searched for clues. Cases are on record where the burglars lost memoranda and left other clues which led to apprehension.

3. *Suburban Dwellings.* Both the amateur and the professional criminal operate against this type of residence in the suburban or sparsely built up sections of city, town, and village. While the burglar generally works during the absence of the homeowner and his family in the day and evening hours, in recent years entrance has been effected after midnight and up until daylight. Entrance may be made at any time by forcing a cellar window or a window on the first floor, usually from the rear yard; by climbing up porch or extension and forcing an upper window; or by the use of skeleton keys.

This class of burglar steals only such property, money, jewelry, silverware, and fur coats as may be concealed on his person or carried away in a suitcase or grip found handy for the purpose. Some also steal radios and television sets, particularly when there is a market for their purchase.

Often the suburban burglar operating after midnight cuts telephone wires as soon as he gains entrance. He may be classed as a very dangerous type who will shoot to effect escape and prevent capture.

Police officers and detectives should be suspicious of the movements of strangers on the streets in suburban sections, especially after midnight.

4. *Penthouse Burglars.* With the advent of the penthouse, the field of activity for the professional residence burglar grew larger. Fair and warm weather helps him. Dwellers in penthouses generally like plenty of fresh air and are accustomed to having windows and doorways screened but open. The technique used by the penthouse burglar is similar to that of the night burglar. Generally only money and jewelry are stolen.

In investigating such cases it is important to determine when and where other penthouses have been burglarized and to lay plans accordingly to effect a capture.

MISCELLANEOUS BURGLARS

Dishonest bellhops, waiters, elevator operators, and janitors form another group. They know when the occupant is out and when return can be expected. Sometimes the keys to the apartment have been left in their care, and keys are easily duplicated. They either commit the burglary or have an accomplice commit it. Loot may be secreted in a storeroom or locker on the premises, to be removed when work is finished.

Degenerates often commit nuisance crimes, taking women's wearing apparel off clotheslines, etc. Their apprehension is desired to prevent them from getting bolder and committing more serious acts. Oftentimes medical treatment may cure them if started early enough.

No matter what the type of the professional burglar, he will be shrewd enough to take almost all precautions to prevent stolen property being found on him and may resort to transferring it by express or to checking it in a self-service or service checking station for a period of time.

CRIMINAL RECEIVERS

The person who earns a livelihood by criminally receiving and disposing of stolen goods is a malignant enemy of society. It has been truthfully said time and again that if there were no receivers of stolen goods there would be very little crime against property and against persons who are attacked and robbed of property. Criminal receivers are responsible for most of the dishonesty and unethical practices in business, for youths committing crime, and for professional criminals continuing in crime. Operating ostensibly as a businessman in a manner to keep away from the arm of the law, the criminal receiver or fence does business only with one man. As a rule that man has a criminal record. Often the fence will operate through a third person designated by him as his lieutenant. Goods purchased are paid for in cash, and rarely is a record made or kept of the purchase.

The finder locates a desirable haul and notes the quality and quantity of the merchandise. This information is given by the finder to the criminal band of burglars or thieves. One of the thieves then locates a receiver and informs him of the amount and quality of the merchandise. The best offer is accepted, and the drop or location of delivery is named. The drop may be a warehouse, a garage, or a loft or store, occupied or unoccupied. The lieutenant sees to it that the drop is set to receive the delivery. The stolen goods are delivered to the drop by one or two of the thieves while others in the band precede the load to the drop to make certain that the way is clear.

With delivery made, the merchandise is examined by the lieutenant. Upon being found satisfactory, identification marks are removed. These marks include selvage markings, stamped numbers or letters, trade marks, tags, wrappings, stencils, or sewed-on marks.

When this task is completed, the receiver is notified. He comes to the drop, pays cash for the loot, and removes it in a truck to his place of business, which has the appearance of a legitimate establishment. From time to time visits are made to the receiver's place by small retail merchants who come from various parts of the city or from suburban towns to purchase marketable merchandise. Thus are stolen goods distributed. The small retail merchant is not the only buyer. Jobbers and merchants doing business on a larger scale are contacted and told of exceptional buys below market quotations and avail themselves thereof, making a quick turnover by underselling reliable competitors.

Sometimes criminal receivers get control over thieves and burglars by lending them money to carry them along while they are awaiting favorable criminal opportunities and by engaging attorneys to defend them in court after arrest. The receiver also busies himself to make advantageous contacts to "fix the case."

In order successfully to prosecute and convict a receiver it is necessary to prove he knew the goods purchased were stolen. This may be brought about by interrogation leading to his admission of the fact or by discovery of the stolen goods on his premises, concealed, re-marked or re-labeled. In making investigations of receivers intelligent interrogation, check, and search play important roles. Conversations are voluble: denials, lies, evasive answers, misstatements are made; false labels and bills or a lack thereof appear; unethical and furtive buying methods show up in combination with very low prices paid.

Criminal receivers may be found in the field occupied by reliable pawnbrokers, secondhand dealers, junk dealers, auctioneers, jewelry merchants, and the like. To the layman the successful prosecution of a man for criminally receiving stolen goods therefore seems a difficult task. It is not. To illustrate with a case:

A few years ago a truckload of silk valued at $20,000 was reported by the driver to have been stolen. It afterward developed that the truck had been turned over by the driver to a thief. The latter drove it to a drop (an unoccupied loft), where the lieutenant for the receiver examined the goods and bought them. Stencil marks on the cases were removed, and the goods were taken out and—after removing the marks thereon—shipped to the receiver. Detectives located the thief and the loft in which the goods were dropped. The thief did not know the receiver nor his place of business, as the only person with whom he had come in contact had been the lieutenant for the receiver. A careful search of the building in which the loft was located was made. In a coal pit of the fireroom parts of the wooden cases, some of which had been burned, were found. It was later determined that the superintendent of the building had received a sum of money for destroying the wooden cases and tags. Continuing the investigation, detectives interrogated the porter in the building, who had helped to carry some of the goods out to the express truck. A description of the expressman and of the truck was obtained. The expressman was located, and he revealed the address of the premises to which he delivered the goods. Here some cases were found on tables, ostensibly in process of manufacture. The receiver produced a lease showing that he had sublet the loft to a man a week previously. The reason for the sublease was that he had received a telegram from a relative in California requesting him to come there. He produced the telegram to substantiate his story. A check-up of associates, home conditions, and his movements before and after receiving the stolen merchandise disclosed that the receiver had slept in a friend's house while the goods were in his loft and that he had informed his friend of anticipated trouble in his loft. The lease and the telegram were proved to be false. It was also ascertained that he told his friend he wanted to stay for two weeks longer in the loft, as he anticipated trouble. This was sufficient to show that the receiver had knowledge that the goods were stolen.

Criminal receivers of stolen goods resort to all sorts of tricks for the purpose of secreting these goods. One trick is to have a trap door through which the stolen merchandise is thrown into a secret compartment. The trap door is then closed, and simulated packages, all wrapped in the same fashion, are placed on the floor over it.

Sometimes criminal receivers visit the homes of thieves for the purpose of inspecting and buying stolen loot. If found satisfactory, a taxicab or closed truck is driven up to the premises and the loot removed.

In cases where jewelry comprises the stolen plunder the burglars or thieves are apt to hire a room in the neighborhood a week or more in advance of the job and continue to occupy it for a few weeks after the job has been committed, the purpose being to have a ready and safe place to hide the stolen goods and keep under cover. Contact is subsequently made with the criminal receiver. The receiver and one of the thieves then may proceed to a bank in which the receiver has a safe-deposit box into which the thief puts the stolen jewelry. Subsequently the receiver returns to the vault, examines the jewelry, places a value thereon, and pays the thief. Shortly thereafter the jewelry is removed to another bank and safe-deposit box.

In one case a merchant was robbed systematically of over one hundred cases of woolen yarn. In a check-up of his employees a shipping clerk was trailed to a shady place and seen conversing with a criminal receiver. The receiver was covered. A few days later, he was seen talking to a truckman and the truckman and his vehicle proceeded to within half a block of the merchant's store. There he was met by the shipping clerk during his lunch hour, and four large cases were taken from the freight elevator of the premises and placed on the truck. Delivery was made to a factory some miles away. Here it was found that the criminal receiver had made many purchases of goods stolen from the same merchant. On the premises were found over fifty cases of merchandise bearing the merchant's name. The criminal receiver could only account for the purchase of ten and refused to explain whence the others came. The shipping clerk was arrested. The truckman and the elevator man in the factory of the receiver told of their work in connection with the stolen cases. This, supplemented by the fact that record books contained no record of the merchandise, as well as by the evasive answers and denials of the receiver, led to successful prosecution and conviction.

SEARCH FOR STOLEN PROPERTY

When property has been stolen, a thorough search should be made of the building from which it has been taken. In many cases the plunder has been recovered on back stairways, in empty rooms or apartments of residences, in empty or occupied lofts in the building in which the crime was committed, or in adjacent buildings, garages, or private homes. Smaller pieces of goods such as jewelry may be concealed almost anyplace. Jewelry may be mixed with sugar and hidden in a sugar bowl, or it may be hung on a string outside the window, etc.

Today many police departments maintain a card system in which to record stolen property, and the cards from this file will often match the cards sent in by pawnbrokers and dealers compelled by law to report pledges and purchases and by banks and honest merchants ready to cooperate with the police. In his quest of stolen goods the efficient detective personally visits and inspects the premises of licensed brokers, accompanied by the victim or complainant, and likewise checks known or suspected fences and drops. Never should the room, apartment, or residence of a prisoner whose arrest is concerned with stolen property or extorted money be overlooked in the quest. The suspect's residence should be visited immediately and a systematic and thorough search made. Automobiles owned or hired by the defendant should also be searched, as well as any garage he may have used.

DESCRIPTION OF PROPERTY

It is essential for the police investigator or detective to secure a complete description of the stolen property. The following gives the main descriptive details for general articles that are subject to theft or loss:

Watches:

Kind of metal; manufacture; description of case and movement and numbers of each; lady's or gentleman's; "h.c." (hunting case) or "o.f." (open face); initials; monograms or inscriptions; value.

Rings:

Kind of metal; lady's or gentleman's; style; setting; kind and number of stones; weight; maker's name; initials or other marks;[4] value.

Kind of metal; lady's or gentleman's; length and weight; kind of link; style; value.

Bonds, currency, etc.:

Identifying numbers such as serial numbers; face amounts, etc.[5]

Earrings or studs:

Kind of metal; style; whether screw, coil, or drop; kind, size, and number of stones; value.

Miscellaneous jewelry:

Name of articles; kind of metal or material; kind and number of stones; design; initials; inscriptions or monograms; maker's name; value.

Table silverware:

Name of articles; solid silver or plated; heavy or lightweight; maker's name; design, such as plain, beaded, or flowered, formal, animal, etc.; initials, inscriptions or monograms; value.

Miscellaneous gold and silver goods:

Name of article; kind of material; plated or solid; size; maker's name; design; number of pieces if set; initials; inscriptions or monograms; plain, chased, etched or engraved; open or solid pattern; value.

Bric-a-brac or antiques:

Name of articles; material or materials; design; size; shape; carved, engraved, enameled, or inlaid; age; value; trade mark on bottom.

Pocketbooks, handbags, suitcases, etc.:

Name of article; material; size; color; shape; initials or other marks; value; contents.

Clothing:

Name of articles; material; style; size; color; maker's name; initials or other marks; value; dry-cleaner's or laundry marks; union label.

Furs:

Name of article; coat; muff; collar, etc.; kind; size; color; value, if coat. Numbers on skins, monogram or name of owner.

Animals:

Kind; size; distinctive color or distinguishing marks; age, sex, etc.

Motor vehicles:

See Chapter XXII.

Motorcycles:

Make; year of model; number of cylinders; manufacturer's number; make of saddle; make and condition of tires; position of speedometer; horn; front and rear lights; distinctive marks; license number.

Bicycles:

Make; color; number; kind of brakes and saddle.

Typewriters:

Kind; serial and model numbers.

SIMULATED BURGLARIES

Although not always susceptible of proof, many burglaries, robberies, and larcenies are prearranged and fraudulent. In character of motive they are in the same category as numerous cases of arson, which is often resorted to for the purpose of concealing insolvency and theft. There is a vast difference, however, between fraudulent claims for indemnification due to alleged burglary or theft and those based on losses by fire. In the former there has been no real loss to the policyholder, whereas in the latter there is a tangible and obvious loss of property which leaves little to be determined but the criminal participation—if there is reason to suspect it of the person insured.

Figure 147.   In the investigation of a burglary where simulation was suspected it was necessary to determine whether a hole drilled through a window frame had been made from the inside or outside. The frame was cut in two through the center of the hole and the fibers in the interior of the hole examined. It was found that the fibers at the right of the hole sloped downward and those at the left sloped upward. Since the fibers around the edges of a drilled hole will turn to the right with the drill, the examination established that in this case the hole had been made in the direction indicated by the arrows.

In either instance the possibilities for fraud are unlimited. For instance, the property alleged to have been stolen or burned may never have been in the possession of the insured, or he may have sold it, or, having guilty knowledge of what was about to transpire, he may have had it transferred elsewhere. The loft districts of metropolitan areas have always been the scene of activity for depredations of the dishonest merchant endeavoring to realize on an insurance policy through burglary, larceny, or arson. So the importance of a careful investigation of the phases referred to in the first part of the chapter is obvious.

A careful investigation of the way of the perpetrator on the scene and of his *modus operandi* will often give information regarding faked burglaries. The owner of a store who simulates a burglary seldom has a correct idea of a burglar's methods, hence he often fails to avoid logical pitfalls. Broken windows will be found to have been smashed from the inside, holes in walls will be too small to allow the entrance of an individual, etc. A case of one of the authors will illustrate:[6]

A jeweler reported to the police that a burglary had been committed in his shop and that goods valued at $40,000 had been stolen. An examination of the scene indicated that the perpetrator had entered through the basement, forced the door of the cellar, and there made a hole in the brick ceiling, which was more than a yard thick. The floor of the shop was occupied by counters and other paraphernalia, but the burglar had been lucky enough to penetrate the open floor space. There were no traces, such as fingerprints. A careful investigation was made, with the following results:

1. The cellar door showed evidence of jimmy marks and evidently had been forced open from the outside. The lock on the inside of the cellar door had been held in place by four screws. Two of the old and rusty screws showed fresh marks of a screwdriver. Smaller pieces of wood were found attached to the threads of the two remaining screws, a sure sign that the screws had been torn away by force. Two of the screws had been removed from the inside with a screwdriver and only two forced away.

Figure 148. These screws have been pulled away by force. This is clearly indicated by the splinters of wood in the pitch.

2. Along the edges of the hole in the ceiling loose pieces of brick and concrete were hanging. Ordinarily they would have fallen down if anyone had tried to go up through the hole.

3. The floor of the shop was covered with encaustic tiles. When examined with a magnifying glass, it was discovered that the slabs had been chiseled from above.

Faced with these overwhelming technical evidences, the jeweler finally admitted that he had committed the burglary to collect insurance. At first he had tried to break open the cellar door but had failed. Then he proceeded to unscrew two of the screws that held the lock from the inside and had succeeded in breaking the door open. He had begun to pierce the ceiling from the cellar but found this operation too tiresome with pieces of brick and concrete constantly falling on his face. Finally he went up to the shop and proceeded to make the hole from above.

1 In olden days safe mobs (more than one is termed a mob in any type of crime, for instance, safe mob, house mob, loft mob, etc.) often used a "finder." The finder was often an employee of the victim or a person who had access to the building. He located the job and gave reports on details. Nowadays the mob generally finds the job itself.

2 Sometimes, however, a criminal will change his *modus operandi* after having learned a trade. Cases are known where former stickup men who worked in shipyards during the war learned how to apply the acetylene torch and after the war turned to safecracking.

3 It is not unusual for criminals to bring a woman along in order to appear more trustworthy, posing as petters.

4 All central private investigating agencies for the different trade associations maintain records of all marks placed on the goods of trade. Secret marks known as scratch marks are placed on pieces of valuable jewelry by many jewelry manufacturers and also on watches in watch repair shops. These places can sometimes furnish information valuable for identification purposes.

5 In the United States the government requires that financial institutions record transactions in which persons cash or deposit bonds or currency of $1,000 and $10,000 denominations.

6 Söderman.[4]

XXII INVESTIGATION OF LARCENY

THE PERSEVERANCE AND INGENUITY OF THE BURGLAR, AS DESCRIBED IN the preceding chapter, are surpassed in degree by the practitioners of the numerous forms of larceny. To cope with the problems of larceny the investigator must be thoroughly familiar with the techniques employed by the professional criminal. To this end we shall describe the methods of operation used in the more common forms of larceny together with the techniques used in setting traps for the thief. Some space has been devoted also to mail thefts, although primary jurisdiction in these offenses is given to the inspectors of the Post Office Department. Nevertheless, a well-rounded investigator should be familiar with the methods used in detecting opened letters, forged seals, and similar problems.

AUTOMOBILE THEFTS

AUTOMOBILE THEFTS. Auto theft is the largest single cause of property loss by criminal means in the United States today. The auto theft, in the majority of cases, occurs on the public highway in contrast to the privacy surrounding most other crimes. In spite of this fact, the arrest clearance rate is very low—in the neighborhood of 20 percent.

Almost half of the automobiles stolen in a large city such as New York are recovered within twenty-four hours after transmission of the alarm. Such early recovery of stolen automobiles is desirable, but only increased apprehensions will serve to discourage the auto thief. The best time to recover a stolen car is while the vehicle is still in the possession of the thief. Because the auto theft prevented, or the auto thief apprehended, may save a life or prevent the commission of a more serious crime, it is of the utmost importance that continued and sustained attention be given to this problem.

Intelligent observation is necessary to combat the auto thief. To escape detection he depends not on concealment, but on simulating the appearance and activity of the average car owner. Observation as relates to auto larceny has three phases: place of theft; the auto thief; and the stolen vehicle.

Place of theft. Automobiles are commonly stolen from the vicinity of:

Places of public assembly—streets and unattended parking lots adjoining sites of sporting events, amusement parks, beaches, motion-picture houses, and theatrical areas where cars are parked close together, giving the thief ideal cover while stealing the auto, and two to four hours before the theft is discovered.

Transit terminals and stations—nearby streets where cars are parked by persons continuing on into the city by public transportation. The car is stolen shortly after being parked, giving the thief six to eight hours' start before the owner returns, discovers the vehicle missing, and reports the loss.

Congested residential areas—streets within the area which are used by residents to store their automobiles because of a lack of available auto storage facilities. Automobiles are parked close together, which gives the thief ideal cover.

The auto thief. Auto thieves come under four general classifications, depending upon the purpose of the theft:

The joyrider—juveniles and youths who steal the auto for a joyride and abandon the car when the gas supply is exhausted. The vehicle is usually abandoned on the day of the theft.

The transportation thief—criminals who steal automobiles for use in the commission of other crimes, for example, stickups, robberies, etc., or intoxicated persons and others who, finding themselves in need of transportation, steal an automobile.

The professional auto thief—persons who steal cars for the purpose of sale. They usually belong to, or are employed by, an auto larceny ring.

The auto accessory thief—persons who steal cars for the purpose of removing and selling the accessories or parts, such as tires, wheels, or radios. The term *car clouting* is used in many areas to describe this particular form of larceny.

Actions of the thief. The behavior and general appearance of persons in or about an automobile should indicate to the alert police officer the possibility of an auto larceny. He should be especially alert for:

General appearance—juveniles or youthful drivers apparently under the age for an operator's license; youths and poorly dressed persons riding in an expensive automobile.

Suspicious behavior. Actions of a driver or a person apparently working on a vehicle may arouse suspicion. For example:

Drivers who violate traffic regulations and refuse to stop when so directed.

Drivers who appear nervous and confused when questioned.

Persons removing parts or accessories from automobiles.

Drivers apparently unfamiliar with the car and accessories.

Persons apparently repairing or, without reason, loitering in the vicinity of a parked car.

Persons trying a number of keys to open a car door.

The vehicle.

Spot-checking. Police officers on patrol duty, especially during the late-evening and early-morning hours, should spot-check motor vehicles in their area in order to establish rightful ownership and to discover and arrest those in unlawful possession of vehicles. These spot-checks should be carried out tactfully and with discretion but also with caution to prevent a possible violent act by a lawbreaker who may be riding in a stolen vehicle.

Registration checks. When a motor vehicle is stopped for a traffic violation or investigation, the police officer should compare the serial number on the registration certificate with the number on the serial plate of the auto. In most models this plate is mounted on the left front door post.

Checking vehicles. In observing automobiles for evidence of possible lar-ceny, particular attention should be given to cars:

With broken windows, especially front vent windows.

With tool marks on the frame around the front vent windows.

Showing evidence of recent tool marks on bolts holding the license plates.

With license plates insecurely mounted.

With ignition short-circuited by means of metal foil or alligator clips on a length of wire.

Showing evidence of alteration of license plates, especially plates containing letters *B, P,* or *R.*

Parked in isolated sections, with or without occupants.

Apparently undamaged, being towed or pushed.

Parked with "For Sale" signs, where alleged owner is standing nearby.

Follow-up investigation. If on initial observation there appears to be reasonable cause for suspicion, further investigation should be conducted as follows:

If persons are observed loitering about parked cars, check their identity and the reason for their presence. Look for coil wires, spoons, beer-can openers, short lengths of pipe—all favorite tools of auto thieves. Check adjacent cars for evidence of attempted larceny.

In cases of persons apparently repairing vehicles, or removing parts or accessories therefrom, such persons should be required to identify themselves and satisfy the officer that they are authorized to perform the work.

If the person is operating a motor vehicle, ask to see operator's license.

If operating a clean vehicle with dirty license plates, or a dirty vehicle with clean license plates, check vehicle and license plate against registration certificate, description and number.

Compare description of driver with that on license and with photograph if chauffeur's license.

If doubtful of identity, compare signature on license with test signature of driver.

A torn license should be examined very carefully. Inspect it for continuity and proper alignment of watermark by holding the license form up to the light.

Check letters and numerals of Department of Motor Vehicles stamp for proper box form and uniformity of size, shape, and thickness.

If the driver appears unfamiliar with operation of the auto or accessories, request him to stop and re-start motor and operate accessories. Note if ignition key is used, and whether he is familiar with controls.

Carefully examine vehicle registration certificate to assure that erasures, changes, or alterations have not been made thereon. If driver is not the owner, seek evidence of operator's identity other than that furnished by operator's or chauffeur's license.

Check current alarms to determine if the vehicle has been reported stolen.

Evidence. Safeguard all evidence. All license plates, tools, papers, matchbook covers, bills for grease, gas, or repairs, found in a car should be regarded as evidence and so marked and safeguarded. Protect fingerprints in car, particularly on rearview mirror, around the window ledges, and on the seat-adjusting lever on the driver's side of the front seat.

Precautions. Some auto thieves are dangerous criminals. A car may have been stolen to provide a getaway car in a robbery. A police officer should approach a suspected car with caution. An approach from the rear or side is preferable. The officer should never walk in front of an occupied vehicle. The operator should be ordered to turn off the ignition and remove the keys. Subsequent action will be dictated by the circumstances. At no time, however, should the officer lean into or upon the vehicle while it is under the control of an occupant.

TRUCK THEFTS

Truck thieves, who operate twenty-four hours a day, are very prevalent nowadays. One mode of working is to steal the truck while the driver parks to make a delivery of merchandise. Sometimes the driver takes the key with him, sometimes he leaves the key in the ignition,[1] and sometimes there is no key at all. It can be stated that 95 percent of the truck thefts are made possible by the carelessness of the driver.

Trucks parked overnight with valuable goods are also stolen. A typical case exemplifies this:

A truck containing valuable goods was parked in downtown Manhattan while the driver went to sleep in a hotel. The truck was stolen and driven off to a garage in the neighborhood. That very night the garage was being watched by detectives for other reasons. When the detectives saw the truck enter, they called headquarters to find out if the truck had been reported stolen but received a negative answer. They continued their watch, however, and saw the truck being driven away in the morning. When the truck driver finally came for the truck that morning, he found it gone and reported it to the police. The detectives were informed that the truck had been stolen and continued to watch the garage discreetly. Three days later, five men entered the garage, and when approached by the detectives were found to be occupied with repacking the stolen goods and taking the marks off. The truck had been found empty and abandoned a few blocks away on the same day it was stolen.

It should be noted that alarms are now on the market which can be mounted on cars and trucks and which give good protection against theft.

SNEAK THIEVES

OFFICE SNEAKS. Lone workers are the rule in this business. The professional sneak makes a survey and inspection of the building; familiarizes himself with the elevators, stairways, fire-escapes, and emergency exits; also names of business firms, so that if questioned he can explain his presence. Firms having a large number of employees in one open office are avoided, as this type has so many persons in constant attendance that opportunity is limited. A small office where there are only one or two persons or a general office subdivided into a number of smaller offices is usually selected. Entry is made on the pretext of business, for instance, as a typewriter or telephone repairman. Told to be seated in an outer office or conducted into an inner office, the thief is frequently left alone for a period of time. During the interim he looks around to locate anything of value, such as pocketbooks or handbags, petty cash, stamps, fountain pens, desk clocks, or other articles of value, which can be secreted on the person. Awaiting opportunity, he takes the property he has selected and departs, either with or without the statement that he cannot wait any longer or that he will call again. If on some pretended business, he concludes it quickly and leaves.

BANK THIEVES. There are two types of bank sneaks: the one who steals from the cashier's cage and the one who loiters around for the purpose of picking up articles put down by persons making deposits, counting money, etc.

Those who steal from the cashier's cage generally work in groups of three. While this type has almost disappeared, it may be mentioned. One of the group engages the paying teller or cashier in conversation under the pretext of transacting some business and while doing so places himself against the window with elbows on the ledge to cover the operations of a confederate who is next in line with a long hooked cane or wire, a straight cane, or a rolled newspaper with a gummy substance on one end,

The wire or hooked cane is inserted into the cage and used to fish out a bundle of banknotes. If the straight cane or rolled newspaper is used, the operation is practically the same, except that the cane or paper is placed on the top of the banknotes and withdrawn. Another confederate has placed himself in a position to observe anyone approaching and give warning.[2]

The other type observes people doing business in the bank, waits until their attention is diverted by filling in a deposit slip, counting money, or other tasks, picks up pocketbook, handbag, or money and departs.

DISHONEST EMPLOYEES. This type includes all classes, from private secretary to night watchman, including the dishonest cashier, bookkeeper, clerk, checker, truckman, loader, stock clerk, and order clerk. Some are professional thieves. Others are occasional thieves.

The professional makes a business of obtaining employment under a false name with faked or forged references. He will work hard and faithfully to win quick approbation of employers. When an opportunity to commit a theft presents itself, the object or money is seized and flight made at a time when the loss is not likely to be discovered for several hours or until the next day.

The dishonest bookkeeper or cashier omits to record bills paid and appropriates the money.

The checker in the mercantile establishment may be in collusion with a customer of the firm and permit a greater quantity of merchandise to be shipped than the order and bill call for.

The truckman may arrange with accomplices to leave his truck, loaded with valuable merchandise, unattended in the street while he is in a restaurant having a meal and permit them to drive off with it.

The loader may arrange to have accomplices drive up to his employer's business location with a truck and permit or assist in the loading and removal of cases standing on the street waiting to be carted away or into the building.

The stock clerk and the order clerk, like the checker, may work in collusion with a customer by sending or wrapping up more merchandise than the order or invoice calls for. They may also steal by secreting merchandise on their persons. Silk houses have had experiences with employees who would wind a bolt of silk around their bodies under their shirts and walk out at closing time undetected.

HOTEL THIEVES. Bogus or ostensible guests of either sex and dishonest chambermaids, bellboys, and other hotel employees having access to rooms may be found among this class of thief. In the case of the dishonest hotel employee the method is much the same as with any other type of dishonest employee. During employment he is constantly on the lookout for an opportunity to steal.

The professional hotel thief registers as a guest. He makes a survey of the hotel to become familiar with the arrangement of rooms, hallways, elevators, and stairways and carefully studies habits of other guests, particularly those known to have money or valuable jewelry, noting when their rooms are occupied and vacant. Entrance is gained to the victim's room by means of an airshaft window, by a false key, or in some instances by forcing the door. Articles of value are usually packed in the victim's own suitcase or bag. The thief takes it to his own room and checks out before the loss is discovered.

Others register in and out of large hotels on a number of occasions. Each time they register they keep the key to the room to which they were assigned. Some hotels pay little attention to such cases, concluding that the guest simply forgot to return the key, and another is made to take its place. With a number of keys accumulated, the thief may reregister at the hotel at any time, go to any of the rooms for which he has a key, and enter and steal. Some thieves have copies made of the keys instead of keeping the original ones. A fairly common type of hotel thief is the one who boldly walks to the desk of the room clerk, ascertains with a glance what keys are in, and asks for one of them.

Another type of professional hotel thief is the ostensible guest who simply walks into a hotel, ascends to an upper floor, walks along the corridor until he finds a door open, enters and steals anything of value, and decamps.

DISHONEST SERVANTS. Among these are domestics, female and male; cooks, maids, laundresses, butlers, footmen, housekeepers, etc. There are two types. One obtains employment with but one idea in mind, and that is to make a good haul and then flee. The other obtains employment and steals intermittently but continues in the employ until discovered. The former secures a position, usually giving a false name and address, with false or forged references. References are seldom investigated. Performing duties well, in a short period of time the domestic is liked and trusted. At the first opportunity, when the family is away, everything of value is packed, with the aid of an accomplice in some cases, and flight taken.

The second type steals one article at a time in such a manner as not to create suspicion. Thefts are timed so that when the loss is discovered it is recalled that a delivery boy, a plumber, painters, or somebody else was in the house at the time, thus diverting suspicion. Some of the articles stolen in the summertime are of the kind that will not be missed for months, such as a fur coat or an overcoat; sometimes jewelry worn only on special and infrequent occasions is taken. As only one article is taken at a time and is frequently taken when it will not be missed for a while, the owners do not as a rule remember putting it in any certain place and conclude it has been lost.

FURNISHED ROOM THIEVES. Both sexes are found in this class. Some work alone; others have a male or female accomplice. A room is hired in a rooming house, and habits of the owner and of the roomers are observed. At an opportune time a room previously selected is entered either by means of a passkey or by forcing the door and wearing apparel and other valuables are packed in the victim's suitcase or handbag. The thief then flees.

CHURCH THIEVES. This kind of thievery is fairly common. The thieves steal ladies' handbags which are placed on the bench while the owners are attending their religious duties.

SHOPLIFTERS. Here we find the occasional thief, who may be a housewife, a shop-girl, business girl, or businessman respectably employed, the kleptomaniac, and also the professional shoplifter.

The occasional thief is one who enters a store for a legitimate purpose but when an opportunity to steal is presented takes advantage of it.

The dress and gown shop thieves usually consist of two or three women operating in a group. One will try on one or more gowns, select a purchase, and ask that an alteration be made. While the salesperson takes the gown to the alteration department, usually located in the rear, another of the women takes a gown, hides it under her dress or coat, and leaves. Sometimes the gown selected is paid for. At other times word is left that it will be called for when alterations are completed. No return call is made. Frequently the loss is not discovered until stock is checked, and the identity or description of the thief is not known. This makes it very difficult to trace the shoplifter.

Professional shoplifters usually work in the larger department stores. They operate with the most success during the winter season when heavy outer clothing is worn. They may have a coat with a very large inside pocket, sometimes extending across the entire width of the garment. An article from a counter is slipped into this without attracting attention, or it may be dropped into an umbrella or other receptacle. If the theft is detected, protest is made that the article must have fallen into it by accident. Cases have been known where the shoplifter inserted an artificial arm into the sleeve of her coat, secured it to the front of the coat, and attached a handbag to the gloved artificial hand to give it a realistic appearance. She then picked up things with the hidden arm and dropped them into an inside pocket provided for that purpose.

Kleptomaniacs have a mania for stealing anything their hands can be placed on, usually without any apparent need for doing so. Very often persons in comfortable circumstances resort to petty thievery, taking articles which they neither need nor want.

Detectives should be aware of a racket not unusual today. In these cases the person acts like a thief but doesn't steal anything. When he has attracted the attention of the department store detectives and is questioned, he is of course able to prove his innocence. He then claims compensation.

SEAT-TIPPERS. This kind of criminal operates in theaters, always taking a seat behind a woman who has placed her handbag on the seat next to her. While the woman is engaged in watching the show, the thief tips the seat next to her, causing the bag to fall to the floor. He then picks it up and pilfers any valuable contents. The experienced detective will easily spot seat-tippers, as they are on the move a great deal of the time and always choose vacant seats behind women.

PENNYWEIGHTERS. These are usually well-dressed adult persons, both male and female, who pose as customers. They sometimes work alone and sometimes with male or female confederates. This type of larceny is nowadays very rare.

The thief operates in jewelry stores during business hours. He enters a store, asks to see a certain article of jewelry, usually a ring, and is shown an assortment of rings on a tray. The thief makes a mental selection of one, carefully noting its design, size, color, etc. He leaves, promising to return later when he is ready to buy it. He then has an imitation made, an exact duplicate of the ring selected. On the second visit to the store he again asks to see the original, switches it for the imitation, advances some reason for not buying it, and leaves. The substitution is so cleverly made and the imitation is such a good one that the loss is often not discovered for days.

BOGUS ADVERTISERS. These are usually male professional thieves and are of all ages. They sometimes work with female accomplices. An advertisement is inserted in a newspaper for an article of furniture, such as a piano, or for a furnished room or an apartment. A post office box number or newspaper box number is given for replies. Upon receiving replies, visits are made to the various places, and if opportunity offers, things of value are stolen.

SNATCHERS. Snatchers are usually young and active men. They operate in quiet residential sections and in business and shopping districts. They loiter on the street until they observe a woman approaching with a handbag, then snatch it from her hand and run. In business districts they get a line on employees conveying money through the streets, meet them in a hallway, grab the money, and make their escape; or with the aid of an automobile they draw up at the curb, leave a man at the wheel with the motor running, snatch the money, and escape in the car. These thieves also snatch pocketbooks, bags, and purses from automobiles just as the car starts with the traffic lights. This type of snatching is very prevalent today.

STREET WOMEN. Thieves of this sort are usually prostitutes. Sometimes they work alone and at other times with a male accomplice. They frequent hallways, furnished rooms, hotels, and parks. They solicit a man for sexual intercourse and take him to a cheap hotel or a furnished room (creep-joint). While he is asleep, money and valuables are taken and departure is made. Others may have an accomplice come in and rifle the victim's pockets while they remain with him to divert suspicion. Where this is done, usually the same room is repeatedly used for the purpose. To avoid notoriety, the victim seldom makes a complaint. This type of thief may use a small dose of chloral or other potion (knock-out drops) to hasten the victim's falling asleep.

OVERCOAT THIEVES. Usually these are young men who work in crowded restaurants where clothing is not checked and where dancing is permitted. The thief enters first, without an overcoat. He locates a coat which is of good quality and similar to one to be hung up by his accomplice. The accomplice follows and hangs his coat alongside the one to be stolen. Both give an order for food which can be supplied quickly. When he is finished eating, the thief leaves, putting on the coat to be stolen. If detected, an apology is offered. If not, the coat left behind is worn by the accomplice as he leaves.

Thieves of this type also operate in theaters. When a woman goes out during intermission and leaves her coat lying over the back of the seat, the thief walks down the aisle, picks up the coat, and saunters out with it. The same method is used in restaurants where dancing is the vogue and no provision is made for checking women's coats.

BAGGAGE THIEVES. These are usually well-dressed young men. They loiter around railroad stations, watch for persons who set down baggage while waiting for a train or buying a ticket, walk alongside, and, when the victim's attention is attracted elsewhere, pick up the bag and walk off.

Others get on a train and sit near a person who has left a bag near the aisle. Just before the train leaves, the thief picks up the bag and leaves, remarking to the trainman that he finds he is on the wrong train.

Others hang around the baggage rack in a hotel lobby. After the doorman has left and while the guest is registering, they pick up a bag and leave. Or while a guest carrying his own bag is registering or paying a bill, they get behind him, pick up his bag, and depart.

GENERAL THEFTS

PACKAGE THIEVERY FROM VEHICLES. Criminals in this business have a get-up to simulate truckmen or delivery boys. They get a line on the vehicle, driver, and kind of merchandise carried and find out the route to be taken and the stops to be made. Sometimes they follow the vehicle. They wait until the driver is in a building making a delivery, then steal a package and escape.

Sometimes they drive alongside of the victim's vehicle and boldly transfer goods from it to their own and drive away. At other times they pretend they are hitching a ride and drop packages off to a confederate who is following.

PARCEL POST PACKAGE THIEVES. This type steals parcel post packages left on top of mail boxes. Some make a practice of stealing express matter from the sidewalk in front of buildings in the wholesale district. Customers deliver a number of packages to an express agent, whose office usually is a small table on the sidewalk or in the freight entrance of a building. As no truck is available at the moment to cart them to the express office, the packages are left on the sidewalk. Opportunity thus presenting itself, the thief walks over, picks up one or two, and departs.

LETTER BOX THIEVES. In addition to stealing checks and money orders sent by mail this type of thief may extract a gas or electric light bill from the box and then go up to the person to whom it is addressed, represent himself as a collector from the company concerned, and collect the bill. He may also take out bank statements containing canceled checks with the idea of studying the signatures and forging checks.

CHECK BOX THIEVES. This type of theft is nowadays fairly common. The thief watches for well-dressed persons checking suitcases or packages in the lockers in railroad terminals. After they leave, he opens the box with a master key or duplicate. Often similar keys will fit several boxes in a section.

THEFTS FROM AUTOMOBILES. This class of thievery has become common in cities in recent years. If the car is locked, the no-draft ventilation window is opened with a beer-can opener; or a pipe about six inches long, which can be fitted over the handle, is used to break the lock and open the door. Anything of value is taken.

Cars having a fabric flap on the rear, which can be raised in warm weather or when passengers are in the rumble seat, are entered by opening the flap.

Automobile accessories that are easily detached, such as mirrors, tires, radios, heaters, bumpers, etc., are also stolen.

PACKAGE THIEVES—READERS. These usually operate in daytime. The "reader" watches for an errand or delivery boy carrying a package on which the label is clearly visible and walks a few feet behind the boy for a short distance, reading the name of the consignor and consignee on the label of the package. He then proceeds to the consignee's address, arriving there before the boy, and removes his coat. When the boy arrives, he is standing at the entrance to the building or the receiving department and admonishes the boy for lateness of delivery. In some instances he directs the boy to return quickly to get and deliver to him another order. He then takes the package, signs a receipt, and, when the boy has departed, recovers his coat and makes his getaway with the package.

Sometimes a package thief acquainted with the operations of a concern and knowing from whom they purchase calls a seller on the telephone and orders merchandise to be delivered immediately. The thief then waits at the premises of the purchasing concern and pretends to represent it when the boy arrives with the package. Receiving this, he departs.

PACKAGE THIEVES—SENDERS. These also usually operate in the daytime. The "sender" stops an errand boy or messenger who is carrying a package and requests him to deliver a message, giving or offering to give him a quarter or fifty cents for doing so. The thief then takes an envelope from his pocket and places a five- or ten-dollar bill in it, instructing the boy to deliver it to the person to whom it is addressed. While the boy's attention is momentarily distracted, the money is switched back to the man's pocket. The empty envelope is then sealed and given to the boy for delivery, with promise of a gift if he will hurry. He is told his package will be guarded until he returns. When the boy returns after being unable to locate the person, he finds the sender has disappeared.

When two or more package thieves are arrested, they generally deny knowing one another and endeavor to place the burden of the larceny on the one who is carrying the bundle. The detective trailing package thieves should make a memorandum of the time and location at which he observed them together and should endeavor to have some other person also witness the pair together.

BOGUS PURCHASES. This class operates by ordering jewelry, furs, or other articles of value and directing delivery to a hotel or business premises C.O.D. Upon receipt the article is taken to another room on a pretext. While the delivery clerk waits, escape is made.

PICKPOCKETS

Among the types of pickpockets[3] may be included patch-pocket workers, fob workers, pants-pocket workers, lush workers, toilet workers, and bag-openers.

PATCH-POCKET WORKERS. This type of thief operates mostly in the spring, fall, and winter but not in the summertime, because then women do not wear coats in which their pocketbooks are carried in an outside pocket. This primary-class pickpocket usually starts his day's work around 7:30 in the morning and continues until about 9 A.M. He starts again about 4:30 P.M. and quits around 7:30 P.M., when the evening rush of homeward-bound working people is over.

The patch-pocket worker's methods vary in some respects, depending upon the amount of experience he has had. He usually carries a newspaper in one hand or has his overcoat over one arm. When he sees a bulging pocket—and usually he picks out a woman's coat pocket—he feels to see whether the bulge is a pocketbook. If it is, he extracts it from the owner's pocket, using the overcoat or newspaper as a shield for his hand.

Some members of this class of thief operate with a newspaper held in the left hand and after they have picked the pocket place the contents between the newspaper pages and back away from the crowd.

The patch-pocket worker usually operates in five-and-ten-cent stores, at parades, or wherever there is a gathering of women. He is particularly easy to catch because of his inexperience, but detectives must nevertheless exercise great care in dealing with this elementary class of dip. The victims are nearly always working people who often prefer to lose the small amount of money the pickpocket has stolen from them rather than go to the trouble and expense of losing a day's work by appearing in court against the thief.

FOB WORKERS. In the main the fob workers are not more than forty years old and generally are much younger. They look and act like mendicants and operate in crowds, usually working in the early afternoon, depending on the season of the year.

There are only two pockets in a person's clothing from which the fob worker can steal: the outside overcoat pocket or the right-hand inner-coat pocket. This class of pickpocket carries a handkerchief in his left hand and, standing beside his victim, covers his own right hand with the handkerchief in his left hand, inserts a couple of fingers in the victim's pocket, takes out whatever money is there, backs out of the crowd, looks around, and edges away. If no one has noticed him, the fob worker looks at his loot, gives the crowd the once-over again, and repeats his illegal activity. Generally the fob worker has a long criminal record.

PANTS-POCKET WORKER. The pants-pocket worker's method calls for the highest degree of skill, and he is recognized by pickpockets as being at the top in this particular class of thievery. The pants-pocket worker often operates alone, although sometimes he has a partner and occasionally he operates in mobs of three or five. His favorite time is during the rush hours of the morning and evening, and he likes motion-picture theaters, subways, piers on a sailing day, or any place where there is a crowd.

Operating by himself, he as a rule carries either a coat over his arm or a newspaper in his hand. Skillful though he very often is, an experienced detective can spot him rather easily because he does not act naturally. He has more purpose in his expression than an honest man, there is a sharper look about him—it's something hard to explain but easy to detect. The lone pickpocket of this class nearly always operates in the subway because most people are in a tremendous hurry getting on and off subway trains.

When pants-pocket workers operate in pairs the one who does the actual pocket-picking is known as a "tool"; his partner is called a "stall." The stall has three objects—to cover the hand of the tool when it is in the victim's pocket, to bump into the victim to divert his attention from the tool, and to receive the pocketbook which the tool has removed from the victim's pocket. When such thieves work in groups of four or five, there are two tools in the outfit. One tool takes his position on either side of the intended victim. This is done so that the tools will not have to shift from one side to the other to locate the victim's pocketbook.

LUSH WORKERS. Thieves of this type usually operate at night. Their field of operation is mainly along subway transportation systems, particularly at terminals. Generally they travel in pairs, but at times there may be three or five thieves operating in concert.

The victim is generally asleep in the car or on a station seat. One of the thieves sits on one side of him and another thief on the other. If there are others, they station themselves in front of the victim, blocking the view of any other person who might be in the station or in the car. One of the thieves sitting alongside the victim opens a newspaper and holds it in such a position as to cover the front portion of the victim's body. The confederate sitting on the opposite side then extracts whatever property he can from the pockets of the victim. In operating in moving trains the thieves generally enter the train by way of different cars and then meet at the point where the victim is asleep. To detect and apprehend this class of thief, trains must be watched as they enter stations, at which time the victim may be seen. In station cases observation should be made from a distance on the platform or from a ticket booth thereon.

TOILET WORKERS—"DONNEGAN WORKERS." This type of thief may operate alone or with a partner, and often there are four or five in a group. Generally, however, they operate in groups of two or three. They enter a washroom, a comfort station, or toilet and one of the thieves stations himself at the urinal, as a lookout, while another goes to a door alongside of an occupied toilet and throws some coins on the floor. The third thief then approaches the toilet, and the second thief starts to pick up what he has dropped. The selected victim does not want to be annoyed and naturally helps to look for the coins or whatever has been dropped. The victim has his coat hanging on a hook in the compartment. The second thief inserts his hand into the pocket of the coat hanging on the wall or door, takes its contents, and passes them to the third thief, who leaves the premises, to be followed by the second thief and then by the lookout. To detect and apprehend this type of criminal, surveillance of comfort stations is necessary. Observation must be made in a natural way without creating suspicion. If the same men are seen making repeated trips into a comfort station, there is ground to suspect criminal intent. It should be added that this type of criminal is nowadays very rare.

BAG-OPENERS. Bag-openers are nearly always women pickpockets who operate in the daytime in department stores. There are three types— all very smart and all very difficult to catch. Bag-openers may be classified as main-floor workers, elevator workers, and upper-floor workers.

The woman pickpocket selects a department store which is having a bargain sale and enters by the last door—that is, the door farthest away from the main entrance. Having entered as inconspicuously as possible, she glances around with assumed carelessness to see if she has been recognized and is being followed. If she is satisfied that no detective has recognized her, she proceeds directly to the crowded sales counter, around which a large number of women are thronged with their bags dangling from their arms.

Most women shopping in department stores are careful buyers. For instance, they will run their hands through stockings before purchasing them, to assure themselves that they are of good quality. They examine other merchandise with equal care. While the honest buyers are thus occupied, the well-dressed bag-opener stations herself beside her chosen victim. The pickpocket's left hand is concealed by a fur piece she is carrying, and with this hand she opens the victim's bag, her act being concealed by the fur. Under pretense of examining the stockings the female dip looks into the opened bag, and while replacing the stockings on the counter she takes the contents.

Since the majority of department store detectives are stationed on the main floor and all persons must enter and depart by that floor, the most astute women pickpockets work the elevators and upper floors. It is hard for a man to get on the same elevator with a woman pickpocket if she wishes to avoid him. When the bag-opener is on the elevator, she gets behind a woman, opens her bag without much trouble, since all are wedged tightly together, and takes the contents without looking at them. Then when the victim steps out of the elevator, the loss is discovered or called to her attention.

Of course, a clever woman pickpocket knows that after she has stolen the contents of two or three bags the store detectives will be on her trail. She therefore leaves immediately after the bell is put on for the shop's sleuths. The elevator picketpocket always departs from the extreme opposite end of the building, as far away as she can get from the elevator in which she made her touch.

There are men as well as women bag-openers, although not so many, and the men do not frequent the department stores because they know they can't get by there as women do. If a male pickpocket went into a department store and approached the stocking counter, the salesgirl would at once give him her undivided attention, because she would expect to sell him more quickly two or three times as much as she could sell to a woman. Also if the male pickpocket operates in a crowd of women and one of them discovers she has been robbed, the first person she will suspect is the lone man. Therefore the masculine bag-opener usually confines his efforts to five-and-ten-cent stores and chain stores, where a good percentage of the purchasers are men. His presence there attracts no special attention.

SWINDLERS AND CONFIDENCE MEN [4]

HOT GOODS RACKET. This racket is still quite prevalent. The swindlers dress as deliverymen and use a delivery car. They stop somewhere in town and ask a passing person if he wants to buy a very cheap fur coat or some similar object, giving him the impression that the object is stolen. In reality the goods were honestly obtained but are of the cheapest sort. If the approached person calls the police, the only thing the swindler can be charged with is unlawful peddling.

DROPPING THE LEATHER—"DROPPING THE PIGEON." This is one of the oldest of confidence games. It is still prevalent, especially among poor people. Its methods have not changed apparently since Smollett was fleeced by this swindle two hundred years ago in London.

In cities the game is usually worked on immigrants and seldom constitutes more than petty larceny. It is worked with two operators. No. 1, striding past, drops a pocketbook in front of the victim, who is not given an opportunity to pick it up for it is instantly seized by No. 2. No. 2 agrees to divide and leads the selected victim to a nearby doorway. When the pocketbook is opened, it is found to contain one or two one-dollar bills and a counterfeit one-hundred-dollar bill. No. 2 points out that it would be unwise to change such a large bill in the neighborhood and as neither has change and he must catch a train suggests that the victim retain the bill until the following day, when they will meet and divide equally. As security the victim gives No. 2 whatever money he may have with him, perhaps adding his watch or other valuables.

LEMON MEN. Lemon men usually hang out around hotels, steamships, or other places where people are enjoying themselves. Some of them dress very nicely and can carry on an intelligent conversation. There is also a lower grade of lemon men who frequent disreputable poolrooms and dress in common with the men of such a neighborhood. The lemon man of today belongs almost inevitably to the last-mentioned class of people. The following case-story involving people of higher circles is still a good example, however, of the *modus operandi* of this type of criminal.

An alumnus of an eastern university went to a metropolitan city to witness a football game between his alma mater and another university. He registered at a first-class hotel and mingled with the football crowd staying there. Conversing with a group of collegians, one of them suggested that they take a walk to get away from the group. They found themselves in the billiard room, still talking about college life. The stranger suggested that they play a few games of pool.

The stranger lost the first few games purposely, letting the alumnus beat him with the agreement that the loser should pay the check. The stranger then suggested playing for a small bet, saying that if he was lucky enough to win a game it would help him toward paying the check.

The stranger lost the first game on which a bet was placed. When he suggested doubling the bet, the visiting alumnus did not hesitate to agree. The stranger won the next game by one point, remarking that he was getting lucky, as he never was very good at pool. He then proceeded to win more than the amount of the check and soon was leading.

The alumnus soon found himself losing money and suggested that they double the amount of the bet to allow him to recuperate his losses. The stranger agreed and kept beating the alumnus by one or two points and losing an occasional game to make it look good.

The alumnus was down to his last few dollars and was on the verge of borrowing some money from his fraternity brothers when a detective making the rounds of the hotels stopped to watch the game and to ask the players some questions. The detective informed the alumnus he was playing with a criminal who belonged to the fraternity of lemon men or pool sharks making a living on winnings from such games. A conviction and jail sentence ensued.

HANDKERCHIEF SWITCH. This is still a fairly prevalent game. The method will be illustrated by the following case-story.

An elderly man seventy years of age, walking on a prominent street of a metropolitan seaboard city shortly after ten o'clock in the morning, was approached by a young fellow in shirt sleeves, who struck up an acquaintance and engaged in a conversation about the weather and business slackness.

The elder showed a patent lock he was endeavoring to sell. After walking a few blocks, they came upon a very bewildered old man who appeared lost.

"I wonder what's the matter with the old fellow," said the young man. So his companion went over to the old man and asked, "What is the matter?"

The stranger, sighing, replied, "I have just arrived from the West and my brother has just died and left me ten thousand dollars in insurance money. If I return to the old country with this money, my mother will wonder where I got it and will soon realize that my brother, whom she loved so much, got killed, and I would not want to grieve her. I don't know what to do with this money. I am a stranger here, and I am afraid to trust it to anybody."

Tears dropped from his eyes as he held the inside pocket of his overcoat open and showed a small canvas bag in which there was something that had the appearance of money.

Both elderly men were natives of the same foreign country. The locksmith arranged with the young fellow for them to be the old man's guardians. They were businessmen and knew the dangers of a big city for strangers who had money.

The old man, still with tears, asked, "How will I know you are honest people?" The young man turned to the locksmith and asked him if he had any money in a bank or on his person. "Yes, I have a bank account," was the reply.

Thereupon the young fellow said to the old man, "We will show you how to keep your money safely by letting you see how banks operate." The old man, glad to meet honest people, wiped the tears from his eyes and promised them a good day's pay of twenty-five dollars for guarding him and his money.

They went to the bank. En route the old man was amazed at the large buildings and asked many questions about landmarks and city life. Holding the locksmith's hand and caressing it, with tears of gratefulness in his eyes, the old man kept repeating his obligation to such honest people.

The locksmith withdrew a thousand dollars. The young fellow suggested that the old man put his money in a package along with the locksmith's so that the latter could carry it safely to the bank for deposit. They repaired to a hallway. The locksmith took the money he had withdrawn from the bank and placed it in a handkerchief. The old man placed his money in the same handkerchief. The handkerchief was tied in a four-cornered knot. While they were doing this, the young fellow kept cautioning the locksmith to be careful with such a large sum of money. With much ceremony the young fellow un-buttoned the locksmith's vest, stressing the matter of carefulness. While this was going on, the old man switched the handkerchief and substituted another. Then the old man excitedly declared, "You got safety pin, I got safety pin, here, here, place it so," and pinned the handkerchief to the inside of the lock-smith's vest, then buttoned the vest and the coat.

The locksmith returned to the bank and discovered that the handkerchief contained clippings from newspapers cut about the same size as paper money.

The thieves were subsequently located by visiting grills in a section of the city occupied by people of that nationality. Arrests and convictions followed.

COIN MATCHERS. This swindle is now fairly rare. The following case-story illustrates the *modus operandi*.

Mr. A. from York, Pennsylvania, stopping at a prominent New York hotel, reported to a detective that while walking west on Forty-second Street he was approached by a man who asked him where the Museum of Natural History was located. Mr. A. replied he was a stranger in the city and was unable to furnish the information.

The man then asked Mr. A. where he was from, and Mr. A. told him. The stranger expressed surprise and told A. that he lived in Wilkes-Barre and was more than glad to meet a fellow Pennsylvanian.

The stranger invited Mr. A. to attend a show as his guest. After the play, they walked north on Broadway. On reaching Forty-seventh Street they were approached by a man who asked them where he could find the Hippodrome. They said they were strangers and did not know.

The newcomer said he was from the South, had been in New York only two days, but found that it was a very funny city. Everybody he spoke to seemed to be a stranger and nobody could direct him to any place he wanted to visit. The Southerner stated that he had been left a large sum of money by his mother, who had died recently, and that he had come to New York to spend part of it having a good time. He said it was hard to get acquainted in New York and proposed that the three of them go to dinner.

They all entered a cigar store and bought cigars. The Southerner insisted on paying for them, and an argument arose on the subject. They finally decided to match coins to determine who should pay. The man from the South lost and paid for the cigars, but he remarked that he had bad luck every time he gambled and pretended that he was sore. He then suggested that they match for five dollars. The three continued to match, and the Southerner continued to lose. The more he lost the angrier he got. They kept walking north on Broadway and entered Central Park.

The Southerner excused himself to go to a lavatory. His confederate said to Mr. A., "Let us work together and get this fellow's money." Mr. A. refused at first, but finally consented when the swindler suggested returning the money after winning it.

After the Southerner's return, they resumed matching. The Southerner lost approximately three hundred dollars and Mr. A. about the same amount. An argument then arose between the so-called Southerner and his confederate, the Southerner claiming that the two were playing in conjunction with each other to swindle him. He threatened to call the police and have them arrested.

Mr. A. became excited and pleaded with them to be quiet, and asked the swindler to return the money to the Southerner and settle the argument. He refused and told Mr. A. to leave the matter in his hands, instructing A. to go to his hotel, where he would meet him later.

Mr. A. then returned to his hotel and waited. After waiting two or more hours, it finally dawned on him that he might have been swindled. He referred the matter to the police. Mr. A. failed to identify any criminal from photographs shown. However, detectives continued working on the case with the information he furnished; and some days later, in a hotel, a detective observed a man—apparently from out of town—conversing with a criminal who had previously been arrested for swindling.

The criminal answered the description of one of the men in Mr. A.'s case. The criminal and victim were trailed to the same cigar store visited in the case of Mr. A. The same mode of procedure was employed by the swindlers in this case. A man who fitted the Southerner's description met them at the cigar store and started to talk to them.

They were followed to luncheon and to Central Park. There the sharpers were placed under arrest. The victim gave the same story as Mr. A. Mr. A. was summoned from York, Pennsylvania, to New York and identified the men. They were convicted and sent to jail.

It might be well to note in cases of this kind that after the swindlers are arrested, identified, and held for trial they usually try to buy the complainant off and send what is generally termed a "fixer," who not only offers reimbursement for the original amount the victim was swindled out of but offers him an additional sum or bonus to drop the charge.

The type of criminal who engages in this racket quite often answers one of the following descriptions:

1. Very well dressed; generally an American twenty-two to thirty-five years of age; affable and friendly; affects English or Southern accent

2. Very well dressed; twenty-five to thirty-five years of age; affable, friendly, polite, affects foreign accent; displays large roll of bills

GAMBLING SWINDLES. This game is now almost obsolete and is only found in remote parts of the country. The routine went somewhat as follows:

Meeting an easy mark with a few thousand dollars, the confidence men staged a fake prize fight, a fake wrestling match, or took the victim to a fake gambling house. Of these, the gambling swindle was the most popular. The victim was introduced to the dealer of a gambling house, who agreed to play into his hand and double-cross the house. He was taught a code of signals and instructed to play his hand according to the dealer's signals. However, during the progress of the game, the signals became mixed and the dupe lost. If it was apparent that he could raise more money, the dealer showed him just how he misinterpreted the signals and his newly made friends induced him to try again, giving him two or three thousand dollars of their money to play with his own to inspire confidence. He fared no better at the second attempt of course and usually lost about the same amount of his own money as the others gave him to play for them.

DIAMOND SWITCH. This game almost belongs to history. The following case-story from the files of the New York City Police Department is a good illustration of how this kind of swindler works.

A woman was walking along a busy street in New York City when she was stopped by a well-dressed man who was talking to a very poor-looking male foreigner. The well-dressed man asked the woman if she could speak Yiddish or Polish. She said she could speak Yiddish. The well-dressed man, pointing to the foreigner, said to the woman, "Ask him what he wants." They conversed.

The foreigner asked the woman how much he could get for a solid gold Russian coin he displayed to her. She explained the situation to the well-dressed man. After negotiating through the woman, he purchased the gold piece, which was alleged to be worth fifty dollars, for five dollars. Thereupon the well-dressed man said to the woman, "Ask this greenhorn if he has anything else to sell." She did. The immigrant brought out a number of diamonds and showed them to the woman, telling her in Yiddish that he had just come over from Russia and these were Russian crown jewels.

The well-dressed man, speaking English, said, "These diamonds are the most beautiful I have ever looked at. However, I wouldn't purchase them unless I had them examined. If they are genuine, there is a fortune in it for us, as this greenhorn doesn't know their value in American money." The woman suggested going to an appraiser whom she knew. The appraiser informed them that they were genuine jewels and were worth plenty of money,

The immigrant then put the jewels back into a bag and slipped the bag carelessly into his coat pocket. Said the well-dressed man to the woman, "This is the greatest break I ever had in my life, but I haven't any money with me. I live in Jersey, and by the time I go to my bank it will be closed. Will you please go to your bank and buy these jewels from this greenhorn before he becomes educated, and I'll come over tomorrow and buy half of them from you. It is only fair that you let me buy half, because he was talking to me when you came along." While this conversation was going on, the immigrant switched the genuine jewels into his hip pocket and put another bag with glass diamonds into his coat pocket.

The woman went to her bank and withdrew $1,500 and gave it to the immigrant for the jewels, agreeing to let the well-dressed man purchase half of the jewels for $750 the following day. Of course, the well-dressed man never returned.

Some days later, while showing her friends the wonderful jewels, the woman was informed that they were not genuine. She immediately ran to the appraiser, and he told her that these were not the stones he had examined a few days previously. The woman described the immigrant to detectives, the description fitted a notorious con man.

A few days later detectives arrested both of the swindlers as they were about to enter a new roadster. Both were tried and found guilty and sentenced to a State prison.

The greenhorn in this swindling game is always poorly dressed and speaks a foreign language very well, often being a genuine foreigner. The well-dressed man is an American and a very convincing talker.

Sometimes three swindlers work this racket, the third being the jeweler, whom they meet rushing out of a jewelry store on the way to the hospital where his wife is sick. He appraises the diamonds in the street, offering the greenhorn a large sum in cash right on the spot. However, the modern swindler who works this game uses genuine diamonds and allows the victim to get them appraised, and the switch comes in after they leave the jeweler or appraiser.

This racket is not confined to Russians; it is used by Italian and Polish confidence men, who pick victims of their own nationality.

MONEY-MAKING MACHINE. This game is rarely seen in the large cities but may still be perpetrated in remote parts of the country. A money-making machine generally simulates a highly polished wood cabinet. Its size is generally about 12 by 12 inches. It contains an electric motor operated by a switch on the right side of the box. The motor has no real purpose other than to make a humming noise when the switch is on. The cabinet also contains about four small electric bulbs, lighted by dry-cell batteries from within, and has a drop-slot drawer which falls to the bottom of the cabinet. A hidden button on the left side, when touched, operates the drop. One hundred pieces of fine white paper cut the size of a twenty-dollar Federal Reserve or National Bank note form part of the paraphernalia.

New bills only are used in the operation of the money-making machine. The confidence man or swindler in demonstrating the machine to a victim places a new bill together with a piece of the white paper in the drop-drawer. The switch is opened and the motor rotates. Pressing the hidden button, he drops the box to the bottom. This brings into view another similar drop-drawer in which two new banknotes are found when the cabinet is opened. The victim believes the machine printed one of them.

The persons who operate this class of swindle are usually foreigners, averaging in age from thirty to fifty years. They work slowly and cautiously. The following illustrates one manner of approach:

The swindler becomes acquainted with a man who in his judgment can be used for his purpose. He imparts little information regarding himself but gains the confidence of the other and gradually finds out whom he knows, his business, and, if possible, his financial standing. Victims are usually foreigners who are not overly sharp or suspicious.

When the victim has been selected, the confidence man usually visits his place of business, spends money freely, and pays for purchases with new twenty-dollar bills. The victim comments on this custom of always paying with new money. The swindler replies cautiously that a relative or friend who formerly worked in a mint in Germany or Austria told him how to duplicate new money, using a chemical and a money-making machine, and that it is very easily done if one is able to get the kind of special paper that the government uses. He then offers to sell the victim a couple of twenties at ten each, or he gives him a couple to pass, warning him to tell no one. The bills he gives him are genuine. After a couple of days, the swindler returns and learns that the victim has passed the two twenty-dollar bills and collects a share thereof. Of course, the victim is interested. An invitation to see the machine follows. The con man tells the victim that if he invests one or two thousand dollars in a machine he will sell him the one he possesses and get the former employee of the mint to make him another. If the victim agrees to enter the deal, the swindler has a confederate watch his movements to see if he informs the police. Everything clear, the swindler gets the machine ready, usually planting it in a furnished room. The room is darkened if he demonstrates it in the daytime, or a very dim light is used if in the evening. The machine is not brought into the room until after the arrival of the victim. This is a precaution. Satisfied that the way is clear, the swindler goes to another room in the premises and returns with the machine. He explains and demonstrates its mechanism and operation. The sale of the machine is accomplished, and the swindler takes leave with the promise that if anything goes wrong he or the former mint employee will fix it.

The more modern criminal paraphernalia used in this type of swindle consists of a number of glass tubes containing colored liquids, a quantity of blank white paper cut to the size of bills, and a simple pressing device. This paraphernalia is generally carried in a briefcase or portfolio.

THE SICK ENGINEER. This swindle may also be regarded as obsolete nowadays, although there is no guaranty that it might not be taken up again.

The dupe is taken by the swindler to a large office building in the financial district and is introduced to a confederate swindler posing as a broker. The broker expresses willingness and even eagerness to buy a particular mining stock that has suddenly become valuable, naming the price he will pay for as much of the stock as he can secure. The guide swindler then leads the victim uptown to a rooming house or hotel, where he is introduced to a sick engineer. The subject of the mining stock is brought up and the engineer, not knowing of the rise in value, offers to sell the lot he holds for a nominal sum. Seeing an opportunity to resell profitably to the broker, the dupe buys the stock. This transaction is generally timed to take place on a Friday or Saturday afternoon, after the broker has left for the day. On Monday, when the victim presents himself at the broker's office, he learns that the man he is looking for had simply hired desk room for one day and that he departed without leaving an address. Returning to the home of the sick engineer, he is informed that that person too has left for parts unknown. He soon finds out that the eagerly sought stock is valueless.

PROBLEMS IN CONNECTION WITH LETTERS

GUM-SEALED LETTERS. The criminal or spy who tampers with a letter may do this for the purpose of reading the contents or of stealing the whole or part of the contents. His procedure will differ according to the purpose in mind.

If his desire is only to read the letter, he may try transillumination by means of a strong light coming from the back, with the hope of reading through the translucent paper. This, however, will not be possible if the paper and envelope are thick. He may then resort to the method of making a print of the contents by putting the letter, instead of a plate, in a frame with sensitive bromide paper behind and using powerful light for some time. The contents will then appear on the print—white on black background. Deciphering the contents will be a difficult matter, however, if the letter is folded and closely written. This difficulty is also encountered when using X-rays for the same purpose. By this latter method a plate is placed in the frame instead of the paper and the letter is then illuminated with very soft X-rays for a short time.

No one of the above-described methods will leave markings, and whoever wishes to protect his mail against such attempts is advised to use thick envelopes and thick paper. In order to make it impossible to read letters by means of X-rays envelopes whose linings contain lead have been put on the market. The lead will not allow penetration by the X-rays.

A frequently used method of opening a letter is to draw the sharp point of a knife across and through a thick printed line on the envelope. When the contents have been removed, the slit is covered with very thin, silky, transparent paper, which is pasted over it.

The classic method, of course, is to let the vapor from boiling water act on the sealed back of the envelope and dissolve the paste, thus allowing the envelope to be opened. This method, however, inevitably leaves traces on the paper in the form of waves. All stamps or marks of indelible ink or pencil writing will also be dissolved to a certain degree, leaving blurs. The clever thief, instead of using water vapor, employs thin strips of blotting paper soaked in water, passing these over the sealed edge of the flap. This method injures only a small part of the flap.

Another method employed by thieves is to roll the flap open. A blunt instrument, such as a lead pencil, is inserted in the opening which almost always occurs at either extremity of the flap, where the paste layer ends. This opening represents the weak spot in the envelope, and it is the starting point of the mail thief's maneuvers. The lead pencil is now carefully and slowly rolled along the edge of the flap, which will open easily in most cases. Many mail thieves start on the under flap because this generally has inferior glue and loosens more readily. In the latter case he opens only one part of the bottom flap and the opposite part of the upper flap.

When this method of opening letters has been used, however, the shrewd investigator can detect it. Fibers from the paper will be detached from the upper as well as the under surface of the layer of glue. Often thin laminæ will be detached from the paper. There is no possibility whatsoever of the thief's hiding these marks. To reseal the envelope a different glue than the one originally present on the envelope is generally used, and if the thief be a clerk he may use the glue of the office. Many post office departments abroad mix their paste or glue with some easily detectable reagent. Generally such reagents have a strong luminescence and an examination of a letter under an ultraviolet light will immediately reveal whether it has been tampered with. Such reagents may also be used to set special traps. If, for example, a clerk is suspected of tampering, his paste may be mixed with some characteristic reagent. If several clerks are suspected, the glue of each may be mixed with a different reagent.

Another difficulty encountered by the thief in sealing the flap for the second time is the production of a double glue line and also, in the case of registered letters, the difficulty, not to say impossibility, of making the divided cancellation stamp, which runs across the edge of the flap, look as it did originally. These difficulties are encountered irrespective of the method used in opening the flap. The double glue line is made when the flap is pressed against the envelope for a second time, because it is almost impossible to match the former edge of the glue line with the new. This can be seen with the magnifying glass or microscope.

Figure 149. An envelope which has been opened by rolling a blunt instrument under the edges of the flap. Note the detached fibers.

Through the above-mentioned opening at the extremity of the flap the contents of the envelope may be taken out without opening it. For this purpose two knitting needles fastened together by means of a cork are used or even a special instrument consisting of a small steel rod having sharp steel points projecting from it. By rotating the knitting needles or the steel rod, the letter, if it is sufficiently thin, is grasped and rolled on the needles or the rod and drawn out through the opening. The letter may then be read, rolled back on the object used, inserted again in the opening, and replaced. Such a procedure will surely leave marks on the letter.

The examination of letters suspected of having been opened and closed again is begun by studying the envelope with a strong illumination from the back. Places where the fiber or thin particles of paper have been detached will show up brighter than the rest of the glued border. Such places are then encircled with a fine lead pencil and later examined closely by the method described below. Next the edge of the flap is carefully examined and any glue there is scrutinized to see if the parts of it match.

To examine the suspected places previously marked with lead pencil, two incisions running at right angles through the edge of the flap are made with a sharp knife so that only the part of the flap between the two cuts can be lifted. A piece of filter paper soaked with water is put on the suspected spot so that it is thoroughly soaked. When the glue has been dissolved, the small flap is carefully lifted with the aid of forceps. Great precautions must be taken in lifting this flap so as not to cause new fibers to become detached. The under surface of the flap and of the envelope is now examined with a magnifying glass. Detached paper fibers and detached thin particles may be easily seen and may be looked upon as a sure sign of previous opening.

Eventually the clues present are photographed. It should be pointed out that although the examination is a simple one a very experienced eye is required. Some mail thieves proceed with the utmost care and leave very few traces of their work, but a careful examination should nevertheless solve the problem in most cases.

The possibility of getting the fingerprints of the suspect on the contents of the letter should not be overlooked.

WAX-SEALED LETTERS. A letter sealed with wax may be opened in exactly the same manner as described above except for the seal. The seal may be removed in many different ways.

The simplest method is to lift the whole seal either by pulling it away directly or by inserting under it a thin electrically heated platinum wire. This method is most likely to succeed if the seal is thick. The seal is then replaced either by pasting it back or by heating its under surface and roughening the paper to bring about better adherence.

The method most commonly used is the one in which a cast of the seal is made and the original later replaced by a new seal made from the cast. This cast is made of plaster of Paris. The thief builds a wall of plastelina around the seal and pours a plaster of Paris mixture on it. When this has dried, the plaster cast reproduces the original seal quite faithfully. Sealing wax of the same color is used by the thief to make the new seals. It has been reported that clever thieves have been able to make a plaster cast of the seal, open a letter, remove the contents, close it, and put on a new seal in about twenty minutes. The fact that the letter has been in the possession of the suspect for only a short time is therefore not proof of his innocence.

The seals made with the plaster cast have some drawbacks. While reproducing all the faults in the original seal, the outlines of the letters are never as sharp and clearcut as when made with the metal signet. Besides, minute traces of plaster lodged in the false seal may be detected by slight enlargement. It should almost always be possible therefore to detect this type of tampering, although an experienced eye is always needed. In order to overcome the drawbacks of the plaster cast some thieves use some dental composition, such as copper amalgam.

In the more crude methods of years ago the thief made an impression of the seal in a soft lead plate. He put a piece of lead plate over the seal and struck it with a strong and absolutely vertical blow with a wooden club. The seal naturally broke in pieces, but a faithful reproduction of it on the lead plate resulted. This was then used to make new seals.

As the thief seldom bothers to open all the seals, the first part of the examination should be directed to the sealing wax. It should be determined if a similarity exists in all the seals. Examination with ultraviolet rays may be very useful, as sealing waxes which look quite alike may have a different fluorescence. Slight differences in the luminescence do not always mean, however, that the seals have been made with different sealing waxes, as the method of melting or burning the sealing wax can alter the fluorescence of the same stick. Experiments must be carried out with the same sealing wax to determine the slight differences. A chemical or microchemical analysis of the sealing wax may also be helpful in this case. When the seals have been lifted away, the thief will in many cases be compelled to repair them by piecing them in place. The different sealing waxes used can then be easily detected by means of the ultraviolet rays.

SETTING TRAPS FOR THIEVES

In places where epidemics of thefts occur, as in schools, offices, clinics, etc., the thief may be detected by setting a suitable trap. This may consist either of some mechanical device or of a dye. It is naturally impossible to describe how the traps should be applied. This depends entirely upon the circumstances of the case and the sagacity and cleverness of the investigator.

The use of the mechanical trap can best be exemplified by an actual case.

Students attending a private school were accustomed to hanging their overcoats and often even their coats in a corridor adjoining a laboratory. Some of them carelessly left their pocketbooks in their coats. Within a few weeks, several thefts were reported. To catch the perpetrator, a coat was rigged with a pocketbook visibly protruding from one of the pockets. The inside of the pocket contained two wires leading to the janitor's room, where they were connected with a battery and a bell. The pocket was also supplied with a contact. Removal of the pocketbook would then cause the bell to ring. The thief was soon apprehended.

The dyes can be mixed with a slowly drying glue and applied under doorknobs and the edges of drawers, on coins, in pockets, etc. Three kinds of dyes may be used for this purpose. The first embraces dyes which will immediately stain the hand; for instance, methylene-blue fuchsin, malachite green, and carbolfuchsin. Of these the methylene-blue and the carbolfuchsin, which has a brilliant red color, are difficult to wash away. The second category embraces less noticeable dyes which by the action of the perspiration, however, stain the hand very markedly. Blue of bromophenol, a light-yellow powder which turns dark-blue after a short time, is used. However, it has the disadvantage that it can be very easily washed away. In recent years nitrate of silver has frequently been used for this purpose. The commercial substance is employed and is ground in a mortar and mixed with vaseline, for instance, or strewn directly in the pocket, purse, etc. When the thief touches the nitrate of silver, there is no immediate reaction, but shortly after by the influence of light, the stain will grow dark and is impossible to wash away.

The third category embraces dyes or, better, chemicals with strong luminescence. In this case the thief gets some white powder on his fingers and does not as a rule pay any attention to it. Even if he washes his hands once, traces of the powder will remain adhered to the skin. If the hands of the suspected person are examined under ultraviolet rays, the particles of powder will be detected by the brilliant luminescence given off. A powder commonly used for this purpose is naphthionate of sodium.[5]

1 In New York it is now unlawful to leave the ignition keys in cars and summonses are issued for the offense.

2 Most modern bank counters are constructed so as to prevent this. In smaller banks in rural areas the method is still possible, particularly if the teller leaves his cage to get a transaction approved.

3 Methods used by pickpockets have not changed much in the last few decades. However, there is a marked decrease of the Caucasian type operating in this game, at least on the East Coast, and pickpockets are generally much younger than before. Also the more refined men of the old school are making way for a cruder type.

4 Swindlers and confidence men belong more or less to the nineteenth century, their activities reaching their peak around the Gay Nineties, when greenhorns of every kind were streaming to this country. Almost all confidence games appealed to the greed and potential criminality of the victim. With the higher education and enlightenment of our days the confidence games are becoming rare. Several of the tricks of the trade here told will now mostly be encountered only in remote parts of the country, but even so the modern detective ought to know the technique of the con men. The days when the Brooklyn Bridge could be sold to a sucker, however, are just about gone.

5 Schade–Widmann.

XXIII ROBBERY

ROBBERY IS ONE OF THE LEADING FORMS OF MAJOR CRIME WITH WHICH the police must deal. There are innumerable types of robbery. Some do not require much planning on the part of the criminal, while others, due to the protective measures taken, not only require a survey of the premises and neighborhood and a study of the habits of the individuals to be attacked, the hour most opportune, and the traffic flow and impediments in the area, but also the organization and assignment of confederates to act definite parts and to swiftly transport the band of robbers from the scene in automobiles stolen weeks in advance and carrying fictitious or stolen license plates. These cars are quickly abandoned at a location where they are unlikely to be found soon, and transportation again taken by other automobiles, airplanes, buses, trains, or steamship.

The main robbers operate in mobs of from two to five. They may specialize in holding up certain classes of persons, stores, or premises. In the following pages many types of robberies are mentioned. It must not be assumed, however, that the list is anywhere near complete. Many volumes could be written without covering the topic completely.

In the investigation of robbery all applicable methods of police science should be useful. Fingerprints may be found on abandoned cars and on other paraphernalia. Filed-off numbers may be revealed on discarded firearms, thereby disclosing at least the original buyer of the weapon Footprints are left at the scene, etc. Even in seemingly hopeless cases a careful investigation will almost always reveal some traces of a technical nature which may be utilized to track down the criminal. The following cases illustrate this.

Some years ago, detectives on motor patrol in New York City noticed and pursued two men driving at a high rate of speed in a Ford sedan. The registration license of the car had been given in a police alarm for a stolen automobile. The car was fired at without avail in an endeavor to make the driver and his companion stop. They escaped.

Later in the same day, the automobile was found abandoned elsewhere in the city, with marks indicating it had been penetrated by bullets. Technicians of the police laboratory were summoned and charted the course of three bullet holes in the car. One bullet had entered the right front-door window, above the doorframe, and struck the occupant of the seat alongside of the driver. A spent bullet was found on the floor of the car. Twenty blond hairs, a particle of glass, and a piece of dark felt clung to the bullet.

A benzidine test applied to the rear cushion on the right of the front seat gave a positive reaction for blood. The handles of the door of the car and the steering wheel had been covered with black tape to avoid leaving fingerprint impressions. The taillight above the license plate was also covered with black tape so that the numerals on the license plate could not be seen.

Seven days later, a patrolman arrested one K. for larceny of this automobile. Before submitting to arrest, K. had been shot in the right hand by the patrolman. Examined by an ambulance surgeon, he was also found to have a recent injury in the back of his head. The strands of hair from the head of K. were compared with the hair found on the spent bullet in the car, and a conclusion was reached that the hairs came from the same head.

K. stood trial and offered an alibi as a defense. Testimony was given regarding the hairs, and a conviction resulted.

In another case N. C., proprietor of a lunch wagon in New York City, was proceeding on foot to his home one night. He carried with him the day's receipts of $300. As he approached the crossing of a railroad, he was struck on the head with a bottle by an unknown male assailant, who, with another man, attempted to rob him. The attempt was unsuccessful. N. C. fired several shots from a revolver which he lawfully possessed and carried. One of the shots hit one of the assailants and led to his arrest when he sought medical aid at a doctor's office.

A search of the overcoat worn by G.—the arrested man—resulted in the discovery of a piece of glass in the right-hand coat pocket. The glass was taken to the laboratory for examination. There it was found to match perfectly particles from the neck of the bottle found at the scene. G. was convicted and sentenced to fifteen years in a State prison.

BANK MESSENGERS. This type of crime is seldom attempted by amateurs but is usually the work of experienced criminals, generally working in groups of from three to six. Sometimes they work in collusion with a dishonest employee who tips them off with information as to movements of messengers, the procedure followed in making deposits and withdrawing funds, and the methods of transportation. The crime is planned in advance. Each criminal is drilled in the part he is to act. Cars are stolen days in advance, the number depending upon the need for escape and transfer. License plates are removed from the stolen cars and other plates which have been secured under a fictitious name and address substituted for them. The cars are stored until the day of the crime. About thirty minutes before the messenger leaves, the robbers drive to a spot adjacent to the bank. One remains at the wheel. Others act as lookouts to prevent interference with the holdup. The motor of the car is left running or, if stopped, is started up a few minutes before the messenger is expected. The holdup men trail the messenger from the bank. If he is riding in an automobile, his car is forced to stop by an argument over some alleged traffic offense or discourtesy in driving. With the messenger off-guard, he is disarmed at pistol point and the money taken.

Another method is for the criminals to await the approach of the messenger in the hallway of the place of delivery and there hold him up at pistol point. This may be done without the knowledge of elevator operators, as flight from the building is by stairway. At other times the elevator operator is brought to the floor on which the holdup is to occur, compelled to remain there until the crime has been committed, and forced to take the criminals to the main floor. Upon letting them out, he is forced to ascend immediately with the elevator.

BANKS. Bank robbers are professional criminals who organize carefully, plan with ingenuity, attack boldly, and are equipped with machine guns, sawed-off shotguns, or rifles and sometimes tear-gas grenades. One of their early morning methods is for a member of the mob—dressed as a letter carrier, telegraph messenger, or policeman—to knock on the bank door and, under a subterfuge, to get the watchman to open it. Upon doing so, he is confronted and subdued with a revolver. The bandit enters the bank, admits his confederates, makes the watchman lock the door, and then handcuffs or ties him.

As other employees and officials arrive, the watchman is compelled to open the door and admit them without giving warning. The robbers take the employees and officials to a certain room or corner until the one who has the combination to the vault arrives. At pistol point he is forced to open the vault at the regular time. In many instances, if he could use the wrong combination and prolong the attempt to open the vault, the robbers would be apprehended.

With the vault opened the money is put into bags and escape made. Officials and employees are covered in the getaway. In some cases the individual covering the getaway has a tear-gas grenade in his hand. As he steps out of the door, he releases the cotter-pin and throws the grenade to the floor, thus distracting the victims' attention from alarm devices until the criminals are on their way.

Another method used by criminals is to drive up to the bank in an automobile, leaving one confederate at the wheel with the motor running and another as a lookout, while the actual robbers enter. Each takes up a definitely planned position. At a signal guns are displayed and employees compelled to move away from alarm devices. Some of the robbers force their way into the cages of the paying and receiving clerks or climb over the partitions. The employees are forced at pistol point to a certain location in the bank. Money is swiftly gathered into bags, and one or two armed robbers cover the getaway.

Small banks not amply protected are sometimes entered at night through an upper floor by forcing a door or window or from an adjoining building by rope or ladder. When the watchman arrives on an upper floor, he is overpowered and disarmed. If he is required to punch a time clock, the criminals compel him to do so under their supervision. In the morning he is compelled to admit the employees without warning. The criminals then follow the same procedure as those who operate with a confederate in uniform, as described above.

Recently there has been an increasing number of lone bank robbers who use the simple technique of passing a note to the teller instructing him to hand over his cash. The criminal is usually an amateur who simulates possession of a weapon. This form of bank robbery is easily discouraged by trained and alert tellers who will delay compliance until they are sure that the robber possesses a real gun.

ARMORED DEALERS. This crime is committed by experienced criminals who go to the greatest pains in planning and preparation. The operation is characterized by a carefully elaborated strategy, supported fully by equipment for transportation, weapons, and disguise. The following case is a classic example:

One of the perpetrators in the guise of a pushcart peddler arrived with a cart and stopped near the curb a few minutes prior to the arrival of the armored car at the premises from which money was to be collected. Others had trailed the armored car to this place. As one guard stepped out of the car and walked toward the premises, the ostensible peddler pushed his cart to the side of the armored car, the door of which was open. A submachine gun was drawn from among the vegetables. The chauffeur on the armored car was covered. Accomplices covered the guard inside the car and the guard who was about to enter the premises to make a collection. Other accomplices entered the armored car and removed money therefrom, and then all escaped. They sped to a nearby waterfront, changing direction on the way. Transfer was made to speed-boats, which were later scuttled and submerged. They had been repainted and the registration number and identification marks changed or removed.

In the robbery of armored cars the technique used is nearly always similar to the method described above. However, the criminal paraphernalia is not always so elaborate.

PAYROLLS. The large payroll entrusted for transport to an officer or paymaster is taken by criminals numbering from four to six men. The small payroll entrusted to the girl cashier who draws it from the bank is taken by a lone worker or criminals who operate in pairs. The large payroll is usually taken from a plant or factory in the manufacturing or industrial section. The smaller one is taken at any time anywhere. The large payroll bandits work in a manner similar to that of the bank messenger robbers. They make a survey of the environs and plan in detail. Sometimes they are supplied with information by a dishonest employee working in collusion with them. If the payroll is delivered by an armored car, their time of operation is a few minutes after the car has left the premises.

Where the cashier is armed and accompanied by a guard, the robbers wait until he returns to the plant. They arrive in a car—usually stolen—carrying fictitious license plates. One criminal remains at the wheel; another at the door as a lookout. In some instances the man in the car has a submachine gun or sawed-off shotgun. The others enter the office, hold up all present, and disconnect the telephone or cut the wires. Seizing the money, they run to the waiting car, covering their escape with guns, and warning their victims not to move for three or four minutes. They either abandon the car in which they take flight for another or separate and go in different directions, taking other cars, a taxicab, a bus, or a train. Where they take a payroll from a cashier riding from a bank in a taxicab or automobile, they operate in a manner precisely the same as that used in robbing a bank messenger.

When they have definite information of a large payroll protected by a guard or policeman who is not on the alert, they approach quickly, shoot the guard, cover other persons with revolvers, take up the payroll, and flee. This type of robbery is always carefully planned and executed for the reason that the robbers have to perform the act and make their getaway in a very short interval to avoid apprehension.

The small payroll criminal is usually a young and active man—not always a professional criminal. He observes a young girl going into a bank and drawing out eight or nine hundred dollars for the week's payroll. Generally she carries this money in an envelope in the same hand with her pocketbook. The robber perhaps precedes her into the building where her office is located. As she approaches, he usually strikes her with his fist or with some blunt instrument, takes the money, and escapes.

This thief seldom has a gun but has been known to use a piece of pipe wrapped in paper. As a rule he is not inclined to resort to grave assault. He mostly works alone and generally attempts to lose himself among pedestrians on the street or runs through alley-ways, buildings, or courts to escape. He may enter the office when the girl is making up the payroll at lunch hour when other employees are out. He applies for a position, or attempts to sell some article. Then, locating the payroll, he seizes the money. If the girl resists, he strikes her with his fist and flees.

JEWELRY STORES. Experienced criminals working in groups of from two to five rob jewelry stores. The better-class store is generally selected. The time chosen is just after opening or just before closing time, when trays of jewelry are being put in or taken out of the window. Criminals of this type generally use a stolen automobile which is provided with fixtitious license plates.

The automobile conveys the robbers to the scene. A confederate remains at the wheel of the parked automobile with motor running. Another acts as a lookout while the others enter. One or two carry small leather bags into which jewelry may be placed. At revolver point they hold up the clerks and owner, remove jewelry from the safe and showcase trays, and decamp, warning that an outcry or pursuit will cause them to shoot. In stores equipped with an alarm system they force the owner or clerks into the rear, tie and bind them, and escape. If two automobiles are used, they ride a few blocks in the first to the point where the second car is waiting for them with a driver accomplice. This type of mob may have one of its members known as a "killer" act as lookout. He generally loiters in a doorway close by. He does not enter the car in which the actual robbers escape after the holdup but casually walks away and enters another car parked in the vicinity and follows along to impede pursuit. Robbers of this type are desperate and dangerous.

Another method is for two criminals to visit a store ostensibly to buy jewelry. A certain piece is selected, and payment by check is offered. The clerk refuses to take the check, and one of the thieves leaves to cash it. The other remains in conversation with the clerk. The thief who left to cash the check phones the store. As the clerk or owner answers the phone, the criminal remaining covers him with a revolver. Then another accomplice enters and steals any jewelry available. Or they may force the clerk to open the safe, tie and gag him, cut telephone wires, and flee from the premises with their plunder.

OUTSIDE SALESMEN. Professional criminals working in groups of two or three operate against the jeweler or salesman calling to show his line to a prospective customer. The criminal operation may occur any time during business hours. Sometimes the thieves are tipped off by a member of the trade working in collusion.

The criminals may hold up the salesman while he is riding in a taxicab or automobile, or again they may hold him up in his hotel room. They may also follow him into a building, hold him up at the point of a gun, assault him if he resists, take the jewels, and direct him to walk up the stairs to the floor above or to the roof. They warn him against making any outcry and flee.

If the jeweler or salesman is riding in a cab or automobile, he is trailed in another. When traffic pauses, the criminals quickly enter his car, cover him with a gun, direct the driver to continue, take the jewels, drive to a distant point, put the victim and driver out, and drive away in the automobile, later abandoning it. In buildings equipped with elevators they may follow the victim into the elevator and, if he is the only other passenger when the car starts up, commit the robbery and order the elevator operator to stop the car at the first floor. There they get out, ordering the operator to proceed up with the car while they escape.

If the salesman is stopping at a hotel, the criminals engage a room on the same floor. They gain the confidence of the salesman, enter his room under some pretext, and commit the robbery. At other times they do not hire a room but gain entrance through disguising one of the gang as a bellboy or other employee.

CHAIN STORES AND SHOPS. All classes of criminals operate in this field. They select stores where there is a large turnover of money in a day, where there are only one or two clerks on duty, or where there is a large weekend business. Time of operation is usually just prior to closing. It may be a Saturday night when banks are closed or when the money is held for pickup by a company collector on Monday. Several such robberies may be committed in succession. The perpetrators drive up to a point near the premises in a car, oftener than not a stolen one. An accomplice remains at the wheel, sometimes accompanied by a woman to avoid suspicion. The motor is kept running. The criminals enter and ask for some article, which the clerk turns to get. When he faces about, he is looking into the muzzle of a gun. In some cases it is an imitation one. Ordered to the rear of the store, he is sometimes tied up or locked in a washroom or icebox and invariably is made to remove his trousers, the legs of which are immediately knotted. In some cases the female accomplice enters alone or with a confederate and removes the money from the cash register while her accomplice handles the revolver.

When two male robbers commit the crime, one usually forces the clerk to the rear of the store with a gun while the other, posing as a clerk, rifles the cash register, even waiting on a customer should one come in. At a favorable moment they run out, get into a waiting car, and escape. While these robbers mainly operate just prior to closing time, police officers may also find them in the field shortly after stores open in the morning.

RESTAURANTS. Criminals robbing small restaurants, lunch wagons,

Figure 150. Weapons used by professional criminals and gangsters, with four so-called bulletproof vests.

and coffee houses work alone or with a partner. The more experienced criminal mob selects the busier and better restaurants, usually operating after eleven o'clock at night. In the former type of robbery the two criminals enter the restaurant, order food, eat, and await an opportunity. They hold up the counterman or cashier at the point of a gun and take the money from the cash register. They will shoot to effect escape. The lone worker seldom has an automobile but hails a taxicab and sometimes at the point of a gun compels the driver to speed away.

In the robbery of larger restaurants the crime is planned in advance, the criminals selecting a place frequented by moneyed clientele. They drive up in an automobile to a spot adjoining the premises and alight. One is left at the wheel of the car and a lookout is on the street. The doorman, if any, is forced to go inside the restaurant. The leader enters and orders the patrons to line up against the wall, after which his confederates go through the pockets and handbags of the diners, taking jewelry and money. The job completed, they escape in the waiting car.

THEATERS AND MOTION-PICTURE HOUSES. The cashier or treasurer of a motion-picture house or continuous vaudeville and burlesque house is apt to be attacked just prior to closing time. In the legitimate playhouse, shortly after curtain time is the hour usually selected. Two or three criminals usually work the motion-picture houses. Previously observing the time for the cashier to transfer the money from the booth to the office, one of the criminals waits at the wheel of a parked car with the motor running while his confederates enter and at the point of a revolver thrust through the wicket of the booth demand and take the receipts. They may also wait inside the door of the theater and hold the employee up as he enters with the money. Again, they may wait until the money is delivered to the office, knock on the door, and, when it is opened, display their guns, subdue the manager and cashier, tie them up, take the money, and flee.

Roughly the same procedures are followed in robbing other amusement houses.

GASOLINE STATIONS. Criminals operate against there stations in groups of from two to four. At times a female accomplice or male so disguised may assist. Gas stations situated on roads in outlying sections or less frequented highways are attacked, generally after eleven o'clock at night. The criminals drive up in a car, which may have fictitious license plates. They order a quantity of oil or gas for the car. When it is time to pay the attendant, guns are displayed. The attendant is forced to enter the station, is tied or bound or handcuffed to an object, or locked in the washroom. The cash register is then rifled and escape effected.

DRUGSTORES. Here may be found the professional and amateur criminal operating alone or with a confederate and with real or imitation pistols. Sometimes a female accomplice enters as an ostensible buyer and orders something; while the clerk is filling the order, the other criminal enters, draws a revolver, and compells him to go to the rear of the store. Thereupon one of the two empties the cash register. The perpetrators may also take narcotic drugs. See Chapter XX on drug addiction.

In other cases the robbers select a store where their actions cannot be observed from the street at night and drive up in a car. One criminal remains at the wheel. The other enters and purchases and pays for an article. As the clerk deposits the money in the cash register, the criminal draws a gun, orders the clerk to the rear behind the partition, and makes him remove his trousers or locks him in the washroom. Returning, the register is emptied. At other times a confederate enters at the moment the clerk is confronted with the gun, and while his partner covers the clerk and forces him to the rear of the store, the confederate rifles the register. They may repeat at another store in the same area, sometimes just when the druggist is closing or the patrol force is changing tours.

CLUBS AND PRIVATE HOMES. The hardened criminal mob commits this type of robbery. Clubs or private homes[1] where gambling is the vogue are a fertile field after 10 P.M. One member of the gang may have frequented the place to make observations of members and players. The number of robbers is in proportion to the number of players to be held up. If known to the players, the criminals mask. If the club has a doorman, he is forced into the clubrooms. One remains at the wheel of a waiting automobile, another at the entrance as a lookout. The players are lined up against the wall at the point of a revolver, and their pockets are rifled. The criminals flee the premises, covering the players until all the robbers are in the waiting car.

These criminals are usually bold and desperate and do not hesitate to shoot to escape. They may overcome resistance by striking a resister over the head with the butt of a revolver.

GAMBLING GAMES. Professional criminals operate on crap and other gambling games conducted in lofts, garages, cellars, poolrooms, wire rooms, piers, and at construction sites on payday if crap games are conducted by the workers. The time usually chosen to stick up such players is when the game is in full swing. Like the club bandits, these criminals have made a survey of the place and laid plans in advance. Their operation is the same.

RESIDENCES. The criminal operating in this field, sometimes with one or two accomplices, selects only homes of the wealthy. In the larger homes and apartments they usually gain entrance without the knowledge of the occupants via a rear door or through a window or by climbing a porch at a time when servants are not about. They try to surprise their victims and catch them when they are dressing or undressing. Money and valuable jewelry is stolen. Sometimes the victims are tied up. If resistance is offered, there is no hesitation to assault. Flight is usually by car. Sometimes the criminals enter the house while the occupants are out and secrete themselves until their victims return.

In smaller apartments and residences the perpetrator, posing as a delivery boy or such, may be admitted by the woman of the house on supposedly legitimate business. Then, distracting attention, he may strike the woman with a blunt instrument or even with his bare hands.

INDIVIDUALS. Criminals use various techniques in robbing individuals. A female accomplice may lure the victim to some secluded place in a building, where a male accomplice is waiting and proceeds to hold up the victim at the point of a gun or with a knife or razor. Together they relieve him of money and valuables and trousers. The woman flees first and her companion follows. Criminals of this type know the neighborhood in which they operate.

Rent collectors, milkmen, and bill collectors may be held up at the point of a revolver by two men waiting in the hallway of the house entered. Sometimes the money is taken in the hallway; at other times the victim is forced to the roof, tied up there, and robbed.

In sparsely settled areas two robbers may wait for a man on his way to a bank, take the money from him at the point of a gun, and flee in an automobile. Other criminals make a practice of following women and girls from subway and elevated stations, market places, or homes late at night. Then either on the street or at the entrance door or in the vestibule of their home, the thief threatens with a revolver, steals money, jewelry, and valuables, or takes a fur piece, and flees. Most cases of this class show only one man operating. Such criminals may assault to overcome resistance.

Some thieves loiter in the vicinity of hotels, restaurants, and saloons and wait for an intoxicated victim, whom they pull into a hallway and rob. They may operate with an automobile, pretend to assist an intoxicated man, get him into the car, strike him over the head with a blunt instrument, remove his money and valuables, and dump him out on an unlighted street or highway.

Others work in groups of two to four. Frequenting the better-class hotels, restaurants, and cabarets as guests, they take special note of a couple spending freely, especially if the woman is wearing valuable jewelry. When the couple leaves, they follow in another car and, with the aid of a gun, commit the robbery in the vestibule or foyer of the victims' home.

Some male criminals dressed in female attire will solicit men on the street. The victim is then taken into a hallway or to the roof of an apartment or tenement house and there robbed. Here indeed is a dangerous robber. Resisted, he may shoot, stab, or throw the victim off the roof. Some have impersonated females with such skill that only after they were in the detention prison undergoing examination was their true sex apparent.

TAXICABS. Amateur criminals sometimes operate in this field. The taxicab robber works mostly at night. He directs the driver to proceed to a lonely spot or street, alights, confronts him with a gun, takes his money, forces him to enter a hallway, and then drives away in the cab, which is abandoned a short time later.

DEPARTMENT STORE DELIVERY TRUCKS. Robbery of trucks and de livery vehicles is usually the work of professionals. Three or four criminals in a stolen or hired car follow the truck to a quiet thoroughfare and force it to the curb; money collected is taken at revolver point. Sometimes the driver and helper are put into the thieves' car, forced to lie on the floor, and driven to a distant point, where they are discharged. In cases of this type the holdup men may drive the vehicle containing merchandise to a "drop," remove the contents, and abandon the vehicle.

RAPID TRANSIT LINES. This type of robbery is usually committed by criminals of experience who work alone or with an accomplice during non-rush hours. The lone robber generally waits for a minute or so after a train has left the station. Then he points a pistol through the window of the ticket booth, orders the agent to open the booth door, seizes the money, and flees to the street. Or he may tie up the agent or knock him unconscious to prevent pursuit. When working with an accomplice, one is the lookout. With the agent covered and the door open, the lookout enters the booth and takes the money. Escape is covered with a revolver. An automobile may be used to expedite flight.

WAREHOUSES. This type of robbery is generally committed by gangs of experienced criminals operating in the early morning. They may work in collusion with one or more employees, or at times the robbery is

planned on information and connections provided by an agent or lieutenant of the fence or receiver. Warehouses or sheds where valuable merchandise such as liquor or tobacco is stored have become a fruitful field
for this type of criminal activity. The place has been previously surveyed,
the habits of the watchmen studied, and the location of merchandise
learned. Heavily armed, some of the criminals proceed to the warehouse
or shed, enter by pretext or force, cover the watchman with a gun, and
assault and subdue him if he resists. Telephone wires may be cut. The
goods are then selected and hand trucks sometimes used to transport
them to the door. The criminals' motor truck (the "switch truck") now
arrives at the premises and lookouts strategically located either give a
warning signal or indicate that the coast is clear. As a sign of danger, the
outer lookout may wipe his face with his handkerchief or give some
other prearranged signal. The inside lookout warns his confederates if
the road is not clear or if a policeman is approaching. If the road is clear,
the truck is loaded and driven away. As this happens about five or six
o'clock in the morning and interstate and market trucks are moving, one
truck more attracts little notice. Generally one or two members of the
band drive the truck away, while the others scatter in various directions.
The merchandise, of course, is taken to a prearranged drop, where marks
of identification are removed. The goods are then sold to a fence or
receiver.

PHYSICIANS AND DENTISTS. Thieves who specialize in this kind of
robbery are experienced criminals, usually operating alone. They select
a time when no patients are likely to be in the office and during the examination draw a revolver and force the victim to turn over money,
valuables, and sometimes gold and certain drugs used by the profession
to lessen pain.

PRIVATE CARS. During recent years, particularly in seasonable
weather, couples parked in secluded spots in outlying areas have been
taken by surprise by lone holdup men who at pistol point relieve them
of their valuables and in some instances the car as well. This type of
criminal may have an accomplice when operating in public parks. Not
content with the plunder secured, one of the pair may attempt a criminal
assault on the female victim. At present this type of crime is fairly prevalent.

The lone criminal also operates by thumbing a ride and shows quick
appreciation by holding up his benefactor, relieving him of his valuables
and forcing him out of the motorcar, with which he makes a getaway.

1 The present high income tax rate has resulted in some cases in large amounts of cash being concealed in homes. This fact has not passed unobserved by criminals. The police are faced with a peculiar problem. In one case, for instance, a man reported that he had been robbed of $3,000 and some valuable jewelry. The perpetrator was arrested, and $30,000 was found in his possession. The victim refused to admit that he had been robbed of the additional $27,000, while the robber insisted that he had stolen the whole amount from that one victim.

XXIV INVESTIGATION OF ARSON

THE SUCCESSFUL PROSECUTION OF AN INCENDIARY DEPENDS MORE THAN in any other crime upon close collaboration between prosecutor and investigator; the final result of such a case rests greatly on the prosecutor.

Although the circumstances may be definitely suspicious, the investigator must eliminate every possibility of natural or accidental causes before he is entitled to build a hypothesis of arson. The important question of motive must be carefully considered from the very beginning. It is quite possible that the questioning may point toward an innocent person who is merely involved in an accidental fire. The utmost skill of the investigator is needed to collect information speedily and discreetly and check oral testimony with the findings of the technical investigation without damage to the reputations of the persons involved. Always remember that in small communities imprudent questioning or statements may do lifelong injury to an innocent person.

ESSENTIAL POINTS IN INVESTIGATING AND CONVICTING

The essential points in connection with the investigation of incendiary fires, the preparation of evidence, and the securing of convictions are the following:[1]

1. It must be established that the fire in question actually occurred. This may be done through witnesses, fire records, photographs, sketches, and other evidence of this sort.

2. A description of the building in which the fire occurred must be given together with a statement of the circumstances which give an accurate picture of the fire.

3. It must be proven that the fire did not occur from accidental causes. This may be done by eliminating the possible sources of accidental origin.

4. It must be indicated that the fire was caused by criminal design. This may be done by positive or circumstantial evidence. Confessions alone are not enough to establish criminal origin, but they must be supported by corroborative facts such as the presence of gasoline, kerosene, or other flammables or explosives, by the presence of more than one (separate and

distinct) fire, by obstructions deliberately placed to impede fire-fighting operations, or by the removal of valuables just prior to the fire. In presenting this corroborative evidence, witnesses are required merely to state facts. A fireman, for example, may testify that there was an unusual amount of black smoke or that the building burned with unusual rapidity. He may not on the witness stand draw the conclusion that this indicates the presence of oils or volatile flammables. He can, however, draw a comparison with the smoke or rate of burning noted with the smoke or rate of burning he has observed in other fires.

5. Establishment of a motive greatly strengthens other evidence. Facts may be presented to show the financial straits of the defendant, or motive may be suggested by proving the existence of a desire to move or to break a lease on the part of the person who had the fire.

6. Responsibility for the fire must be directly connected with an individual. This may be done by a confession if suitably corroborated. Evidence of the circumstances of the fire may also be used to establish the guilt of an individual. Possession of the only available keys to a locked building, for example, might constitute evidence of the sort which may be used to connect a given individual with the fire.

THE MOTIVE

To achieve success in the investigation of the crime of arson, the investigator must have a clear understanding of the motives which inspire its commission. The usual and general underlying motives are listed here and discussed briefly below.

1. To defraud insurance companies by the collection of fire insurance
2. To conceal a previous crime
3. To destroy books, records, or other incriminating evidence
4. For revenge, intimidation, extortion, racketeering, or sabotage
5. For purposes due to business rivalry or competition
6. For no particular motive except the thrill of seeing the blaze—the pyromaniac

It is most important for the investigator to ascertain the motive on the part of the suspect or accused, but the establishment of the motive is not absolutely necessary for the prosecution. It often serves as a guide to the guilty person, however.

INSURANCE FRAUD. The insurance angle of arson cases is most important and should be carefully investigated. It goes without saying that the financial status of the suspect, as well as the dates of any embarrassing payments due about the time of the fire, should be ascertained.

The intent to defraud the insurer may not always be manifested by the increasing of the insurance just before the commission of the crime. Cases are known where the insurance was reduced to some extent before the setting of the fire in order to avoid suspicion.

The motive to defraud insurance companies may be inspired by any of the following reasons:

1. To liquidate a business enterprise
2. To dispose of obsolete merchandise
3. To avoid bankruptcy or financial failure in business
4. To destroy manufactured articles that are nonsalable because of cancellation of orders or because of defects in the product
5. To destroy unsalable merchandise which is out of style because of changes in fashions
6. To avoid complying with building and health laws which would necessitate making structural changes, etc., entailing considerable expenditure in money
7. To destroy old or obsolete machinery or fixtures because it would be too expensive to repair or improve them and maintenance costs are too high
8. To avoid the cost of moving merchandise from one locality to another
9. To dispose of an unprofitable or worthless building
10. To quickly acquire cash to meet obligations
11. Because of failure to meet date of delivery of goods contracted for, particularly where there is a penalty for nondelivery on a stipulated date
12. To cancel a lease on property

Arson fires that are indirectly due to trade conditions are commonly referred to as trade or business fires. A change in the fashion of wearing apparel finds the merchant overstocked. A financial loss confronts him. If unscrupulous, the merchant may resort to arson and sell his unwanted goods to the fire insurance company. He may also surreptitiously remove the most valuable goods from the premises on a bogus sale or shipment, leaving the unwanted goods to be damaged or destroyed by the fire.

The unsuccessful or fraudulent merchant sometimes employs a professional arsonist to apply the torch. In order to avoid having what is known as a fire record he may arrange to have the fire started on the floor above his own, where another business is conducted, so that he will sustain a water loss and collect insurance therefor.

CONCEALMENT OF CRIME. Arson is sometimes employed to conceal a previously committed crime. A murderer will set fire to a building to destroy all traces of the homicide, and make it appear that the victim perished in the fire accidentally. It should be pointed out that when a person burns to death, the charred body—owing to the contraction of the tissues caused by the heat—often assumes the most peculiar positions, sometimes indicating that the person died defending himself. Only an autopsy can furnish any foundation for such a suspicion. (Figure 126.)

Arson has also been committed to cover a burglary, and therefore all locks should be carefully inspected. These will not have been destroyed by the fire.[2]

To DESTROY BOOKS AND RECORDS. The fraudulent businessman will plan the setting of a fire to destroy his account books, etc., when he is expecting a checkup from income tax authorities or for some other reason wishes his records destroyed. In such cases the account books are very often opened at the pages which the businessman wants destroyed, as it is well known that it is almost impossible to burn a thick account book if it is closed. Hence, if the account books are found opened at an incriminating place, there is reason to suspect arson and a thorough investigation should be conducted.

FOR INTIMIDATION OR RACKETEERING PURPOSES. Another motive for arson may be intimidation. For instance, the fire may be set to intimidate a witness in a civil or criminal case. Fires of this type are usually set at the entrance door of the intended victim.

Racketeers may resort to the torch in their extortion rackets when they want to intimidate contractors or other firms or individuals in various building or other trades and thus force the victims to meet their illegal demands.

BUSINESS RIVALRY OR COMPETITION. Arson may also be committed in cases of trade rivalry, one competitor burning out another in order to get his business.

PYROMANIA. Pyromaniacs are often found among the first onlookers at a fire or at least in the neighborhood. It is not uncommon for such persons to be members or patrons of the local fire association.

As a rule, the pyromaniac commits arson for no reason other than the abnormal impulse which urges him on. In explanation of his act in nearly every instance he will state that he did it to get a thrill, to create excitement. Whenever a series of fires of mysterious origin occur under similar circumstances in any particular district—in unoccupied or isolated buildings or in a particular part of a building, such as cellars, storage rooms, hallways, etc.—it is safe to conclude that a pyromaniac is operating.

The alcoholic pyromaniac usually operates at night and frequently wanders a considerable distance from his home or place of employment to apply the torch.

Pyromaniacs, by turning in alarms and aiding firemen or helping persons from the building they have set afire, often avert suspicion from themselves. The pyromaniac is the most difficult arsonist to detect because of the lack of motive.

There has been a good deal of discussion as to whether pyromania is a special psychopathological condition or can be attributed to other sources, generally of a sexual nature. Pyromaniacs often are found to be mentally defective boys and girls of youthful ages, as well as half-witted tramps, farmhands, maid servants, alcoholics, etc. Outstanding characteristics are that they always work alone and are usually of the non-sociable type. Several cases have also been noted in which fires have been set by hysterical, pregnant, or menstruating women or by women whose minds are affected by menopause.

VANITY. Strange as it may seem, vanity sometimes plays a part as a motive for arson. There are cases on record, for instance, where a proud member of a voluntary fire brigade or company has set fires in order to be able to wear his uniform and operate as a fireman.

THE TECHNICAL INVESTIGATION

Arson is a major felony calling for a most thorough and careful examination of the scene and environs at the earliest possible moment.

Regardless of the cause, from the viewpoint of the technical examination fires may be divided into three categories, namely: (1) those extinguished without having caused too much damage, (2) those extinguished quickly but after causing some damage, for instance to one room, and (3) those causing total destruction. In the first case it should almost always be possible to establish the cause of the fire; in the second case it should usually be possible to establish the cause of the fire; and in the third case the combined investigatory and technical evidence may furnish sufficient information so that there is a fair chance of establishing the cause of the fire.

The scene of the fire should be kept intact until the examination is completed. If necessary, the walls and chimneys must be supported with beams or similar objects; and if circumstances call for it, the scene should be guarded day and night until it has been examined thoroughly.

If the cause of the fire cannot be determined at the first examination, the investigator should eliminate, step by step, all natural and accidental causes until the actual cause has been found. Not only should stoves, flues, and the electric system be tested, but in many cases ashes and debris should also be sifted and minutely examined. Before anything is touched at the scene, the possible presence of flammable oils should be sought out by smell and samples of objects suspected of being soaked in inflammable oils should be collected.

In all cases the scene should be thoroughly photographed and sketched. All traces (fingerprints, footprints, traces of tires, hairs, fibers, toolmarks, paint, etc.) should be searched for in the usual manner. Soil samples should be taken to compare with soil on the clothing or shoes of the suspect. In many cases it will be found useful to search the environment for lost or discarded objects and footprints. In rural areas the use of a police dog may be helpful.

Doors and windows must be examined to determine whether or not they were locked when the fire was discovered. If found forced, the identity of the firemen or persons who forced them must be learned. Witnesses must be interviewed without delay. Occupants, if absent, must be located and questioned immediately to ascertain the time of their departure; who locked doors and windows; who had keys to the premises; where insurance policies are or were at time of fire; financial status; outstanding liabilities, business and personal; time, date, and manner of last receipts and shipments of goods, and so forth. An inspection and inventory of stock should be made by an expert appraiser for the purpose of determining the possibility of overinsurance or overstock of unseasonable goods.

The outcome of the investigation of the scene depends, of course, on the degree to which the premises have been left undisturbed. The work of the fire brigade often destroys important evidence. Sometimes furniture and other objects have been hurled some distance by the powerful streams of water. Flooring may have been chopped and seriously damaged in order to extinguish the fire. In such cases everything must be done to reconstruct the original aspect of the scene if this be possible, as it should be if the fire was confined to only one room. Even if the reconstruction is a very painstaking and time-consuming task, it should be done, as it may pay astonishing dividends. The aim should be to return everything in the room to the exact place it occupied before the fire started.

WHERE DID THE FIRE START? Regardless of the statements of witnesses, the point where the fire originated must also be determined from the examination of the premises. Often it may be advisable to work backward by asking oneself: Where was the last place reached by the fire? From where did it spread to that place? And so on. Traces of smoke and charring will help indicate the reverse route of the fire. Keep in mind the fact that the natural path of fire is upward and that it travels vertically— elevator shafts and staircases—rather than horizontally.

SMOLDERING. If the air supply is insufficient, a phenomenon called smoldering fire may occur. The smoldering fire is characterized by the fire slowly creeping along the surfaces of walls and ceiling: paint and resins in the wood are incompletely consumed, the room is filled with a nauseating black smoke of tar products which will settle as a brown, tarry film on the cold windowpanes. If the windows are smashed or the door opened and air enters, the whole room will immediately burst into flames.

The inexperienced investigator might mistakenly think that the film on the windowpanes originated from turpentine, linseed oil, or some other liquid which fumes strongly when burning. Also the smoldering fire may eat its way into another room with more favorable air conditions and there start a fire which may easily be mistaken for the original one.

Reconstruction of such scenes will as a rule give good results.

ACCIDENTAL CAUSES OF FIRE

LIGHTNING. Lightning as a rule strikes high points and places con- nected with subsoil water. It may strike several places at the same time and may pass from one object to another. Very often the sulfurlike odor of ozone may be detected, and the lightning is often accompanied by a sound of rustling. The traces are very characteristic, especially on metallic objects, which melt or show beads of melted metal or deformations. Iron objects may become magnetic, as evinced by the compass. The traces of lightning in brick walls may also be very characteristic: pieces of plaster are broken and shattered, whole bricks may be scattered about, some of them may be glazed on the surface, etc.

When there is a suspicion of arson, the lightning-rod should be exam- ined carefully, especially as to traces of lightning and as to the rod's effi- ciency. Ascertain that there really was a thunderstorm at the time of the fire. Lightning is very often used as a pretext by the arsonist.

ACTION OF THE SUN. We know that the rays of the sun concentrated in a lens or in a concave mirror may set fire to inflammable material. Such lenses may be furnished by tumblers, glasses, or eyeglasses, as well as by certain mirrors displayed in store windows. (A bubble in a window- pane will not act as a lens.) Such cases are very rare, however, and yet it is not uncommon to hear an arsonist use this as an explanation for the origin of the fire. When such a question arises, the sun's position at the time of the fire (if possible, the day after the fire), the focus of the supposed lens, and the position of the inflammable material in relation to the focus should be determined. It must be borne in mind that the rays of the sun can be concentrated by such a lens for only a short time each day and in certain latitudes only at certain times of the year.

SPARKS. Sparks result not only from incendiary fires, of course, but can also come from flues, locomotives, locomobiles, etc. If a fire is alleged to have been ignited by sparks, there must be a plausible time relation between the moment the spark was thrown and the moment the fire started. If sparks ignite a house, the roof must be of inflammable material or there must have been openings in the walls or in the roof.

EXPLOSIONS. These may be caused by unstable explosives, fireworks, kerosene or gasoline lamps, cooking gas, gasoline, alcohol, ether, acetylene, dust of flour, sugar, starch, coke, wood, silicon, magnesium, and aluminum. Explosions may also occur as the result of leaking gas pipes or gas containers, from the careless use of gasoline, or from fires originating from other causes in premises where explosive materials are stored. Arsonists seldom use explosives for their purposes.

In recent years several violent explosions have resulted from the washing of gloves or other articles in gasoline. When this is done in a small room, for instance a kitchenette, the minimum limit of the gas mixture is speedily reached. Any open flame, such as a pilot light on the gas stove or refrigerator or even a spark emanating from an electric doorbell when ringing, is then sufficient to ignite the gas mixture.

When an explosion is suspected, the investigator should determine the position of the origin of the explosion in relation to the place where the fire started, ascertain the nature of the explosive material (which can sometimes be determined by a chemical analysis of surrounding material), and look for the characteristic traces of explosions. The aid of a specialist on explosives is essential, and the investigator should confine himself to gathering the traces.

ANIMALS. All animals fear fire to such an extent that only by pure accident will they come near it. Animals therefore rarely cause fire. Sometimes a dog or a cat will accidentally upset a carelessly placed lamp or cooking device. A kerosene lamp generally goes out when upset and only in rare cases explodes. If it does happen to explode, the traces of the explosion and the remains of the lamp will always be found if the room has not been destroyed by the fire.

A few cases have been reported where insects, birds, and mice, by

contacting bare electric wires, have caused short circuits and thereby en-
dangered a house. In all such cases, however, the fuses have functioned
and broken the circuit.

"Rats and matches" as a cause of fire is not accepted nowadays. Match
heads are not attractive to rats or mice, and experiments have shown
that they would rather starve to death than gnaw them.

SPONTANEOUS COMBUSTION. The common phenomenon of spontaneous combustion is almost always accompanied by strong smoke and acrid
gas fumes. The material subject to spontaneous combustion may sometimes partly remain after the fire and has a very characteristic appearance.
Burned waste which has been soaked in linseed oil looks like some kind
of a bird's nest. A spontaneous combustion of, for instance, waste soaked
in linseed oil must, in an inhabited house, draw the attention of the occupants by the smell and smoke escaping through the flues and the ventilation openings. In cases where the fire was extinguished at an early stage,
the time of the outbreak of the fire may be approximately determined by
experiments carried out under identical circumstances. Spontaneous combustion is staged with the same material in the same room and observation made of the time the fire is discovered from the outside. During such
an experiment, the temperature inside and outside should be approximately the same as during the fire.

Several materials have the property of retaining and concentrating the
oxygen of the air on their surfaces. This phenomenon is followed by the
generation of heat which, because of the insufficient circulation of air,
finally leads to spontaneous combustion. Coal dust, charcoal, flour, hay,
grain, and other plant products; and vegetable oils such as linseed soaked
in porous materials such as cotton waste, paper, etc., are specially susceptible to spontaneous combustion.

It should here be mentioned that certain materials may, under certain
circumstances, ignite at temperatures far below their normal ignition
temperatures. This phenomenon is called semi-spontaneous combustion.
For instance, wood is normally ignited at about 570° F., yet wood in a
wall near a steampipe or a flue or wooden logs piled in an oven for drying will ignite at a considerably lower temperature; in fact, a temperature
as low as about 250° F. may be sufficient. There will form on the surface
of the wood a microscopic charcoal film, which at first is light yellowish-
brown and later darkens to black. The charcoal film is oxidized by the
oxygen in the air, and the process gradually increases the temperature
until the 570° F. necessary for the ignition stage is reached and the fire
starts. Under certain conditions, Celluloid, which consists chiefly of nitro-

cellulose and camphor and normally ignites at about 350° F., may ignite if subjected a certain time to only about 160° F.

In the spontaneous combustion of hay the origin of the heat is not the same as in the other materials, because the development of the heat here depends on fermentative processes in the hay, which will occur only when the hay has been stored before drying. The combustion of hay does not start with an open flame. The heat begins in the interior of the pile. A heavy odor arises, the hay begins to smolder in the interior, and the fire slowly finds its way to the outside.

When spontaneous combustion of hay or other vegetable matter is suspected, it must be ascertained when the hay was cut, how it was dried, how the weather was on the day it was stacked, and, if it was still moist, if any odor of fermentation was apparent or if any sinking of parts of the stack was observed; also how long a time elapsed between the day of the cutting and the day of the stacking, between the day of the cutting and the day of the fire, and between the day of the stacking and the day of the fire. It is important to ascertain whether any neighboring farmer cut his hay on the same day and stacked it under the same circumstances. If so, his hay can be used for comparison. It is generally held that spontaneous combustion in a haystack cannot occur before eight to ten days after the stacking and that the danger of spontaneous combustion is passed after seventy to eighty days.

Spontaneous combustion of oil-soaked waste is a fairly common occurrence; hence plants, garages, etc., where it is found have strict regulations regarding the disposal of such waste. Spontaneous combustion of oil-soaked waste may occur after a few hours if the waste is in a small pile and the circumstances are favorable. If such combustion is suspected, the presence of vegetable oils on the premises must be established and reconstructions and experiments under the same circumstances as prevailed at the time of the fire must be made.

A necessary condition for spontaneous combustion of oils is, as said above, that they be spread out in a very thin film over extensive surfaces such as those furnished by the innumerable fibers of cotton waste, rags, wood shavings, and even lampblack (the latter, though, only in exceptional cases). Even fine metal shavings soaked with oil or fat may be subject to spontaneous combustion.[3]

Coal may be subject to spontaneous combustion, especially if finely screened and piled in large heaps. As a rule heaps of finely screened coal must be two or three yards high and heaps of coarsely screened coal three to four yards high before they are subject to spontaneous combustion.

The capacity of coal for spontaneous combustion may be determined experimentally, and samples should be taken and submitted to an expert. Coke cannot ignite spontaneously. Freshly processed charcoal, even if it seems cool, will fairly often ignite spontaneously simply because the charcoal is still smoldering. There may be a real spontaneous combustion in charcoal, however, owing to its capacity to absorb oxygen from the air. Unslaked lime which is piled in heaps may develop strong heat when water is poured over it. Small amounts of lime mixed with water equal to about a third of the weight of the lime will develop a temperature of about 300° F. in large heaps of unslaked lime the temperature may rise to 1100° F. If piles of unslaked lime are covered with sacks, straw, or similar material and moisture enters, a fire may easily start.

New observations about substances susceptible to spontaneous combustion are made constantly. In one case, for instance, a bottle containing laundry ink began to burn and set fire to some paper in its vicinity. Laundry ink is made by dissolving nitrate of silver in ammonia. When such an ammonia-silver compound evaporates, the remainder is the highly explosive nitride of silver (AgN_3). In this case the cork must have been loose, the ink dried up, and the explosive silver compound caught fire because of the presence of gum arabic or dextrose in the ink. In another case a box of rat poison was the origin of a fire. Rat poison is generally made by dissolving phosphorus in lukewarm water. The oily layer which forms on the surface of the water is then stirred with flour until a thick porridge results. In the case just mentioned some of the poison had been used in 1921 and the remainder had been stored near a window and forgotten. Some barrels containing kerosene and oil had been placed below this window. By July, 1933, the porridge had become absolutely dry, and under the action of the sun the phosphorus caught fire and the fire was communicated to the kerosene barrels. This "time burner" then acted after twelve years.

The chlorate of sodium or chlorate of calcium used to clear grass from railroad banks may, even in such weak solutions as 1 to 2 percent, make the grass and pieces of wood and paper along the banks highly inflammable.

Lists of the more common materials subject to spontaneous heating, and therefore potentially dangerous, may be found in publications of fire prevention organizations.[4]

Many oxidizing agents used in industry and agriculture can cause combustion if they are improperly handled or negligently stored. Concentrated nitric acid, which is in common use throughout the country, can cause combustion if it comes in contact with sawdust or wood shavings. Potassium permanganate, a substance widely used in chemistry and medicine, will cause combustion in contact with glycerine. Ordinary quicklime, in contact with water, generates sufficient heat to ignite straw, paper, and excelsior. In general, substances which are used for low-explosive homemade bombs are dangerous because of their capacity for rapid oxidation. These include ammonium nitrate, ammonium dichromate, chromic acid, metallic peroxides, metallic potassium, metallic sodium, potassium chlorate, potassium nitrate, the powdered forms of aluminum, iron, magnesium, and zinc, sulfur, and sulfuric acid.

FAULTY STOVES AND FLUES. In cases where the origin of the fire is supposed to have been in a faulty stove, the position of the stove in relation to the wall, the kind of substructure upon which the stove stands, leakages in the pipes, faults in the stove itself, and the position of inflammable material in relation to the stove should be determined.

In the case of gas stoves the working order of the pipes, the position of the jet, how the burner functioned, whether the rubber hose was on, and whether there had been any perceptible odor of gas before the fire should be ascertained. The facilities which the fire had to spread from place to place also should be carefully examined.

If necessary, reconstructions and experiments should be made to determine the origin of the fire.

In most cases the flue will be preserved after the fire, and faults in it can be ascertained by the presence of holes and smoky places. The position of the faults in the flue in relation to the place where the fire originated should be determined.

In examining flues it is recommended that experiments be made to determine their faults. Dry wood should be ignited at the base of the flue, directly in the flue, or in the stove if this is preserved. When the air in the flue is sufficiently warm, some moist material should be placed on the fire and the smoke permitted to escape. If the top of the flue is now covered for a moment, the smoke will find its way out of all faulty places. The distances between the faults in the flue and the inflammable material should also be noted.

SHORT CIRCUITS. It has become almost a habit today to blame the electric system of a house as being the cause of fire when no other plausible explanation can be found. The electric system, however, is seldom to blame, especially when the installation is up to date and the fuses are working.

Examination of the electric system in an arson case demands much knowledge, theoretical as well as practical, and preferably should be done by a specialist.

Fires caused through an electric system may be due to *overloading* (short circuit, grounding, exaggerated consumption), *faulty contacts* (high resistance), *sparks* (by short circuits, grounding or breaking of the current), *carelessness* in the handling of electrical apparatus, or *intentional acts*.

The most important thing to check when the electric system is suspected is the condition of the fuses. See if they have functioned, if they have been replaced by heavier fuses, if they have been bridged over, and if they were in the right proportion to the diameter of the wires and the consumption.

A fire may sometimes occur without reaction from the fuses. Such an occurrence is possible where, for instance, the insulation of the wires is faulty and a bridge is formed where a part of the current passes. This may be regarded as a hidden short circuit. The part of the current which passes through this point is so feeble that the fuse will not react. The resistance at the point is so high, however, that under certain circumstances fire may result. Certain resistances used in commercial apparatus may also be put into the circuit and heated to a danger point without reaction from the fuses.

Sometimes the armature windings of electric motors are partially removed to cause overheating and subsequent fire at a time when the premises are vacant (electric fans, water-coolers, oil-furnace motors, etc.).

The investigator should sketch the circuit throughout the house, looking for traces of short circuits and other suspicious places, and these should be noted on the sketch.

MISCELLANEOUS CAUSES. It is naturally impossible to give a list of all the accidents that may cause a fire. Besides the ones already mentioned there are of course numerous other accidental ways of igniting a fire; for instance, by carelessness in smoking, careless handling of inflammable material, children's playing with matches or fire, leaking gas pipes, forgetfulness in the use of electric irons or electric heating pads, drying clothes too near a hot stove, carelessness with firearms, carelessness in the use of blowtorches, friction caused by insufficient lubrication of machines, etc. Anyone can lengthen the list. In effect, the introduction of new products, like new plastic materials in the home or new metals in industry, adds to the list and should be considered where a more ordinary cause has not been established.

INVESTIGATIVE OUTLINE

In an arson inquiry the investigator must gather facts which tend to establish the willful and malicious burning of property. The fact that the act was intended may sometimes be shown by excluding all accidental causes. Proof of motive, although not required, may contribute to the evidence of malice as well as willfulness. The elementary facts of the burning itself should not be neglected; that is, the dwelling or structure must be shown or described, its approximate value established, and the charring or other damage described.

The following list is suggestive of the facts and data which should be included in the investigative report:

INCIDENT. The fact that a burning did occur must be established. The following information is necessary:

The date and time of the burning.
The address or location where the burning occurred (official designation).
A brief, accurate description of the building, structure, or premises, including:
The kind of material of which constructed.
The age, or approximate age.
The dimensions or approximate dimensions.
The first station that received the alarm.
The time that the fire station received the alarm.
The fire apparatus, if any, that attended the fire, and the time that the fire apparatus was officially in operation.
The time that the fire apparatus was withdrawn from the burning, or the time that the fire department declared the burning extinguished.
The official designation of the incident by fire department records.

VALUE. The fact that the dwelling or structure was of a given value and belonged to a certain person must be established. The following information is necessary:

The approximate value of the property.
The insurance coverage on the property.
The inventory of stock, fixtures, equipment, and other items of value within the premises, and the damage as a result of the fire.
The name of the occupant at the time of the fire; if the dwelling was vacant, the length of time that the premises had remained unoccupied.
The name of the owner of the property, including all aliases.
The name of the insured, whether owner or tenant.

FACTUAL EVIDENCE. The basic facts necessary to the commission of the crime must be established. The following information is necessary:

The name of the person who discovered the fire, and his observations concerning:

    The building or room that was the first to burn.

    The exact origin of the fire.

The time that the fire was discovered.

The name of the person who turned in the alarm.

The means by which the fire was reported.

How the burning occurred, if known.

Significant noises that were noticed before or during the burning.

The direction in which the burning spread.

The name of the person who was in the building at the time of the burning or who was in the building last.

The area that suffered the greatest damage.

The physical evidence discovered.

If a death occurred, all the important data and facts revealed by the autopsy.

Photographs and impressions of evidence of forced entry at any of the doors, windows, hatches, skylights, or other points of entry.

The condition and location of fire-fighting equipment such as hoses, extinguishers (full or empty), damaged alarm mechanisms, and sprinkler systems.

Evidence of the careless storing or placing of such flammable materials as gasoline, paint, oils, chemicals, lighter fluid, and cleaning fluid.

The location and condition of all electric lights, drops, extensions, appliances, and fuses.

The condition of electric wiring, including exposed wiring; evidence of recent repairs, inside and outside; evidence of splices, connections, or alterations, and when, if known, such alterations were made and by whom; load carried by the wires; prescribed load of the fuses through which the lines were fed; testimony as to whether or not heat was ever noticed in the wires or terminals before the fire.

The number and type of machines, if any, in the room or building; when they were last used; the amount of power they consumed; and when they were last tested and serviced.

The number of electric motors in the room or building; how they were safeguarded against dust; their horsepower, voltage, and purpose; whether they were the "open" or "sealed" type; the length of time they were generally in operation; and their defects, if any.

The condition of gas pipes, bottled-gas pipes, steam pipes, air pipes, and water pipes.

The number and type of stoves within the room or building; whether fires were in the stoves; the kinds of fuel that were used; the locations of the sources of fuel in relation to the stoves; whether the stoves were well insulated; when the ashes were last removed; where removed ashes were placed; when the stoves were last cleaned or serviced; and whether they had pilot lights or similar continually burning flames.

Glass objects that may have accidentally caused the fire by concentrating the rays of the sun.

The facts pertaining to the devices that may have been found among the debris.

The methods used to extinguish the burning; e.g., water, foam, and carbon dioxide. (Such data are sent to the criminal investigation laboratory when evidence is forwarded for identification.)

CIRCUMSTANTIAL EVIDENCE. In the prosecution of arson, although circumstantial evidence may convict, it must be established that a suspect was directly or indirectly connected with the crime. Many of the factors listed under *Factual Evidence* above may also be considered under this heading; conversely, several of the items listed under this heading may subsequently be developed into factual points. The following circumstantial evidence may connect a suspect with arson:

Hearsay, corroborated by evidence, and coupled with the investigator's appraisal at the scene.

The testimony of the first person on the premises after the fire was discovered:

His observations.

His opinion as to the origin of the fire.

The circumstances under which the fire was first discovered.

The testimony of personnel of the fire department who entered the building.

The time interval between the discovery of the fire and the report to the fire department.

The type of burning; e.g., flash fire, explosion, smoldering fire, or rapidly spreading fire; the approximate intensity of the burning; and whether there were separate fires.

The presence, color, and odor of smoke during the fire.

The color, height, and intensity of the flames.

Alterations or changes made in the building while it was occupied by the latest tenant, such as the addition of partitions, electric wiring, or stoves.

Evidence of possible devices or means by which the burning was started: candle, match, timing device, or flammable material.

Evidence of the presence of a suspicious person, particularly a loiterer, in the immediate area of the burning during the twenty-four-hour period preceding the fire.

Evidence that any articles were removed from the premises or were recently repaired, altered, or adjusted in any way.

Blistered paint, charred wood, melted metal, glass, or other material that may be found at the suspected or known point of origin.

Evidence that a liquid chemical, such as alcohol or turpentine, was used to start the burning; or evidence found in the crevices of a table, box, or floor that a candle or similar item may have been used.

Records, financial or otherwise, or items or materials that the arsonist might have wished to destroy.

Information relative to the insurance coverage of the building, structure, premises, or property, or of items and articles of particular value; data as to mortgages, liens, loans, and the financial status of the suspect; and any action, pending or past, against the suspect or against any member of his family.

Information from inspections of the premises which may have been made prior to the fire. (Such data may be obtained from city or local fire departments, insurance carriers, city or local construction permits and accompanying inspections, and from insurance underwriters' groups.)

The direction of any air current within the building during the burning, as deduced from partially burned wallpaper, depth of charring, or soot deposits.

The availability of air within the building during the fire, as revealed by the heaviest concentrations of smoke and soot.

Evidence that the heat created by the inspected igniting agent was sufficient to kindle the material.

The identification of the material burned; e.g., oils or chemicals. The laboratory examination of samples of soot may supply this information.

The presence among the debris of peculiarly colored ashes and clinkers, or of traces of paraffin, saturated rags, waste excelsior, or other fire spreaders.

Evidence indicating who was responsible for the security of the building, who possessed the keys to the building, and who could have had additional keys made.

Information as to whether windows or doors were normally closed and locked; whether some windows were closed, but without locks; or whether some, or all, of the windows were normally left open.

Weather data such as the atmospheric temperature and the direction of the wind at the time of the burning, and the information concerning any electrical storm that may have occurred at that time.

Evidence that a suspect is a known arsonist and that the *modus operandi* employed in the case under investigation is similar to that employed by the suspect in the past.

Evidence that the fire resulted from spontaneous combustion.

Additional circumstances that may either tend to prove or disprove the burning to be the work of an arsonist.

Scaled photographs or sketches of the scene, interior and exterior, during the burning and after the burning has been extinguished, supplemented with notes and evidence.

THREATS. Any pertinent statements, utterances, or declarations of a threatening nature made by the suspect or by others concerning the building, the owner, or the tenant who occupied the property should be considered by the investigator.

MOTIVE. A motive for setting a fire may be established by determining the following:

That a person or a group of persons would benefit from the burning.

That another crime, such as theft, larceny, or unlawful disposition of funds or property, has been committed on the premises previous to the fire, and that the burned building contained evidence of the crime.

That there were money, stock, or equipment shortages.

That worthless items had been substituted for valuable items alleged to have been consumed in the fire.

That an impending apprehension, inventory, audit, inspection, investigation, or transfer of custody might have revealed evidence of crime, shortages, improper activity, or negligence.

That there was jealousy, ill will, or friction between an employer and an employee or between a superior and a subordinate.

INTENT. Intent to set fire to a building may be established by determining the following:

That a person removed property of value from a building or attempted wrongfully to dispose of items that were not his own before the fire started.

That previous to the fire and contrary to normal habit or practice, personal property was either left in or moved into a building.

That measures were taken to deny normal access to the building or area or to impede the entry of firemen or the utilization of their equipment.

That fire-fighting equipment and fire control systems on the premises were moved from their normal locations or were rendered unserviceable previous to the fire.

That contrary to normal practice, flammable materials were allowed to accumulate where they would start or accelerate the spread of a fire.

That a heating or electrical device or system was tampered with in such a way as to make a fire likely.

That doors, windows, transoms, and ventilating systems were, contrary to normal practice, opened or shut so as to facilitate the spread of a fire.

That devices or materials capable of starting or accelerating a fire were placed in the building.

That communicating systems or automatic warning devices were tampered with or rendered unserviceable previous to the burning.

That firemen were deliberately not summoned immediately after the fire was discovered; that firemen were summoned but misdirected so as to delay their arrival; or that a person attempted to prevent or delay watchmen or guard personnel from reporting the fire.

That a person made a statement or committed an act that was witnessed, indicating his intention to set a fire.

That a person attempted to hire or to procure through coercion, threats, or appeals to friendship the assistance of another person in the setting of a fire.

ACCOMPLICE. Evidence that tends to connect a suspect with the crime may also tend to connect an accomplice with the crime.

INCENDIARY FIRES

Having discussed briefly the major ways in which accidental fires may be started, we proceed now to the work of the arsonist: the circumstances indicating he may have been at work; his *modus operandi* and the tools of his trade.

SUSPICIOUS CIRCUMSTANCES

There are numerous circumstances which may justify a suspicion of arson, some of which are the following:

1. Broken windows. (To differentiate between smashed windows and windows burst by the heat, see Chapter XV.)
2. Smell of gasoline, Celluloid, phosphorus, acetone, kerosene, or turpentine. (The amateur may mistake the characteristic smell of the fire debris with, for instance, kerosene.)
3. The presence of combustible materials around the combustion point (inflammable oils, fat, straw, wood shavings, paper, excelsior, sulfur, matches, candles, etc.). (The presence of these materials may, however, be innocent.)
4. Several combustion points.
5. Open drawers and cupboard doors. (This may also indicate a burglary.)
6. Fire-extinguishing paraphernalia put out of function (chemical fire-extinguisher emptied, firehoses cut, hose openings stuffed with rags, etc.).
7. The presence of time fuses.
8. Materials delivered just prior to closing time and not opened.

The presence of oil-soaked rags or waste in premises with doors and windows locked, the departure of the occupant shortly before the fire was discovered, coupled with the fact that insurance was recently taken out on the property or chattels, presents opportunity for prosecution on the basis of exclusive opportunity and circumstantial evidence.

THE ARSONIST'S MATERIALS

The following are some of the inflammable and volatile liquids, chemicals, materials, and articles used by incendiaries in their nefarious work:

Kerosene	Naphtha	Ether
Benzine	Turpentine	Banana oil
Gasoline	Alcohol	Lacquers
Combustible liquids used	Gunpowder	Phosphorus
in the household, such	Flashlight powder	Cigarettes

as cleaning fluid, liquid stove polish, and insect spray	Trailers of various materials	Pig's bladders
	Electric light bulbs	Bologna casings
Cotton	Illuminating gas	Rubber hot-water bags
Excelsior, shavings and sawdust	Movie film	Cardboard containers
	Celluloid	Chinese punk and matches
Oakum	Candles and tapers	Wooden containers
Cord and twine	Metallic sodium	Electric heating elements

TIME FUSES. The whole technique of the arsonist is concentrated on the problem of establishing an alibi. Direct ignition with matches is therefore not so common, as the fire would start almost immediately. A match will not burn more than twenty seconds before it burns the fingers. A full box of matches is consumed in sixty to eighty seconds after it has been lighted. A match may be lighted and thrown in three to five seconds, but it is impossible to be certain that it will continue to burn after having been thrown more than one yard. A simple time fuse consisting of a ring of matches tied around the lower part of a cigarette with a thread has sometimes been used.

If a candle is used as a time fuse, it may be placed in a container of inflammable oil or in a heap of excelsior or paper soaked with kerosene or surrounded by Celluloid scraps.[5]

There are many variations in the methods used to place the candle in the most favorable position. The widespread idea that a candle will burn slower if it has been rolled in salt has no foundation in fact. On the contrary, this process will make the candle burn faster.

Candles now on the market are made of stearin, paraffin, or a mixture of both. The wick consists of braided cotton thread, and its arrangement varies. In the times of tallow candles and wax candles the wick used to present a problem, as it was not automatically consumed and always had to be trimmed. Nowadays the wick is soaked in sulfate of ammonia and phosphate of ammonia. The sulfate of ammonia, together with the braiding, causes the point of the wick to curl toward the outer part of the flame, where it is consumed by the fire. The phosphate of ammonia and the ashes of the wick melt into small balls which drop down into the crater of the candle. In this way the wick is automatically and completely destroyed as the candle burns. This chemical compound also keeps the wick from smoldering.

The wick of a candle is completely consumed, however, only if the candle burns normally. If the whole candle is consumed at once (for instance, when a time fuse functions too early and the stearin melts, it will, under the influence of the surrounding heat, burn at once), the wick, although charred, will be preserved. Such a charred wick may be of surprising toughness, doubtless because of the supporting salt skeleton. When such leftovers of wicks are found at the scene, they should be put into a test tube supported by cotton and taken to an expert. In many cases the expert may be able to tell from the wick what type candle it came from.

Candles often leave traces of paraffin which penetrate deep into the wood. When this happens, suspected spots should be cut out and submitted to an expert examination. Even fairly small quantities may enable the expert, with the aid of the micromelting point, by examination of the crystal forms, and by examination in polarized light, to compare traces of stearin with the certain kind of candle bought by the suspect. If larger quantities are present, other common analytical methods may also be helpful.

If a whole piece of candle has been preserved, the manufacturers can in many cases be determined by examining the pressing, lathing, and stamping on the surface of the candle, and it can thus be identified with the corresponding traces on seized candles.

As has already been mentioned, explosives are not commonly used by arsonists. Fuses generally burn approximately a little more than one half a yard a minute. In order to have time to get away the arsonist must use quite a long fuse; for instance, to burn half an hour, about fifteen yards of fuse would be needed. Burned fuses are fairly tough and may resist

Figure 151. A three-story wooden building was destroyed by fire, and there was a suspicion of arson. After painstakingly sifting the ashes for about three weeks, investigators finally found a small piece of fuse in the cellar of the building. The make of the fuse was determined by an examination of the threads in the different layers. It was discovered that this make fuse was sold only by a certain hardware dealer in the vicinity and had been purchased only by a particular individual. Confronted with this evidence, the arsonist confessed.

even a devastating fire. Some cords used in Venetian blinds may, when charred, have the same appearance as a burned fuse. It is generally easy to determine the make of a burned fuse by examining the braiding and the arrangement of the layers. Such an identification has often played an important role in arson cases. Usually the arsonist attaches the fuse to a small bag or sack filled with black powder. When the flame reaches the bag, the black powder will ignite. Explosives stronger than black powder, such as dynamite or TNT, will ordinarily not cause fire, because the explosions occur too quickly. Instances are known in which TNT has been exploded in a heap of gasoline-soaked waste and no fire has occurred.

A lot of chemical time fuses have been invented by arsonists and also by military agencies for war uses. For a person with some knowledge of chemistry the possibilities are almost unlimited in this field. Here are some examples of chemical time fuses used by arsonists.

Phosphorus dissolved in disulfide of carbon. When the disulfide of carbon has evaporated, the phosphorus will start to burn. The time necessary for ignition may vary from some minutes to several hours, depending on the concentration of the solution. The traces pointing to arson in such cases are the thick white smoke of pentoxide of phosphorus, the typical phosphorescence in the debris, and the acrid smell.

Sulfuric acid, potassium chlorate, and powdered sugar. If concentrated sulfuric acid is dropped upon a mixture of potassium chlorate and powdered sugar, a violent fire will start immediately. Generally a small bottle containing the acid is placed upside-down over the chlorate mixture. The bottle is sealed by a thin cork or thick paper. After a certain time, the acid will corrode the cork or the paper and the acid will drip down on the mixture and thereby start a fire.

Phosphide of calcium, metallic sodium, and *metallic potassium.* These have also in some cases been used by arsonists as time fuses.

MECHANICAL DEVICES AND CHANCE FUSES. Mechanical devices are nowadays seldom used by arsonists. They have often proved dangerous to the inventors, as they often escape the fire and are found afterward more or less intact.

Among the mechanical devices should be included the chance fuses. These are put into action by some innocent person opening a door or walking down the road and picking up a cord, etc. A form of chance fuse is the one consisting of two boards, one on top of the other. The upper board is connected with the cord. Matches are fastened to the underside of the bottom board.

Figure 152.   A mechanical device used in an attempted arson case. A contractor-bachelor who had a home in the suburbs decided to destroy the house by fire and collect the insurance on it. The contractor laid his plans very carefully. First he rigged up the ignition device (shown in the picture at left), which was to be placed in the drawing-room. The idea was that when the hands of the clock reached a certain position the trap would be released, igniting the matches, which in turn would set fire to a small pile of oil-soaked waste. The fire would be spread from the ignition device to different strategic points in the house by means of strings of oil-soaked waste along the floor. These strategic points were a sideboard and a chest of drawers in the drawing-room and a heap of waste in the smoking-room.

When all was set, the contractor set off on a trip so he would not be near the scene when the fire started. The ignition device was to be set off by the clock sometime during the night, about twelve hours after the contractor left on his journey. According to plan, the fire was started at the proper time and immediately spread to the sideboard. However, suspended over the sideboard was a heavy oil painting; and when the cord supporting it was burned through, the painting fell onto the sideboard with a crash.

One of the rooms adjoining the drawing-room was rented to a telegraph operator, who was asleep when the fire started. The noise made by the falling picture partially aroused him, and he debated whether he should try to determine its origin. In the meantime the fire had spread to the chest of drawers, above which another heavy oil painting was hung. Again the supporting cord was burned, and there was another loud crash. When he heard the second painting fall, the telegraph operator ran to investigate and succeeded in extinguishing the fire.

The plan of the house and the route of the first across the drawing-room and smoking-room are shown in the illustration at the right.

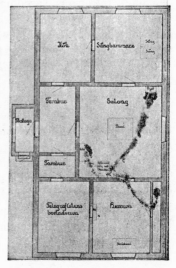

ELECTRICAL DEVICES. When electricity is used in arson, generally the heat emanating from an electric bulb is used. A suspended electric bulb may reach a temperature of from 210° F. to 480° F., according to the watt consumption. If suspended in the room, a 100-watt electric bulb will reach a temperature of about 210° F. If wrapped in wool, the temperature will rise to 360° F. If the bulb is wrapped in rayon, the temperature will go over 300° F. Wrapped in a veil, the temperature will rise to about 400° F. and in chiffon to possibly 500° F. In one arson case, for instance, an electric bulb was wrapped in chiffon and surrounded with Celluloid objects. The fire was started in another part of the building by placing the fuse of the electric system back into position.

In recent years many firebugs have resorted to the practice of leaving an electric iron in circuit on a table, close to which is a quantity of combustible material. The electric iron generates sufficient heat to set fire to the material. Gas irons have also been used in the same way. Of course, the accident excuse is offered, but it has not been as successful as arsonists expected.

OILS AND OTHER INFLAMMABLE MATERIALS. Inflammable oils, such as gasoline or kerosene, and materials with similar effects, such as motion-picture film, etc., are often used by arsonists to facilitate the spreading of the fire. The arsonist then generally calculates that the fire will destroy all traces of the inflammable material. In many cases, however, enough of it remains in the coals and ashes and soaks into unburnt wood to allow a determination by chemical analysis.[6]

Sometimes, too, an examination of the soot will lead to a determination of the material used, as the appearance of the soot is highly characteristic for different inflammable oils. It is recommended that the arson investigator experiment with different inflammable oils in order to familiarize himself with the appearance of their soot and smoke.

Sometimes the smell of the inflammable oil will allow an immediate determination. If kerosene, for instance, has been used, the coals will have an odor of kerosene for quite a while. There is a simple method of examination based upon the odor. Pieces of charred wood from the suspected places are put into a wide-mouthed glass container which is carefully closed and heated in water to 60° or 70° C. When the container is then opened, it is often possible to determine by the odor if an inflammable oil has been used. Naturally such an examination should be made as soon as possible.

A simple and very effective method to determine the presence of kerosene is to *taste* it. The investigator chews a piece of bread until he has the taste of the bread in his mouth. Another piece of bread is now rubbed against the suspected place and then also chewed. The presence of even very small quantities of kerosene or other inflammable oil will be noticeable.

Other signs of the presence of inflammable oils are spots of dissolved paint, wave-shaped charrings on the floor, and a coating of smoke on the ceiling. (Not to be mistaken for the smoldering fire mentioned above.) When kerosene has been put on the floor, the fire will be stronger at the periphery and will gradually work its way from there to the center. It often happens that the almost unburned center is left surrounded by wave-shaped charrings.

Gasoline will normally not leave any traces after a fire except a possible edge formation around the spot if the place where it was is left unburned. Methylated spirit evaporates also but may leave traces of ingredients with a higher cooking point, for instance, acetone, the presence of which may be determined by a chemical analysis. When used in arson cases, kerosene is usually soaked into upholstered furniture, paper, wood shavings, cotton waste, or rags at the point of origin of the fire. Inexperienced arsonists are known to have poured kerosene into pails, buckets, bottles, and other containers, placing them at the origin of the fire. Even if the surface of the floor is charred, the kerosene may have penetrated into the wood and may be found underneath the charring in the interior of the double floor or may have penetrated into the mortar or plaster. It is of the utmost importance that test samples of places suspected of being saturated with inflammable oils be taken immediately. The test samples are cut, sawed, or sliced, according to circumstances, and should be put immediately into airtight glass containers. A separate container is needed for each sample.

If there is enough kerosene available at the scene to compare with another kerosene, identification may be approximately determined by an expert examination in the laboratory. If, under certain circumstances, a kerosene or gasoline lamp or stove could have started a fire, this also may often be determined by an expert examination.

Ordinary commercial kerosene must be heated to about 100° F. before it starts to emanate inflammable gas. A fuse led into kerosene does not ignite it. Gasoline, however, has a flash point far below 32° F. and is always ignited by an open flame or spark, though a glowing cigar butt thrown into gasoline may not ignite it. However, owing to the fact that when circulated (as in a washing machine or a tube) it becomes heavily charged with positive electricity, thereby creating sparks, gasoline is very dangerous. Some unfortunate women have been burned to death while combing their hair with an ebonite comb after having washed the hair in gasoline. (A horn comb will not produce sparks.)

RECONSTRUCTION OF BURNT PAPER

It is often possible to read writing on burnt paper if the remains are carefully collected. If, in searching a house or in an arrest, burnt paper is found in a stove, the damper should be closed immediately, also the window; if necessary an armful of wet rags, towels, or something similar should be put in the stovepipe. Under no circumstances should water be used to extinguish the fire. When the fire is choked, the paper is removed in the following manner. A glass pan is taken in the left hand, and, keeping the pan as near the paper as possible, the ash is gently fanned over to the glass pan. The ash is now moistened with fixative (a mixture of shellac and alcohol such as artists use on charcoal drawings), using an atomizer. Then, with the utmost precaution, the ash is flattened and another glass pan placed on the top, so that the ash is pressed between the two, and the whole is placed in a printing frame. It is then photographed on an orthochromatic plate and printed on compression paper.

Another method consists of preparing a hot solution of 1 percent gelatin in water. This solution is put in a flat developing pan. The ash is placed on a glass plate in the above-described manner, and the plate is sunk in the pan so that the surface is just covered with the solution. When the ash has been so moistened, it is flattened, another glass plate is put on the top, and the whole is pressed firmly together in order to prevent the appearance of air bubbles.

If charred documents are immersed in a 25 percent solution of chloral hydrate in alcohol, then dried at 140° F., and the process repeated until the surface is a mass of small white crystals, and are then treated with the same solution plus 10 percent glycerin, the writing shows up very well in a number of cases. The document should then be photographed using a contrasting non-color sensitive plate. If writing is on both sides of the document, this method develops both sides in those cases where it is successful.[7]

Another method utilizes a treatment in a 5 percent silver nitrate solution, and it is claimed that this method reveals more details than are visible to the naked eye. The specimen, supported on a glass plate, is lowered into the silver nitrate solution and left there for about three hours. At the end of this time the writing is reconstituted as a black image on a gray background, and after washing well in distilled water several times

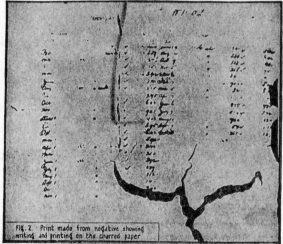

Figure 153.   Deciphering charred records by chemical action and photography. It will be seen from the tear that Fig. 2 is a print of the reverse side of the sheet shown in Fig. 1.

and drying rapidly, it can be photographed. The method seems to have a limited application, however.[8]

In still another method the document is soaked in benzyl alcohol for two weeks and then mounted on a glass sheet coated with a solution of Canada balsam in benzyl alcohol. Another glass sheet is placed on top, care being taken to allow all air bubbles to escape by placing in a large vacuum desiccator with a heavy weight on it and gently applying the vacuum. The plates are then removed and clamped together, after which the document is photographed using a panchromatic plate and a combination filter consisting of a red screen and a gelatin filter tinted with a green dyestuff. This cuts out all radiation having wavelengths below 7,300 angstroms, and the writing becomes clearly legible.[9]

This sort of work must be done with the utmost care if any success is to be expected. The ashes must be handled very gently, and sometimes the process may take several hours.

1 Used by permission from Crosby–Fiske–Forster, *Handbook of Fire Protection,* Boston, 1948, National Fire Protection Association.

2 Do not open safes before they have had time to cool off, and remember that the insulation will store the heat inside the safe. If a safe has been exposed to a big fire and is opened too soon, the contents will burn immediately when exposed to the air.

3 The tendency of oils to spontaneous combustion is measured in the laboratories by the very simple Mackey test, whereby the test sample is placed under the influence of a certain temperature in a standard apparatus for a certain period of time. A possible and spontaneous rise in the temperature of the test sample will indicate its tendency to spontaneous combustion.

4 Based upon the report of the Committee on Spontaneous Heating and Ignition, adopted by the National Fire Protection Association, 1947.

5 There has been some discussion in recent years as to the possibility of using some modern plastic materials in this way. The term plastics includes a large group of synthetic materials which may be fabricated into various shapes. The oldest synthetic plastic is pyroxylin (Celluloid). The pyroxylin plastics have a high degree of inflammability. All other plastics, however, have a slow burning rate and are very stable chemical compounds. (See *Bulletin of Research,* No. 22, Underwriters' Laboratories, Inc.)

6 Usually a simple distillation process is used in the laboratories to detect inflammable oils in materials from the scene of a fire. Attention should be called, however, to the so-called Mass Spectrometer, with which infinitely small quantities of inflammable oils can be detected. Some of the large oil companies are supplied with this costly and elaborate device and will certainly aid the investigator.

7 Taylor–Walls and Grant.[1]

8 Murray.

9 Amy–Melissinos.

XXV SABOTAGE

THE PRESENT ERA HAS BROUGHT INTO THE HANDS OF THE CRIMINAL NEW weapons with which to force the merchant, manufacturer, or businessman to accede to unlawful demands for money or to force him to join a "protective" organization, to which he must pay monthly, bimonthly, or semiannual dues. When he refuses to submit to this kind of extortion, he is threatened with violence or at least with serious annoyance.

USE OF STENCH BOMBS BY RACKETEERS

In the larger cities chemical bombs have frequently been used to cripple the business of restaurants, dress shops, and other mercantile establishments. Some of these are the so-called stench bombs. The chemicals are carried in tightly corked bottles or glass vials which, when thrown, will break upon striking the ground or floor. The disagreeable odors thus produced compel the discontinuance of business, sometimes for several days.

MATERIALS USED. Some of the agents commonly used for stench bombs are valerian, valeric acid, butyric acid, hydrogen sulfide, asafetida, and ethyl mercaptan. The first three are the ones generally used, because of their heavy, lingering, disagreeable odor and the difficulty in getting rid of it.

By far the most commonly used materials in stench bombs are the *valerian* preparations. Valerian itself consists of the rhizome and roots of *Valeriana officinalis,* a large perennial plant of which there are two varieties—the European or Asiatic, which is also cultivated to some extent in New Jersey and New York, and the Mexican. Valerian has a strong, characteristic, disagreeable odor. The most common valerian preparations used for stench bombs, and easily obtainable on the market, are *zinc valerate,* a pure-white powder; *valeric acid,* small, water-white crystals; *tincture of valerian* (the alcoholic extract); the *fluid extract;* and *ammoniated valerian.*[1] In these preparations the characteristic smell of valerian is still more penetrating and repulsive.

436

Butyric acid is a colorless thick liquid with a disagreeable odor and a taste resembling rancid butter. It is obtained from a double fermentation whereby milk and sugar are transformed through lactic and butyric ferments into butyric acid. The final product is obtained through distillation.

Hydrogen sulfide in aqueous solution is a slightly yellowish light fluid with an unpleasant odor similar to rotten eggs or putrid fish. The gas emanating from the liquid is poisonous and the presence of large quantities in the air may be dangerous. Mixed with 1½ volumes of oxygen and ignited, it explodes. The gas is easily obtained by treating iron sulfide with an acid.

Mercaptans (also known as *thioalcohols*) are organic compounds with an exceedingly offensive odor. Even the slightest trace of mercaptan in the air may be detected by smell.

PREPARATION OF THE BOMBS. The following methods have been used by racketeers in preparing powdered valerian, zinc valerate, and valeric acid for use in stench bombs:

1. The powder is dissolved in a small quantity of alcohol or ether, to which warm water may or may not be added.
2. The powder may be mixed with warm water.
3. Another method is to mix the valerian preparations with water and put the mixture into a glass container. Some ether is then carefully poured on top of it so that it remains unmixed, thus preventing the valerian fumes from escaping around the cork or stopper.

Sometimes instead of using bombs the powdered or crystallized substance is scattered on the floor about the revolving door of the entrance, and as persons enter through the door, the powder or its odor is taken up by the air current and carried throughout the interior of the premises.

The mixing is generally done in a thin-glass bottle, a vial, or the glass container of a Thermos bottle. The container is corked, sealed with wax, carried to the premises, and thrown with enough force to break it. In the case of a Thermos bottle the outer metal protection is discarded.

Cases are also known in which the obnoxious liquid has been put in a bottle with a fulminating cap and a short piece of fuse. Another method which has been used is the following. Concentrated sulfuric acid and tincture of valerian are put in the stench bomb bottle, the tincture of valerian rising to the top. Two strips of zinc plate are inserted in that part of the cork which goes inside the bottle, and when the bottle is tipped on its side, the sulfuric acid can get to the zinc plates and hydrogen is produced.

The pressure of the gas causes the bottle to explode in from ten to fifteen minutes.

Butyric acid, hydrogen sulfide, and ethyl mercaptan are also put into containers.

Certain staining chemicals are sometimes added to cause damage in addition to the disagreeable odor. Sometimes strong ammonia is put in a separate vial which is broken at the same time as the stench bomb. As a result of the ammonia fumes, the occupants of the premises may also suffer from a severe smarting of the eyes.

TREATMENT OF DAMAGED PROPERTY

A neutralizer or counteracting agent used to overcome the odor of a stench bomb should, from a practical viewpoint, have the following qualities:

1. It should act not only on the basic body but on the disagreeable vapors in the air as well.
2. It should not be injurious to health, property, merchandise, or food to any greater extent than the stench bombs themselves.
3. It should be noninflammable and nonexplosive.

The agent used in counteracting stench bombs must be placed on every particle of the offensive chemicals. It should also be sprayed in the air to neutralize the disagreeable fumes. If possible, electric fans should be placed on the floor to drive the odor to the windows, as the fumes, being heavier than air, remain at low levels. The following procedures have been found practical in dealing with stench bombs:

1. Remove all affected material outside the building. If the offensive agent is on the carpet, cut out all affected pieces and remove them to the open air (fire-escape, street, etc.).
2. Confine the fumes to the one space or room if possible.
3. Ventilate quickly by opening all windows and doors leading to the outside.
4. Place electric fans on the floor to blow the fumes out through open doors or windows. Strong ammonia can be used to advantage during this operation, sprinkling it on the floor to neutralize the odor.
5. Spray the counteracting agent—such as oil of wintergreen, etc.—on the air affected.
6. Objects which cannot be removed, such as floors or walls, may be covered with a paste made from caustic soda and water.
7. If the odor is too disagreeable, a cotton-fabric pad impregnated with dilute caustic soda in glycerin should be put over the mouth and nostrils. The

pad should be wrung out before applying it in order not to cause injury to the skin. Care should be taken not to bring the pad in contact with the eyes.

8. To prevent the offensive odor from getting into another room, a heavy cotton cloth should be placed over closed doors, window crevices, and other openings; and the paste of caustic soda placed against the lower cracks will help to keep the odor out.

9. A rubber raincoat and old clothing should be worn in the premises affected, as it requires several hours in the open air to get rid of the odor on the clothing.

The following agents will counteract to a certain extent the offensive chemicals and their fumes: (1) a solution of alcohol and sodium hydroxide; or (2) a solution of sodium carbonate or milk of lime. Other agents which give good results if placed over the offensive agent and sprayed into the air are activated charcoal, which absorbs all gases, and copper sulfide, which absorbs ammonia.

To counteract the action of valeric acid, asafetida, butyric acid, hydrogen sulfide, and similar substances, one of the following procedures may also be used:

1. Wash the premises with denatured alcohol and absorb as much of it as possible with absorbent cotton.

2. Wash the affected object with 20 percent ammonia and allow to stand for five minutes. A diluted alkali solution (for instance, 5 percent sodium hydroxide solution) can be used instead of the ammonia. If the material used in the stench bomb is entirely volatile, this treatment is certainly of no use.

3. Soak up the offending solution with some absorbent material, and when as dry as possible, cover the area which has been in contact with the obnoxious agent with carbon tetrachloride. There must be ample provision for ventilation, as the fumes of this substance are poisonous.

4. Rub dry with newspapers and remove all the materials used in the cleaning process to the open air.

5. Spray the area of the entire room with oil of rosemary. This pleasant odor will disappear within two days.

When mercaptans have been used in the stench bombs, it is extremely difficult to remove the odor. Treatment with carbon tetrachloride should prove to be of value, and the damaged area can also be covered with chloride of lime, which tends to neutralize the odor. This substance must be handled with caution, since, after releasing chlorine, lime is left as a residue. Every particle or object must be covered.

EXPLOSIVES

For obvious reasons a description of the most common bombs likely to be encountered by police forces and other law enforcement agencies is not given here. It must be constantly borne in mind that there will always be a hazard in handling bombs, infernal machines, and other forms of explosives. To reduce the hazard to a minimum, the New York City Police Department has issued orders that whenever the attention of a

Figure 154.   Effect of bombing resulting from labor troubles.

member of the force is called to a suspected container of this kind, the premises on which it is found must be evacuated of all persons immediately and the investigating officer must notify police headquarters by telephone of his findings. The telegraph bureau (which is the central office for communication service by telephone, radio, teletype, and telegraph) at Police Headquarters immediately dispatches an emergency service squad motor truck, with a police crew, to the scene and also notifies the bomb squad, the police laboratory, and the desk officer of the

Figure 155.   Bomb Squad detectives equipped with protective armor remove a suspected bomb, using a steel mesh bag.

Figure 156.   Fluoroscoping a package bomb in the field.

precinct concerned, in addition to making other routine departmental and extradepartmental notifications. Upon arrival at the scene, the officer in charge of the emergency service squad orders a sufficient quantity of lubricating oil—which is carried on the truck at all times for such purposes—to be brought to the place where the suspected container was found and designates one member of the squad to immerse the container in the oil. The lubricating oil will stop the works of a clock while in the oil and will desensitize a number of chemicals provided the oil can penetrate the package. All others present, except the member so designated, are kept at a safe distance. Any bomb, upon explosion, will cause damage

Figure 157.   Applying the tritongs preparatory to tearing apart a suspected suitcase bomb.

to property and fatal or serious injury to persons within three hundred feet of the point of explosion. If there is a vacant lot or a roadway nearby which can be closed to traffic and which will furnish a free radius of three hundred feet from a central selected point, the officer in charge of the emergency service squad orders the container of lubricating oil in which the bomb, suspected bomb, infernal machine, or other explosive has been immersed to be removed there. Under no circumstances is the suspected container removed from the oil by anyone other than a member of the bomb squad or of the police laboratory.

When lifting a suspected bomb to transport it or immerse it in lubricating oil, extreme care must be exercised to keep it in the identical position in which it was found, so that it will not be jarred, tilted, or turned. Police safety lines must be established and maintained at proper distances by the officer in charge until the removal of the suspected explosive by proper authority. Suspected bombs should not be immersed in containers of water.

Metropolitan and State police departments have personnel especially assigned to the investigation of suspected bombs or infernal machines and also technical equipment, including the fluoroscope and an X-ray unit for radiographing purposes, available for use by the specialists assigned to this class of work. Police officers should always remember that the investigation or handling of bombs or suspected infernal machines of any kind requires the services of an expert. Disposition of the suspected container should be made under the direction of the expert.

RADIOACTIVE MATERIALS

The increased use of radioactive materials in medicine, research, and industry has resulted in the transportation and storage of these substances in populated areas. The constant traffic in radioactive materials necessarily implies a police problem, since an "accident" involving spillage of these substances can result in the isolation of an area for a considerable period of time. In the space of a few minutes these materials can be tracked over a large area of a plant where they will represent a serious danger until appropriate decontamination procedures are effected. Lost radioactive isotopes, ruptured containers, improperly packed materials, and a number of other hazardous contingencies must be considered in police planning. As a matter of record, occurrences of this nature have already taken place in large cities. The consequent dangers to health and even life are well known. The sabotage potential of a serious "radioactive incident" is difficult to overestimate. A fire involving a few cans of uranium oxide, for example, may result in airborne contamination over a wide area.

Initial police action in a radioactive incident should be concerned with isolating the area surrounding the radioactive material to prevent the entry of unauthorized persons within the danger zone and to check for contaminated persons leaving the area. A frozen area of 100-foot radius should be created with the radioactive source as a center. If the radioactive material is located within a building, the room containing the source should be evacuated.

In dealing with these incidents the police must work closely with members of the Atomic Energy Commission and with the city's office of radiation control, which is usually part of the city's health department. Equipment is necessary, and appropriate training, if the police at the scene are to be effective. In New York the Emergency Service Units are equipped with Geiger-Müller Counters, ion chambers, dosimeters, and dosimeter chargers. The Police Laboratory responds to the scene with additional instruments of greater sensitivity which can detect alpha and beta as well as gamma radiation and permit close monitoring for slight contamination. Suitable protective clothing and shielding are provided, as well as a lead container in which the radioactive source can be placed.

Police officers entering a frozen area to perform necessary police duty must carry a film badge affixed to the outermost garment. At the conclusion of a radiation incident, the film badge is returned to the Police Laboratory where a report is subsequently made of the degree of radiation exposure for each officer. Police officers emerging from a frozen area are checked instrumentally for possible contamination. At a prolonged incident a schedule is drawn up on the basis of radioactivity measurements of the area to limit the exposure time of each policeman assigned to work within the area. To avoid accidental ingestion of dangerous material, smoking, eating, and drinking are forbidden within the area.

Police vehicles are parked on the windward side of an incident and, if possible, on high ground so as to avoid contamination from dust, smoke, or flow-off water. Vehicular traffic is detoured away from the radiation incident until the area is declared safe by the office of radiation control.

1 The New York Department of Health has included these products in a Sanitary Code, restricting them to sale by prescription only.

XXVI   QUESTIONED DOCUMENTS

OF THE MANY PROBLEMS CONNECTED WITH QUESTIONED HANDWRITING we shall discuss only a few which have special importance in detective work.

DETERMINING THE KIND OF INK USED

Three types of ink are chiefly used today in the United States, namely gallotannic, chromic (logwood), and aniline (nigrosine) inks. In addition there are the colored inks, India ink, and a small number of rare dark inks, such as vanadium and wolfram. The most widely used writing materials, however, are the "ballpoint inks," which are not true inks in the chemical sense. The following treatment will be confined, for reasons of space, mainly to the conventional types of ink.

The gallotannic ink was originally an Arabic invention—a solution of iron salt and nutgall. When these substances were mixed, a thick black precipitate consisting of tannic acid, gallic acid, and iron was obtained. The inconvenience of this precipitate was conquered in the middle of the nineteenth century when small amounts of hydrochloric and sulfuric acids were added. These dissolved the precipitate, giving a clear, almost colorless liquid which turned black as a result of the oxidizing action of the atmosphere. However, it took some time before the ink turned black, so in order to make it visible and usable for writing, a so-called primary dye —an aniline dye resistant to acids—was added. When this ink oxidized, the color of the primary dye was obscured by the deep-black color which resulted.

Modern gallotannic inks may be regarded as sulfuric or hydrochloric solutions of tannic and gallic iron salts with some aniline dye and a quantity of sugar and gum arabic or similar substances added to prevent rapid drying. Copying ink contains greater quantities of dye and glue. Gallotannic ink is regarded as the most stable of all inks.

Chromic ink consists of a watery solution of logwood, dichromate of potassium or chromate of potassium, and alum. Logwood contains a blue-

445

red dye, hematoxylin, which is turned black by dichromate of potassium.

Aniline inks are water solutions of aniline dyes. Generally they also contain a small quantity of sugar and an acid to make the color more brilliant.

The different classes of inks may be determined by many different methods. Among them are the use of reagents on the ink lines, the spectrographic method, and the photographic method of Miehte.

In the reagent method the reagents are applied on unimportant parts of the document with a glass rod and the resultant color permits a determination of the nature of the ink used.[1]

Spectrography may be used to some advantage for the differentiation of aniline dyes. A microspectrograph is used. The different aniline dyes will show absorption bands at different places in the spectrum.

The old method of Miehte consists of photographing a text which is suspected of having been written with two different inks. The document is photographed in transparency if only one side of the paper was written on and with reflected light if it shows writing on both sides. To make the paper transparent, Vaseline or tetrachloride ethane is used. The text is first photographed on an ordinary film with a blue filter. Then it is photographed with a specially prepared film sensitive to red and with a red filter. If the ink shows up differently on the two different films, it may be assumed that two different inks were used on the document.

With the aid of the above-mentioned methods it may be determined that two inks are chemically different but it cannot be proved that a document was written with only one ink, because within the types there are innumerable compositions. Inks of the same type but of different manufacture may differ as to the strength and depth of the color, as to the contrast of color between the different parts, as to their secondary color by oblique reflected light, and as to the appearance of the borders of the ink lines, which may be even or irregular. They may also differ as to the amount of pigments shown in thin or blotted strokes and as to their glossiness. A careful examination of these properties will sometimes show differences or similarities between two inks of the same type.[2]

Determination of the color of the ink with the naked eye is difficult because of the personal element involved. There are at least three objective methods for determining the colors of inks, i.e., filter photography, examination in an Osborn-Lovibond tintometer, and by photometric examination.

In filter photography the writing is photographed through a light filter, which allows only certain colors to pass onto the film. If one color is to be made stronger than the others, a filter having its complementary color[3] is used. As the filter with the complementary color does not allow the color of the object to pass through, the sensitive film will be lighter on the place in question and the print darker. On the other hand, to remove a color, a filter of the color to be suppressed is used, which allows the light to pass through. A thick, black precipitate will then be found on the sensitive film and the print will be light-colored. The ink specimens to be examined are photographed on the same film. The difference in the colors will be shown on the film. With proper filters and panchromatic film some good results may be achieved.

The Osborn-Lovibond tintometer is built on the same principle as the comparison microscope used in examining bullets. Each lens has an opening in which a Lovibond filter glass may be inserted. These consist of red, yellow, and blue stained-glass slides representing all gradations of these colors. The specimen of writing to be examined is placed under one of the lenses. The various stained slides are inserted in a groove placed immediately above the opposite lens until the same color as that of the ink is obtained. This procedure is repeated with comparison specimens, and if there is a difference, this may be ascertained by means of the numbered slides. This method is delicate, however, and can only be applied in a limited number of cases.

Another method of determining the color of ink is by the photometer. As microphotometric methods have been developed to a great extent, dependable ways of determining the colors of minute objects such as ink lines have now been found.

DETERMINING THE AGE OF THE INK

Efforts to determine the age of ink are seldom successful. It is chiefly possible when the ink has been recently applied and when it is of the gallotannic type. There are also some possibilities of determining the age if other inks have been used, especially if they have been applied only a few days before the examination.

In order to understand the possibility of determining the age of gallotannic ink the alterations taking place in the writing during a lapse of time must be described. As already stated, the color of the gallotannic ink before use is due to the presence of an aniline dye. When applied to the paper, the ink still shows this primary color. The process of oxidation in time turns the ink to deep black. In summer the ink will seem black to the eye after a few weeks and in winter after one to several months. During these periods, however, the black color is only superficial; the pure, dense-black color is only obtained later. Gallotannic inks require from one to two years to attain their intensest blackness, and this will then last for several years more. After that period the ink begins to turn yellow along the traces made by the penpoint. This discoloring will continue for several years more, until the writing becomes a dark yellowish-brown. This latter color will last indefinitely. The above-mentioned periods of time can be stated only approximately, because the oxidation processes are retarded or accelerated according to the degree of atmospheric humidity, the light, the ink itself, and the paper.

If the ink under examination still shows the fresh primary color, it cannot be more than a few weeks old. This may be ascertained in the following manner. The document to be examined is covered with a thin metal plate having an aperture through which only one letter is exposed. The plate is then flooded with ultraviolet rays, without filter, for about a quarter of an hour at a distance of about five inches. The unfiltered light is not only very rich in all of the actinic rays of the sunlight but during the exposure ozone is also developed.

During this time the exposed letter undergoes an artificial oxidation, which causes it to appear blacker than the surrounding letters if the ink is of recent application.

If a few weeks have elapsed since the writing and the ink is already fairly black, its property of dissolving in water may be put to use to determine its approximate age. A recently applied ink is immediately dissolved in a drop of water placed on the writing, the drop assuming a blue color. This may be due either to the fact that the ink is fresh or that it contains a dye soluble in water. In the first case the occurrence is temporary, as the ink will not be dissolved when oxidized. In the second case the occurrence is constant, as the ink colors the drop regardless of its age. To determine whether the ink is fresh or whether it contains a soluble aniline dye, the process of oxidation must be completed. The quartz-lamp method (see Chapter XXVII) may be used for this purpose. A drop of distilled water is put on the already treated portion of the writing. If the ink does not become dissolved after twenty minutes, while the other untreated parts of the writing do, it must be concluded that the document has been written recently. On the other hand, if the ink on both the treated and untreated parts is dissolved, the test is negative.

The chloride method of Mezger and Heess[4] may also be used to determine the approximate age of the ink. The shape of the chloride picture will give some indication as to the age of the ink. The chloride picture of ink not more than a few days old corresponds exactly to the form of the original writing. With the lapse of time the chloride picture is blurred because of the spreading of the chloride ions. After a period of one-half to one year, the chloride picture is entirely blurred. Naturally with this method it is chiefly possible to determine the difference in age between two writings which are supposed to have been subject to the same influences from the moment of the writing. If no comparison material is at hand, one can repeat the test after, for instance, a month in order to observe a possible change of the chloride picture. This method has been subject to much criticism in recent years. We shall cite only the following by two research workers: [5] "Since so many factors are concerned in the chloride test for age of inks, any conclusions regarding the age of writing, as determined by this test, should be viewed with extreme suspicion."

Errors may arise both when determining the age of an ink and when comparing inks. These errors may be due either to the writing having been dried with blotting paper or to the fact that the ink was diluted. Writing dried with a blotter never becomes deep black but looks light and dull. The blotting can be recognized by the blurring of certain lines. The blotted writing contains a reduced quantity of the ink substance, but it will nevertheless show the characteristic reaction.

Writing made with diluted ink looks like blotted writing. It is uniformly light, however, and there are no traces of blotting. Microscopic examination shows small black grains due to the settling of the ink.

Handwriting experts are often able to arrive at conclusions as regards the age of a document or the age of additions in relation to the text by other means besides the studying of the ink.[6] Examination of the sequence of strokes and the writing on the folds, as well as examination of slants, position while writing, watermarks, and other signs of the manufacture of the paper, etc., may lead to definite conclusions.

ERASURES

Ink may be erased with a knife, rubber, or ink eradicator. When the erasure has been made with a knife or rubber, it is generally easy to detect the area involved, as it is translucent. A microscopical examination of the surface of the paper may also give results. This can be seen by holding the paper against the light. A simple method consists in putting a few drops of benzine in the vicinity of the suspected area. The benzine spreads to the border of the erased portion of paper, continues to spread along the border, and later penetrates the erased spot. The iodine-fumes treatment described in Chapter IX may also give good results and even allow the reading of the erased writing. However, the best iodine method for the detection of erasures is the one in which Moser's solution is used. Moser's solution consists of 0.75 gram of iodine, 1.5 grams of potassium iodide, 60 grams of aluminum chloride, and 90cc. of distilled water. The solution is applied by means of a pad of cotton wool or a brush. The stains caused by Moser's solution may be removed by applying a saturated solution of sodium thiosulphate and magnesium sulphate with some cotton wool.

If the erasure has been made with ink eradicators, it may be difficult to detect, especially if a great deal of time has elapsed. Newly applied ink eradicators can be easily detected with ultraviolet rays, which bring out the contrast quite sharply. As clever forgers have been known to wash away all residue of the eradication with distilled water, the examination with ultraviolet rays should not be too much relied upon.

If the eradicated ink is a gallotannic one, it is almost always possible to bring out at least some traces of the original writing, because small particles of ink will always adhere to the paper. The suspected area is treated with sulfide of ammonia. A quantity of the sulfide of ammonia is then put in a glass container, which is covered with the document to be examined, the suspected spot pointing downward. The sulfide of ammonia gas is allowed to act on the paper from five to fifteen minutes, until the invisible residue of iron oxide is transformed to black sulfide of iron and thereby made plainly visible. Liquid sulfide of ammonia may also be applied directly on the paper, using a piece of cotton. The developed writing must in both cases be photographed immediately.

The sulfocyanic acid method [7] may also be used to detect iron-containing inks. Crystalline potassium sulfocyanate is placed between wads of cotton wool and glass wool in a Gooch funnel and moistened with a few drops of dilute hydrochloric acid (10 percent). The document bearing the erasure is held before the mouth of the funnel, and the operator blows through the stem, causing the vapor of sulfocyanic acid generated in the tube to be sprayed over the surface of the paper. If iron is present in the erasure, it will react with the vapor, forming blood-red ferric sulfocyanate. Because of the extreme sensitivity of the method it is especially useful in dealing with not only the blue-black inks but also with the inks containing very small amounts of iron, such as certain blue and jet-black inks. The coloration obtained is not permanent but is quite persistent, remaining for a period of from two days to several weeks. Even if fading occurs, the restoration can be made repeatedly by fresh application of the vapor. If it is desirable to make the recovered writing disappear, this can be accomplished by fuming with ammonium hydroxide vapor.

PROBLEMS OF LEAD-PENCIL WRITING

It may be said at the outset that it is very difficult to determine whether two lead-pencil writings have been made with the same sort of pencil or not. There are different proportions of graphite and clay in "lead" pencils, but because of the very small quantities of material at the disposal of the expert the proportions cannot be determined. It is almost impossible to get pure material free from foreign substances in the paper itself. However, it may sometimes be possible to reveal foreign substances in the lead pencil by the application of different reagents on the pencil lines in the same manner as that used when dealing with inks. The presence of such a foreign substance in lead-pencil writing should at least be able to furnish negative proof, i.e., the presence of such a substance in one lead-pencil writing and its absence in another indicates nonidentity. The most common foreign substances in lead-pencil writing are titanium, chlorides, sulfides, and iron. Owing to the fact that the paper itself may sometimes contain titanium, iron, and chlorides, control experiments must be carried out on the paper.[8]

The German scientist Kögel has invented a method which differentiates one indelible-pencil writing from another to a certain degree and distinguishes indelible-pencil writing from lead-pencil writing with certainty. A filtered ultraviolet light is played obliquely on the writing to be examined. The lead-pencil writing will reflect the ultraviolet light in such a manner that it appears chalk-white, while the indelible pencil, which contains only aniline dyes, shows up jet-black. The writing of indelible pencils of inferior quality, which contain graphite in addition to the aniline dyes, disappears more or less completely by blending in with the violet tone of the paper.

Lead-pencil writing often shows traces of having been written on an uneven substructure, and it is possible in some cases to show that a certain sheet has been written on a certain substructure or that several writings have been written on the same underlying surface. For this purpose a piece of paper is put over the suspected surface and the pencil writing made on it is compared. It is not possible to compare the substructure directly with the paper.

Erased lead-pencil writing may be made visible by different methods, i.e., iodine fumes, as described previously; "contrast photography"; examination in polarized light; and photography in oblique light.

By "contrast photography" the erasure is photographed with a hard film which is developed in a hard developer. Appropriate filters are used, for instance a red filter for white paper.

Examination in polarized light with crossed Nicol prisms will sometimes give good results. All mirroring is prevented through the polarization when the Nicol prisms are crossed, so that the particles of graphite remaining in the paper appear jet-black.

If the paper on which the writing appears is very dirty, it may be bleached by treating it for a short time with a strong solution of peroxide of hydrogen. This must be done very carefully, however, to prevent the particles of graphite from being loosened by the oxygen liberated by the hydrogen peroxide.

If there are any traces of writing on the front or the back of the paper, reconstruction of the original writing is possible by photographing this in an oblique light, thus giving relief to the impressions.

SEQUENCE OF STROKES IN WRITING

When two ink lines cross one another, it is often of great importance to determine which is superimposed on the other.[9] The solution of such a problem often answers the question as to whether a number has been altered, whether words or sentences have been added to a document, or whether the whole text has been written after the signature was affixed. There is no absolutely infallible method for arriving at such conclusions, but in the majority of cases a solution will be found. In all examinations of the sequence of strokes comparison tests should be made with the same paper and with the same ink if possible.

If the second line is superimposed on the first before the latter has become completely dry, the ink from the second stroke will spread out on the first line at the crossing in such an obvious manner that there can be no doubt about the second line lying over the first one. This, however, is true only when the lines have about the same content of ink. One reason for this is that the paper covered by the first line, being moist, is more absorbent and therefore causes the ink from the second stroke to spread more pronouncedly than on dry paper. Another is that the paper has been roughened by the penpoint during the act of making the first stroke and is thus rendered more porous. This is also shown by the fact that the additional ink spreads out only along the traces of the first stroke. This part of the phenomenon may be observed even when the first stroke is entirely dry. It should be noted that if the first line is thick and very wet when crossed by a thin line, the phenomenon may be reversed so that the ink from the first line will enter into the second.

The appearance of the crossing is quite different if the second stroke is immediately blotted. If the second stroke was made before the ink in the first line was dry, a part of the ink from the first stroke will dissolve in the ink from the second stroke. In blotting, however, pigments will be absorbed from the second as well as the first stroke. The first one will then appear lighter at the crossing than the rest of the same stroke, but the second will be uniform. If the two strokes were each blotted immediately after writing, it is almost impossible to determine the sequence. If the traces at the penpoint from the second stroke show up more clearly at the crossing than the traces from the first one, however, there is a possibility of determining the sequence.

If the first stroke was not blotted and was fully dry but the second was blotted immediately, there are great possibilities of making mistakes. In most cases the dark stroke underneath will look as if it were over the blotted one. Such mistakes often occur when the strokes are of different width and intensity of color, even if there has been no blotting. At first sight a broad line looks as if it were superimposed over a thin one. A thin light line also often does not spread out on the broad one.

Ink lines over lead-pencil lines will show the same spreading underneath as has been described above. The penpoint will also smooth the graphite at the crossing, so that the grains of graphite acquire a glossy surface. If the ink line is under the lead-pencil line, the latter will show a continuous metallic glossiness even at the crossing.

Ink lines over rubber stamps will spread out if the stamp is not dry. The reverse is true if the stamp is dry. Ink lines over typewriting will not spread even if the typewriting is still wet. On the contrary, the typewriting repels the ink in the same manner as does oily paper, so that the sequence may often be determined. In most cases it is impossible to determine the sequence of strokes in lead-pencil writing which crosses rubber stamps or typewriting.

Examination of the sequence of strokes should be done by slight enlargement and with the light from behind the paper, in front, or obliquely, according to circumstances. In examination with the light placed back of the paper it is often necessary to make the paper transparent. This is done by depositing a drop of resin oil or some similar substance on the back of the paper at the crossing. The minutest possible quantity of oil should be used.

CROSSINGS IN FOLDS

When a paper has been folded, the fibers in the fold are broken, and as paper does not possess elastic qualities, it is not able to return to its normal position. The properties of absorption are altered in the fold, which can be regarded as a strip of blotting paper over the surface of the folded document. In most cases it is easy to show that an ink line running over the folded part has been written before or after the fold was made. If the line is first drawn and the paper is subsequently folded, the line over the fold will be even and uniform, and if the paper in the fold is very much worn, the protruding paper fibers will not appear stained. If the ink line, on the other hand, is written over an already existing fold, the ink will not only spread out over the fold but the protruding paper fibers will become stained. Thin inks show this phenomenon more clearly than thick inks, and different papers also give different results. It is therefore often necessary to make practical tests with similar ink and similar paper.

It is almost impossible to determine whether a lead-pencil line was drawn before or after the folding of the paper.

Crossings in folds are very important in questioned documents. Most documents will be written on unfolded paper, and if the incriminated part of the text appears to have been written after the paper has been folded, this fact certainly makes the document more open to suspicion.

There are many cases on record in which forgeries of this kind have been solved entirely by the examination of ink lines running over folds.

TRACING

By tracing we mean a forgery in which the original writing was traced on a forged document. In most cases the tracings apply only to signatures, but in a few cases larger pieces of text have been copied. The latter procedure, however, is not a tracing in a real sense of the word but could be called forgery by piecing words or letters together. The forger picks out words or letters from a written communication or other document, arranges them in the order in which he wishes to have them, and traces them on another paper.[10] Such forgeries should be examined with very strong enlargements. In the original writing the height of the letters and the distances between words will be more or less uniform, etc.; but when the forger picks out letters from different parts of the document and rearranges them, there will be slight variations in height and other differences. These cannot be observed on the forgery unless the document is greatly magnified.

Different methods are used in common tracing. The simplest is that of copying the signature with the aid of carbon paper and filling in the tracing with ink. Such a procedure can be detected immediately by microscopic examination, as parts of the carbon tracing will be seen under the ink. Another method is to put the paper containing the genuine signature against a windowpane, place the document to be forged upon it, and draw the signature. We use the word draw to describe the writing made by the forger while in this unnatural position. A tracing of this sort is conspicuous because of the strained writing obtained. Clever forgers use the apparatus which photographers employ in retouching—an oblique ground glass with an electric bulb underneath. The hand will then be in a natural position when writing, and if the tracing is repeatedly made, so that the forger acquires familiarity, it may be very similar to the original. Upon close examination, however, it should be possible to detect the forgery.

The forger will often lift the pen away from the paper, pausing for a moment to gaze at his handiwork or to determine the manner in which he has to continue. These interruptions in the writing are hidden through a retracing, so that the new stroke is begun over the previously unfinished stroke. Such a retrace differs from the normal lifting of the pen not only in its unnatural position—often in the middle of a letter—but also in that the natural retracing is not hidden.

The forger will often retouch his work, especially when the tracing has not closely followed the outlines of the original. These retouches should not be mistaken for the retouches which many persons, called retouchers, do on their own writing. Such normal retouching may be the result of exaggerated carefulness or of a nervous affliction. Quite often, however, the retoucher's handwriting is not very legible, so that he improves parts of it which seem indistinct to him. Here we also see the difference between the forger and the normal retoucher: the forger retouches even parts of letters which are clear and understandable in order to obtain similarity with the original, but the normal retouchers retouch only illegible letters.

Traced strokes do not show the speed and steadiness of normal handwriting, consequently the letters often show that they have been written by a hand affected with more or less pronounced trembling. The trembling may be natural, however, so it is necessary to differentiate the trembling of the forger from that due to age, cold, or certain illnesses. The trembling of the forger will be especially noticeable on the upward strokes and on the places where the pen, during its tracing, covers the original writing. Furthermore, this trembling is irregular. The trembling due to old age is mostly noticeable in the initial strokes, while cold, rigid fingers often cause angular writing. The pathological trembling of different illnesses, such as paralysis and Parkinsonism, may be very characteristic.

The wrong starting-point in the tracing of a letter is often quite evident. If the forger, for instance, is writing a closed "o," it seems unimportant to him whether he begins to trace from the top or elsewhere.

Sometimes it is possible to obtain the original of the tracing. This is especially true in cases of forged due bills and checks. It is then very simple to detect the forgery, because two signatures can never be alike

Figure 158.   An examiner consults the fraudulent check file in the Document Section of the FBI laboratory, Washington, D. C.

in all their proportions. It is impossible to write a second signature absolutely similar to the first. If two such signatures are found, one of the two must be a forgery. The shape of the initial strokes and the punctuation may be found to vary if the original and the tracing are compared, because the forger will often trace them after having completed his work. The end strokes may also vary. However, the distances between the letters and between important parts of the signature are absolutely alike. This may be shown to the court by photographing the original and the tracing on exactly the same scale and printing them on a network, which will show the similarity. This similarity may also be put in evidence if the print is made by superimposing the two films. The tracings above mentioned are shown by photomicrographs moderately enlarged. The trembling is shown in common photographic enlargements.

THE COMPARISON OF HANDWRITING

The examination of forged and disguised handwriting is one of the most difficult problems in police science.[11] The expert must not only have an extensive theoretical knowledge of the manifold problems connected with questioned documents and a long practical experience but also the ability to detect small differences in shape. The last is not the least important, because many persons are blind to forms and cannot perceive the slight differences upon which the handwriting expert bases his conclusions.[12]

Examinations of handwriting in former days were based almost exclusively on the calligraphic method, i.e., the comparison of the outer shapes of the letters. It is precisely these shapes, however, which the forger seeks to imitate, and it was only natural that the experts sometimes made mistakes. The most widely known miscarriage of justice based on an examination of questioned handwriting is the famous Dreyfus case. In recent decades, however, the examination of questioned handwriting has attained a more scientific character owing to the work of Locard, Schneickert,[13] Osborn,[14] and others. We cannot within the scope of this book give a comprehensive account of the methods employed in the comparison of handwritings, and we therefore refer the student to special textbooks on the subject.[15]

PROBLEMS CONNECTED WITH TYPEWRITING

In connection with typewritten documents questions may arise as to whether the whole document was written with the same typewriter in the same continuous writing, whether the typewriting was done on a certain machine, or whether the make of the typewriter corresponds with the date of the writing. Most of these problems can be solved.

It can be said that each typewriter gives an individual writing which, if properly enlarged and measured, can be identified with the machine in question. Pioneer work regarding the identification of typewriting has been carried out by Albert Osborn in New York. The glass measures invented by him have facilitated the work of the expert to a high degree.

It can almost always be shown when part of a document is an ad-

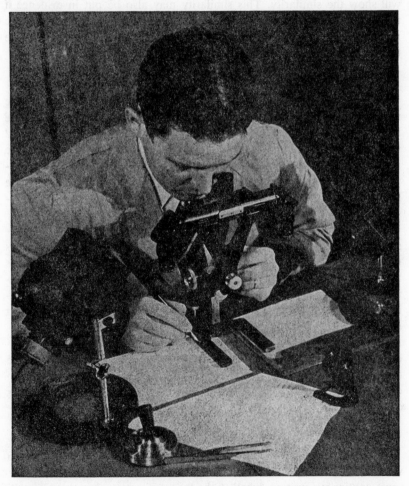

Figure 159.   Technician making typewriter comparisons in the FBI laboratory.

dition to the original. It is almost impossible to insert the paper in the typewriter exactly as it was before. Appropriate enlargements and measurements will clearly show such a forgery. The identification of typewriting done with a certain machine is also almost always possible if the incriminated writing is sufficient to show the constant peculiarities of the typewriter. In order to determine whether the age of the machine used corresponds to the date of the writing it is necessary to have a comprehensive collection of specimens from the various typewriters, with notes showing the dates when the different manufacturers changed letters and other signs of identification in their typewriters. It should be the aim of each police laboratory to build up such a collection. For further study of this question we refer to the previously cited work of Osborn.

STANDARDS OF COMPARISON [16]

STANDARDS OBTAINED THROUGH DICTATION. In the taking of standards of comparison by dictation the circumstances prevalent in the original writing should be reproduced as much as possible.

The same sort of paper should be used, as, for instance, letterheads, postcards, telegraph blanks, money order blanks, bills, receipts, etc. If the suspected handwriting is written on lined paper, the standards should also be written on lined paper having the same spacing. In emergencies the lines may be drawn with lead pencil.

The same writing material should be used, i.e., the same ink; lead pencil; crayon; fine, broad, hard, or soft steel pen; ballpoint pen; and smooth or rough paper.

If the handwriting in question has been written very slowly and carefully, very quickly and carelessly, very slantingly or upright, or very large or small, the standards from the suspect should also embrace specimens written correspondingly (slowly, quickly, slantingly, etc.). The investigator should note the manner of writing on each sheet of paper.

If the suspect tries to disguise his handwriting, he should not only be made to write as fast as possible but also a considerable quantity of text should be written.

When the writing under investigation appears on doors or walls, a sufficiently large paper is put on the wall at the same height as the suspected writing and the suspect made to write thereon. (It should be noted that persons writing on walls will hold the pencil at a height corresponding to the height of their eyes, thereby furnishing a clue as to their stature.)

The standard should reproduce the entire text, or at least a considerable part of its beginning and end. Special attention should be paid to parts of the text in which errors in spelling are common.

Short texts should be written several times, especially when dealing with forged signatures or brief additions to the text. It is advisable to have the suspect write the signature twenty to thirty times. It is also advisable to have him write a short continuous text in which the words or letters from the forgery appear in other connections, as, for instance, a short autobiography.

Standards of comparison should always be dictated. The suspect should not be allowed to see the document either before or after the dictation, and words should not be spelled for him. Foreign words should be dictated with their usual pronunciation.

If the suspect declares that he cannot print, for instance, block letters, have him make the standards with a newspaper as a copy. In important cases it is advisable to obtain standards from the schools attended by the suspect, especially when he denies his ability to write.

Exceptional circumstances prevalent at the time of the writing of the standards of comparison, as, for example, strong agitation of the writer, imperfect light facilities, cold, heat, inferior writing material, etc., should be noted and recorded by the investigator.

OTHER STANDARDS OF COMPARISON. In addition to the standards obtained by dictation other samples of handwriting, such as from letters, notebooks, income tax returns, checks, account books, automobile registrations, leases, receipts, marriage licenses, voting registration, applications for gas and electric service, public library registrations, purchases made on the installment plan, etc., should be sought.

If there are any doubts as to the origin or age of the standards of comparison, these should be noted. The standards should, if possible, have been made at the same time as the suspected document. It is preferable that the standards embrace the time of the origin of the document, so that one part comes from the time before the origin and one part from the time after the origin.

In major cases when a raid on the house of the perpetrator or suspected person is necessary in order to gather standards of comparison, special attention should be paid to the seizing of writing materials, such as paper, lead pencils, crayons, ink, blotting paper, stamps, carbon paper, hectograph pads, and envelopes, and of writing experiments on discarded paper, torn or burnt paper in the waste-paper basket, furnace, or stove, etc.

As specimens for ink testing, some words written with the suspect's ink and with a clean pen are sufficient. If the bottles of ink are not seized, each specimen of ink should be taken on special paper.

If the original document was a sheet in a book or a part of another sheet, search for the book or sheet in question should naturally be made.

WHEN AND HOW SHOULD STANDARDS OF COMPARISON BE TAKEN? The taking of standards of comparison should be done at the first interrogation if determining the identity of a writer—whether he be a suspect, anonymous complainant, or merely a witness. They should also be taken then in all cases where the suspect may seek to avoid further interrogation by changing his residence or by disappearing.

In order to facilitate the work of the handwriting expert the standards of comparison should be written on one side of loose sheets, which are then put in a special envelope. Suspected documents and anonymous complaints, together with their corresponding envelopes, should also be put in a special envelope and not attached to the record. Under no circumstances should suspected or incriminated documents be pasted to the record, as is sometimes seen, or have their words underlined or annotations added by others, thus making the work of the expert very difficult. The standards of comparison should have no other notes than those already described.

In important cases a handwriting expert should always be consulted before obtaining the standards of comparison.

If several anonymous letters originate from the same person and there is reason to believe that more will be received, the recipient should be advised to turn them over to the police laboratory unopened in order to determine the presence of fingerprints.

CONTACT DETECTION

Writing which has been in contact with any paper for at least a few hours may leave invisible traces. For instance, the envelope containing a letter often carries a latent picture of the writing which has touched it.[17] Such traces are left only by gallotannic inks. The latent picture may be made visible by the method of Paul Ermel. The surface of the paper or envelope is treated in the dark room by red light with a solution composed of 5 grams of silver nitrate, 1 gram of citric acid, 0.5 gram of tartaric acid, and three drops of nitric acid in 100 grams of distilled water. The writing is developed in ordinary daylight and fixed with ordinary fixation. Since the process of fixation weakens the intensity of the letters it is advisable to photograph the writing first.

RESTORATION OF TORN AND CHEWED PAPER

Paper can be torn in only a few ways, so that it is possible to detect the manner by examining the layers of paper fragments, which, experience shows, always adhere to one another. The number of fragments and the succession of smooth and torn edges give the clues to the system of tearing. There is a special table made by Friedendorff for the purpose of reconstructing torn paper. The use of this table will save time in more complicated cases.[18]

It is also possible to reconstruct the fragments when the paper has been destroyed by chewing or otherwise. Water should not be used, as the paper will easily become putrefied. The dry pieces of paper should be soaked in some thin clear lacquer, as, for instance, sapon lacquer, which will be absorbed very readily, making the pieces resistant and elastic. They can then be handled with microscopic preparation needles, unfolded, put on a glass slide, and covered with another glass slide in the same manner as a mounted lantern slide.

1 O'Hara–Osterburg and *Inks,* Circular C 426, National Bureau of Standards, Washington, D. C., 1940.

2 See also Osborn.[3]

3 Two colors which by being mixed produce a white light are called complementary colors. They may be simple or complex. Simple complementary colors are, for instance, orange/blue, gold-yellow/blue, yellow/indigo blue, greenish-yellow/violet, etc. Green, on the contrary, has a complex complementary, purple.

4 Türkel.[3]   5 Finn–Cornish.   6 Sannié.[2]   7 O'Neill.

8 J. Locard, *"L'Analyse des traits de crayon en criminalistique"* (thesis), Lyons, 1936.

9 Mitchell–Ward.

10 E. Locard.[3]

11 E. Locard.[2]

12 It should perhaps be pointed out that graphology and the examination of handwriting from the viewpoint of criminal investigation are two quite different things. Graphology in its worst form is a quack science similar to astrology; such graphologists think they can read the past and future of a person by studying his handwriting.

13 Hans Schneickert, born 1876, died 1944. Doctor of Law (Tübingen), director of the identification bureau of the police department of Berlin until 1928; instructor in criminology at the University of Berlin from 1920. Schneickert was a well-known handwriting expert on the Continent.

14 Albert S. Osborn, born at Sharon, Michigan, 1858, died 1946. Examiner of questioned documents in New York City from 1887.

15 See Osborn,[3] E. Locard,[10] Schneickert,[7] Mayer, and Conway and Hilton.

16 Partly from the excellent *Regulations of the Berlin Police Department,* September 1, 1911, by Dr. Hans Schneickert and Dr. Georg Meyer.

17 See Schneickert,[2] Mayer, and O'Hara–Osterburg.

18 Friedendorff.

XXVII THE POLICE LABORATORY

THE FUNCTION OF THE POLICE LABORATORY IS NOW WELL INTEGRATED with the crime detection process. A growing appreciation of his range of useful skills has gained for the scientist a place as a regular and effective member of the law enforcement team. Criminalistics—a term which has come to mean the work of the police laboratory—is no longer viewed with an invidious suspicion or subjected to the specious criticisms of those with little knowledge of its nature and even less understanding of its proper applications. In the past these critics have followed a common pattern of argument: "How often does the laboratory 'break' the case—how often does it come up with a suspect or with the proof that will clinch the case?"

The detective's common sense has seen through the fallacy implicit in this argument. Criminalistics is a supplement, not a substitute for the work of the field investigator. The business of the police laboratory is with physical evidence. At a crime scene where no physical evidence of value is present, the laboratory representatives can avail nothing, however great their proficiency or however elaborate their equipment may be. The laboratory has not yet developed the methods or equipment to discover evidence that does not exist, and the facts of the matter point out that more crimes than we would care to contemplate are committed without leaving physical clues that will have probative significance or even provide useful leads.

Employed in its proper domain, however, criminalistics serves an essential function in crime detection. Its value is readily conceded in cases where the physical evidence is itself part of the *corpus delicti*. An arrest for a narcotics offense or for violation of an alcoholic beverage control law requires a laboratory analysis of the narcotic or beverage submitted in evidence as an essential part of the offense. Similarly, to support a charge of forgery, the altered or simulated writing must be submitted to the laboratory's document examiners. It should be noted in passing that work of this nature—specifically, the analyses of narcotics and beverages and the examination of questioned documents—accounts for a majority of the cases in a municipal police laboratory.

Despite their number and importance, however, tasks such as chemical analyses in which a specific test is requested are not truly representative of the crime detection function that the police laboratory should perform. A more characteristic police purpose is served by the laboratory at crime scenes where the evidence must first be uncovered and its relationship to the criminal act established. Here the detective-scientist must employ to the full his powers of analytic deduction and his capacity for imaginative synthesis.

The full significance of the physical evidence can only be realized if the laboratory representative is sufficiently astute to "diagnose" from the available traces the conditions that must have existed at the time of occurrence and the manner in which the criminal act must have been performed. His knowledge of criminalistics must be broad enough to enable him to recognize evidence of value and to form a sound judgment as to the information such evidence can provide and its probable worth to the detectives in their assessment of the case.

Figure 160.	John J. O'Connell.[1]

Finally, his scientific knowledge, training, and experience must be equal to the demands made by the evidence—performing suitable field tests, selecting the proper solvents, collecting evidence in sufficient quantity, intelligent sampling, obtaining standards for comparison, separating and protecting specimens, preserving perishable substances, and the many other ministrations that insure the full probative value of the physical clues.

The most important work of the police laboratory, then, is often performed in the field. In a major case the effectiveness of the work accomplished at the laboratory will depend to a great extent on the sampling done at the crime scene. This is not to say that the work in the laboratory itself is necessarily routine in nature or wholly dependent on the persons submitting the evidence. In the laboratory, too, there is equal opportunity for the application of scientific acumen and even broader fields for the development of new methods and techniques. In the area of analysis alone there will be found a lifetime of challenge for the chemist of imagination and initiative. The "unknowns" submitted to him are too often truly unknowns with few or no clues to their general nature or probable origin such as serve the industrial chemist as a starting point. The limitations of available quantity of the evidential sample impose special requirements of experience and knowledge in the separation and preparation of the substance. The method of analysis must be chosen with equal care and the findings interpreted with a scrupulously objective temperament and an intelligent awareness of the limitations and full implications of the method used.

PERSONNEL OF THE LABORATORY

A description of the demands made upon the talents of the physicist or the biologist by the police laboratory would require a similar emphasis upon breadth of experience, depth of professional knowledge, and integrity of scientific character, and would lead naturally into the problems of personnel and recruiting. How do the police departments manage to people their laboratories with these paragons? Which is to ask, how, at a time when scientifically trained personnel are in great demand for industrial work and government-sponsored projects, does the police laboratory fare in the employment market? Not too well, unfortunately. The intrinsic interest and challenge offered by police laboratory work, the mystique of crime detection, and the satisfactions derived from social service of a high order—these attractions and many other advantages too often fail to outweigh the simple charms of industry's high wages and regular hours.

Recruiting is but one of the problems that must be dealt with in forming the personnel policy of a large police laboratory. Difficulties arise also from the mixed nature of the staff, since there is usually a component of civilian specialists in addition to the detailed members of the uniformed force. Technically trained detectives are obviously better suited than civilians for the rigors of laboratory field work, which requires response to a crime scene at any hour of any day or night. Full control of personnel is necessary at the scene, where the work of the various service units must be coordinated by a single detective supervisor. At the laboratory itself civilian specialists are needed as well as detectives selected for their scientific background. Their qualifications should be appropriately related to the nature of the cases and the specialized equipment of the laboratory.

The selection of a director or commanding officer presents another personnel problem on which opinion, as well as practice, varies widely. Many police departments—particularly those which have happened to find within their ranks detective supervisors with suitable training in the sciences—take the view that a chemist or other civilian scientist is seldom the right man to be chosen as the commanding officer of a police laboratory. A policeman, they maintain, with a thorough training in the detective division will act more effectively in this capacity because of

his familiarity with the investigative aspects of the problems and his closer relationship to the line of command. Special training, however, including a degree in science, should be a requisite for this position, since the detective supervisor heading a police laboratory must work in close harmony with a civilian scientific adviser and maintain directive control over the other technical workers.

Some police departments look upon the directorship of a laboratory as simply another administrative position which may be adequately filled by a policeman who has qualified for promotion to the supervisory level and has been trained in the general principles of administration. Other

Figure 161.   Harry Söderman.[2]

departments, viewing the laboratory as a service unit out of the direct line of operations, have not hesitated to staff it with civilians under a civilian head. Still others have found a happy solution in selecting a director from civilian ranks, making him a peace officer, and conferring an appropriate rank, such as lieutenant, to provide him with the necessary controls over uniformed members, as well as civilians, assigned to the laboratory.

This variance in approach to a personnel policy arises from the problem of attracting competent civilians to an organization in which the controls and promotional opportunities are for the greater part in

Figure 162.   An examiner in the FBI laboratory, Washington, D. C., conducts a petrographic examination of an abrasive substance found in a motor bearing. Boxes at right contain abrasive specimens for comparison.

the hands of police officers. Civilians rightly consider themselves career scientists and tend to look upon police officers assigned to the laboratory as detailed men engaged in an avocation while preparing for promotion to other assignments or evading the rigors of patrol duty. This viewpoint has an impeccable logic and would enjoy a greater currency were its validity not brought into question by the paradox of the history of the police laboratory in this country: the major contributions to the planning, design, and operational theory of the modern police laboratory, as well as to the literature of criminalistics, have been the work of members of the uniformed force of the police departments.[3]

OUTLINE OF LABORATORY WORK

Police laboratories designed for large departments are generally organized along the following lines: (1) chemical and physical section, (2) biological section, (3) field work section, (4) firearms section, (5) questioned documents section, (6) photographic section, (7) instrument section (design, construction, maintenance, and repair of apparatus). These operational units are, of course, under the control of an administrative office and are supported by a supply unit and provided with suitable library facilities.

To indicate the general nature of the work conducted by the various divisions of a police laboratory, some typical case-file headings are given in the following list:

Chemical examinations:

Narcotics
Alcohol
Explosives
Incendiary materials
Toxic substances
Analysis of unknown specimens—for identification and tracing
Analysis for comparison—the evidence specimen is compared with specimens of known origin

Physical examinations:

Automobile parts—broken ornaments, lenses, and other parts
Broken windows—and other glass problems
Electrical appliances
Locks and keys
Tool marks and other impressions
Etching deleted numbers

Personal markings for identification purposes:

Fingerprints
Foot and shoe impressions
Laundry and dry-cleaning marks

Documentary examinations:

Questioned handwriting
Typewriting
Erasures and obliterations
Paper, ink, and pencil problems

Firearms problems:

Identification of bullets and cartridges

Firearms examination
Trajectories

Biological examinations:

Blood
Semen
Hair and fibers

Photography

Contrast and filter photography
Infrared and ultraviolent photography
Photomicrography
Radiography

Figure 163.   Measuring the refractive index in order to identify an oil.

EQUIPMENT FOR THE CHEMICAL AND
PHYSICAL LABORATORIES

The chemical laboratory should be equipped for the general work of
analysis. There is a need, of course, for specialized instrumentation in
certain areas. For example, it is apparent from the brief descriptions
of the work given above that michrochemistry plays an important role in
criminalistics. Evidentiary traces discovered at the crime scene are usu-

ally found only in minute quantities. A paint streak left by a colliding automobile or a lipstick smear on a suspect's hand represents at best a meager sample after it has been collected and prepared for examination. To deal with the wide range of minute specimens encountered in this work the police laboratory should be suitably equipped for microanalysis. Since the physical aspects of chemistry are especially important in micro-work, the equipment should include a microbalance, a specific gravity balance, and the various instruments of optical analysis such as the refractometer, colorimeter, polarimeter, and units for spectrochemical work.

In the laboratories of large municipal police departments it will be found that a great many of the cases involve narcotics offenses and violations of alcoholic beverage control laws. The volume of such cases warrants the assignment of special sections of the laboratory with appropriate equipment for these examinations. In some jurisdictions possession of a specified quantity of the pure narcotic is considered *prima facie* evidence of a selling offense; hence a quantitative analysis is required. Since the narcotics are sold in a highly diluted form, with adulterants casually selected and unpredictable in nature, wet methods are ordinarily used in the analysis and a great deal of the chemist's time is taken up with the processes of separation.

THE SPECTROGRAPH [4]

The spectrograph is ideally suited to the analysis of minute quantities of evidentiary materials. A grating spectrograph or an instrument of the Quartz-Littrow type is particularly effective in microanalysis of inorganic substances. Its great sensitivity enables it to show even the slightest impurities—an advantage that is not unmixed with danger unless the results are interpreted against a background of sound training, broad experience, and delicate judgment. Impurities such as trace elements unavoidably or accidentally present in the manufacturer's product often provide the basis for distinguishing among successive runs of the same product. For example, the spectrograph can be used to determine the composition of a small paint stain left on a bicycle frame by a hit-and-run vehicle. If a suspect vehicle is found, the spectroscopist can compare the compositions of both samples of paint and, if the incidence of trace elements permits, he may be able to establish a much closer identity. Similarly, metal fragments found on a file or material found on the blade of a jimmy or on some other tool discovered in a suspect's possession can be compared with specimens taken from tool-

Figure 164.   Technician examining evidence on the grating spectrograph, FBI laboratory.

Figure 165.   Infrared spectrophotometer.

mark areas at the crime scene to establish similarity of composition. Lipstick, rouge, inks, gunpowder traces, glass particles, and other evidentiary traces of an inorganic nature can be analyzed and compared with standards from known sources.

SPECTROPHOTOMETERS

Absorption spectrophotometry as a method of analyzing organic materials has gained increasing favor in recent years with the development of the infrared recording spectrophotometer. Spectrographs employing the ultraviolet end of the spectrum record a picture of the substance in which the constituent molecules are in an excited and abnormal state. The infrared instrument, however, presents a record of the characteristics of the molecular arrangement in relative repose, thus permitting the identification of narcotics, alkaloidal poisons, and other organic substances of complex structure.

The reflecting spectrophotometer is also in use in some police laboratories. Where the basis of an identification or comparison depends primarily on color, this instrument is particularly effective, since it permits the specification of color in the more exact terms of trichromatic coefficients.

X-RAYS

X-rays and the associated techniques of fluoroscopy and radiography have found a number of important applications in criminal investigation. We have already seen the value of X-rays in the examination of suspected bombs. Other uses of X-rays include the testing of metallic parts of machinery in cases of suspected sabotage; the examination of paintings to determine whether the substructure is consistent with other known works of the painter; and searches for hidden objects such as weapons secreted in upholstered furniture or contraband concealed in a locked suitcase. In general, X-radiation is applicable where it is necessary to acquire information about the interior of an opaque container or object. The penetration of a metallic object can be accomplished by means of gamma rays, sources of which have been made available in the form of isotopes such as cobalt-60.

SOFT X-RAYS.[5] The region from 4 to 25 kilovolts is usually referred to as the soft X-ray region. Since the wavelengths of soft X-rays are longer than those of the hard X-rays discussed above, they are less penetrating and by employing the proper technique can be made to

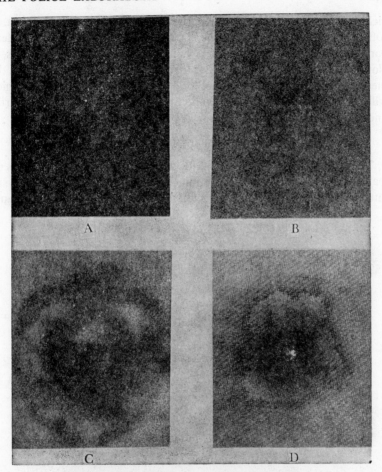

Figure 166. Examination of powder residue. A. Gunshot through sailor's dark-blue middy blouse, as seen by the unaided eye. The unburnt powder particles are revealed only because of the reflected illumination and are not normally visible. B. Contrast and details have been somewhat improved by using process ortho film, making a transparency of this negative on commercial type emulsion, and printing the transparency. C. Contrast and details have been considerably improved by using infrared film (Wratten 87 filter). D. Additional detail may be obtained by means of soft X-rays. (Type M Eastman Kodak film, 12 kv. peak, 50 ma., 20-inch focus-film distance, 5-second exposure.)

yield information concerning the surface and subsurface of an object. A soft X-ray picture will reveal the distribution of lead fouling and lead particles about the entrance of a bullet hole in clothing. Surfaces of cloth, fabrics, paper, and leather can be studied and compared by means of these rays. A radiograph of a painting in the soft X-ray region will provide considerable information about the technique of the artist and will also reveal latent images below the visible surface.

X-RAY DIFFRACTION ANALYSIS

The extremely short wavelength of X-rays permits their use in chemical analysis of crystalline and semiamorphous substances. The crystal lattice or characteristic configuration of the molecules of a substance

Figure 167.   X-ray diffraction unit.

serves to diffract a beam of X-rays, thus producing the same phenomenon as the diffraction of light rays by a grating. By recording the image of a beam of X-rays diffracted by a small, powdered specimen of a clue material, the analyst is able to identify the substance through the characteristics of its crystalline form. Since the method is nondestructive, the evidence sample, however minute, is still preserved. X-ray diffraction has been used in the analysis of a wide variety of clue materials, including poisonous mixtures, narcotics, rubber, glass, dust, soil, clay, ceramics, and safe-lining.

ULTRAVIOLET LIGHT

One of the oldest and best publicized of police laboratory instruments, the ultraviolet lamp owes much of its popularity to the apparent simplicity of its theory and operation as well as to the startling effects which it presents to the layman's eye. The effectiveness of ultraviolet radiation depends upon the fact that the appearance of an object under this light may be quite different from its ordinary appearance. This effect is one of *luminescence,* a general term denoting the absorption of energy by a substance and its re-emission as visible or near-visible radiation. If the emission occurs during excitation, the process is commonly called *fluorescence.* If the emission occurs after excitation has ceased, the process is called *phosphorescence.* Fluorescent effects, then, must be observed in a darkened room with the object under examination a few feet away from the ultraviolet lamp and filter.

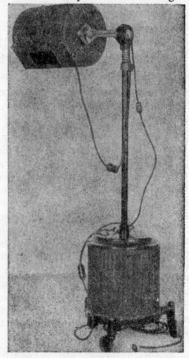

Specimens such as ink writings or paper can be quickly compared under ultraviolet light in this manner. Differences in fluorescence are immediately apparent. Some substances fluoresce, other do not. Among the large number of fluorescent substances there are differences in the color and intensity of the emitted

Figure 168. Hanovia ultraviolet lamp.

light. An altered document can sometimes be detected in this manner. If additions have been made with a different ink, there may be comparable variations in the fluorescence. Erasures may be detected by a disturbance in the fluorescent image.

Some materials, invisible in ordinary light because of a neutral background, become visible under the ultraviolet radiation. Stains such as those of urine or semen can be readily located on cloth. Minute particles of fluorescent powders remain invisible on the hands or garments of a suspect until they are exposed to ultraviolet light. The use of such powders is particularly effective in trapping thieves, since it eliminates the necessity for constant surveillance. With the rapid development of phosphors in recent years powders have now become available which exhibit an afterglow or phosphorescence in a darkened room without the aid of an ultraviolet lamp.

ORDINARY FLUORESCENCE PHENOMENA. Listed below are a number of the more common examinations that can be made under ultraviolet radiation. A lamp such as the Hanovia or the General Electric should be used with suitable filter. Since the wavelength at 3,650 angstroms is especially effective, the filter used cuts off the visible radiation emanating from the lamp a little below 4,000 angstroms. A filter should be available also for the transmission of the 3,130-angstrom wavelength, another rich source of fluorescence.[6]

Questioned documents. If an ink eradicator has been used and the treated part has not been washed in water, it will show up dark under the quartz lamp. Often also the eradicated writing may be read.

Mail thefts and examinations of mail in general. If a paste other than the original has been used to close the envelope the second time, this will often be seen in the ultraviolet light. Gum arabic has no fluorescence, but textiles on the contrary have a very strong one. Sealing waxes which in daylight may look alike may have different fluorescences.

Secret inks. Several secret inks will be visible in ultraviolet light. It is especially useful in detecting the one commonly used in prisons, urine. As mentioned above, the wavelength 3,130 angstroms should also be used in such cases. Modern spies are well aware of the possibility of being discovered by the quartz lamp and after writing with secret inks will often treat the paper with some substance which gives uniform fluorescence to the whole surface. They will also write with a soft paint brush so that there will be no derangement of the fibers on the surface of the paper, as will aways be the case when a pen is used.

Forged bills and stamps. If an authentic and a forged bill or stamp are placed side by side under a quartz lamp, the differences in the paper and dyes used will often be plainly discernible.

Paintings. The painting over and repair of oil paintings can often be seen in ultraviolet light.

Search for stains. Stains on textiles originating from greasy material, semen, etc., which cannot be seen in daylight will often show a strong fluorescence under ultraviolet light. The clothes should be put under the quartz lamp, a sketch made of the article of clothing in question, and the position of the stains marked on the sketch.

Miscellaneous. Gums may show different fluorescences, depending on their purity and origin. Drugs, foodstuff, clothing, etc., may be preliminarily examined by putting a suspected sample side by side with an authentic one under the quartz lamp.

FLUORESCENCE MICROSCOPY.[7] The use of ultraviolet light as a source of illumination for the ordinary microscope is one of the most interesting and recent applications of fluorescence as a testing method.

The applications of fluorescence microscopy to police laboratory work are very numerous. Many microstructures—invisible to the naked eye— become visible by inspection in ultraviolet light under the microscope. The fluorescence microscopy of animal and vegetable tissues has been extensively studied and found to be of prevailing importance in differential analysis. Many poisons present in minimal amounts may also be identified by fluorescence microscopy, e.g., belladonna colchicine, morphine, procaine, quinine, and strychnine. The method may also be of great help in distinguishing between certain kinds of ink.

PHOTOGRAPHY OF FLUORESCENCE PHENOMENA. All visible phenomena of fluorescence can be photographed with an ordinary camera and lens. Since there is a great amount of reflected ultraviolet radiation in addition to the fluorescence, a yellow filter such as the Wratten 2A should be placed over the lens to screen out the excess of blue light. The photography should be performed in a darkened room with the ultraviolet lamp a few feet away from the object. A medium-contrast panchromatic film is used with an exposure varying from a few seconds to a minute, depending on the distance of the lamp, the magnification, and the aperture stop.

REFLECTED ULTRAVIOLET LIGHT.[8] The image formed by the reflected ultraviolet radiation in the invisible region of the spectrum sometimes provides useful information in document examinations such as those involving erasures and sequence of strokes in writing. To eliminate visible rays a filter such as the Wratten 18A should be used over the lens. This filter affords a means of obtaining ultraviolet radiation of a fairly narrow band having its maximum at 3,600 angstroms. Since the ordinary glass lens cuts off most of the ultraviolet radiation, a quartz

Figure 169. Secret writing made visible by ultraviolet light. The paper on the left apparently contains only the message written in black ink, but ultraviolet light brings out the words written in salicylic acid.

lens is better suited to this type of photography. Other filters must be used to obtain the effects of ultraviolet radiation in the shorter regions about 2,750 angstrom line. The choice of filter will depend on the nature of the lamp used. Special emulsions sensitive to the shorter ultraviolet can be obtained in 4 by 5 size from Eastman Kodak Co. The results obtained by the reflected ultraviolet technique rarely justify the effort.

INFRARED LIGHT

At the other side of the spectrum the visible region ends in the red wavelengths at 7,800 angstroms. The invisible infrared region from 8,000 to 9,000 angstroms sometimes proves useful in deciphering illegible inscriptions, such as erasures and obliterations, and in rendering visible markings which are obscured by a dark background. The method depends on the different capacities of dyes and materials for the reflection of infrared rays. Thus, an altered document in which two different inks may have been used will provide an infrared picture showing one ink fainter than the other because of their differing reflectivities in the infrared. Powder residue from a shot fired within a few inches

Figure 170. Infrared photograph reveals contents of suicide note. Picture taken in the FBI laboratory, Washington, D. C.

may not be visible on a black garment; an infrared photograph, however, will reveal a halo of black particles against a lighter background.[9]

The infrared method is most commonly applied photographically. Infrared film, a special emulsion sensitive to this region, is used with a Wratten 87C filter to cut off the visible region. An incandescent light source such as the Photoflood is rich in infrared radiation. Instruments similar to the Snooperscope of World War II have recently been marketed to provide a rapid, visual method of infrared examination. This viewing device converts the infrared rays forming the image of the object under examination into visible wavelengths. It is applicable, also, to nighttime surveillance.

MICROSCOPES

The wide applicability and effectiveness of the microscope in the detection and evaluation of physical evidence have made this instrument a symbol of scientific crime detection. A well-equipped police laboratory will have a variety of microscopes available: hand magnifiers such as the ordinary "magnifying glass," the linen tester, a fingerprint magnifier, and

Figure 171. Apparatus for making a microscopic determination of the melting point. This may be an important factor in analysis.

a magnifier with a built-in light source for latent fingerprint searches; low-power compound microscopes, particularly stereomicroscopes such as the Greenough binocular instrument with magnifications ranging from 7X to about 35X; and high-power microscopes providing magnifications up to 600X. A comparison microscope for firearms and tool mark examinations is desirable.

The versatility of the high-power microscope and its effective application to modern methods of optical analysis cannot be realized without considerable auxiliary equipment. Oil immersion objectives, dark-field condensers, and monochromatic light sources are required for the highest magnification. Special stages, polarizing eyepieces, and other accessories are required for petrographic work as well as for the crystallographic examination that often accompanies an X-ray diffraction analysis. A set of special-purpose oculars should be available, including a filar micrometer eyepiece. Effective illumination, an essential to good microscopy as well as photomicrography, is achieved by a selection of illuminants, condensers, and diaphragms which offer flexible arrangements and can be readily adjusted on stands or aligned on an optical bench.[10]

PHOTOGRAPHIC EQUIPMENT

The camera is the most widely used instrument in the police laboratory.[11] In expert hands it serves to discover new aspects of evidence by means of controlled lighting, special filters and films, or by appropriate magnification. It provides, too, a permanent record of the initial appearance of the evidence and of the significant findings of the laboratory analyst. Finally, the camera enables the expert to present his findings in court through the medium of pictorial exhibits, readily understood by the layman juror and available for scrutiny by the judges and defense counsel.

A reproduction camera with a set of good lenses and an adaptable lighting system is the nucleus of the laboratory's photographic equipment. Since document cases constitute a large part of the laboratory's workload, the arrangement for copy work should provide uniform lighting and correct focus over the whole document area and should insure convenience and ease of operation.

A small camera using 35mm. film can be used for many laboratory purposes, especially if it is equipped with extension tubes, focusing frames, and other accessories.

In the larger laboratory a permanent setup should be provided for photomicrography—and photomacrography as well, since the equipment is to a great extent common to both techniques. For satisfactory work, lenses especially designed for photomicrography should be used, particularly in the regions of low-power magnification where there is a tendency to select lenses solely on the basis of short focal length rather than specific design. A comparison microscope or a bridge eyepiece with matched objectives is a desirable convenience for firearms identification work and tool mark comparisons. A suitable camera arrangement should be associated with this optical system.[12]

CASTING METHODS

Like photography, casting methods play a role in police science. Both serve the same purpose; namely, to preserve the appearance of a thing in an objective way. Both have been subjected to criticism in the courts. For many years the value of photographs as evidence was attacked by defending attorneys on the ground that the lens and plate could not reproduce facts in true fashion. Today the fidelity of the photographic picture is uniformly acknowledged when problems of distances and perspectives have no influence in the matter.

Casting methods, however, are in a quite different position, being often criticized even by criminologists. This criticism is based on the fact that in all casting methods a medium is employed which has countless more sources of error than the rays of light which, assembled through the lens, produce chemical reactions in the photographic plate. It is true that casting methods will not reproduce in faithful fashion under *all* circumstances. All traces should therefore be photographed before the casting is done.

It must also be said that, owing to the development of modern photography, casting methods are not used so much nowadays as before, being chiefly employed for footprints, prints of cloth, prints of teeth, and prints of burglars' tools. Casting methods formerly employed in forensic ballistics have practically disappeared.

Casting methods generally employ plaster of Paris for footprints and prints of cloth, and plastelina for tooth prints and prints of burglars' tools. In recent years the casting materials used by dentists have been useful in special cases.

In the different chapters on tooth prints, footprints, and prints of burglars' tools we deal with the employment of plaster. In this chapter we shall chiefly discuss the moulage method.

THE MOULAGE METHOD. In this method at least two materials are used, namely, one for the negative casts and one for the positive. A third reinforcing material may be used in order to support the brittle cast.

The negative materials are generally semi-elastic substances. They come in small lumps and must be heated in enamelware before the casting process. They should be brought to a temperature of approximately 100° C. (212°F.). If possible, a double boiler should be used, but if necessary the material can be heated directly over the flame. In this case it should be stirred gently to avoid burning. On the other hand, the stirring should not be excessive, as the mass will become "dead" and useless. The negative material, even if kept in airtight containers, will eventually lose water and become too thick. When purchased, it is of the proper consistency, and the addition of water will preserve it in its natural state. At any rate, there is no harm in putting a half or a whole cupful of water to each pound when heating it. Some of the negative materials may be heated at least a hundred times before losing their elasticity and may be used a few hundred times if carefully heated.

As soon as the positive form has been made the negative material should be cut in small pieces and ground in a common meat grinder. When the negative mass is even and fairly thin, it is spread with a common paintbrush over the surface which is to be reproduced. The spreading is the most difficult part of the operation. The mass begins to congeal rather soon, and when this occurs it does not adhere to the fresh layer. The spreading must therefore proceed rapidly so as to prevent the layers from congealing. At the same time air bubbles must be avoided. The proper application of these substances calls for a great deal of experience.

In most cases it is not necessary to prepare the surface of the trace except when dealing with wood and porous materials, such as fabric or felt. The trace on wood should be painted with a solution of paraffin and benzene. With the evaporation of the benzene a very fine film of paraffin covers the wood, preventing the negative material from sticking. Porous materials must be soaked with water to prevent the loss of water from the negative material and the lessening of its elasticity and binding properties. Without this soaking the material would adhere to the negative mass.

The coat of the negative mass should be at least half an inch thick. Larger casts require reinforcement. This can be made of pieces of soft brass wire inserted into the mass while it is being spread; or pieces of gauze soaked with plaster of Paris can be placed on top of the cast and allowed to dry before the cast is taken off.

The negative cast is carefully lifted from the trace and the positive material applied as soon as possible. Long-distance transportation should be avoided. The cast must be kept moist. In dry air it commences to dry after one or two hours. If it is to be kept for some time it should be placed in a container filled with water or surrounded by wet towels.

The positive casting material is generally marketed in large prisms of different colors. It should be melted in an enamel pan directly over the fire. The melting point is between 120° and 150° C. (say, 275° F.). Common brushes cannot be used for stirring or spreading: the strong heat would destroy them. A special brush made of so-called "Chinese hair," capable of withstanding high temperatures, should be used.

The positive mass is spread over the negative in a layer not thicker than one tenth of an inch. It hardens immediately. Before the spreading, if there are air bubbles in the negative cast they should be filled with a special "correction" paste. The second layer of positive material should be reinforced with gauze. This is placed on the first layer and soaked with the aid of a brush. The whole surface must be covered with this soaked gauze. Three or four layers of soaked gauze are applied. This is followed by the final reinforcement.

The reinforcement materials in the market generally have a melting point of over 300° F. They are melted in the same manner as the positive material. Gauze is also used for reinforcement.

The disadvantage of this method lies in the fact that the substances must be melted and that a certain amount of time is required.

In recent years the moulage method has chiefly been used for making casts of the heads of unknown dead, when the case seems to warrant such a procedure.

The field outfit for making moulages should consist of a Thermos bottle containing liquid negative mass, a small enamel pan for heating the positive material, a small lamp, positive material, gauze, and two brushes, one for the negative and the other for the positive mass.

When the moulage method is used to make casts of the heads of living and dead persons, it is recommended that casts of living persons be made at first to gain practical experience. About two pounds of negative material will suffice to make a cast of an adult's face extending back to the ears. It is also possible to make a cast of the entire head, in separate parts, which are later molded together. On the living person the negative material should not be applied at temperatures higher than about 120° F. A thermometer should be the guide. It is possible to make a cast of a living person with his eyes open, although a great deal of experience is necessary. The negative mass is applied so as to surround both eyes. With the aid of artificial eyes a positive cast of the eyes is then molded in the eye-sockets of the negative cast. Usually, however, casts of living persons are made with the eyes closed. The only precaution necessary is to allow the person to breathe freely by leaving an opening for each nostril. The negative mass should be applied quickly with a thick brush, and the layer should be at least one inch thick. Reinforcements are made with plaster-coated gauze, which is placed on the surface of the cast, forming a "basket."

When making casts of the faces of dead bodies, the temperature of the negative mass may be higher, although, especially in the cases of floaters, too much heat may loosen the skin and cause it to adhere to the cast.

The natural appearance of the face and its vivid expression may be better brought out by painting it in natural colors. With the aid of water colors or oil pigments any artist may easily accomplish this feat. If the face is deformed, positive material or plaster may be used to correct the deformities, but some artistic talent is required.

COLLECTIONS FOR COMPARISON PURPOSES

Some types of work in the police laboratory require complete collections of different specimens for comparison purposes. Such collections range, for instance, from laundry marks to typewriter writings to samples of soil. The success of such a collection is entirely dependent upon (1) its completeness and (2) its classification. The classification is sometimes very obvious; for instance, typewriting is classified according to the year when the type was first put on the market and samples of soil as to the geologic provenance. In other cases the classification may be more complicated, as, for instance, tires. The following is a list of the most common collections.

Typewriting	Laundry marks	Soils	Drugs
Watermarks on paper	Matches	Firearms	Rubber soles and heels
Munitions	Powders	Automobile head-	
	Cigarettes	light lenses	Animal and human
Textile fibers	Inks	Paper	hairs

Each specimen should be carefully marked with provenance and year of manufacture, as well as other dates of interest.

At present the FBI laboratory in Washington, D.C., has certainly the largest collection of this kind in the country.

Figure 172.   Photographic Unit of the New York Police Department.

EQUIPMENT FOR A SMALL POLICE LABORATORY

The choice of equipment must be made in accordance with the size of the department and funds available. For a medium-sized department the following suggestions are given:

One 5-by-7-inch all-round reproduction camera with stand for reproduction and a stable tripod.

A set of spotlights for illumination.

A complete set of filters.

A miniature camera using 35mm. film, with copying attachments and fixed-focus reproduction arrangement.

An enlarger for smaller film sizes.

An enlarger accepting 5-by-7-inch and 4-by-5-inch film.

A 16mm. motion picture projector.

A microscope for general work with three parfocal objectives.

A low-power binocular miscroscope.

Microscope accessories such as a filar micrometer eyepiece, a stage micrometer, eyepieces for photomicrography, and illuminants.

A photomicrographic camera.

An ultraviolet lamp.

A fingerprint outfit.

A fingerprint camera.
Casting materials (moulage and plaster of Paris).
Draftman's instruments.
Measuring devices such as tape measures and micrometer calipers.
Darkroom equipment for developing and printing.
Equipment for biological work and for the preparation of specimens for microscopic examination.
Equipment for a small chemical laboratory.
Equipment for the construction, maintenance, and repair of apparatus.

PORTABLE OUTFIT

A portable outfit should be available for the examination of crime scenes and the collection of evidence. A small law enforcement unit will, for example, have a basic kit which will include a fingerprint outfit, flashlights, a hand magnifier, a tape measure, a folding rule, and appropriate tools.

Organizations whose duties include the investigation of homicides in rural districts should be more fully equipped than the detectives of a large urban police department, where the resources of specialized units are always available. The following list of equipment is suggested for a police agency working in rural areas. The equipment is divided into a photographic outfit and a technical outfit for sketching, measuring, searching, casting, elementary testing, and the collection and preservation of evidence.

Photographic Outfit. A 5-by-7-inch view camera with three lenses as described in Chapter VIII; black-and-white film and color film; photoflood lamps and flash equipment; filters, tripod, meter, and other accessories; a fixed-focus fingerprint camera.

Technical Outfit. Self-illuminated sketchboard; compass; tape measure and folding rule; pencils, chalk, and crayon; graph paper—rectangular and polar coordinates types; level; fingerprint development kit; fingerprint recording kit; footprint kit (see pp. 167-168); two dozen tests tubes; small test-tube stand; hand magnifier; biology kit; set of tools (screwdriver, saw, hammer, pliers, cutters, wood chisel, steel jimmy, knives, tweezers, forceps, compass saw, and files); rubber gloves; rubber policemen and eyedroppers; blood-testing reagents; saline solution; litmus paper; filter paper; pillboxes, transparent envelopes, and other containers for evidence; plastelina; plaster of Paris unit (to be stored separately).

Mobile Laboratory Unit. In a large city prompt response to the crime scene requires one or more mobile units. The equipment for this purpose is usually transported in a small truck or a station wagon.

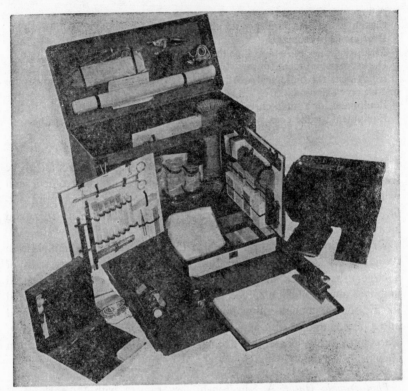

Figure 173. Portable kit for detecting and collecting evidence.

The mobile units of the New York Police Laboratory contain the following equipment:

Photographic equipment: 4-by-5 press camera, 8-by-10 view camera, fingerprint camera, and camera for 35mm. film; photoflash units, photoflood lamps and voltage regulator, light meter, and set of filters; black-and-white film and color film.

Portable X-ray unit; fluoroscope viewer, cassettes, and X-ray film; lead-lined gloves and apron, lead-lined protective screen with built-in fluoroscope; 110-volt A.C. generator, gasoline-driven, (supplies power for X-ray unit and floodlights); survey meter and Geiger counter for detection of gamma and beta radiation, dosimeters, and film badges.

Ultraviolet lamp.

Permanent magnet retrieving arm, Alnico type.

General Kit. Tweezers; forceps; scalpels; spatulas; scissors; needles; filter paper; acetic acid; saline solution; benzidine; known blood samples; finger-

Figure 174.   Police Laboratory mobile unit.

print powders and equipment; lifting tape; test tubes and rack; pill boxes, square boxes, and envelopes for holding samples of evidence.

Plaster-Casting Kit. Including shellac or sprayer and casting materials such as plaster, Hominit, Celerit, Plastico, paraffin, plastelina, plastic gun and foot-casting form and face-casting form, vacuum cleaner and filters (for collecting dust).

General Supplies. Various size test tubes, dropper, bottles, litmus paper, medicine droppers, tongue depressors, specimen bottles, tissue-building kit, iodine-fuming kit, rubber gloves, lens tissues, etc. Complete set of workman's tools, including saws, screwdrivers, hammer, rule measures, pliers, chisels, files, drills, crowbar, wrenches, etc.

1 John J. O'Connell, former chief inspector of the Police Department of the City of New York, was born in 1884 and died in 1947. After finishing college, he entered the New York police in 1905 as a patrolman and held practically all positions in the department, including that of first-grade detective, from 1911 to 1920. In 1929, having attained the top position on the eligible list for captain, he became a deputy inspector, rising subsequently to the highest position on the force, the chief inspectorship, in 1942. O'Connell was known as one of the most brilliant and experienced policemen in the United States, his chief achievements being connected with the education of New York policemen. From 1930 to 1942 he was in charge of the New York Police Academy and from 1933 to 1942 was also in charge of the technical research laboratory, one of the first of its kind in the United States, which he built up in collaboration with the co-author of this book. In the dry words of a recommendation from the Police Department in 1933 he was cited as follows: "For the creation and adoption by the Department, in cooperation with the Board

of Education, the parochial school systems and other public and private service organizations, of unique, practical and scientific methods of police technique in safety education, accident and crime prevention and crime detection, thereby the efficiency of police work was enhanced and official relations promoted."

2 Dr. Harry Söderman, the eminent Swedish criminologist, died on March 16, 1956, in Tangier, at the age of 53. Born in Stockholm, he received his early schooling in northern Sweden. He studied chemistry in Germany and France, receiving a degree of doctor of science from the University of Lyons after working as an assistant under the famed Edmond Locard. Söderman's career in law enforcement was notable for his contributions to the literature of police science as well as for his active work in the development of police administration and the application of scientific methods to the investigation of the numerous cases on which he was consulted. Widely traveled, fluent in several languages, and professionally acquainted with the leading criminologists of Europe, Söderman was well suited to become a moving force in the International Criminal Police Commission and to serve as an adviser in the reorganization of a number of police departments. In the United States his ideas on investigative training were communicated mainly through the present book, which was an outcome of a fruitful collaboration with Chief Inspector John J. O'Connell. In Sweden Dr. Söderman was the founder and later the Chief Director of the Swedish National Institute of Technical Police. Throughout his career he remained active in the work of Interpol, serving initially as Technical Adviser and later as Reporter General.

3 The *Journal of Criminal Law and Criminology* is the best source of original articles on laboratory methods and techniques. *Fingerprint and Identification Magazine,* in addition to its special studies of dactyloscopy, carries many articles of interest to laboratory personnel and field investigators. The *Journal of Forensic Sciences,* although primarily a medico-legal publication, contains special sections devoted to police laboratory work. The journal *Police* covers a wide range of law enforcement topics which usually includes several articles of interest to the scientific investigator. The *FBI Law Enforcement Bulletin* and the numerous pamphlets on different aspects of the FBI laboratory issued by the Federal Bureau of Investigation are helpful in explaining the laboratory services which the FBI makes available to other law enforcement agencies. In the areas of fingerprint identification, plaster casting, crime-scene photography, and similar elementary techniques, these publications are of special value to police officers in smaller communities. *Chemical Abstracts* will be found to treat criminalistics under a number of headings. To keep abreast of developments in police laboratory work both here and abroad, and new methods which may be applied to the field of criminalistics, the police scientist will find *Chemical Abstracts* invaluable. Other scientific abstracting services and periodical indexes will also be found helpful.

4 The use of the spectrograph in the service of police science dates from the early years of this century, when it was applied by R. W. Wood to actual criminal case work. In the twenties, E. Bayle, head of the Paris police laboratory, worked with it, and in 1927 H. Söderman,[5] then associated with the police laboratory of Lyons, published the results of his spectrographic analysis of powder residues.

5 Pavlovsky lists a number of uses of grenz rays. See also Hours–Miédan and Eastman Kodak.[5, 6]

6 See Bäckstrom and the Eastman Kodak Data Book, *Wratten Filters.*

7 Radley–Grant, Haitinger, and De Menthe.

8 See Langenbruch.

9 For further information about the use of infrared radiation in criminology see Clark and Hours-Miédan.

10 The books on the subject by Allen and Shillaber are recommended.

11 For laboratory work there are some especially useful books published by Eastman Kodak [1, 3, and 5]. Also recommended are Radley,[2] Scott, Clerc, and Neblette.

12 For the study of photomicrography the textbooks of the following are recommended: Hind–Randles, Barnard–Welch, Eastman Kodak,[4] and Shillaber.

XXVIII SOME PROBLEMS OF THE
UNIFORMED POLICE

It is difficult to tell exactly where the work of the detectives ends and the work of the uniformed police begins. The two branches overlap considerably. In theory and practice both are peace officers, and the duty of both categories is to protect life and property and to maintain order. Thus a detective should have a working knowledge of the functions and governing principles of the uniformed police force, as he will quite often be called upon to cooperate with them. In this chapter it is our intention to outline those duties of the uniformed police in which cooperation with the plain-clothes man is essential.[1]

HANDLING OF CROWDS

A crowd is possessed of a dormant power that has an inestimable potential for destruction. A slight spark may explode this destructive power into action. An excited, panic-stricken mob is like a tornado, which forms only under certain atmospheric conditions. To change the simile, crowds are also similar to a flock of sheep: They will follow a leader aimlessly, but without a leader they become individuals endowed with a sole purpose—self-preservation. A fire, an accident, even a sudden, unexpected shower or squall may transform a happy, cheerful group into a selfish, frantic mob.

The foremost considerations in handling crowds are the rights and interests of the great majority; the safety of life and property and the convenience of the participants, spectators, business people, and residents; and the preservation of order in the vicinity.

In preparing for functions at which crowds of people can be expected to gather, extensive surveys of the territory should be made and diagrams prepared showing the location of fire-alarm boxes, telephones, etc. In making such surveys special consideration should be given to the physical and functional aspects of buildings and business concerns in the vicinity, so that police details may be properly assigned.

Adequate police protection must be provided at all times for both "the crowds and the crowded." Each and every crowd, large or small, presents a specific police problem, depending upon its location and character.

In policing crowds the general procedures outlined below should be followed:

Preparation:

Responsibility of command must be placed. Surveys and diagrams of the locale should be made, including, among other things, the following:

1. Entrances and exits—if an enclosure
2. Principal traffic and intersecting streets
3. Railroad, subway, and El stations in the vicinity
4. Construction of buildings adjoining and adjacent
5. Parking spaces, taxicab and bus stands
6. The location of police and fire-alarm boxes and public telephones
7. Street-car lines, ambulance streets, and fire-run streets

Other factors which must be considered include:

1. Information as to the nature and purpose of the crowd or assembly
2. Whether trouble in the nature of riots or disorder is anticipated
3. Facilitation of traffic
4. Protection against fire, accidents, storms, hazards, etc.
5. Prevention of operation by ticket speculators, beggars, panhandlers, peddlers, pickpockets, etc.

Cooperation:

Cooperation of public and private service corporations such as the following should be sought as needed:

1. Railway and bus companies
2. Fire department
3. Department of hospitals for ambulances and surgeons
4. Department of sanitation for cleaning of streets and removal of encumbrances
5. Public utilities
6. Any other organizations the circumstances may require, such as Federal police agencies

Policing the Scene:

Instructions should be given members of the assigned force beforehand if time and circumstances permit. The instructions should include general information as to the nature and purpose of the gathering.

Assignments:

Assignments must be allotted and orders given in advance. These assignments should include:

1. A general headquarters, in direct communication with the telegraph bureau
2. Sector headquarters at points within the designated zones, in communication with general headquarters
3. Reserves at strategic points, including foot, mounted, motorcycle, and police emergency wagons
4. Special assignments to cover:
   a. General policing
   b. Traffic streets, street cars, and ambulance streets
   c. Parking, bus, and hack stands
   d. Subway and El stations, to prevent congestion
   e. The speaker's stand, entrances to and exits from enclosures, aisles, galleries, and platform-entrance area
   f. Special hazards, such as excavations, building material, explosives or inflammables in vicinity, including gas stations, entrances to and exits from buildings, roofs of buildings in area, etc.
   g. If meeting and conditions warrant it, stenographers to make notes
   h. Detectives and plain-clothes men to mingle with the crowd
   i. Men skilled in the use of emergency equipment, stationed at tactical points

Transportation:

Transportation must be available for assembling additional forces in case of emergency. Designated wagons should be given specific assignments for transporting additional men from designated points if the need arises. Radio and patrol cars should be on call.

Communication Lines:

Communication lines should be maintained between headquarters and the various units, including:

1. Telephone, teletype
2. Radio
3. Liaison officers on motorcycles
4. Foot messengers
5. Motor vehicles and airplanes equipped with radio

Special Problems:

Special emergencies that may arise and should be provided for include:

1. First aid to, removal of, and establishment of identity of persons accidentally or otherwise killed or injured
2. Arrest of, and collection of evidence against, law-breakers
3. Lost children and missing persons
4. Frantic and hysterical persons seeking children, relatives
5. Thievery in adjacent premises or on the streets

THE HANDLING OF PARADES AND LARGE
PUBLIC MEETINGS IN NEW YORK

In New York City there is a special Parade Board consisting of the Chief Inspector, the Assistant Chief Inspector of the borough concerned, and the commander of the Safety (formerly Traffic) Division. The Assistant Chief Inspector of the borough and the commander of the Traffic Division have direct charge of police preparations for the parade.

The traffic inspector in charge of the borough concerned must go over the route of the parade at least twenty-four hours in advance and report conditions and locations requiring special police attention. The route of the parade is divided into "parade sectors," specified areas bounded by designated streets and railroad terminals, Els, and subway stations within one block of either side of the route of parade.

Each parade sector has a commanding officer, who must establish headquarters within his sector and notify the Telegraph Bureau of the borough of the location of his headquarters and its telephone number. He must also notify the Telegraph Bureau when the parade enters and leaves his sector. The commanding officer of the sector is responsible for assigning patrolmen to railroad terminals, Els, and subway stations within the sector whenever such action is necessary; for excluding all vehicular traffic from the route of the parade when notified to do so by the motorcycle detail; for keeping all cross-streets except those designated as traffic streets clear of cars and other vehicles within one block of either side of the line of march; and for seeing that fire apparatus are only permitted on fire-run streets, ambulances only on ambulance-run streets, and buses and surface cars only on streets designated for traffic. He must also be sure that the number of spectators does not exceed the sidewalk capacity, and when he judges that the sidewalk is becoming overcrowded must assign one or more of his details to intersections of cross-streets one block from either side of the line of march with instructions to divert all pedestrian traffic from these streets. This is continued until the sidewalk congestion along the line of march is relieved.

The commanding officer of the Traffic Division is responsible for the policing of all intersections along his sector of the route of the parade and all intersections within one block on either side of the route. The commanding officers of precincts along the route and at formation and dismissal points of the parade are responsible for preventing the parking of vehicles along the route sufficiently in advance of the time of the parade.

(At large parades parking is not permitted within one block of either side of the line of march.)

Whenever possible, the same inspectors and captains should have charge of the same sector of the line of march of parades regardless of the division to which they are attached.

Spectators are not permitted to stand within one hundred feet of inter-section corners nor to congregate on the sidewalks of side streets crossing the parade route but are kept to the sidewalks along the line of march.

Figure 175.   Use of wooden barriers on Fifth Avenue, New York, at Saint Patrick's Day parade.

They are not allowed to gather on building excavations nor to climb on buildings under construction, fire-escapes, subway kiosks, trees, or other such things, and are not permitted to stand on barrels, boxes, or other portable stands during the time of the parade. No person is allowed to approach within one hundred feet of the route of the parade, and spec-tators and pedestrians who attempt to trail along behind or alongside the marches are removed from the line of march at the first intersection. The sale of programs, flags, etc., is prohibited within police lines.

Patrolmen assigned to the periphery of the line of march must face the spectators. Enough policemen are assigned to take places on the sidewalk behind the spectators to assist pedestrians who wish to pass through and to prevent pushing and shoving, which may endanger or break the police lines. Sufficient space is kept clear along the house lines to permit free entrance to and exit from buildings and to provide passageway for pedestrians who may decide to leave the line of march.

At large public meetings or parades a sufficient area (about fifty square feet) is kept clear at the immediate entrance to the hall or stand to permit the free and unobstructed entrance and departure of distinguished per-

Figure 176. An example of perfect order. President Truman addressing one million people in Central Park, New York.

sonages. This restricted area is flanked on three sides by closely aligned uniformed patrolmen and no one, except the personal bodyguard of the distinguished personage, police officials, or assigned detectives, is allowed within the area until after the arrival or departure of the distinguished person. Motorcycle escorts assigned to accompany distinguished personages must identify each vehicle used by the party to the commanding officer of the restricted area at the entrance of the hall or stand. Part of the escort forms a rear guard, whose duties are to afford necessary protection, to prevent other vehicles from breaking in on the party, and, when entering the police lines, to notify the officer in immediate command that the vehicles of the official party have entered. On arriving at the restricted area, the escort requests the guests to remain in their cars until they are inside the police lines flanking the restricted area. Only one vehicle at a time is permitted in this area to discharge or take on passengers. Inside the hall or stand an inspector and a detail of policemen maintain an unbroken passageway from the entrance to the stage or seats to be occupied by the official party. No other persons are permitted in this passage except detectives or especially assigned Secret Service men.

At large public meetings and at the official stand at parades, press cards, shields, etc., are not accepted as identification for admittance to police lines. Reporters, policemen in civilian clothes, etc., must show evidence from those in authority that they are assigned to the specific event.

FRANCE

It may be of interest to give a short survey of how the French police handle the problem of parades and visiting distinguished personages and their security.[2]

The French police handling parades are divided into two groups: the police of order and the police of security. The police of order at such occasions consist of troops, gendarmes, and uniformed policemen. These are assigned to the periphery of the line of march and face the paraders, with their backs to the spectators. The police of security are divided into two categories. One of these is in uniform and is entrusted with the task of keeping order among the spectators. They face the spectators, with their backs toward the parade or cortège. One man out of every five, however, turns his face to the parade when it passes. The other category of the police of security consists of plain-clothes men who mix with the crowd.

Among the preventive measures taken, the tailing of any suspect for some time beforehand plays an important role. The suspected individual is either continuously tailed or taken into custody for the time necessary. For this latter measure a prefectorial warrant is needed. All places to be visited by the distinguished visitor and his attendants are thoroughly searched in advance by official architects, fire marshals, and other appropriate experts. The hotels in which the distinguished person or persons will stay are especially searched, particularly the basement, and are put under round-the-clock surveillance.

The tenants of the apartments facing the route of the cortège are warned against receiving unknown persons and are told that if they do so, it will be on their own responsibility and at the risk of being prosecuted for aiding and abetting. Inquiries are made as to the persons who will serve the distinguished visitor or his attendants (head waiters, waiters, maids, bellboys, drivers, florists, etc.). All gifts, flowers, parcels, etc., arriving for the distinguished personage are closely examined. Under no circumstances may a letter, flowers, or a gift of any kind be given directly to the distinguished visitor.

Offensive writing on walls or signs placed in windows are immediately removed by the police.

The measures for traffic control and the dividing of the route of the parade into sectors, each with responsible officers, are very similar to those used in the United States. Armed policemen are also placed on the roofs of the houses along the route of the cortège. For days before the cortège or the arrival of the distinguished person all trains and cars are closely watched.

ASSASSINATIONS

The French police have studied about one hundred attempted assassinations of sovereigns, heads of states, ministers, and other distinguished persons during the last eighty years. The conclusions to be drawn from the analyses are that the attacks have generally been attempted outside of buildings or at stopping points along the route of the cortège and that the weapon used has in most cases been a revolver, pistol, or submachine gun.

Points at which distinguished personalities have been killed in most cases have been on stairways leading into buildings, on sidewalks while taking leave, at traffic stops, or when entering or leaving cars. The traffic stops were caused either by some flaw in the traffic organization, by an act of the criminal, or by an official act (cortège stopping to receive military honors, etc.). It follows that every stop constitutes a danger point.

Statistics of 104 attacks on important personalities in the last hundred years in the United States, Latin America, and Europe show that the following weapons were used: revolvers and automatic pistols, 68; explosives, 18; stabbing, 12; rifles, 5; poison, 1.

Political assassinations are always planned far in advance, and the criminal will place himself in a convenient position quite a while before the passing of the cortège.

From what has been said above it will be clear that political assassinations as a rule are carried out in the following way: (1) They are planned a long time in advance, (2) the place of attack is generally outside a building when (3) a momentary stop occurs, and (4) the criminal will generally use a small arm.

CONTROL OF RIOTS

IMMEDIATE CAUSES OF RIOTS. A riot may be defined as a large assemblage of persons whose concerted action for an unlawful purpose lead to violence and disorder. The causes of riots are many and varied. Social conditions such as widespread unemployment, poor housing, and limited educational and recreational facilities may be underlying sources of a disturbance that appears to have begun with a simple altercation. A riot may be incited by the desire of a group to accelerate the processes of justice. In wartime the possibility of a riot as a form of sabotage must be carefully investigated. Subversive propaganda is spread among alien groups. In areas of heterogeneous population racial discrimination is urged by this type of saboteur as a motive for disorderly demonstrations. Religious minorities may also be the victims of these propaganda campaigns. Labor troubles leading to widespread strikes and extensive picketing are a fruitful source of disorder. Looting following a catastrophe such as a hurricane, flood, fire, or even an air raid or civil disturbance may lead to mob violence.

A disorderly assemblage may, for our purposes, be divided into three groups: the active ringleaders, the active members of the assemblage, and the passive onlookers. The ringleaders may consist of paid propagandists, professional labor agitators, fifth-columnists, or simply a few citizens more spirited and determined than the rest. If the group of leaders is intelligently organized, it will be found that they circulate throughout the assemblage urging on the more passive members and constantly encouraging acts of violence. The active members of the assemblage are not necessarily of the criminal element but are usually normal citizens who have been psychologically disturbed. To the unbalanced mentality of the mob mind, the riot is a worthy demonstration against manifestly unjust conditions. If this mental condition is fully understood by the police, it will guide their actions in restoring the crowd to normalcy.

It must be remembered that the active participants form only a small section of the mob. By far the majority of a disorderly crowd consists of passive onlookers whose presence is due to curiosity and a desire to witness trouble. The aim of the ringleaders is to infuse this element with the mob spirit and to whip it into a homogeneous mass blindly obeying their lawless urgings. Conscious personality disappears, and the subconscious mind, highly susceptible to suggestion, comes to the fore and rules the actions of the crowd.

With the collective mind of the crowd in this highly sensitive state, suggested ideas are easily transformed into action. One rash and violent gesture may be the catalytic agent which will turn a restless crowd into a fearsome mob, eager for violence. It is important for the police, at this threshold stage, to refrain from the indiscriminate use of force. The ringleaders may place women and children in the front of the crowd to taunt the police with jeers and abuse. If the police respond with force, the delicate balance may be disturbed and the crowd will become a rebellious, lawless mob.

THE PSYCHOLOGY OF THE MOB. A sound knowledge of the mob mentality is essential to any effort at riot control. It is a mistake on the part of police officers to look on the mob as a homogeneous group of lawless troublemakers and to employ force indiscriminately. Such an attitude reduces the forces of law and order to the status of another mob opposing the first with equal viciousness and lack of discrimination. As in other forms of police work, a scientific approach must be brought to the study of crowd control.

TACTICAL METHODS. A fundamental error in the control of riots is the dependence on sheer weight of numbers. The concept of overwhelming an unlawful assemblage by pouring into the area large numbers of patrolmen and detectives, without plan or organization, has led in the past to unnecessary violence. Such methods succeed only in arousing resentment on the part of the rioters and in sowing the seeds of further disorders by supplying the propagandists with grievances for future use. Unnecessary injuries to the public and to the police occur from intemperate and unplanned use of force. Police authorities should keep in mind that their aim is not to subdue a mass of people but to correct a condition. The confidence of the public is essential to this task. This aim can be achieved by the police authorities only if they have fully anticipated occurrences of this nature in carefully detailed plans. The following may be considered the cardinal principles in the control of riots:

1. Possession of a specific plan of action
2. Rapidity of its execution
3. Firmness in its prosecution

A plan for the control of riots will follow, in general, standard military tactical principles. Festering spots for civil disturbances should be clearly marked on the maps of a central bureau of operations. These areas will usually include sections where heterogeneity of population may give rise to troublesome issues or where subversive political philosophies and racial or religious propaganda are most likely to find adherents. Superior officers in these areas should be instructed to notify headquarters immediately of incidents likely to create mob disorders.

At headquarters danger spots should be mapped strategically into zones and the zones marked off in accordance with the precinct conventions as regards sectors and posts. The plan should be detailed in regard to the number of men necessary to control a potential riot. Strategic spots and controlling points should be marked off and directions given for the assembly of men at these points. The sources from which reserve forces are to be moved must be carefully selected.

As soon as definite information is received concerning the incipient riot, the machinery of mobilization must be set in action immediately. All officers of the rank of captain and above should be notified to report for duty, and members of the force off duty should be notified to report to the affected zones forthwith. Trucks and patrol wagons should be dispatched for the transportation of reserves. Two-way radio cars and trucks equipped with loudspeakers should proceed to strategic points and mounted patrolmen should be moved into the zone. The precincts should be notified to assemble at the station house the required number of reserves.

At the scene of the riot the officer in command should have a situation map of the affected area, showing the location of major industrial establishments, armories, storage places for munitions, hospitals, organizations that might foster a civil disturbance, public utility installations, jewelry and liquor stores, and societies representing law and order.

Before deploying his forces, the commanding officer should first assign trustworthy subordinates to report on the number of rioters, their state of mind, the location of ringleaders and dangerous nuclei, and the direction of motion and the intent of the mob. (This reconnaissance force should not be disbanded after the preliminary survey but maintained intact for further such duties.) When he has the results of this survey, the commanding officer is then in a position to make decisions concerning the disposition of available forces and the necessity for reserves. Field headquarters are set up at a strategic spot, not too far from the center of disorder, and equipped with all communication facilities: telephone, short-wave radio, motorcycle messenger, and a two-way radio car.

Mobilization of the patrol force will usually take place at a station house and the force be transported by truck or patrol wagon to the scene. Detrucking should take place at some distance from the scene so that the force will not be surrounded and overwhelmed. In marching through crowded streets close formations should be avoided. Platoon wedge formations should be used.

It is beyond the scope of this chapter to describe the various military formations that are suited for dispersing crowds in narrow streets, wide streets, open areas, and other terrain. Police officers are referred to FM 19–15 Basic Field Manual, Infantry Drill Regulations, on Domestic and Civil Disturbance of the U. S. Army, where an exhaustive treatment will be found.

A critical phase in the dispersal of crowds is the first contact. A disorderly assembly should be treated as a crowd, not a mob, until actual physical violence is met. Superior officers should first order the crowd to disperse. No bluffing should be used. Any threats made must be fulfilled by action to maintain the respect and fear of the crowd. Members of the police force must be instructed to use only as much force as is needed and should not engage in any discussion with civilians. In the case of strikes and other factional disputes, a completely neutral attitude must be maintained. If the crowd fails to obey the order of dispersal, the commanding officer must take decisive action. Surprise is now his greatest weapon; hesitation is his chief enemy. If the mob is not too deep, an attack from the front using the platoon wedge is the best tactic. In the case of a wide street a double platoon wedge is necessary. Mounted patrolmen are useful at this stage.

When the mob is quite deep, an attack on the flank, rear, or both sides is advisable. The rear is usually made up of spectators and lukewarm supporters of the mob, and on being confronted with a rear attack they will give way immediately and take flight. Just as the spirit of violence is contagious in crowds, so also is the feeling of fear. Flight will usually suggest the same procedure to immediate neighbors and spread confusion and demoralization. The attack should not be made on more than two sides because of the danger of panic when the crowd feels itself surrounded. Once the crowd is broken up, it should be kept moving. Units should be placed in the rear to prevent reorganization. These rear patrols will also serve to protect the main force from a flanking movement on the part of the crowd.

Lesser disorders in the vicinity of the riot may be quelled by small detachments of not less than five men. The size of detachments will naturally be governed by the available supply of men and also by the necessity of maintaining a reserve. This reserve must not be tapped except in extreme need and should then be replaced as soon as possible.

Traffic regulation throughout a riot should be an integral part of the control plan. The situation map should show clearly the location of all main arteries and bus, street-car, subway, elevated, and other railroad lines. The judgment of the commanding officer must be used in determining which streets are to be closed off and which transportation lines are to be stopped. Guards, signs, or wooden barriers properly marked must be placed at the entrance of all streets leading to the closed-off area. Plans for the diversion of traffic should then be put into operation.

The commanding officer should not rely with blind faith upon the preconceived plans. The results of active reconnaissance and intelligence work should supplement his existing knowledge. The intelligence force should be composed mainly of detectives, distributed throughout the mob to report plans of the ringleaders to the commanding officer. This police function is quite important, because without the evidence of unlawful intent, subsequent proof of guilt will be extremely difficult.

Plans for seizing the ringleaders should center around the detectives. A group of six or more can usually surround a leader and hurry him out of the crowd. If resistance is met, a squad wedge should be brought into action at double time.

INDIVIDUAL PROBLEMS

Many varied problems arise in the control of riots because of the individual character of the persons involved or the area in which the disorder takes place. The tactics used will vary considerably with the nature of the problem. A few of these situations will be discussed briefly.

OUTBREAKS IN PRISONS OR PRISON CAMPS. In this situation plans for the suppression of a riot should be put into effect with all possible speed. Because of the disparity between the number of guards and the number of prisoners, any appearance of loss of control will be disastrous. A firm hand must be shown from the start, and complete control must be demonstrated by the operation of a carefully conceived plan. In prison riots it is possible to devise plans anticipating in detail almost any emergency. Frequent drills are feasible and advisable.

RACE RIOTS. These are usually aimed not only at personal injury but at destruction or removal of property. A serious problem of looting arises from such disturbances. After tornadoes and floods, the practice of the military has been to shoot looters on sight. In race riots, however, most participants are swayed by emotion rather than desire for material gain.

Show windows will be shattered, merchandise will be damaged or scattered, and some members of the mob will seize all valuables within reach. As in other riots, mob suggestion will urge the rest of the crowd to follow the leaders and widespread looting will follow. Obviously, in these situations the proper remedy is not indiscriminate shooting of all persons carrying merchandise. Many normally honest citizens will be thus injured and the condition that gave rise to the rioting will be aggravated.

One plan for preventing looting is to assign detachments to key points on the periphery of the looted area. All persons emerging from the streets with merchandise can then be arrested and the property deposited in a designated spot and put under guard. Surveillance must cover rear exits to adjoining houses and streets. It is important to centralize, as far as possible, the collection of property.

LABOR DISTURBANCES. This type of riot often presents delicate problems requiring careful judgment on the part of police authorities. The duty of the police is to observe a strict neutrality until a definite, overt act of violence to person or property demands firm action. In each State court rulings and tradition have established with some clarity the lines along which picketing may be legally conducted. Superior officers must be thoroughly instructed in the rules for lawful picketing and must convey this information to their subordinates.

Industrial plants likely to be involved in strikes should be carefully studied in regard to the strategy of riot prevention in conference with the plant's own protective force. The detective division can be used to great success in the investigation of the characters of strike leaders. Very often it is possible to anticipate labor trouble by noting the arrival in town of characters notorious for strike activities. The criminal element is sometimes hired as strikers or strike-breakers. If the detective force has kept a careful file on these persons, it is possible to nip in the bud an incipient riot by establishing firm control of leaders with criminal intent.

1 This chapter was to a certain extent prepared by the late Chief Inspector O'Connell of the New York City Police Department, co-author of this book. It is partly the outcome of his experiences in the Harlem riots of 1944, and it will mainly reflect conditions prevailing in New York City, where the greatest crowds in the world may gather. (The New York City area is now inhabited by almost ten million people of all races and creeds.) Nowhere else in the world is there equal experience in the handling of crowds. The principles and the underlying trends of thought, however, can certainly be applied to any other place.

2 "*Vade-Mecum à l'usage des autorités devant participer à l'organisation des mesures d'ordre et de sécurité relative aux voyages officiels des hautes personnalités françaises et étrangères,*" Bulletin du Ministère de l'Intérieur, June 1, 1947.

XXIX PLANT PROTECTION

THE PRIMARY PURPOSES OF PLANT PROTECTION ARE TO FACILITATE IN every way possible the operation of factories, public utilities, and other business enterprises and to protect such facilities at all times (during peace and war) against any activities which would slow down, interfere with, or halt production or prevent the facility from performing its intended function.

When we speak of plant protection, we must consider the category of security that this type of work involves. Primarily it comes under the title of preventive enforcement, and this type of enforcement must include all of those measures necessary to lessen illegal entry by the careful checking of all employees and the screening of all material transported in and out of the plant area.

While some of the measures taken during war are unnecessary during peacetime, generally the methods and organization are very similar. This particularly applies to transportation of materials, fire protection, control of personnel, and general security measures. However, since plant protection is of primary importance in wartime, in this chapter the basic principles of this phase of the subject will be emphasized.

Although limited protection of plants was maintained during World War I, it was not until World War II that plant protection became of prime importance to the security of the country. An example of the easy-going attitude toward plant protection in the first World War is the great explosion which occurred at New York on July 30, 1916. Shortly after 2 A.M. on that day, two million pounds of munitions stored on Black Tom Island (a headland jutting from the New Jersey shore into Upper New York Bay, nearly opposite the Statue of Liberty) exploded. Three men and a child were killed and the damage was estimated at $14,000,000. It was subsequently determined that the explosion was a planned act of destruction. The guard assigned to protect the site consisted of six guards and four private detectives—not much security for a stretch of land nearly a mile long. There was no screening of personnel, nor was there any fencing or lighting. The semi-island was easily reached either by boat or by a walkway over the fill that connected with the mainland.

Prior to World War II, plant protection was primarily a job given to older employees who performed watch duties and, where the system was in use, carried time clocks throughout the plant on a preplanned route punching the clock with keys that had been installed at strategic locations throughout the building area. Other similar check methods were sometimes employed. While such measures helped to prevent losses by theft and pilferage, they were primarily instituted to prevent fires or to insure the reporting of fires before they reached uncontrollable proportions. The existence of this type of guard was a definite factor in the insurance rates available for plant properties.

With the advent of World War II, there was a growing awareness of the necessity of keeping factories and plants functioning smoothly and uninterruptedly, and today plant protection has grown into an important full-time profession.

THE SABOTEUR

One of the most important problems with which plant protection is concerned is the saboteur. The first anti-sabotage[2] legislation in the United States was passed in 1918 and was called in part "an act to punish the wilful injury or destruction of war material or war premises or utilities used in connection with war materials and for other purposes." The act defines *war material* as armament, ammunition, livestock, stores, clothing, food, foodstuff, and fuel; *war premises* as all buildings, grounds, mines, or other places where war materials are being manufactured, repaired, mined, or transported, and all defense forts, arsenals, navy yards, camps, and prisons; and *war utilities* as all utilities and transportation that are used in connection with a war effort. The legislation covered the destruction of material intended for the use of the United States or any of its allies.

In order to understand the problem better we must know the type of person to be dealt with—the types of saboteurs. These may be classified in three groups:

1. Enemy agents: professionally trained and equipped personnel of a hostile country.

2. Traitorous agents: persons sympathetic to the cause of a hostile country or those bearing hatred for or who are prejudiced against their own country.

3. Irresponsible persons: those who through ignorance and lack of understanding of a wartime situation place personal situation above that of their country. These are the people who for some personal motive commit acts of carelessness or fail to live up to their job responsibilities. There might also be included in this group those persons who through thoughtless actions cause the destruction of property by fire or other property damage detrimental to a national war effort.

In considering security against trained saboteurs there must be taken into consideration the fact that these agents are a selected group, thoroughly indoctrinated, and well briefed in the art of organized destruction. They are trained in the art of decoy and are experts in capitalizing on the element of surprise. The trained saboteur knows where to find the vital spots and how the most destruction can be wrought without drawing attention to his own activity.

Sabotage during wartime or as a prelude to war is both destructive to military supplies needed by a fighting force and paralyzing to morale. The Germans were the first to appreciate the fact that munitions were as vital to war as were the men who fight it. Sabotage was first used as a tactic of warfare by the Germans in World War I. But it was a new phase of warfare and its success was limited due to lack of experience. In World War II, however, sabotage was a major force used by the Germans during the invasions of Poland, Norway, The Netherlands, Denmark, Belgium, and France. Trained saboteurs preceded the army; in many cases some had been at their assigned places long before the war. Then shortly before an invasion, these agents for destruction were unleashed to carry out their plans both for physical destruction and for psychological sabotage.

Sabotage is not directed toward any particular stage of the manufacturing process but is aimed at any or all the steps along the way—from the sources of raw material to the making and delivery of the end product. Thus plant protection must cover all these points: receipt of raw materials, manufacture, and delivery. Another related security aspect lies in the protection of and prevention of destruction of communication and transportation facilities, such as motor vehicle equipment, rail, and water carriers. (See also Chapter XXV.)

GOVERNMENT SECURITY REQUIREMENTS

Who requires that security measures be taken by plants engaged in the manufacture of war materiel and how extensive should these meas·ures be? When a manufacturer is awarded a contract by either the Department of Defense or its components, security measures are normally stipulated in the contract. To insure compliance, an inspection team of the component that awarded the contract makes a security survey of the plant some time before work is actually begun. Such an inspection team usually consists of an investigator who is an expert on measures of police security and investigation and an inspector who is an expert on all phases of fire protection, fire-protection equipment, and organizing fire-prevention programs. After the initial inspection, a detailed report as to any inadequacies is given to the plant. The report also contains recommendations for the standardizing of these conditions. Follow-up inspections are made periodically to insure that the recommended measures are complied with and to assist the supervisor of plant protection to attain maximum security. Failure to comply with security requirements often results in the cancellation of the contract.

In the case of larger plants or in those engaged in highly classified projects a government representative may be assigned full-time to the plant. He works closely with the plant protection supervisor, assisting him in fulfilling his responsibilities. The plant protection supervisor maintains close liaison with the area inspectors who are specially trained to coordinate contract requirements and the related individual and general protection problems. Any act of sabotage or an act that may be one of sabotage is reported to them immediately.

VULNERABILITY

In determining the vulnerability of a plant or facility, the fundamental consideration is the relationship of the materials and the machines which are necessary for its operation. Any place or point in the series of operations where the flow of production would be blocked is a vulnerable point. All points at which an act of sabotage would materially cripple plant operation should be noted in the plan for protection. These points should be correlated with telephone lines, power lines, generators, shipping and receiving platforms, entrances and exits.

No generalizations can be made concerning the points of vulnerability of an industrial plant. Each industry will have spots peculiar to its own production methods and to the nature of the machinery used in production. Cable concentrations and emergency power units are vital points for utilities providing communication facilities. Railroads consider tunnels, bridges, and key switching yards to be of primary importance. Generators in power plants, material stores of explosive nature in arms and ammunition production are other examples. It is necessary, therefore, that each industry determine its most vital points by examining each link in the chain of production from raw materials to the finished component or product. Diagrams and maps must be drawn to indicate the relative positions of vulnerable points. Oftentimes arrangements can be then made for emergency or standby facilities.

Certain types of facilities will require a protection plan much wider in scope than others. For instance, large plants that include harbor installations must protect the following: (1) docks, warehouses, and shipping points, (2) oil and gasoline storage points, (3) steam plants for generating electrical power, (4) underwater cables and crossing pipe lines, (5) bridges, tunnels, and other dangers of channel stoppage, (6) floating oil and gasoline, (7) lumber yards, (8) danger to ships from floating contact and magnetic bombs.

A further example of a protective scheme that must include larger areas would be the defense plan of water supply facilities. The plan in this case must include: (1) pipe lines, (2) pumping and filter units, (3) protection of small reservoirs from pollution, (4) reserve water supplies, (5) power plants for pumping, (6) distribution reservoirs, (7) dams, (8) water system valves.

OUTLINE OF A PLANT PROTECTION PLAN

It is thus understood that each protection plan has its own peculiar problems and that no formal set of rules may be fully applicable to all. However, to establish the fundamentals, let us follow the steps taken by a newly appointed supervisor of plant protection with a company that has secured its first government contract for manufacturing war materiel. The contract will stipulate that the materiel to be made is of great importance and "maximum security" will be maintained.

Therefore, the assigned supervisor will at once draw up a detailed outline of the measures to be taken needed for compliance with the contractual requirement. To aid in preparing the final plans, a check list that includes all possible security requirements will be set up. Let us look first at such a check list and then examine each point in further detail.

SECURITY PLAN CHECK LIST

I. PERIMETER SECURITY
   A. Area fencing
   B. Parking-lot fencing
   C. Entrance and exit gates
   D. Guard towers

II. FIRE PROTECTION
   A. Availability of public fire-fighting personnel and equipment
   B. Availability of water
   C. Sprinkler systems
   D. Special equipment (for electrical and inflammable-material fires)
   E. Alarm systems
   F. Fire point inspections
   G. Housekeeping
   H. Liaison with appropriate public officials

III. GUARD FORCE
   A. Gate guards
   B. Tower guards
   C. Critical-area guards
   D. Static guards
   E. Foot patrols
   F. Motor patrols
   G. Delivery guards
   H. Checkroom guards
   I. Total guard requirements
   J. Guard equipment
      1. Uniforms
      2. Firearms
      3. Special equipment

IV. PERSONNEL SCREENING AND IDENTIFICATION SECTION
   A. Investigation
   B. Fingerprint and photograph section
   C. Identification badges (employees)
   D. Identification cards (employees)
   E. Identification cards (visitors)
   F. Investigation—general
   G. Liaison with appropriate public officials

V. LIGHTING
   A. Perimeter lighting
   B. Gate lights
   C. Blackout lights

VI. COMMUNICATIONS
    A. Telephone requirements
    B. Intercommunications systems
    C. Radio requirements

VII. EDUCATIONAL PROGRAM
    A. Morale
    B. Saboteur methods
    C. Merit awards

I. PERIMETER SECURITY

The foremost thought in the prevention of sabotage is the elimination of unauthorized entry. Therefore, perimeter security is one of the most important aspects of plant protection. Peripheral protection is generally afforded by a combination of mechanical devices and guard personnel. All perimeter security measures should be checked at frequent intervals.

Area fencing.   There are many types of fencing available for perimeter security. A heavy-gage, chain-link cyclone type, six to eight feet in height, topped by three to five strands of barbed wire mounted on steel arms extended at a 45° angle away from the fenced area, is a recommended type. Posts should be of steel and set in a concrete base with frequent anchorage between posts to prevent entry under the fence.

In extremely large fenced areas it is desirable to install an alarm system. There are many types of these devices and they should be chosen according to the needs of the situation. Alarm systems are not a substitute or replacement for guard personnel but an implementation.

The standard recommended fence is not adequate in many situations and must be implemented with additional devices or be reset in a new location. If a factory-site fence line borders light or telephone poles or trees which may be used to surmount the fence obstacle, sufficient clearance must be made so that the poles or trees cannot be used for illegal entry. Another example is a fence line running close to another building, where by the use of a rope entry may be gained from a window or roof of the adjoining building. In this case if enough clearance cannot be allowed, it may be necessary to put man-proof bars on the adjoining building's windows or fencing devices on the roof. If this is necessary for security and difficulty is experienced with the owner of the building, forced compliance might be possible through the area security officer or through due process of law.

In many cases the use of fencing may not be feasible because of adjacent sidewalks, alleys, railroad tracks, etc. In such cases windows should be equipped with bars and heavy mesh wire, the latter to eliminate the possibility of bombs or incendiary devices being thrown into the building from the outside and to prevent the passing of objects from someone on the inside to a confederate waiting in the street.

Parking-lot fencing. Parking of employees' vehicles should never be permitted inside the factory perimeter area. Many factories provide other fenced areas for this purpose. This area should be separated from the factory or storage area by fencing, so that all employees are required to enter the factory area through regulated pedestrian entrances.

Gates. The number of gateways in a perimeter area should be kept at a minimum to conserve guard personnel and provide better security. Considerations in this respect are based on the number of employees to be admitted for each shift and the number of gates required for vehicular transportation, taking into consideration loading and unloading areas and railway spur gates. When in use all gates must be manned by guards. When not in use they should be securely chained and locked. All gate keys should be in the custody of the guard supervisor on duty and a permanent record maintained of their use by a sign-in, sign-out register.

Guard towers. The use of guard towers is a controversial issue; however, in some instances they are of definite value. Where continued observation is essential, they provide a maximum range of vision with a minimum of personnel. When periodic patrols are sufficient, the use of such towers becomes unnecessary. Height of towers is governed by the natural terrain, constructed obstacles, and other pertinent circumstances. The minimum recommended height is fifteen feet. Frequency of the towers is governed by the same conditions that figure in their height plus ease of vision between them and firearm range. For proper surveillance each tower guard should be in full view to his counterpart to the left and right.

II. FIRE PROTECTION

Fires are one of the favorite weapons of the saboteur, because they can be a result of normal safety failures or carelessness and are not immediately traceable to sabotage. In view of this added importance all fire-protection planning should be made with the assistance of a trained expert.

Availability of equipment and personnel. Information as to all public fire-fighting facilities in the vicinity is essential and can be secured from the local municipal safety representative. The municipal engineer can furnish data on the location of fire hydrants and their capacities and also the location of water-storage points.

Sprinkler systems and other special equipment. What the requirements are for installation is a technical problem and should be discussed and planned with a fire technician; this also applies to the use of special equipment essential to combat fires involving electricity or inflammable materials.

Alarm systems. Fire-alarm systems are of great benefit in fire prevention, but they are not always tamper-proof. They should be used to implement other fire-prevention measures, but not to replace them.

Fire point inspections. These should be made frequently. It is recommended that each piece of fire-fighting equipment be equipped with locking seals so that the inspector may quickly check the equipment for tampering. The seal check, however, does not cover those inspections needed for hose condition nor for fullness of extinguishers.

Good housekeeping. This is a very important factor in the prevention of fires. The use of canisters for waste material and trash and continuous policing is necessary to eliminate this threat. In the storage of inflammables, follow the rules established for the prevention of fires. Plan so that critical inflammables are stored in small quantities in order that losses will be minimized in case of fire.

Liaison. Cooperation with and by community and other public officials must be arranged for, to secure full range for emergency action and mutual understanding. This includes use of local police files (fingerprints, arrest records, etc.).

III. GUARD FORCE

The plant protection force usually operates as a part of the plant personnel department. This is an advisable setup since it is imperative that close coordination be maintained between the employment office and the personnel security and identification section of the guard force.

As there are many types of plant guard organizations let us outline two of the most acceptable in as much as they cover most situations adequately. The first may be called *duty organization* where a supervisor is in charge of guard personnel performing particular functions. In smaller plants with limited personnel, a supervisor may be assigned two or more functions, while in larger plants assistant supervisors may be advisable for particular-area functions. The second may be called *area organiza-*

tion; here again variations in area-size function-coverage may apply, but it is usually best used whenever the plant area is very large or where two or more areas separately developed are used. The latter type is the more widely used and is perhaps the more practical.

Gate guard. This is one of the most critical guard assignments. It includes the employees' and visitors' gates, and the truck and railroad gates. Each has special security requirements. Employee and visitor gates require expeditious entry and exit procedures, yet precaution must be taken to forestall many types of hazardous entries. Among them are: the "prankster," flashing a picture of a monkey or public figure, or a pack of cigarettes; the "forgetter," arriving at the last minute with a "forgotten" pass and a good excuse; the "traveler," attempting entry with traveling bag or package. Such as these usually require utmost scrutiny— have they been discharged the day before for questionable loyalty with pass lifted? Is the "forgetting" genuine and supported by correlative identification or is it a ruse? Is the proposed "evening visitor's" status verifiable?

Each gate guard should receive written instructions and orders on the procedures and duties of each post. Alert guards with proper vision, proper official employee identification, controlled ingress and egress are essential. All questionable cases must be referred to the supervisor for checking and decision for either entry or exit.

A special visitors' gate is usually necessary. Full information as to the visitor and the person visited must be supplied and recorded in a *register,* including time of entry and departure, telephonic or other verbal clearance for the visit, purpose of visit, etc. Visitors should be *escorted* to and from the place of the visit, signing out on departure. A list of authorized visitors, kept up to date, should be furnished to all gate guards.

Other guards. Items B, C, D, E, F, G, and H of the plan should each have its guard functions thoroughly analyzed and with detailed instructions and procedures provided to each guard. The patterns are not dissimilar to that of the gate guard and will be dictated by the physical plant layout and the operational procedures of the plant's or facility's administrative and productive objective.

Guard equipment. This equipment should be carefully selected for various use requirements. Flashlights, keys, and notebooks are standard. A distinctive uniform should be utilized for duty use. Care must be taken that such uniforms do not resemble closely those of the various branches of the armed forces. Special items such as raincoats, overcoats, boots, etc., should be made available. Firearms should be selected according to particular need, issued and checked in by the guard supervisor daily at the beginning and end of the tour of duty.

IV.   PERSONNEL SECURITY AND
IDENTIFICATION SECTION

Personnel selection is equally as important for the plant guard as for plant operating personnel. The actual selection for guard personnel should be left to the manager of plant protection who will best know his own needs. His supervisory staff should have qualifications similar to his own, while each guard, patrolman, or special policeman must be mentally and physically capable of performing his duties and actively willing to accept the responsibility of assignment. Qualities to be sought include traits such as loyalty, diplomatic firmness, trustworthiness, discreetness, ability to carry out orders and use sound judgment in emergencies, faithfulness in making reports, etc.

In all cases the screening of plant guards should consist of unusually thorough checking and pre-employment investigation. After the plant employment office has interviewed and accepted an applicant as meeting the job requirements, he receives the requisite checking and investigation before final acceptance; on final approval he receives the necessary identification called for in the overall plant protection plan. As the job is usually one of monotony, hard work, and little credit, the morale problem is always present; and a high standard of morale must be maintained and kept constantly in mind by the manager and supervisors of the plant protection organization.

A question frequently asked is what authority guards have in making an arrest. In some cases the guard force receives its authority by becoming a military auxiliary; in others, the authority is vested by the state, county, or local government where the plant is located. Where a city vests authority it is as a "special police"; in counties, it is deputized as members of the sheriff's office. The area plant protection authority should be consulted for advice on procedure.

Investigation.   Background checks are made from personal history statements by trained investigators of the guard force or by private investigators who have been certified as thoroughly responsible by local authorities or police. Birth record, citizenship status, arrest record, employment record, all places of residence, educational records, club and organization membership, are all essential to background investigation and check. A sufficient number of copies should be made for required action and for quick employment approval or disapproval to maintain the plant operating personnel efficiently. In critical job placements where employees have access to high-classification documents or work in areas of manufacture of materiel of high classification, special investigation should be immediately conducted.

Fingerprint and photograph section. Extreme care should be taken that prints are clear and legible for quick local police checking. A fingerprint check by the FBI usually requires considerable time and legibility facilitates this work. Files and records within the plant must be accurate and up to date and well guarded.

Identification badges. Badges and credentials are the employees' authorization for entry and exit and are issued only after full investigation and approval. To issue an identification badge which can be easily counterfeited defeats the effectiveness of personnel screening and of plant security. The pass and badge combination is one of the more widely accepted types of personnel identification. It is of tamper-proof construction which cannot be easily interchanged without obvious mutilation. Usually it bears a ¾ inch photo of the employee, his time-clock or payroll number, and an identifying serial number on the badge metal. The last is of importance as a serial guide number for the identification section when the badge is reported lost. All employees should be required to wear their badges in plain view when on duty. Different badge colors may be used to confine workers to proper work areas and for quick identification by guards.

Identification cards. The card supplements the badge: the obverse bears the employee's photo, identification number, company name, date of issue, employee's signature, countersignature of certifying official; the reverse bears physical description including height, weight, coloring (hair, eyes, complexion), identifying marks, fingerprints of thumb and index finger of both hands. It is recommended that cards be enclosed and sealed in transparent acetate or plastic cases for preservation of the card and immediate visibility of data on either side. The same color system used for badges is equally valid for identification cards. These too should be carried on the person at all times by the employee, whether within or outside the plant.

Visitors' identification cards. Even though escorted within the plant by guards, all visitors should be issued distinctive cards on signing in. Casual visitors' cards should be picked up on exit. Where continuing cards are issued, the list of holders should be constantly checked for validity and all gate guards notified of all changes. The period of valid use of the latter card should be of short term.

V. LIGHTING

Interior and exterior lighting should be used so that advantage may not be taken of darkened areas to gain admittance. When possible a wall of illumination can be placed around restricted areas with the interior darkened so that an intruder must pass through the lighted area. A number of electronic protective devices are also available to supplement human vigilance.

Perimeter. Exterior area lighting should be installed in such a way as to illuminate the entire ground area of the premises. By well-planned and well-spaced lighting it will be possible for any guard to observe easily the movements of any person in his guard area. All lights should be installed within the perimeter to forestall tampering.

Gates. This lighting should be installed to provide full visibility and shadowless observation for checking employee identification, for necessary record taking, and for all vehicular and rail traffic. At all vehicle entrances lighting should be planned to eliminate any driving hazard, such as those that may blind drivers or obscure road marking. Guard towers should be equipped with swivel searchlights.

Blackout. Blackout control of the lighting system should be regulated from a central control switch, located within the plant and with guarded yet easy accessibility; if not within the plant proper, the switch should be well within the perimeter.

VI. COMMUNICATION

Each post should be equipped with some means of communication with direct connection to the office of the supervisor so that all alarms may be reported immediately and emergency help requested for any point in the protective system. Guard planning calls for periodic reporting to an assigned supervisor, and any failure to report at the scheduled time requires immediate investigation. It may indicate foul play, illness, technical difficulty, or plain man-failure for which corrective measures must promptly be instituted to maintain the security system.

The telephone, intercommunication systems, and two-way radio systems are used variously as equipment is available and as the practical effectiveness of the device used can be employed at the various types of guard posts. For motor patrols the two-way radio provides the best coverage. All installations are to be made so that any individual unit which becomes inoperative can be quickly spotted and checked. No guard post should be established that does not have protected communication and the guards thoroughly instructed in its use.

VII. EDUCATIONAL PROGRAM

This training is both specific and general: specific as to the guard job itself, general as to factors of *morale, saboteur methods, meirt awards* for work well done as a part of the overall war effort of which plant protection is an integral part. The general aspect applies to the plant guard force itself and more broadly to the entire plant personnel.

Each guard should receive a course of training prior to receiving any assignment. Such a course should be well planned and presented by trained and competent instructors. Refresher courses should be scheduled at stated intervals. The following topics are suggested for the initial course:

1. Geography of the plant and its environment
2. Brief outline of the plant operations
3. Methods and techniques of the saboteur
4. Search of persons, vehicles, etc.
5. Authority of the guard personnel
6. Laws of arrest
7. Fire prevention, fire fighting, and fire-fighting equipment
8. Nomenclature of assigned weapons
9. Target practice
10. Badge and pass regulations
11. Reports and forms
12. Established guard procedures
13. Topic related to individual guard assignments
14. Organization of the plant protection system of which he is a part.

An exact record of this training program should be maintained and kept up to date in the personnel file of the guard and used as a basis for determining refresher course needs.

The problems of morale require astute judgment on the part of the plant supervisor and his assistants. A definite appreciation of this overall problem and good planning to keep the situation well in hand are requisite.

While the plant guard or police force are readily recognized as essential components in plant protection, other subsidiary assignments for special purpose may be required of plant personnel. Such assignment may include: shutting down machinery and conveyors, opening emergency doors, closing fire doors, directing workers to proper exits, etc.

A program to educate all personnel should be established so that they will become alert-minded, safety-trained, and security-conscious. Such a program may well encompass:

1. Organizing assignment details and establishing sound conduct patterns for every employee;
2. Training in handling of confidential information and material;
3. Alerting personnel to the dangers of loose talk both within and without the plant;
4. Developing a high degree of morale to forestall objection on the part of employees who may resent seemingly excessive precautions for security and who must be made to realize that strict investigation procedures are designed for their protection rather than for persecution.

To achieve a successful security educational program, plant publications and posters are helpful; as are group meetings where overall measures and procedures can be discussed, purposeful questions answered, and films shown from governmental sources or others, such as the National Board of Fire Underwriters, insurance companies, equipment manufacturers, safety bureaus. Meetings, with outside speakers from local or state government, government agents, army and navy security men, are sure to effect the desired understanding which creates wholehearted employee cooperation. Awards for individuals, groups, departments, are an effective device to stimulate pride in effort and work and in cooperative effectiveness throughout the plant or facility.

Any individual plant or facility will use all or the majority of these devices in preparing its security program. From the administrative point of view the selection of the manager of plant protection is of first importance as on his planning and the effective carrying out of that planning will depend the entire structure of efficient, effective protection in time of any national emergency.

1 This chapter was prepared in collaboration with Lt. Col. Carl E. Grimsley, formerly of the Ohio State Patrol and investigator with the Defense Production Service, U. S. Air Force. At the time, Col. Grimsley was serving with the U. S. Army as Provost Marshal, Stuttgart Military Post.

2 The word "sabotage" is from the French word *sabot,* a type of wooden shoe worn by French peasants. In the mid-nineteenth century French workmen became obsessed with the belief that machinery would soon replace them in the factory. In order to eliminate this threat the French workers were said to have used their *sabots* to wreck the machinery. The word "sabotage" thus came to describe the destruction of property by persons who wilfully and deliberately commit such acts.

XXX QUESTIONS

I ASPECTS OF DETECTIVE WORK

1. Describe the phases of modern criminal investigation discussed so far.
2. Give four examples of *corpus delicti* in crimes other than homicide.
3. What do you understand a simulated crime to be? Describe one or more from experiences of your own or others.

II POLICE ORGANIZATIONS HERE AND ABROAD

1. Tell briefly the difference between ordinary police and political police.
2. What are the general qualifications of an American sheriff?
3. What does the expression prosecutor's detective mean?
4. Describe briefly the qualifications for a good detective.
5. What is the jurisdiction of the Bureau of Narcotics?
6. What is the jurisdiction of the Post Office inspectors?
7. What is the jurisdiction of the Immigration Border Patrol?
8. Describe the development of the FBI.
9. What does the expression Scotland Yard signify?
10. Describe the role of the *Préfecture de Police* in Paris.
11. What is the difference between the Russian MVD (Cheka) and similar agencies in the western world?
12. Describe briefly the aim of the ICPC.

III PSYCHOLOGY IN DETECTIVE SERVICE

1. How should the interrogation of witnesses be conducted?
2. What is a suggestive question?
3. Why is it essential in many cases to visit the scene before questioning a suspect?
4. Enumerate methods for detecting deception.
5. Describe the principles of the lie detector.
6. Describe a case where in your opinion the lie detector can be applied.
7. Describe some different types of witnesses.
8. What are the stages of testimony?
9. What is your opinion of aural experiences in testimony?
10. Describe some case out of your own or others' experience where witnesses were mistaken in good faith.
11. What circumstances tend to promote mistakes in the identification of persons through witnesses?
12. What is the difference between sadism and masochism?

13. What is transvestitism and how does it affect police work?
14. Describe briefly the influences of epilepsy and hysteria on testimony.
15. What is meant by mass suggestion?

IV TRACING THE FUGITIVE

1. What is the crime index?
2. Describe briefly the different registers and indices in your department.
3. Describe briefly the steps to be taken to obtain information about an alien.
4. Enumerate the channels of intelligence at your disposal for the tracing of a fugitive.

V IDENTIFICATION OF INDIVIDUALS

1. Describe briefly the history of criminal identification.
2. Why was the anthropometrical system abolished?
3. Describe the most important details of the human ear.
4. What are the most important elements in the description of a wanted person?
5. On what parts of the body do the friction ridges appear?
6. Describe briefly the history of fingerprinting.
7. Give reasons for the first rule of dactyloscopy: There are no two identical fingerprints.
8. Are fingerprint patterns inherited?
9. Give reasons for the second rule of dactyloscopy: Fingerprints are not changeable.
10. What is the difference between a principal registration and a single-fingerprint registration?
11. What do the terms inner and outer terminus mean?
12. What is meant by ridge tracing?
13. Does modern plastic surgery represent a danger to criminal identification?

VI PROBLEMS WITH MISSING PERSONS

1. Describe some methods of making a dead body look more natural.
2. What information is to be gained from a human skull?
3. How is a body found in water fingerprinted?

VII SKETCHING THE SCENE OF A CRIME

1. Enumerate the different kinds of sketches used in police work.
2. What is the coordinate system?
3. What is triangulation?
4. Describe how heights are measured from the sketchboard.

VIII PHOTOGRAPHING THE SCENE OF A CRIME

1. Give some examples out of your own or others' experience of a photograph of the scene of a crime having been of great importance.
2. Can you mark important spots on the scene with white chalk?
3. Enumerate the necessary photographs to be taken in case of an ordinary homicide in an apartment house.
4. What is metric photography?

IX FINGERPRINTS AT THE SCENE OF THE CRIME

1. Describe the different types of chance impressions.
2. How are chance impressions produced?
3. Describe methods for developing fingerprints on paper.
4. How would you photograph a fingerprint on a multicolored background?
5. Which are the most common fingerprint patterns?
6. Describe the characteristic points found in the pattern of friction ridges.
7. Has the absolute size of the fingerprint any importance in identification?
8. What is your opinion of the value of fingerprints as evidence?
9. What is poroscopy?
10. Is there any possibility of identification if the criminal used gloves?

X FOOTPRINTS

1. Describe the elements of the walking picture.
2. Describe briefly Müller's system of measuring the walking picture.
3. How is a cast of a footprint in dust made?
4. Which are the most important points in the identification of a footprint made by a shoe?

XI TRACES OF TOOLS

1. Describe some types of crime where traces of tools will have special importance.
2. How is a cast made of the trace of a tool?
3. Describe briefly how a trace of a tool is identified by the microscope.

XII THE EXAMINATION OF PAINTINGS

1. What is a "dating pigment"? What is its probative value?
2. Describe the four layers of a typical Renaissance painting.
3. Describe three kinds of forgery evidence that might be detected by means of X-rays.
4. What are the three general methods of proving authenticity?

XIII HAIR

1. In what types of crime is the examination of hair especially important?
2. When and how should comparison hairs be obtained?
3. What information can be obtained from the roots of the hair?
4. What is the medulla index and what is its importance in identification?
5. Describe some cases where dirt adhering to the hair will give information.
6. Tell briefly what information can be obtained from deformations of the hair.
7. What are the general differences between human and animal hair?
8. On what factors is the identification of hairs based?

XIV PROBLEMS OF ATTACKS WITH FIREARMS

1. What revolver calibers are used in the United States?
2. How is the caliber of a fired bullet determined?
3. Describe briefly the methods used in identifying a bullet with the firearm from which it was shot.

4. On what factors is the determination of the make of an unknown firearm by a bullet founded?
5. Describe briefly the traces left by an automatic pistol on a shell.
6. On what factors is the determination of the make of an unknown firearm by a shell founded?
7. Is there any possibility of determining, from examination of the gun, how long a time has elapsed since the last shot was fired?
8. Describe the appearance of powder tattooing around a wound and explain how the distance from which the shot was fired is determined.
9. What is a bow-wave report and how does it help determine the direction of the shooting?

XV PROBLEMS OF BROKEN WINDOWS

1. Tell briefly how it is determined through which side of a windowpane a bullet was fired.
2. Describe briefly the role of the radial and concentric fractures in determining from which side a windowpane was shattered by a blunt object.

XVI STAINS OF BLOOD, SEMEN, ETC.

1. Describe briefly where one should look for bloodstains in a room in an ordinary homicide case.
2. What is meant by the leuco-malachite test?
3. Tell how to determine whether a bloodstain is of human or animal origin.
4. Is there any possibility of determining from what part of the body the blood originated?
5. What is blood grouping?
6. Describe the precautions to be taken when transporting stains of semen.
7. Are there any stains other than those of blood and semen which may be of importance in criminal investigation?

XVII MISCELLANEOUS TRACES

1. What information may be obtained from the earwax of a person?
2. What information may be obtained from dust in a suspect's wearing apparel?
3. How is the dust gathered?
4. Has the analysis of tobacco or tobacco ash any importance in criminal investigation? Give reasons.
5. What part of the brain is of importance in criminal investigation?

XVIII INVESTIGATION OF HOMICIDE

1. Give some examples out of your own or others' experience where seemingly insignificant details played a part in tracking down a murderer.
2. If you arrived at the scene of a homicide and found that the position of the body and of several pieces of furniture had been altered, what would you do?
3. If you arrived at the scene of a homicide together with two fellow officers, enumerate briefly the duties which would devolve upon the three of

you, and describe especially how you would organize the investigation and divide the duties among you.

4. If you arrested a suspect, what would you look for upon his body and wearing apparel?

5. Describe the steps to be taken in a poison case to gather evidence.

6. What authorities should you notify in case of a homicide?

7. Build up and describe an alarm system in your community to be used in case of an escape of the perpetrator. Make a map of your community with all adjoining roads and put in the names of the gasoline-station attendants, bridge tenders, ferry captains, railroad-crossing attendants, station agents, bus drivers, etc., whom you would have to instruct and immediately notify by an alarm. (Such a plan of general alarm should be built up as soon as possible if it does not exist.)

8. What is meant by *res gestæ* evidence?

9. What questions should be asked to obtain a dying declaration?

10. How is the identity of the deceased proven?

11. Describe how you would remove and dispose of the body in a homicide case in your community.

12. Outline the role of the medical examiner or coroner in a homicide case.

13. Describe the typical appearance of the wound of a suicide by shooting.

14. Describe the examination to be made of the rope in a case of strangulation.

15. In case of a slit wound, is there any possibility of determining whether it was caused by suicide or by homicide?

16. State briefly the means of determining at what time death occurred.

17. Tell briefly what information may be gained from the appearance of bloodstains.

18. Describe the methods of locking a door from the outside with the key on the inside.

19. What information can be gained from the skid marks in fatal motor-vehicle accidents?

20. What is a decelerometer?

21. Enumerate the steps of investigation to be taken in hit-and-run cases.

22. Enumerate briefly the steps to be taken in the investigation of a railroad accident.

23. Describe briefly a case of abortion in which a conviction was obtained, giving special attention to the evidence offered.

24. How is the direction in which a car has traveled determined from its tracks?

XIX ELEMENTS OF TOXICOLOGY

1. Describe some occurrences in connection with the death of a person which would make you suspicious of poisoning.

2. What do you know about knockout drops?

3. Enumerate the four stages of drunkenness.

XX DRUG ADDICTION

1. Explain the difference between addiction to narcotic drugs and habituation to tobacco.
2. What plant is the major source of narcotics? Name three drugs derived from it.
3. Why is heroin preferred to other narcotic drugs?

XXI INVESTIGATION OF BURGLARIES

1. What role does the perseverance of a criminal play in the investigation of burglary?
2. Enumerate the methods commonly used by safe burglars.
3. What are the most common ways used by burglars to dispose of their loot?
4. Enumerate briefly the steps to be taken in searching for stolen property.
5. How would you describe your own watch, your own motorcar, and your own clothing?
6. If you suspected a simulated burglary, what would you especially look for in the way of technical evidence?

XXII INVESTIGATION OF LARCENY

1. Describe some different methods of automobile thievery.
2. What is a sneak thief? Describe two types from your own experience.
3. How would you operate if you were sent out to look for pickpockets?
4. Describe briefly the psychological conditions which make a switch game possible.
5. How would you examine a letter which you suspected had previously been opened?
6. What would you look for on a seal which you had reason to suspect was forged?
7. Describe some of the traps which may be set for thieves.

XXIII ROBBERY

1. Enumerate some elements of procedure and strategy employed by bandits in one or more robberies which have occurred in your locality.
2. Can you expect to use any method of police science in the investigation of robbery?

XXIV INVESTIGATION OF ARSON

1. What facts are necessary in building up an arson case?
2. Describe how spontaneous combustion may occur.
3. State briefly how a flue is examined.
4. Tell what should be looked for in the electric system in an arson investigation.
5. Describe out of your own or others' experience some chemical time fuses.
6. Describe some methods of detecting inflammable oils.
7. Why is it necessary to reconstruct all circumstances prevailing at the time of the fire?

XXV SABOTAGE

1. What are the most common chemicals used in stench bombs?
2. State briefly how you would deal with the situation when stench bombs have been used in a store.
3. Describe briefly some other sabotage methods.

XXVI QUESTIONED DOCUMENTS

1. Describe briefly different types of inks used in this country.
2. Are there any possibilities of distinguishing between different classes of ink?
3. Is it possible to distinguish between inks of the same class?
4. What are the possibilities of determining the age of ink?
5. Is there any way to determine the difference between several lead-pencil writings?
6. Describe a case in which the sequence of strokes would be important.
7. What is graphology?
8. Describe some methods of making erased ink writing reappear.
9. What is contact detection?

XXVII THE POLICE LABORATORY

1. Describe briefly the advantages and the limitations of police science.
2. Tell briefly the use of spectrography in the police laboratory.
3. What does ultraviolet light signify?
4. Describe some cases where ultraviolent light can be used in police work.
5. What is stereophotography?
6. Describe some use of the moulage method.

XXVIII SOME PROBLEMS OF THE UNIFORMED POLICE

1. Enumerate some special assignments to cover in handling a great crowd.
2. Why should a patrolman assigned to a parade face the spectators?
3. Describe how you would, from a police viewpoint, organize a parade in your locality.
4. How should a distinguished visitor be protected in his hotel?
5. Where is it most likely that an assassination of a distinguished visitor will be attempted?
6. Enumerate some causes of rioting.
7. In general, when and how should force be applied to suppress rioting?
8. What tactical principles are followed in attacking a crowd?

XXIX PLANT PROTECTION

1. What is the purpose of antisabotage legislation?
2. What are the types of saboteur? Describe their characteristics.
3. Who sets the standard for plant security requirements?
4. What are the points of plant vulnerability?
5. What are the six phases of plant security planning?
6. Enumerate the types of guard duty.

GLOSSARY OF TERMS COMMONLY USED
IN CONNECTION WITH FIREARMS

GLOSSARY OF TERMS COMMONLY USED
IN CONNECTION WITH FIREARMS

action. The mechanism of a firearm.

alloy. Metals mixed by fusing.

antimony. Used to alloy lead in bullets for hardening the projectile.

anvil. A small piece of metal, arrowhead in shape, which is placed inside the primer cup and forms the point of resistance as the firing-pin strikes the primer, thereby creating friction which discharges the priming composition.

ballistics. The science of the flight of projectiles.

barrel time. Measured from the fall of the hammer to the muzzle of the gun.

battery cup. The small cup which contains the primer.

bore. The diameter of the gun barrel; the gage.

breech. The rear extremity of the rifle.

bulging. The swelling of a gun barrel.

bullets. Cannelured Bullet: An elongated bullet with grooves around it. These grooves are used for holding the lubricant or for crimping purposes.

Elongated Bullet: Longer than it is wide, the opposite type from the round bullet.

Flat-Point Bullet: One with a flat nose.

Hollow-Point Bullet: One with a hollow point for the purpose of increasing the mushrooming effect upon impact.

Metal Bullet Point: Bullet having lead bearing and metal tip.

Metal-Cased Bullet: One with a jacket of metal which completely encases the nose.

Soft-Point Bullet: A metal-cased bullet with a tip of lead, so that it will mushroom on impact, thereby increasing the striking energy.

caliber. A term synonymous with gage (diameter of bore measured in hundredths of an inch).

chamber. The rear end of a barrel, which receives the shell or cartridge.

chilled shot. Refers to hard shot. Hard shot is produced by mixing antimony with the lead.

choke. The decreased diameter of a shotgun barrel toward the muzzle—for the purpose of regulating the spread or pattern of the shot.

combustion. Burning of the powder in the barrel.

cone. The reduction of diameter in a barrel where the chamber joins the bore.

corrosion. The deterioration on the inside of the barrel caused by the chem-

531

ical action of the products of combustion after firing; usually due to neglect.

crimping. A mechanical operation employed in loading metallic cartridges which consists in turning over slightly or compressing the mouth of the metallic shell or case to hold the bullet securely in its place. Applied also to shot shells.

drop. As applied to a gunstock, it means downward bend.

drop shot. Soft shot.

ejector. Mechanism which throws the fired shell or cartridge from the arm.

energy. The force or power of a charge.

erosion. The actual wear on the inside of a barrel produced by the flame and gases of the ignited powder.

extractor. The part of the gun mechanism that withdraws the shell or cartridge from the chamber.

fulminate. One of the ingredients of the priming mixture.

gage. Diameter of the gun barrel; "12 Ga.," for instance, means that 12 round lead balls of this diameter weigh one pound; lead balls the size of a 10-gage gun weigh ten to the pound; of a 16-gage gun, sixteen to the pound, etc.

gallery load. A light or reduced charge in cartridges for use indoors.

grooves. The cavities inside a rifle barrel, usually spiral, by which a bullet, when expanded and forced forward, receives a spinning motion, making its flight accurate.

hangfire. Delayed or slow combustion.

impact. A blow. The force of a bullet striking an object.

jacket. A covering for a bullet.

keyhole. Refers to the shape of the hole made by a bullet that has been traveling off its long axis.

lands. A rifle barrel is bored to a desired size; the inside of the barrel is then called the surface; the grooves are cut into this surface. The raised spiral surfaces left by this operation are the lands.

leading. The term used to designate the presence of lead on the inside of a barrel.

leed. See *twist.*

machine rest. An arrangement to which a rifle is affixed, or on which it rests, when tested for accuracy.

mid-range. The distance between short range and long range.

mushrooming. The upsetting or expanding of a bullet on impact.

muzzle velocity. The velocity of a bullet at the muzzle.

o'clock. To illustrate, face the target with watch in hand, and with back of watch toward target. A shot in the line of figure XII would be a 12 o'clock shot; one in the line of III, a 3 o'clock shot, etc.

pattern. Refers to the distribution of the shot charge after leaving the muzzle.

percentage of pattern. Number of pellet marks in a thirty-inch circle, over a forty-yard range, divided by number of pellets in the load.

powder charge. The amount of powder used in a load.

powders. The powders used in loading are of three types: black, semismokeless, and smokeless. Smokeless powders are divided into two types: the first is known as "bulk," meaning that its charge corresponds, or nearly so, in bulk to the charge of black powder; the second is the "dense" type, which means that it is denser and of much less bulk.

Single-base: A powder containing nitrocellulose as the only explosive ingredient.

Double-base: A powder containing nitrocellulose and nitroglycerin as the principal explosive ingredients.

primer. A metallic cup charged with a priming composition. A blow from the hammer or plunger striking the primer ignites the powder charge.

recoil. The backward movement of a gun in the act of discharge.

ricochet. Ricochet shot—a glancing shot, rebounding from a flat surface.

rim-fire. A term applied to a cartridge fired by a blow on the rim of the cartridge-head. A rim-fire rifle or pistol is one that fires a rim-fire cartridge.

Semismokeless powder. See *powders.*

shocking power. The energy delivered by the projectile on impact; the result brought about through combination of momentum and penetration.

squib, squib load. A defective load. An extremely weak-sounding load.

striking energy. The energy impact measured in foot-pounds.

take-down system or *take-down rifle.* An arm in which the barrel can readily be taken from the action; employed for securing compactness in carrying the arm.

trajectory. As applied to a bullet, the curve it describes in its flight.

trigger pull. The applied force necessary to release the trigger. Riflemen refer to this as a one-pound pull or two-pound pull, i.e., requiring a force of one or two pounds to release the trigger. A hair-trigger pull is a very light pull; other terms are a creeping pull, a dragging pull, a still pull, a hard pull, a smooth pull, a fine pull, etc.

twist. The pitch or rate of twist in the rifling of a pistol or rifle barrel.

uncrimped. Ammunition that is not crimped.

velocity. The speed of a projectile in its flight.

wad. A yielding substance, usually of felt, placed over the powder of a shot shell for the purpose of controlling the gas blast.

windage. The allowance made for drift of a bullet.

wobble. A term applied to the unsteady rotation or spin of a bullet; usually caused by insufficient twist in the rifle barrel.

BIBLIOGRAPHY

BIBLIOGRAPHY

Books and articles of the same author have been numbered in sequence. However, only where a work is referred to in the text notes do the numbers actually appear.

ANNALS, ARCHIVES, PERIODICALS, and PAMPHLETS

American Journal of Police Science, 1:4:423

Amy–Melissinos, "Sur l'identification des papiers imprimés carbinisés," *Annales de Médecine Légale, de Criminologie et de Police Scientifique,* 16, 14 (1936)

Bäckström, "Über die Ultraviolett-Absorption der Kobaltsalze und über einige Lichtfilter für das ultraviolette Strahlgebiet," *Arkiv för Kemi. Mineralogi och Geologi,* 13 A., No. 24 (1940)

Balthazard–Rojas, "Examen des taches d'urine," *Annales de Médecine Légale, de Criminologie et de Police Scientifique,* 2, 23 (1922)

Berg, in *Deutsche Zeitschrift für gerichtliche Medizin,* 39283 (1949)

Boller, "Vorschlag einer neuen forensischen Haaruntersuchungsmethode," Inaugural-Dissertation, 1936

Britton, "Dusts and Their Importance in Crime Detection," *The Police Journal* (London), 12, 352 (1939)

Brüning–Schnetka, "Uber die chemische Untersuchung und die Beurteilung von Einschussen," *Archiv für Kriminologie,* 101, 81 (1937)

Burd–Greene, "Tool Mark Comparisons," *Journal of Criminal Law and Criminology,* October (1948)

Dauber, "Die Gleichförmigkeit des psychischen Geschehens und die Zeugenaussagen," *Fortschritt der Psychologie* (1913)

De Rechter–Mage, in *Revue de Droit Pénal,* March (1927)

Dupré, "Le Témoignage: Étude psychologique et médico-légale," *Revue de Deux Mondes* (1910)

Duquenois, "Contributions à l'examen médico-légal des débris végétaux recueillis sur les vêtements," *Annales de Médecine Légale, de Criminologie et de Police Scientifique,* 18, 104 (1938)

Finn–Cornish, in *Industrial and Engineering Chemistry,* Analytical Edition, 10, 524 (1938)

Freud, "Tatbestandsdiagnostik und Psychoanalyse," *Archiv für Kriminologische Anthropologie* (1906)

Friedendorff, "Zusammensetzen zerrissenen Papiers," *Archiv für Kriminologie* (1906)

Gamble–Burd–Kirk, "Glass Fragments as Evidence," *Journal of Criminal Law and Criminology,* 33, 416 (1943)

Gettler, "Method for Determination of Death by Drowning," *Journal of the American Medical Association,* 77, 1650 (1921)

Gettler–Blume, "Chloroform Content of the Brain Following Anesthesia," *Archives of Pathology,* 11, 841 (1931)

Goddard, "Scientific Identification of Firearms and Bullets," *Journal of Criminal Law and Criminology,* Vol. XVII–2 (1926)

Goddefroy, "Les Empreintes de pattes de chiens comme moyen d'identification," *Revue Internationale de Criminalistique* (1929)

Grant,[1] "Deciphering Charred Documents: Some Recent Work and a New Method," *Analyst,* 67, 42 (1942)

Hansen, "Acid Phosphatase as a New Method of Demonstrating Sperm Spots," *Acta Pathologica et Microbiologica Scandinavica,* 23, 187 (1946)

Hansen, in *Nordisk Kriminalteknisk Tidskrift*

Hanson, "L'Examen microchimique des taches d'urine en criminalistique," *Svensk Kemisk Tidskrift,* 57, 235 (1945)

Hellwig,[1] "Einige merkwürdige Fälle von Irrtum über Identität von Sachen und Personen," *Archiv für Kriminologische Anthropologie* (1907)

Hooker–Boyd, in *Immunology,* 16, 451 (1939)

Kaye,[1] "The Collection and Preservation of Biological Materials and General Procedure for Toxicological Analysis," *Journal of Criminal Law and Criminology,* 38, 670 (1948)

——,[2] "Law and Criminal," *Journal of Criminal Law and Criminology,* 38, 79 (1947)

Keefe–Bailey, in *Cornell Law Quarterly,* 34, 72, September (1948)

King–Armstrong, "A Convenient Method for Determining Serum and Bile Phosphatase Activity," *Journal of the Canadian Medical Association,* 31, 376-361 (1934)

Kippel, "Zur Beurteilung von Halsschnittwunden," *Archiv für Kriminologie,* Bd. 79, H. 2/3

Kirk–Magagnose–Salisbury, "Casting of Hairs—Its Technique and Application to Species and Personal Identification," *Journal of Criminal Law and Criminology,* August (1949)

Kirk–Roche, "Differentiation of Similar Glass Fragments by Physical Properties," *Journal of Criminal Law and Criminology,* 18, 104 (1947)

Kockel,[1] in *Vierteljahrschrift für gerichtliche Medizin,* Bd. XXVII, II Suppl. (1909)

Koehler, "Technique Used in Tracing the Lindbergh Kidnapping Ladder," *Journal of Criminal Law and Criminology,* 27, 5 (1937)

Kraft, "Critical Review of Forensic Ballistics," *American Journal of Police Science* (1931)

Krogman,[1] "A Guide to the Identification of Human Skeletal Material," *FBI Law Enforcement Bulletin* (1948)

——,[2] "Role of the Physical Anthropologist in the Identification of Human Skeletal Remains," *FBI Law Enforcement Bulletin* (1943)

Krogman–McGregor–Frost, "A Problem in Human Skeletal Remains," *FBI Law Enforcement Bulletin* (1939)

Kutscher–Wolberg, "Prostataphosphatase," *Zeitschrift für physiologisch Chemie,* 236, 237 (1935)

Landsteiner–Levine, in the *Journal of Experimental Medicine* (1928)

Langenbruch, "Kriminalistische Ultraviolett-Reflex-Mikrophotographie mit einer neuen nach Angaben des Verfassers hergestellten Optik," *Archiv für Kriminologie,* Vol. 99, part 1/2 (1936)

——, "Die Technik der Ultraviolett-Reflex-Mikrophotographie," *Archiv für Kriminologie,* Vol. 102, part 1/2 (1938)

Law, "The Restoration of Numbers on Metal," *The Police Journal* (London), 17, 44 (1944)

Lindquist, "Medico-Legal Identification of Seminal Stains Using the Acid Phosphatase Test," *Archives of Pathology,* 50, 395-396 (1950)

Locard, E.,[1] "The Analysis of Dust Traces," *American Journal of Police Science,* 1, 276; 401; 496 (1930)

——,[2] "L'Expertise des écritures," *L'Avenir Médical* (1922)

——,[3] "Les Faux sur découpage," *Revue de Droit Penal* (1927)

——,[4] "L'Hastoscope," *Revue Internationale de Criminalistique,* August (1929)

——,[5] "La Poroscopie, procédé nouveau d'identification des criminels par les traces des orifices sudoripares," *Archive d'Anthropologie Criminalistique* (1913)

Locard, J.,[6] "Contribution à l'analyses des taches de matières colorantes," *Revue Internationale de Criminalistique,* 9 (1937)

——,[7] "La Determination de sang par le leucovert malachite," *Revue Internationale de Criminalistique* (1931)

Lochte, in *Archiv für Kriminologie,* Vol. 88

Madsen, "Bidrag til Undersögelsestekniken for Skaarspor: Traevaerk," *Nordisk Kriminalteknisk Tidskrift,* No. 12 (1933)

Matwejeff, in *Archiv für Kriminologie,* Vol. 2–3 (1930)

May, "The Identification of Knives, Tools and Instruments: A Positive Science," *American Journal of Police Science,* Vol. 1, No. 3 (1930)

Medinger, "Contributions au diagnostic de traces minimes de sang," *Revue Internationale de Criminalistique,* No. 7 (1931)

Mitchell–Ward, "The Sequence of Strokes in Writing," *Analyst* (1927)

Muehlberger, "The Investigation of Deaths Due to Highway Accidents," in Snyder, *Homicide Investigation,* Springfield (1951)

Müller, in *Kriminalistische Monatshefte,* No. 1 (1932)

Murray, "Examination of Burnt Documents," *Nature,* 148, 199 (1941)

O'Neill, "The Restoration of Obliterated Ink Writing," *Journal of Criminal Law and Criminology,* 27, 574 (1937)

Ottolenghi, in *Bollettino della scuola di polizia scientifica e dei Servizi tecnici annessi* (1925)

Pavlovsky, "Use of Grenz Rays in the Laboratories," *Journal of Criminal Law and Criminology,* June (1949)

Piédelièvre, "Les Empreintes de vêtements relevées sur les balles de plomb," *Études Criminologiques* (1927)

Piédelièvre–Desoille, "Blessures par coups de feu," *Études Médico-légales* (1939)

Plesters, "The Preparation and Study of Paint Cross Sections," *The Museum Journal*, 54, 4 (1954)

Puranen, in *Deutsche Zeitschrift für gerichtliche Medizin*, 26, 366 (1936)

Putkonen, in *Acta Societatis Medicinalis*, Duodecim, 14, 2 (1930)

Riifeldt, "Acid Phosphatase Employed as a New Method of Demonstrating Seminal Spots in Forensic Medicine," *Acta Pathologica et Microbiologica Scandinavica*, Supp. 58, 1-80 (1946)

Sannié,[1] "Une Cause d'erreur dans l'identification des douilles," *Annales de Médecine Légale*, May–June (1944)

——,[2] "La Détermination de l'âge des traces manuscrits à l'encre," *Acta Médecine Légalis et Socialis*, Vol. I, No. 2

——,[3] "L'Identification par analyse spectrographique des orifices de projectiles sur les vêtements," *Annales de Médecine Légale*, February (1939)

——,[4] "Les Taches et les traces d'origine biologique," *Annales de Médecine Légale*, No. 6, November–December (1946)

Sannié–Guérin,[1] "Le Classement monodactylaire du service de l'identité judiciaire de Paris," *Annales de Médecine Légale*, July (1937)

Sasaki, in *Zeitschrift für Immunitätsforschung.*, 77, 101 (1932)

Schade–Widmann, "Die Verwendung von Farbstoffen als Diebesfälle," *Archiv für Kriminologie*, 108, 58 (1941)

Schneickert,[1] "Massensuggestion," *Archiv für Kriminologie*, Vol. XVIII (1905)

——,[2] "Sichtbarmachung latenter Abdrücke eisenhaltiger Tintenschriftzüge," *Archiv für Kriminologie* (1921)

Severine–Maurel, in *La Nature*, No. 2457, May 7 (1924)

Simon, "Pyromania and Kleptomania," *Annals of the International Association of Chiefs of Police* (1949)

Söderman,[1] "Détermination d'un système de pistolet à l'aide des balles et des douilles déchargées," *Revue Internationale de Criminalistique*, 5, 90 (1933)

——,[2] "En ny apparat för uppsamling av damm i förbrytares kläder," and "Ett bidrag till frågan om den kriminaltekniska dammsugningens teknik," *Nordisk Kriminalteknisk Tidskrift* (1931)

——, "Science and Criminal Investigation," *Annals of the American Academy of Political and Social Science*, November (1929)

Sternack, "Über die Täuschungen bei der Schätzung von Entfernungen," *Archiv für Kriminologische Anthropologie*, Vol. XVI (1906)

Stockis,[1] "Le Classement monodactylaire," *Revue de Droit Penal*, April (1914)

——,[2] "Les Empreintes palmaires," *Archives de Médecine Légale* (1910)

Tage–Jensen, "Under sökelser paa gerningssteder," *Tidskrift för Strafferet* (1923)

Tatum, et al., "Drug Addiction," *Physiological Reviews*, II, 107 (1931)

Taylor–Walls, "A New Method for the Decipherment of Charred Documents," *Nature*, 147, 417 (1941)

Tryhorn,[1] "The Examination of Glass," *The Police Journal* (London), 12, 301 (1939)

——,[2] "Scientific Evidence in Cases of Motor Accidents," *The Police Journal* (London), 13, 288 (1940)

Türkel, "Über Pollenanalyse," *Archiv für Kriminologie,* 88, 69 (1931)

U. S. Army Technical Bulletin, P.M.G.[1] 1, "Narcotics, Marihuana" (1951)

——[2] 8, "Narcotics—Opium and other Dangerous Drugs" (1952)

——[3] 13, "Dangerous Nonnarcotic Drugs" (1953)

——[4] 22, "Use of the Lie Detector" (1954)

——[5] 18, "Hit-and-Run Accidents" (1953)

——[6] 21, "Crimes Involving Poisons" (1955)

——[7] 23, "Crimes Involving Explosives" (1956)

Vance, "The Medicolegal Examination of Hairs," *New England Journal of Medicine* (1938), pp. 914–918

Van Itallie,[1] "La Fixation du moment de l'administration du poison en cas d'intoxication chronique par l'arsenic," *Journal de Pharmacie et de Chimie,* 25, 97 (1937)

——,[2] "Het arseengehalte van haaren," *Pharmazeutisch Weekblad,* 69, 1134 (1932)

Wachtmeister, "Vittnespsykologi," *Svenska Dagbladet,* July 30 (1929)

Werner, "The Scientific Examination of Paintings," *The Royal Institute of Chemistry,* 4 (1952)

Wiener,[1] in *Bulletin New York Academy of Medicine,* 25: 255 (1949)

——,[2] in *Proceedings of the Society of Experimental Biology and Medicine,* 34: 316, December (1943)

BOOKS

Abderhalden, *Handbuch der biologischen Arbeitsmethoden.* Berlin, 1932

Abrahamsen, *Crime and the Human Mind.* New York, 1944

Allen, *The Microscope.* Boston, 1945

Anuschat, *Pistolen und Revolverschiessen.* Berlin, 1928

Anderson, *Criminals and Crime.* Edinburgh, 1907

Arther–Caputo, *Interrogation for Investigators.* New York, 1959

Askins, *The Art of Handgun Shooting.* New York, 1945

Atcherly, *Criminal Investigation and Detection.* Wakefield, 1932

Avé–Lallemant, *Das deutsche Gaunertum.* Berlin, 1858

Balthazard, *Précis de police scientifique.* Paris, 1934

Bamford, *Poisons; Their Isolation and Identification.* Philadelphia, 1951

Barnard–Welch, *Practical Photomicrography.* New York, 1925

Barnes–Teeters, *New Horizons in Criminology.* New York, 1945

Battley, *Single Fingerprints.* New Haven, 1931

Bebie, *Manual of Explosives, Military Pyrotechnics and Chemical Warfare Agents.* New York, 1943

Bensing & Schroeder, *Homicide in an Urban Community.* Springfield, 1960

Bertillon, A., *Identification anthropométrique.* Melun, 1885

——,[2] *Photographie judiciaire.* Paris, 1890

Bertillon, S., *Vie d'Alphonse Bertillon.* Montrouge, 1941

Best, *Crime and Criminal Law in the United States.* New York, 1930
Biderman–Zimmer, *The Manipulation of Human Behavior.* New York, 1961
Birnbaum, *Kriminalpsychopathologie.* Berlin, 1921
Bischoff, *La Police scientifique.* Paris, 1938
Bleuler, *Lehrbuch der Psychiatrie.* Berlin, 1923
Bock, *Moderne Faustfeuerwaffen.* Neudamm, 1923
Branham–Kutash, *Encyclopedia of Criminology.* New York, 1949
Brend, *A Handbook of Medical Jurisprudence and Toxicology.* London, 1941
Bridges, *Practical Fingerprinting.* New York, 1942
Brill, *Fundamental Conceptions of Psychoanalysis.* New York, 1932
Brookes–Alyea, *Poisons.* New York, 1946
Brotteaux, *Hachich: Herbe de folie et de rêve.* Paris, 1934
Brown, *The Enigma of Drug Addiction.* Springfield, 1961
Brunswig, *Das rauchlose Pulver.* Berlin, 1926
Burk–Grummitt, *Recent Advances in Analytical Chemistry.* New York, 1949
Burrard, *Identification of Firearms and Forensic Ballistics.* New York, 1934
Burroughs, *Criticism from a Laboratory.* Boston, 1938
Burtt, *Legal Psychology.* New York, 1931
Cahalane, *Policeman.* New York, 1923
Callan, *Police Methods for Today and Tomorrow.* Camden, 1939
Camps–Purchase, *Practical Forensic Medicine.* London, 1956
Casier–Delaunois, *L'Intoxication par l'alcool éthylique.* Paris, 1947
Cennini, *Libro dell'Arte*
Chandler, *The Policeman's Manual.* New York, 1922
Chapel, *Fingerprinting.* New York, 1941
Chavigny, *L'Expertise des plaies par armes à feu.* Paris, 1918
Clark, *Photography by Infrared.* New York, 1946
Clerc, *Photography, Theory and Practice.* London, 1937
Collins, *A Telegraphic Code for Fingerprint Formulae.* London, 1921
Conway, *Evidential Documents.* Springfield, Ill., 1959
Crew–Gibson, *A Dictionary of Medico-legal Terms for Criminal Lawyers and Police Officers.* London, 1937
Cummins–Midlo, *Fingerprints, Palms and Soles.* Philadelphia, 1943
Cutler, *Successful Trial Tactics.* New York, 1949
Davis, *The Chemistry of Powder and Explosives.* New York, 1943
Davison, *Manual of Toxicology.* New York, 1939
De Menthe, *Fluorescent Substances.* New York, 1951
Dennstedt–Voigtlander, *Der Nachweis von Schriftfälschungen.* Braunschweig, 1906
Déribéré, *Les Applications pratiques de la luminescence.* Paris, 1943
De River, *The Sexual Criminal.* Springfield, 1949
Dérobert–Duchene, *L'Alcoolisme aigu et chronique.* Paris, 1942
Dérobert–Hausser, *La pratique médico-légale.* Paris, 1938
Dérome, *Expertise en armes à feu.* Montreal, 1929
Dervieux–Leclercq, *Le Diagnostic des taches.* Paris, 1912
de Wild, *The Scientific Examination of Paintings.* London, 1929
Duncan, *An Introduction to Fingerprints.* Aberdeen, 1942
Eames–MacDaniels, *An Introduction to Plant Anatomy.* New York, 1948

Eastman Kodak Co.,[1] *Elementary Photographic Chemistry*. Rochester, 1941
——,[2] *Photography in Law Enforcement*. Rochester, 1959
——,[3] *The Photography of Colored Objects*, 14th Edition. Rochester, 1938
——,[4] *Photomicrography*. Rochester, 1958
——,[5] *Wratten Light Filters*, 7th Edition, revised. Rochester, 1951
Elster–Lingemann, *Handwörterbuch der Kriminologie*. Berlin, 1933
Erdman, *Pollen Analysis*. Waltham, 1945
Fabre, *Leçons de toxicologie*. Paris, 1945
Federal Bureau of Investigation, *The Science of Fingerprints*. Washington, D.C., 1961
Ferrer,[1] *La identificación personal por medio de las impresiones palmares*. Madrid, 1917
——,[2] *Manuel de identificación judicial*. Madrid, 1921
Fisher, *Incendiary Warfare*. New York, 1946
Fleury–Silvera, *Determination de la date d'usage des armes à feu et des munitions*. São Paolo, 1926
Forgeot, *Les Empreintes latentes*. Lyon, 1891
Fortunato, *Las impresiones digitales y palmares del recien nacide*. La Plata, 1943
Fortunato–Albarracin, *Procedimiento indirecto para la identificación de cadavres*. Buenos Aires, 1938
Fosdick, *European and American Police Systems*. New York, 1920
Frazer, *American Pistol Shooting*. Marshallton, 1930
Fuld, *Police Administration*. New York, 1910
Gaddum, *Pharmacology*. London, 1948
Gage, *The Microscope*. Ithaca, 1932
Gaines, *Elementary Cryptanalysis*. Boston, 1944
Galton, *Decipherment of Blurred Fingerprints*. London, 1893
——, *Fingerprints*. London, 1892
Geipel, *Anleitung zur erbbiologischen Beurteilung der Finger- und Handleisten*. Nördlingen, 1935
Glaister, *Medical Jurisprudence and Toxicology*. Edinburgh, 1945
Goddefroy,[1] *La Police technique et les recherches judiciaires*. Bruxelles, 1923
——, *Manuel elementaire de police technique*. Bruxelles, 1922
Gonzales–Vance–Halpern, *Legal Medicine and Toxicology*. New York, 1940
Gonzales *et al.*, *Legal Medicine and Toxicology*. New York, 1956
Gorphe, *L'Appréciation des preuves en justice*. Paris, 1947
——,[2] *La Critique du témoignage*. Paris, 1927
Grant, *Science for the Prosecution*. London, 1941
Graper, *American Police Administration*. New York, 1921
Greenwood, *Document Photography*. Chatham, 1943
Griffin, *Introduction to Mathematical Analysis*. Boston, 1921
Gross, *Criminal Investigation*, 4th Edition (Ronald Howe, editor). London, 1949
——, *Criminal Psychology*. Boston, 1911
——,[3] *Handbuch für Untersuchungsrichter*. München, 1943
Guiral, *La Valeur de la prueve dans l'expertise des écritures*. Lyon, 1927
Gunther, J. D. and C. O., *The Identification of Firearms*. New York, 1935

Hahn, *The Rape of La Belle.* Kansas City, 1946
Haitinger, *Die Fluoreszenzanalyse in der Mikrochemie.* Vienna, 1937
Harbitz, *Laerebok i retsmedicin.* Oslo, 1950
Harder–Brüning, *Die Kriminalität bei der Post.* Berlin, 1924
Harley, *Medicolegal Blood Group Determination.* London, 1943
Harrison, *Police Administration in Boston.* Cambridge, 1934
Hatcher, *Textbook of Firearms Investigation, Identification and Evidence.* Plantersville, 1959
Heindl, *Die Daktyloskopie.* Berlin, 1927
——,[2] *System und Praxis der Daktyloskopie.* Berlin, 1927
Hellwig,[2] *Psychologie und Vernehmungstechnik.* Berlin, 1927
Henry, *Classification and Uses of Fingerprints.* London, 1928
Herzog–Erickson, *Camera, Take the Stand!* New York, 1940
Hesse, *Narcotics and Drug Addiction.* New York, 1946
Hilton, *Scientific Examination of Documents.* Chicago, 1956
Himmelwright, *Pistol and Revolver Shooting.* New York, 1928
Hind–Randles, *Handbook of Photomicrography.* New York, 1927
Horoszowski, *Kryminalistyka.* Warsaw, 1955
Hours–Miédan, *A la Découverte de la Peinture.* Paris, 1957
Howe, *The Modern Gunsmith.* New York, 1941
Inbau, *Lie Detection and Criminal Interrogation.* Baltimore, 1953
Jeserich, *Chemie und Photographie im Dienste der Verbrechensaufklärung.* Berlin, 1930
Jones, *Photographic Sensitometry.* Rochester, 1934
Jörgenson,[1] *Distant Identification and One-Finger Registration.* New York, 1923
——, *Forbrydelsens efterforskning.* Köbenhavn, 1920
Kahn, *Psychopathic Personalities.* New Haven, 1931
Kaye, *Handbook of Emergency Toxicology.* Springfield, 1961
Kinberg, *Brottslighet och sinnessjukdom.* Stockholm, 1908
Kirk, *Crime Investigation.* New York, 1952
Kleinschmidt–Schneickerling, *Der Verkehrs-Unfall.* Berlin, 1930
Kley–Schneickert, *Die Kriminalpolizei.* Lübeck, 1924–26
Kockel, "Die gerichtliche Sektion," in Abderhalden's *Handbuch der biologischen Arbeitsmethoden.* Berlin, 1932
Kögel, *Die unsichtbaren Strahlen im Dienste der Kriminalistik.* Graz, 1928
Kohn–Abrest, *Précis de toxicologie.* Paris, 1948
Krafft-Ebing, *Grundzüge der Kriminalpsychologie für Juristen.* Stuttgart, 1882
Kratter, *Lehrbuch der gerichtlichen Medizin.* Stuttgart, 1927
Kuhne, *Fingerprint Instructor.* New York, 1916
Kunkele, *Intern. Kongress für gerichtliche Med.* Bonn, 1938
Lambert, *Traité théorique et pratique de police judiciaire.* Lyon, 1947
Lambert–Balthazard, *Le Poil de l'homme et des animaux.* Paris, 1910
Larson, *Single Fingerprint System.* New York, 1924
Lattes, *Die Individualität des Blutes.* Berlin, 1925
Lee, *The Instrumental Detection of Deception.* Springfield, 1951
Leers, *Gerichtsärtzliche Untersuchungen.* Berlin, 1913

Leibig, *Kriminaltechnik*. München, 1937
Lewin, *Gifte und Vergiftungen*. Berlin, 1929
——, *Phantastica*. Berlin, 1927
Lichem, *Die Kriminalpolizei*. Graz, 1935
Lindesmith, *Opiate Addiction*. Bloomington, 1947
Locard, E.,[8] *L'Enquête criminelle et les méthodes scientifiques*. Paris, 1934
——, *Manuel du philatéliste*. Paris, 1942
——,[10] *Manuel de technique policière*. Paris, 1948
——, *La Police et les méthodes scientifiques*. Paris, 1934
——,[12] *Traité de criminalistique*, Tomes I–VII. Lyon, 1930–40
Lochte, *Atlas der menschlichen und tierischen Haare*. Leipzig, 1938
Louwage, *Police Criminelle technique et tactique*. Bruxelles, 1944
——, *Psychologie et criminalité*. Bruxelles, 1945
——, *Technique de quelques vols et escroqueries*. Bruxelles, 1932
Lucas, *Forensic Chemistry and Scientific Criminal Investigation*. London, 1943
Macdonald, *The Murderer and His Victim*. Springfield, Ill., 1961
McHenry–Roper, *Hand Guns*. Huntington, 1945
McNally, *Medical Jurisprudence and Toxicology*. Philadelphia, 1939
——,[2] *Toxicology*. Chicago, 1937
Maliniak, *Sculpture in the Living*. New York, 1934
May, *Scientific Murder Investigation*. Seattle, 1933
Mayer, *Die gerichtliche Schriftuntersuchung*. Berlin, 1933
Mayor's Committee on Marihuana, "The Marihuana Problem in New York City." Lancaster, 1944
Mees, *The Fundamentals of Photography*. Rochester, 1934
Mellor, *La Torture*. Paris, 1949
Merck Manual, Rahway, 1960
Merck Veterinary Manual, Rahway, 1961
Meyer, *Explosives*. New York, 1943
Mezger–Heess–Hasslacher, *Atlas of Arms*. Berlin, 1931
Mitchell, *Documents and Their Scientific Examination*. London, 1922
——, *Inks*. Glasgow, 1937
——, *The Expert Witness*. New York, 1923
——, *The Scientific Detective and the Expert Witness*. Cambridge, 1931
Moriarty, *Police Procedure and Administration*. London, 1930
Moritz, *Pathology of Trauma*. Philadelphia, 1942
Moylan, *Scotland Yard*. London, 1934
Münsterberg, *On the Witness Stand*. New York, 1933
National Board of Fire Underwriters, "Suggestions for Arson Investigators." New York, 1950
NFPA, *Handbook of Fire Protection*. Boston, 1948
Naudin, *L'Enquête criminelle*. Paris, 1927
Neblette, *Photography, Its Principles and Practices*. Lancaster, 1945
Nelkin, *Die Brandstiftung*. Berlin, 1928
——, *Publikum und Verbrechen*. Berlin, 1925
Neuberger, *Echt oder Fälschung?* Leipzig, 1924
Newman, *Acute Alcoholic Intoxication*. Stanford University, 1941

Niceforo–Lindenau, *Die Kriminalpolizei und ihre Hilfswissenschaften.* Berlin, 1940

Nolte, *Psychologie für Polizeibeamte.* Berlin, 1928

Norsk Brandvern Forening, *Handbok i brandefterforsking.* Oslo, 1934

O'Hara, *Fundamentals of Criminal Investigation.* Springfield, Ill., 1956

O'Hara–Osterburg, *Introduction to Criminalistics.* New York, 1949

Osborn, *The Mind of the Juror.* Albany, 1937

———,[2] *The Problem of Proof,* 2nd Edition. New York, 1922

———,[3] *Questioned Documents.* New York, 1929

Ottolenghi, *Polizia scientifica.* Rome, 1907

Parry, *Tattoo.* New York, 1933

Partridge, *A Dictionary of the Underworld.* London, 1950

Paul, *Handbuch der kriminalistischen Photographie.* Berlin, 1900

Perkins, *Elements of Police Science.* Chicago, 1942

Peters Cartridge Co., *American Rifleman's Encyclopedia.* Cincinnati, 1902

Phillipp, *Kriminalistische Denklehre.* Berlin, 1927

Pollard, *A History of Firearms.* New York, 1926

Polzer, *Handbuch für den praktischen Kriminaldienst.* Berlin, 1922

———, *Praktischer Leitfaden für kriminalistische Tatbestandsaufnahmen.* Berlin, 1921

Porot, *Les Toxicomanies.* Alger, 1945

Possehl, *Moderne Betruger.* Berlin, 1928

Pringsheim–Vogel, *Luminescence of Liquids and Solids.* Baltimore, 1943

Quirke, *Forged, Anonymous and Suspect Documents.* London, 1930

Radley, *Photography.* Chatham, 1948

———,[2] *Photography in Crime Detection.* London, 1948

Radley–Grant, *Fluorescence Analysis in Ultra-violet Light.* Aberdeen, 1948

Rehfeldt, *Zum Selbstmordsproblem.* Berlin, 1929

Reid, *Detection of Deception.* Springfield, 1952

Reiss, *Manuel de police scientifique.* Paris, 1911

———,[2] *La Photographie judiciaire.* Paris, 1903

Rethoret, *Fire Investigations.* Montreal, 1945

Reuter, "Naturwissenschaftlich-kriminalische Untersuchungen menschlicher Ausscheidungen" in Abderhalden, *Handbuch der biologischen Arbeitsmethode.* Berlin, 1938

Rhodes, *Forensic Chemistry.* London, 1946

Ribeiro, *Policia scientifica.* Rio de Janeiro, 1934

Rose–Cirino, *Jewelry Making and Design.* Worcester, 1946

Sannié,[5] *Le Méthodes scientifiques de l'identification judiciaire.* Paris, 1940

Sannié–Guérin,[2] *Instructions pratiques pour le relevé correct des empreintes digitales.* Paris, 1940

———,[3] *Notice sur le service de l'identité judiciaire.* Paris, 1949

Schatkin, *Disputed Paternity Proceedings,* 2nd Edition. New York, 1947

Schiff–Boyd, *Blood Grouping Technic.* New York, 1942

Schneickert, *Die Bedeutung der Handschrift in Zivil- und Strafrecht.* Leipzig, 1906

———, *Der Beweis durch Fingerabdrucke.* Berlin, 1923

———, *Kriminalistische Spurensicherung.* Berlin, 1925

——, *Kriminaltaktik und Kriminaltechnik.* Berlin, 1927
——,[7] *Leitfaden der gerichtlichen Schriftvergleichung.* Berlin, 1918
——, *Die Verstellung der Handschrift.* Jena, 1925
Schneickert–Geissel, *Einbruch und Diebstahl und ihre Verhütung.* Berlin, 1923
Schneickert–Meyer, *Regulations of the Berlin Police Department.* Berlin, 1911
Scott, C., *Photographic Evidence.* Kansas City, 1942
Scott, Walter R., *Fingerprint Mechanics.* Springfield, Ill., 1951
Shalloo, *Private Police.* Philadelphia, 1933
Sheehan, *General and Plastic Surgery.* New York, 1945
Shillaber, *Photomicrography in Theory and Practice.* New York, 1944
Shore, *Crime and Its Detection.* London, 1931
Skehan, *Modern Police Work Including Detective Duty.* Brooklyn, 1939
Smart, *The Technology of Industrial Fire and Explosion Hazards.* Bristol, 1947
Smith, B., *American Police Systems.* New York, 1940
——,[2] *Police Systems in the U.S.* New York, 1949
——, *Rural Crime Control.* New York, 1933
——, *The State Police.* New York, 1925
Smith, O., *Identification and Qualitative Chemical Analysis of Minerals.* New York, 1946
Smith, S.,[6] *Forensic Medicine.* London, 1945
Smith, W. H. B., *Basic Manual of Military Small Arms.* Harrisburg, 1945
——, *Mannlicher Rifles and Pistols.* Harrisburg, 1947
——, *Mauser Rifles and Pistols.* Harrisburg, 1946
——, *Walther Pistols.* Harrisburg, 1946
Smith–Glaister, *Recent Advances in Forensic Medicine,* 2nd Edition. Philadelphia, 1939
Snyder, *Homicide Investigation.* Springfield, 1951
Söderman,[4] *Brottets värld.* Stockholm, 1927
——,[5] *L'Expertise des armes à feu courtes.* Lyon, 1928
Söderman–Fontell, *Handbok i kriminalteknik.* Stockholm, 1930
Stettbacher, *Spreng- und Schiesstoffe.* Basel, 1948
Stevens, *Microphotography.* New York, 1951
Strasmann, *Lehrbuch der gerichtlichen Medizin.* Stuttgart, 1937
Streicher, *Die kriminologische Verwertung der Maschinschrift.* Graz, 1919
Stringaris, *Die Haschischsucht.* Berlin, 1939
Ther, *Pharmakologische Methoden.* Stuttgart, 1949
Thienes–Haley, *Clinical Toxicology.* Philadelphia, 1948
Thompson, *The Materials and Techniques of Medieval Painting.* London, 1936
Tramm–Hellwig–Rhode, *Brandstiftungen und Brandursachen.* Kiel, 1933
Türkel, *Atlas der Bleistiftschrift.* Graz, 1927
——,[3] *Beiträge zur kriminalistischen Symptomotologie und Technik.* Graz, 1931
——, *Fälschungen.* Graz, 1930
Turner–Hilton, *Forensic Science and Laboratory Technics.* Springfield, 1949
Underhill–Koppanyi, *Toxicology.* Philadelphia, 1936
Vogel, *Brandstiftungen und ihre Bekämpfung.* Berlin, 1929

Vollmer, *The Police and Modern Society.* Berkeley, 1936

Vollmer–Parker, *Crime and the State Police.* Berkeley, 1935

Von Hentig, *Crime, Causes and Conditions.* New York, 1947

Von Neureiter–Pietrusky–Schütt, *Handwörterbuch der gerichtlichen Medizin und naturwissenschaftlichen Kriminalistik.* Berlin, 1940

Vucetich, *Dactiloscopia comparada.* La Plata, 1904

Wadsworth, *Post-Mortem Examinations.* Philadelphia, 1916

Walton, *Marihuana.* Philadelphia, 1938

Webster, *Legal Medicine and Toxicology.* Philadelphia, 1930

Wehde–Beffel, *Fingerprints Can Be Forged.* Chicago, 1924

Weingart, *Kriminaltaktik.* Leipzig, 1904

Weiss, *Publikum und Verbrechen.* Berlin, 1928

Wendel–Svensson, *Handbok i brottsplatsundersökning.* Stockholm, 1949

Wentzell, *Der Schriftindizienbeweis.* Berlin, 1927

Widmark, *Die Theoretischen Grundlagen und die praktische Verwendbarkeit der Alkoholbestimmung in der gerichtlichen Medizin.* Berlin, 1932

Wiener,[3] *Blood Groups and Transfusions,* 3rd Edition. Springfield, 1943

Wilder–Wentworth, *Personal Identification.* Boston, 1918

Wilson, *Police Planning.* Springfield, Ill., 1958

Wilton, *Fingerprints, History, Law and Romance.* Edinburgh, 1938

Wolfgang, *Patterns in Criminal Homicide.* Philadelphia, 1958

INDEX

INDEX